C000054477

STREE

Gloucestershire
South Gloucestershire
and Bristol

First published in 2001 by

Philip's, a division of
Octopus Publishing Group Ltd
2-4 Heron Quays, London E14 4JP

Second edition 2005
Second impression with revisions 2007
GLOBB

ISBN-10   0-540-08761-0 (pocket)
ISBN-13   978-0-540-08761-7 (pocket)

© Philip's 2007

Ordnance Survey®

This product includes mapping data licensed from
Ordnance Survey® with the permission of the
Controller of Her Majesty's Stationery Office.
© Crown copyright 2007. All rights reserved.
Licence number 100011710.

Printed by Toppan, China

Contents

III   **Key to map symbols**

IV   **Key to map pages**

VI   **Route planning**

X   **Administrative and Postcode boundaries**

1   **Street maps** at 2⅔ inches to 1 mile

140   **Street maps** at 1⅓ inches to 1 mile

190   **Street maps** at 2⅔ inches to 1 mile

193   **Street maps of centres of Cheltenham, Bristol and Gloucester** at 5⅓ inches to 1 mile

197   **Index** of towns and villages

201   **Index** of streets, hospitals, industrial estates, railway stations, schools, shopping centres, universities and places of interest

Digital Data

The exceptionally high-quality mapping found in this atlas is available as digital data in TIFF format, which is easily convertible to other bitmapped (raster) image formats.

The index is also available in digital form as a standard database table. It contains all the details found in the printed index together with the National Grid reference for the map square in which each entry is named.

For further information and to discuss your requirements, please contact james.mann@philips-maps.co.uk

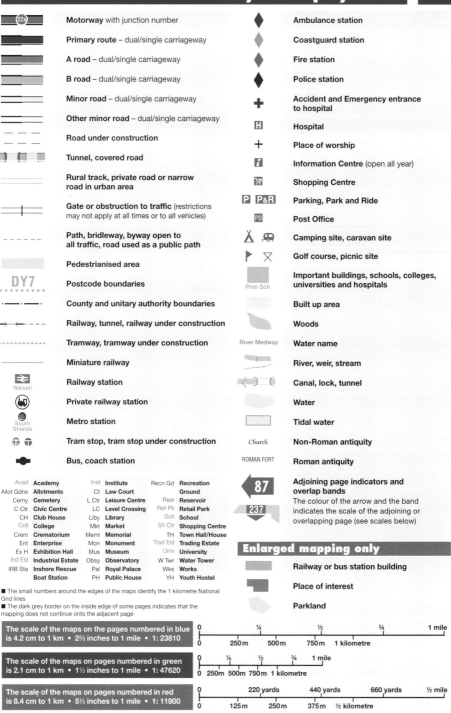

	Motorway with junction number			**Ambulance station**
	Primary route – dual/single carriageway			**Coastguard station**
	A road – dual/single carriageway			**Fire station**
	B road – dual/single carriageway			**Police station**
	Minor road – dual/single carriageway			**Accident and Emergency entrance to hospital**
	Other minor road – dual/single carriageway		H	**Hospital**
	Road under construction		+	**Place of worship**
	Tunnel, covered road		i	**Information Centre** (open all year)
	Rural track, private road or narrow road in urban area			**Shopping Centre**
	Gate or obstruction to traffic (restrictions may not apply at all times or to all vehicles)		P P&R	**Parking, Park and Ride**
	Path, bridleway, byway open to all traffic, road used as a public path		PO	**Post Office**
	Pedestrianised area			**Camping site, caravan site**
DY7	**Postcode boundaries**		Prim Sch	**Golf course, picnic site**
	County and unitary authority boundaries			**Important buildings, schools, colleges, universities and hospitals**
	Railway, tunnel, railway under construction			**Built up area**
	Tramway, tramway under construction			**Woods**
	Miniature railway		River Medway	**Water name**
Walsall	**Railway station**			**River, weir, stream**
	Private railway station			**Canal, lock, tunnel**
South Shields	**Metro station**			**Water**
	Tram stop, tram stop under construction			**Tidal water**
	Bus, coach station		Church	**Non-Roman antiquity**
			ROMAN FORT	**Roman antiquity**

Acad	**Academy**	Inst	**Institute**	Recn Gd	**Recreation Ground**	
Allot Gdns	**Allotments**	Ct	**Law Court**			
Cemy	**Cemetery**	L Ctr	**Leisure Centre**	Resr	**Reservoir**	
C Ctr	**Civic Centre**	LC	**Level Crossing**	Ret Pk	**Retail Park**	
CH	**Club House**	Liby	**Library**	Sch	**School**	
Coll	**College**	Mkt	**Market**	Sh Ctr	**Shopping Centre**	
Crem	**Crematorium**	Meml	**Memorial**	TH	**Town Hall/House**	
Ent	**Enterprise**	Mon	**Monument**	Trad Est	**Trading Estate**	
Ex H	**Exhibition Hall**	Mus	**Museum**	Univ	**University**	
Ind Est	**Industrial Estate**	Obsy	**Observatory**	W Twr	**Water Tower**	
IRB Sta	**Inshore Rescue Boat Station**	Pal	**Royal Palace**	Wks	**Works**	
		PH	**Public House**	YH	**Youth Hostel**	

87 **Adjoining page indicators and overlap bands**
The colour of the arrow and the band indicates the scale of the adjoining or overlapping page (see scales below)

237

Railway or bus station building

Place of interest

Parkland

■ The small numbers around the edges of the maps identify the 1 kilometre National Grid lines
■ The dark grey border on the inside edge of some pages indicates that the mapping does not continue onto the adjacent page

The scale of the maps on the pages numbered in blue is 4.2 cm to 1 km • 2⅔ inches to 1 mile • 1: 23810	0 ¼ ½ ¾ 1 mile 0 250m 500m 750m 1 kilometre
The scale of the maps on pages numbered in green is 2.1 cm to 1 km • 1⅓ inches to 1 mile • 1: 47620	0 ¼ ½ ¾ 1 mile 0 250m 500m 750m 1 kilometre
The scale of the maps on pages numbered in red is 8.4 cm to 1 km • 5⅓ inches to 1 mile • 1: 11900	0 220 yards 440 yards 660 yards ½ mile 0 125m 250m 375m ½ kilometre

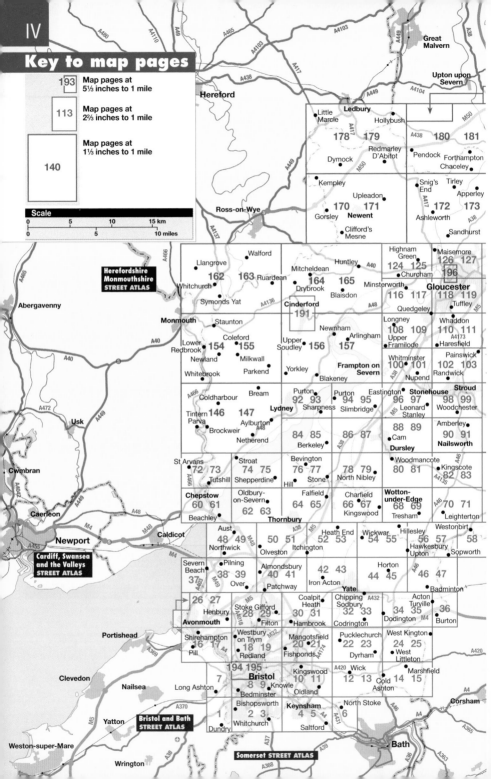

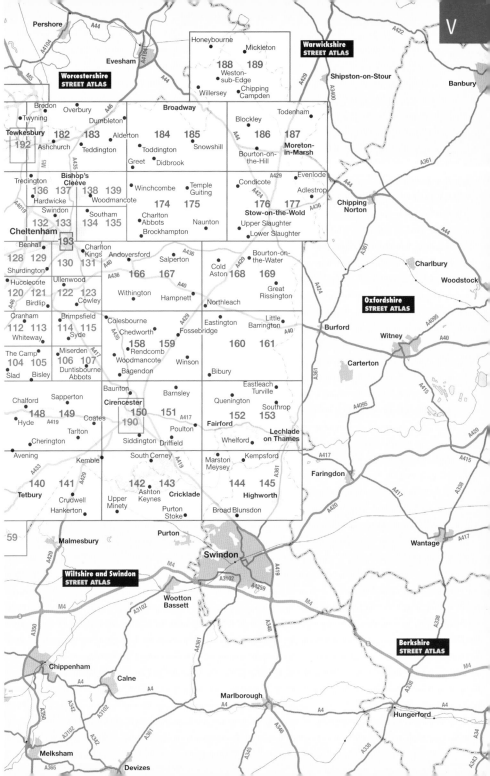

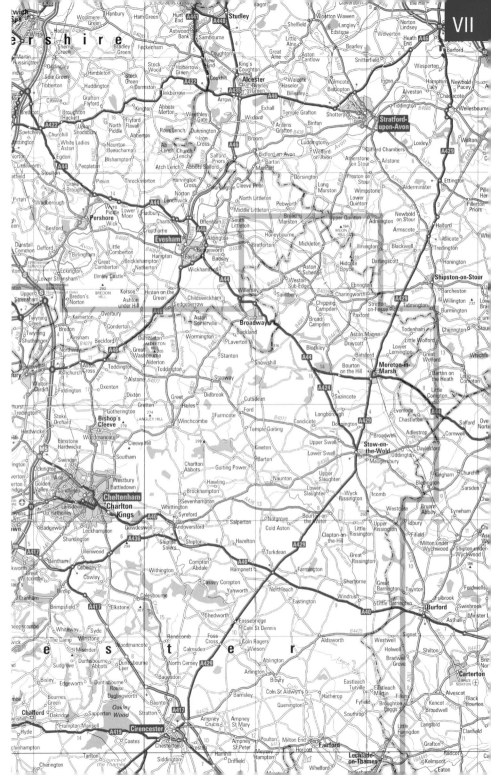

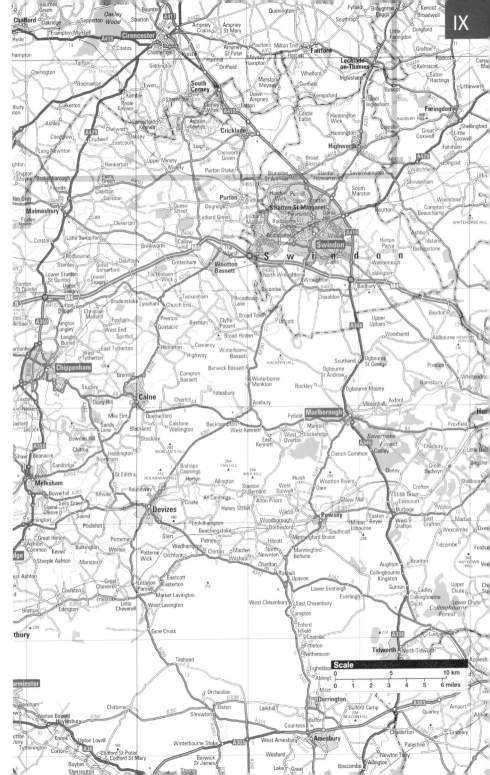

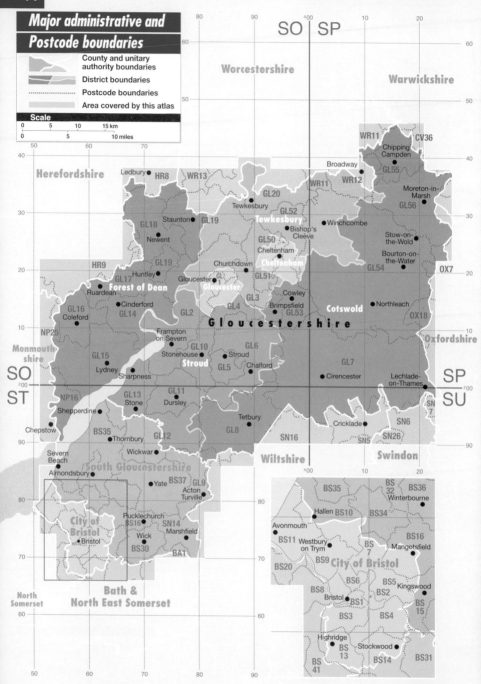

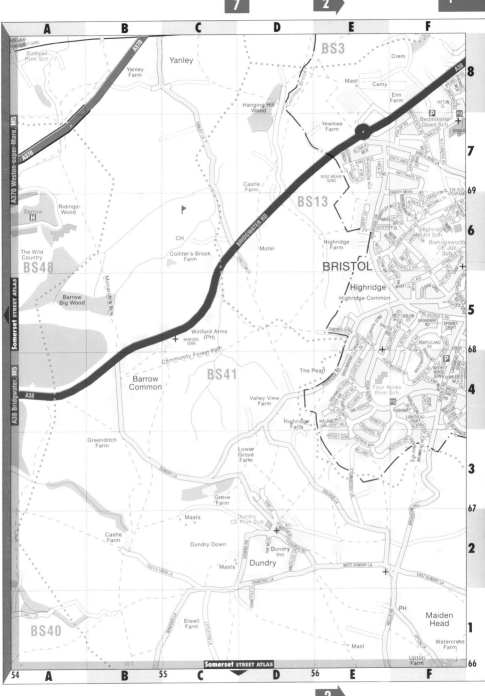

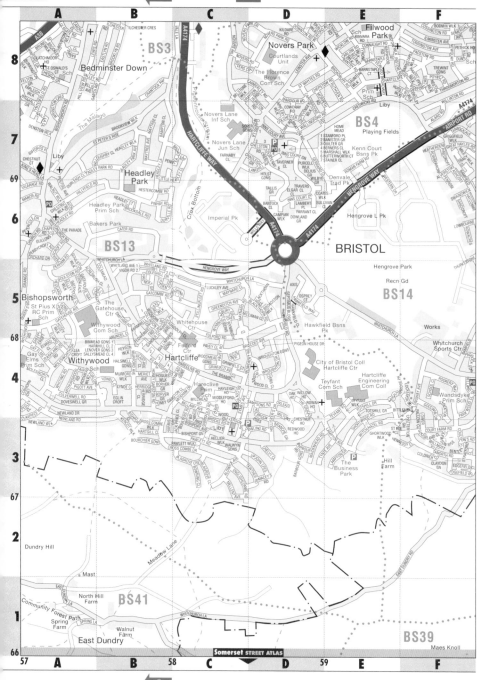

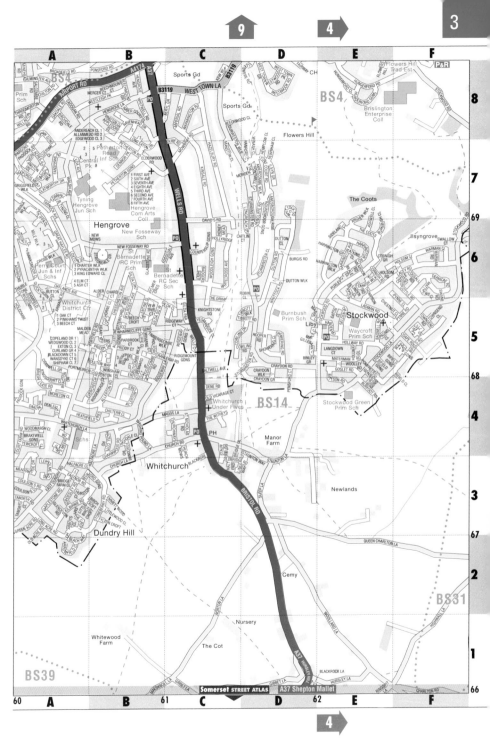

3

10

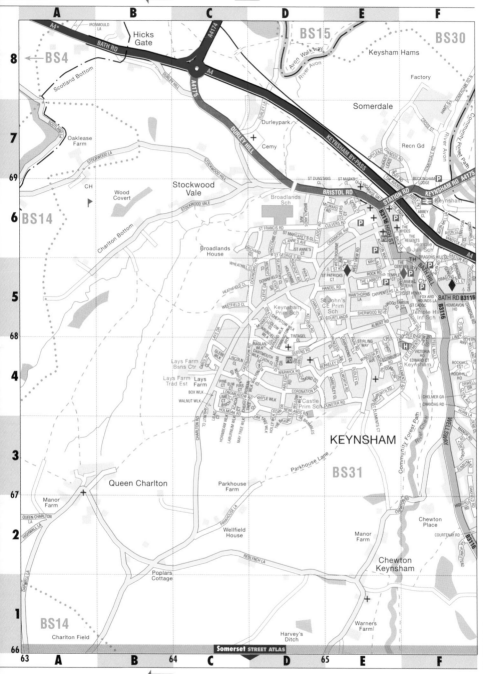

3

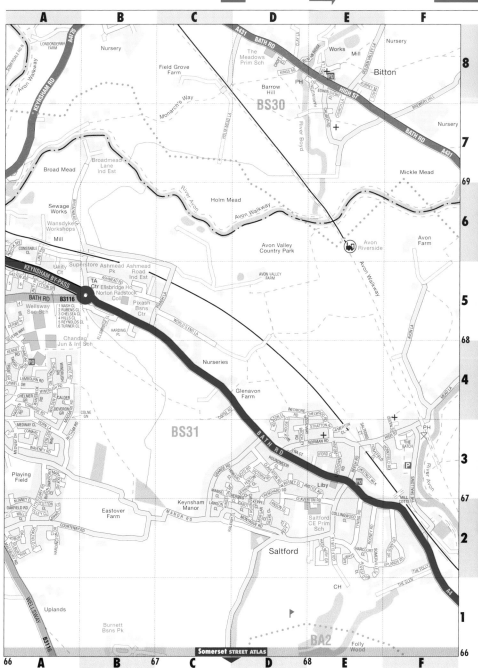

A **B** **C** **D** **E** **F**

Monarch's
Way

Upton Cheyney

LANSDOWN LA

LANSDOWN LA

PH

BS30

Congrove
Wood

8

NORTH STOKE LA

Pipley
Bottom

BREWERY HILL

SPRINGFIELD
COT'S

Nursery

Further
Slate

Brockham
End

Pipley
Wood

Cotswold Way

7

P

PH

Swineford

A431

69

North Stoke

Mast

Weir

Bath
Race Course

6

Saltford
Mead

Little
Down

B A T H   R D

Weston
Wood

5

Sewage
Works

River Avon

Prospect
Stile

BS31

Foxhall
Farm

68

MEAD LA

Weir

Coombe
Barn

4

BA1

Midridge

BROCKHAM FOR LA

Kelston Round
Hill

Roundhill
Barn

Cotswold Way

Kelston

BLACKSMITHS LA

3

PH

67

Sandpit
Shrubbery

Dean
Hill

Manor
Farm

2

Dean Hill
Manor

Pendean
Farm

DEANHILL LA

Bristol & Bath Rly Path

Tennant's
Wood

River Avon

KELSTON RD

A4

BATH RD

Avon Walkway

BA2

Oldfield Girls
Sch

1

Kelston
Park

River Avon

A431

66

A4 Bath

Bristol & Bath STREET ATLAS

Avon Walkway

A431 Bath

69 **A** **B** **70** **C** **D** **71** **E** **F**

Bristol & Bath STREET ATLAS

F5
1 Bristol Gate
2 Faraday Rd
3 Dowry Pl
4 Little Caroline Pl
5 Grenville Chapel
6 Humphry Davy Way

7 Grenville Pl
8 Ashmead Way
9 Cumberland Rd
10 Brunswick Pl

F6
1 Haberfield Ho
2 Albermarle Terr
3 Dawes Ct
4 Cleve Ct
5 Browne Ct
6 Adams Ct

7 Cumberland Pl
8 Carrick Ho
9 South Green St
10 Albermarle Row
11 Hopechapel Hill
12 North Green St
13 Hinton La

F6
14 Windsor Ct
15 Victoria Terr
16 The Polygon
17 Glendale
18 Wellington Terr
19 Oxford Pl

F7
1 Clifton Cl
2 Harley Mews
3 Harley Ct
4 Harley Pl
5 Glendower Ho
6 Clifton Down Rd

7 Gloucester Row
8 Beaufort Bldgs
9 Beaufort Mews
10 Guardian Ct
11 Waterloo St
12 Gloucester St
13 Carter's Bldgs

17 **8** **7**

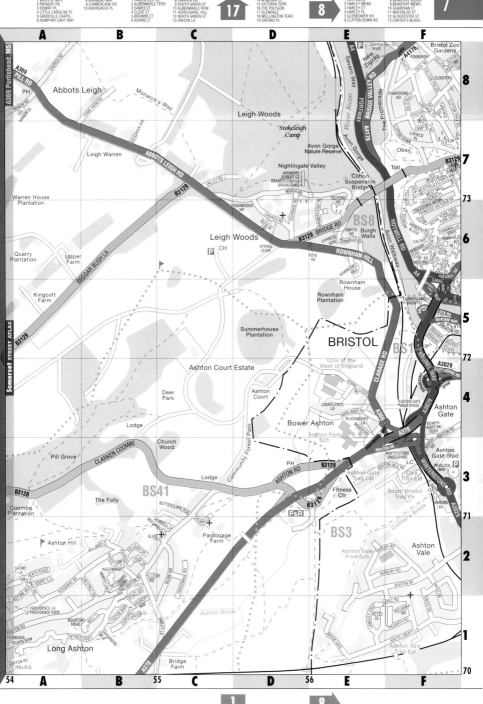

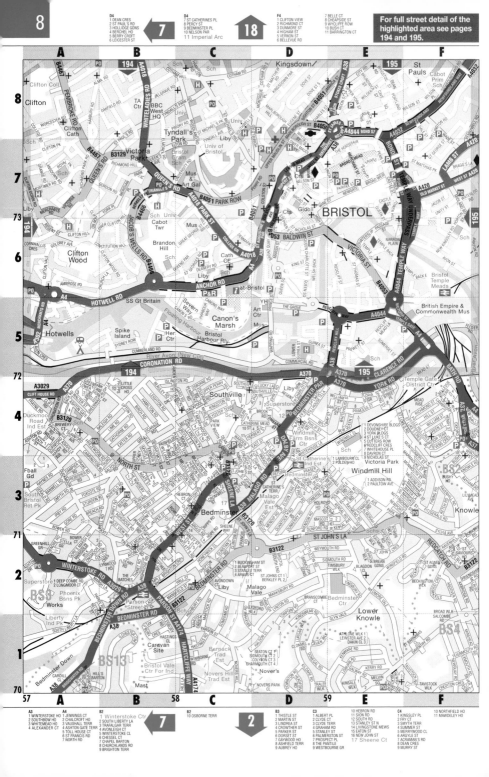

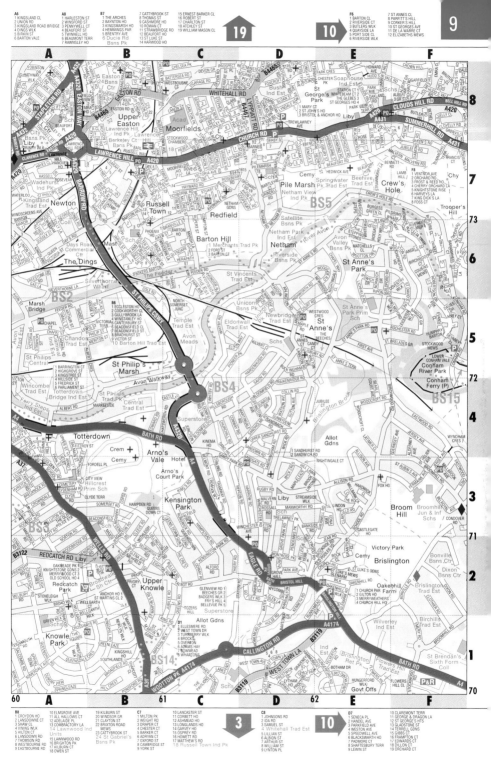

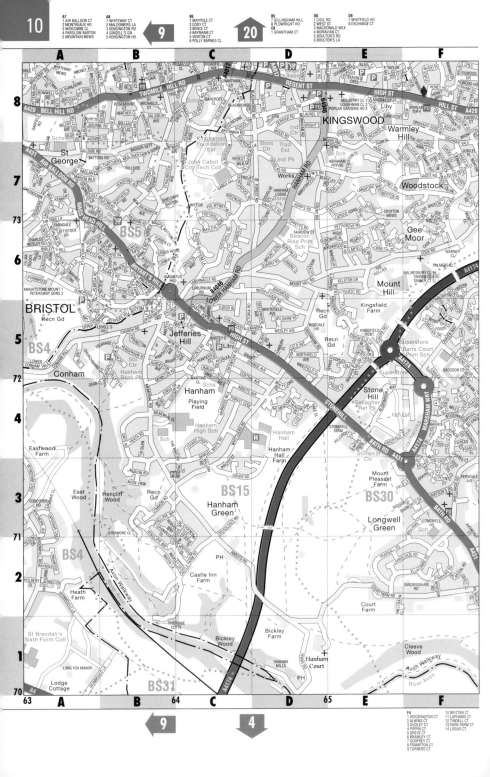

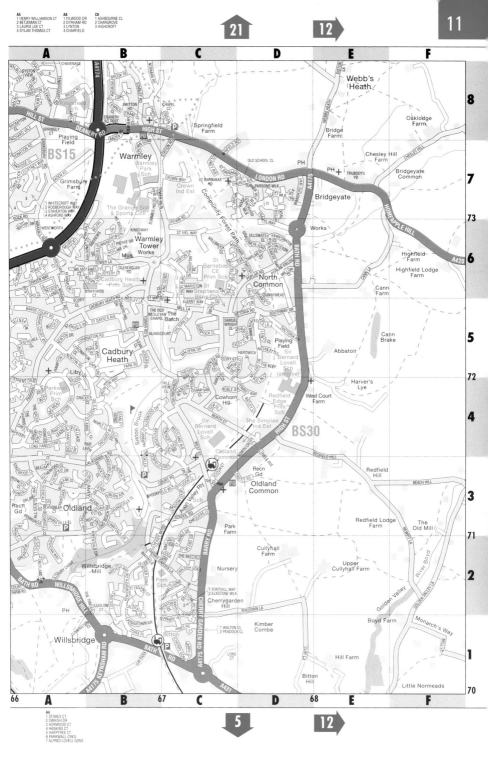

A B C D E F

8

Ketcheshill Farm

Sewage Works

Doynton House

Cleeve Bridge

Hill Farm

Ketcheshill

LODGE RD

Holbrook Common

Wick Rocks

ROCK RD

ABSON RD

BURY LA

Perry's Farm

HORSECROFT LA

7

HOLBROOK LA

New House Farm

Holbrook Farm

WINDSOR CT

Naishcombe Hill

ST. JAMES CT

SANDLEWAY

ST. ANNE'S DR

PAINTERS AVE

MAISHCOMBE HILL

Horsepool Farm

FROGMARSH LA

Brockwell Park

SUNNY BANK

ST. FRANCIS RD

VINE CRESCENT

BOYD CL

73

Bury Manor

Wick CE Prim Sch

COURT VIEW

CHURCH RD

Dog Brook

Limebrook Farm

P

Wick

LONDON RD

6

A420 RIDING BARN HILL

CHURCH RD

Boyd Bridge

River Boyd

Works

HIGH ST

Wick

Wick Court

PH

LONDON RD

A420

COURT LA

Court Farm

MANOR RD

Old Manor Farm

OLDBURY LA

Greenway Farm

BARROW HILL

BS30

Highfield Park Farm

The Manor

5

Monarch's Way

72

Sewage Works

Tracy Park

CH

BATH RD

4

Coldharbour Farm

Grandmother's Rock

Fifteen Acres Farm

3

Mount Pleasant

Upland House

71

Copperfield Farm

West Tyning

BACK LA

Beach

WICK LA

Britton's Farm

GRANDMOTHER'S ROCK LA

2

Barton Farm

Beach House

Beach Farm

Hanging Hill Cottages

MARSHFIELD LA

Beach Wood

1

Mount Pleasant

Cotswold Way

Mast

BA1

Upton Farm

ST. TYE'S LA

Cotswold Cottage

LANSDOWN LA

Hanging Hill

70

69

A B 70 C D 71 E F

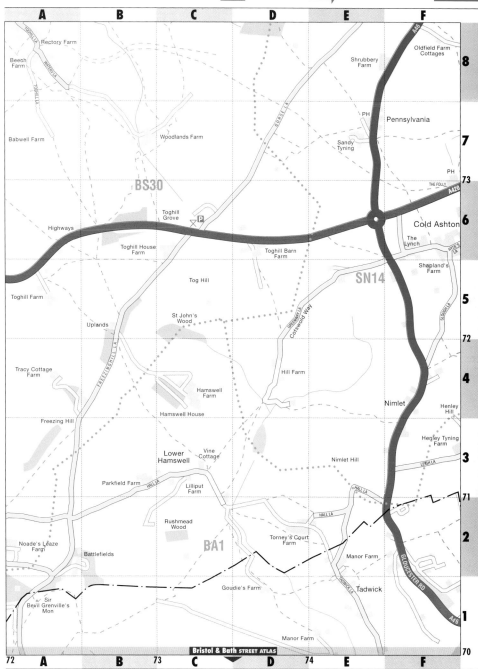

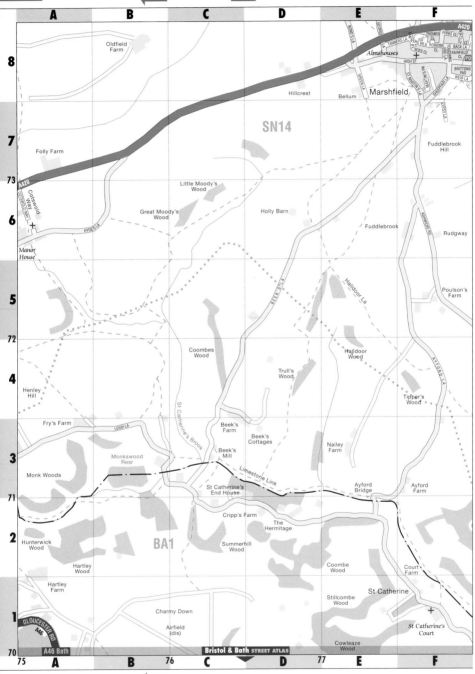

A **B** **C** **D** **E** **F**

8

Oldfield Farm

SN14

Hillcrest

Bellum

Marshfield

Almshouses

Fuddlebrook Hill

7

Folly Farm

Fuddlebrook

Rudgway

73

A420

Cotswold Way

Little Moody's Wood

Holly Barn

6

Great Moody's Wood

Manor House

Poulson's Farm

HYDE LA

BEEK'S LA

Halldoor La

5

Coombes Wood

Halldoor Wood

72

Henley Hill

Trull's Wood

Tipper's Wood

4

St Catherine's Brook

Nailey Farm

LEIGH LA

Beek's Farm

Beek's Cottages

3

Monkswood Resr

Beek's Mill

Limestone Link

Ayford Bridge

Ayford Farm

Monk Woods

St Catherine's End House

71

Cripp's Farm

The Hermitage

2

Hunterwick Wood

Summerhill Wood

Coombe Wood

Court Farm

Hartley Wood

BA1

Stillcombe Wood

St Catherine

Hartley Farm

1

Charmy Down

St Catherine's Court

GLOUCESTER RD

A46

Airfield (dis)

Cowleaze Wood

70

A46 Bath

Bristol & Bath STREET ATLAS

75 **A** **B** 76 **C** **D** 77 **E** **F**

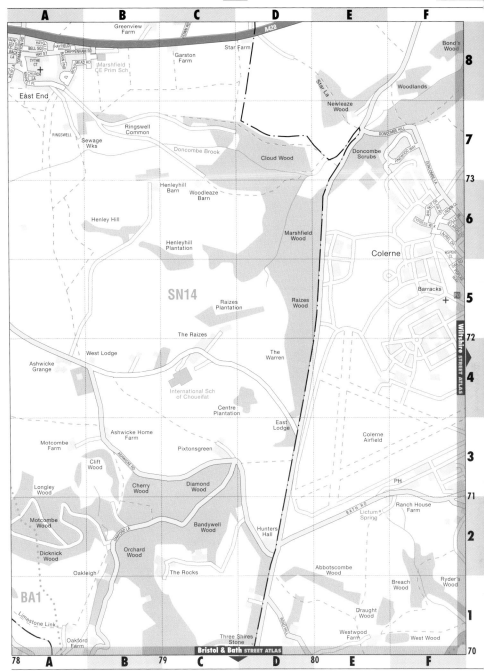

East End

Greenview Farm

Garston Farm

Star Farm

Marshfield CE Prim Sch

A420

Bond's Wood

Star La

Woodlands

Newleaze Wood

Ringswell

Sewage Wks

Ringswell Common

Doncombe Brook

Cloud Wood

Doncombe Hill

Doncombe Scrubs

Henleyhill Barn

Woodleaze Barn

Henley Hill

Henleyhill Plantation

Marshfield Wood

Colerne

Barracks

SN14

Raizes Plantation

Raizes Wood

The Raizes

West Lodge

The Warren

Ashwicke Grange

International Sch of Choueifat

Centre Plantation

East Lodge

Colerne Airfield

Ashwicke Home Farm

Motcombe Farm

Pixtonsgreen

Clift Wood

Cherry Wood

Diamond Wood

PH

Longley Wood

Bath Rd

Lictum Spring

Ranch House Farm

Motcombe Wood

Bandywell Wood

Hunters Hall

Dicknick Wood

Orchard Wood

Abbotscombe Wood

Breach Wood

Ryder's Wood

Oakleigh

The Rocks

BA1

Draught Wood

Westwood Farm

West Wood

Limestone Link

Oakford Farm

Three Shires Stone

Beach Hill

Wiltshire STREET ATLAS

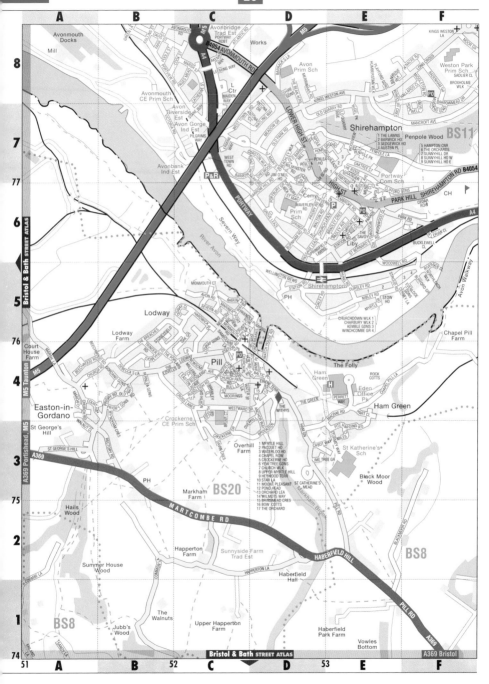

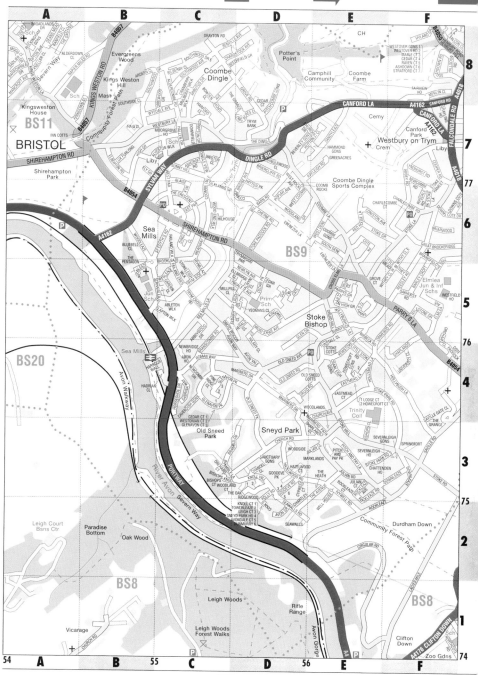

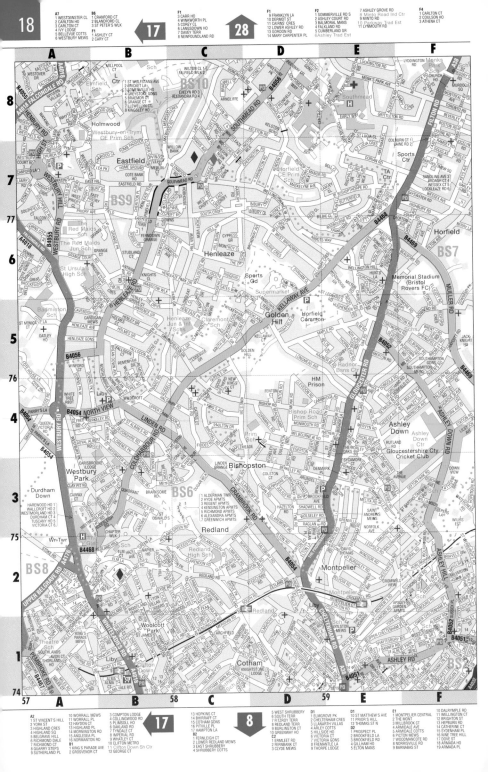

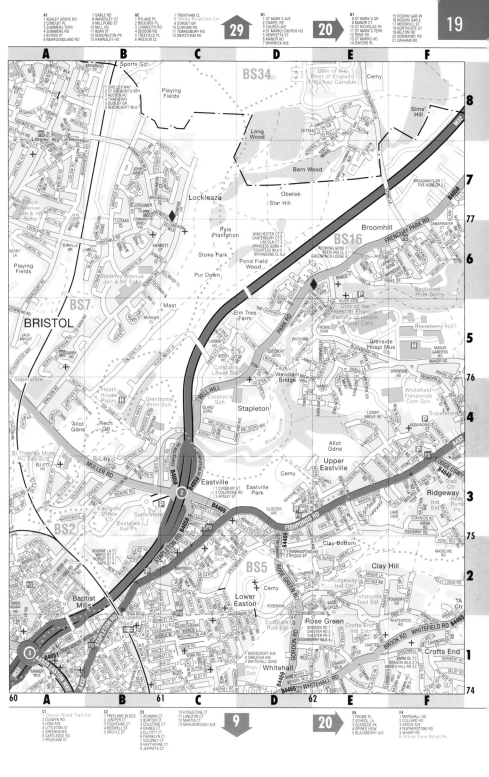

A1
1 ASHLEY GROVE RD
2 CONDUIT PL
3 SUMMERS TERR
4 SUMMERS RD
5 BYRON ST
6 NEWFOUNDLAND RD

7 GABLE RD
8 WAVERLEY ST
9 MILLPOND ST
10 MILL HO
11 BEAN ST
12 KENSINGTON PK
13 RAWNSLEY HO

A2
1 RYLAND PL
2 BOUCHER CT
3 PLYMOUTH RD
4 SEDDON RD
5 TREEFIELD PL
6 WEEDON CL

7 TRENTHAM CL
8 Minto Road Ind Ctr
9 DORSET GR
10 DURHAM RD
11 TEWKESBURY RD
12 MERSTHAM RD

B1
1 ST MARK'S AVE
2 CHAPEL RD
3 CHURCH AVE
4 ST MARKS CHURCH HO
5 HENRIETTA ST
6 MANOR HO
7 WARWICK AVE

B1
8 ST MARK'S GR
9 ST NICHOLAS PK
10 ST NICHOLAS CL
11 ST MARK'S TERR
12 IRENE RD
13 ST MARKS HO
14 OXFORD PL

15 ROSHNI GAR W
16 ROSHNI GAR E
17 MOORHILL ST
18 NORTHCOTE ST
19 BELTON RD
20 NORMANBY RD
21 GRAHAM RD

29

20

19

C1
1 Devon Road Trad Est
2 COLWYN RD
3 LENA AVE
4 LITTLETON ST
5 GREENHAVEN
6 CARTLEDGE RD
7 PRUDHAM ST

C2
1 FREELAND BLDGS
2 JUNIPER CT
3 FOUNTAINE CT
4 BOSWELL ST
5 ARGYLE ST

E3
1 ASHMAN CT
2 BURTON CT
3 COLSTONE CT
4 DAINES CT
5 ELLYOTT CT
6 FRANKLYN CT
7 GOLDNEY CT
8 HAYTHORNE CT
9 JEFFREYS CT

10 KYNGSTONE CT
11 LANGTON CT
12 MARTIN CT
13 MARLBOROUGH AVE

9

20

E5
1 FROME PL
2 SCHOOL LA
3 GLENSIDE PK
4 SPIRES VIEW
5 BLACKBERRY AVE

F4
1 MARSHALL HO
2 COLLARD HO
3 GROVE AVE
4 FEATHERSTONE RD
5 WHARF RD
6 Stoke View Bsns Pk

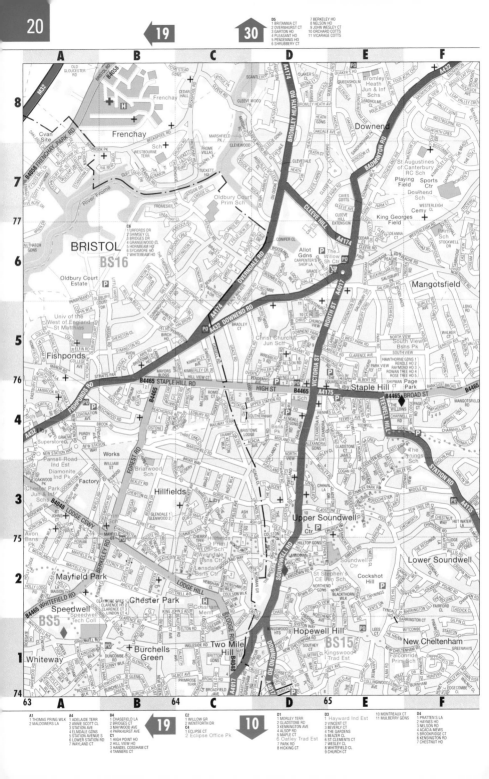

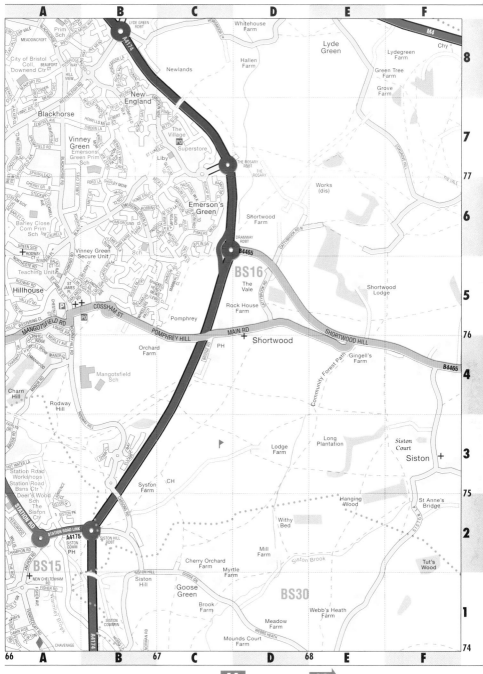

21
32

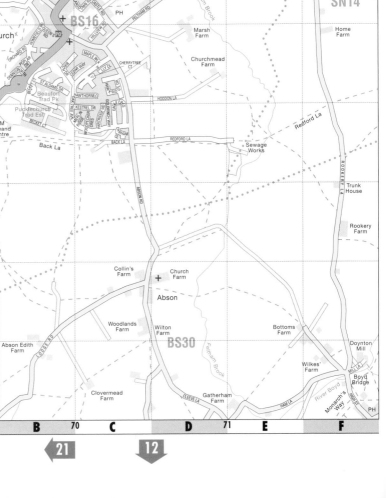

21
12

BS37

BS37

M4

Monarch's Way

M4

Park Farm

Ivy Cottage

St Aldam's Ash Farm

Barleyclose Farm

Lower Fields Farm

Bridehill Farm

8

7

Parkfield

PARKFIELD BANK

PARKFIELD RD

PH

King's La

WESTERLEIGH RD

BATCHFIELD LA

Pucklechurch CE Prim Sch

Cranford Farm

Feltham Brook

Feltham Farm

SN14

Home Farm

77

6

PH

BS16

Pucklechurch

Dennisworth Farm

Marsh Farm

Churchmead Farm

CHERRYTREE CT

5

Beaufort Trad Pk

Pucklechurch Trad Est

HAWTHORNE CT

KESTREL DR

HODDON LA

Redford La

76

HM Remand Centre

SHORTWOOD RD

B4465

BECKET CT

Back La

BACK LA

REDFORD LA

Sewage Works

Trunk House

ROOKERY LA

4

Primrose Wood

Northmead Farm

ABSON RD

Rookery Farm

3

Overscourt Farm

Collin's Farm

Church Farm

75

2

Abson

BS30

LOSSE RD

Abson Edith Farm

Woodlands Farm

Wilton Farm

Bottoms Farm

Fennum Brook

Doynton Mill

Wilkes' Farm

Boyd Bridge

MILL LA

1

Blue Lodge

Clovermead Farm

CLEEVE LA

Gatherham Farm

HAM LA

River Boyd

Monarch's Way

Boyd

PH

74

69   **70**   **71**

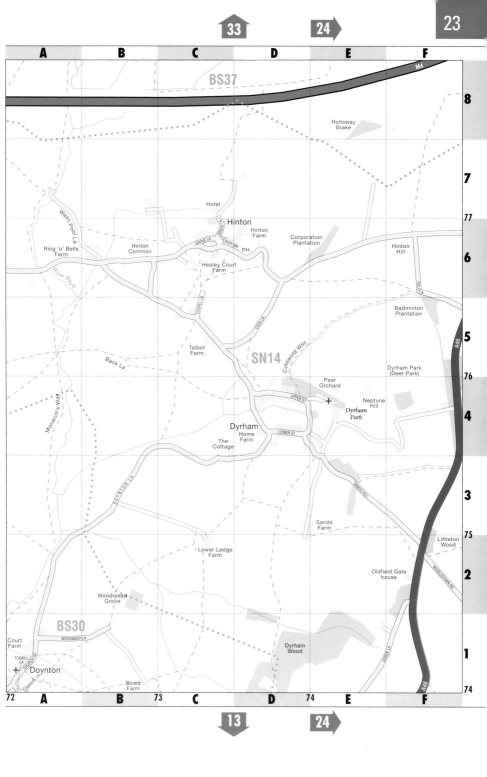

23
34

A **B** **C** **D** **E** **F**

8

Beacon Lane
Plantation
Cotswold Way
Mast

BS37

Beacon La

Lower Lapdown
Farm

MANSFIELD RD

Turnpike
Cottage

Turnpike
Farm

GL9

West Littleton Down

Rownham
Farm

7

77

PH Tolldown
Farm

6

Ebbdown
Farm

Camp Barn

Harcombe
Wood

5

Dunsdown
House

DUNSDOWN LA

Whiteshill
Barn

Harcombe
Farm

76

Dunsdown
Beeches

4

BUTT'S LA

Church
Farm

CAMP LA

Manor
Farm

Home
Farm

West
Farm

West Littleton

SN14

Broadmead Brook

3

Upper
Farm

Slait La

Cadwell Hill

75

Littleton Wood
Barn

Cadwellhill
Barn

WEST LITTLETON RD

RUSHMEAD LA

CASTLE
COTTS

2

Springs
Farm

Middledown
House

MIDDLEDOWN RD

Westend Town
Farm

Castle
Farm

Westland
Farm

CASTLE LA

GEORGE LA

NORTHWICK LA

1

Oldfield
Copse

Westend
Farm

BIRD'S LA

74

A **B** **C** **D** **E** **F**
75   76   77

23
14

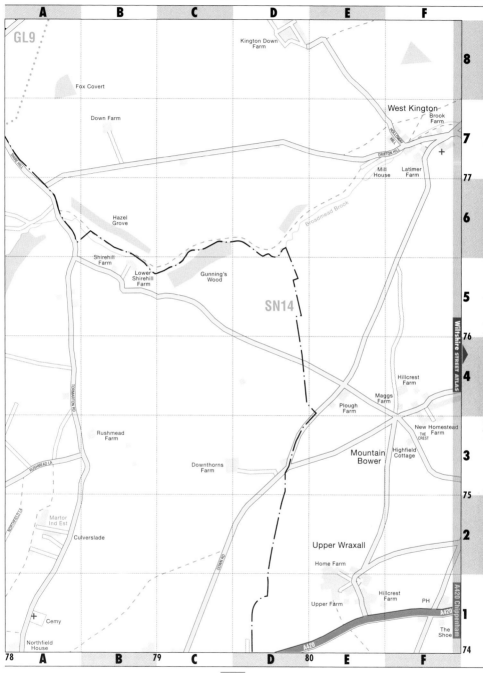

GL9

8

Kington Down Farm

Fox Covert

Down Farm

West Kington

Brook Farm

7

HOLLOWAY HILL

DRIFTON HILL

77

Mill House

Latimer Farm

Broadmead Brook

6

Hazel Grove

Shirehill Farm

Lower Shirehill Farm

Gunning's Wood

SN14

5

76

4

Hillcrest Farm

Maggs Farm

TORMARTON RD

Plough Farm

New Homestead Farm

THE CREST

Rushmead Farm

RUSHMEAD LA

Downthorns Farm

Mountain Bower

Highfield Cottage

3

75

NORTHFIELD LA

Martor Ind Est

DOWN RD

Upper Wraxall

2

Culverslade

Home Farm

Hillcrest Farm

PH

A420 Chippenham

Upper Farm

A420

A420

The Shoe

1

Cemy

Northfield House

74

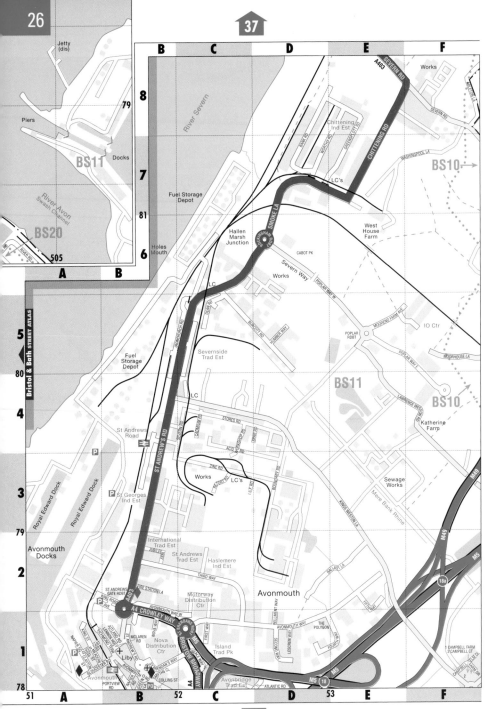

Bristol & Bath STREET ATLAS

Jetty (dis)

Piers

BS11

Docks

79

8

7

81

6

River Severn

Fuel Storage Depot

Holes Mouth

Hallen Marsh Junction

SMOKE LA

A4018

BRISTOL RD

CABOT PK

Severn Way

Works

LC

A403

SEVERN RD

Works

SEVERN RD

Chittening Ind Est

BRAN RD

ROUSH RD

CHELSTON RD

CHITTENING RD

LC's

WASHINGPOOL LA

BS10

West House Farm

POPLAR WAY W

IO Ctr

MOOREND FARM AVE

POPLAR RDBT

POPLAR WAY E

MOORHOUSE LA

BS11

BS10

LAWRENCE WESTON RD

Katherine Farm

Sewage Works

Mere Bank Rhine

KINGS WESTON LA

River Avon Swash Channel

BS20

505

5

80

4

79

3

2

1

78

Fuel Storage Depot

Severnside Trad Est

LC

DEAN RD

BRUNSWICK RD

BENNETT RD

PEMBER WAY

St Andrews Road

St Andrew's Rd

P

LC

CHADMOUTH RD

STORES RD

WORKSHOP RD

BEMSTED RD

BOUNDARY RD

ACID RD

ZINC RD

Works

BEDFORD RD

LC's

I.S.E. RD

P

St Georges Ind Est

International Trad Est

St Andrews Trad Est

Haslemere Ind Est

JUBILEE RD

THIRD WAY

Avonmouth

BALLARD LA

FIFTH WAY

Royal Edward Dock

Royal Edward Dock

Avonmouth Docks

P

St Andrews Gate RDBT

A403

FIRE STATION LA

Motorway Distribution Ctr

P

A4 CROWLEY WAY

McLAREN RD

Nova Distribution Ctr

FIRST WAY

AVONMOUTH WAY W

AVONMOUTH WAY

Island Trad Pk

THE POLYGON

LESCREN WAY

WILLMENT WAY

MILLENNIUM WAY

FIFTH WAY

M49

M5

18a

M5

M5

18

Campbell Farm
Campbell Ct

CAMPBELL FARM DR

M49

Liby

Avonmouth

PORTVIEW RD

KING ST

COLLINS ST

NOVA SCOTIA PL

M5 BRISTOL BRIDGE DIVING

Avonbridge Trad Est

ATLANTIC RD

A4

P

51

A

B

52

C

D

53

E

F

A

B

C

D

E

F

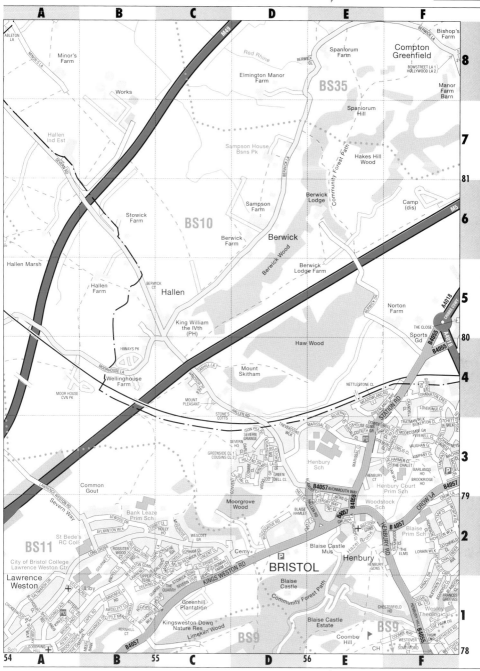

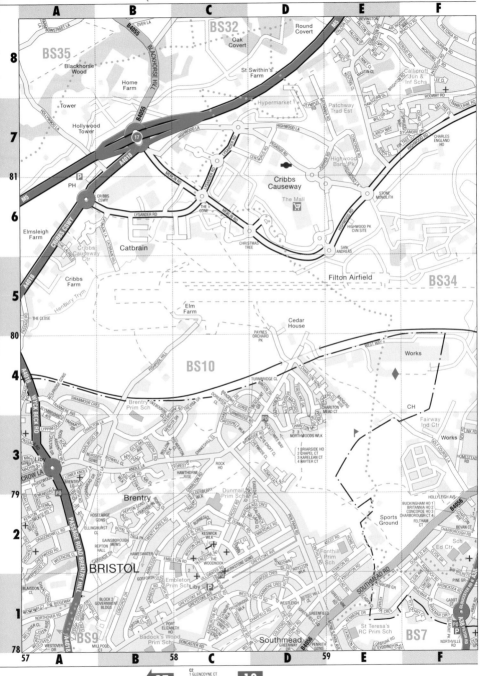

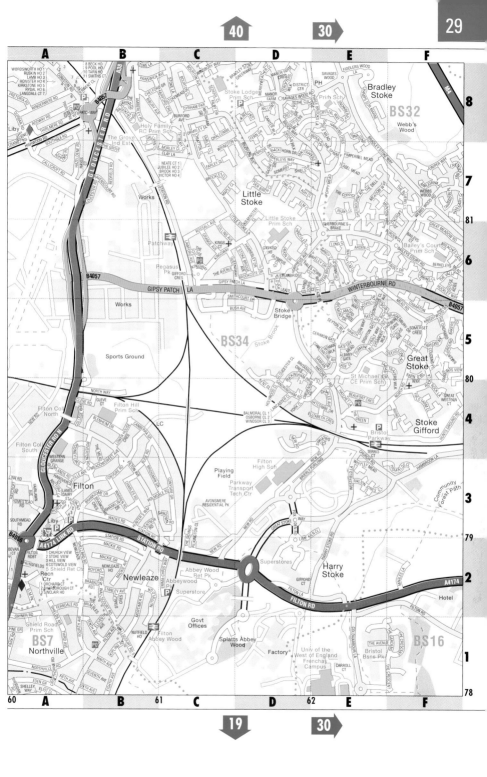

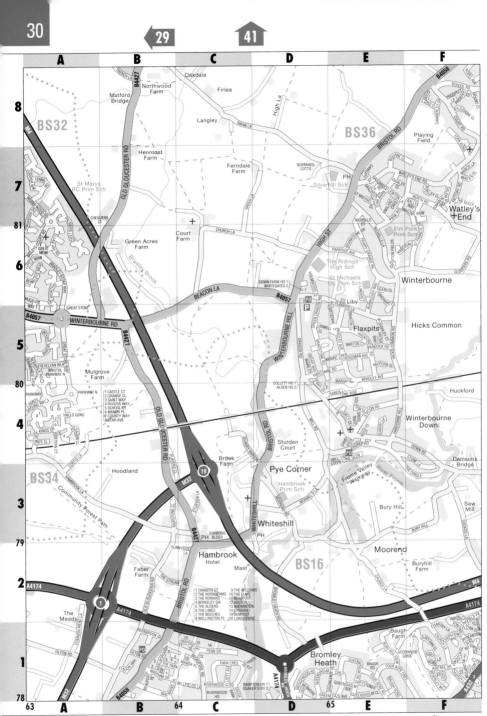

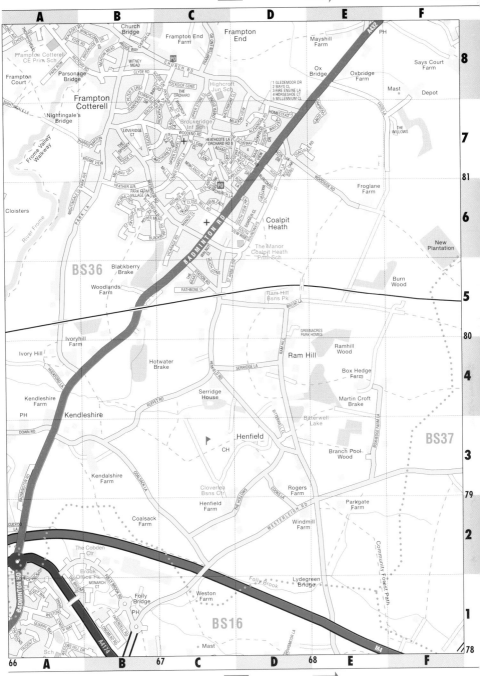

31
43

D7
1 MINSTER CT
2 FOUNTAIN CT
3 MONKS HO
4 FRIARS HO
5 ABBEY HO
6 PRINKNASH CT

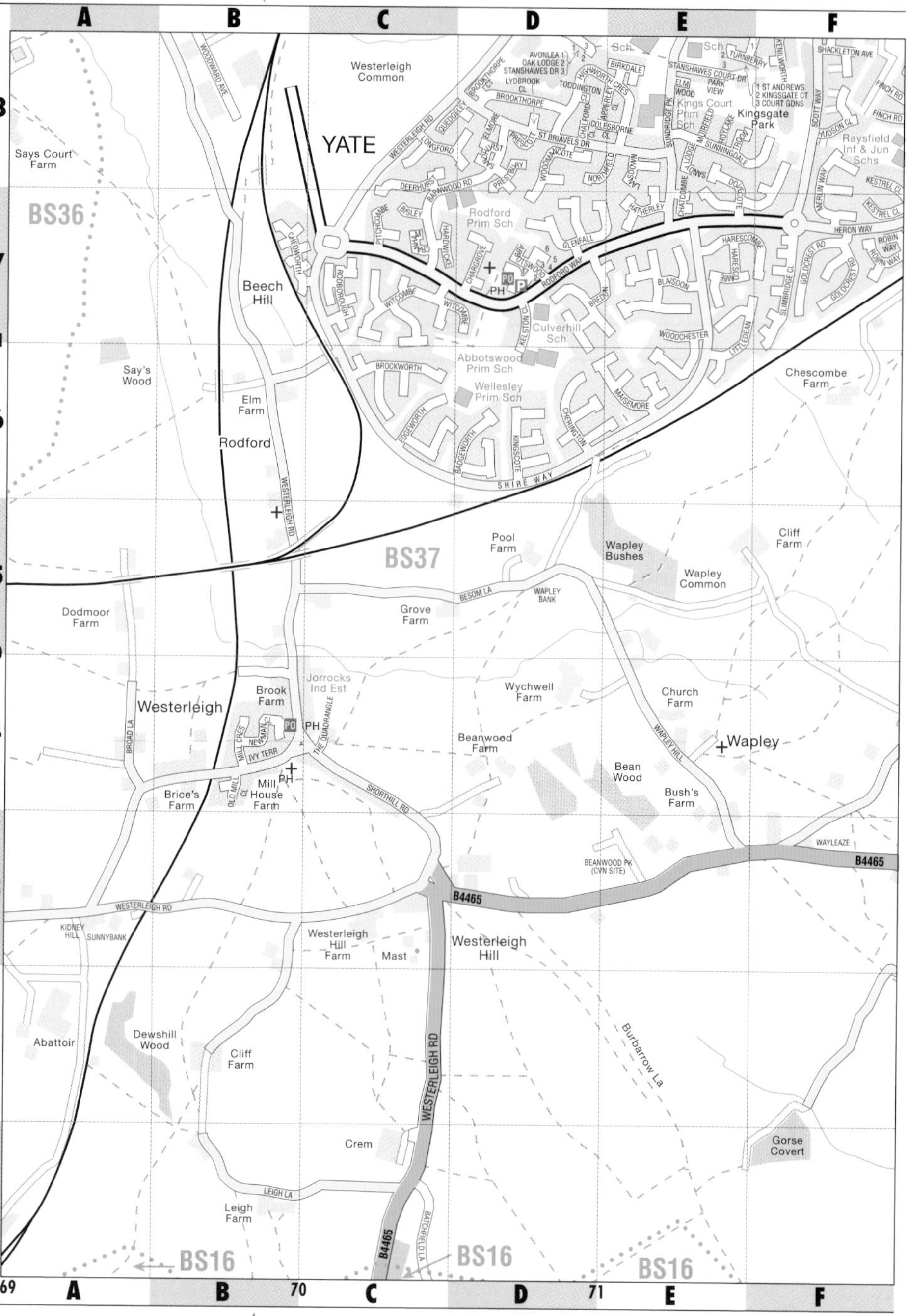

A   B   C   D   E   F

8

Says Court Farm

BS36

7

Westerleigh Common

YATE

Beech Hill

81

Say's Wood

Elm Farm

Rodford

6

Westerleigh Common

Rodford Prim Sch

Culverhill Sch

Abbotswood Prim Sch

Wellesley Prim Sch

Chescombe Farm

Kingsgate Park

Raysfield Inf & Jun Schs

1 ST ANDREWS
2 KINGSGATE CL
3 COURT GDNS

SHIRE WAY

5

BS37

Dodmoor Farm

Pool Farm

Wapley Bushes

Wapley Common

Cliff Farm

80

Grove Farm

BESOM LA

WAPLEY BANK

4

Westerleigh

Brook Farm

Jorrocks Ind Est

THE QUADRANGLE

Wychwell Farm

Beanwood Farm

Bean Wood

Church Farm

Wapley

Bush's Farm

Brice's Farm

Mill House Farm

SHORTHILL RD

WAPLEY HILL

WAYLEAZE

B4465

3

Kidley Hill   Sunnybank

WESTERLEIGH RD

Westerleigh Hill Farm   Mast

Westerleigh Hill

BEANWOOD PK (CVN SITE)

B4465

79

2

Abattoir

Dewshill Wood

Cliff Farm

Burberrow La

Gorse Covert

1

Crem

WESTERLEIGH RD

LEIGH LA

Leigh Farm

78

BS16   BS16   BS16

69   70   71

A   B   C   D   E   F

31
22

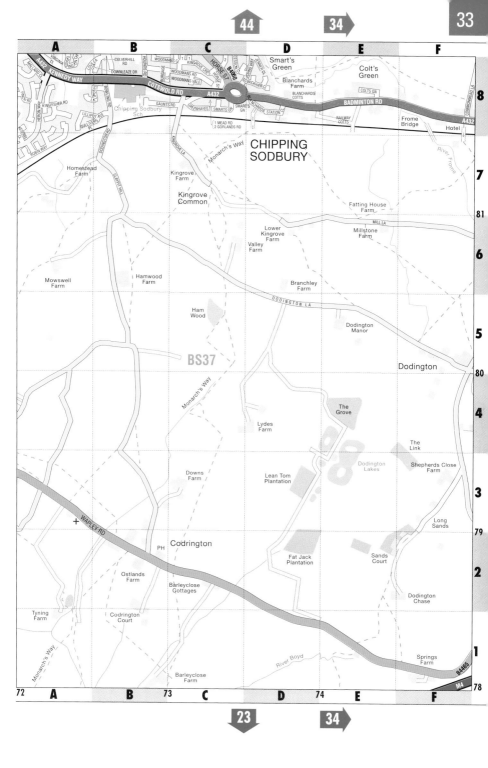

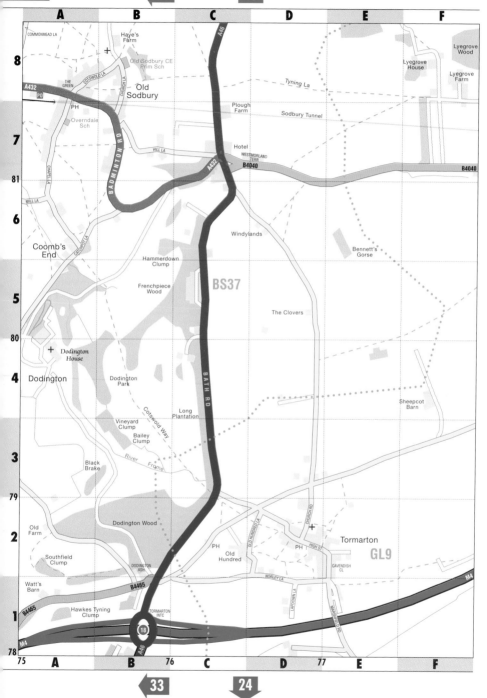

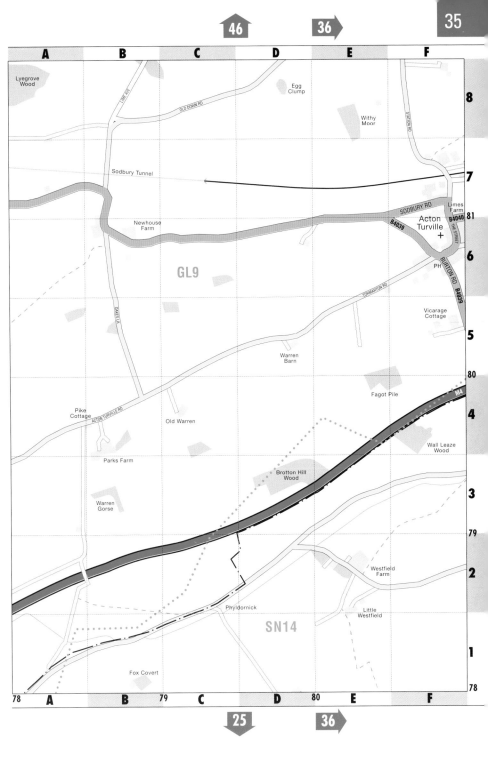

Map labels:

8
7
81
6
5
80
4
3
79
2
1
78

A   B   C   D   E   F

Lyegrove Wood

Egg Clump

Withy Moor

STATION RD

LIME AV

OLD DOWN RD

Sodbury Tunnel

Limes Farm

SODBURY RD

B4040

Acton Turville

B4039

THE STREET

Newhouse Farm

GL9

PH

BURTON RD

B4039

TORMARTON RD

Vicarage Cottage

OAKES LA

Warren Barn

M4

Fagot Pile

Pike Cottage

ACTON TURVILLE RD

Old Warren

Wall Leaze Wood

Parks Farm

Brotton Hill Wood

Warren Gorse

Westfield Farm

Phyldornick

Little Westfield

SN14

Fox Covert

78   A   B   79   C   D   80   E   F

Centre Walk Brake

B4040

Cranhill Wood

8

Alderton Grove Farm

Macmillan Way

Alderton Grove

7

B4040

81

1 CHESTNUT CL
2 LITTLETON DREW LA
3 HOLLYBUSH CL

GL9

Trinity CE Prim Sch

Goulter's Gorse

Hollybush Farm

6

ALDERTON RD

YINGER'S LA

Ivy Leaze

Manor Farm

Littleton Drew

5

B4039

Withy Beds

Townsend Farm

80

M4

MARSH LA

Mast

4

HILLSIDE

New House Farm

PH

New Town

M4 Swindon

THE STREET

DOWN WAY

FREDERICK'S PL

BURTON FARM CL

Burton

SN14

Horsedown

The Gibb

3

THE MEADS

Step Hill Plantation

SUMMER LA

Goulter's Hill Farm

PH

B4039

The Piggeries

Littleworth Plantation

Fosse Bridge

FOSSCOMBE LA

79

NETTLETON RD

Macmillan Way

Gatcombe Plantation

2

Green Farm

Priory Farm

Lugbury Longbarrow

Mill

Gatcombe Hill

Nettleton Green

PH

Gatcombe Wood

1

Hanger Wood

Elm Tree Farm

Manor Farm

Square Plantation

LONG LEASE

78

Garrick Wood

Wiltshire STREET ATLAS

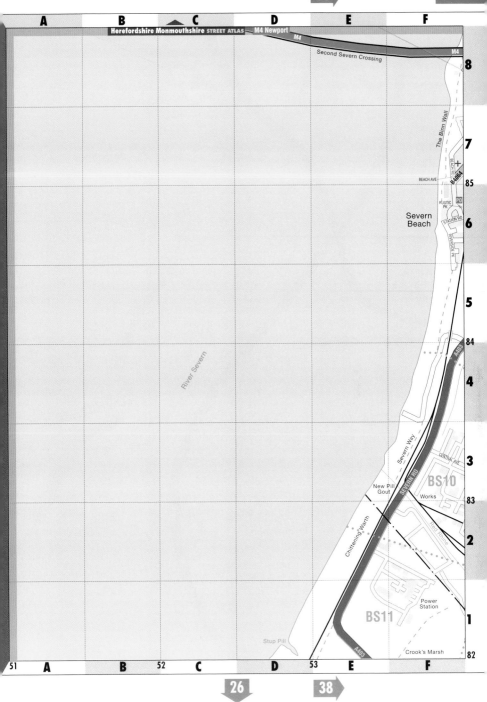

M4 Newport

M4

Second Severn Crossing

M4

The Binn Wall

8

7

BEACH RD

BEACH AVE

B4064

85

RUSTIC PK

PO

STATION RD

Severn Beach

6

RIVERSIDE PK

5

A403

84

River Severn

4

Severn Way

CENTRAL AVE

3

SEVERN RD

BS10

New Pill Gout

Works

83

Chittening Warth

Rail Rd Line

2

Power Station

BS11

1

Stup Pill

Crook's Marsh

A403

82

51

52

53

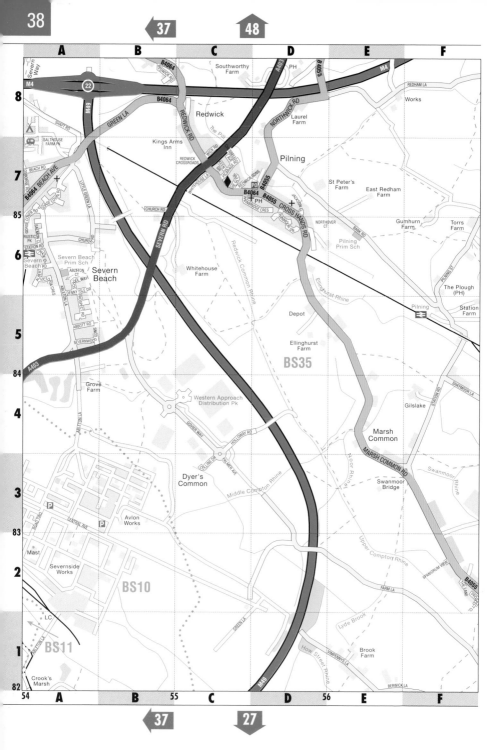

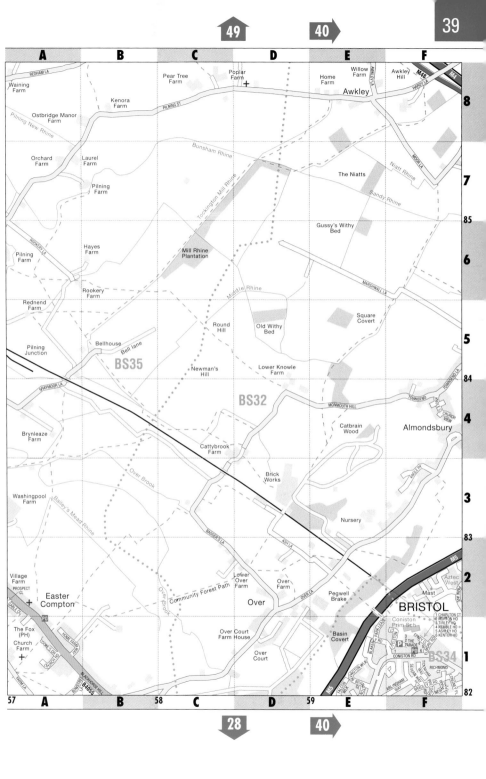

A B C D E F

8

M4
M48
Sewage Works
MOOR LA
LOWER TOCKINGTON RD
The Roundabout
Lower Woodhouse Farm
Harts
A38
BS35
Gatten's Brake
TOCKINGTON PARK LA
Tockington Park Farm

7

Woodcock Hill
Woodhouse
FERNHILL
Fernhill Farm
FERNDALE CL
Woodhouse Down
WOODHOUSE AVE
Tockington Park wood

85

Sewage Works
Meerbrook Farm
FERNHILL CT
WOODHOUSE CL/THE CL
Hortham Wood

6

Cemy
Lower Almondsbury
THE QUODRIE/WEST/BISHOP'S WOOD
GLOUCESTER RD
HORTHAM LA
Hortham Farm
M5

5

Lower Court Farm
CHESTERMASTER CL
WALNUT TREE CL/COURT FARM CL
ALMONDSBURY
CHURCH RD
THE SCOP
FLORENCE
CHURCH LA
GLEN FIELD
PO
Woodlands Wood
WOODLANDS LA
Colony Farm

84

Almondsbury CE Prim Sch
MARSHWALL LA
LOWER COURT CL
THE POUND
CHURCH RD
SUNDAYS HILL
HOLLOW RD
OVER LA
THE HILL
RED HOUSE LA
PH
BS32

4

Almondsbury Hill
OAKLANDS DR
Mast
Sports Gd
WEST POINT ROW
RAC Twr
BROTHERSWOOD
20
15
ALMONDSBURY INTC
Hortham Brook

3

A38
16
PO
Orpen Pk
Mast
Interplex 16
WOODLAND MEAD LA
WEST POINT ROW
HEMPTON LA/FONTHILL
ASTBY PARK RD
Almondsbury Bsns Ctr
ST JAMES
Equinox Eagles Wood Bsns Pk
Mast
NORTH CT
SOUTH CT
BUCKINGHAM CT
EAGLES WOOD
BLENHEIM
CROWS DR
HAWKLEY DR
Mast

83

A38
The Quadrant
PO
WOODLANDS
WOODLANDS LA
Holy Trinity Prim Sch
COOKS CL
FOX CLOSE
PADDOCK CL
PELICAN CL
MERLIN LEAZE
TRENCH LA
CH
West Country Water Park

2

PARK AVE
Aztec West
The Aztec Ctr
PARK AVE
HEMPTON LA
COURTNEY CRES
Patchway
PATCHWAY BROOK
PATCHWAY BROOK
BOWLAND WAY
PENROSE
HIGHAM
BOWLAND
Sch
BOWLAND
Patchway Brook
BS36

1

Playing Field
Patchway High Sch
AWNELL DR
THE CLOSE
THE COMMON
ALBION TERR
STAVERTON
HIGHWOOD
PATCHWAY CE Prim Sch
SAXON WAY
Wheatfield Prim Sch
BRADLEY STOKE WAY
BOWLAND
SACKVILLE
Community Forest Path
Savage's Wood
Superstore
L Ctr & Liby

82

BRISTOL
WATERSIDE RD
LONGWAY
COLERIDGE RD
CONISTON RD
SHELLEY RD
BS34
MAISEMORE AVE
SANDHURST CL
SHELLMOR MANOR LEAZE
A38
M4

60 A B 61 C D 62 E F

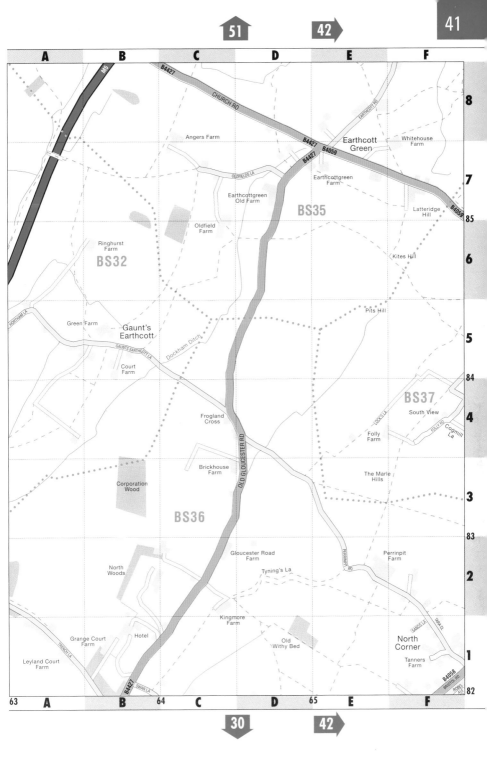

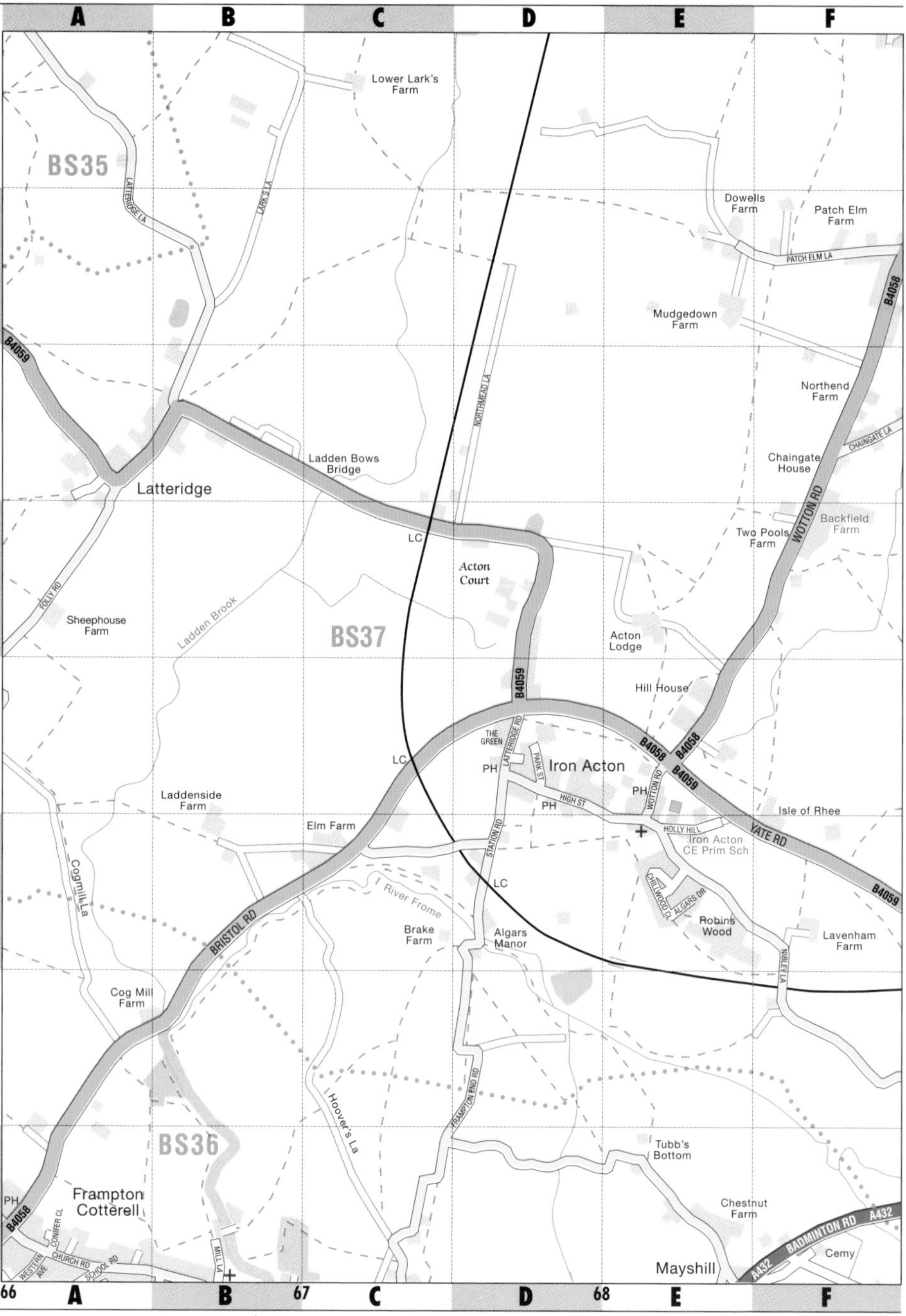

A B C D E F

8
7
85
6
5
84
4
3
83
2
1
82

66 67 68

BS35

LATTERIDGE LA

LARKS LA

Lower Lark's Farm

Dowells Farm

Patch Elm Farm

PATCH ELM LA

B4058

Mudgedown Farm

Northend Farm

B4058

NORTHMEAD LA

Ladden Bows Bridge

Latteridge

CHAINGATE LA

Chaingate House

Backfield Farm

WOTTON RD

Two Pools Farm

LC

Acton Court

BS37

Acton Lodge

Hill House

Isle of Rhee

B4058

B4058

B4058

B4059

TOLL RD

Sheephouse Farm

Ladden Brook

LC

THE GREEN

PH

LATTERIDGE LA

Iron Acton

PH

GATE RD

B4059

Laddenside Farm

Elm Farm

HIGH ST

PH

Iron Acton CE Prim Sch

HOLLY HILL

NIBLEY LA

COGMILL LA

BRISTOL RD

STATION RD

River Frome

LC

Brake Farm

Algars Manor

CHURCH RD

ATLAS DR

Robins Wood

Lavenham Farm

B4059

Cog Mill Farm

HOOVER'S LA

FRAMPTON END RD

Tubb's Bottom

BS36

PH

B4058

Frampton Cotterell

WESTON AVE

CONNER CL

CHURCH RD

SCHOOL RD

MILL LA

Chestnut Farm

Mayshill

BADMINTON RD

A432

A432

Cemy

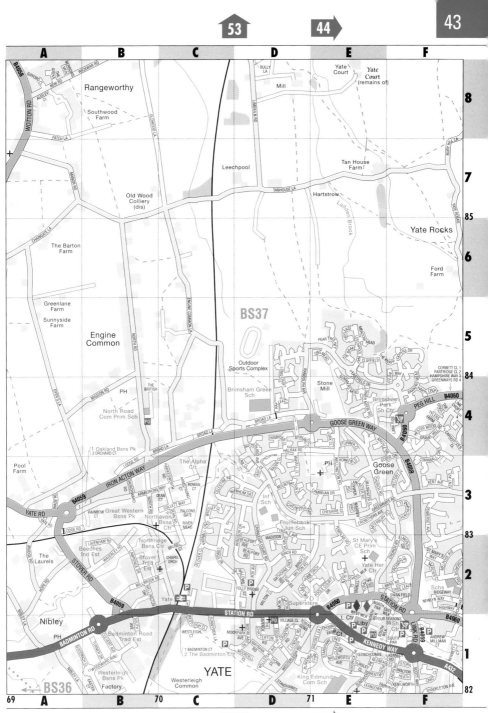

43
54

A **B** **C** **D** **E** **F**

8

Oxwick Farm

Lady's Wood

Horwood Riding Farm

B4060

BURY HILL LA

The Chase

Springfield Farm

VINNEY LA

Bury Hill

Lattimore Farm

Little Wood

7

Brinsham Wood

85

Hares Farm

Brinsham Farm

Brinsham Bridge

MAPLERIDGE LA

Ashlea Farm

BRINSHAM LA

6

WICKWAR RD

Horton Bushes

Quarry

GRAVEL HILL RD

5

Home Farm

Quarry

Quarry

BS37

Sodbury Common

Totteroak

Rockwood

84

ROCKWOOD HO

Totteroak Farm

B4060

PEG HILL

SOUTHFIELD WAY

Star Vale Farm

Winchcombe Farm

4

LOVE LA

LIME CROFT

BARNHILL CL

HORTON RD

Little Sodbury End

Greystone Ct

CARMARTHEN CL

PETTER WAY

WILLOW

Stub Riding

Mead Riding

CH

The Windmill

Great House Farm

3

YATE

Monarch's Way

Lodge

DORSE

BROADWAY

JUBILEE CL

MELROSE CL

83

PRIMROSE

2

PORTWAY LA

Hardwoodgate Farm

DOWNING'S CL

CAROLINE CL

COUZENS CL

BROOKFIELD CL

JOHN WAY

JOHNS WAY

River Frome

Park's Farm

Works

Bowling Hill Bsns Pk

Mill

Cemy

BARNHILL RD

STONE HOUSE MEWS

Chipping Edge Est

BEAUFORE MEWS

ROGERS

COTTEN CT

Trad Est

CHIPPING SODBURY

1

B4060

BOWLING HILL

ROUNCEVAL ST

THE PARADE

HIGH ST

TH

BROAD

WALSHE CT

HARTLEY CL

WHITEFIELDS

GESSON CL

Liby

Prim Sch

COPSWOLD

HORSESHOE LA

BARNOLD

HOUNDS CL

ABBEYFIELD HO

MEAD RD

82

GRASSINGTON DR

HIGHFIELD

A **B** **C** **D** **E** **F**

72 73 74

43
33

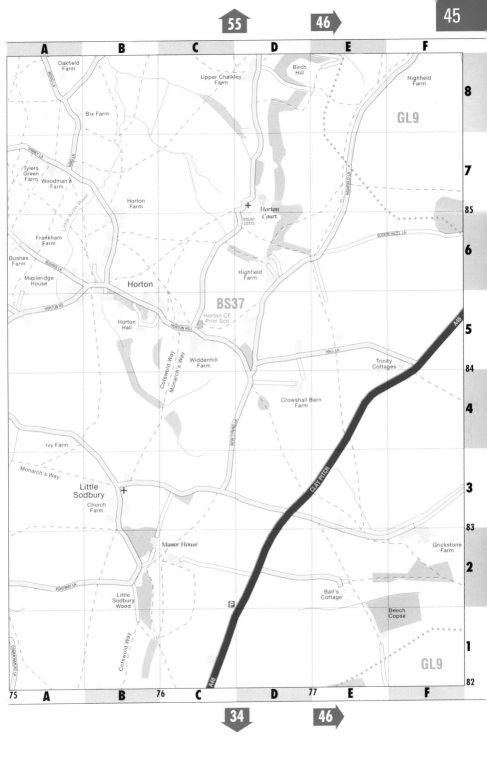

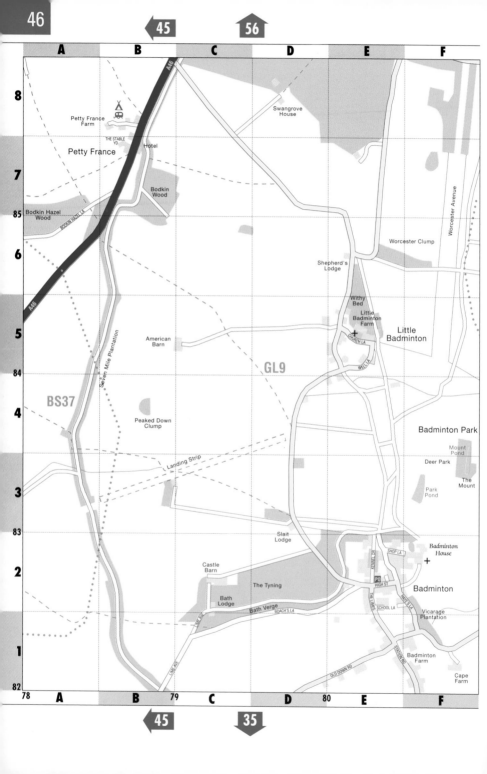

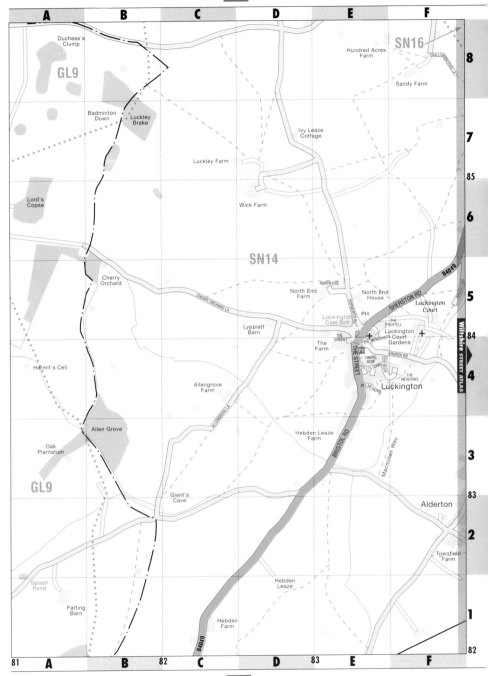

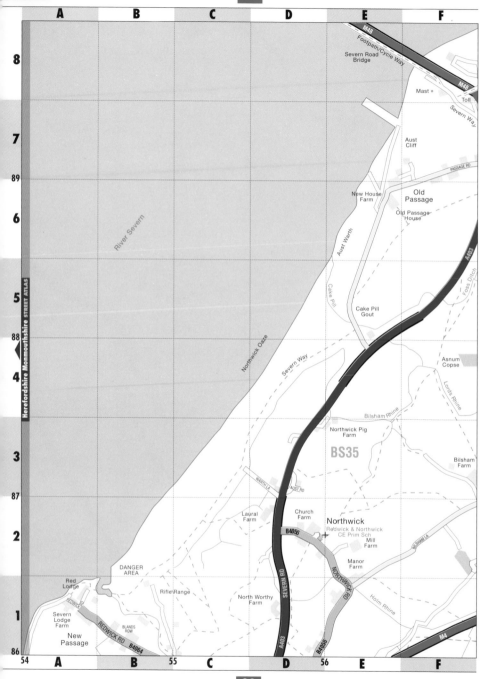

A **B** **C** **D** **E** **F**

8

7

89

6

5

88

4

3

87

2

87

1

86

54 **A** **B** 55 **C** **D** 56 **E** **F**

Herefordshire Monmouthshire STREET ATLAS

M48
Footpath/Cycle Way
Severn Road Bridge
M48
Mast
Toll
Severn Way
Aust Cliff
PASSAGE RD
New House Farm
Old Passage
Old Passage House
A403
Aust Warth
Foss Ditch
Cake Pill
Cake Pill Gout
Asnum Copse
River Severn
Northwick Oaze
Severn Way
Lords Rhine
Bilsham Rhine
Northwick Pig Farm
BS35
Bilsham Farm
WARTH LA
AUST RD
Laural Farm
Church Farm
Northwick
Redwick & Northwick CE Prim Sch
B4055
Mill Farm
SHAW LA
Manor Farm
DANGER AREA
Red Lodge
Rifle Range
North Worthy Farm
SEVERN RD
NORTHWICK RD
Holm Rhine
REDWICK RD
Severn Lodge Farm
BLANDS ROW
New Passage
B4064
B4055
A403
M4

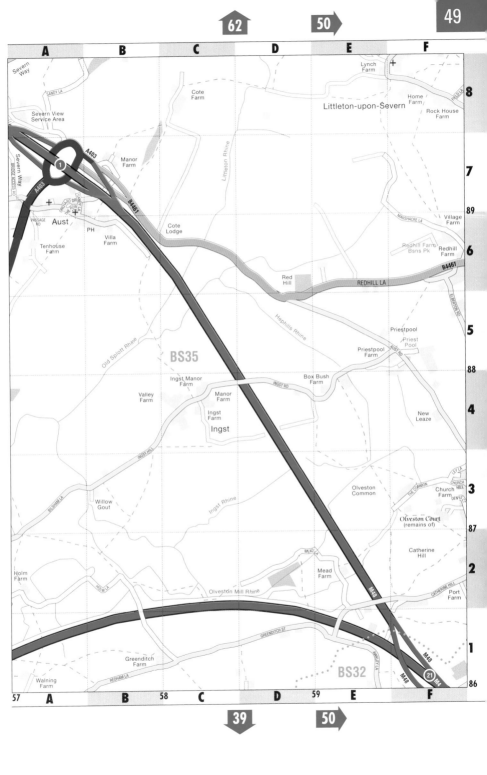

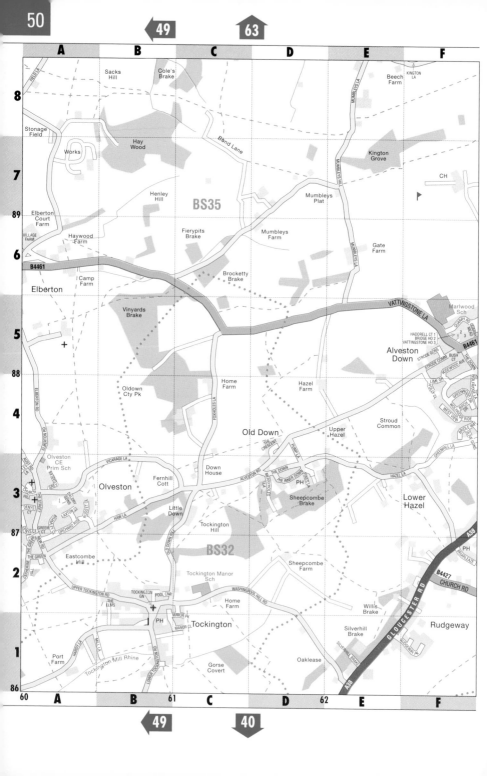

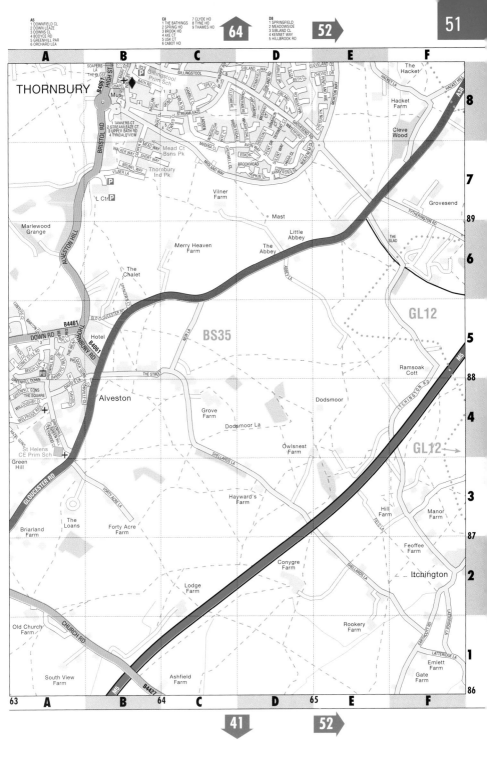

A5
1 DOWNFIELD CL
2 DOWN LEAZE
3 DOWNS CL
4 BODYCE RD
5 GREENHILL PAR
6 ORCHARD LEA

C8
1 THE BATHINGS
2 SPRING HO
3 BROOK HO
4 AXE CT
5 USK CT
6 CABOT HO

7 CLYDE HO
8 TYNE HO
9 THAMES HO

D8
1 SPRINGFIELD
2 MEADOWSIDE
3 SIBLAND CL
4 KENNET WAY
5 HILLBROOK RD

64

52

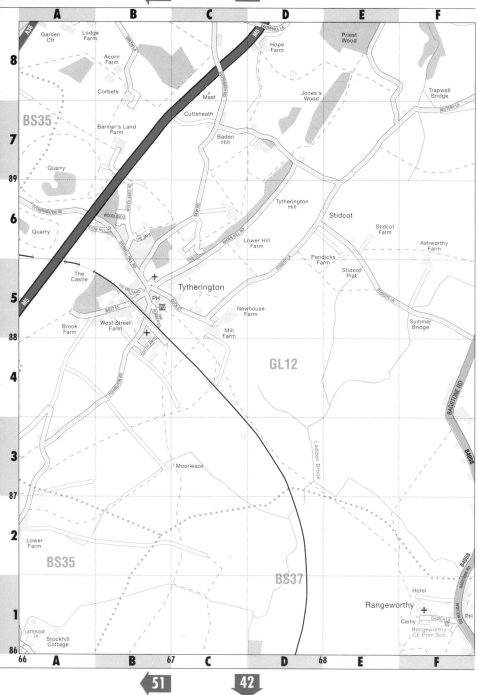

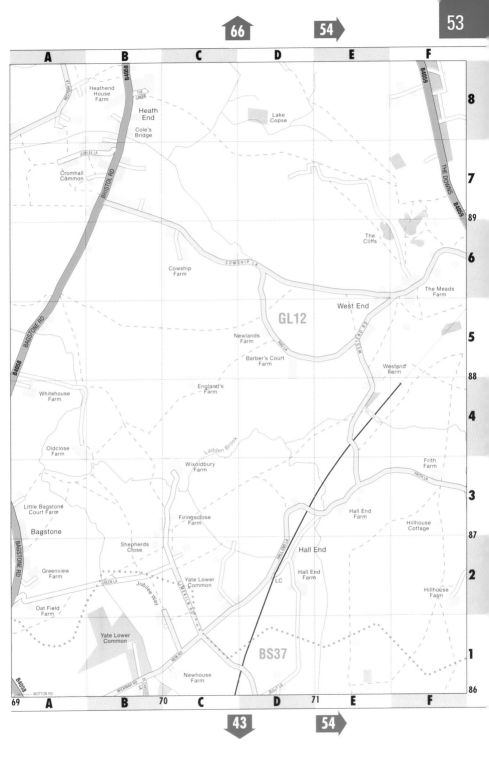

	A	B	C	D	E	F

8

Southwood Farm

Bunsall Bridge

Archfield Nursery

B4060

Cherryrock Farm

Cherryrock Brake

Haroldsfield Farm

Mounteney's Farm

7

Station House
Trad Est

STATION RD

Chasehouse Farm

Kites Farm

Mounteney's La

89

CHURCH LA

CHASE LA

Chaselane Farm

Chase Hill

Ingleslone Farm

6

B4058

WESTEND RD

THE DOWNS

B4060

PH

NORTH ST

Saltmoors Ditch

South Moon Ridings

GL12

Arnolds Field
Trad Est

TH

Alexander Hosea Prim Sch

HIGH ST

COTSWOLD VIEW

The Walk

Sturt Farm

5

SOUTHEND HO

SOUTHEND RD

Wickwar

Sturt Bridge

Little Stanley Wood

Lower Woods Lodge

88

Little Avon River

GL9

4

South Farm

Poplar Farm

POPLAR LA

HORWOOD LA

Horwood Farm

Wetmoor Nature Reserve

Littley Wood

3

FRITH LA

SODBURY RD

Hill View Farm

Bishop's Hill Wood

Upper Wetmoor

Lower Wetmoor Wood

87

Pincots Farm

PINCOTS LA

Bishop's Hill Brook

Sturgeon Wood

Burnt Wood

2

WICKWAR RD

Bedford's Wood

Bays Wood

BS37

Stonybridge Wood

1

Little Shortwood Farm

Shortwood Farm

Haskin's Farm

WOOD LA

86

B4060

Birdsbush Farm

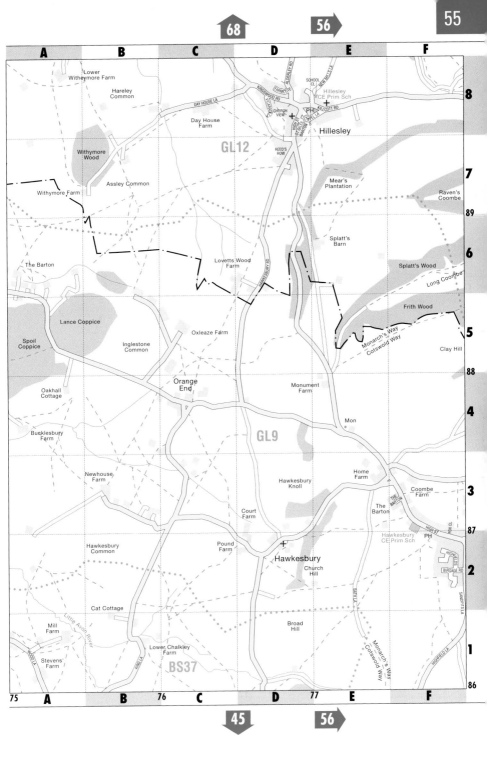

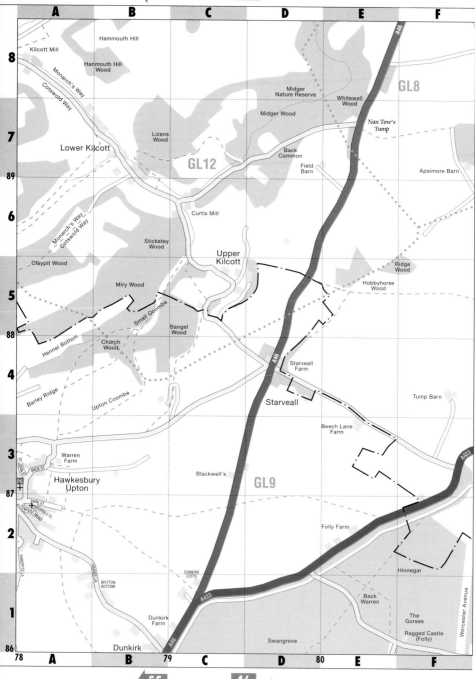

55
69

A B C D E F

8

Kilcott Mill

Hammouth Hill

Hanmouth Hill
Wood

Monarch's Way

Cotswold Way

Midger
Nature Reserve

GL8

7

Lizens
Wood

Midger Wood

Whitewell
Wood

Nan Tow's
Tump

Lower Kilcott

GL12

Back
Common

89

Field
Barn

Apsimore Barn

6

Monarch's Way
Cotswold Way

Curtis Mill

Cfaypit Wood

Sticksley
Wood

Upper
Kilcott

Ridge
Wood

5

Miry Wood

Small Coombe

Hobbyhorse
Wood

88

Hennel Bottom

Church
Wood

Bangel
Wood

4

Barley Ridge

Upton Coombe

A46

Starveall
Farm

Starveall

Tump Barn

3

Warren
Farm

ST JOHN

BACK ST

Blackwell's

Beech Lane
Farm

87

PO

MALEYPOLE CL

PARK ST

Hawkesbury
Upton

GL9

2

ST PEALS ROAD

SANDPITS LA

FRENCH LA

BRITTON
BOTTOM

Folly Farm

Hinnegar

1

Dunkirk
Farm

DUNKIRK
COTTS

A433

Back
Warren

The
Gorses

Ragged Castle
(Folly)

Worcester Avenue

86

Dunkirk

Swangrove

78 A B 79 C D 80 E F

55
46

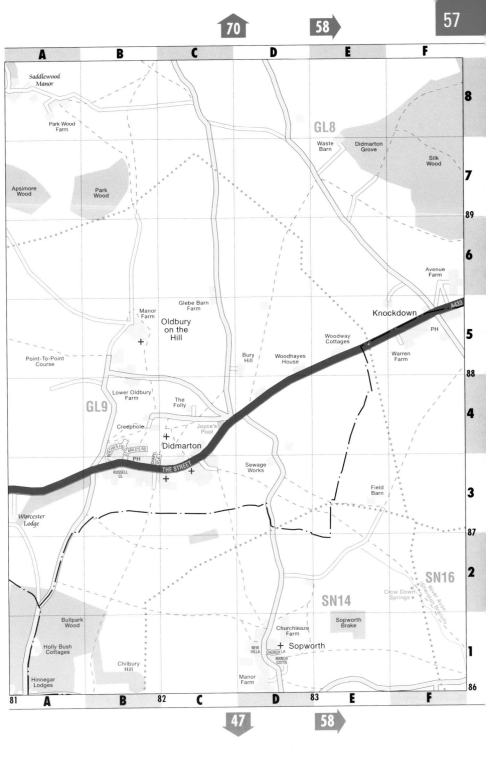

57
71

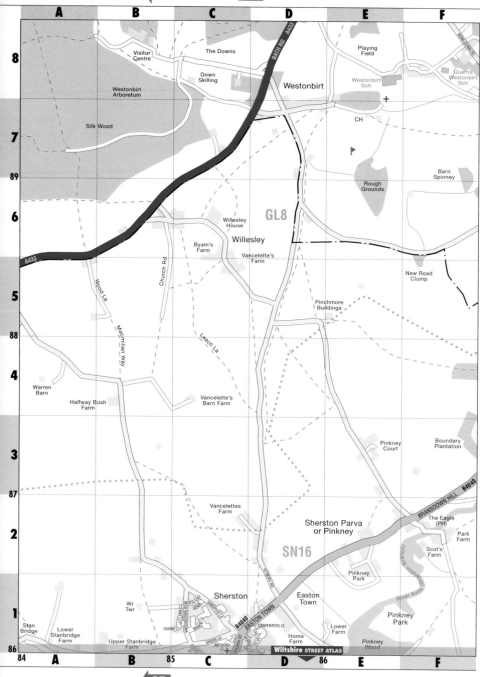

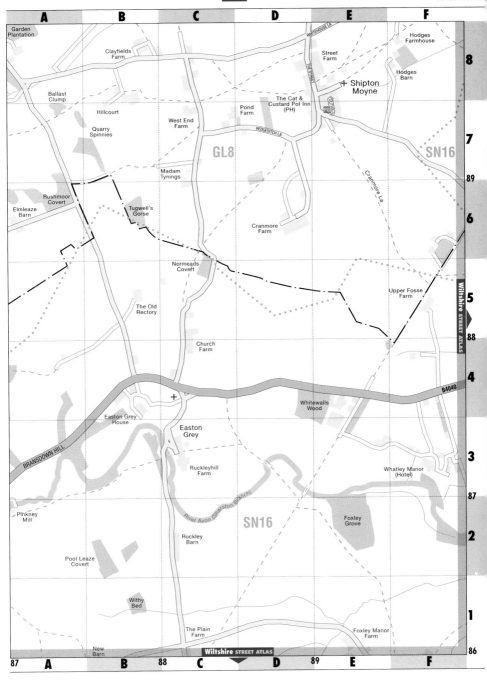

Garden
Plantation

Clayfields
Farm

Ballast
Clump

Hillcourt

Quarry
Spinnies

West End
Farm

Madam
Tynings

Rushmoor
Covert

Elmleaze
Barn

Tugwell's
Gorse

Normeads
Covert

The Old
Rectory

Church
Farm

Easton Grey
House

Easton
Grey

Ruckleyhill
Farm

BRANSDOWN HILL

Pinkney
Mill

Pool Leaze
Covert

Ruckley
Barn

Withy
Bed

New
Barn

The Plain
Farm

WHITEHOUSE LA

THE STREET

Street
Farm

✛ Shipton
Moyne

The Cat &
Custard Pot Inn
(PH)

Pond
Farm

HEDGEDITCH LA

GL8

Cranmore
Farm

Whitewalls
Wood

River Avon (Sherston Branch)

SN16

Foxley
Grove

Whatley Manor
(Hotel)

Foxley Manor
Farm

B4040

Hodges
Farmhouse

Hodges
Barn

Cranmore La

SN16

Upper Fosse
Farm

Wiltshire STREET ATLAS

A   B   C   D   E   F

8
7
89
6
5
88
4
3
87
2
1
86

87   88   89

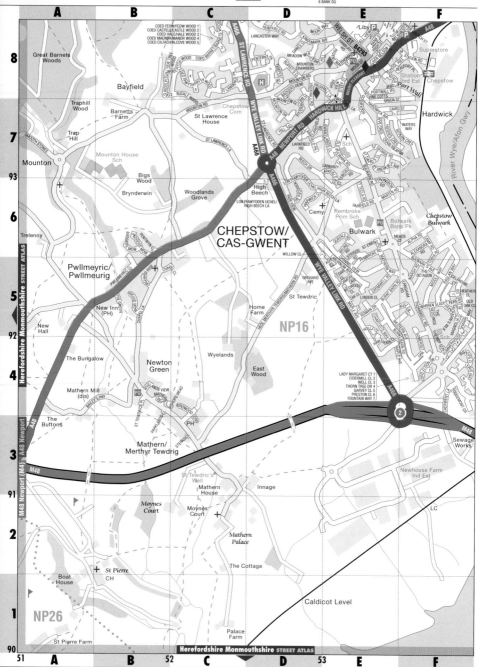

E8
1 ALBION SQ
2 LIBRARY PL
3 OLD BELL CHAMBERS
4 HOCKER HILL ST
5 BEAUFORT SQ
6 BANK SQ
7 MIDDLE ST
8 ST MARY ST
9 ST MARY STREET ARC
10 OXFORD ST
11 RESTWAY WALL
12 GARDEN CITY WAY
13 School Hill Ind Est
14 EXEMOUTH PL

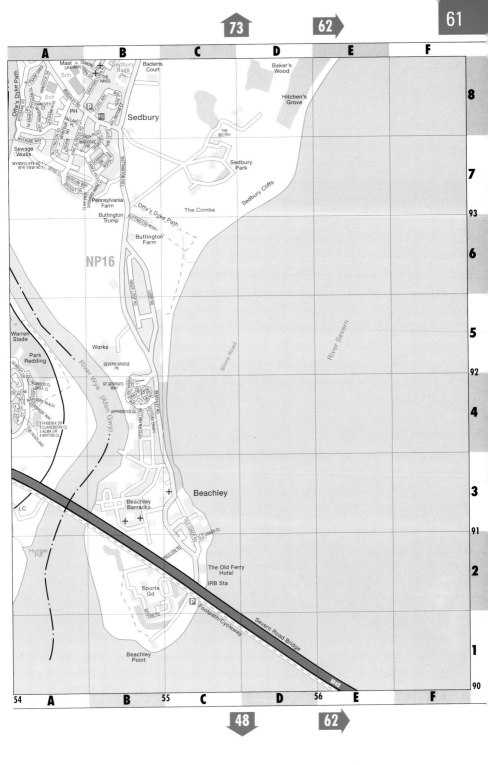

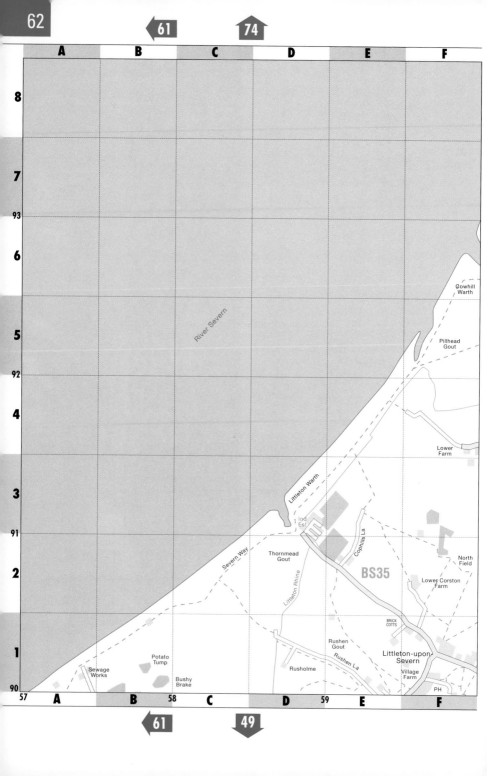

61
74

A   B   C   D   E   F

8

7

93

6

Cowhill
Warth

5

Pillhead
Gout

92

4

Lower
Farm

River Severn

3

Littleton Warth

91

Ind
Est

Severn Way

Thornmead
Gout

Cophills La

North
Field

2

BS35

Littleton Rhine

Lower Corston
Farm

BRICK
COTTS

1

Rushen
Gout

Littleton-upon-
Severn

Potato
Tump

Rusholme

Rushen La

Village
Farm

Sewage
Works

Bushy
Brake

PH

90

57   A   B   58   C   D   59   E   F

61
49

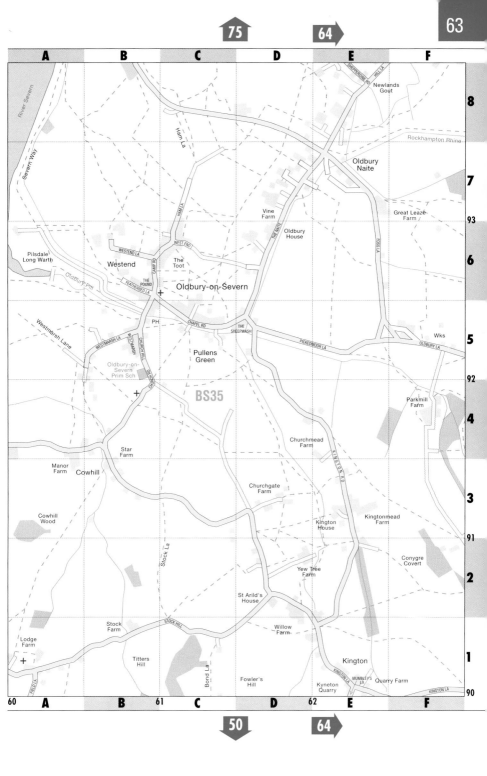

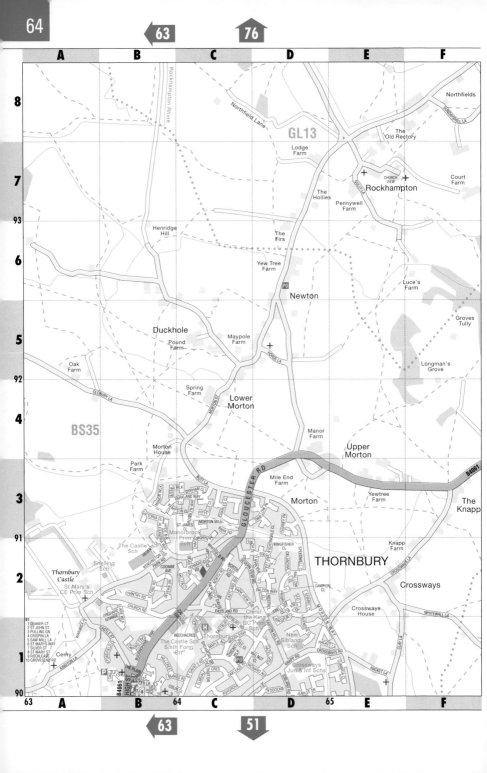

A   B   C   D   E   F

8

Northfields

Northfield Lane

GL13

The Old Rectory

7   CHURCH VIEW   Rockhampton   Court Farm

Lodge Farm

The Hollies

93   Pennywell Farm

Henridge Hill   The Firs

6   Yew Tree Farm   PO   Newton   Luce's Farm

Groves Tully

Duckhole   Maypole Farm

5   Pound Farm   HORSE LA   Longman's Grove

Oak Farm

92   OLDBURY LA   Spring Farm   Lower Morton

BS35

4   Manor Farm

Morton House   Upper Morton

Park Farm   B4061

3   Mile End Farm   Morton   Yewtree Farm   The Knapp

MORTON MILL   GLOUCESTER RD

91   Manorbrook Prim Sch   KINGFISHER CL   Knapp Farm

The Castle Sch   Sheiling Sch

THORNBURY

2   Thornbury Castle   St Mary's CE Prim Sch   COOMBE AVE   Crossways

CAMPION CL   Crossways House

FALCON CL

CHANTRY RD   CHURCH RD   EASTLAND RD   Christ the King RC Prim Sch   New Siblands Sch   WHITEWALL LA

H   Thornbury   Crossways Jun & Inf Schs

1   The Castle Sch Sixth Form Ctr   BEECHACRES   HACKET LA

Cerny   PO

ORCHARD CL

P   HACKET LA

90   B4061   HIGH ST

1 QUAKER CT
2 ST JOHN ST
3 PULLINS GN
4 CRISPIN LA
5 SAW MILL LA
6 ST MARYS WAY
7 SILVER ST
8 ST MARY ST
9 ROCKLEAZE
10 GROVESEND RD

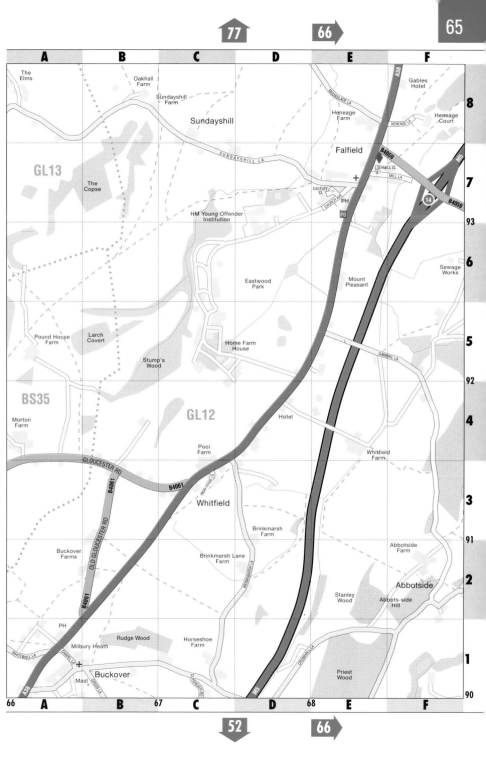

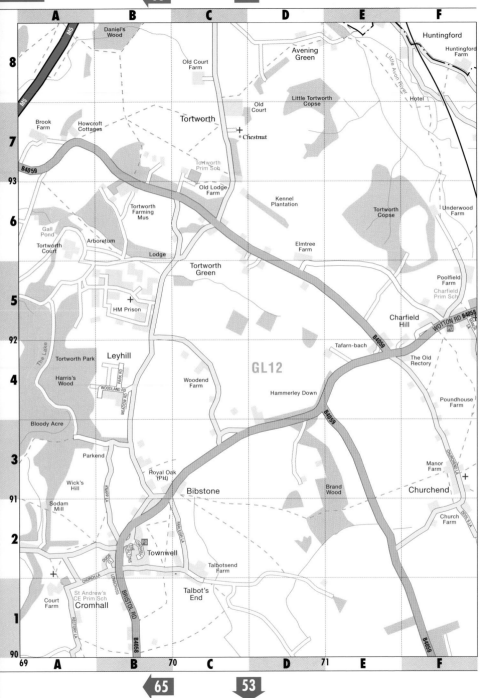

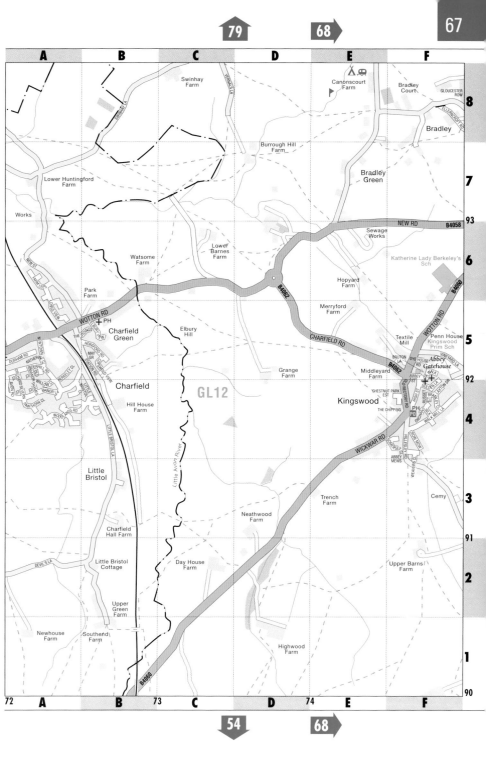

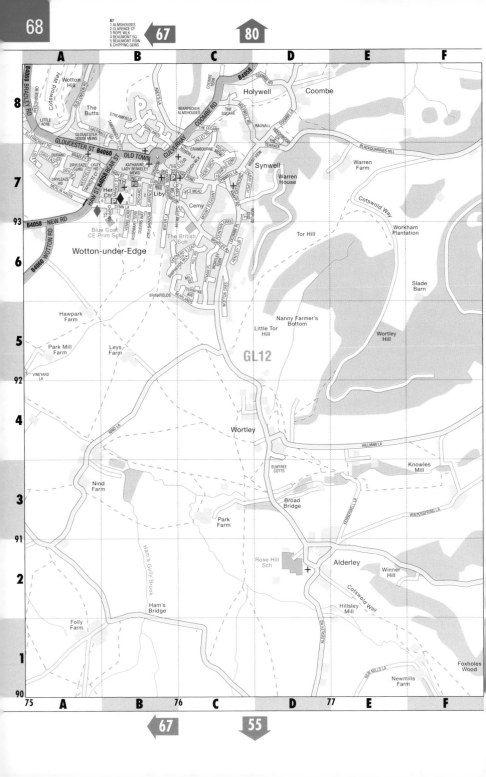

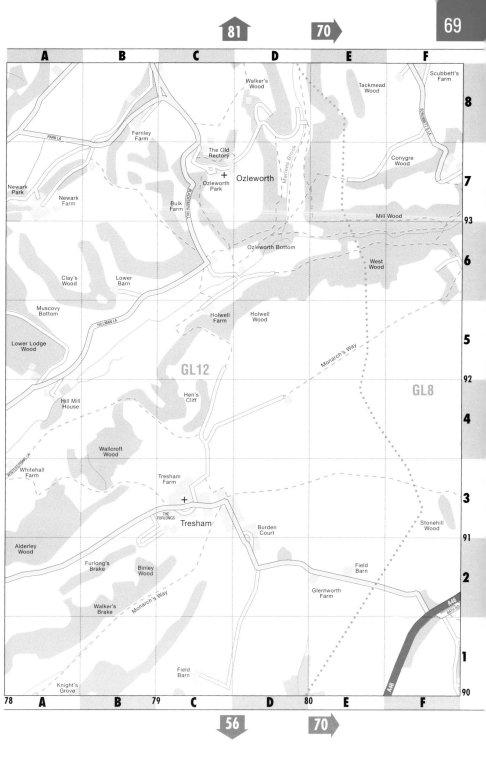

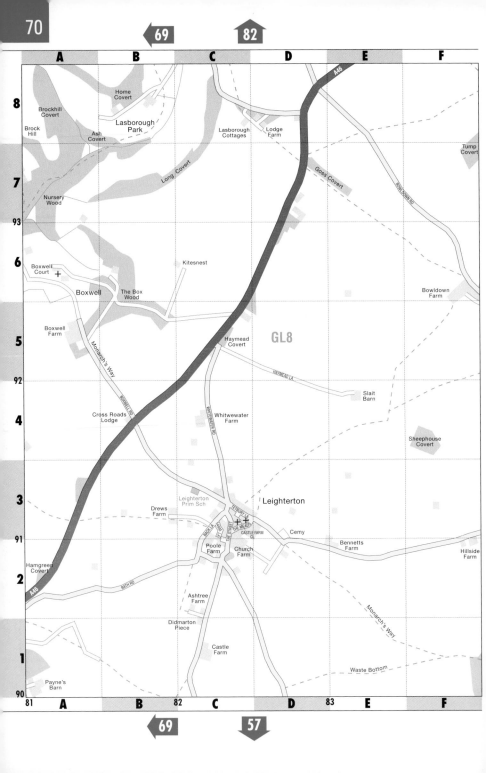

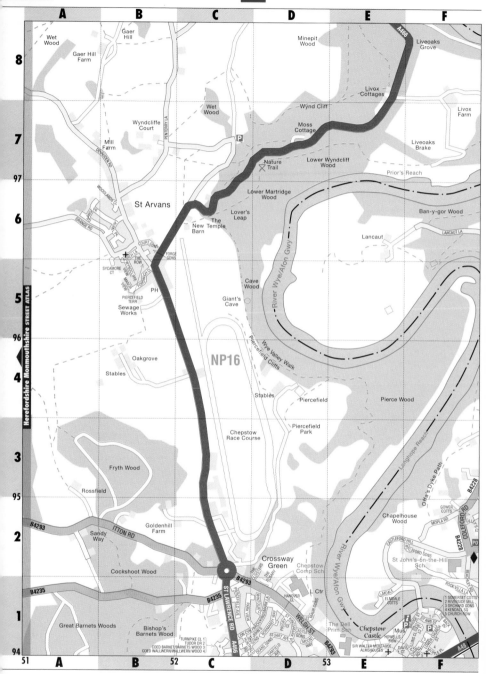

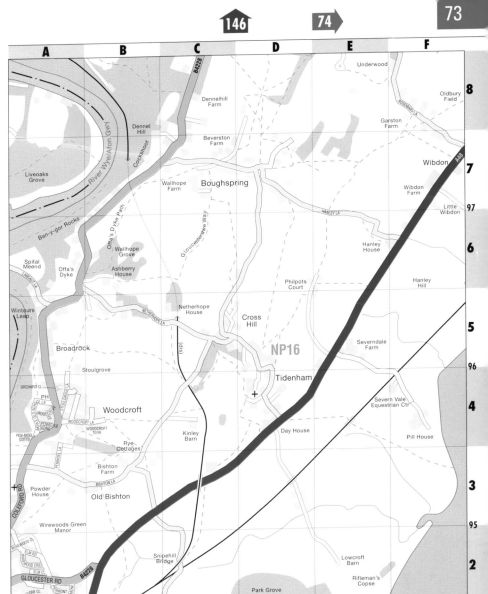

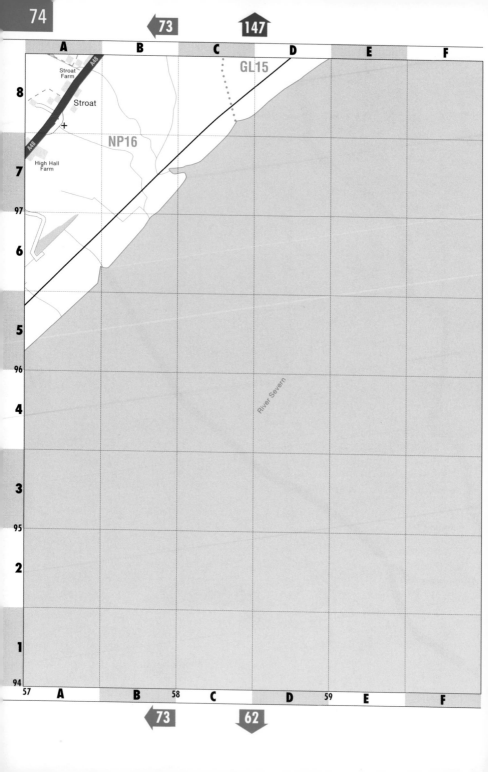
73
147

A B C D E F

8

7
97
GL13

6

River Severn

White House

Chapel House

Seven Way

Manor Farm

NUPDOWN RD

The Laurels

5

96

PH

Shepperdine Farm

North Ham Corner

Shepperdine Farm

4

Shepperdine

Brickhouse Farm

Shepperdine Withybed

3

95
GL13
Harecrest La

BS35

Jobscreen Farm

SHEPPERDINE RD

Lowgoods Farm

2

Oldbury Power Station

Knight's Farm

LA HILL

Visitor Ctr

Mast

1

94

60 A B 61 C D 62 E F

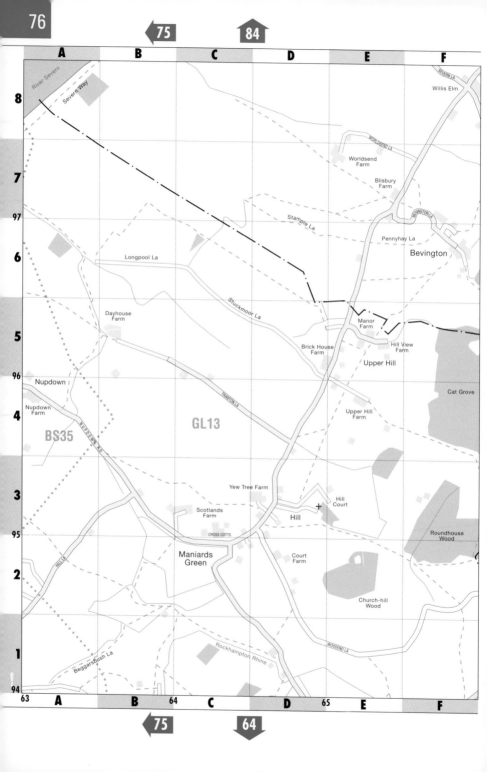

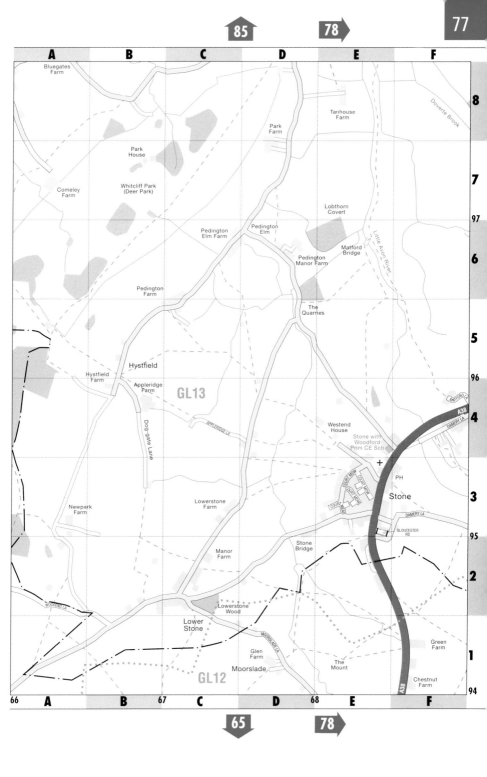

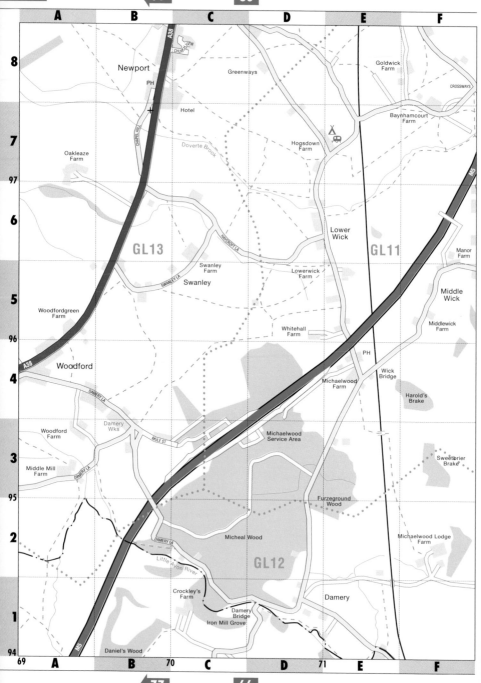

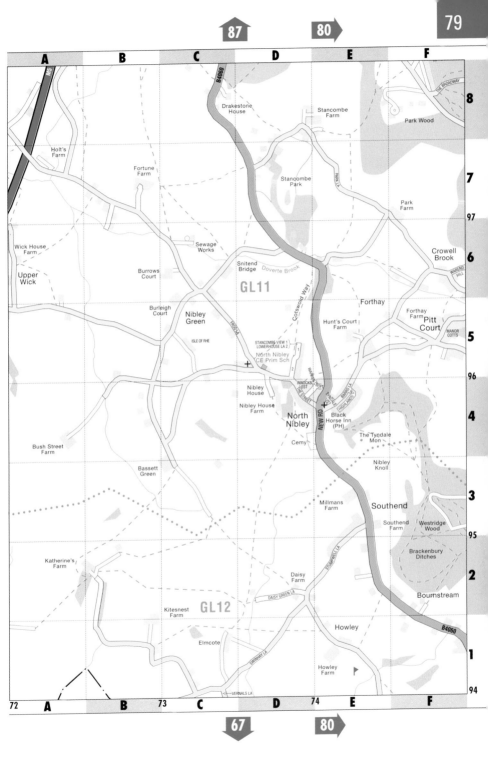

79
88

A B C D E F

8

THE BROADMEAD
FIVE ACRES
HUNGER'S HILL
APRIL CL
THE SLADE
BOULTON LR 2
CHAMPIONS CT 3
BULL PITCH 4
FORTFIELDS 5
HILLSIDE CT 6
REINE BARNES CL 7
UPPER POOLE
MELKSHAM
POOLE
FORT LA
FORTRESS

ELMLEIGH
NEW SLANG
B4066
A4135
GYFORD CL
PO
FIRST AVE
EWELME CL
ULEY RD
River Ewelme
Rockstowes Hill
B4066

SECOND AVE
DOWNHAM
DOWNHAM

1 FERNEY
2 YELLOW HUNDRED CL
3 STANTHILL DR
4 ROSEBERY MOUNT
5 ANVIL CT
6 HEATH CT

1 CASWELL CT
2 CASWELL MEWS
3 RIVERSMILL
4 RIVERSMILL WLK
5 RIVERSMILL CT
6 DOWNHAM WLK

Rockstowes

Hermitage Wood

DURSLEY

Woodmancote

Dursley CE Prim Sch

ROSEBERY PK
THIRD AVE
SCHOOL RD
Highfields

Castle Stream Farm

Sheephouse Farm

7

WOODMANCOTE
HERMITAGE RD
SOMERSET AVE
KINGSHILL RD

BLACK MEAD
NUNNERY LA
PT MOUNTJOY

TENNYSON RD
SHAKESPEARE RD
LOWER PAGANHILL LA
CHAUCER RD
WORDSWORTH RD
GANZELL LA
THE RANGERS

Folly Wood

Cooper's Wood

97

WHITEWAY

Dursley Wood

Whiteway

Dingle Farm

A4135

6

Millend Wood

Whiteway

Tumbleyhill Wood

WATSON'S HILL

Breakheart Hill

PH

GL11

Ashen Plains Wood

Sandfields Wood

Millend

Waterley Bottom

Ridings Wood

5

Smart's Green

Sandfield Farm

Waterley Farm

96

4

Binley Farm

Spuncombe Bottom

Half Way Farm

Monkcombe Wood

B4058

Hamlin Brake

Laycombe Ditch Wood

CH

3

Westridge Wood

Upper Rushmire Farm

The Ridings

Briery Wood

95

Cotswold Way

Lower Rushmire Farm

Wimley Barn

2

GL12

Wimley Hill

OLD LONDON RD

Bradley Barn

Wimley Hill

Tyley Bottom

B4060
BRADLEY RD

Conygre Wood

POLE LA

Coombe Hill

B4058

94

75 A B 76 C D 77 E F

79
68

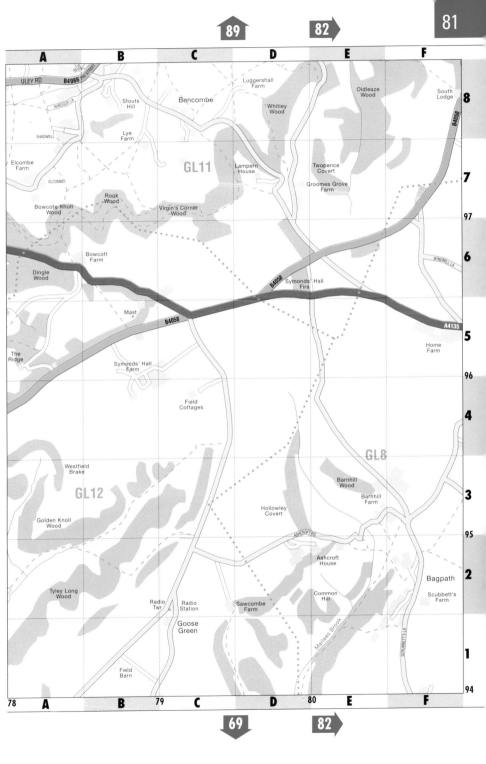

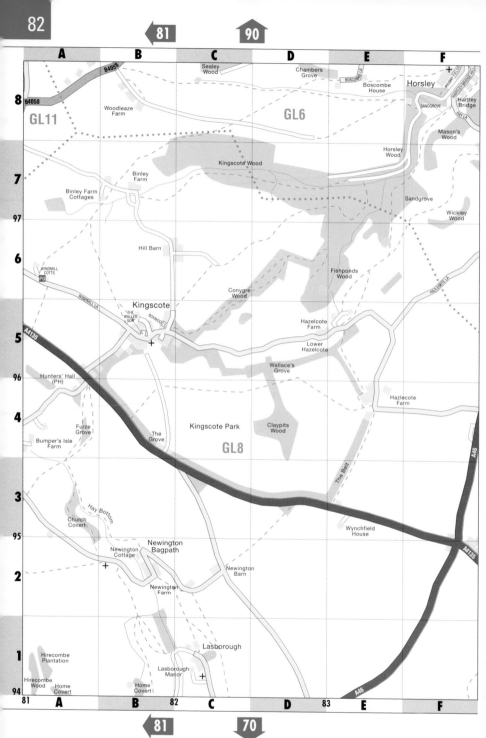

A B C D E F

8

GL11

GL6

Horsley

B4058

B4058

Sealey
Wood

Chambers
Grove

Boscombe
House

Hartley
Bridge

Woodleaze
Farm

SANDGROVE

Mason's
Wood

Horsley
Wood

7

Kingscote Wood

Binley
Farm

97

Binley Farm
Cottages

Sandgrove

Wickley
Wood

6

Hill Barn

WINDMILL
COTTS

Fishponds
Wood

Conygre
Wood

5

A4135

WINDMILL LA

Kingscote

THE WALLED GDN

BOXWOOD CL

Hazelcote
Farm

Lower
Hazelcote

96

Hunters' Hall
(PH)

Wallace's
Grove

Hazlecote
Farm

4

Furze
Grove

Bumper's Isle
Farm

The
Grove

Kingscote Park

Claypits
Wood

GL8

The Bett

A46

3

Hay Bottom

Church
Covert

Wynchfield
House

A4135

95

Newington
Cottage

Newington
Bagpath

Newington
Barn

2

Newington
Farm

1

Hirecombe
Plantation

Lasborough

Hirecombe
Wood

Home
Covert

Lasborough
Manor

Home
Covert

94

81 A B 82 C D 83 E F

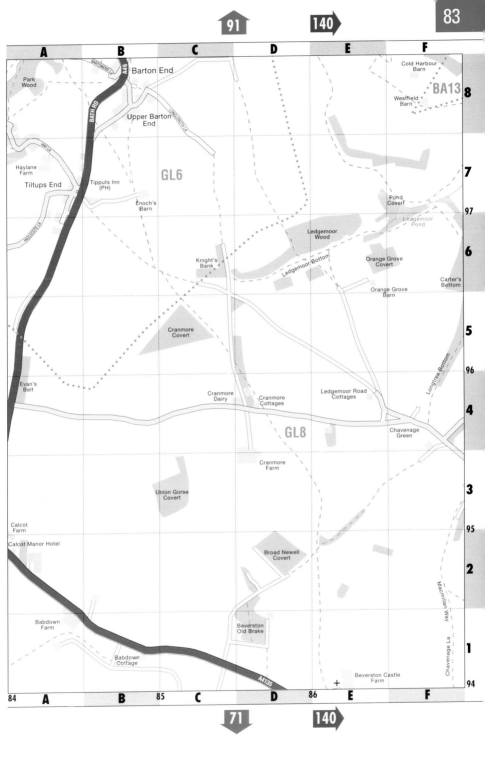

A   B   C   D   E   F

8

Ward
Ind Est

Lydney
COOKSON
TERR
LC
RAILWAY
TERR

THE MARINA

HARBOUR RD

GL15

Lydney
Ind Est

Naas
House

7

Lydney Marsh

Lydney Harbour

HARBOUR RD

01

New Grounds

6

5

River Severn

00

4

3

99

2

GL13

Severn Way

1

Severn House
Farm

SEVERN LA

98

63   A   B   64   C   D   65   E   F

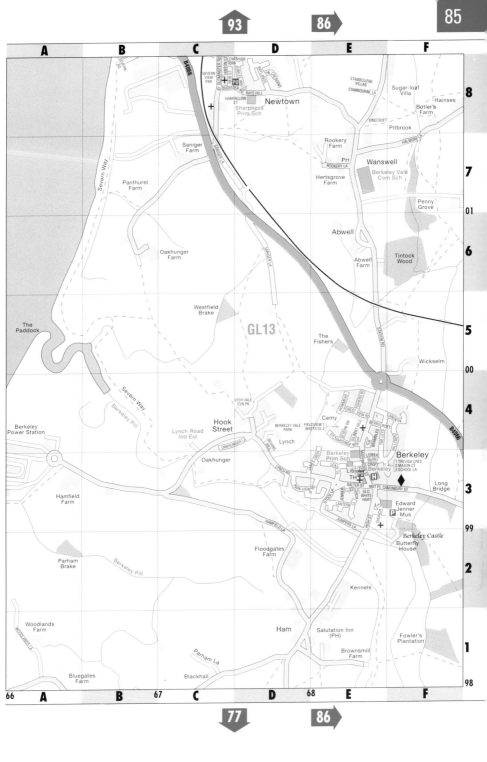

A **B** **C** **D** **E** **F**

8
7
01
6
5
00
4
3
99
2
1
98

66 67 68

GLEWISHAM TERR
GLOUCESTER ST
THE CRESCENT
BAYS LANE
HAMFALLOW CT
BAYS HILL
PH
SEVERN VIEW PAR

Severn Way
B4066
SANIGER LA

Saniger Farm

Panthurst Farm

Oakhunger Farm

Westfield Brake

The Paddock

STAMBOURNE VILLAS
STAMBOURNE LA
Sugar-loaf Villa
Hainses
Botler's Farm

Newtown
Sharpness Prim Sch

Rookery Farm
PH
ROOKERY LA
Wanswell
Berkeley Vale Com Sch
VINECROFT
Pitbrook
HALMORE LA

Hertsgrove Farm

Penny Grove

Abwell

Abwell Farm

Tintock Wood

Wickselm

STATION RD

GL13

The Fishers

LYCH VALE CVN PK
Hook Street
Lynch Road Ind Est
Berkeley Vale Park
FIELDVIEW 1 WATTS CL 2
Cemy
HOWARD CL
FISHERS RD
FOREST VIEW RD
CANN PK
Lynch
OAKHUNGER LA
Oakhunger
LYNCH RD
DENNIS
SEVERN DR
MARYBROOK ST
HEMPONDGE WAY
BERKELEY
JAMES DOCK
AXH VIEW
LOWER BERRY CROFT
Berkeley Prim Sch
Library
TH
H
MKT PL
Berkeley
1 TREVISA CRES
2 MASON CT
3 SCHOOL LA
CANONBURY ST
THE BRAMBLES
THE LYS ST
BERRYCROFT
Long Bridge
MARTIN CL
SALTER ST
OLD WHITE HART
HIGH ST
LANTERN CL
Edward Jenner Mus
P
JUMPERS LA
Berkeley Castle
Butterfly House
Kennels

Berkeley Power Station

Hamfield Farm
HAMFIELD LA

Parham Brake
Berkeley Pill

Floodgates Farm

Woodlands Farm
WOODLANDS LA

Bluegates Farm

Blackhall
Parham La

Ham

Salutation Inn (PH)

Brownsmill Farm

Fowler's Plantation

B4066

Severn Way
Berkeley Pill

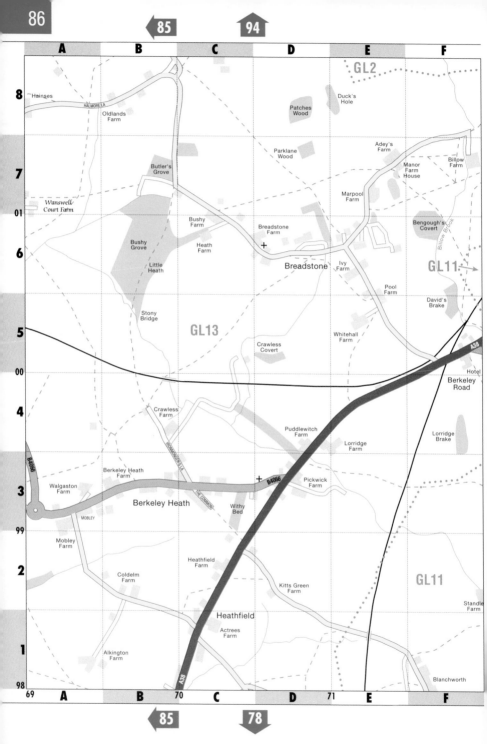

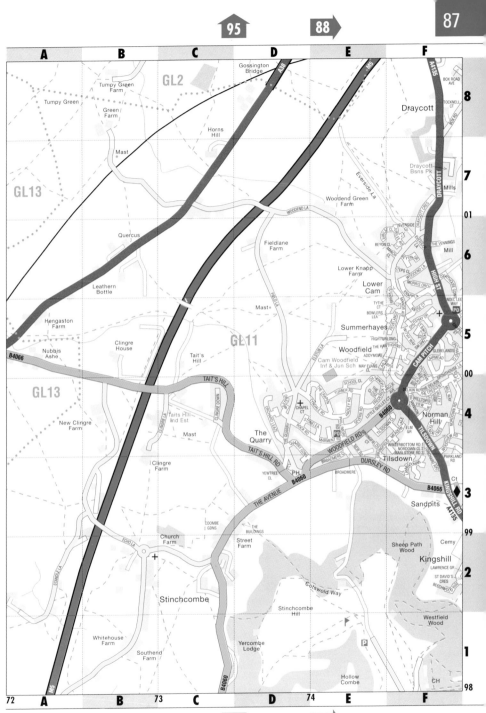

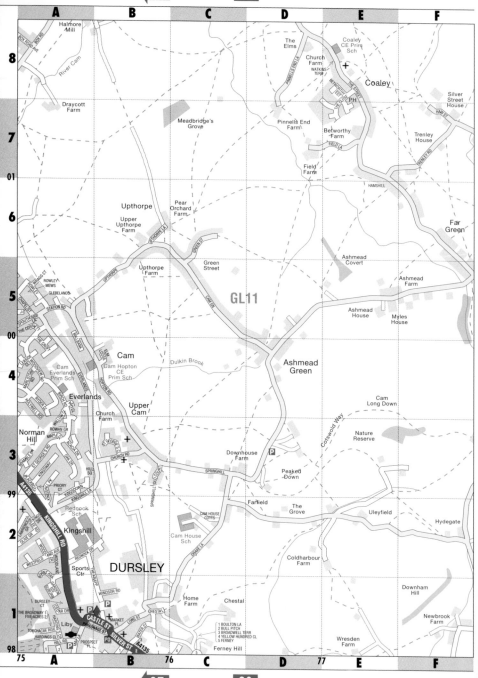

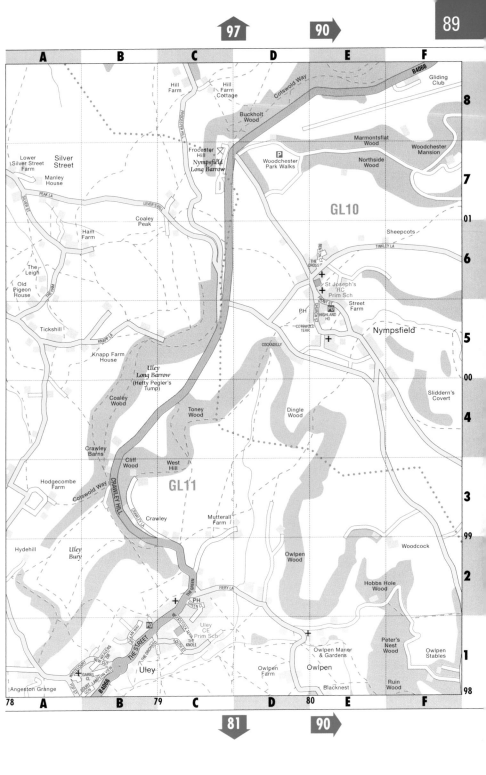

89
98

A   B   C   D   E   F

8

Longwood Farm

The Tower

Colepark Wood

Bownhill Farm

Atcombe Court

Break-heart-hill Wood

Honeywell Pond

Atcombe Court Farmhouse

GL5

Old Pond

Atcombe Wood

7

Leaze Wood

Woodchester Park

Convent of Poor Clares

Stoneshard Wood

Middle Pond

01

Pontin's Plantation

Kennel Pond

Parkmill Pond

PARK LA

GL10

Kennel Plantation

MILLBROOK WLK 1
INCHBROOK WAY 2
INCHBROOK CT 3

6

Collier's Wood

Windsoredge

WINDSOREDGE LA

Lynch Knoll

TINKLEY LA

NORTON CT 1
ROWAN WAY 2
HAWTHORN RIDGE 3
BADGERS WAY 4
WOODPECKER WLK 5
CRADDOCK CT 6
HIGHWOOD CT 7

5

Partstreet Farm

Partfield Farm

Wood Farm

Nailsworth CE Prim Sch

00

Tinkley Farm

NYMPSFIELD RD

Forest Green Rovers FC

Bunting Hill

4

High Wood

Newmarket

Bowlas Wood

Miry Brook

LOWER NEWMARKET RD

Field Farm

Lower Lutheredge Farm

Waghill

MERTON COTTS 1
COTSWOLD COTTS 2

SPORTWOOD RD

GL6

Shortwood

3

Twatley

99

Upper Lutheredge Farm

Sallywood Farm

WALLOW GB

Wallow Green

2

GL11

SUGLEY LA

Tickmorend

Sugley Farm

Downend

Ragged Barn

SUGLEY LA

1

Horsley

B4058

THE STREET

THE CROSS

Owlpen Lodge

Nupend

PRIORY FIELDS 1
HARTLEY BRIDGE HILL 2

Sch

PH

B4058

98

81   A   B   82   C   D   83   E   F

89
82

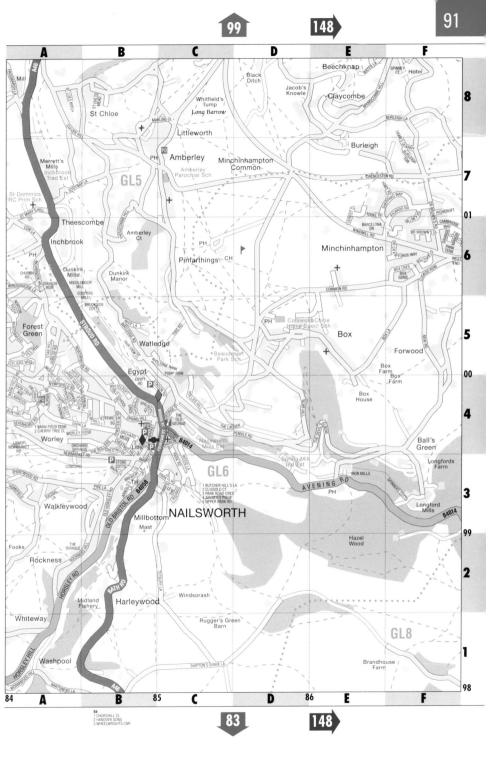

147   156

	A	B	C	D	E	F

Shaphouse Farm

Oldcroft

1 BRIERLEY WAY
2 CHURCH WLK

8

Needs Top

Little Purlieu

Hulks Farm

Soilwell Farm

Purlieu End Farm

7

Soilwell Manor

The Purlieu

Ten Acre Wood

Allaston Meend

Tingley Wood

Plummer's Brook

05

Little Allaston

6

Billings Barn

NEW MILLS

Allaston

Driffield Farm

Mast

Nursehill Wood

Nursehill

Millrough Wood

Allaston Court

Primrose Hill CE Prim Sch

GL15

5

HIGHFIELD RD

04

Primrose Hill

Middle Forge

Warren

4

Highfield

1 NODENS WAY
2 NERO CL
3 CAESARS CL

Rodley Manor

Hurst Farm

Wellhouse Grove

B4234

NEW RD

Newerne

Lydney

Warren Grove

Severnbanks Prim Sch

Lydney CE Com Sch

FOREST RD

3

Liby

1 TUTHILL RISE
2 THE FOLDERS
3 HAWTHORN CT
HIGHFIELD RD

MANOR CT

Crump Farm

Kears Wood

Lydney Town

HAMPTON MEWS FAIRFIELD RD

ST MARY'S SQ. CL

BATH PL

ELMS RD

03

PYLERS WAY

Purton Pl

B4231 HIGH ST

B4231

1 WYNTOUR'S PAR
2 DARTERS CL
3 HERBERT HOWELLS CL
4 STEEPLE VIEW
5 VICARAGE CL

RUSHY EAZE

Plummer's Farm

Cliff Farm

Superstore

2

Bathurst Park

Tutnalls

ORCHARD RD

COURT PLEASANT

1 THE BUNGALOWS
2 MOUNT PLEASANT CL

Whitecross Sch

CHURCH RD

LAKESIDE AVE

SUMMERLEA

CH

A4231

LEAZE

SUMMERLEAZE

St Mary's

CHURCH GDNS

Iron Foundry

Naas Crossing (LC)

1

A48

B4231

Naas Court

Naas

Lydney Junc

02

LC

63	A		B	64	C		D	65	E		F

A3
1 RAGLAN GDNS
2 GOODE CT
3 CAVENDISH BLDGS
4 FOREST PAR
5 REGENTS WLK

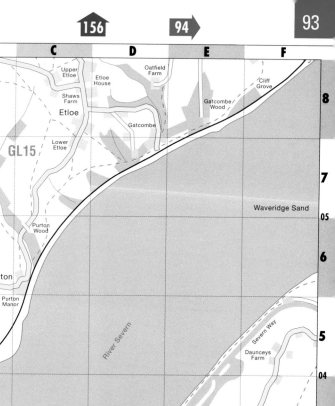

A B C D E F

8
7
05
6
5
04
4
3
03
2
1
02

Purlieu
Farm

Oldstreet
House

A48

LENSBROOK

Lensbrook
Farm

Lanes Brook

Upper
Etloe

Shaws
Farm

Etloe

Etloe
House

Oatfield
Farm

Gatcombe
Wood

Cliff
Grove

Gatcombe

GL15

Lower
Etloe

Hill Farm

Purton
Wood

Waveridge Sand

Gurshill
Farm

Purton

Purton
Manor

The
Wards

River Severn

Severn Way

Daunceys
Farm

Wellhouse Bay

The Ridge Sand

Kingshill
Farm

The Gloucester & Sharpness Canal

Ironwells
Grove

IRB
Sta

SUNNYBROOK
TERR

Hinton

Hinton
Farm

GL13

Sharpness

PO

DOCK RD

Luggs
Farm

The Malthouse

GLOUCESTER RD

OAKFIELD DRIVE

BRIDGE RD

Severn Way

Brookend
Farm

CHURCH LN

Docks

WESTERN RD

B4066

Pier View Hotel
(PH)

Bucketts Hill
Farm

Brookend

Lammastide Inn
(PH)

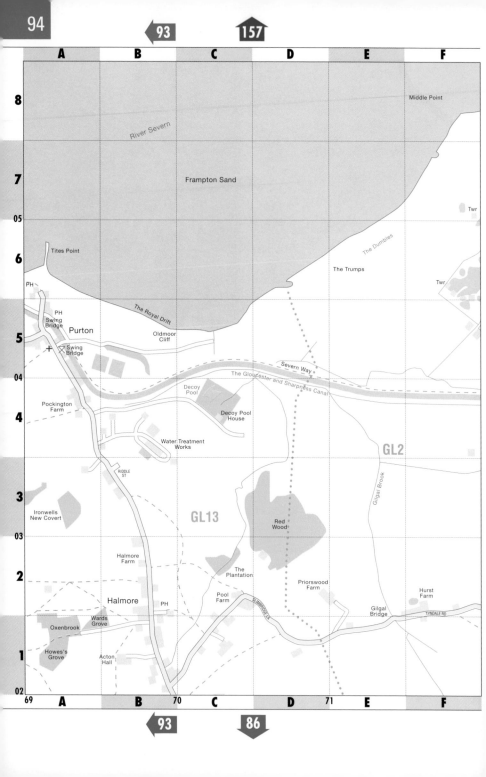

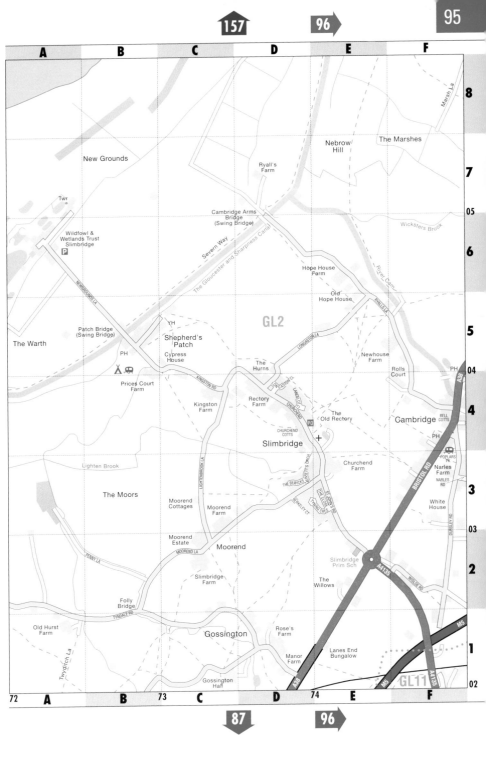

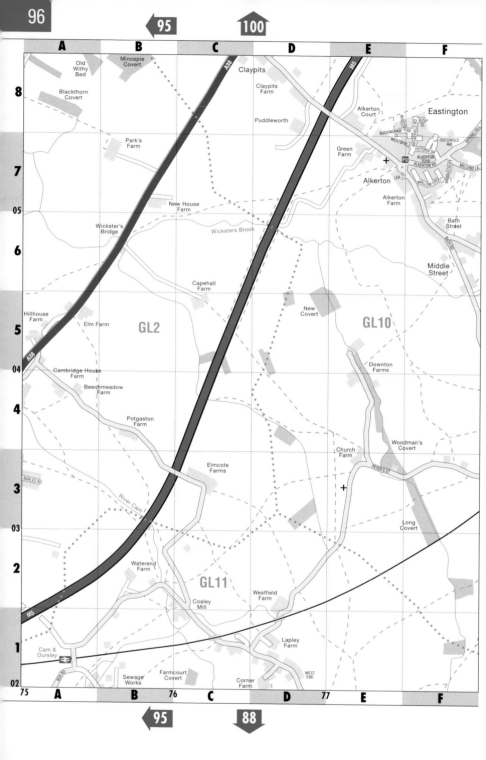

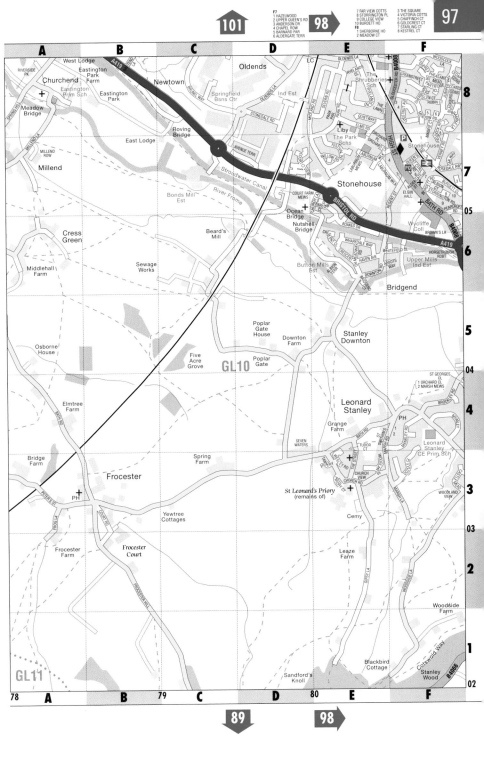

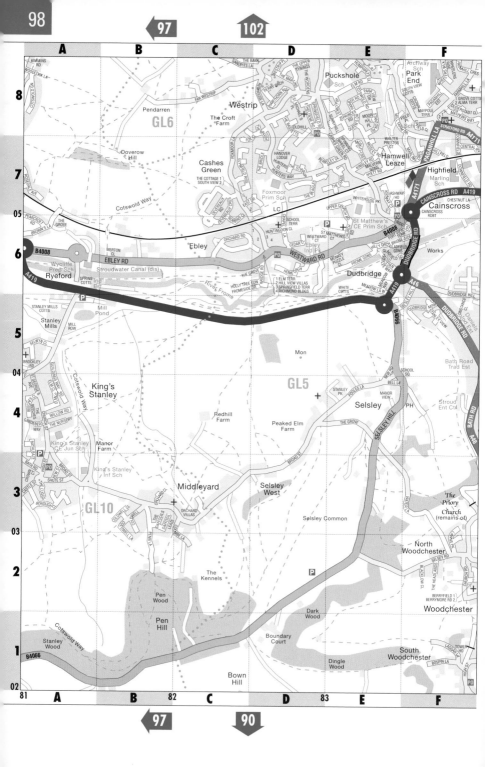

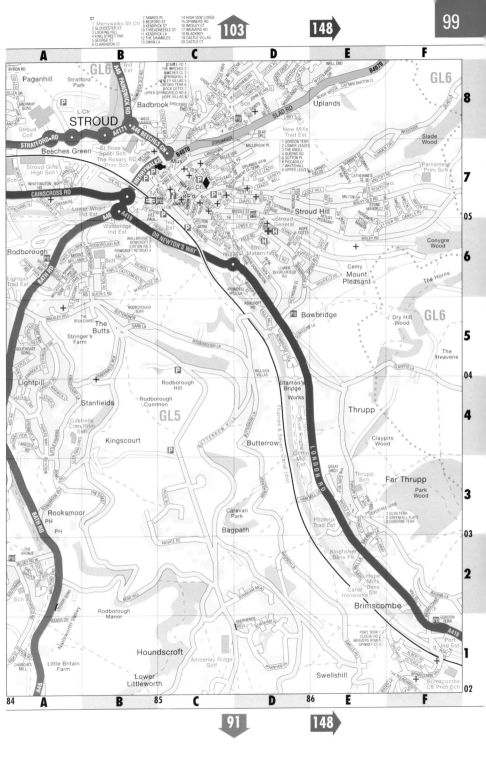

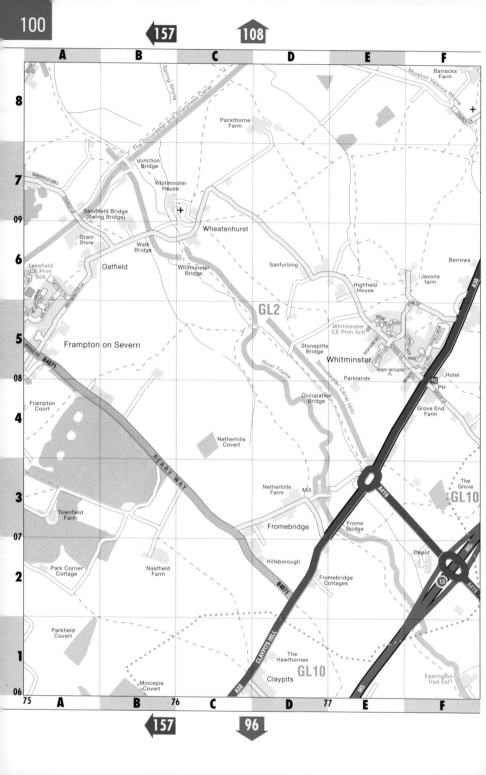

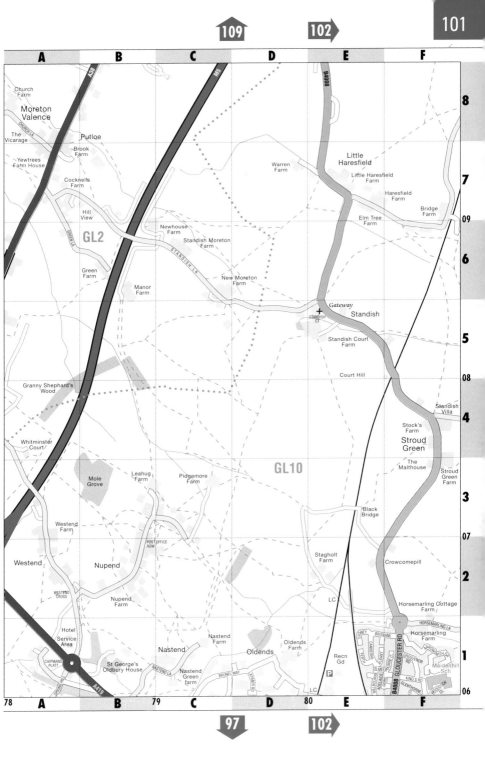

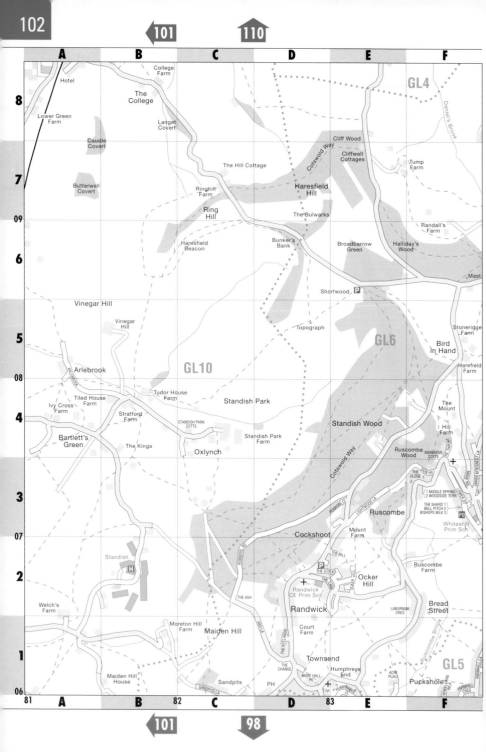

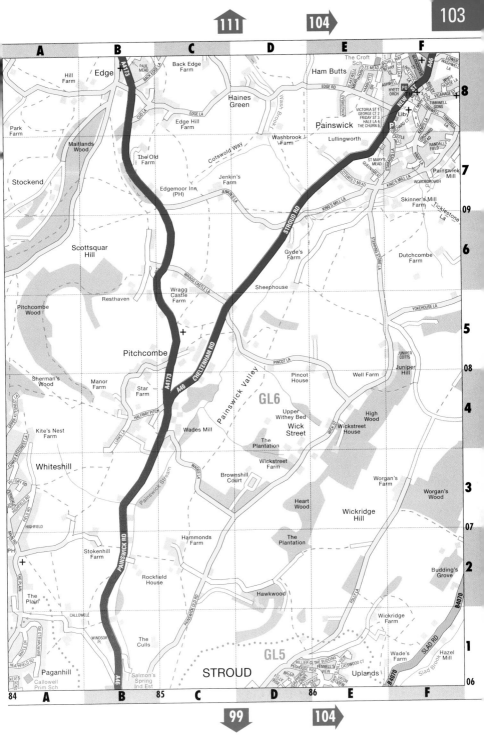

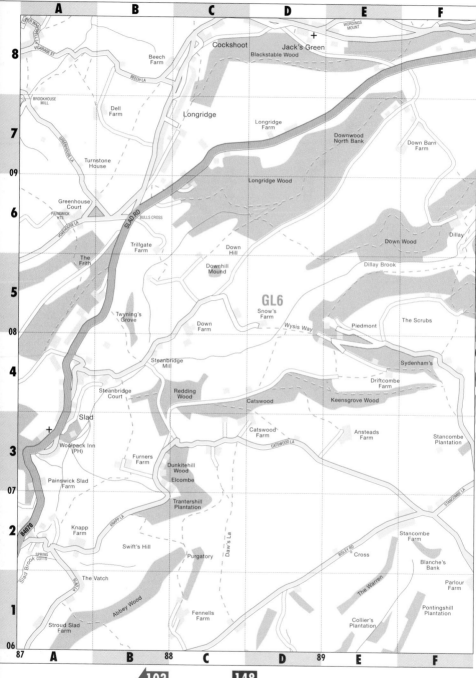

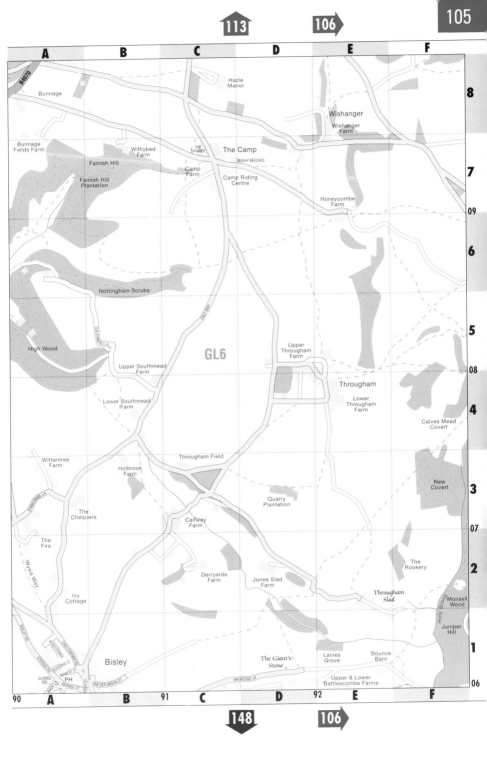

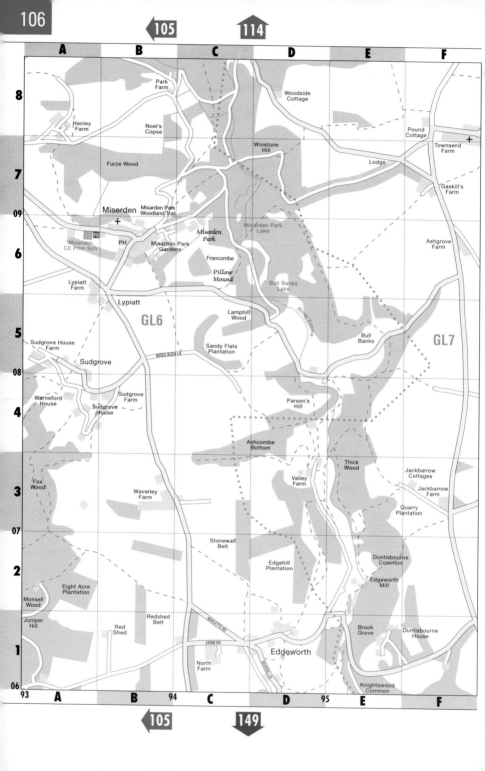

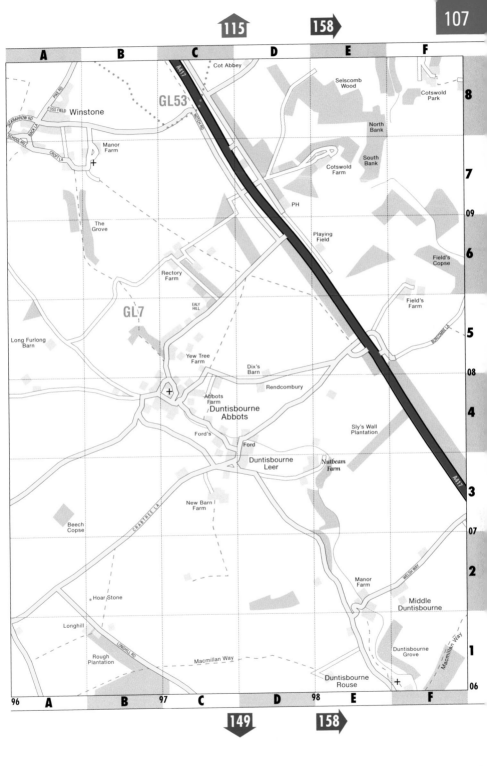

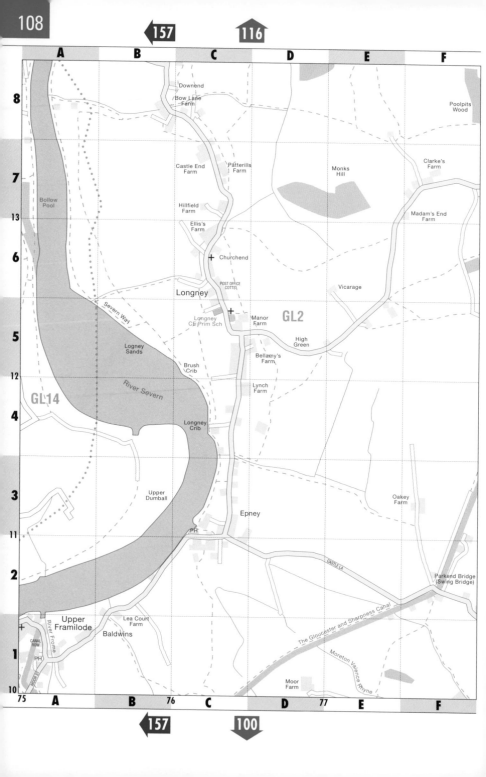

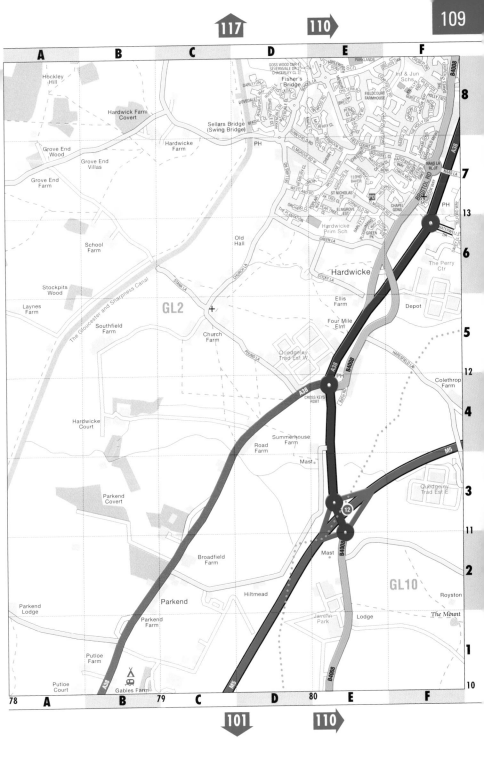

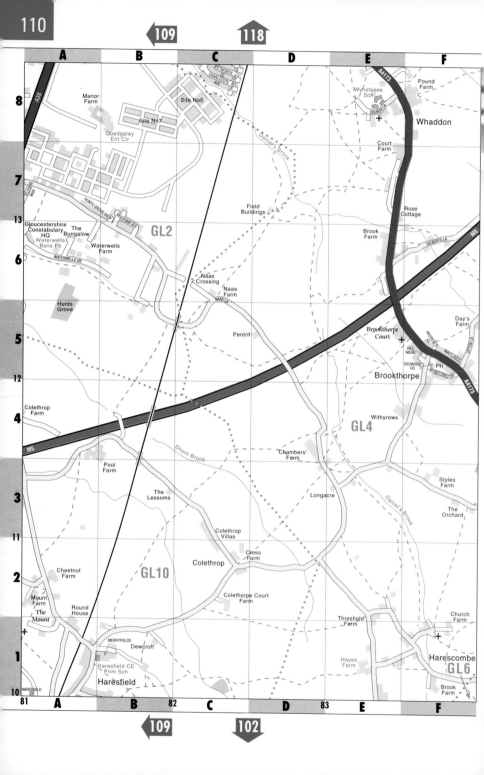

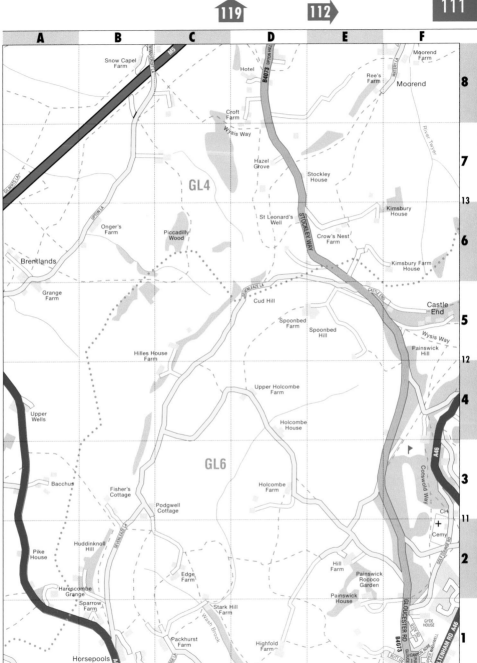

8

7

13

6

5

12

4

3

11

2

1

10

111
120

	A	B	C	D	E	F

8

Gastrell's Farm

Prinknash Abbey

Upton Wood

GL3

High Brotheridge

Brotheridge Farm

The Buckholt

GL3

Prinknash Pottery

Prinknash Bird and Deer Park

PAINSWICK RD

A46

Rough Park

BUCKHOLT RD

Buckholt Wood Nature Reserve

7

Prinknash Park

PRINKNASH

GL4

P

13

Cotswold Way

Cranham Corner

Woodside Farm

P

Black Horse Inn (PH)

PO

Kites Hill

Cranham Mill

6

Pope's Wood

Royal William (PH)

GL LA

Cranham Hall Farm

Simmonds Hall Farm

Cranham

Cranham CE Prim Sch

Cranham Common

CHURCH CL

5

Castle End

BEACON CL

Freams Farm

Mann's Court

Brook Farm

Painswick Hill

Overtown

12

Tocknells House

A46

Olivers Farm

4

Castle Godwyn

Olivers

Tocknells Court

Batch Farm

Saltridge Common Wood

GL6

Damsells Farm

3

Paradise House

Saltridge Wood

Saltridge Hill

The Old Ebworth Centre

11

A46

CLATTERGROVE

Damsells Mill

Wysis Way

Lady's Wood

Lord's Wood

Ebworth Plantations

2

CHELTENHAM RD

Damsells Cross

The Park

Painswick Lodge

Butchers Arms (PH)

Far End

PARKFIELD COTTS

Sheepscombe Cty Prim Sch

1

Highgrove

Sheepscombe

Phyll House Farm

The Green

Clissold Farm

10

87	A	B	88	C	D	89	E	F

111
104

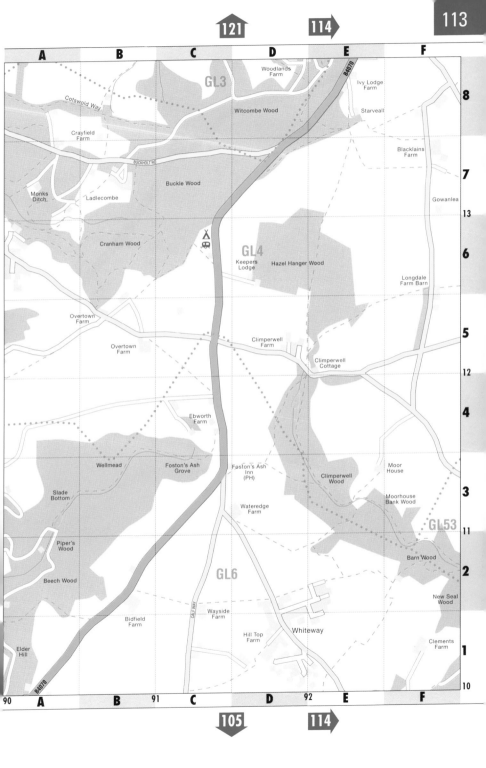

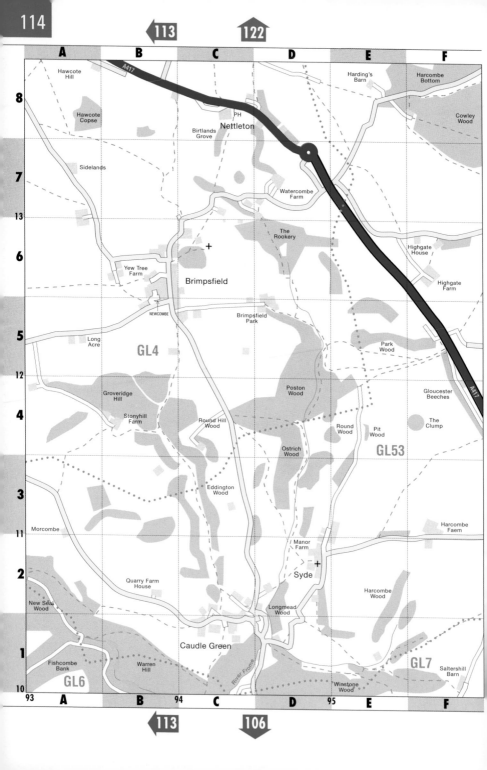

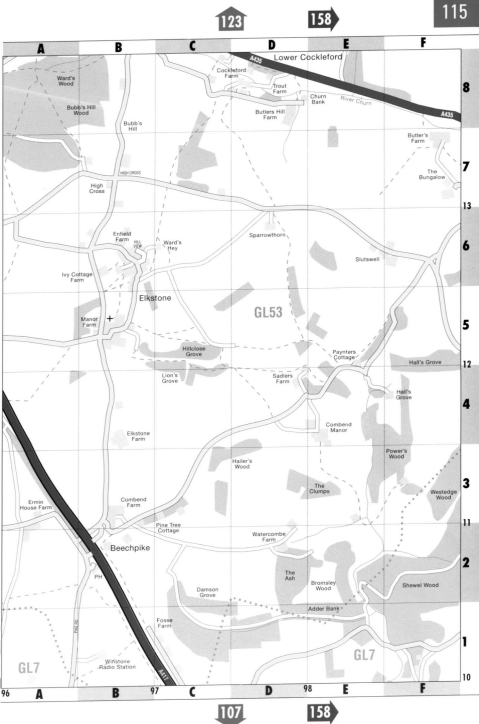

A B C D E F

8
7
13
6
5
12
4
3
11
2
1
10

96 A B 97 C D 98 E F

Lower Cockleford
A435
Cockleford Farm
Trout Farm
Ward's Wood
Bubb's Hill Wood
Butlers Hill Farm
Churn Bank
River Churn
A435
Butler's Farm
The Bungalow
Bubb's Hill
HIGH CROSS
High Cross
Enfield Farm
HILL VIEW
Ward's Hey
Sparrowthorn
Slutswell
Ivy Cottage Farm
Elkstone
GL53
Manor Farm
Hillclose Grove
Paynters Cottage
Hall's Grove
Lion's Grove
Sadlers Farm
Hall's Grove
Combend Manor
Power's Wood
Elkstone Farm
Hailer's Wood
The Clumps
Westedge Wood
Ermin House Farm
Combend Farm
Pine Tree Cottage
Watercombe Farm
Beechpike
PH
The Ash
Bromsley Wood
Shewel Wood
Damson Grove
Adder Bank
Fosse Farm
GL7
Winstone Radio Station
A417
GL7
PYKE RD

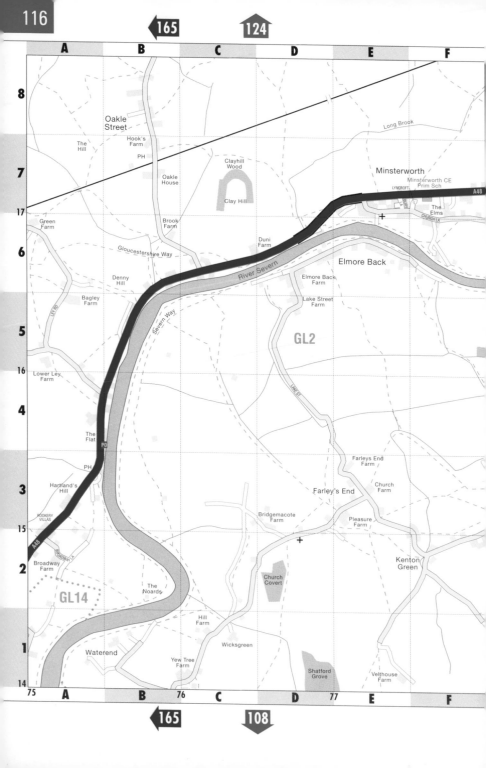

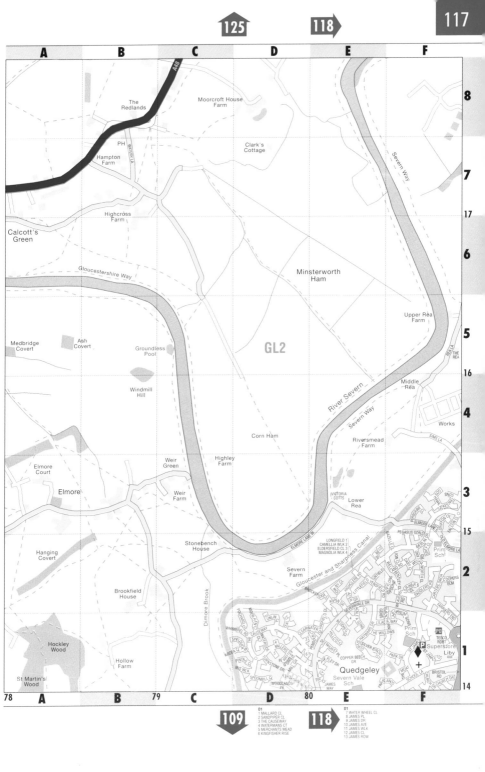

A   B   C   D   E   F

8

The Redlands
Moorcroft House Farm

A48

PH
Hampton Farm

WATER LA

Clark's Cottage

Severn Way

7

17

Highcross Farm

Calcott's Green

6

Gloucestershire Way

Minsterworth Ham

Medbridge Covert

Ash Covert

Groundless Pool

Upper Rea Farm

5

GL2

Windmill Hill

THE REA

Middle Rea

16

River Severn

Works

4

Severn Way

Corn Ham

Highley Farm

Riversmead Farm

SIMS LA

Elmore Court

Weir Green

VICTORIA COTTS
Lower Rea

3

Elmore

Weir Farm

ELMORE LANE W

15

Hanging Covert

Stonebench House

LONGFIELD 1
CAMELLIA WLK 2
ELDERSFIELD CL 3
MAGNOLIA WLK 4

Prim Sch

COOPERS ELM

2

Brookfield House

Dimore Brook

Severn Farm

Gloucester and Sharpness Canal

Prim Sch

Hockley Wood

Quedgeley

Severn Vale Sch

PO
TESCO
Superstore

P

Liby

BRISTOL RD

1

St Martin's Wood

Hollow Farm

JAMES WAY

WOODLANDS

CHURCH RD

14

78 A   B 79 C   D 80 E   F

D1
1 MALLARD CL
2 SANDPIPER CL
3 THE CAUSEWAY
4 WATERMANS CT
5 MERCHANTS MEAD
6 KINGFISHER RISE

D1
7 WATER WHEEL CL
8 JAMES PL
9 JAMES DR
10 JAMES AVE
11 JAMES WLK
12 JAMES CL
13 JAMES ROW

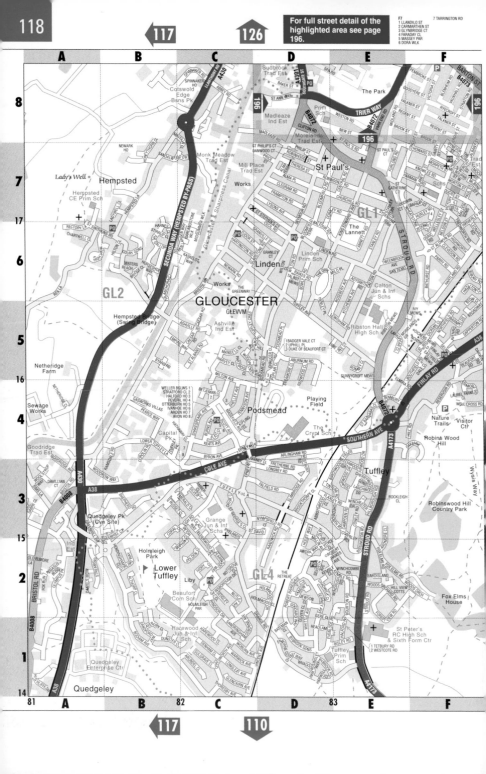

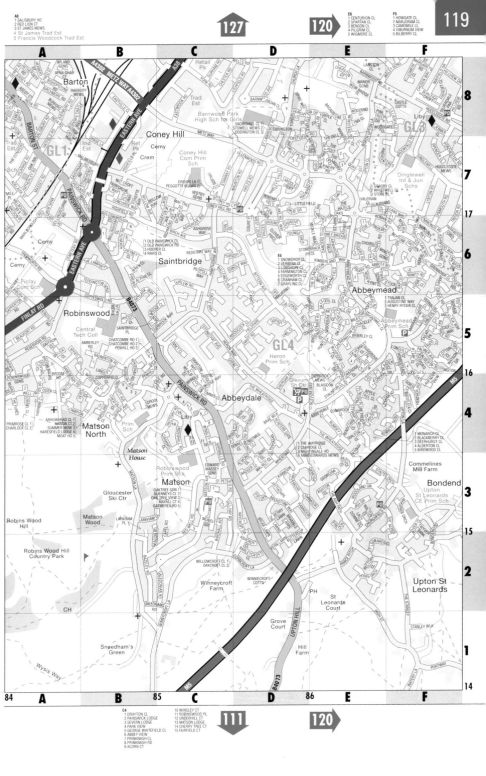

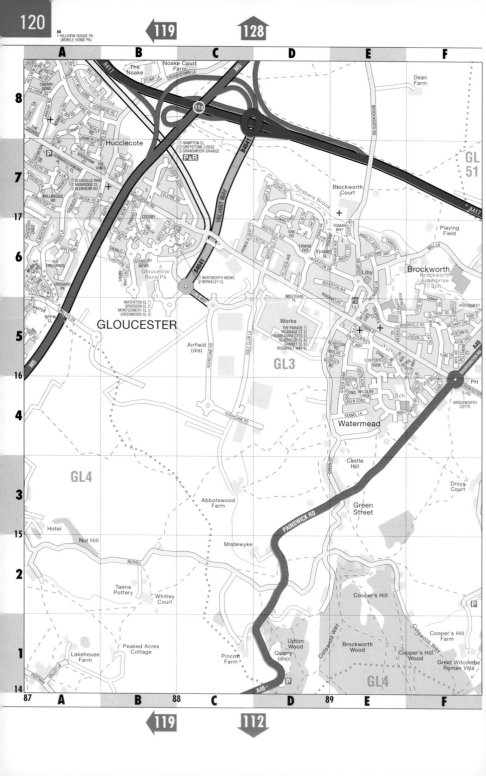

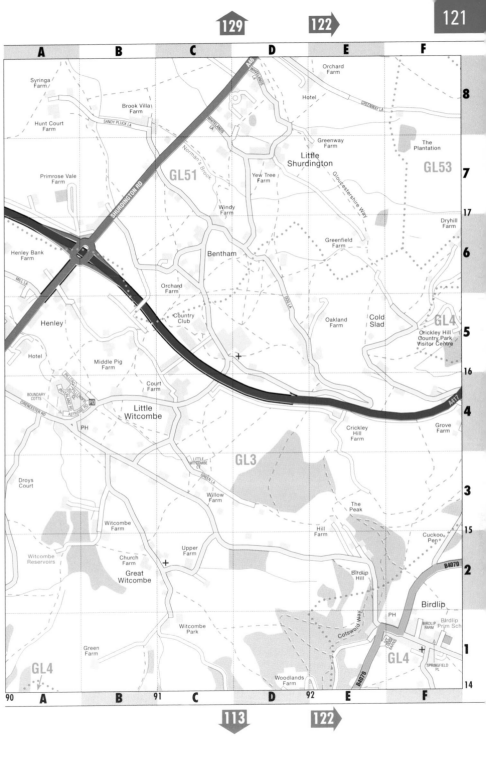

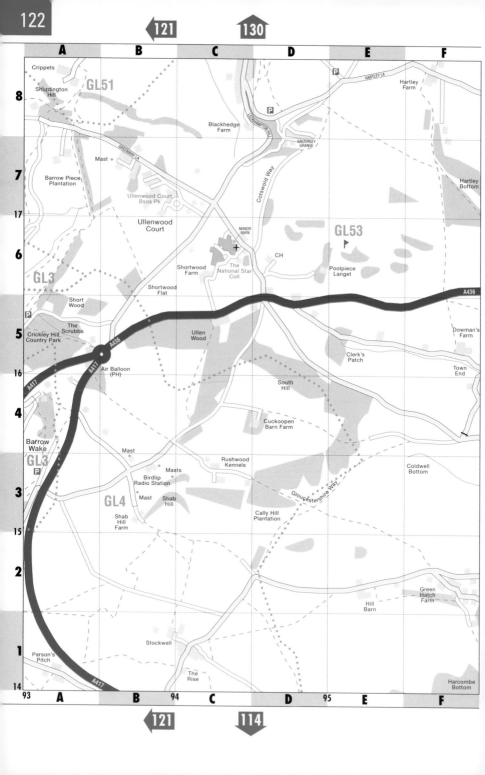

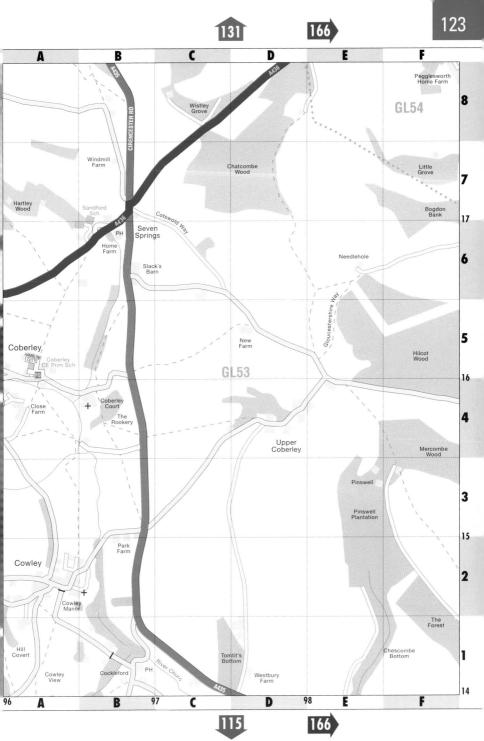

A B C D E F

GL54

Pegglesworth
Home Farm

Wistley
Grove

Chatcombe
Wood

Little
Grove

CIRENCESTER RD

A435

Windmill
Farm

Hartley
Wood

Sandford
Sch

A436

PH

Seven
Springs

Cotswold Way

Bogdon
Bank

Home
Farm

Slack's
Barn

Needlehole

Gloucestershire Way

Coberley

HAMBLING
COTTS

Coberley
CE Prim Sch

PO

New
Farm

GL53

Hilcot
Wood

Close
Farm

Coberley
Court

The
Rookery

Upper
Coberley

Mercombe
Wood

Pinswell

Pinswell
Plantation

Park
Farm

Cowley

Cowley
Manor

Hill
Covert

Cowley
View

Cockleford

PH

River Churn

A435

Tomtit's
Bottom

Westbury
Farm

The
Forest

Chescombe
Bottom

96 A B 97 C D 98 E F

8 7 17 6 5 16 4 3 15 2 1 14

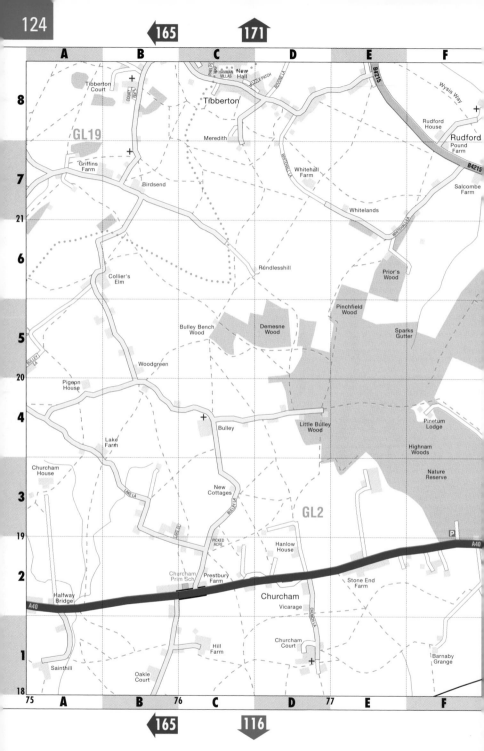

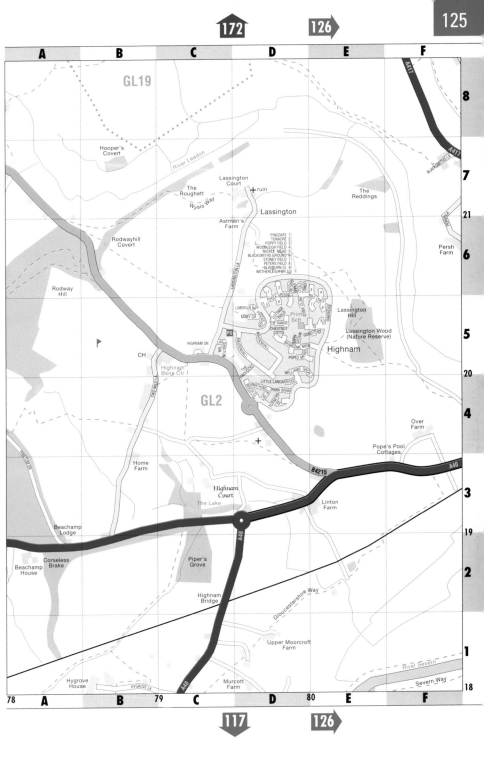

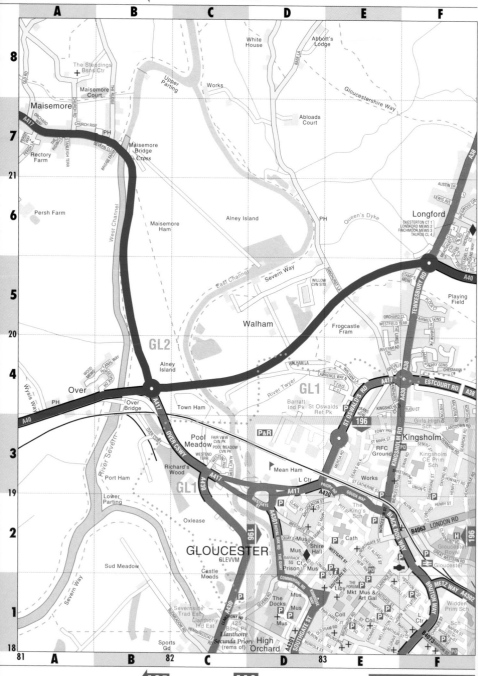

For full street detail of the highlighted area see page 196.

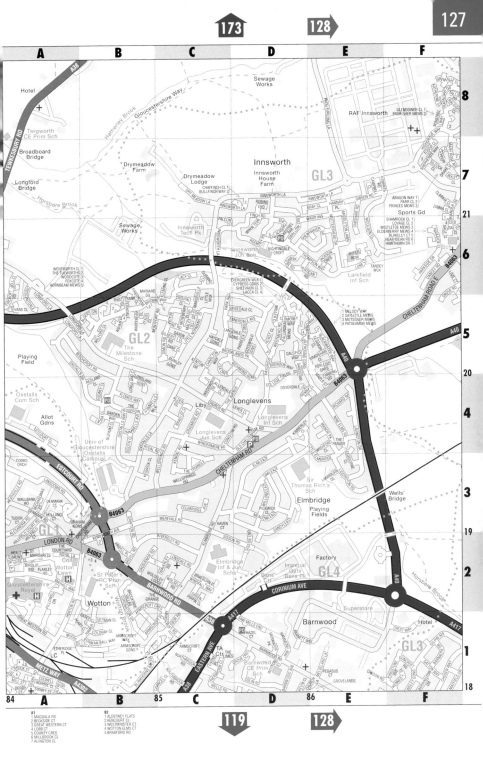

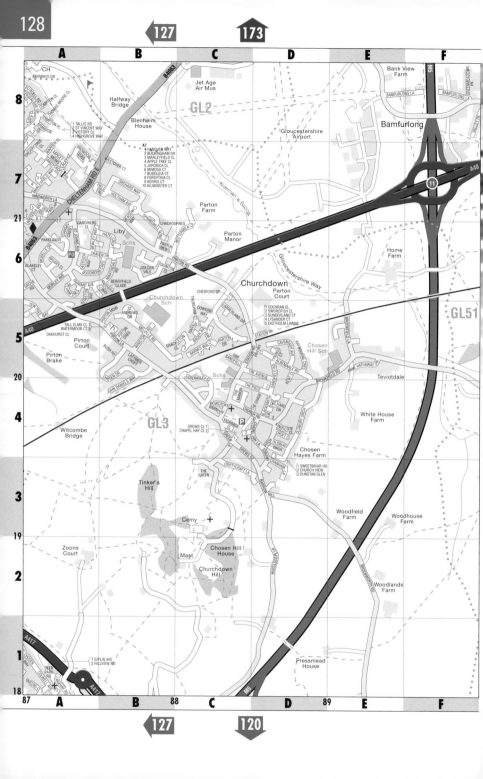

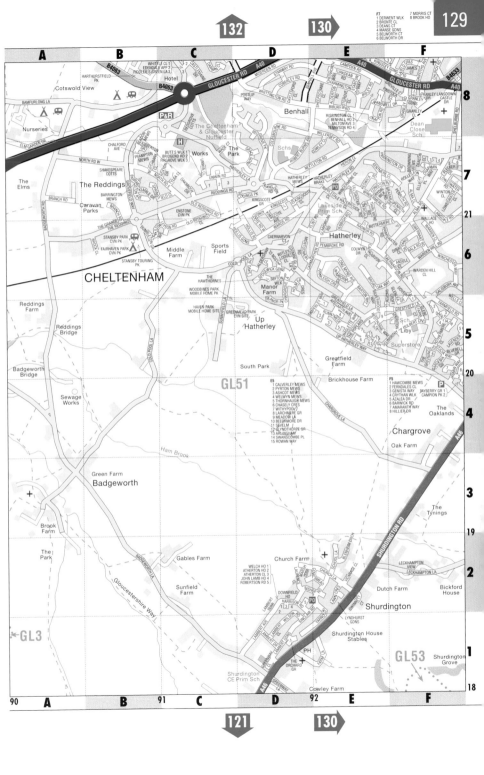

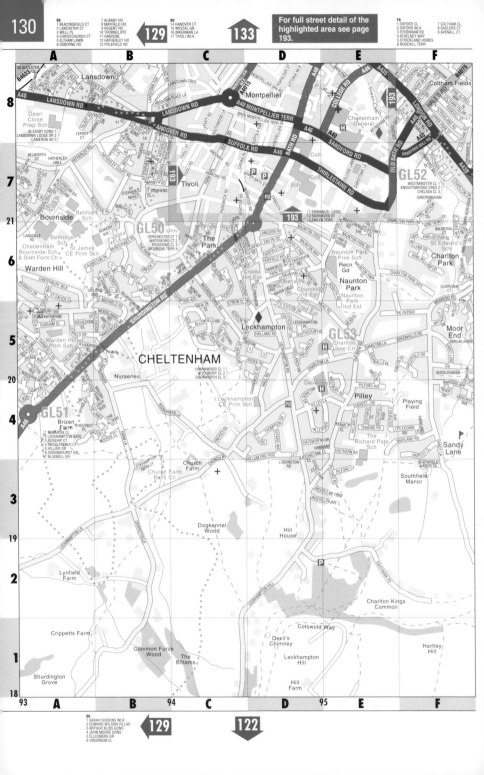

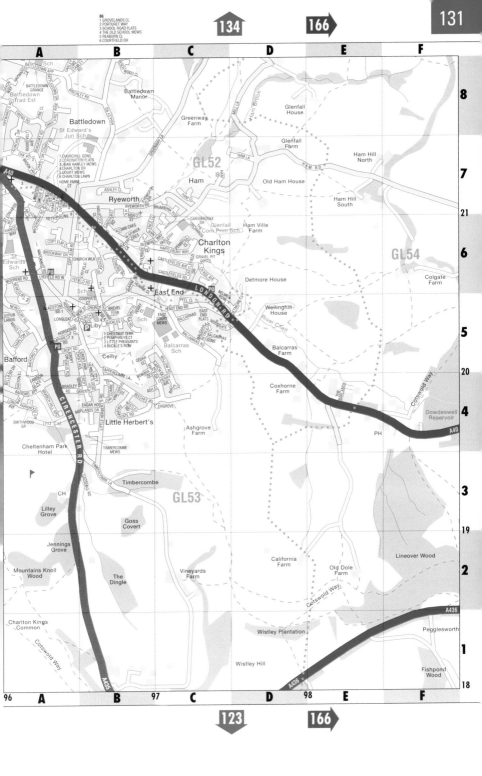

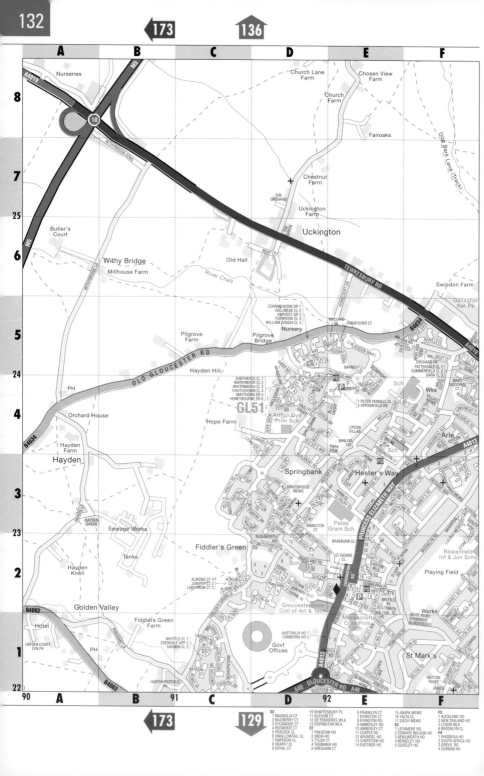

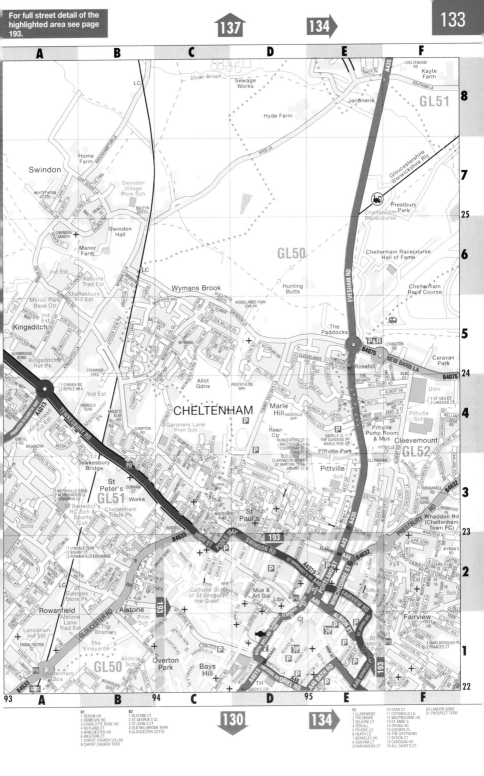

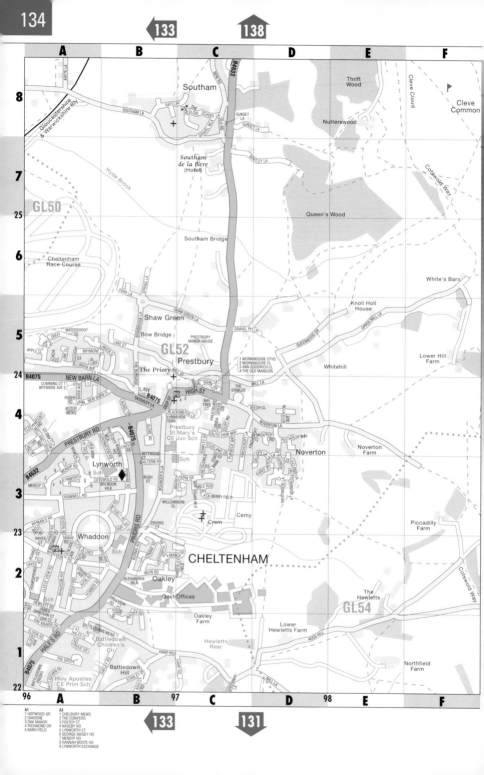

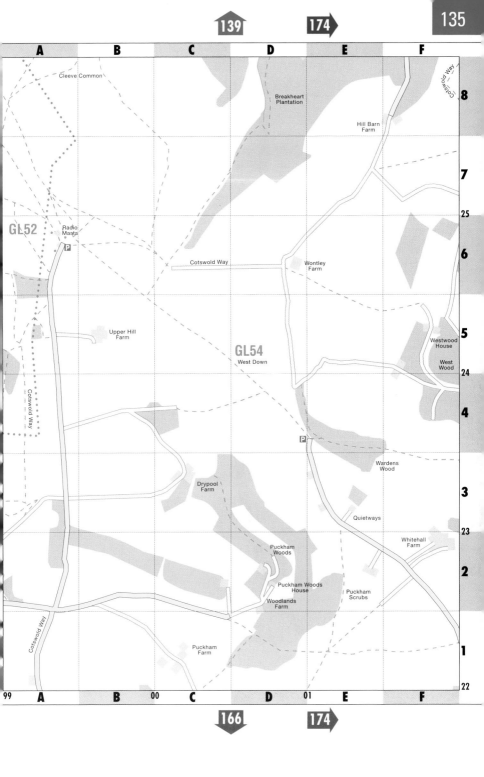

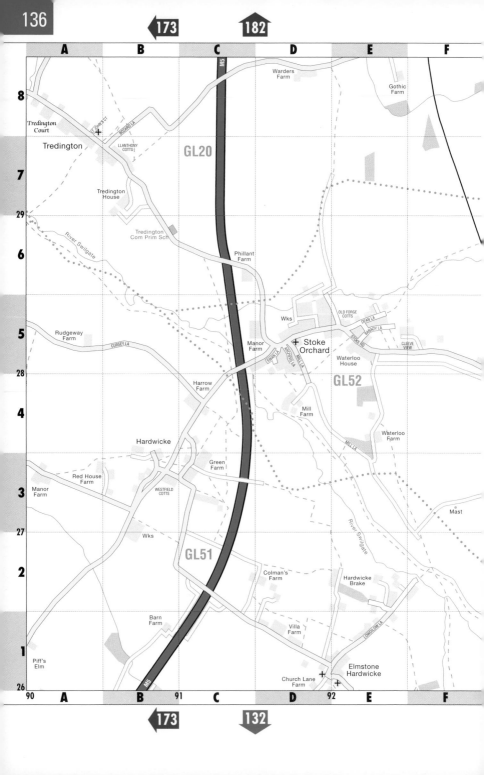

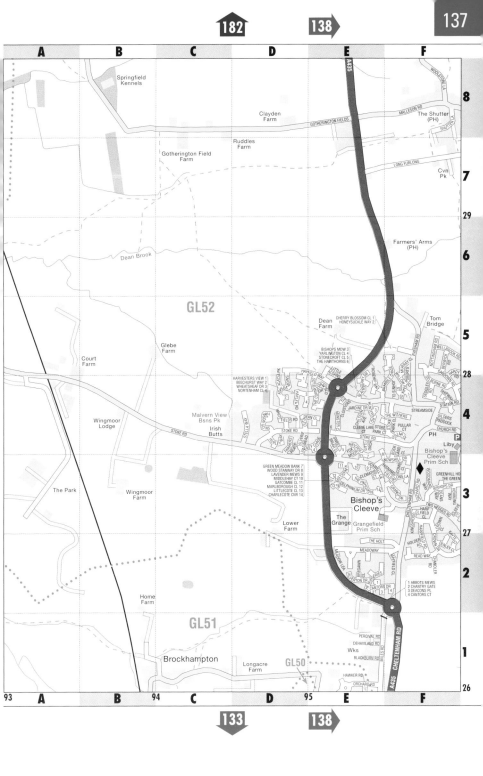

A　B　C　D　E　F

8

Gotherington

Gotherington
Greenway
Farm

Pardon Hill
Farm
Motor Museum
(The Bugatti Trust)

GRETTON RD

GRANNA LA

MALLESON RD

Truman's
Farm

Chapel Close
Farm

7

THE COBBLER'S CL

THE LAWNS

Gotherington
Prim Sch

PO

Manor
Farm

Prescott

Prescott
House

Manor
Farm

CLEEVE RD

MARLE LA

29

Gotherington
Farm

6

Homelands
Farm

Gotherington
Wood

Gloucestershire & Warwickshire Rly

GOTHERINGTON LA

Bushcomb
Wood

Wickfields
Farm

GL54

5

The
White House

Nottingham
Hill

Bishop's
Cleeve

Slades
Farm

28

HARDY RD

OLDACRE DR

Bushcombe House
Farm

BUSHCOMBE LA

P

Longwood
Farm

HORSEFAIR LA

B4632

HERTFORD RD

MILLHAM RD

STATION RD

PINE CL

OXBUTTS
CVN PK

Oxbutts
Ind Est

1 WILLOW DR
2 SYCAMORE CRES
3 BIRCH CL
4 POPLAR CRES
5 COLLYBERRY RD
6 KNAPPS CRES

GL52

4

PRIORY LA

LONG
LANDS

ROSEWOOD
WLK

Woodmancote

PH

CHURCH RD

PO

Sch

BROMFIELD

STOCKWELL LA

CH

P

3

Sch

CLEEVECROFT
AVE

MINETTS AVE

THE
GREEN

BESFORD RD

FIRST AVE

PREST

Cleeve
Hill

27

SUNNYCROFT CL

Cleeve Sch

TWO HEDGES RD

POTTERS FIELD RD

APPLE TREE CL

1 HAWTHORN DR
2 DRAPERS CT
3 ANDERSON CL
4 WILLCOX DR

BYFC

Cotswold Way

2

LYNWORTH RD

DELABERE RD

Haymes
Farm

GAMBLES LA

NEW RD

Hotel
RISING SUN LA

Ben's
Tump

The Ring

SPRING LA

1

HAYMES DR

HAYMES LA

LYE LA

ASHLEIGH LA

B4632

26

96　A　B　97　C　D　98　E　F

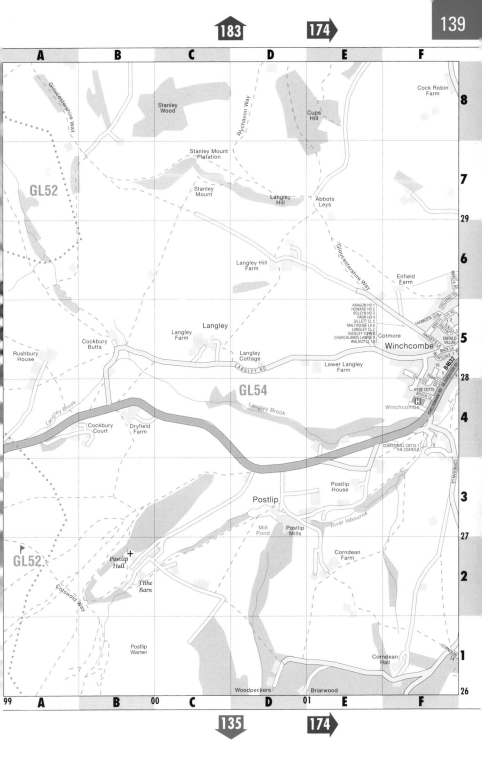

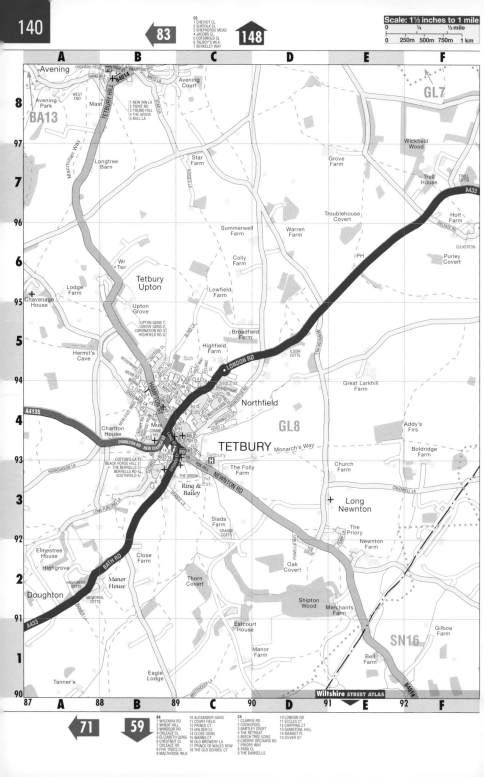

Scale: 1⅓ inches to 1 mile

0 ¼ ½ mile
0 250m 500m 750m 1 km

C5
1 CHEVIOT CL
2 SUFFOLK CL
3 SHEPHERDS MEAD
4 JACOBS
5 COTSWOLD CL
6 TALBOY'S WLK
7 BERKELEY WAY

Avening

ORCHARD FIELD FARM
HIGH ST
HAMPTON RD
B4014
TETBURY HILL
MAYS LA
Avening Court

BA13
Avening Park
WEST END
Mast
1 NEW INN LA
2 POINT RD
3 POUND HILL
4 THE GROVE
5 MILL LA

Macmillan Way

Longtree Barn

Star Farm

GL7

Wickfield Wood

Trull House

TRULL COTTS

A433

Grove Farm

Holt Farm

OXLEAZE RD

Wr Twr

Tetbury Upton

Lodge Farm

Chavenage House

Upton Grove

Summerwell Farm

Warren Farm

Troublehouse Covert

PH

CULKERTON

Purley Covert

Colly Farm

Lowfield Farm

UPTON GDNS 1
GROVE GDNS 2
CORONATION RD 3
HIGHFIELD RD 4

Broadfield Farm

Hermit's Cave

BLIND LA

Highfield Farm

Sch

LONDON RD

ILSOM COTTS

Ind.Est

Great Larkhill Farm

WOODWARD'S
WEBB RD
BERKELEY CL
HAMPTON ST

NORTHAMPTON HILL

Charlton House

Mus

Northfield

GL8

Addy's Firs

A4135

COMBE
NEW CHURCH ST

TETBURY

Tetbury
H

Monarch's Way

Boldridge Farm

HOOKSHOUSE LA

CHARLTON RD

COTTON'S LA 1
BLACK HORSE HILL 2
THE BERRELLS 3
BERRELLS RD 4
SOUTHFIELD 5

PO

THE GREEN

Ind.Est

FOX HILL

NEWTON RD

Church Farm

CRUDWELL LA

LONG FURLONG LA

Ring & Bailey

The Folly Farm

Long Newton

Slads Farm

GRANGE COTTS

The Priory

Newnton Farm

Elmestree House

Close Farm

BATH RD

Thorn Covert

POWELL'S WAY

THE DRIVE

The Priory

Highgrove

Manor House

Oak Covert

HIGHGROVE COTTS

MEMORIAL COTTS

Shipton Wood

Merchants Farm

SN16

Gilboa Farm

Doughton

A433

BARNFIELD LA

Tanner's

Eagle Lodge

WHITENDGE LA

Estcourt House

Manor Farm

Bell Farm

B4014

B4
1 WISTARIA RD
2 WHEAT HILL
3 WINDSOR RD
4 OXLEAZE CL
5 ELIZABETH GDNS
6 CHESTNUT CL
7 OXLEAZE RD
8 FIVE TREES CL
9 MALTHOUSE WLK
10 ALEXANDER GDNS
11 COURT FIELD
12 PRINCE CT
13 HOLDER CL
14 CLOSE GDNS
15 WARNS CT
16 OLD BREWERY LA
17 PRINCE OF WALES ROW
18 THE OLD SCHOOL CL

C4
1 CLARRIE RD
2 COOKSPOOL
3 BARTLEY CROFT
4 THE RETREAT
5 BEECH TREE GDNS
6 CHERRY ORCHARD RD
7 PRIORY WAY
8 PARK CL
9 THE DAMSELLS

D
10 LONDON RD
11 ECCLES CT
12 CHIPPING CT
13 GUMSTOOL HILL
14 MARKET PL
15 SILVER ST

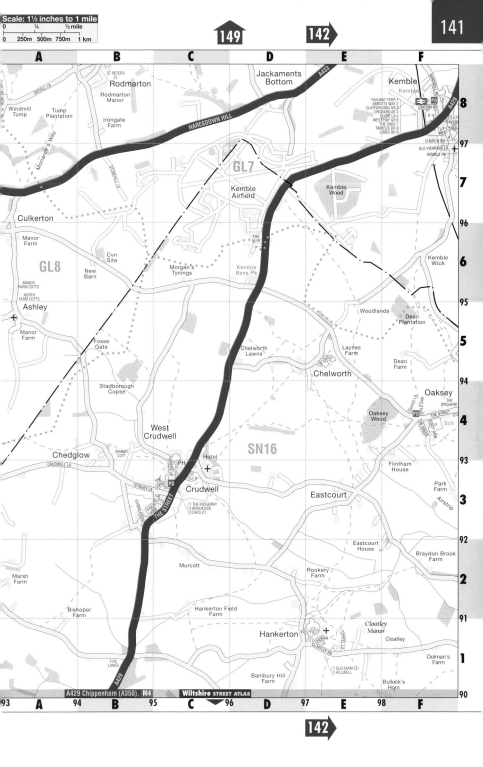

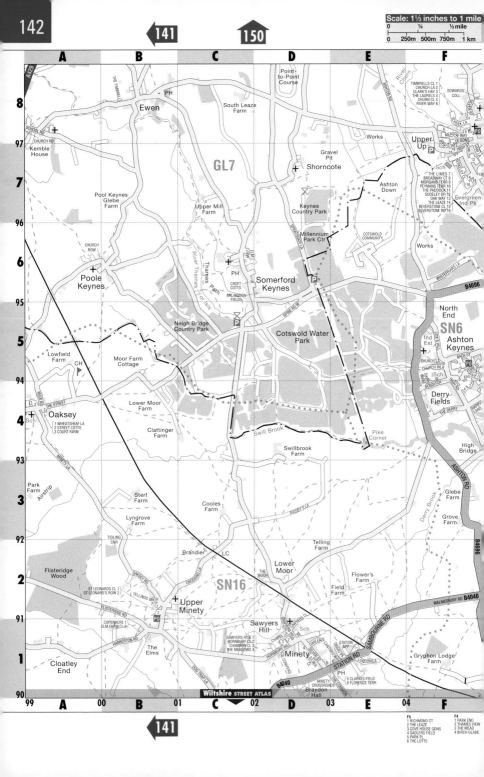

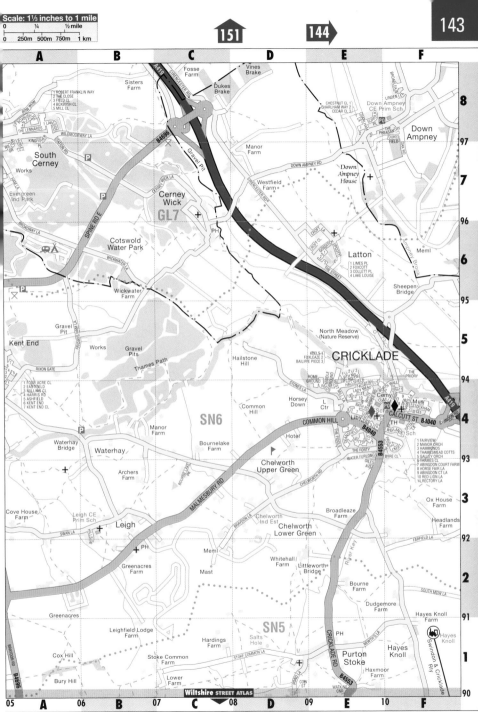

A   B   C   D   E   F

8

1 ROBERT FRANKLIN WAY
2 THE CLOSE
3 FIELD CL
4 BOXBUSH CL
5 MILL CL

THE LENNARDS

Fosse Farm

Vines Brake

Dukes Brake

Sisters Farm

Manor Farm

CHESTNUT CL 1
SHARLHAM WAY 2
CEDAR CL 3

Down Ampney CE Prim Sch

LINDEN CL

THE PHEASANTS

DUKES FIELD

Down Ampney

97

South Cerney

Cerney Wick

GL7

Westfield Farm

Down Ampney Rd

Down Ampney House

Meml

7

Cotswold Water Park

PH

Latton

1 LIMES PL
2 FOXCOTT
3 COLLETT PL
4 LAKE LOUISE

Sheepen Brook

96

Wickwater Farm

THE STREET

Sheepen Bridge

6

Works

Kent End

Gravel Pit

Works

Gravel Pits

Thames Path

RIXON GATE

1 FOUR ACRE CL
2 EASTFIELD
3 MILLING CL
4 HARRIS RD
5 ASHFIELD
6 KENT END
7 KENT END CL

Hailstone Hill

North Meadow (Nature Reserve)

KBELS 1
FOXLEAZE 2
BAILIFFE PIECE 3

CRICKLADE

95

Horsey Down

HOME GROUND

STONES LA

THE PRIORY

94

SN6

Common Hill

L Ctr

Mus

CALCUTT ST

B4040

5

Manor Farm

Waterhay Bridge

Waterhay

Bournelake Farm

Hotel

COMMON HILL

Liby

TH

B4040

B4553

BYRE CL

1 FAIRVIEW
2 MANOR ORCH
3 HAMMONDS
4 THAMESMEAD COTTS
5 GALLEY ORCH
6 THAMES CL
7 ABINGDON COURT FARM
8 HORSE FAIR LA
9 ABINGDON CT LA
10 RED LION LA
11 RECTORY LA

4

Cove House Farm

Archers Farm

Leigh CE Prim Sch

Leigh

Chelworth Upper Green

THE FORTY

WATER FURLONGS

Broadleaze Farm

Ox House Farm

Headlands Farm

FAIRFIELD LA

93

3

SWAN LA

PH

Greenacres Farm

Meml

Mast

Chelworth Ind Est

Chelworth Lower Green

Whitehall Farm

Littleworth Bridge

River Key

Bourne Farm

Dudgemore Farm

SOUTH MDW LA

92

2

Greenacres

Leighfield Lodge Farm

Hardings Farm

Salts Hole

SN5

PH

Bourne Farm

Hayes Knoll Farm

Hayes Knoll

Swindon & Cricklade Rly

91

Cox Hill

Bury Hill

B4696

Stoke Common Farm

Lower Farm

STOKE COMMON LA

CRICKLADE RD

Purton Stoke

Haxmoor Farm

B4553

WATKINS CNR

COW ST

90

05   A   06   B   07   C   08   D   09   E   10   F

E4
1 HOPKINS ORCH
2 BISHOPFIELD
3 PARSONAGE FARM
4 PORTWELL
5 CHURCH LA
6 HEBERDEN HO
7 DOUBLEDAYS
8 CLIFFORDS
9 VALE CT

10 FULLERS AVE
11 CULVERHAY
12 CHERRY TREE RD
13 PIKE HOUSE CL
14 FAIRFIELD
15 KITEFIELD
16 PLEYDELLS
17 BRANDERS

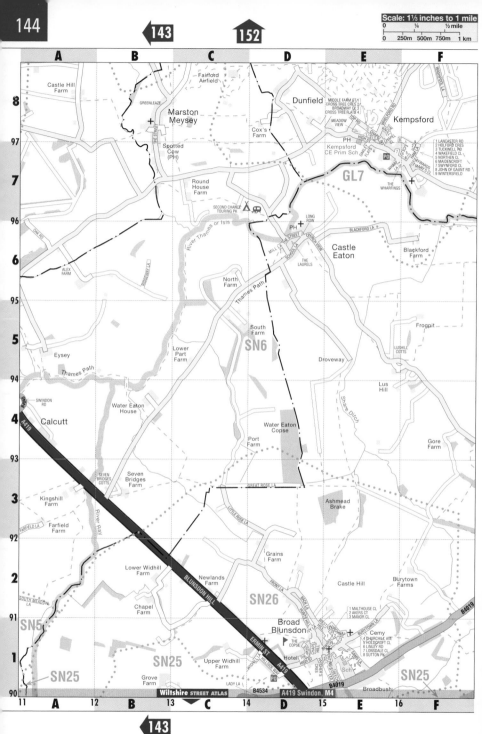

Castle Hill Farm

GREENLEAZE

Fairford Airfield

Dunfield

MIDDLE FARM ST 1
CROSS TREE CRES 2
BROADWAY CE 3
CROSS TREE FLATS 4

MEADOW VIEW

Kempsford

1 LANCASTER RD
2 HOLFORD CRES
3 TUCKWELL RD
4 WAKEFIELD CL
5 NORTHEN CL
6 MAIDENCROFT
7 SWYNFORD CL
8 JOHN OF GAUNT RD
9 WINTERSFIELD

Marston Meysey

Cox's Farm

THE STREET

Kempsford CE Prim Sch

PH

PO

ST MARY'S CE

HIGH ST

CHAPEL

WHARF LA

HAYWARDS

Spotted Cow (PH)

GL7

THE WHARFINGS

Round House Farm

SECOND CHANCE TOURING PK

LONG ROW

River Thames or Isis

PH

BLACKFORD LA

Blackford Farm

MILL LANE

THE STREET

OXEN LEAZE

SCHOOL LA

Castle Eaton

THE LAURELS

OAK RD

ALEX FARM

RIDGEWAY LA

North Farm

Thames Path

Frogpit

LUSHILL COTTS

Eysey

Lower Part Farm

SN6

South Farm

Droveway

Lus Hill

Thames Path

Water Eaton House

Water Eaton Copse

Share Ditch

Gore Farm

SWINDON RD

Calcutt

A419

Port Farm

SEVEN BRIDGES COTTS

Seven Bridges Farm

GREAT ROSE LA

Ashmead Brake

Kingshill Farm

River Ray

LITTLE ROSE LA

FARFIELD LA

Farfield Farm

Grains Farm

Lower Widhill Farm

BLUNSDON HILL

Newlands Farm

FRONT LA

JACK'S LA

Castle Hill

Burytown Farms

B4019

SOUTH MEADOW LA

SN5

Chapel Farm

SN26

1 MALTHOUSE CL
2 AKERS CT
3 MANOR CL

Cemy

4 CHURCHILL AVE
5 HODGCROFT CL
6 LINLEY RD
7 LONSDALE CL
8 SUTTON PK

BURYTOWN LA

ERMIN ST

Broad Blunsdon

THE COPSE

Hotel

PO

HIGH ST

Sch

SN25

SN25

Grove Farm

Upper Widhill Farm

LADY LA

SN25

Broadbush

A419

B4534

A419 Swindon, M4

B4019

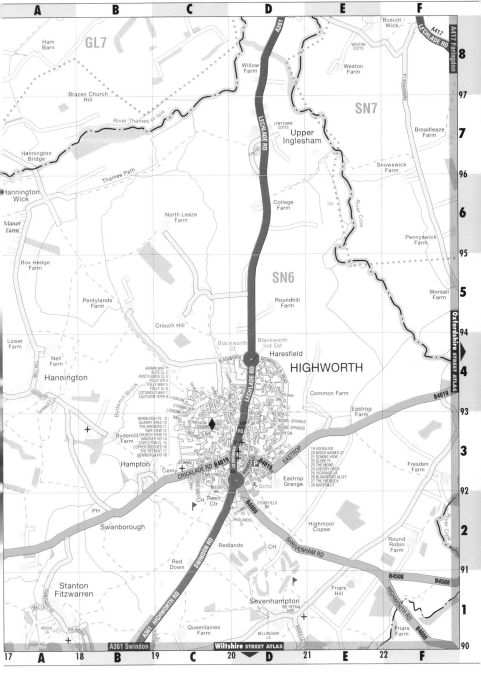

GL7

Ham
Barn

Brazen Church
Hill

River Thames or Isis

Thames Path

Hannington
Bridge

Hannington
Wick

Manor
Farm

Box Hedge
Farm

Lower
Farm

Nell
Farm

Hannington

Pentylands
Farm

Crouch Hill

Bydemill Brook

Willow
Farm

Upper
Inglesham

LECHLADE RD

A361

WESTON
COTTS

Weston
Farm

LYNT FARM
COTTS

LYNT

College
Farm

North Leaze
Farm

Roundhill
Farm

Blackworth
Ct

Blackworth
Ind Est

Haresfield

HIGHWORTH

Buscot
Wick

LECHLADE RD

A417

A417 Faringdon

SN7

Broadleaze
Farm

Snowswick
Farm

River Cole

Pennyswick
Farm

Worsall
Farm

SN6

ARRAN WAY 1
BUTE CL 2
PENTYLANDS CL 3
FOLLY DR 4
FOLLY WAY 5
FOLLY CL 6
COTSWOLD WAY 7
EASTVIEW TERR 8

NEWBURGH PL 9
QUARRY CRES 10
THE ARCHERS 11
FAIR VIEW 12
CHURCH VIEW 13
HANOVER HO 14
STAPLETON CL 15
COPPER BEECHES 16
THE RETREAT 17
NEWBURGH RD 18

Common Farm

Eastrop
Farm

Biddel Springs

Biddel Springs

EASTROP

Eastrop
Grange

19 VORDA RD
20 MIDDI HAINES CT
21 DOWNS VIEW
22 GLEBE PL
23 THE MEWS
24 CHERRY ORCH
25 VICARAGE LA
26 BLANDFORD ALLEY
27 THE PADDOCK
28 BARTON CT

B4019

Fresden
Farm

Bydemill Gdns

Hampton

Cemy

CRICKLADE RD

B4019

P

SHRIVENHAM RD

Highmoor
Copse

Round
Robin
Farm

River Cole

Swanborough

PH

Red
Down

Redlands

CH

B4508

B4508

HIGHWORTH RD

B4000

Stanton
Fitzwarren

SWINDON RD

A361 HIGHWORTH RD

Queenlaines
Farm

Sevenhampton

THE REEMA
HO

Friars
Hill

Friars
Farm

B4000

Oxfordshire STREET ATLAS

8
97
7
96
6
95
5
94
4
93
3
92
2
91
1
90

Scale: 1⅓ inches to 1 mile

0   ¼   ½ mile
0   250m   500m   750m   1 km

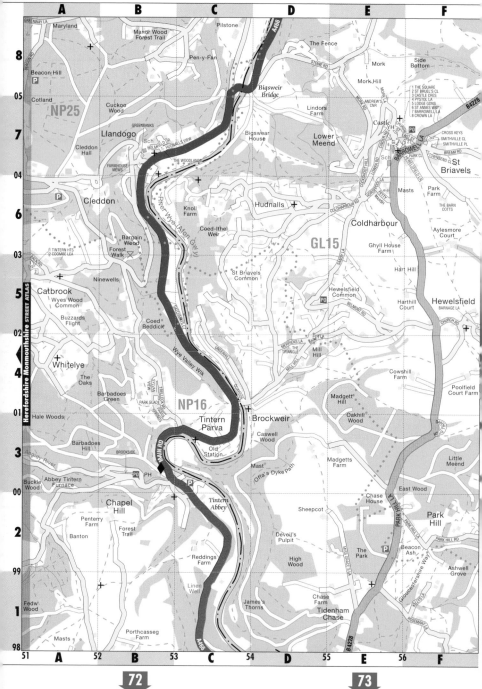

1 THE SQUARE
2 ST BRUEL'S CL
3 CASTLE CRES
4 PYSTOL LA
5 LODGE GDNS
6 ST ANNES WAY
7 BARROWELL LA
8 CROWN LA

Herefordshire Monmouthshire STREET ATLAS

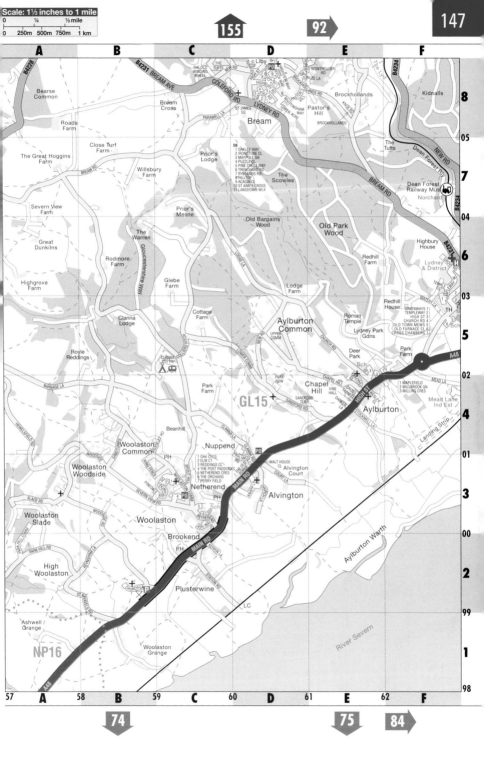

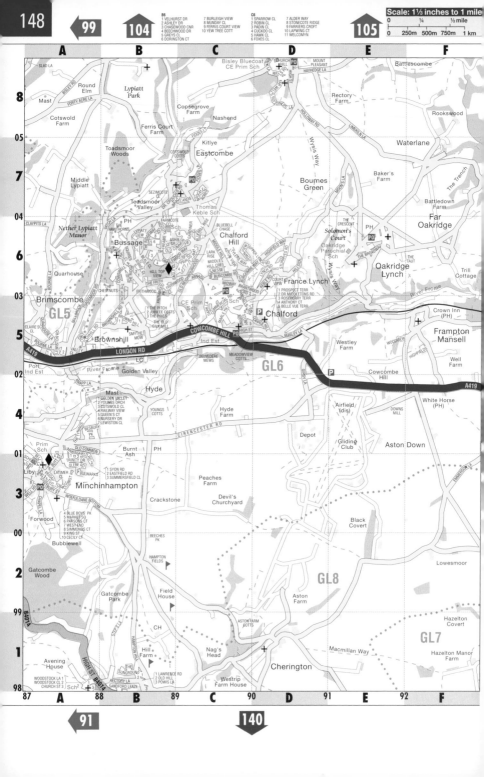

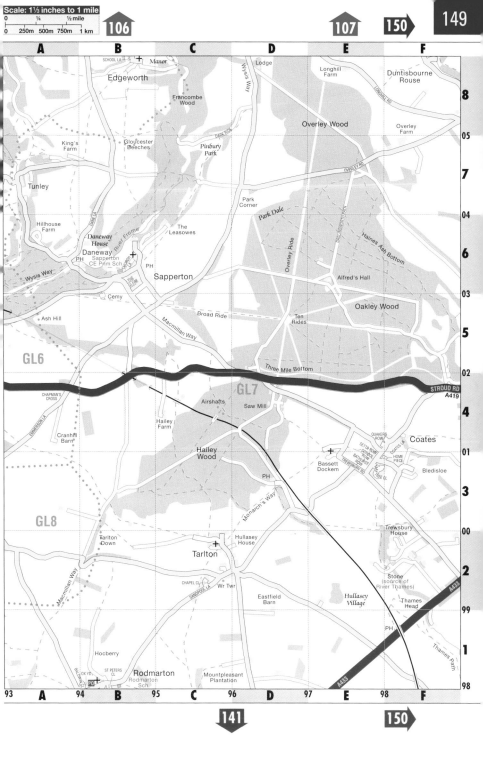

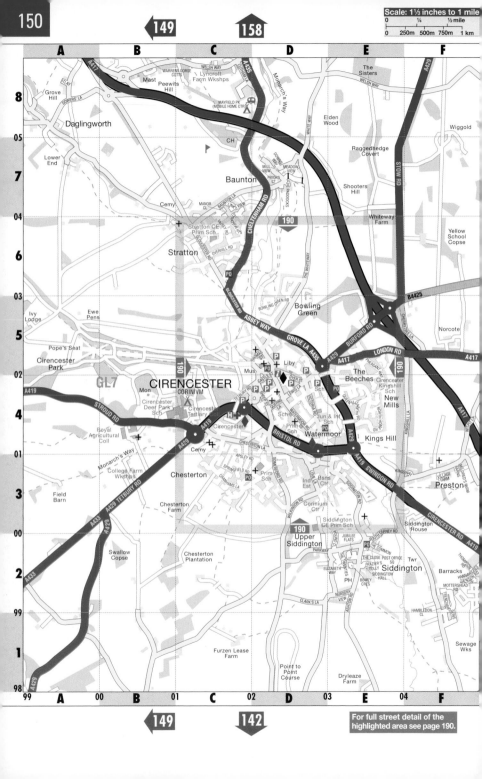

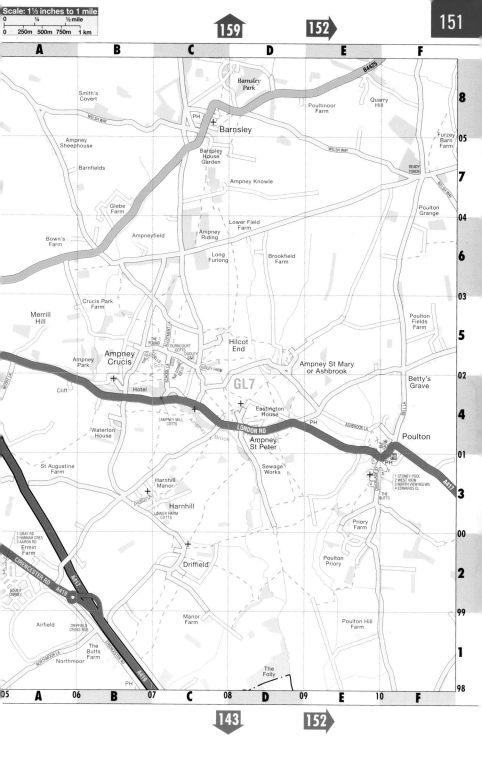

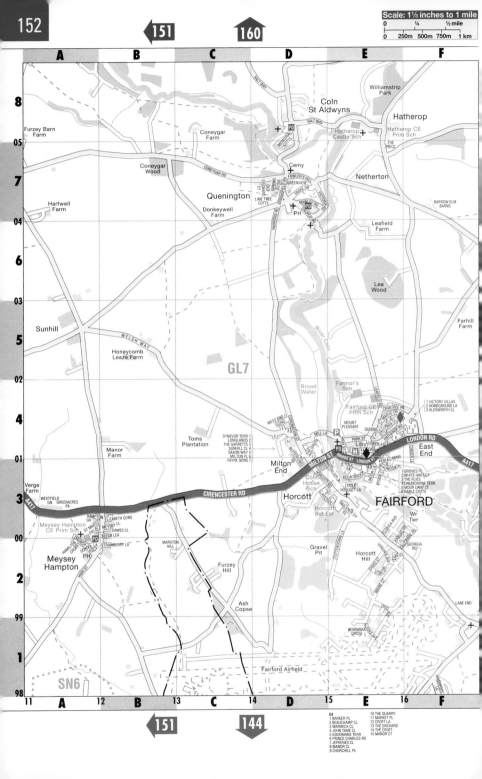

Scale: 1⅓ inches to 1 mile

0   ¼   ½ mile
0   250m 500m 750m 1 km

A **B** **C** **D** **E** **F**

8

05

7

04

6

03

5

02

4

01

3

00

2

99

1

98

Furzey Barn
Farm

Coneygar
Farm

Coln
St Aldwyns

Williamstrip
Park

Hatherop

Hatherop CE
Prim Sch

Hatherop
Castle Sch

THE PIECE

Coneygar
Wood

Cemy

Netherton

Quenington

Donkeywell
Farm

Leafield
Farm

BARROW ELM
BARNS

Hartwell
Farm

Lea
Wood

Farhill
Farm

Sunhill

WELSH WAY

Honeycomb
Leaze Farm

GL7

Broad
Water

Farmor's
Sch

River Coln

Fairford CE
Prim Sch

1 VICTORY VILLAS
2 HOMEGROUND LA
3 ALDSWORTH CL

Toms
Plantation

WEST END

DYNEVOR TERR 1
LONGLANDS 2
THE GARRETTS 3
SUNHILL CL 4
SAXON WAY 5
MILTON PL 6
FAYRE GDNS 7

MOUNT
PLEASANT

QUEENS

PARK ST

Lib

LONDON RD

East
End

Manor
Farm

Milton
End

MILL LA

MILTON ST

BRIDGE ST

LONDON ST

1 GROVES PL
2 WHITE HART CT
3 THE PLIES
4 EASTBOURNE TERR
5 MOOR LANE CT
6 GABLE COTTS

CIRENCESTER RD

Horcott

FAIRFORD

Wr
Twr

Verge
Farm

A417

A417

WESTFIELD
GN GREENACRES
PK

Coln
Hoúse
Sch

Horcott
Ind Est

Hampton

Meysey Hampton
CE Prim Sch

ELIZABETH GDNS

WARWICK CL
DAWES CL

BELCH LEA

Gravel
Pit

Horcott
Hill

GEORGIA
RD

Meysey
Hampton

PH

MARSTON
HILL

STRAWBERRY LA

Furzey
Hill

Ash
Copse

MEBRASKA
CIRCLE

LANE END

SN6

Fairford Airfield

A **B** **C** **D** **E** **F**
11   12   13   14   15   16

E4
1 BARKER PL
2 BEAUCHAMP CL
3 WARWICK CL
4 JOHN TAME CL
5 GOODMANS TERR
6 PRINCE CHARLES RD
7 JEFFERIES CL
8 MANOR CL
9 CHURCHILL PL
10 THE QUARRY
11 MARKET PL
12 CROFT LA
13 THE ORCHARD
14 THE CROFT
15 MANOR CT

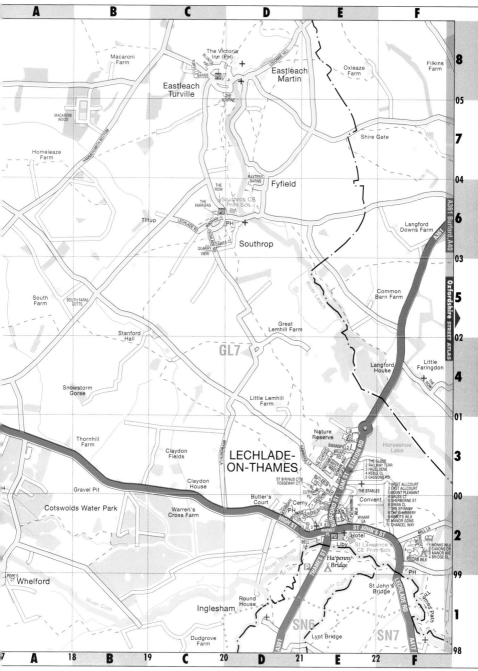

A6
1 MONKSWELL RD
2 MONKSWELL CL
3 JONES HO
4 BURGAGE
5 Hadnock Rd Ind Est

A7
1 NEWLAND WAY
2 CHURCH FARM
3 ORCHARD CT
4 RHODFA WYESHAM/WYESHAM AVE
5 CLAYPATCH RD
6 Y PADDGAU/ THE PADDOCKS

7 CHESTNUT TERR
8 CILGANT DEFNI/OAK CRES
9 LIMETREE AVE
10 CHESTNUT CT
11 HEATH ST
12 READE ST
13 BLAKE ST

A7
14 THE DOWNHAMS
15 HILLCREST CL
16 GREENLANDS CL
17 WYESBRIDGE ST
18 ST JAMES ST
19 WHITECROSS ST

20 ST JAMES' SQ
21 GRANVILLE ST
22 YR HEN HEOL/THE OLD RD
23 RIVERSIDE PK
24 Mayhill Ind Est
25 Wyeside Com Ctr

Herefordshire Monmouthshire STREET ATLAS

MONMOUTH TREFYNWY

Dixton
Haberdashers Sch for Girls

May Hill
The Garth
BLESTIVM
Kymin
Naval Temple
Wyesham
Sewage Works

Lord's Grove
Otfa's Dyke Path
Troypark Wood
Wye Valley Walk
Penallt
Peny-garn Farm
Pen-twyn
Moorcroft
Bush Inn (PH)

Common Farm
GREEN PASTURES
CROSS VANE
The Argoed
Lower Meend Farm

Hoop
Tre-gagle
Newmills
Hael Woods

Trelleck Common
The Narth
FOREST VIEW
Trekkers (PH)
Vicar's Allotment
Manor Wood
Whitebrook
Forest Walks

Redding's Inclosure
Highmeadow Woods
Wysis Way
WELL MEADOW
Beaulieu Farm
Buck Stone
Birchen Wood
Bunjups Wood
Knockalls Inclosure

Upper Redbrook
1 MILL COTTS
2 BREWERY COTTS
Redbrook CE Print Stu
WYE VIEW TERR
WYE'S GN
Lower Redbrook
Highbury Terr
Highbury Farm
Glyn Farm
LONE LA
Glyn Farm

The Grove
Coxbury Farm

Wyeseal Farm

HR9
Mailscot Wood
Forest Trails
Braceland Adventure Centre
Christchurch
Coalpit Hill
Broom Hill
Broom Hill Forest Trail
Staunton
STAUNTON HO 1
TILLIS VIEW 2
THE OLD RECTORY 3
Marian Inclosure
ROBIN HOOD JUNC
STAUNTON RD
GL16
Stowfield Quarry
Scowles
Cemy
Whitecliff
High Meadow Farm
The Ostrich (PH)
ALMSHOUSES RD
Newland
Millend
Sewage Works
Scatterford Farm
Inwood Farm
COUNCIL VILLAS
LOWER CROSS
HYDE VIEW 1
TANNERY GDNS 2
CARPENTER COTTS 3
Lodges Farm
Caudwell Farm
Lodges Barn Farm
GL15
Clearwell Quarries
The Traveller's Rest (PH)
STOWE LA
Stow Greer
Quarry
Stowe
Wyegate Green
Wyegate Hill

NP25

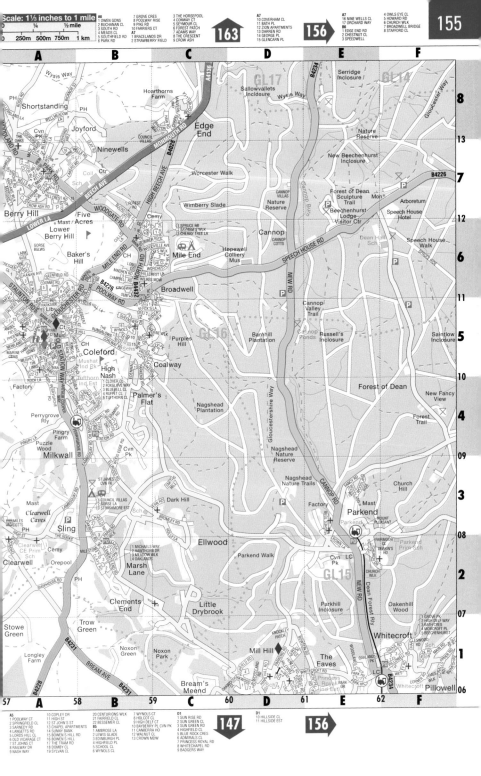

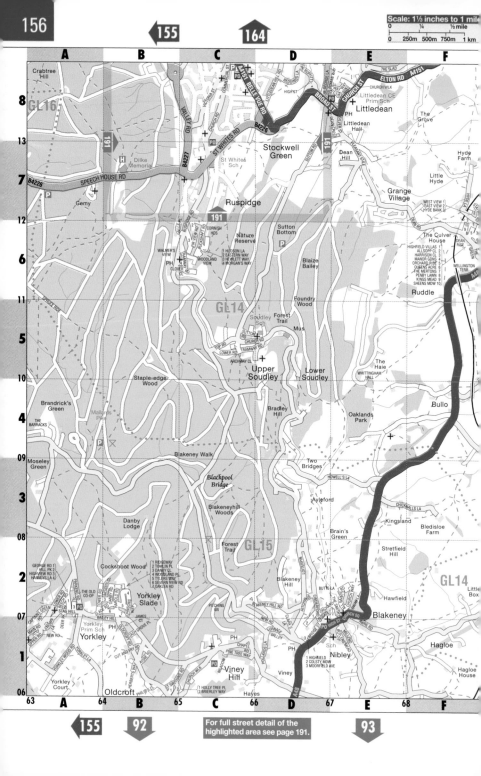

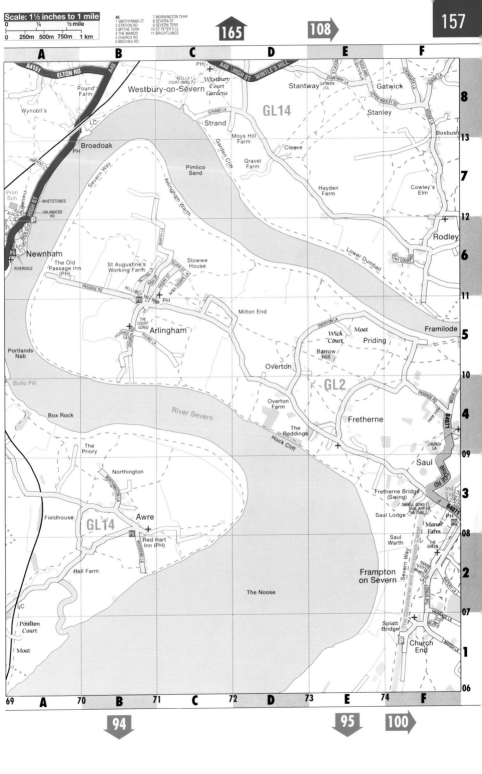

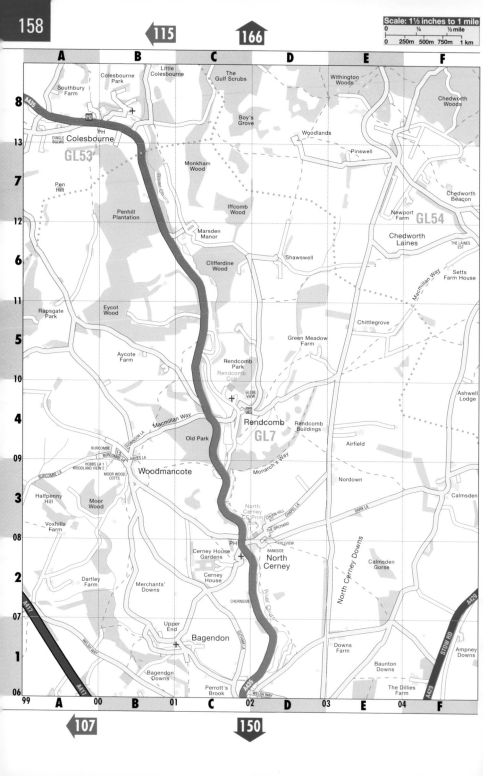

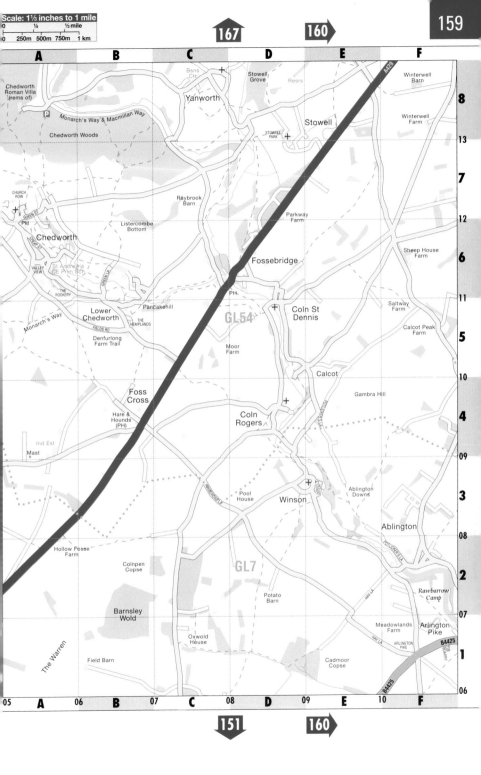

Scale: 1⅓ inches to 1 mile

0   ¼   ½ mile
0   250m 500m 750m 1 km

A **B** **C** **D** **E** **F**

Chedworth
Roman Villa
(rems of)

Bsns
Ctr

Yanworth

Stowell
Grove

Resrs

Winterwell
Barn

A429

8

Monarch's Way & Macmillan Way

Stowell

Winterwell
Farm

Chedworth Woods

STOWELL
PARK

13

CHURCH
ROW

Raybrook
Barn

Parkway
Farm

7

PH

Chedworth

Listercombe
Bottom

12

VALLEY
VIEW

St Andrew's
CE Prim Sch

Fossebridge

Sheep House
Farm

6

THE
ROOKERY

Pancakehill

PH.

GL54

Coln St
Dennis

Saltway
Farm

11

Lower
Chedworth

FIELDS RD

THE
HEMPLANDS

Moor
Farm

Calcot Peak
Farm

5

Denfurlong
Farm Trail

Monarch's Way

Calcot

10

Foss
Cross

Gambra Hill

Hare &
Hounds
(PH)

Coln
Rogers

4

Ind Est

Mast

09

Pool
House

Winson

Ablington
Downs

3

Ablington

Hollow Posse
Farm

Colnpen
Copse

GL7

08

Barnsley
Wold

Potato
Barn

Rawbarrow
Camp

2

07

Oxwold
House

Meadowlands
Farm

Arlington
Pike

The Warren

Field Barn

Cadmoor
Copse

ARLINGTON
PIKE

B4425

1

B4425

06

A 06 **B** 07 **C** 08 **D** 09 **E** 10 **F**

05

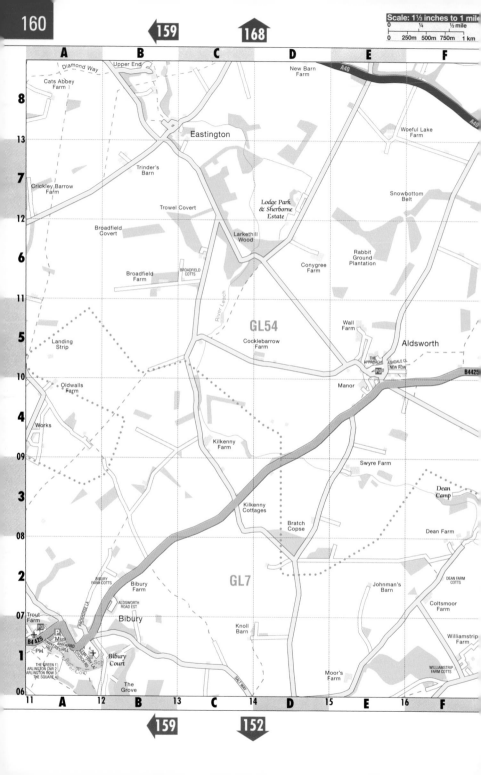

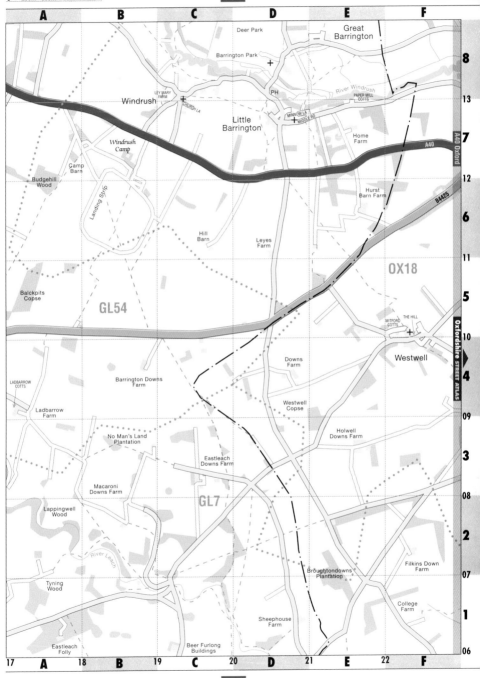

Scale: 1½ inches to 1 mile

Deer Park

Great
Barrington

Barrington Park

8

River Windrush

Windrush

LEY MARY
FARM

CHURCH LA

PH

PAPER MILL
COTTS

13

Little
Barrington

MINNOW LA
MIDDLE RD

Home
Farm

7

A40 Oxford

Windrush
Camp

A40

Camp
Barn

12

Budgehill
Wood

Hurst
Barn Farm

Landing Strip

B4425

6

Hill
Barn

Leyes
Farm

11

OX18

Balckpits
Copse

5

GL54

THE HILL

MITFORD
COTTS

10

Westwell

Downs
Farm

4

Oxfordshire STREET ATLAS

LADBARROW
COTTS

Barrington Downs
Farm

Westwell
Copse

Ladbarrow
Farm

Holwell
Downs Farm

09

No Man's Land
Plantation

Eastleach
Downs Farm

3

Macaroni
Downs Farm

GL7

08

Lappingwell
Wood

2

River Leach

Filkins Down
Farm

07

Tyning
Wood

Broughtondowns
Plantation

College
Farm

1

Eastleach
Folly

Beer Furlong
Buildings

Sheephouse
Farm

06

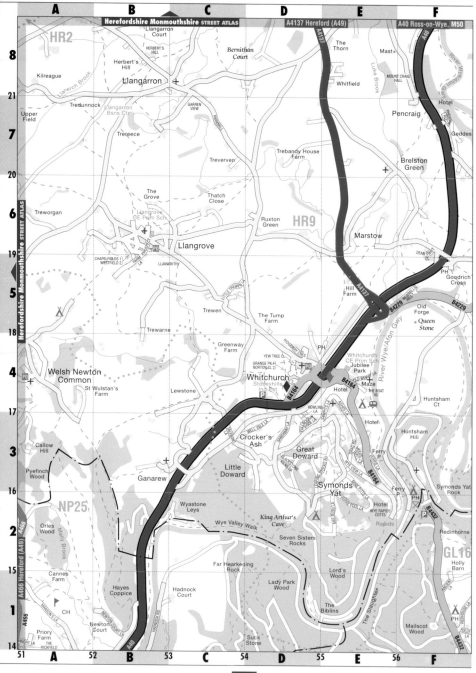

Herefordshire Monmouthshire STREET ATLAS

A4137 Hereford (A49)

A40 Ross-on-Wye, M50

HR2

Llangarron Court

Herbert's Hill

Bernithan Court

The Thorn

Mast

Luke Brook

Mount Craig Hall

Kilreague

Herbert's Hill

Llangarron

Whitfield

Llanerch Brook

Tredunnock

Llangarron Bsns Ctr

GARREN VIEW

Pencraig

Hotel

Geddes

Upper Field

Trereece

Trebandy House Farm

Brelston Green

HR9

The Grove

Thatch Close

Ruxton Green

Marstow

Treworgan

Llangrove CE Prim Sch

Llangrove

DEAN SWIFT

PH

Goodrich Cross

CHAPELFIELDS 1 WESTFIELD 2

LLANWRTHY

Little Trevel La

Hill Farm

Old Forge

Queen Stone

B4229

Trewen

The Tump Farm

RIDGEWAY CRES

B4137

Welsh Newton Common

St Wulstan's Farm

Greenway Farm

YEW TREE CL

PH

Whitchurch CE Prim Sch

River Wye/Afon Gwy

Lewstone

Whitchurch

Stoneyhills Ind Est

Jubilee Park

Maze

The Boat Ho

Hotel

Huntsham Ct

Crocker's Ash

Great Doward

Hotel

Huntsham Hill

Callow Hill

Pyefinch Wood

Ganarew

Little Doward

Ferry

Symonds Yat

Ferry

PH

Symonds Yat Rock

NP25

Orles Wood

Wyastone Leys

King Arthur's Cave

Hotel WYE RAPIDS COTTS

Rapids

GL16

Redinhorne

Cannes Farm

Wye Valley Walk

Seven Sisters Rocks

Holly Barn

Hayes Coppice

Far Hearkening Rock

Lady Park Wood

Lord's Wood

The Slaughter

Priory Farm

Newton Court

Hadnock Court

Suck Stone

The Biblins

Mailscot Wood

PH

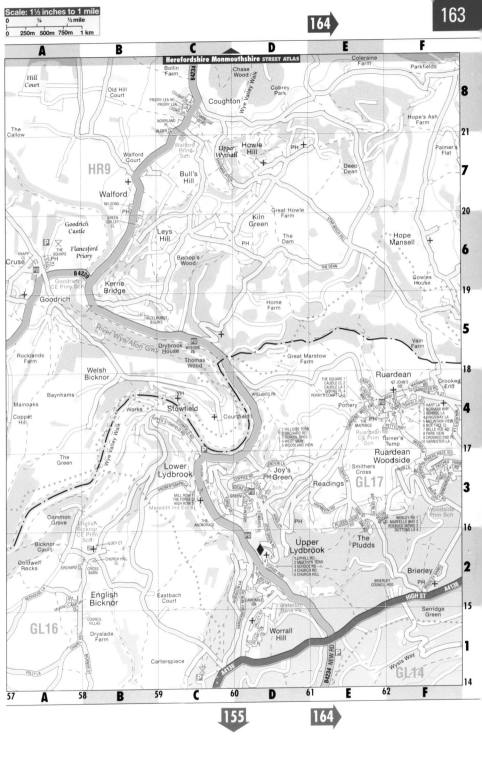

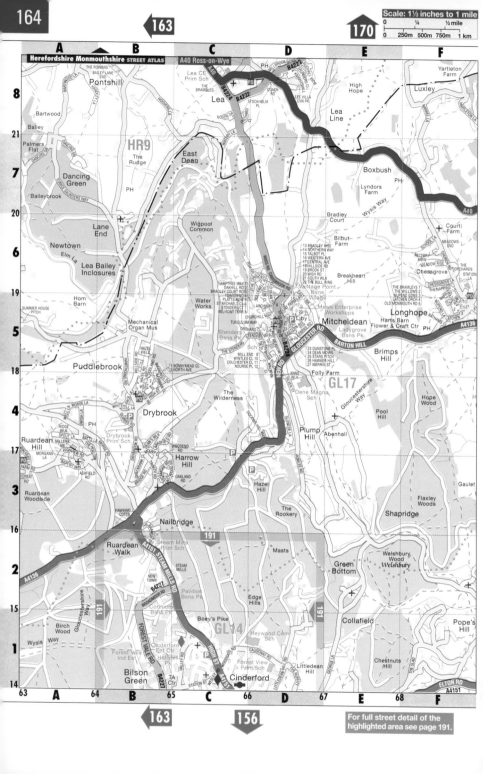

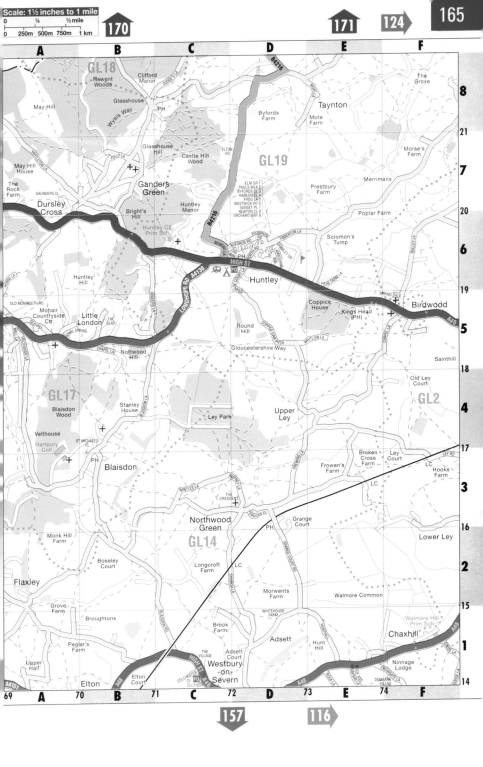

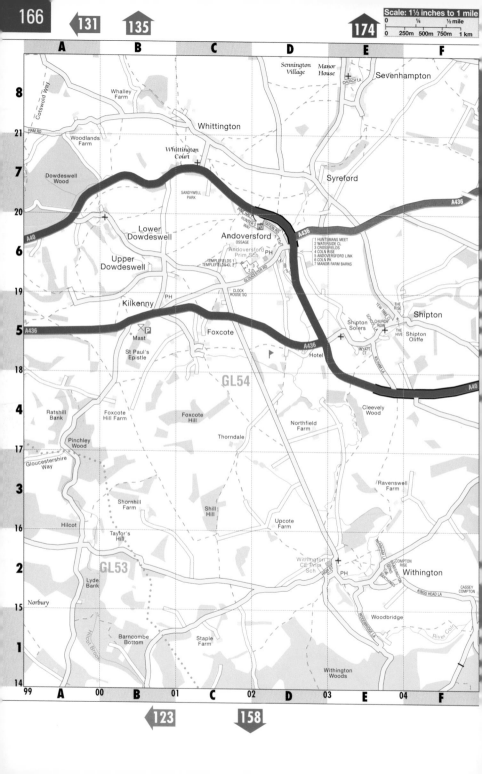

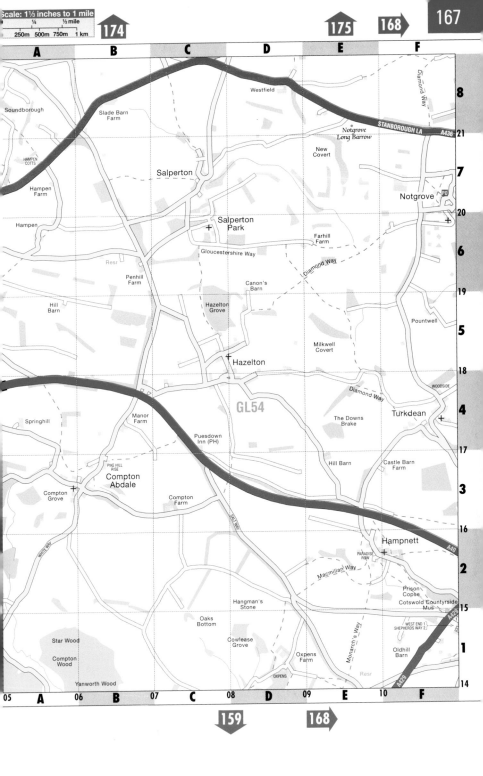

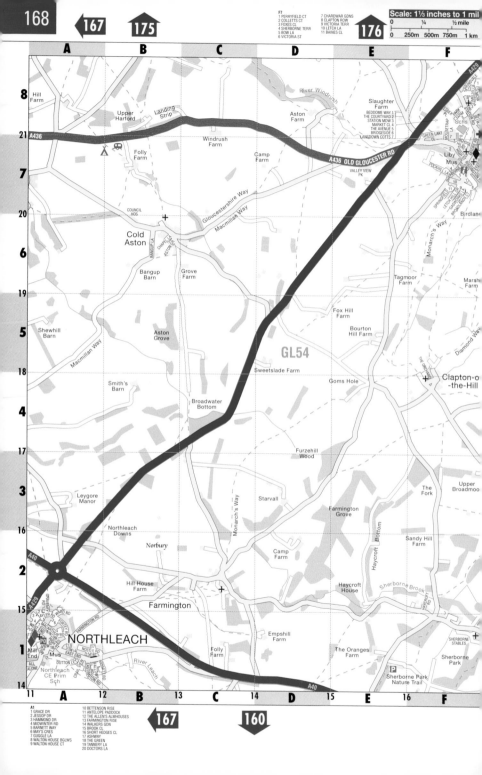

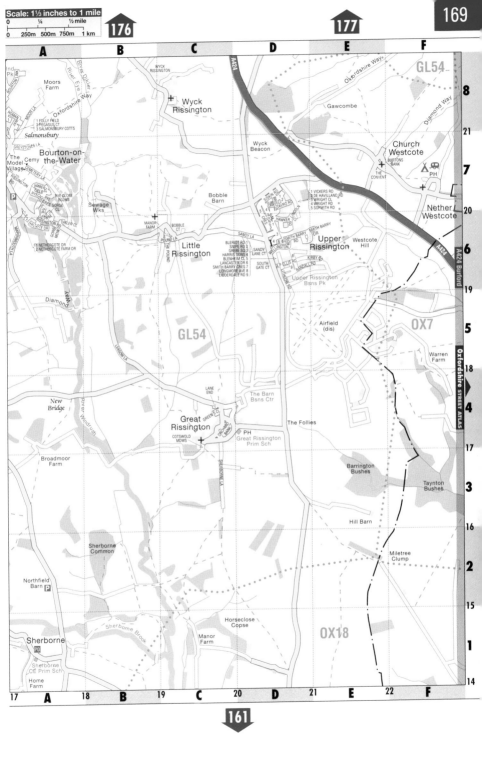

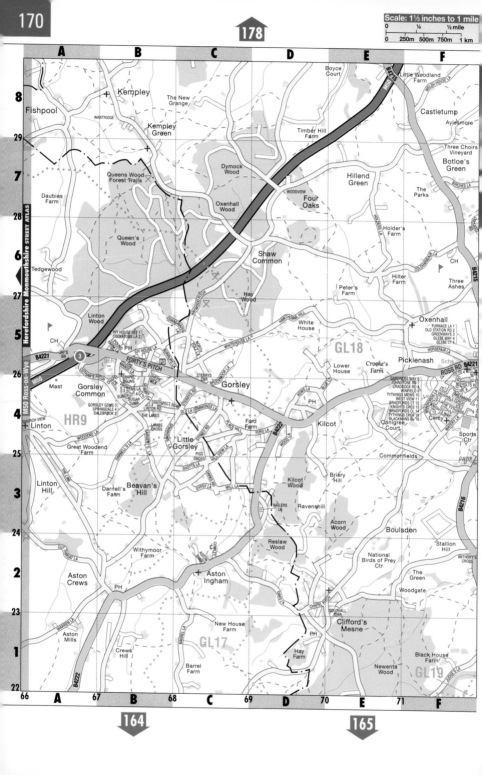

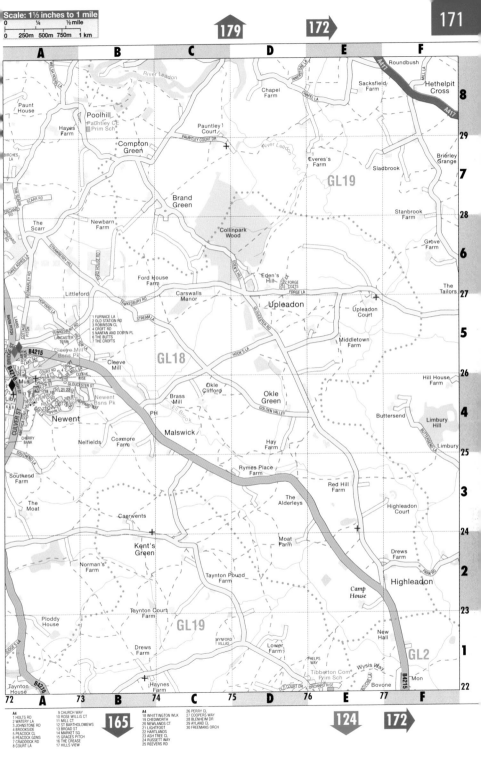

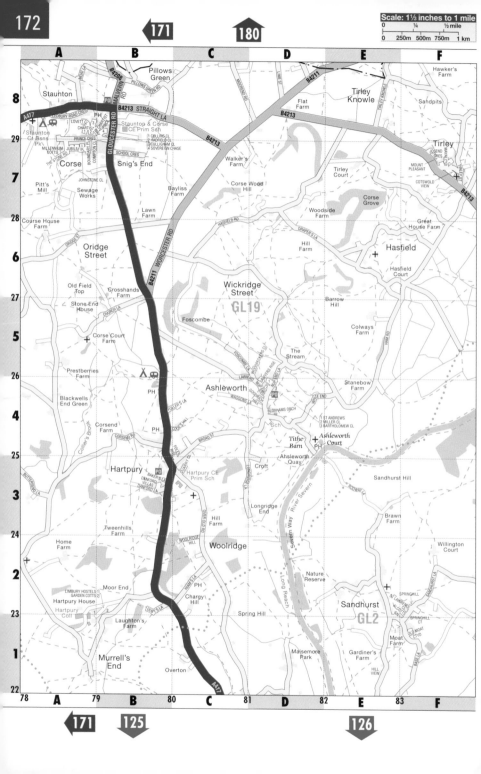

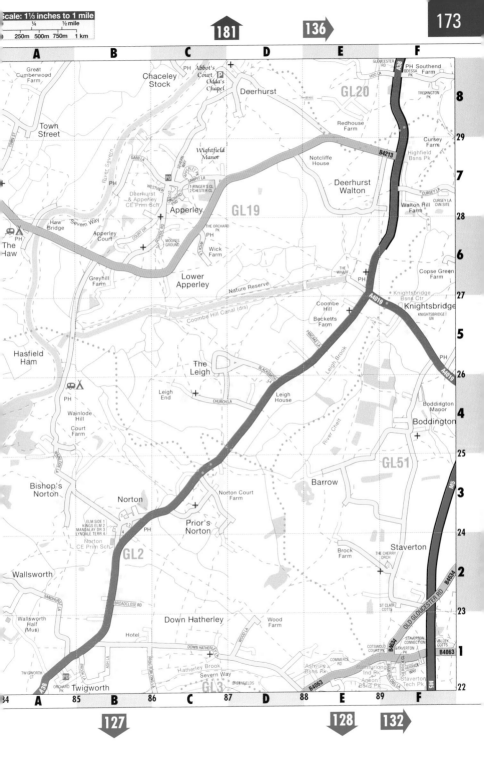

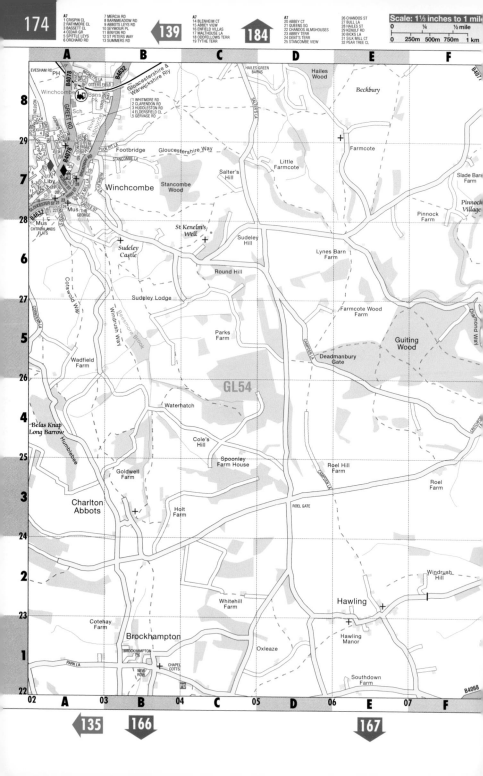

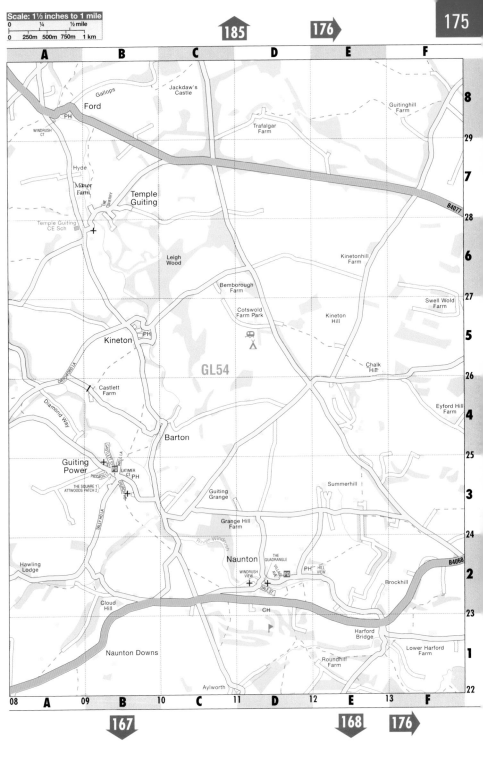

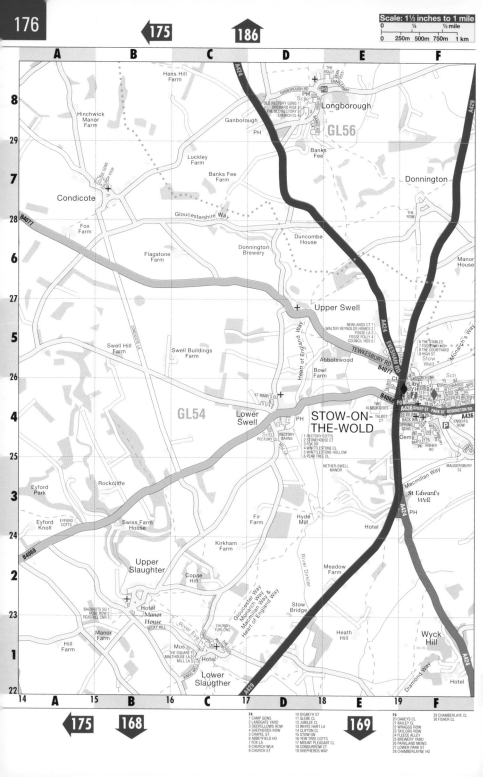

Scale: 1½ inches to 1 mile
0 ¼ ½ mile
0 250m 500m 750m 1 km

A B C D E F

8

THE FOLLY
Longborough
GL56

29

Hans Hill Farm

Hinchwick Manor Farm

Luckley Farm

Ganborough

PH

OLD RECTORY GDNS 1
ORCHARD RISE 1
THE OLD RECTORY
CHURCH CL 4

Banks Fee

7

Banks Fee Farm

Donnington

28

Condicote

Fox Farm

Gloucestershire Way

THE ROW

B4077

6

Flagstone Farm

Donnington Brewery

Duncombe House

Manor House

27

Swell Hill Farm

Swell Buildings Farm

Upper Swell

NEWLANDS CT 1
WALTER REYNOLDS HOMES 2
FOSSE LA 3
FOSSE FOLLY 4
COUNCIL HO 5

6 THE STABLES
7 FOSSEWAY HO
8 THE COURTYARD
9 HIGH ST
Stow Well

5

TEWKESBURY RD

B4077

Abbotswood

Bowl Farm

Sch

26

GL54

Lower Swell

ST MARY'S CL
1 ST 2

Library
Sch

PARSON'S CNR
PO
B4068
THE ALMSHOUSES
A436 SHEEP ST
22 23 24
SPRING GDNS
BARTLETTS

PARK ST ODDINGTON RD
A436
ENOCH'S ROW
PK FISHER HO

4

STOW-ON-THE-WOLD

RECTORY COTTS
RECTORY CL

PH

TALBOT CT

1 RECTORY COTTS
2 STONEHOUSE CT
3 FOX DR
4 WHITTLESTONE CL
5 WHITTLESTONE HOLLOW
6 PEAR TREE CL

Cemy
CHAPEL

25

Rockcliffe

NETHER-SWELL MANOR

St Edward's Well

MAUGERSBURY CL

Eyford Park

Eyford Knoll

EYFORD COTTS

Swiss Farm House

Fir Farm

Hyde Mill

Hotel

Macmillan Way

St Edward's Well

PH

3

24

B4068

Kirkham Farm

Hotel

Meadow Farm

2

Upper Slaughter

Copse Hill

Gloucester Way
Monarch Way &
Macmillan Way &
Heart of England Way

Stow Bridge

Wyck Hill

Hotel

23

BAGSHOTS SQ 1
ROSE ROW 2
PEAS HILL CNR 3

Hotel
Manor House

BECKY HILL

CHURCH FURLONG

River Eye

Heath Hill

Diamond Way

1

Manor Farm

Hill Farm

Mus

THE SQUARE 1
MALTHOUSE LA 2
MILL LA 3

KINGS CL

Hotel

Lower Slaughter

Hotel

22

14 A 15 B 16 C 17 D 18 E 19 F

F4
1 CAMP GDNS
2 LANDGATE YARD
3 ODDFELLOWS ROW
4 SHEPHERDS ROW
5 CHAPEL ST
6 ABBEYFIELD HO
7 FOX LA
8 CHURCH WLK
9 CHURCH ST

10 DIGBETH ST
11 GLEBE CL
12 JUBILEE CL
13 WHITE HART LA
14 CLIFTON CL
15 STOW GN
16 YEW TREE COTTS
17 MOUNT PLEASANT CL
18 CONDURROW CL
19 SHEPHERDS WAY

F4
20 OAKEYS CL
21 BAILEY CL
22 WRAGGS ROW
23 TAYLORS ROW
24 FLEECE ALLEY
25 BREWERY YARD
26 PARKLAND MEWS
27 LOWER PARK ST
28 CHAMBERLAYNE HO

29 CHAMBERLAYE CL
30 FISHER CL

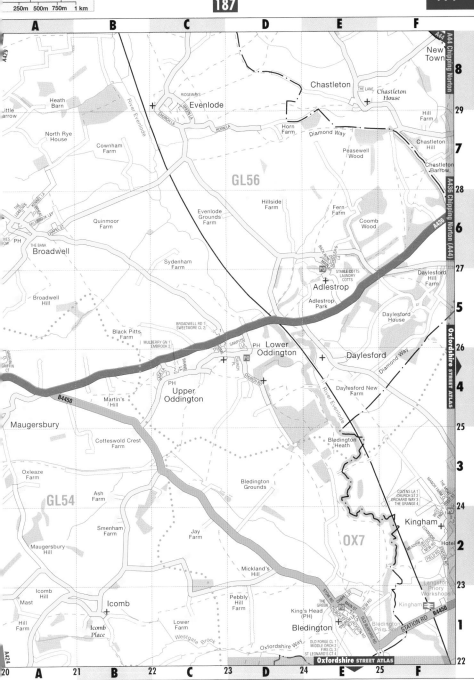

Scale: 1⅓ inches to 1 mile

¼ ½ mile
250m 500m 750m 1 km

Oxfordshire STREET ATLAS

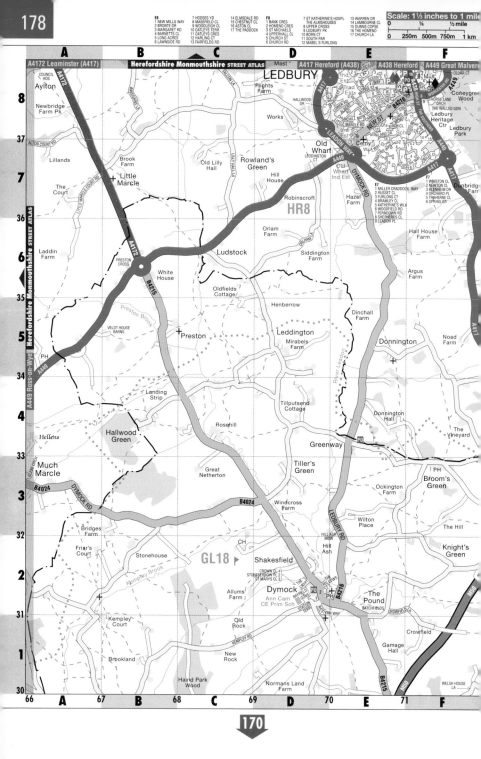

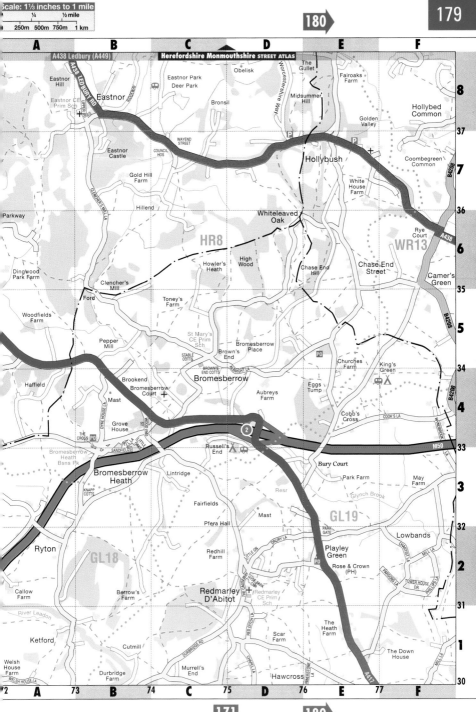

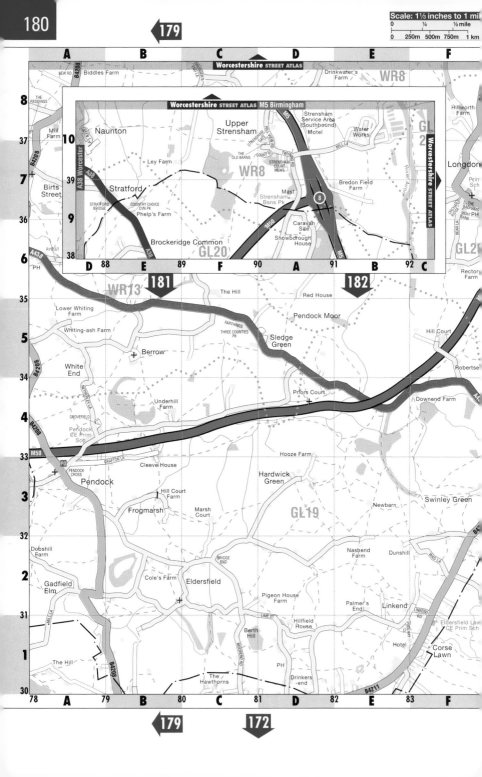

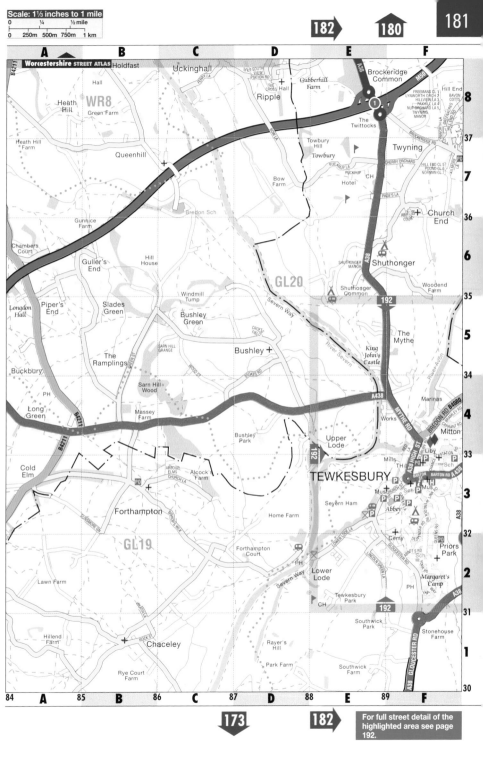

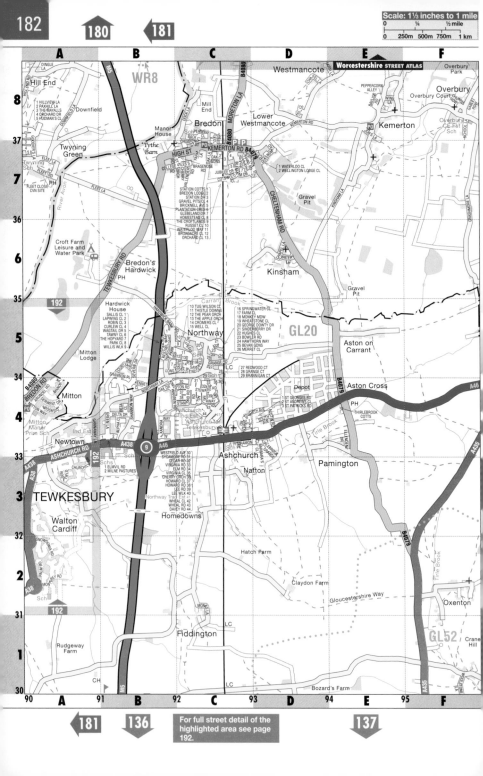

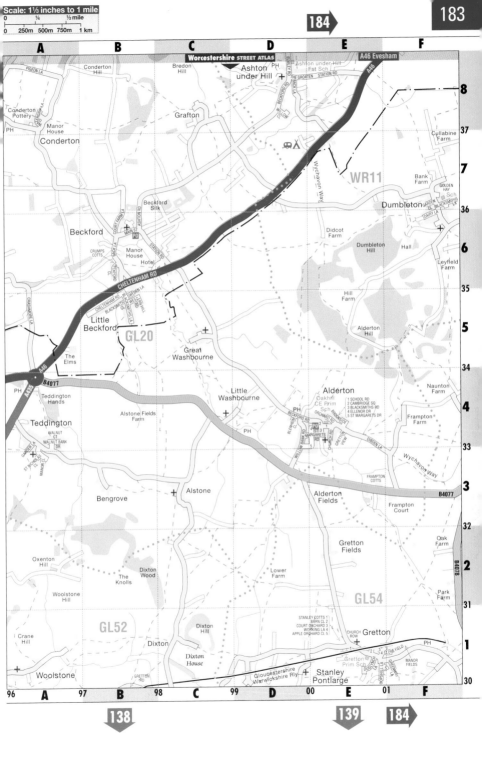

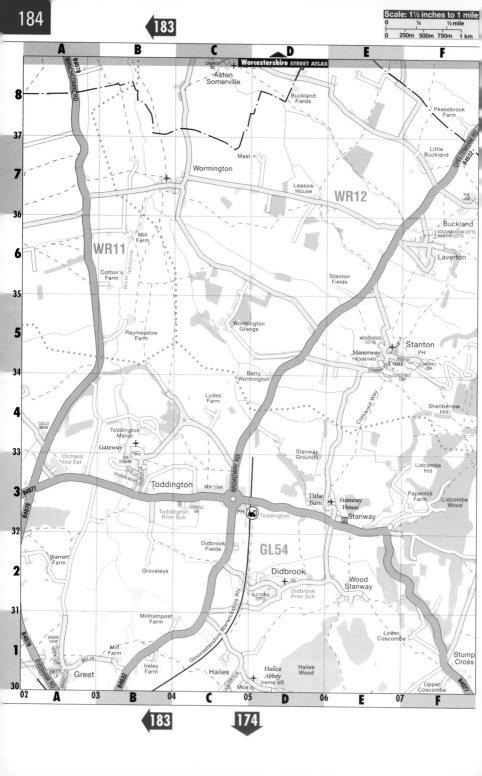

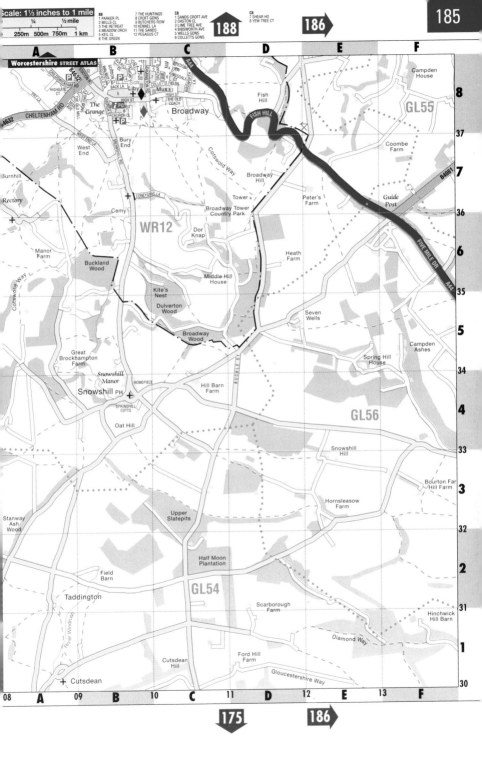

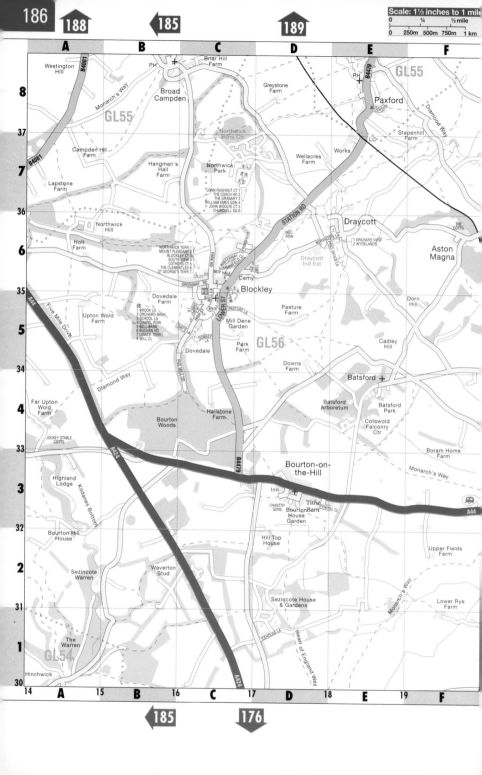

Scale: 1½ inches to 1 mile

0   ¼   ½ mile
0   250m 500m 750m 1 km

A429 Warwick **Warwickshire** STREET ATLAS

Paddle Brook

CV36

High Furze

Middle Ditchford

Ditchford Frary

Neighbrook

Lower Farm

Ditchford Hill

Knee Brook

STONE BRIDGE PH

BECKET CL

Todenham

THE BYRES

1 WOOLAWAY BGLWS
2 CHURCH VIEW
3 CHURCH FARM LA

Oldborough Farm

Aston Hale

Mount Sorrell

Great Wolford

THE GREEN

CARTERS LEAZE PH

Woodhills Farm

INGRAM CL

NETHERCOTE

Lower Lemington

Lemington Manor

CV36

DORN

Lemington Grange

GL56

NORTH CIRCULAR RD

Wolford Wood

Rectory Farm

Stanford Brook

BARTON RD

Old Covert

Moreton-in-Marsh District

Moreton-in-Marsh

The Fire Service Coll

Gravels Coppice

Barton-on-the-Heath

MAIDEN CL

Inn

Mus

HIGH ST

London Rd

Cotswold Bsns Village

The Four Shire Stone

PH

Moreton-in-Marsh

Wells Folly

Kitebrook

Coldicote Farm

Brookend House

Salter's Well Farm

Frogmore Farm

Middle Brookend Farm

DEERHURST CL 1
CHAPEL ROW 2
BREWERY ROW 3

Diamond Way

River Evenlode

Grove Farm

Little Compton

A44

Diamond Way

Chaselton Glebe

Inn

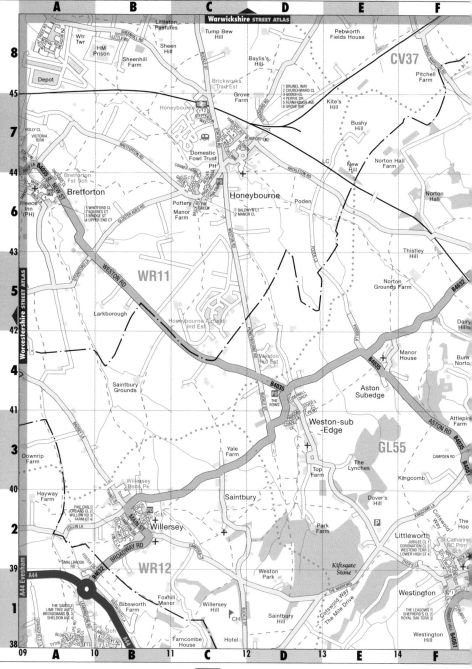

Scale: 1⅓ inches to 1 mil

0   ¼   ½ mile
0 250m 500m 750m 1 km

A   B   C   D   E   F

8
45
7
44
6
43
5
42
4
41
3
40
2
39
1
38

Worcestershire STREET ATLAS

Fleet Rd
Royal Rd
Wtr Twr
HM Prison
Depot
Sheenhill Farm
Littleton Pastures
Sheen Hill
Tump Bew Hill
Baylis's Hill
Pebworth Fields House
CV37
Pitchell Farm
Brickworks Trad Est
Grove Farm
Kite's Hill
Bushy Hill
Honeybourne
1 BRUNEL WAY
2 CHURCHWARD CL
3 GOOCH CL
4 PERRIE DR
5 FERNIHOUGH AVE
6 GROVE AVE
Norton Hall Farm
HOLLY CL
VICTORIA TERR
STATION RD
Bretforton
Bretforton Fst Sch
Fleece Inn (PH)
1 WHITFORD CL
2 SQUIRES CT
3 BRIDGE ST
4 UPPER END CT
ORCHARD CL
Corner Farm
Domestic Fowl Trust
BEAUFORT END
LC
New Hill
Norton Hall
Honeybourne
Pottery
Manor Farm
THE GREEN
1 BALDWYN CT
2 MANOR CL
Poden
Thistley Hill
Norton Grounds Farm
WR11
Larkborough
Honeybourne Airfield Ind Est
Weston Ind Est
B4035
Manor House
Burn Norto
Dairy Hills
Saintbury Grounds
CHERMILL ORCH
DOVER'S HILL
Aston Subedge
Attlepin Farm
Downrip Farm
Yale Farm
Weston-sub-Edge
GL55
The Lynches
Kingcomb
CAMPDEN RD
ASTON RD
Hayway Farm
Willersey Bsns Pk
PIKE CNR
1 JORDANS CL
2 WILLOW RD
3 FARM CT
Top Farm
Dover's Hill
Cotswold Way
The Hoo
Willersey
Saintbury
Park Farm
Littleworth
1 JUBILEE CL
2 CORONATION CL
3 WESTEND TERR
4 LOWER HIGH ST
St Catharine RC Prim Sch
COLLIN LA
BROADWAY RD
WR12
SMALLBROOK RD
Weston Park
Kiftsgate Stone
Cotswold Way
The Mile Drive
Westington
A44 Evesham
A44
THE SANDS
1 LIME TREE AVE
2 BRIDGEMANS RD
3 SHELDON AVE
Bibsworth Farm
Foxhill Manor
Willersey Hill
CH
Saintbury Hill
THE MARROWS
THE LEASOWS
1 SHEPHERD'S CL
2 ROYAL OAK TERR
Westington Hill
Farncombe House
Hotel
B4632
B4081

185   186

A   B   C   D   E   F

8

CV37

Lower Clopton

Lower Meon

Meon Hall

Meon Hill

Admington Hall

Top Farm

York Farm

45

Admington Lane Units

Admington La

7

Stratford Rd

Heart of England Way

Orchard Rd
Hill View
Cedar Rd
Granbrook La

Upper Clopton Farm

Coleman's Hill

Park La

Centenary Way

Mickleton Rd
Old Manor Gdns

Hidcote Combe

Lower Lark Stoke

Ilmington CE Prim Sch

44

Campden Rd B4632

Broad Marston Rd
Long Marston Rd
Beaunash Rd
Whatcote Rd
Spirley Rd

Cotswold Edge 1
Gloucester La 2
Greyrick Ct 3
Mill La 4
Alveston Grange 5
Garden Ct 6
Proum La 7
Arbour Cl 8
Norton View 9

Mickleton

The Leasows

Chapel

Mickleton Wood Farm

Lark Stoke

CV36

Ilmington

Front St

6

High St

Baldens

Broadway Rd

B4081

Kiftsgate Court Gardens

Baker's Hitt

Monarch's Way

Campden Pitch

Campden Hill

Groo Hill

43

Nineveh Farm

Baker's Hill

Hidcote Manor Garden

Hidcote Bartrim

Mast

Woodmeadow Farm

Nebsworth

Masts

The Downs House

5

Hidcote House

Campden Rd

Hidcote Boyce

Windmill Hill

42

Middle Norton Farm

Longlands Farm

Ebrington Hill

Foxcote Farm

4

Campden Tunnel

Everel La

GL55

Diamond Way

Hoarston

Longmoor House

41

Mickleton Hills Farm

Bidford Rd

3

Heart of England Way

The Old Orchard 1
Church Cl 2
Keytes Acre

Ebrington CE Prim Sch

Ebrington

Goose Hill

40

Chipping Campden Sch

Sports Ctr

Gainsborough Rd

Orchard Cotts

Battledene Farm

Campden Rd

PH

Charingworth Manor (Hotel)

Charingworth

2

Aston Rd

Cidermill

Station Rd

Paxford Rd

Braxfield House

B4035

B4479

39

Chipping Campden

St James CE Prim Sch

Pudlicott La

Marfurlong Farm

1

The Green

Catbrook

1 Haysum's Cl
2 Pear Tree Cl
3 Gainsborough Terr
4 Sheep St
5 Cherry Orchard Cl
6 Catbrook Gdns

Briar Hill Farm

GL56

B4479

GL56

Black Downs

38

15   A   16   B   17   C   18   D   19   E   20   F

A2
1 BARRELS PITCH
2 WOLDS END CL
3 GRIGGS CL
4 ROLLING STONES
5 SEYMOUR GATE
6 THE SQUARE

7 COLDICOTTS CL
8 NOEL CT
9 THE OLD GRAMMAR SCHOOL MEWS
10 GLEBE FOLD
11 ALMSHOUSES
12 VICARAGE COTTS
13 CHURCH COTTS

Warwickshire STREET ATLAS

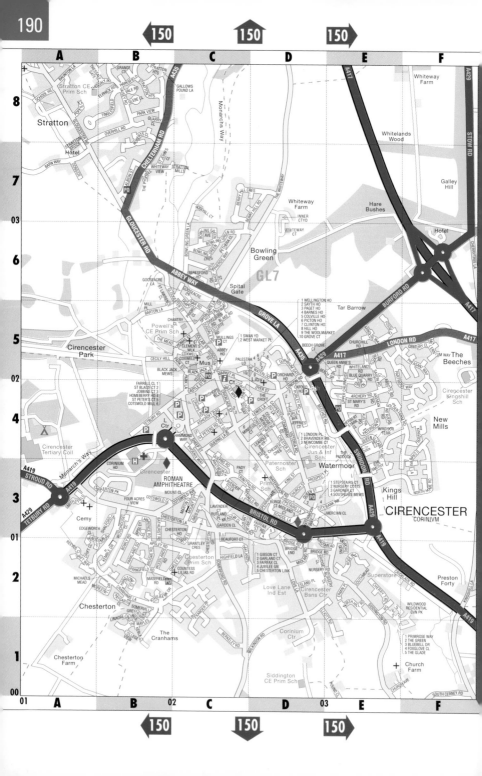

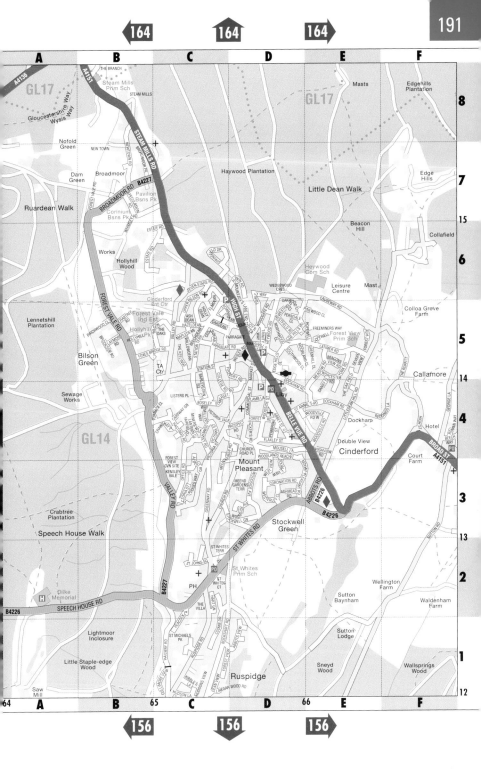

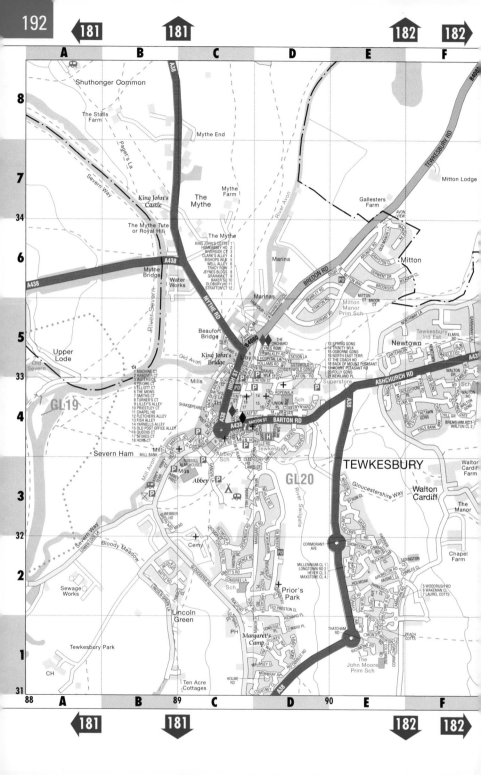

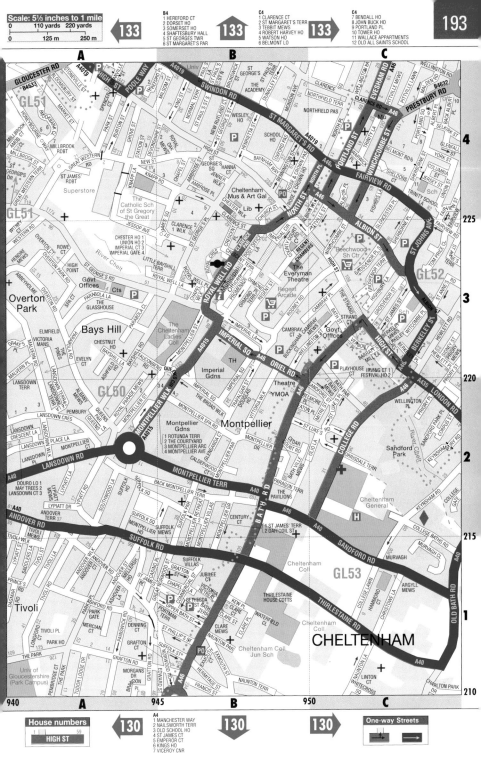

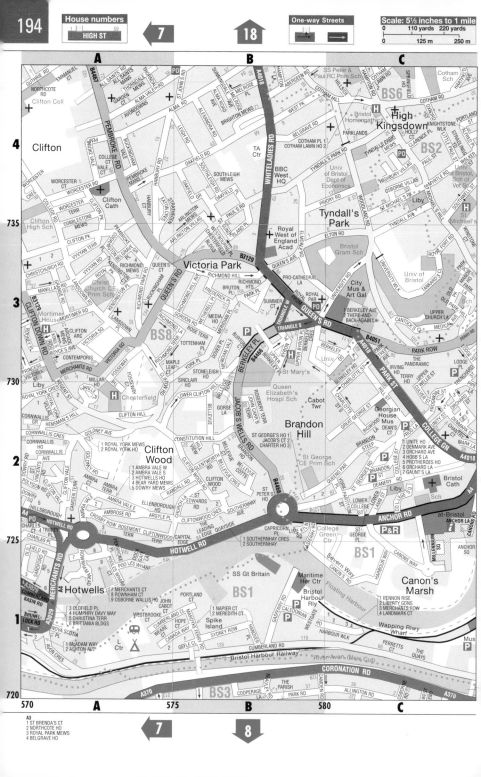

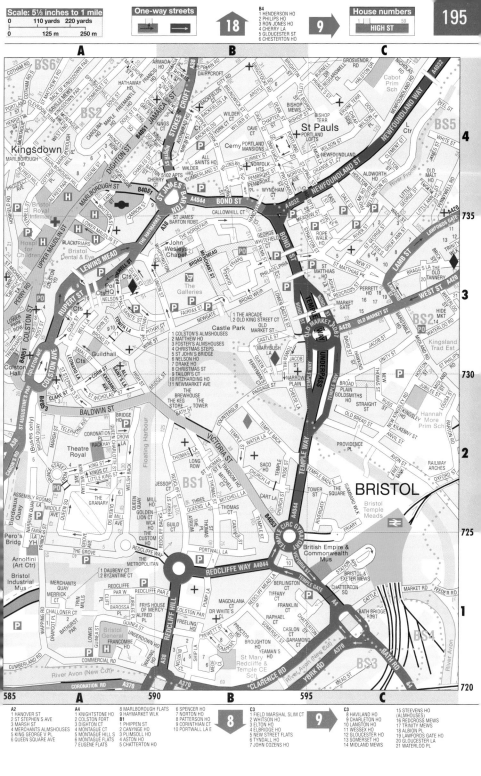

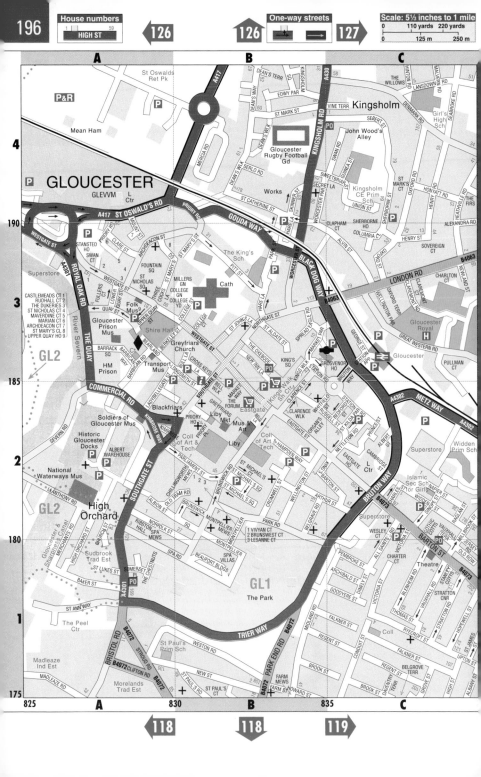

Index

Church Rd **6** Beckenham BR2......... **53** C6

Place name	**Location number**
May be abbreviated on the map	Present when a number indicates the place's position in a crowded area of mapping

Locality, town or village	**Postcode district**
Shown when more than one place has the same name	District for the indexed place

Page and grid square
Page number and grid reference for the standard mapping

Public and commercial buildings are highlighted in magenta   **Places of interest** are highlighted in blue with a star ★

Abbreviations used in the index

Acad	**Academy**	Comm	**Common**	Gd	**Ground**	L	**Leisure**	Prom	**Promenade**
App	**Approach**	Cott	**Cottage**	Gdn	**Garden**	La	**Lane**	Rd	**Road**
Arc	**Arcade**	Cres	**Crescent**	Gn	**Green**	Liby	**Library**	Recn	**Recreation**
Ave	**Avenue**	Cswy	**Causeway**	Gr	**Grove**	Mdw	**Meadow**	Ret	**Retail**
Bglw	**Bungalow**	Ct	**Court**	H	**Hall**	Meml	**Memorial**	Sh	**Shopping**
Bldg	**Building**	Ctr	**Centre**	Ho	**House**	Mkt	**Market**	Sq	**Square**
Bsns, Bus	**Business**	Ctry	**Country**	Hospl	**Hospital**	Mus	**Museum**	St	**Street**
Bvd	**Boulevard**	Cty	**County**	HQ	**Headquarters**	Orch	**Orchard**	Sta	**Station**
Cath	**Cathedral**	Dr	**Drive**	Hts	**Heights**	Pal	**Palace**	Terr	**Terrace**
Cir	**Circus**	Dro	**Drove**	Ind	**Industrial**	Par	**Parade**	TH	**Town Hall**
Cl	**Close**	Ed	**Education**	Inst	**Institute**	Pas	**Passage**	Univ	**University**
Cnr	**Corner**	Emb	**Embankment**	Int	**International**	Pk	**Park**	Wk, Wlk	**Walk**
Coll	**College**	Est	**Estate**	Intc	**Interchange**	Pl	**Place**	Wr	**Water**
Com	**Community**	Ex	**Exhibition**	Junc	**Junction**	Prec	**Precinct**	Yd	**Yard**

Index of localities, towns and villages

A

Abbeydale 119 D4
Abbeymead 119 E6
Abbotside 65 F2
Abbots Leigh 7 A8
Ablington 159 F3
Abwell 85 E6
Acton Turville 35 F6
Adlestrop 177 E5
Adsett 165 D1
Alderley 68 E2
Alderton
  Luckington 47 F2
  Tewkesbury 183 E4
Alderton Fields 183 E3
Aldsworth 160 E5
Alkerton 96 E7
Allaston 92 B6
Almondsbury 40 B5
Alstone
  Cheltenham 133 B4
  Tewkesbury 183 C3
Alveston 51 B4
Alveston Down 50 F5
Alvington 147 D3
Amberley 91 C7
Ampney Crucis 151 B5
Ampney St Mary 151 E5
Ampney St Peter 151 D4
Andoversford 166 C6
Apperley 173 C7
Apsley 132 C4
Arlebrook 102 A5
Arlingham 157 B5
Arlington Pike 159 F1
Arno's Vale 9 B4
Ashbrook 151 E5
Ashchurch 182 C4
Ashleworth 172 C4

Ashley 141 A5
Ashley Down 18 F4
Ashmead Green 88 D4
Ashton Court Estate 7 C4
Ashton Gate 7 F4
Ashton Keynes 142 F5
Ashton under Hill 183 D8
Ashton Vale 7 F2
Aston Crews 170 A2
Aston Cross 182 E4
Aston Down 148 E4
Aston Ingham 170 C2
Aston Magna 186 F6
Aston on Carrant 182 E5
Aston Somerville 184 C8
Aston Subedge 188 E4
Aust 49 A6
Avening 140 A8
Avening Green 66 D8
Avonmouth 26 D2
Awkley 39 E8
Awre 157 B3
Aylburton 147 E4
Aylburton Common ..147 D5
Aylton 178 A8

B

Badbrook 99 B8
Badgeworth 129 B3
Badminton 46 F2
Badminton Park 46 F4
Bafford 131 A5
Bagendon 158 C1
Bagpath
  Stroud 99 C3
  Wotton-under-Edge ..81 F2
Bagstone 53 A3
Baker's Hill 155 B6
Baldwins 108 B1

Ball's Green 91 F4
Bamfurlong 128 F8
Baptist Mills 19 A2
Barnsley 151 C8
Barnwood 127 E1
Barrow 173 E3
Barrow Common 1 B4
Barrow Wake 122 A4
Bartlett's Green 102 A4
Barton
  Cheltenham 175 C4
  Gloucester 119 A8
Barton End 83 B8
Barton Hill 9 C6
Barton-on-the-Heath ..187 F3
Batsford 186 E4
Battledown 131 B8
Baunton 150 C7
Bayfield 60 B8
Bays Hill 193 A3
Beach 12 C2
Beachley 61 C3
Beavan's Hill 170 B3
Beckford 183 B6
Bedminster 8 C3
Bedminster Down 2 B8
Beeches Green 99 A7
Beech Hill 32 B7
Beechknap 91 E8
Beechpike 115 B2
Bencombe 81 C8
Bengrove 183 B3
Benhall 129 D8
Bentham 121 C6
Berkeley 85 F3
Berkeley Heath 86 B3
Berkeley Road 86 F4
Berrow 180 B5
Berry Hill 155 A7
Berwick 27 D6
Betty's Grave 151 F4

Bevington 76 F6
Bibstone 66 C3
Bibury 160 B1
Bilson Green 191 B5
Bird in Hand 102 F5
Birdlip 121 F2
Birdwood 165 F5
Birts Street 180 A7
Bishop's Cleeve 137 E3
Bishop's North 173 A3
Bishopston 18 D3
Bishopsworth 2 A5
Bisley 105 B1
Bitton 5 E8
Blackhorse 21 A7
Blaisdon 165 B3
Blakeney 156 E2
Bledington 177 E1
Blockley 186 C6
Boddington 173 F4
Bondend 119 F3
Botloe's Green 170 F7
Boughspring 73 C7
Bouldson 170 E3
Bournes Green 148 D7
Bournside 130 A7
Bournstream 79 F2
Bourton-on-the-Hill ..186 D3
Bourton-on-the-Water 169 A7
Bowbridge 99 D5
Bower Ashton 7 E4
Bowling Green 190 D6
Box 91 E5
Boxbush 164 E7
Bradley 67 F8
Bradley Green 67 F8
Bradley Stoke 29 E8
Brand Green 171 C7
Brandon Hill 194 B2
Breadstone 86 D6
Bread Street 102 F2

Bream 147 D8
Bream's Meend 155 C1
Bredon 182 C8
Bredon's Hardwick ..182 B6
Bredon's Green 162 F7
Brentlands 111 A6
Brentry 28 B2
Bretforton 188 A6
Bridgend 97 F6
Bridgeyate 11 E7
Brierley 163 F2
Brimpsfield 114 C6
Brimps Hill 164 E5
Brimscombe 99 E2
Brislington 9 E2
Bristol 195 C2
Broad Blunsdon 144 D1
Broad Campden 186 B8
Broadoak 157 B7
Broadrock 73 A5
Broadway 185 C8
Broadwell
  Coleford 155 C6
  Stow-on-the-Wold ..177 A6
Brockeridge Common ..180 E9
Brockhampton 174 B1
Brockweir 146 D3
Bromesberrow 179 C4
Bromesberrow Heath ..179 B3
Bromley Heath 30 D1
Brookend
  Berkeley 93 E1
  Lydney 147 C2
Brookthorpe 110 F1
Broomhill 19 E6
Broom Hill 9 F3
Broom's Green 178 F3
Brownshill 148 B5
Buckbury 181 A5
Buckland 184 F6

Buckover 65 B1
Bullo 156 F4
Bull's Hill 163 C7
Bulwark 60 E6
Bunting Hill 90 F4
Burchells Green 20 B1
Burleigh 91 E7
Burton 36 B3
Bushley 181 D5
Bushley Green 181 C5
Bussage 148 B6
Butterrow 99 D4

C

Cadbury Heath 11 B5
Cainscross 98 F7
Calcot 159 E5
Calcott's Green 117 A6
Calcutt 144 A4
Callamore 191 F5
Cam 88 B4
Cambridge 95 F4
Camer's Green 179 F6
Cannop 155 D6
Canon's Marsh 194 C1
Cas-Gwent/Chepstow ...60 D6
Cashes Green 98 C7
Cassey Compton 166 F2
Castle Eaton 144 E6
Castle End 111 F5
Castletump 170 F8
Catbrain 28 B6
Catbrook 146 A5
Caudle Green 114 C1
Cerney Wick 143 C7
Chaceley 181 B1
Chaceley Stock 173 C8
Chalford 148 D5
Chalford Hill 148 C6
Chapel Hill
  St Arvans 146 B2
  Lydney 147 E4
Charfield 67 B4
Charfield Green 59 F2
Charfield Hill 66 F5
Chargrove 129 F4
Charingworth 189 F2
Charlton Abbots 174 A3
Charlton Kings 131 C6
Charlton Park 130 F6
Chase End Street 179 E6
Chase Hill 54 D6
Chastleton 177 E8
Chaxhill 165 F1
Chedglow 141 A4
Chedworth 159 A6
Chedworth Laines 158 F6
Cheltenham 193 C1
Chelworth 141 E5
Chelworth Lower Green 143 D3
Chelworth Upper Green 143 D3
Chepstow/Cas-Gwent ...60 D6
Cherington 148 D1
Chester Park 20 B2
Chesterton 190 B2
Chewton Keynsham 4 E2
Chipping Campden 189 A2
Chipping Sodbury 44 D1
Christchurch 154 E8
Churcham 124 D2
Churchdown 128 D6
Churchend
  Charfield 66 F3
  Stonehouse 97 A8
Church End
  Frampton on Severn ..157 F1
  Tewkesbury 181 F7
Church Westcote 169 F7
Cinderford 191 E4
Cirencester 190 F3
Clapton-on-the-Hill 168 F4
Claycombe 91 E8
Clay Hill 19 E2
Claypits 100 D1
Clearwell 155 A2
Cliddon 146 A6
Cleeve Hill 138 E2
Cleevemount 133 F4
Clements End 155 B2
Clifford's Mesne 170 E1
Clifton 194 A4
Clifton Wood 194 A2
Cloatley End 142 A1
Coaley 88 E8
Coalpit Heath 31 D6
Coalway 155 C5
Coates 149 F4
Coberley 123 A5
Cockshoot
  Bisley 104 C8
  Stroud 102 D3
Codrington 33 C2
Cold Ashton 13 F6
Cold Aston 168 B6
Cold Elm 181 A3
Coldharbour 146 E6
Cold Slad 121 E5
Coleford 155 B5

Colerne 15 F6
Colesbourne 158 A8
Colethrop 110 C2
Collafield 164 E1
Coln Rogers 159 D4
Coln St Aldwyns 152 D8
Coln St Dennis 159 D5
Coltham Fields 130 F8
Colt's Green 33 E8
Compton Abdale 167 B3
Compton Green 171 B7
Compton Greenfield ..27 F8
Conderton 183 A7
Condicote 176 A7
Coney Hill 119 C8
Conham 10 A5
Coombe 68 D8
Coombe Dingle 17 C8
Coomb's End 34 A6
Corse 172 A7
Corse Lawn 180 F1
Cotham 181 C1
Coughton 163 C8
Cowhill 63 B3
Cowley 123 A2
Cranham 112 F6
Cress Green 97 A6
Crew's Hole 9 F7
Cribbs Causeway 28 D6
Crickdale 143 E5
Crocker's Ash 162 D3
Crofts End 19 F1
Cromhall 66 A1
Cross Hill 73 D5
Crossway Green 72 D2
Crossways 64 F2
Crowell Brook 79 F6
Cudwell 141 C3
Cruse 163 A6
Culkerton 141 A7
Cutsdean 185 A1

D

Daglingworth 150 A8
Damery 78 E1
Dancing Green 164 A7
Daneway 149 B6
Daylesford 177 E4
Deerhurst 173 D8
Deerhurst Walton ...173 E7
Derry Fields 142 F4
Dobbreook 184 D2
Didmarton 57 C4
Dixton
  Monmouth 154 A8
  Winchcombe 183 C1
Dodington 34 A4
Donnington
  Ledbury 178 E5
  Stow-on-the-Wold ..176 F7
Doughton 140 A2
Down Ampney 143 F8
Downend
  Bristol 20 E8
  Nailsworth 90 F1
Down Hatherley 173 C1
Doynton 23 A1
Draycott
  Dursley 87 F8
  Moreton-in-Marsh ..186 E6
Driffield 151 C2
Drybrook 164 B4
Duckhole 64 C5
Dumbleton 183 F7
Dundry 1 D2
Dundry Hill 3 B3
Dunfield 144 D8
Duntisbourne Abbots ..107 C4
Duntisbourne Leer ..107 C3
Duntisbourne Rouse ..107 E1
Dursley 88 B2
Dursley Cross 165 A7
Dyer's Common 38 C3
Dymock 178 D2
Dyrham 23 D4

E

Earthcott Green 41 E7
Eastcombe 148 A4
Eastcourt 141 E3
East Dean 164 C7
East Dundry 2 B1
East End
  Cheltenham 131 C6
  Fairford 152 F4
  Marshfield 15 A8
Easter Compton 39 A2
Eastfield 18 B7
Eastington
  Northleach 160 C8
  Stonehouse 96 F8
Eastleach Martin ...153 D8
Eastleach Turville ..153 C8
Eastnor 179 B8
Easton Grey 59 C3
Easton-in-Gordano ..16 A4

Easton Town 58 D1
Eastville 19 C3
Ebley 98 C6
Ebrington 189 E3
Edge 103 B8
Edge End 155 C8
Edgeworth 106 D1
Egypt 91 B5
Elberton 50 A6
Eldersfield 180 C2
Elkstone 115 B5
Ellwood 155 C2
Elmbridge 127 E3
Elmore 117 A3
Elmore Back 116 E6
Elmstone Hardwicke .136 E1
Elton 165 B1
Emerson's Green ...21 C6
Engine Common 43 B5
English Bicknor 163 B2
Epney 108 C3
Etloe 93 C8
Evenlode 177 C8
Everlands 88 A4
Ewen 142 B8

F

Fairford 152 E3
Fairview 133 F1
Falfield 65 E7
Far Green 88 F6
Farley's End 116 E3
Farmington 168 B2
Far Oakridge 148 F1
Far Thrupp 99 F3
Fiddington 182 C1
Fiddler's Green 132 C2
Filton 29 A3
Filwood Park 2 E8
Fishponds 20 A5
Fishpool 170 A8
Five Acres 155 B7
Flaxley 65 A2
Flaxpits 30 E5
Ford 175 B8
Forest Green 91 A5
Forthampton 181 B3
Forthay 79 E5
Forwood 91 F5
Foss Cross 159 B4
Fossebridge 159 D6
Four Oaks 170 D7
Foxcote 166 C5
Framilode 157 F5
Frampton Cotterell ..31 B7
Frampton End 31 D8
Frampton Mansell ..148 F5
Frampton on Severn ..100 A5
France Lynch 148 D6
Frenchay 20 B8
Fretherne 157 E4
Frocester 97 B3
Frogmarsh 180 B3
Frombridge 100 C3
Fyfield 153 D6

G

Gadfield Elm 180 A2
Ganarew 162 B3
Ganders Green 165 B7
Gatwick 157 F8
Gaunt's Earthcott ..41 B5
Gee Moor 10 F6
Gloucester 196 A4
Golden Hill 18 D5
Golden Valley 132 A2
Goodrich 163 A5
Goose Green
  Bristol 21 C1
  Wotton-under-Edge ..81 C1
  Yate 43 E3
Gorsley 170 C4
Gorsley Common ..170 A4
Gossington 95 C1
Gotherington 138 B8
Grafton 183 C8
Grange Village ...156 E7
Great Barrington ..161 E8
Great Doward 162 D3
Great Rissington ..169 C4
Great Stoke 29 F5
Great Washbourne ..183 C5
Great Witcombe ..121 B2
Great Wolford ...187 F5
Green Bottom 164 E2
Green Street 120 E3
Greenway 178 E4
Greet 184 A1
Gretton 183 E1
Gretton Fields ...183 E2
Guiting Power ...175 A3
Guller's End 181 B6

H

Hagloe 156 F1
Hailes 184 C1
Haines Green 103 D8
Halen 27 C5
Hall End 53 E2
Hallwood Green ..178 B4
Halmore 94 B2
Ham
  Berkeley 85 D1
  Cheltenham 131 C7
Hambrook 30 C2
Ham Butts 103 E8
Ham Green 16 E4
Hampnett 167 F2
Hampton 145 B3
Hamshill 88 E6
Hamwell Leaze ...98 E7
Hanham 10 C4
Hanham Green 10 C3
Hankerton 141 D1
Hannington 145 A4
Hannington Wick ..145 A6
Hardwick 60 F7
Hardwicke
  Cheltenham 136 B4
  Gloucester 109 E6
Hardwick Green ..180 D3
Haresfield
  Gloucester 110 B1
  Highworth 145 D4
Harleywood 91 B2
Harnhill 151 C3
Harrow Hill 164 C3
Harry Stoke 29 E2
Hartcliffe 2 C4
Hartpury 172 B3
Hasfield 172 E6
Hasfield Ham 173 A5
Hatherley 129 E6
Hatherop 152 E8
Hawcross 179 D1
Hawkesbury 53 B6
Hawkesbury Upton ..56 A3
Hawling 174 E2
Hayden 132 A3
Hayden Green ...132 A3
Hayes Knoll 143 F1
Hazelton 167 D5
Headley Park 2 B7
Heath End 53 A8
Heathfield 86 C1
Heath Hill 181 A8
Hempsted 118 B7
Henbury 27 E2
Henfield 31 D3
Hengrove 3 B6
Henleaze 18 C6
Henley 121 A5
Hester's Way 132 E3
Hethelpit Cross ..171 F8
Hewelsfield 146 F5
Hicks Gate 4 B8
High Botheridge ..112 E8
Highfield
  Lydney 92 C4
  Stroud 98 F7
Highfields 80 D7
High Kingsdown ..194 C4
Highleadon 171 F2
Highnam 125 E5
Highnam Green ...125 C5
High Nash 155 B5
High Orchard 196 A2
Highridge 1 E5
High Woolaston ..147 A2
Highworth 145 D4
Hilcot End 151 D5
Hill 76 D3
Hill End 182 A8
Hillend Green ...170 E7
Hillesley 55 E8
Hillfields 20 B3
Hillhouse 21 A5
Hinton
  Berkeley 93 E3
  Bristol 23 C6
Holbrook Common ..12 A8
Holdfast 181 B8
Hollybed Common ..179 F8
Holwell 68 C8
Holywell 145 C4
Homedowns 182 C3
Honeybourne 188 C6
Hook Street 85 C4
Hoop 154 A2
Hope Mansell ...163 F6
Hopewell Hill 20 D1
Horcott 152 D6
Horfield 18 F6
Horsepools 111 B1
Horsley 90 F1
Horton 45 B6
Hotwells 194 A1
Houndscroft 99 C1
Howle Hill 163 D7
Howley 79 E1
Hucclecote 120 B7
Hudnalls 146 D6

Huntingford 66 F8
Huntley 165 D6
Hyde 148 B4
Hystfield 77 B5

I

Icomb 177 B1
Ilmington 189 F6
Inchbrook 91 A6
Inglesham 153 C2
Ingst 49 C4
Innsworth 127 D7
Iron Acton 42 D4
Itchington 51 F2

J

Jackaments Bottom ..141 D8
Jack's Green 104 D8
Jefferies Hill ...10 C5
Joyford 155 B8
Joy's Green 163 D3

K

Kelston 6 C3
Kemble 141 F8
Kemerton 182 E8
Kempley 170 B8
Kempley Green ...170 B8
Kempsford 144 E8
Kendleshire 31 A4
Kensington Park ..9 C3
Kent End 143 A5
Kenton Green ...116 E2
Kent's Green 171 B2
Kerne Bridge 163 B6
Ketford 179 A1
Keynsham 4 E3
Kikemry 166 C8
Kilcot 170 D4
Kiln Green 163 D6
Kineton 175 B5
Kingham 177 F2
Kingrove Common ..33 C7
Kingscote 82 B5
Kingscourt 99 B4
Kingsditch 130 A5
Kingsdown 193 A5
Kingshill 87 F2
Kings Hill 190 E3
Kingsholm 196 C4
King's Stanley ..98 A4
Kingswood
  Bristol 10 E8
  Wotton-under-Edge ..67 E4
Kington 63 E1
Kinsham 182 D6
Kitebrook 187 E2
Knightsbridge ...173 F5
Knight's Green ..178 F2
Knockdown 57 F5
Knowle 8 F3
Knowle Park 9 A1
Kymin 154 B7

L

Lane End 164 B6
Langley 139 C5
Lansdown 130 B8
Lark Stoke 189 E6
Lasborough 82 C3
Lassington 125 D2
Latteridge 42 A6
Latton 143 E6
Laverton 184 F6
Lawrence Weston ..27 A3
Lea 164 C3
Lea Line 164 E6
Lechlade-on-Thames ..153 D5
Leckhampton 130 D3
Ledbury 178 D7
Leddington 178 B5
Leigh 143 B6
Leighterton 70 D3
Leigh Woods 7 D3
Leonard Stanley ..97 E3
Leyhill 66 E4
Leys Hill 163 C6
Lightpill 99 A1
Lincoln Green ...192 C4
Linden 143 A5
Linkend 180 E1
Linton 170 A6
Linton Hill 170 A7
Little Badminton ..46 E1
Little Barrington ..161 C7
Little Beckford ..183 B5
Little Bristol 67 E3
Little Compton ..187 F5
Littledean 156 A6
Little Dovard ...162 E2
Little Drybrook ..155 C8
Little Gorsley ...170 C

ittle Haresfield 101 E7
ittle Herbert's 131 B4
ittle London 165 B5
ittle Marcle 178 B7
ittle Rissington 169 C6
ittle Shurdington 121 D7
ittle Sodbury 45 B3
ittle Sodbury End 44 E4
ittle Stoke 29 D7
ittleton Drew 36 E5
ittleton-upon-Severn ..49 E8
ittle Washbourne 183 D4
ittle Witcombe 121 B4
ittleworth
  Chipping Campden 188 F2
  Nailsworth 91 C8
iandogo 146 B7
iangarron 162 B8
iangrove 162 C6
ockleaze 19 C7
odway 16 B5
ong Ashton 7 A1
ongborough 176 E8
ongdon 180 F7
ongford 126 F6
ong Green 181 A4
onghope 164 F5
onglevens 127 D4
ong Newton 140 E3
ongney 108 C6
ongridge 104 C7
ongwell Green 10 E3
owbands 179 F2
ower Almondsbury 40 A6
ower Apperley 173 C6
ower Berry Hill 155 A6
ower Cam 87 E6
ower Chedworth 159 B5
ower Cockleford 115 D8
ower Dowdeswell 166 B6
ower Easton 19 D2
ower Hamswell 13 C3
ower Hazel 50 F3
ower Kilcott 46 D4
ower Knowle 8 E1
ower Lemington 187 B5
ower Ley 165 F2
ower Littleworth 99 B1
ower Lydbrook 163 C3
ower Meend 146 D7
ower Moor 142 D2
ower Morton 64 C4
ower Oddington 177 D4
ower Redbrook 154 D4
ower Slaughter 176 C1
ower Soudley 156 D5
ower Soundwell 20 F2
ower Stone 77 C1
ower Swell 176 D4
ower Tuffley 118 B2
ower Westmancote 182 D8
ower Wick 78 E6
uckington 47 E4
udlow Green 102 F3
udstock 178 C6
uxley 164 F8
yde Green 21 E8
ydney 92 C3
ynworth 134 B3
ypiatt 106 B5

M

Maiden Head 1 F1
Maisemore 126 A7
Maiswick 171 C4
Mangotsfield 20 F6
Maniards Green 76 C2
Marle Hill 133 D4
Marshfield 14 B3
Marsh Common 38 E4
Marsh Lane 155 B2
Marston Hill 152 B2
Marston Meysey 144 C8
Marstow 162 E6
Mathern/Merthyr Tewdrig 60 C3
Matson 119 C3
Matson North 119 B4
Maugersbury 177 A4
Mayfield Park 20 A2
May Hill 134 A8
Mayshill 42 E1
Merthyr Tewdrig/Mathern 60 C3
Meysey Hampton 152 A2
Mickleton 189 B6
Middle Duntisbourne ..107 F2
Middle Street 96 F6
Middle Wick 78 F5
Middleyard 98 C3
Mile End 155 C6
Milkwall 155 A4
Millbottom 91 B3
Millend
  Easington 97 A7
  Monmouth/Trefynwy ..154 F4
Mill Hill 155 D1
Milton End 152 D3

Minchinhampton 91 E6
Minety 142 D1
Minsterworth 116 E7
Miserden 106 B7
Mitcheldean 164 E5
Mitton 192 F6
Monmouth/Trefynwy 45 B3
Montpelier 18 E2
Montpellier 193 B2
Moorend
  Dursley 95 C2
  Gloucester 111 F8
  Winterbourne 30 E2
Moor End 130 F5
Moorfields 9 C8
Moorslade 77 D1
Moreton-in-Marsh 187 B2
Moreton Valence 101 A8
Morton 64 D3
Mountain Bower 25 E3
Mount Hill 10 E6
Mounton 60 A7
Mount Pleasant
  Cinderford 191 D3
  Stroud 99 E6
Much Marcle 178 B7
Murrell's End 172 B1

N

Naas 92 D1
Nailbridge 164 B3
Nailsworth 91 C3
Narth The 154 A1
Nastend 101 C1
Naunton
  Stow-on-the-Wold 175 D2
  Tewkesbury 180 D10
Naunton Downs 175 B1
Naunton Park 130 E6
Nebsworth 189 E5
Netham 9 D6
Netherend 147 C3
Netherton 152 E7
Nether Westcote 169 F7
Nettleton 114 C8
Nettleton Green 36 B1
New Cheltenham 20 F1
New England 21 B7
Newent 171 A4
Newerne 92 B3
Newington Bagpath 82 B2
Newland 154 E4
Newleaze 29 B2
Newmarket 90 F4
New Mills 190 F4
Newnham 157 A6
New Passage 48 A1
Newport 78 B8
Newton
  Bristol 9 A7
  Sharpness 85 D8
  Thornbury 64 D6
Newton Green 60 B4
Newtown
  Lea 164 A6
  Stonehouse 97 C8
  Tewkesbury 192 F5
New Town
  Moreton-in-Marsh 177 F8
  Winchcombe 184 C3
Nibley
  Blakeney 156 E5
  Yate 43 A1
Nibley Green 79 C5
Ninewells 155 B7
Norman Hill 87 F4
North Cerney 158 D2
North Common 11 D6
North Corner 41 F1
North End 142 F5
Northfield 140 D4
Northleach 168 A1
North Nibley 79 D4
North Stoke 6 C6
Northville 29 A1
Northway 182 C5
Northwick 48 E2
North Woodchester 98 F2
Northwood Green 165 C3
Norton 173 B3
Notgrove 167 F7
Novers Park 2 D8
Noverton 134 D4
Nupdown 76 A4
Nupend
  Nailsworth 90 E1
  Stonehouse 97 C4
Nuppend 147 C4
Nympsfield 89 E5

O

Oakle Street 116 B8
Oakley 134 B2
Oakridge Lynch 148 E6
Oaksey 141 F4
Oatfield 100 B6

Ocker Hill 102 E2
Okle Green 171 D4
Old Bishton 73 B3
Oldbury Naite 63 E7
Oldbury-on-Severn 63 C6
Oldbury on the Hill 57 C5
Oldcroft 92 E8
Old Down 50 D4
Oldends 101 D1
Oldland 11 A3
Oldland Common 11 D3
Old Passage 48 F6
Old Sodbury 34 B8
Old Wharf 178 D7
Olveston 50 B3
Orange End 55 C4
Oridge Street 172 A6
Over
  Bristol 39 D2
  Gloucester 126 A4
Overbury 182 F8
Overton 157 D5
Overton Park 193 A3
Owlpen 89 E1
Oxenhall 170 F5
Oxenton 182 F2
Oxlynch 102 C4
Ozleworth 69 D7

P

Paganhill 103 A1
Painswick 103 E8
Palmer's Flat 155 B4
Pamington 182 E3
Parkend
  Coleford 155 E3
  Gloucester 109 C2
Park End 98 F8
Parkfield 22 A7
Park Hill 146 F2
Patchway 40 B2
Paxford 186 E8
Penalt 154 B5
Pencraig 162 F7
Pendock 180 A3
Pendock Moor 180 D5
Pennsylvania 13 F7
Pen-twyn 154 B4
Petty France 46 B7
Pibey Marsh 176 F5
Pile Marsh 9 D7
Pill 16 C4
Pilley 130 E4
Pillowell 155 F1
Pillows Green 172 B8
Pilning 38 D7
Pinfarthings 91 C6
Piper's End 181 A5
Pitchcombe 103 B5
Pitt Court 79 F5
Pittville 133 E3
Playley Green 179 E2
Plump Hill 164 D4
Plusterwine 147 C2
Podsmead 118 D4
Pontshill 164 B8
Poole Keynes 142 A6
Poolhill 171 B8
Pool Meadow 126 C3
Pope's Hill 164 F1
Postlip 139 D3
Poulton 151 F4
Prescott 138 E7
Prestbury 134 C5
Preston
  Cirencester 150 F3
  Ledbury 178 C5
Priding 157 E5
Prior's Norton 173 C3
Prior's Park 192 D2
Puckelchurch 22 B5
Puckshole 98 E8
Puddlebrook 164 B5
Pullens Green 63 C5
Purton 94 A5
Purton Stoke 143 E1
Putloe 101 B8
Pwllmeurig/Pwllmeyric ..60 B5
Pwllmeyric/Pwllmeurig ..60 B5
Pye Corner 30 D3

Q

Quedgeley 117 E1
Queen Charlton 4 B3
Queenhill 181 B7
Quenington 152 C7

R

Randwick 102 D2
Rangeworthy 43 B8
Readings 163 E3
Redfield 10 A7
Redland 18 C3
Redmarley D'Abitot 179 C2

Redwick 38 C8
Rendcomb 158 D4
Reybridge 131 B7
Ridgeway 19 F3
Ripple 181 D8
Robinswood 119 B5
Rockhampton 64 E7
Rockness 91 A2
Rockstowes 80 F8
Rodborough 99 A6
Rodford 32 B6
Rodley 157 F6
Rodmarton 149 B1
Rooksmoor 99 A3
Rose Green 19 E1
Rowland's Green 178 C7
Ruardean 163 F4
Ruardean Hill 164 A4
Ruardean Woodside 163 F3
Ruddle 156 F6
Rudford 124 F8
Rudgeway 50 F1
Ruscombe 102 E3
Ruspidge 191 D1
Russell Town 9 B7
Ryton 179 A2

S

St Anne's 9 E5
St Anne's Park 9 E6
St Arvans 72 B6
St Briavels 146 F7
Saintbridge 119 C6
Saintbury 188 C2
St Catherine 14 F1
St Chloe 91 B8
St George 10 A7
St Mark's 132 F1
St Pauls
  Bristol 195 C4
  Cheltenham 133 D3
  Gloucester 118 D7
St Peter's 133 B3
St Philip's Marsh 9 B5
Salperton 167 C2
Salperton Park 167 C6
Salterley Grange 122 D7
Saltford 8 E8
Sandhurst 172 E2
Sandpits 87 F3
Sandy Lane 130 F4
Sapperton 149 C6
Saul 157 F3
Sawyers Hill 142 D1
Scowles 154 F5
Sea Mills 17 B6
Sedbury 61 B8
Selsley 98 E4
Selsley West 98 D3
Sevenhampton
  Cheltenham 166 E8
  Highworth 145 D1
Seven Springs 123 B6
Severn Beach 37 F6
Shakesfield 178 D2
Shapridge 164 E3
Sharpness 93 B2
Shaw Common 170 D6
Shaw Green 134 B5
Sheepscombe 112 F1
Shepherd's Patch 95 C5
Shepperdine 75 D3
Sherborne 169 A1
Sherston 58 C1
Sherston Parva or Pinkney 58 E2
Shipton 166 F5
Shipton Moyne 59 E8
Shirehampton 16 E7
Shorncote 142 D7
Shortstanding 155 A8
Shortwood
  Kingswood 21 D4
  Nailsworth 90 F3
Shurdington 129 E2
Shuthonger 181 E6
Siddington 150 E3
Silver Street 89 A7
Siston 21 F3
Slad 104 A3
Slades Green 181 B5
Sledge Green 180 D5
Slimbridge 95 D4
Sling 155 A3
Smart's Green 33 D8
Sneyd Park 17 D3
Snig's End 172 B7
Snowshill 185 B4
Somerdale 4 E7
Somerford Keynes 142 D6
Sopworth 57 D1
Southam 134 C8
South Cerney 137 E8
Southend 79 E3
Southmead 28 D1
Southrop 153 D6
Southville 8 C4

South Woodchester 98 F1
Speedwell 20 A2
Springbank 132 D3
Standish 101 E5
Stanfields 99 B4
Stanley 157 F8
Stanley Downton 97 E5
Stanley Pontlarge 183 E1
Stanton 184 F5
Stanton Fitzwarren 145 A1
Stantway 157 E8
Stanway 184 E3
Staple Hill 20 E4
Stapleton 19 D4
Starveall 56 D4
Staunton
  Gloucester 172 A8
  Monmouth/Trefynwy 154 E7
Staverton 173 F2
Stidcot 52 E6
Stinchcombe 87 C2
Stockend 103 A7
Stockwell Green 191 D3
Stockwood 3 E5
Stockwood Vale 4 C6
Stoke Bishop 17 C5
Stoke Gifford 29 F4
Stoke Orchard 136 D5
Stone 77 F3
Stone Hill 10 E4
Stonehouse 97 E2
Stowe 154 F1
Stowe Green 154 F1
Stowell 159 E8
Stowfield 163 C4
Stow-on-the-Wold 176 E4
Strand 157 C8
Stratford 180 E9
Stratton 190 A8
Stroat 74 A8
Stroud 99 B8
Stroud Green 101 F4
Stroud Hill 90 D7
Stump Cross 184 F1
Sudgrove 106 A5
Summerhayes 87 E5
Sundayshill 65 C8
Sunhill 152 A5
Swanborough 145 B2
Swanley 78 C5
Swellshill 99 E1
Swindon 133 A7
Swineford 6 A7
Swinley Green 180 F3
Syde 114 D2
Symonds Yat 162 E3
Synwell 68 D7
Syreford 166 E7

T

Taddington 185 A2
Tadwick 13 E1
Talbot's End 66 C1
Tarlton 149 C2
Taynton 165 E8
Teddington 183 A4
Temple Guiting 175 B7
Tetbury 140 C4
Tetbury Upton 140 B6
Tewkesbury 192 E3
The Beeches 190 F5
The Butts 99 B5
The Camp 105 D7
The College 102 B8
The Dings 9 A6
The Eaves 155 E1
The Gibb 36 F3
The Haw 173 A6
The Knapp 64 F3
The Leigh 173 C5
The Mythe 192 C7
The Park 130 C6
The Pludds 163 E2
The Pound 178 E2
The Quarry 87 D4
The Ramplings 181 B5
The Reddings 129 B7
Thornbury 51 B8
Threescombe 91 A6
Throughham 105 E4
Thrupp 99 E4
Tibberton 124 C8
Tickmorend 90 E1
Tidenham 73 D4
Tidenham Chase 146 E1
Tiller's Green 178 B3
Tilsdown 87 F3
Tiltups End 83 A7
Tintern Parva 146 C3
Tirley 172 F7
Tirley Knowle 173 A4
Tivoli 193 A1
Tockington 50 C1
Toddington 184 B3
Todenham 187 B6
Tormarton 34 E2
Tortworth 66 C7
Tortworth Green 66 C5

1
1st Ave GL56 ....187 B4

2
2nd Ave GL56 ....187 B4

3
3rd Ave GL56 ....187 B3

5
5th Ave GL56 ....187 C4

6
6th Ave GL56 ....187 B4

7
7th Ave GL56 ....187 B3

8
8th Ave GL56 ....187 B3

1
125 Bsns Pk GL2 ....126 C1

5
5102 Apts BS1 ....195 B4

A

A P Ellis Rd GL54 ....169 D6
Aaron Rd GL7 ....150 F2
Abbenesse GL6 ....148 C6
Abbey Cl BS31 ....4 F6
Abbey Ct Bristol BS4 ....9 F5
  Tewkesbury GL20 ....192 B3
  20 Winchcombe GL4 ....174 A7
Abbey Ho
  Cirencester GL7 ....190 C5
  5 Yate BS37 ....32 D7
Abbey La BS35 ....51 D6
Abbey Mdw GL20 ....192 D1
Abbey Mews GL4 ....67 F4
Abbey Pk BS31 ....4 F6
Abbey Prec GL20 ....192 B3
Abbey Rd Bristol BS9 ....17 F7
  Abbey Sch GL20 ....192 C4
Abbey St Cinderford GL14 ....191 D4
  Kingswood GL12 ....67 F5
Abbey Terr
  Tewkesbury GL20 ....192 B3
  22 Winchcombe GL54 ....174 A7
Abbey Tintern Furnace*
  NP16 ....146 A3
Abbey View
  6 Gloucester GL4 ....119 C4
  15 Winchcombe GL54 ....174 A7
Abbey Way GL7 ....190 C6
  Abbey Wood Ret Pk
  BS34 ....29 C2
Abbeydale GL3 ....30 E6
Abbeydale Ct GL4 ....119 E4
Abbeyfield Ho
  Chipping Sodbury BS37 ....44 C1
  6 Stow-on-t-W GL54 ....176 F4
Abbeyholme GL53 ....193 A3
Abbeymead Ave GL4 ....119 E6
  Abbeymead Prim Sch
  GL4 ....119 F5
Abbeywood Dr BS9 ....17 C5
  Abbeywood Pk BS34 ....29 C2
Abbot's Rd GL20 ....192 C2
Abbots Ave BS15 ....10 C4
Abbots Cl Bristol BS14 ....3 A3
  Cheltenham GL51 ....133 D3
Abbots Court Dr GL20 ....181 F7
Abbots Leigh Rd BS8 ....7 C2
Abbots Leys Rd GL54 ....139 D3
Abbots Mews GL52 ....137 E2
Abbots Rd Bristol BS15 ....10 C2
  Cinderford GL14 ....191 E3
  Cirencester GL7 ....190 E4
  Gloucester GL4 ....119 E6
Abbots View GL14 ....191 D1
Abbots Way Bristol BS9 ....16 D1
  Stonehouse GL10 ....97 E6
Abbots Wlk GL7 ....153 E2
Abbotsford Rd BS6 ....18 B1
Abbotswood Bristol BS15 ....10 D7
  Yate BS37 ....32 D7
Abbotswood Prim Sch
  BS37 ....32 D6
Abbotswood Rd GL4 ....120 F4
Abbott Rd BS35 ....38 A5
Abbotts Way GL17 ....141 F8
Aberdeen Rd BS6 ....194 B4
Abingdon Court La SN6 ....143 F4
Abingdon Rd BS16 ....20 A3

Ableton Ct BS35 ....38 A6
Ableton La
  Compton Greenfield BS10 ....38 A1
  Severn Beach BS35 ....38 A5
Ableton Wlk BS9 ....17 C5
Abnash GL6 ....148 C6
Abon Ho BS9 ....17 C4
Abraham Cl BS5 ....9 B8
Abraham Fry Ho BS15 ....10 E7
Abson Rd
  Pucklechurch BS16 ....22 C3
  Wick BS30 ....12 C8
Acacia Ave BS16 ....20 D4
Acacia Cl 9 Bream GL15 ....147 D8
  Bristol BS16 ....20 D3
  Cheltenham GL52 ....134 A5
  Newnham GL14 ....157 A7
Acacia Ct
  Cheltenham GL51 ....132 C2
  Keynsham BS31 ....4 C1
Acacia La HR8 ....88 A3
Acacia Mews 4 BS16 ....20 D4
Acacia Pk GL52 ....137 E8
Acacia Rd BS16 ....20 D4
Academy The GL50 ....193 B4
Acer Gr GL2 ....117 E2
Acid Rd BS11 ....26 C4
Acomb Cres GL52 ....131 B6
Acorn Ct 9 GL4 ....119 C4
Acorn Gr BS13 ....1 E6
Acraman's Rd 7 BS3 ....9 E4
Acre Pl GL6 ....102 E1
Acre St GL5 ....99 C7
Acresbush Cl BS13 ....2 A5
Acton Rd BS16 ....20 A3
Acton Turville Rd GL9 ....35 B4
Adams Ct 6 BS8 ....7 F6
Adams Hay 8 BS4 ....9 D1
Adams Land BS36 ....14 E7
Adams Way 7 GL16 ....155 A7
Adderly Gate BS16 ....21 B7
Addis Rd GL51 ....133 B3
Addiscombe Rd BS14 ....3 B5
Addison Rd BS3 ....8 E3
Addymore GL11 ....87 F5
Adelaide Gdns GL10 ....101 F1
Adelaide Pl
  Bristol,Fishponds BS16 ....19 F4
  Bristol,Upper Easton BS5 ....9 B8
Adelaide St GL1 ....119 A7
Adelaide Terr 1 BS16 ....20 A4
Adelante Cl BS34 ....30 A4
Adey's La GL12 ....68 B8
Admington La CV36 ....189 D7
  Admington Lane Units
  CV36 ....189 E7
Admiral Cl Bristol BS16 ....19 E7
  Cheltenham GL51 ....132 D2
Admirals Cl 6 GL15 ....155 D1
Adryan Ct 8 BS5 ....9 C7
Aesops Orch GL52 ....138 C3
Agate St BS3 ....8 B3
Aggs Cl GL52 ....138 A8
Aggs Hill GL54 ....134 D1
Aggs La GL52 ....138 A8
Aiken St BS5 ....9 B6
Aintree Dr BS16 ....30 F1
Air Balloon Ct BS16 ....10 A7
  Air Balloon Hill Jun & Inf
  Schs 10 A7
Air Balloon Rd BS5 ....10 A7
Airport Rd BS14 ....3 A8
Airthrie Sch GL50 ....133 B1
Aisne Rd GL15 ....156 B1
Akeman Rd BS16 ....20 A7
Akeman Way BS11 ....16 C8
Akermans Orch GL18 ....170 F4
Akers Ct SN26 ....144 E1
Alanscourt BS30 ....11 E6
Alard Rd BS4 ....2 F7
Alaska Ave GL7 ....152 E1
Albany GL10 ....101 E1
Albany Gate BS34 ....29 E5
Albany Ho 7 GL50 ....130 B8
Albany Mews GL50 ....193 A2
Albany Rd Bristol BS6 ....18 E1
  Gloucester GL1 ....118 F7
Albany St GL50 ....130 C8
  Gloucester GL1 ....118 F7
Albany St BS16 ....11 C5
Albemarle Gate GL50 ....133 E4
Albemarle Rd BS8 ....128 D5
Albemarle Row 10 BS8 ....7 F6
Albemarle Terr 2 BS8 ....7 F6
Albert Cres BS2 ....9 D8
Albert Ct GL52 ....133 F3
Albert Gr BS5 ....9 F8
Albert Gr S BS5 ....9 F8
Albert Par 8 BS5 ....9 D8
Albert Park Pl BS6 ....18 F1
Albert Pl
  1 Bristol,Bedminster BS3 ....8 C3
  Bristol,Eastfield BS9 ....18 A7
  Cheltenham GL52 ....193 C4
Albert Rd Brimscombe GL5 ....99 F1
  Bristol,Hanham BS15 ....10 D5
  Bristol,St Philip's Marsh BS2 ....9 D4
  Bristol,Staple Hill BS16 ....20 D4
  Cheltenham GL52 ....133 F3
  Cinderford GL14 ....191 D3
  Coleford GL16 ....155 A5
  Keynsham BS31 ....4 E5
  Ledbury HR8 ....178 E8
  Severn Beach BS35 ....38 A6
Albert St Bristol BS5 ....9 E8
  Cheltenham GL50 ....133 D3

Albert St continued
  Gloucester GL1 ....196 C2
  Lydney GL15 ....92 B3
Albert Terr BS16 ....19 F4
Albert Warehouse GL1 ....196 A2
Alberton Rd BS16 ....19 F6
Albion Cl BS16 ....20 F5
Albion Ct GL10 ....97 F7
Albion Pl 18 Bristol BS2 ....195 C3
  Cheltenham GL52 ....193 C4
Albion Rd Bristol BS5 ....19 B1
  Cinderford GL14 ....191 D6
Albion Sq 1 NP16 ....60 E8
Albion St 6 Bristol BS5 ....9 C8
  Cheltenham GL52 ....193 C3
  Gloucester GL1 ....196 A2
  Stratton GL7 ....190 B7
Albion Terr Bristol BS34 ....40 B1
  Stonehouse GL10 ....97 F6
Albion Wlk GL50 ....193 C4
Albright La HR8 ....179 D4
Alcotts Gn GL2 ....172 F2
Alcove Rd BS16 ....19 F3
Alcove Wood/Coed Cilfach
  NP16 ....60 C8
Alden Ho BS36 ....30 D4
Alder Cl Gloucester GL2 ....127 D4
  Walford HR9 ....163 C8
Alder Ct Bristol BS14 ....3 B5
  Cheltenham GL51 ....129 F7
Alder Dr BS5 ....9 E7
Alder Way 7 GL6 ....148 C6
Aldercombe Rd BS9 ....17 C8
Alderdale GL15 ....92 B4
Alderdown Cl BS11 ....17 A8
Aldergate St GL10 ....97 F7
Aldergate Terr 6 GL10 ....97 F7
Alderley Rd GL12 ....68 D1
Alderman Knight Sch
  GL20 ....182 B4
Alderman Twr BS6 ....18 C3
Aldermoor Way BS30 ....10 E4
Alderney Ave BS4 ....9 F4
Alderney Flats 1 GL2 ....127 B5
Alders Gn GL2 ....127 B5
Alders The Bristol BS16 ....30 B1
  Cheltenham GL53 ....130 B4
Aldershaw Cl GL51 ....129 D6
Alderton Cl GL4 ....119 E4
Alderton Rd Bristol BS7 ....18 E8
  Burton SN14 ....34 D6
  Cheltenham GL51 ....129 E8
Aldridge Cl GL50 ....133 C3
Aldsworth Cl GL7 ....152 F4
  Aldsworth Road Est
  GL7 ....160 B2
Aldwick Ave Bristol BS13 ....2 C3
Aldworth Ho BS2 ....195 C4
Alex Farm SN6 ....144 A6
Alexander Ct 4 BS3 ....8 A3
Alexander Dr GL7 ....190 C2
Alexander Gdns 10 GL8 ....140 B8
  Alexander Hosea Prim Sch
  GL12 ....54 B5
Alexandra Apartments
  BS6 ....18 C3
Alexandra Cl BS16 ....20 D4
Alexandra Ct BS16 ....19 F4
Alexandra Pl BS16 ....20 D4
Alexandra Pk
  Bristol,Cotham BS6 ....18 C2
  Bristol,Ridgeway BS16 ....19 F4
Alexandra Pl BS16 ....20 D4
Alexandra Rd
  Bristol,Clifton BS8 ....194 B4
  Bristol,Eastfield BS10 ....18 C8
  Bristol,Hanham BS15 ....10 D5
  Bristol,Highridge BS13 ....1 F7
  Chepstow/Cas-Gwent NP16 ....60 F6
  Coalpit Heath BS36 ....31 D7
  Gloucester GL1 ....127 A3
Alexandra St GL50 ....130 B7
Alexandra Way
  Northway GL20 ....182 B4
  Thornbury BS35 ....64 B3
Alexandra Wlk GL52 ....132 B4
Alford Rd BS4 ....9 C2
Alfred Hill BS2 ....195 A4
Alfred Lovell Gdns 7
  BS30 ....11 A4
Alfred Par BS2 ....195 A4
Alfred Pl Bristol BS1 ....195 A1
  Bristol,Tyndall's Park
  BS1 ....194 C4
Alfred Rd
  Bristol,Moorfields BS5 ....9 B8
  Bristol,Newton BS2 ....9 A6
  Gloucester GL1 ....127 A3
Algars Dr BS37 ....42 E3
Algiers St BS3 ....8 D3
Alice Cres NP16 ....61 A4
Alington Cl 7 GL1 ....127 A1
Alkerton Rd GL10 ....96 F7
Alkerton Terr GL10 ....96 F7
All Alone GL16 ....168 A1
All Hallows Ct 11 BS5 ....9 B8
All Hallows Rd BS5 ....9 B8
All Saint's Cl 10 GL52 ....133 F2
All Saint's La GL52 ....193 A2
All Saints Cl BS30 ....11 A3
All Saints Fields GL5 ....99 E7
All Saints Mans GL52 ....194 A4
All Saints Rd
  Blakeney GL15 ....156 E2

All Saints Rd continued
  Stroud GL5 ....99 D8
All Saints' Rd Bristol BS8 ....194 A4
  Cheltenham GL52 ....133 F2
  Gloucester GL1 ....196 C1
All Saints' St BS1 ....195 A3
All Saints' Terr GL52 ....133 F1
All Saints' Villas Rd
  GL52 ....133 F2
Allanmead Rd BS14 ....3 B8
Allaston Rd GL15 ....92 B6
Allen Dr GL15 ....91 D1
Allen's Almshouses The 12
  GL54 ....168 A1
Allendale Cl GL2 ....127 C4
Allenfield Rd GL53 ....130 C5
Allengrove La SN14 ....47 C3
Allerton Cres BS14 ....3 B4
Allerton Gdns BS14 ....3 B5
Allerton Rd BS14 ....3 B4
Allfoxton Rd BS7 ....19 A3
Allington Dr BS30 ....10 F4
Allington Rd BS3 ....194 C1
Allison Ave BS4 ....9 E4
Allison Rd BS4 ....9 E3
Allotment La GL7 ....151 C5
Allsopp Cl GL14 ....156 F6
Alma Cl Bristol BS15 ....10 E8
  Cheltenham GL51 ....129 F7
Alma Ct BS8 ....18 B1
Alma Dr NP16 ....61 A7
Alma Pl GL1 ....118 D7
Alma Rd
  Bristol,Clifton BS8 ....194 B4
  Bristol,Kingswood BS15 ....10 E1
  Cheltenham GL51 ....129 F7
Alma Road Ave BS8 ....194 B4
Alma St GL51 ....18 B1
Alma Terr
  Gloucester GL1 ....118 D7
  Stroud GL5 ....98 F8
Alma Vale Rd BS8 ....194 A4
Almeda Rd BS5 ....10 A5
Almhouses GL7 ....190 C4
Almond Cl GL4 ....119 D3
Almond Ct GL51 ....132 C2
Almond Way BS16 ....20 F5
Almond Wlk GL15 ....92 B4
Almondsbury Bsns Ctr
  BS32 ....40 D3
Almondsbury CE Prim Sch
  BS32 ....40 A4
Almondsbury Intc BS32 ....40 E4
Almorah Rd BS3 ....8 E3
Almshouses
  11 Chipping Campden
  GL55 ....189 A2
  Marshfield SN14 ....14 E8
  1 Wotton-u-E GL12 ....68 B7
Almshouses Rd GL14 ....156 F6
Almshouses The GL54 ....176 F4
Alney Terr GL1 ....126 C3
Alpha Ctr The BS37 ....43 C3
Alpha Rd BS3 ....8 D4
Alpine Cl GL4 ....119 B6
Alpine Rd BS5 ....19 C1
Alsop Rd 3 BS15 ....20 D1
Alstone Ave GL51 ....133 B2
Alstone Croft GL51 ....133 B2
Alstone Ct 1 GL51 ....133 B2
Alstone La GL51 ....133 A2
  Alstone Lane Trad Est
  GL51 ....133 B2
Alstone Mews GL51 ....133 B2
Althorp Cl GL4 ....118 B2
Alton Court Rd HR8 ....178 A7
Alton Rd BS7 ....18 F5
Altringham Rd BS5 ....9 D8
Alverstoke BS14 ....2 F7
Alverton Dr GL52 ....137 E2
Alveston Grange GL55 ....189 A4
Alveston Hill BS35 ....51 A6
Alveston Rd BS32 ....50 D2
Alveston Wlk BS9 ....17 B2
Alvin St GL1 ....196 C3
Alwins Ct 3 GL50 ....193 C4
Amaranth Way 7 GL51 ....129 F5
Amazing Hedge Puzzle The*
  HR9 ....162 E4
Amber Cl GL4 ....119 A6
Amberley Cl Bristol BS16 ....20 D7
  Keynsham BS31 ....4 E4
Amberley Ct 11 GL52 ....132 E2
  Amberley House Sch
  BS8 ....18 A1
Amberley Parochial Sch
  GL5 ....91 C7
Amberley Rd
  Bristol,Kingswood BS16 ....20 B8
  Bristol,Patchway BS34 ....29 B8
  Cheltenham GL51 ....132 E2
  Gloucester GL4 ....119 A3
  Amberley Ridge Sch GL5 ....99 C1
Amberley Way GL12 ....54 B4
Amble Cl BS15 ....10 F7
Ambleside Ave BS10 ....28 B2
Ambra Ct BS8 ....194 A2
Ambra Terr BS8 ....194 A2
Ambra Vale BS8 ....194 A2
Ambra Vale E BS8 ....194 A2
Ambra Vale S BS8 ....194 A2
Ambra Vale W BS8 ....194 A2
Ambrose La 1 GL16 ....155 B5
Ambrose Pl GL50 ....193 B4
Ambrose Rd BS8 ....194 A3
Ambrose St GL50 ....193 B4

Amercombe Wlk BS14 ....3 D7
America Gdns GL18 ....171 A4
Amos Cl GL50 ....193 A4
Ampney Crucis CE Prim Sch
  GL7 ....151 C5
Ampney La GL14 ....165 D3
Ampney Mill Cotts GL7 ....151 C4
Anapa Mews 15 GL51 ....132 E2
Anbrook Cres GL4 ....119 E7
Anchor Cl BS5 ....9 F6
Anchor Ho BS4 ....9 B2
Anchor La BS1 ....194 C2
Anchor Rd
  Bristol,Canon's Marsh
  BS1 ....194 C2
  Bristol,Kingswood BS15 ....21 A2
Anchor Sq BS1 ....194 C2
Anchor Way BS20 ....16 D4
Anchorage The
  Gloucester GL2 ....118 B6
  Lower Lydbrook GL17 ....163 C3
Ancient Rd GL16 ....162 F1
Andereach Cl BS14 ....3 B8
Anderson Cl GL52 ....138 B3
Anderson Dr 3 GL10 ....97 F7
Andorra Way GL3 ....128 B6
Andover Cl GL51 ....132 C2
Andover Rd Bristol BS4 ....8 F2
  Cheltenham GL50 ....193 A1
Andover St GL50 ....193 A1
Andover Terr GL50 ....193 A1
Andover Wlk GL50 ....193 A1
  Andoversford Link
  GL54 ....166 D6
  Andoversford Prim Sch
  GL54 ....166 D6
Andrew Millman Ct BS37 ....43 F1
Andrew's Cl GL4 ....110 F5
Andrew's Cnr GL15 ....146 E7
Andruss Dr BS41 ....1 D2
Angel Field GL16 ....155 A5
Angelica Way GL4 ....119 F5
Angels Rd BS4 ....9 F6
Angers Rd BS4 ....9 A4
Anglesea Pl 18 BS8 ....18 A2
Anlaby Ct GL52 ....132 E2
  Ann Cam CE Prim Sch
  GL8 ....168 A2
Anthea Rd BS5 ....19 E2
Anthony Cl SN16 ....58 C1
Anthony Ct GL4 ....148 C5
Antona Ct BS11 ....16 D7
Antona Dr BS11 ....16 D7
Antrim Rd BS9 ....18 B6
Anvil Cl GL11 ....80 C8
Apex St BS32 ....195 C2
Apex Ct BS32 ....40 D3
Apna Ghar Ct GL1 ....119 A8
Apperley Cl BS37 ....32 E8
Apperley Dr GL2 ....117 E1
Apperley Pk GL19 ....173 C7
Apple Cl GL54 ....134 A5
Apple Orch BS37 ....32 E8
Apple Orch The GL20 ....182 C5
Apple Orchard CI GL54 ....183 C1
Apple Tree Cl
  4 Churchdown GL3 ....128 A7
  Gloucester GL4 ....119 E4
  Woodmancote GL52 ....138 C2
Appleby Wlk BS4 ....2 D7
Appledore Cl BS14 ....3 B8
Applegate BS10 ....28 B3
Appleridge La GL13 ....77 C4
Appleton Ave GL51 ....129 B6
Appleton Way GL3 ....120 A6
Applin Gn BS16 ....21 C6
Apprentice Ct NP16 ....61 B4
Approach The GL4 ....160 C5
Apsil Ct GL11 ....80 A8
Apseleys Mead BS32 ....40 C2
Apsley Cl GL4 ....190 B3
Apsley Garden Apartments
  BS6 ....18 E2
Apsley Mews BS8 ....18 A2
Apsley Rd Bristol BS8 ....18 A1
  Cheltenham GL50 ....190 B2
Apsley St BS5 ....19 C3
Aragon Ho GL54 ....139 F5
Aragon Way GL3 ....127 F7
Arbour Cl GL55 ....189 A6
Arbour Elms GL19 ....181 C3
Arbutus Dr BS9 ....17 C8
Arcade Mews BS8 ....194 A3
Arcade The GL1 ....196 B3
Archdeacon Cl GL1 ....195 A3
Archdeacon St GL1 ....196 A3

Archer Ct BS30 . . . . 10 F3
Archer Wlk BS14 . . . . 3 E6
Archers La GL52 . . . . 136 D5
Archers The **1** BS6 . . . . 9 B7
Archfield Ct BS6 . . . . 18 E1
Archfield Rd BS6 . . . . 18 C1
Archibald St GL1 . . . . 196 C1
Archway Cl GL14 . . . . 156 C5
Archway Ct GL17 . . . . 164 D5
Archway Gdns GL5 . . . . 99 A8
Archway Sch GL5 . . . . 98 F8
Ardagh Ct BS7 . . . . 18 F7
Ardea Cl GL2 . . . . 117 D1
Arden Cl BS32 . . . . 29 E6
Arden Ho GL2 . . . . 118 C4
Arden Rd GL53 . . . . 130 D5
Ardenton Wlk BS10 . . . . . . 28 A3
Ardern Cl BS9 . . . . 17 B8
Ardmore BS8 . . . . 7 D7
Ardmore Cl GL4 . . . . 118 E2
Argus GL3 . . . . 8 C2
Argus Rd BS3 . . . . 8 C2
Argyle Ave BS5 . . . . 19 C2
Argyle Dr BS37 . . . . 43 E4
Argyle Pl BS8 . . . . 194 A2
Argyle St
 5 Bristol,Eastville BS5 . . . . 19 C2
 6 Bristol,Southville BS3 . . . 8 C4
Argyll Mews GL53 . . . . . . 193 C1
Argyll Pl GL2 . . . . 127 B2
Argyll Rd
 Cheltenham GL53 . . . . 130 F8
 Gloucester GL2 . . . . 127 B2
Ariel Lodge Rd GL52 . . . . 133 F2
Arkells Ct GL12 . . . . 54 A6
Arkendale Dr GL2 . . . . 109 D8
Arkle Cl GL50 . . . . 133 C5
Arle Ave GL51 . . . . 133 B2
Arle Cl GL51 . . . . 133 B2
Arle Cotts GL51 . . . . 132 F4
Arle Ct Dr GL51 . . . . 133 A3
Arle Gdns GL51 . . . . 133 A3
Arle Rd GL51 . . . . 133 A3
Arlebrook GL10 . . . . 102 A5
Arley Cotts **4** BS6 . . . . . . 18 D1
Arley Hill BS6 . . . . 18 D1
Arley Pk BS6 . . . . 18 C1
Arley Terr BS5 . . . . 19 E1
Arlingham Fields GL7 . . . 142 D6
Arlingham **3** GL51 . . . . . 129 C5
Arlingham Rd GL4 . . . . . . 118 D4
Arlingham Way BS34 . . . . . 39 F1
Arlington Cnr GL7 . . . . . . 160 A1
Arlington Ct NP16 . . . . 61 B8
Arlington Mews BS4 . . . . 194 B4
Arlington Mill Mus*
 GL7 . . . . 160 A2
Arlington Pike GL7 . . . . . 159 F1
Arlington Rd Bristol BS4 . . . 9 D5
 Tewkesbury GL20 . . . . 192 E2
Arlington Row* GL7 . . . . 160 A1
Arlington Villas BS8 . . . . 194 B3
Armada Cl GL3 . . . . 127 F7
Armada Ho BS2 . . . . 195 A4
Armada Pl BS1 . . . . 195 B4
Armada Rd BS14 . . . . 3 A6
Armidale Ave **4** BS6 . . . . 18 E1
Armidale Cotts **5** BS6 . . 18 E1
Armoury Sq BS5 . . . . 9 A8
Armscroft Cres GL2 . . . . . 127 B2
Armscroft Cl GL2 . . . . 127 C1
Armscroft Gdns GL2 . . . . 127 B1
Armscroft Pl GL2 . . . . 127 B1
Armscroft Rd GL2 . . . . . . 127 C1
Armscroft Way GL2 . . . . . 127 B1
Armstrong Cl BS35 . . . . 51 D7
Armstrong Dr BS37 . . . . . . 43 C3
Armstrong Dr BS30 . . . . . . 11 B5
Armstrong Way BS37 . . . . . 43 B3
Arnall Dr BS10 . . . . 27 F1
Arncliffe BS10 . . . . 18 C8
Arneside Rd BS10 . . . . 28 E4
Arno's St BS4 . . . . 9 A3
Arnold Ct BS37 . . . . 44 B1
Arnolds La GL6 . . . . 91 B3
Arnolds Field Trad Est
 GL12 . . . . 54 A5
Arnolds Way GL7 . . . . 190 E5
Arnolfini (Art Ctr)*
 BS1 . . . . 195 A1
Arran Way SN6 . . . . 145 C4
Arreton Ave GL4 . . . . 119 C6
Arrowfield Cl BS14 . . . . 3 A2
Arrowhead Cl GL4 . . . . . . 119 B4
Arrowsmith Dr GL10 . . . . 101 F1
Arthur Bliss Gdns **3**
 GL50 . . . . 130 B6
Arthur Cooper Way
 GL16 . . . . 155 A4
Arthur Dye Prim Sch*
 GL51 . . . . 132 D4
Arthur Skemp Cl BS5 . . . . 9 B7
Arthur St
 7 Bristol,Moorfields BS5 . . 9 C8
 Bristol,St Philip's Marsh BS2 . 9 A5
 Gloucester GL1 . . . . 196 B2
Arthurs Cl BS16 . . . . 21 C6
Arthurswood Rd BS13 . . . . 2 A4
Arundel Cl Bristol BS13 . . . 2 B5
 Gloucester GL4 . . . . 118 C1

Arundel Ct BS7 . . . . 18 D3
Arundel Dr GL5 . . . . 99 B6
Arundel Ho **12** GL51 . . . . 132 E2
Arundel Rd
 Bristol BS7 . . . . 18 D3
 Tewkesbury GL20 . . . . 192 E6
Arundel Wlk BS31 . . . . 4 D5
Arundel Mill La GL5 . . . . . 99 D6
Ascot Cl BS16 . . . . 30 F1
Ascot Ct GL11 . . . . 119 A8
Ascot Rd BS10 . . . . 28 E2
Ash Cl
 Bristol,Hillfields BS16 . . . . 20 C3
 Bristol,Little Stoke BS34 . . 29 D7
 Charlton Kings GL53 . . . . 131 C4
 Chepstow/Cas-Gwent NP16 . 60 F5
 Dursley GL11 . . . . 88 A4
 Lydney GL15 . . . . 92 B4
 Yate BS37 . . . . 43 D3
Ash Ct BS14 . . . . 3 A6
Ash Dene Rd GL17 . . . . . . 163 E3
Ash Gr
 Bristol BS16 . . . . 20 D3
 Bussage GL6 . . . . 148 B6
 Mitcheldean GL17 . . . . . . 164 D6
 Upton St Leonards GL4 . . 119 E3
 Ash Grove Pl GL15 . . . . . . 156 B1
Ash La
 Down Hatherley GL2 . . . . 173 B1
 Over BS32 . . . . 39 D2
 Randwick GL6 . . . . 102 D1
Ash Path The GL4 . . . . 119 E3
Ash Rd
 Bristol BS7 . . . . 18 E5
 Northway GL20 . . . . 182 C4
 Stroud GL5 . . . . 99 A4
Ash Ridge Rd BS32 . . . . . . 40 B3
Ash The GL6 . . . . 102 C2
Ash Tree Cl **2** GL18 . . . . 171 A4
Ash Way GL15 . . . . 147 C3
Ash Wlk BS10 . . . . 28 B3
Ashbed Cl GL4 . . . . 147 C3
Ashbourne Cl **1** BS30 . . . 11 C6
Ashbrook La GL4 . . . . 151 E4
Ashburton Rd BS10 . . . . . . 28 C1
Ashchurch for Tewkesbury
 Sta GL20 . . . . 182 C4
Ashchurch Ind Est GL20 . 182 C4
Ashchurch Prim Sch
 GL20 . . . . 182 C4
Ashchurch Rd GL20 . . . . 192 E4
Ashcombe Cres BS30 . . . . 11 D6
Ashcot Mews **3** GL51 . . . 129 E5
Ashcott BS14 . . . . 2 F7
Ashcroft Ave BS31 . . . . 4 D5
Ashcroft Cl GL4 . . . . 119 D2
Ashcroft Gdns GL2 . . . . . 190 C4
Ashcroft Rd GL5 . . . . 99 D5
Ashcroft Rd
 Bristol BS9 . . . . 17 C7
 Cirencester GL7 . . . . 190 C4
 Wotton-u-E GL8,GL12 . . . . 81 D3
Ashdale Cl GL51 . . . . 160 E5
Ashdean GL1 . . . . 191 C5
Ashdene Ave BS5 . . . . 19 D3
Ashdown Ct BS9 . . . . 17 F8
Asher La BS2 . . . . 195 C3
Ashes La HR9 . . . . 162 E4
Ashfield SN6 . . . . 143 A5
Ashfield Cl GL52 . . . . 138 A3
Ashfield Ho GL50 . . . . 193 A3
Ashfield Pl BS6 . . . . 18 F1
Ashfield Rd Bristol BS3 . . . 8 B3
 Ruardean Hill GL17 . . . . . 164 A3
Ashfield Terr **3** BS3 . . . . . 8 B3
Ashford Rd Bristol BS34 . . 29 A7
 Cheltenham GL50 . . . . . . 193 A1
Ashford Way BS15 . . . . 11 A7
Ashgrove
 Charlton Kings GL53 . . . . 131 C4
 Thornbury BS35 . . . . 64 C1
Ashgrove Ave
 Abbots Leigh BS8 . . . . 7 B7
 Bristol BS7 . . . . 18 F4
 Gloucester GL4 . . . . 119 C6
Ashgrove Cl Bristol BS7 . . 18 F4
 Hardwicke GL2 . . . . 109 E7
Ashgrove Cotts GL6 . . . . . 102 F4
Ashgrove Rd
 Bristol,Ashley Down BS7 . . 18 F4
 Bristol,Bedminster BS3 . . . 8 B3
Ashgrove Way GL4 . . . . . . 119 C6
Ashland Rd BS13 . . . . 2 A4
Ashlands Cl GL51 . . . . 132 E3
Ashlands Rd GL51 . . . . . . 132 E3
Ashlea Mdws GL52 . . . . . . 137 D4
Ashleigh La GL52 . . . . 138 D1
Ashletts Rd GL6 . . . . 106 C1
Ashleworth CE Prim Sch
 GL19 . . . . 172 D4
Ashleworth Gdns GL2 . . . 109 E8
Ashleworth Tithe Barn*
 GL19 . . . . 172 D4
Ashley BS15 . . . . 10 F8
Ashley Cl Bristol BS7 . . . . 18 E4
 Charlton Kings GL53 . . . . 131 B7
Ashley Court Rd **2** BS7 . 18 F2
Ashley Ct BS2 . . . . 18 F1
Ashley Down
 BS7 . . . . 18 F5
Ashley Down Rd BS7 . . . . 18 F4
Ashley Dr **2** GL6 . . . . . . 148 B6
Ashley Grove Rd
 1 BS2 . . . . 18 F2
 1 BS2 . . . . 19 A1
Ashley Hill BS6,BS7 . . . . . 18 F2
Ashley Ho BS34 . . . . 39 F1
Ashley Lo BS53 . . . . 130 C6

Ashley Par BS2 . . . . 18 F2
Ashley Pk BS6 . . . . 18 F3
Ashley Rd
 Bristol BS6 . . . . 18 E1
 Cheltenham GL52 . . . . . . 131 B8
Ashley St BS2 . . . . 19 A1
Ashley Trad Est **1** BS2 . . 18 F2
Ashman Cl BS5 . . . . 9 A8
Ashman Ct **1** BS16 . . . . . 19 E3
Ashmead GL2 . . . . 127 B5
Ashmead Dr GL52 . . . . . . 138 A8
Ashmead Ho **5** BS5 . . . . . 9 C7
Ashmead Pk BS31 . . . . 5 B5
Ashmead Rd
 Cinderford GL14 . . . . 191 D3
 Keynsham BS31 . . . . 5 B5
Ashmead Road Ind Est
 BS31 . . . . 5 B5
Ashmead Way **1** BS1 . . . 7 F5
Ashmore Rd GL4 . . . . 118 F4
Ashover La GL50 . . . . 193 A1
Ashton BS16 . . . . 30 C1
Ashton Ave GL4 . . . . 194 A1
Ashton Cl GL4 . . . . 119 E3
Ashton Court Stf* BS41 . . . 7 C4
Ashton Dr BS3 . . . . 7 F2
Ashton Gate Prim Sch
 BS3 . . . . 8 A4
Ashton Gate Rd BS3 . . . . . . 8 A4
Ashton Gate Stad(Bristol City
 FC) BS3 . . . . 8 A4
Ashton Gate Terr **4** BS3 . . 8 A4
Ashton Gate Trad Est BS3 . 7 E3
Ashton Gate Underpass
 BS3 . . . . 7 F3
Ashton Keynes CE Prim Sch
 SN6 . . . . 142 F5
Ashton Park Sch BS3 . . . . . 7 E4
Ashton Rd
 Ashton Keynes SN6 . . . . 142 F3
 Beckford GL20 . . . . 183 B6
 Bristol,Ashton Gate BS3 . . . 7 F4
 Bristol,Bower Ashton BS3, . .
 BS41 . . . . 7 D3
 Siddington GL7 . . . . 150 E1
Ashton under Hill Fst Sch
 WR11 . . . . 183 D8
Ashton under Hill BS3 . . 7 F2
Ashton Vale Rd BS3 . . . . . . 7 F3
Ashton Vale Trad Est BS3 . 7 F1
Ashton Way BS31 . . . . 4 F6
Ashville Bsns Pk GL2 . . . 173 E1
Ashville Ind Est GL2 . . . . 118 C5
Ashville Rd Bristol BS3 . . . 8 A4
 Gloucester GL2 . . . . 118 C5
Ashville Trad Est GL51 . . 133 B6
Ashway GL7 . . . . 168 A1
Ashway Cl GL5 . . . . 98 E7
Ashway Ho GL5 . . . . 98 F7
Ashwell Cl BS14 . . . . 3 E6
Ashwell Rd BS14 . . . . 3 E6
Ashwicke BS14 . . . . 3 A6
Ashwicke Rd SN14 . . . . . . 15 B3
Ashwood Way GL3 . . . . . . 119 F6
Askham Ct **8** GL52 . . . . 133 F2
Askwith Rd GL4 . . . . 119 B6
Aspen Cl SN14 . . . . 15 F6
Aspen Dr GL2 . . . . 117 E2
Asquith Rd GL53 . . . . 130 E6
Assembly Rooms La
 BS1 . . . . 195 A2
Aston Bank HR9 . . . . 170 C2
Aston Bridge Rd GL17 . . 163 E3
Aston Cl **2** Berry Hill GL16 . 155 A7
 10 Eckington BS35 . . . . . 15 F8
Aston Farm Cotts GL8 . . 148 C1
Aston Gr
 Cheltenham GL51 . . . . . . 132 D2
 Cold Aston GL54 . . . . 168 B6
Aston Ho **4** BS1 . . . . . . 195 B1
Aston Rd GL55 . . . . 188 F3
Aston View GL6 . . . . 148 C6
Astor Cl GL3 . . . . 120 D6
Astridge Rd GL4 . . . . 121 A4
Astry Cl BS11 . . . . 27 A1
at–Bristol* BS1 . . . . 194 C2
Atchley St **18** BS5 . . . . 9 B7
Atcombe Rd GL5 . . . . 80 F8
Athelney Way GL4 . . . . . . 130 F8
Athena Ct **3** BS7 . . . . . . 18 F4
Atherstone BS30 . . . . 11 D5
Atherstone Cl GL1 . . . . . . 132 C3
Atherton Cl GL51 . . . . 129 D2
Atherton Ho GL51 . . . . . . 129 D2
Athlone Wlk BS4 . . . . 8 E1
Atkins Cl BS14 . . . . 3 E6
Atlantic Rd BS11 . . . . 16 C8
Atlas Cl BS5 . . . . 20 B8
Atlas Rd BS3 . . . . 8 E3
Atlas St BS2 . . . . 9 B5
Atrium The BS1 . . . . 195 B2
Attwood Cl GL51 . . . . 132 F5
Attwoods Patch GL54 . . . 175 B3
Atwell Dr BS32 . . . . 40 B1
Atwood Dr BS11 . . . . 27 B2
Atyeo Cl BS3 . . . . 7 E1
Aubrey Ho **9** BS3 . . . . 8 B3
Aubrey Meads BS30 . . . . . . 5 E8
Aubrey Rd BS3 . . . . 8 B3
Auburn Ave BS30 . . . . 11 B3
Auburn Rd BS6 . . . . 18 B1
Auckland Ho **1** GL51 . . 132 F3
Audley Cl BS37 . . . . 43 A8
Audley Wlk BS9 . . . . 17 D6
Augustine Way GL4 . . . . . 119 F6
Augustus Ho BS10 . . . . . . 10 B6
Augustus Way GL15 . . . . . 92 B4
Aust Cres NP16 . . . . 60 F5

Aust La BS9 . . . . 18 A8
Aust Rd
 Northwick BS35 . . . . 48 D3
 Olveston BS35 . . . . 49 F5
Austen Gr BS7 . . . . 19 A8
Austen Ho BS7 . . . . 19 A8
Austen Pl BS11 . . . . 16 E7
Austin Dr GL2 . . . . 126 F6
Austin Rd
 Ashchurch GL20 . . . . 182 D4
 Cirencester GL7 . . . . 190 E4
Australia Ho GL51 . . . . . . 132 E1
Avalon Lo BS5 . . . . 10 B6
Avalon Rd BS5 . . . . 10 B6
Avebury Cl GL4 . . . . 118 B1
Avebury Rd BS3 . . . . 7 F2
Avenall Ct **9** GL52 . . . . . 130 F8
Avenall Par GL53 . . . . 130 F8
Avening Prim Sch GL8 . . 148 A1
Avening Rd Bristol BS15 . . 10 A8
 Gloucester GL4 . . . . 118 F5
 Nailsworth GL6 . . . . 91 E3
Avenue Terr GL10 . . . . 97 D7
Avenue The
 Bourton-on-t-W GL54 . . . 168 F8
 Brimscombe GL6 . . . . 148 B5
 Bristol BS4 . . . . 40 B2
 Bristol,Ashley Down BS7 . . 18 E3
 Bristol,Clifton BS8 . . . . . . 18 A1
 Bristol,Chew's Hole BS5 . . . 9 F8
 Bristol,Frenchay BS16 . . . 29 E1
 Bristol,Little Stoke BS34 . . 29 C6
 Bristol,Sneyd Park BS9 . . . 17 E3
 Cheltenham GL53 . . . . . . 130 F5
 Churchdown GL3 . . . . . . 128 D5
 Cirencester GL7 . . . . 190 D4
 Dursley GL11 . . . . 87 D3
 Gloucester GL2 . . . . 127 C4
 Keynsham BS31 . . . . 4 E6
 Stanton Fitzwarren SN6 . . 145 A1
 Woodchester GL5 . . . . 99 A2
 Yate BS37 . . . . 43 D1
Averil Cl GL4 . . . . 119 C4
Averill Ct WR12 . . . . 185 B8
Avon Bsns Pk GL2 . . . . 20 A3
Avon Cl Bristol BS15 . . . . . . 9 F6
 Keynsham BS31 . . . . 4 F6
Avon Cres Bristol BS1 . . . 194 A1
 Brockworth GL3 . . . . 120 F5
 Wickwar GL12 . . . . 54 B6
Avon Ct Bristol,Clifton BS8 . 18 A1
 Bristol,Fishponds BS16 . . . 20 B5
Avon Gorge Ind Est **1** . . 16 C7
Avon Gorge Nature Reserve*
 BS8 . . . . 7 E7
Avon Gr BS9 . . . . 17 D2
Avon Ho GL2 . . . . 118 C4
Avon La BS31 . . . . 5 F5
Avon Meads BS2 . . . . 9 D5
Avon Mill La BS31 . . . . 4 F6
Avon Pk BS5 . . . . 9 D7
Avon Prim Sch BS11 . . . . . 16 D8
Avon Rd Bristol BS13 . . . . . 2 A6
 Charfield GL12 . . . . 67 A4
 Cheltenham GL52 . . . . . . 134 A2
 Keynsham BS31 . . . . 4 F5
Avon Rise SN14 . . . . 47 E4
Avon Riverside Est BS11 . 16 C7
Avon Riverside Sta* BS11 . 5 E6
Avon St BS2 . . . . 195 C2
Avon Trad Est BS2 . . . . 9 A5
Avon Vale BS9 . . . . 17 D4
Avon Valley Bsns Pk BS4 . 9 E6
Avon Valley Ctry Pk*
 BS31 . . . . 5 D6
Avon Valley Farm BS31 . . . 5 D5
Avon Valley Rly* BS30 . . . 11 C3
Avon View Bristol BS15 . . . 10 B3
 Tewkesbury GL20 . . . . 192 E6
Avon Way
 Bristol,Sneyd Park BS9 . . . 17 C4
 Bristol,Southmead BS10 . . 18 D7
 Thornbury BS35 . . . . 51 D7
Avonbank Ind Est BS11 . . 16 B7
Avonbridge Trad Est
 BS11 . . . . 16 C8
Avondale Bsns Ctr BS15 . 20 C2
Avondale Ct
 Bristol,Oldland BS30 . . . . 10 F3
 Bristol,Sneyd Park BS9 . . . 17 D3
Avondown Cl BS10 . . . . . . 28 D2
Avondown Ct BS3 . . . . 8 C2
Avondowns Ct BS8 . . . . . 194 A4
Avonlea Bristol BS10 . . . . . 10 C5
 Yate BS37 . . . . 32 D8
Avonlea Ct BS30 . . . . 11 A3
Avonleaze BS9 . . . . 17 B5
Avonleigh Ct **4** BS3 . . . . . 8 B2
Avonleigh Rd BS3 . . . . 8 B2
Avonmead Ho BS1 . . . . . . 195 B4
Avonmouth CE Prim Sch
 BS11 . . . . 16 C8
Avonmouth Rd
 Avonmouth BS11 . . . . 16 C8
 Avonmouth BS11 . . . . 26 B1
Avonmouth Way
 Avonmouth BS11 . . . . 26 D1
 Bristol BS10 . . . . 27 E3
Avonmouth Way W BS11 . 26 B1
Avonside Ind Est BS2 . . . . 9 C6
Avonside Rd BS2 . . . . 9 C6
Avonside Way BS4 . . . . 9 E6
Avonsmere Residential Pk
 BS34 . . . . 29 C3
Avonvale Rd BS5 . . . . 9 C7
Avonwood Cl BS11 . . . . . . 16 E6

Avro Rd GL54 . . . . 169 D7
Awdelett Cl BS11 . . . . 27 B1
Awdry Way GL4 . . . . 118 D2
Awebridge Way GL4 . . . . 119 C4
Awkward Hill GL7 . . . . . . 160 A2
Awre Rd GL15 . . . . 156 E1
Axbridge Rd BS4 . . . . 8 F2
Axe Ct **4** BS35 . . . . 51 C8
Axis BS14 . . . . 2 D5
Aycote Cl GL4 . . . . 119 B5
Ayford La SN14,BA1 . . . . . 14 F4
Ayland Rd GL2 . . . . 171 A4
Ayland Gdns GL1 . . . . 119 A8
Aylburton CE Prim Sch
 GL15 . . . . 147 C5
Aylesbury Cres BS3 . . . . . . 8 B1
Aylesbury Rd BS3 . . . . 8 B1
Aylmer Cres BS14 . . . . 3 B6
Aylminton Wlk BS11 . . . . . 27 B2
Aylton Cl GL51 . . . . 129 D6
Aysgarth Ave GL51 . . . . . 129 E5
Azalea Dr GL51 . . . . 130 A5
Azalea Gdns GL4 . . . . 117 E1
Aztec Ctr The BS32 . . . . . . 40 A2
Aztec W BS32 . . . . 40 A2

B

Back Albert Pl GL52 . . . . . 193 C4
Back Edge La GL6 . . . . . . 103 B8
Back Ends GL15 . . . . 189 A2
Back La
 Ashton under Hill WR11 . . 183 D8
 Beckford GL20 . . . . 183 B6
 Bisley GL6 . . . . 148 D8
 Bredon GL20 . . . . 182 C8
 Bretforton WR11 . . . . 188 A6
 Broad Blunsdon SN26 . . . 144 D2
 Broadway WR12 . . . . 185 B8
 Drybrook GL17 . . . . 164 B4
 Fairford GL7 . . . . 152 E3
 Keynsham BS31 . . . . 4 E6
 Leighterton GL8 . . . . 70 C3
 Marshfield SN14 . . . . 14 F8
 Mickleton GL55 . . . . 189 A6
 Pill BS20 . . . . 16 C5
 Pucklechurch BS16 . . . . . 22 C4
 Upper Oddington GL56 . . 177 C4
 Wickwar GL12 . . . . 54 A5
 Winchcombe GL54 . . . . . 174 A7
 Woodchester GL5 . . . . . . 107 A8
Back Montpellier Terr
 GL50 . . . . 193 B2
Back Of Avon GL20 . . . . . 192 C4
Back Of Kingsdown Par
 BS6 . . . . 195 A4
Back Of Mount Pleasant
 GL20 . . . . 192 D4
Back Rd
 Bristol BS3 . . . . 8 A4
 Llandogo NP16 . . . . 146 A5
Back Row GL56 . . . . 177 E6
Back St
 Ashton Keynes SN6 . . . . 142 F5
 Hawkesbury Upton GL9 . . 56 A3
 Timington CV36 . . . . 189 F6
 Newnham GL14 . . . . 157 A6
Back Stoke La BS9 . . . . . . 17 F6
Back The NP16 . . . . 72 F1
Back Walls GL54 . . . . 176 F4
Backfield Farm BS37 . . . . 42 F5
Backfields BS2 . . . . 195 B4
Backfields Ct BS2 . . . . . . 195 B4
Backfields La BS2 . . . . . . 195 B4
Backwell Wlk BS13 . . . . . . 1 F8
Baden Hill Rd GL12 . . . . . 52 C6
Baden Rd
 Bristol,Kingswood BS15 . . 11 A7
 Bristol,Redfield BS5 . . . . . 9 C7
Badenham Gr BS11 . . . . . . 16 F8
Bader Ave GL3 . . . . 128 C5
Bader Cl BS37 . . . . 43 D3
Badger Cl
 Bristol BS30 . . . . 10 F3
 Gloucester GL4 . . . . 119 D3
Badger Sett BS5 . . . . 10 B7
Badger Vale Ct GL2 . . . . . 118 C5
Badger's La BS32 . . . . 39 C3
Badgers Cl BS32 . . . . 40 D3
Badgers Dene
 Chepstow/Cas-Gwent NP16 . 60 D8
 Narth The NP25 . . . . 154 B1
Badgers Field GL55 . . . . . 189 A2
Badgers Holt BS14 . . . . 3 C6
Badgers Mow NP10 . . . . . 60 B6
Badgers Rise BS10 . . . . . . 28 E4
Badgers Way
 9 Bream GL15 . . . . 155 D1
 Nailsworth GL6 . . . . 90 F5
Badgers Wlk BS4 . . . . 9 D2
Badgeworth BS37 . . . . 32 D6
Badgeworth La GL51 . . . . 129 B2
Badgeworth Rd GL51 . . . 129 A7
Badhams The GL20 . . . . . 180 F7
Badminton Cl BS16 . . . . . . 30 C1
Badminton Ct BS37 . . . . . 43 C2
Badminton Ctr The BS37 . 43 C2
Badminton Rd
 Bristol,Downend BS16 . . . 20 D7
 Bristol,Montpelier BS2 . . . 18 F1
 Chipping Sodbury BS37 . . 34 B7
 Frampton Cotterell BS36, . .
 BS37 . . . . 31 C6
 Gloucester GL4 . . . . 119 B5
Badminton Road Trad Est
 BS37 . . . . 43 B3

Badminton Sch BS9 ......18 A5
Badminton Wlk BS16 ....20 E7
Badock's Wood Prim Sch
BS10 ....28 B1
Badsey La WR12 ....188 A3
Bafford App GL53 ....131 A4
Bafford Gr GL53 ....130 F4
Bafford La GL53 ....131 A5
Baglyn Ave BS15 ....20 F3
Bagnell Cl BS14 ....3 E5
Bagnell Rd BS14 ....3 E5
Bagpath GL5 ....99 D2
Bagshots Sq GL54 ......176 B2
Bagstone Rd BS37,GL12 ..53 A2
Bagworth Dr BS30 ....10 F3
Bailey Cl GL54 ....176 F4
Bailey Hill GL15 ....156 B1
Bailey La NP16,GL15 ....146 D4
Bailey's Court Prim Sch
BS32 ....29 F6
Bailey's Hay NP16 ....60 B4
Bailey's Court Rd BS32 ..29 F6
Baileys Ct BS32 ....29 F6
Bailey Mead Rd BS16 ....19 C5
Bailiffe Piece SN6 .....143 E5
Baines Cl GL54 ....168 F7
Bakehouse La GL50 ......130 B7
Baker Sq GL20 ....192 D5
Baker St
Cheltenham GL51 ....133 C3
Gloucester GL2 ....196 A1
Baker's Hill GL55 ......189 B5
Baker's La GL19 ....172 B3
Bakers Ground BS34 ......30 A5
Bakers Hill GL16 ....155 B6
Bakers Piece Rd GL17 ..163 F3
Bakers Pk BS13 ....2 B6
Bakersfield BS30 ....11 E3
Bala Rd GL51 ....129 F6
Balaclava Ind Est BS16 ..19 F3
Balaclava Rd BS16 ....19 F3
Balcarras GL53 ....131 C5
Balcarras Gdns GL53 ....131 C5
Balcarras Rd GL53 ......131 C5
Balcarras Retreat GL53 ..131 C5
Balcarras Sch GL53 .....131 C5
Baldwin Cl GL7 ....149 B1
Baldwin St BS1 ....195 A2
Baldwyn Ct WR11 ....188 C6
Balfour Rd Bristol BS3 ...8 B3
Gloucester GL1 ....118 D6
Ballards Cl GL55 ....189 A6
Ballast La BS11 ....26 E2
Ballinode Cl GL50 .....133 E5
Ballinska Mews GL2 ....127 D5
Balmain St BS4 ....9 A4
Balmoral Cl BS34 ....29 D4
Balmoral Cl Bristol BS16 ..21 A5
Cheltenham GL53 ....130 F6
Balmoral Mans 3 BS7 ...18 F2
Balmoral Rd
Bristol,Longwell Green
BS30 ....10 F2
Bristol,Montpelier BS7 ..18 F2
Keynsham BS31 ....4 E4
Baltic Pl BS20 ....16 D4
Bamfield BS14 ....3 A6
Bamfurlong Ind Pk
GL51 ....173 E1
Bamfurlong La
Bamfurlong GL51 ....128 F8
Bamfurlong GL51 ....129 A8
Bamfurlong GL51 ....173 F1
Bampton Cl
Bristol,Emerson's Green
BS16 ....21 C6
Bristol,Headley Park BS13 ..2 B7
Bampton Croft BS16 .....21 C6
Bampton Dr BS16 ....30 D1
Banady La GL52 ....136 E5
Baneberry Rd GL4 ......119 A4
Banfield Cl BS11 ....17 A8
Bangor Dr BS4 ....9 F5
Bangrove Wlk BS11 ......16 E8
Bangup La GL54 ....168 B6
Banister Gr BS4 ....2 D7
Bank Cres 1 HR8 ....178 F8
Bank Leaze Prim Sch
BS11 ....27 B2
Bank Pl BS20 ....16 D4
Bank Rd Avonmouth BS11 ..26 D7
Bristol BS15 ....20 D2
Pilning BS35 ....38 E6
Bank Sq 6 NP16 ....60 E8
Bank St
Chepstow/Cas-Gwent NP16 ..60 E8
Coleford GL16 ....155 A5
Bank The Broadwell GL56 ..177 A6
Cheltenham GL52 ....134 C4
Stroud GL6 ....98 D8
Banks Fee La GL56 .....176 D8
Bankside Bristol BS4 ....9 D3
North Cerney GL7 ......158 D3
Bankside Ind Est HR8 ..178 E8
Bankside Rd BS4 ....9 D3
Banner Rd BS6 ....18 E1
Bannerleigh La BS8 ......7 E6
Bannerleigh Rd BS8 .....7 E6
Bannerman Rd BS5 ....9 A8
Bannerman Road Prim Sch
BS5 ....19 B1
Bannetts Tree Cres BS35 ..51 A5
Bantock Cl BS4 ....9 D2
Bantry Rd BS4 ....2 E8
Banwell Cl Bristol BS13 ..2 A8
Keynsham BS31 ....5 A2
Banwell Rd BS3 ....8 A3
Banyard Cl GL51 ....132 D2

Baptist Cl GL4 ....119 F6
Baptist St BS5 ....19 A1
Baptist Way GL17 ......164 A3
Baranwheel Ct BS5 ......9 F6
Barber La GL8 ....140 A2
Barberry Cl GL50 ......130 B6
Barbican Rd GL1 ....196 A3
Barbican Way GL1 ......196 A3
Barbour Rd BS13 ....2 D3
Barbour Rd BS13 ....2 D3
Barbridge Rd GL51 .....132 E3
Barcelona Dr GL6 ....91 F6
Barcroft Cl BS15 ....10 C8
Baregains La HR8 ......178 E8
Barker Cl 5 BS35 ....9 C7
Barker Pl 1 GL7 ....152 E4
Barker Wlk BS5 ....19 A1
Barker's Leys GL52 ....138 B4
Barkers Mead BS37 ......43 F4
Barkleys Hill BS16 .....19 C5
Barlands Ho BS10 ....27 F3
Barlands The GL52 .....131 E4
Barley Cl Bristol BS16 ..21 A6
Cheltenham GL51 ....132 D5
Frampton Cotterell BS36 ..31 C8
Hardwicke GL2 ....109 E6
Barley Close Com Prim Sch
BS16 ....21 A6
Barleycorn Sq GL14 ...191 C4
Barleycroft Cl GL4 ....119 D2
Barlow Cl GL10 ....97 E7
Barlow Rd GL51 ....132 F4
Barn Bsns Ctr The GL54 ..169 D4
Barn Cl Bristol BS16 ....21 B6
Gloucester GL4 ....119 E4
Gretton GL54 ....137 A6
Nailsworth GL6 ....91 B3
Barn Cotts The GL15 ...146 F6
Barn End SN14 ....15 A8
Barn Field 5 GL52 .....134 A1
Barn Field Ave GL6 .....91 A4
Barn Field Rd GL6 ....91 A4
Barn Field Terr GL6 ....91 A4
Barn Ground GL2 ....119 E4
Barn Hill Rd GL16 .....155 C6
Barn La GL17 ....163 F3
Barn Owl Way BS34 .....29 F5
Barn Way 7 GL4 ....190 A7
Barnabas St 9 BS2 .....18 E1
Barnaby Cl GL1 ....118 F7
Barnack Trad Est BS3 ...8 C1
Barnard Par BS4 ....9 D3
Barnage La GL15 ....147 A4
Barnard Par 5 GL10 ....97 F7
Barnard Wlk BS31 ....4 D4
Barnes Ho GL7 ....190 D5
Barnes St BS5 ....9 D8
Barnes Wallis Way GL3 ..128 C5
Barnets Wood/Coed Barnet
NP16 ....60 C8
Barnett Ave HR8 ......178 E8
Barnett Cl GL51 ....132 E5
Barnett Way
Gloucester GL2 ....127 C2
Yate BS37 ....32 C7
Barons Cl BS3 ....7 F3
Barossa Pl BS1 ....195 A1
Barra Cl SN6 ....145 C3
Barrack Sq GL11 ....196 A3
Barrack's La BS11 .....16 D8
Barracks The GL15 ....156 A4
Barratt Ind Pk GL11 ..126 D4
Barratt St BS5 ....19 C1
Barratt's Mill La GL3 ..193 C3
Barrel La GL17 ....164 F8
Barrels Pitch 1 GL51 ..189 A2
Barrington Ave BS15 ...20 F3
Barrington Cl GL51 ....129 B7
Barrington Ct BS15 ....20 F2
Barrington Ct
1 Bristol,Knowle BS2 ....8 F4
Bristol,New Cheltenham
BS15 ....20 E1
Barrington Dr GL51 ....119 F8
Barrington Mews GL51 ..129 B7
Barrow Cl GL12 ....109 F8
Barrow Elm Barns GL7 ..152 F7
Barrow Hill
Churchdown GL3 ....128 D3
Wick BS30 ....12 B5
Barrow Hill Cres BS11 ..16 C7
Barrow Hill Rd BS11 ....16 D6
Barrow Hospl BS48 .....1 A6
Barrow Rd BS2 ....9 A7
Barrowell La GL15 .....146 F7
Barrowfield Rd GL5 ....103 A1
Barrowmead Dr BS11 ...16 F7

Barrs Court Ave BS30 ...11 A5
Barrs Court Prim Sch
BS30 ....10 F5
Barrs Court Rd BS30 ....11 A5
Barrs La GL11 ....79 E4
Barry Cl BS30 ....11 C1
Barry Rd BS30 ....11 C2
Barstable Ho BS2 .....195 C3
Bartholomew Cl GL19 ..172 D4
Bartholomew Sq BS7 ...18 F7
Bartlett's Rd BS3 ....8 C2
Bartletts Pk GL54 .....176 F4
Bartley Croft 3 GL8 ...140 C4
Bartley Ct BS5 ....9 D7
Bartley St BS3 ....8 D4
Barton Cl Alveston BS35 ..51 A5
1 Bristol BS4 ....9 F6
Charlton Kings GL53 ...131 A4
Winterbourne BS36 .....30 E5
Barton Ct Bristol BS5 ...9 C6
Highworth SN6 ....145 D3
Barton Gn BS5 ....9 C6
Barton Hill GL17 ......164 E5
Barton Hill Prim Sch BS5 ..9 B6
Barton Hill Rd BS5 .....9 B7
Barton Hill Trad Est 10
BS5 ....9 B6
Barton Ho BS5 ....9 C6
Barton La GL7 ....190 B5
Barton Manor BS2 ......9 A6
Barton Mews GL20 .....192 D4
Barton Rd
Barton-on-t-H GL56 ...187 F3
Bristol BS2 ....195 C2
Tewkesbury GL20 ......192 D4
Barton St Bristol BS1 ..195 A3
Gloucester GL1 ....119 A8
Tewkesbury GL20 ......192 C4
Barton The Bristol BS15 ..10 C4
Hawkesbury Upton GL9 ..55 F3
Barton Vale 6 BS2 ......9 A6
Barton Way GL54 ......137 A6
Bartonend La GL6 ....91 A1
Bartonia Gr BS4 ....9 D1
Bartwood La HR9 ......164 A8
Barwick Ho BS11 ....16 E7
Barwick Rd 8 GL51 ....129 F5
Barwood Cl BS15 ....10 F8
Base La GL2 ....172 F1
Basil Cl GL4 ....119 E4
Bassett Cl 3 GL54 ....174 A7
Bassett Rd GL54 ....168 A1
Bassetts The GL5 ......98 D8
Batch The BS31 ....8 B2
Batches The GL7 ....8 B2
Batchfield La BS16,BS37 ..22 D8
Batchfields GL4 ....178 E2
Bateman Cl GL4 ....118 D2
Bates Cl BS5 ....19 A1
Bath Bldgs BS6 ....18 E1
Bath Cres GL15 ....155 C1
Bath Hill BS31 ....4 F5
Bath La GL9 ....55 C2
Bath Mews GL53 ....193 C2
Bath Par GL53 ....193 C2
Bath Pl
1 Berry Hill GL16 .....155 A7
Lydney GL15 ....92 B3
Bath Race Course* BA1 ..6 F6
Bath Rd Bitton BS30,BA1 ..5 F7
Bristol BS3 ....195 C1
Bristol,Longwell Green
BS30 ....10 F3
Bristol,North Common BS30 ..11 D6
Bristol,Totterdown BS4 ..9 B4
Bristol,Upper Knowle BS4 ..9 D2
Bristol,Willsbridge BS30 ..10 E1
Cheltenham GL50,GL53 ..193 B2
Chipping Sodbury BS37,GL9 ..34 C4
Colerne SN14 ....15 C2
Cricklade SN6 ....143 E4
Eastington GL10 ......105 D8
Hardwicke GL2 ....109 E4
Leighterton GL8 ....70 B2
Leonard Stanley GL10 ..97 E4
Nailsworth GL6 ....91 B2
Salford BS31 ....5 D1
Stonehouse GL10 ....97 F7
Tetbury GL8 ....68 A2
Thornbury BS35 ....51 B8
Wick BS30 ....12 E4
Woodchester GL5 ....91 A2
Bath Road Trad Est GL5 ..98 A5
Bath St Bristol BS1 ....195 A2
Bristol,Ashton Gate BS3 ..8 A4
Bristol,Staple Hill BS16 ..20 A4
Cheltenham GL50 ......193 C3
Stroud GL5 ....193 B1
Bath Terr GL53 ....193 B1
Bath Ville Mews GL53 ..193 B2
Bathams Ct GL17 ......164 F5
Bathings The 2 BS35 ..51 C8
Bathleaze GL10 ....97 E4
Bathurst Par BS1 .....195 A1
Bathurst Park Rd GL15 ..92 A5
Bathurst Rd
Cirencester GL7 ......190 B3
Gloucester GL1 ....118 F6
Bathwell Rd BS4 ....9 A3
Batley Ct BS30 ....11 D7
Batsford Arboretum*
GL56 ....186 E4
Batten Cl BS37 ....44 C1
Batten's La BS5 ....10 A6
Battenburg Rd BS5 .....10 A8

Battens Rd BS5 ....10 B7
Battersby Way BS10 ....27 E2
Battersea Rd BS5 ....9 C8
Battle Rd GL20 ....192 B2
Battlebrook Dr GL55 ..189 B2
Battledown App GL52 ...131 A8
Battledown Childrens Ctr
GL52 ....134 A1
Battledown Cl GL52 ...134 A1
Battledown Dr GL52 ...131 A8
Battledown Grange
GL52 ....131 A8
Battledown Mead GL52 ..134 A1
Battledown Priors GL52 ..134 A1
Battledown Trad Est
GL52 ....131 A8
Batts La GL17 ....164 A4
Battson Rd GL54 ....3 E4
Baugh Gdns BS16 ....30 E1
Baugh Rd BS16 ....30 E1
Baunton La GL7 ....150 C7
Baxter Cl BS20 ....181 F8
Baxter Cl BS13 ....10 F8
Baxters Barns GL7 ....153 D6
Bay Gdns BS5 ....19 C2
Bay Tree Cl BS34 ....28 F7
Bay Tree Rd GL4 ......119 F5
Bayberry Pl Cvn Pk 10
GL16 ....155 B5
Bayfield Gdns GL18 ...178 D2
Bayham Rd BS4 ....9 A3
Bayham's Wlk GL16 ...155 C6
Baylands GL13 ....85 D8
Bayleys Dr BS15 ....10 C6
Bayliss Ho GL51 ......132 E4
Bayliss Rd GL20 ......182 E8
Baynham Ct 4 BS15 ....10 B5
Baynham Rd GL17 .....164 D5
Baynham Way GL50 ...193 B4
Baynham's Wlk GL16 ..155 B6
Baynton Ho 2 BS5 ......9 B7
Baynton Rd BS3 ....8 B2
Bays Hill GL13 ....85 D8
Bayshill La GL50 ......193 A3
Bayshill Rd GL50 .....193 A3
Bayswater Ave BS6 .....18 B3
Bayswater Rd BS7 .....18 F7
Bazeley Rd GL4 ....119 B2
Beach Ave BS35 ....38 A7
Beach Ho BS35 ....11 F3
Beach La BS30 ....12 C2
Beach Rd BS35 ....37 F7
Beachgrove Gdns BS16 ..20 D2
Beachgrove Rd BS16 ...20 D2
Beachley Rd
Beachley NP16 ....61 B4
Tutshill NP16 ....73 A1
Beachley Wlk BS11 .....16 E7
Beacon Cl GL6 ....112 A5
Beacon La BS16 ....30 C6
Beacon Rd
Gloucester GL4 ....119 B2
Llandogo NP25 ....146 A8
Beacon Rise Prim Sch
BS15 ....10 D6
Beaconlea BS15 ....10 D6
Beacons View Rd GL14 ..191 D5
Beaconsfield Cl 6 BS37 ..26 D8
Beaconsfield Ct 1
GL50 ....130 B8
Beaconsfield Rd
Bristol,Clifton BS8 ....18 A1
Bristol,Crew's Hole BS5 ..9 F7
Bristol,Kensington Park BS4 ..9 B6
Beaconsfield St 7 BS5 ..9 B6
Beagles The GL5 ....98 D7
Beale Cl Bristol BS14 ...3 E6
Beale Rd GL51 ....132 D3
Beam Acre The BS11 ...16 D8
Bean Hill BS56 ....176 E8
Bean 11 BS5 ....19 A1
Beanhill Cres BS37 .....19 A1
Beanwood Pk (Cvn Site)
BS37 ....32 E3
Bear Hill GL5 ....99 B2
Bear La GL20 ....180 F6
Bear St GL8 ....68 B7
Bearbridge Rd BS13 ....1 F4
Bearcroft Gdns GL55 ..189 B6
Beard's La GL5 ....99 A7
Bearland GL1 ....196 A3
Bearlands GL7 ....68 C6
Bearpacker Almshouses
GL12 ....68 C8
Bearsfield GL6 ....105 A1
Beauchamp Cl 2 GL7 ..152 E4
Beauchamp Mdw GL15 ..92 C4
Beauchamp Rd BS7 ....18 D4
Beaudesert Park Sch
GL6 ....91 C5
Beaufort Cl BS5 ....9 B8
Beaufort Ave BS37 .....43 D2
Beaufort Bldgs
8 Bristol BS8 ....7 F7
Gloucester GL1 ....196 B1
Beaufort Cl BS5 ....9 D7
Beaufort Com Sch GL4 ..118 B2
Beaufort Cres BS34 ....29 E4
Beaufort Ct Bristol BS16 ..21 A8
Cirencester GL7 ......190 C3
Beaufort Dr GL15 ......92 B2
Beaufort End WR11 ...188 C7
Beaufort Ho 12 BS5 ....9 B7

Beaufort Hts BS5 ....9 E7
Beaufort Mews
9 Bristol BS8 ....7 F7
Chipping Sodbury BS37 ..44 B1
Beaufort Pl
Bristol,Frenchay BS16 ..30 B1
Bristol,Upper Easton BS5 ..9 A8
Chepstow/Cas-Gwent NP16 ..60 E8
Tewkesbury GL20 ......192 C2
Beaufort Rd
Bristol,Clifton BS8 ....18 A1
Bristol,Horfield BS7 ...18 F6
Bristol,Kingswood BS15 ..20 C1
Bristol,Pile Marsh BS5 ..9 F7
Bristol,Staple Hill BS16 ..20 E5
Bristol,Vinney Green BS16 ..21 A8
Cheltenham GL52 ......131 A7
Frampton Cotterell BS36 ..31 A8
Gloucester GL4 ....119 A5
Yate BS37 ....43 D2
Beaufort Sq 5 NP16 ....60 E8
Beaufort St
Bristol,Bedminster BS3 ..8 C2
4 Bristol,Upper Easton BS5 ..9 A8
Beaufort Trad Pk BS16 ..22 B5
Beaufort Way BS10 ....18 D8
Beauley Rd BS3 ....8 B4
Beaufort Dr GL31 ......11 A3
Beaumont Dr GL51 ....132 D4
Beaumont Pl GL15 .....92 A2
Beaumont Rd
Cheltenham GL52 ......132 D3
Gloucester GL2 ....127 C5
Beaumont Row 5 GL52 ..68 B7
Beaumont Sq 4 GL12 ...68 B7
Beaumont St BS5 ......10 B5
Beaumont Terr 8 BS5 ...9 A8
Beaumoor Pl GL7 ......152 E3
Beaver Cl BS36 ....30 F7
Beazer Cl 5 BS16 ......20 D3
Beceshore Cl GL56 ....187 A3
Beck Cl BS16 ....21 C7
Beck Ho BS34 ....29 A8
Becket Cl GL56 ....187 F7
Becket Ct BS16 ....22 B5
Becketts La GL54 .....174 A8
Beckford Cl GL20 .....183 B6
Beckford Gdns BS14 ....3 A3
Beckford Rd
Alderton GL20 ....183 D4
Ashton under Hill WR11 ..183 D8
Gloucester GL4 ....119 B2
Beckford Silk* GL20 ..183 B6
Beckington Rd BS3 ......8 F2
Beckington Wlk BS3 ....8 F2
Beckside Ct 2 GL1 ....127 A1
Beckspool Rd BS16 .....30 C1
Becky Hill GL54 ....176 B1
Beddome Way GL54 ....168 F8
Bedford Cres GL51 ....133 A2
Bedford Cres BS37 ....18 F5
Bedford St
Gloucester GL1 ....196 C2
3 Stroud GL5 ....99 C7
Bedminster Down Rd BS3,
BS13 ....8 B1
Bedminster Down Sch
BS13 ....1 F7
Bedminster Par 8 BS3 ..8 D4
Bedminster Pl 9 BS3 ...8 D4
Bedminster Rd BS3 .....8 C2
Bedminster Sta BS3 ....8 D3
Beech Ave BS16 ....155 B7
Beech Cl Alveston BS35 ..51 A5
Bristol BS30 ....11 A5
Cheltenham GL52 ......134 D1
Hardwicke GL2 ....109 E7
Highnam GL2 ....125 D4
Beech Croft BS14 ......3 B5
Beech Ct BS14 ....3 A5
Beech Gr
Chepstow/Cas-Gwent NP16 ..60 D7
Cirencester GL7 ......190 E5
Highworth SN6 ....145 C3
Woodchester GL5 ......99 A2
Beech Green Prim Sch
GL2 ....117 F1
Beech Grove Ct GL7 ..190 E5
Beech Ho BS16 ....19 C5
Beech La GL16 ....104 B8
Beech Lea
Broad Blunsdon SN26 ..144 E1
Meysey Hampton GL7 ..152 B3
Beech Rd Bristol BS7 ..18 E5
Salford BS31 ....5 E3
Yorkley GL15 ....156 A2
Beech Tree Gdns 5
GL8 ....140 C4
Beech Way Bream GL15 ..147 D8
Littledean GL14 ......156 E8
Beech Well La GL16 ...155 C8
Beechacres BS35 ....64 C1
Beechbank BS41 ....1 D2
Beechcroft Rd GL52 ...127 B5
Beechcroft Wlk BS7 ...19 A8
Beechdean GL14 ......191 C5
Beeches Cl GL10 ....98 A4
Beeches Gn GL5 ....99 B8
Beeches Gr BS4 ....9 D2
Beeches Ind Est BS37 ..43 B2

Beeches Pk GL6 .....148 B2
Beeches Rd
Charlton Kings GL53 .....131 B4
Cirencester GL7 .....190 D4
[6] Newnham GL14 .....157 A6
Beeches The
Bristol,Bradley Stoke BS32 ..29 D8
Bristol,Frenchay BS16 .....30 B1
Bristol,Oldland Common
BS30 .....11 C2
Bristol,St Anne's BS4 .....9 E5
King's Stanley GL10 .....98 A4
Beechfield Cl BS41 .....7 C2
Beechfield Gr BS9 .....17 C8
Beechmore Dr [10] GL52 ..129 E5
Beechmount Ct BS14 .....3 B8
Beechmount Gr BS14 .....3 B8
Beechurst Ave GL52 .....133 F1
Beechurst Way GL52 .....137 D4
Beechwood Ave BS15 .....10 D5
Beechwood Cl Bristol BS14 ..3 C8
Cheltenham GL52 .....131 B8
Beechwood Dr [4] GL6 ..148 B6
Beechwood Gr
Gloucester GL4 .....118 E3
Wotton-u-E GL12 .....68 D8
Beechwood Rd
Bristol BS16 .....20 B4
Easton-in-G BS20 .....16 A4
Beechwood Rise GL11 .....87 F2
Beechwood Sh Ctr
GL50 .....193 C3
Beehive Trad Est BS5 .....9 E7
Beek's La SN14,BA1 .....14 D5
Beesmoor Rd BS36 .....31 B6
Begbrook La BS16 .....19 F6
Begbrook La BS16 .....19 F6
Begbrook Pk BS16 .....20 A7
Begbrook Prim Sch BS16 ..19 F6
Beggar Bush La BS8 .....7 B6
Beggarswell Cl BS2 .....195 C4
Bekdale Cl GL2 .....109 D8
Belas Knap Long Barrow*
GL54 .....174 A4
Belfast Wlk BS4 .....2 E7
Belfry BS30 .....111 B6
Belfry Ave BS5 .....10 A8
Belfry Cl GL4 .....119 E8
Belfry The NP16 .....61 C8
Belgrave Hill [5] BS8 .....18 A2
Belgrave Ho [4] BS8 .....194 A3
Belgrave Pl BS8 .....194 A3
Belgrave Rd Bristol BS8 ..194 B4
Gloucester GL1 .....196 B2
Belgrove Terr GL1 .....196 C1
Bell Bank [6] GL56 .....186 C5
Bell Barn Rd BS9 .....17 D6
Bell Cl BS10 .....18 E7
Bell Cotts GL2 .....95 F4
Bell Hill BS16 .....19 C4
Bell Hill Rd BS5 .....9 F8
Bell La Blockley GL56 ...186 C5
Bristol BS1 .....195 A3
Bromesberrow Heath
GL18 .....179 B4
Gloucester GL1 .....196 B2
Lechlade on GL7 .....153 E2
Minchinhampton GL6 ...148 A3
Poulton GL7 .....151 F4
Stroud GL5 .....98 E4
Westbury-on-S GL14 ...157 C8
Bell Orch GL2 .....157 B6
Bell Pitch GL6 .....102 F3
Bell Rd BS36 .....31 C6
Bell Sq SN14 .....15 A8
Bell Wlk GL1 .....196 B2
Bella Vista GL52 .....138 B3
Bellamy Ave BS13 .....2 C4
Bellamy Cl BS15 .....10 A5
Belland Dr Bristol BS14 ...2 F4
Charlton Kings GL53 ...131 A4
Belle Ct [7] BS2 .....8 F4
Belle Vue Cl GL5 .....99 C7
Belle Vue Rd Bristol BS5 ..19 C1
Cinderford GL14 .....191 D4
Ruardean GL17 .....163 F4
Stroud GL5 .....99 C7
Belle Vue Terr GL6 .....148 C5
Bellevue Cotts
[5] Bristol BS8 .....18 A7
Bristol,Clifton Wood BS8 ..194 B2
Bellevue Cres BS8 .....194 B2
Bellevue Ct BS8 .....194 B2
Bellevue Pk BS4 .....9 D2
Bellevue Rd
Bristol,Kingswood BS15 ..10 F7
Bristol,St George BS5 ...10 A8
[6] Bristol,Windmill Hill BS2 ..8 F4
Bellevue Terr
Bristol,Brislington BS4 ...9 D2
Bristol,Clifton Wood BS8 ..194 B2
Bristol,Windmill Hill BS2 ..8 F4
Bellfields La BS16 .....30 C1
Bellflower Rd GL20 .....192 E2
Bellhouse Wlk BS11 .....27 B1
Bellingham La SN6 .....145 D1
Bells Pl Cinderford GL14 ..156 C6
Coleford GL16 .....155 A5
Belluton Rd BS4 .....9 A3
Belmont Ave GL3 .....120 B7
Belmont Dr BS34 .....29 C5
Belmont La GL16 .....155 A8
Belmont Ct [6] GL52 ....193 C4

Belmont Pk BS7 .....28 F1
Belmont Rd
Bristol,Arno's Vale BS4 .....9 C3
Bristol,Montpelier BS6 ...18 E2
Cheltenham GL52 .....193 C4
Hewelsfield GL15 .....146 E5
Stroud GL5 .....99 E6
Belmont Sch GL51 .....130 A7
Belmont St BS5 .....19 B1
Belmont Terr GL17 .....164 D5
Belmore Pl GL53 .....193 B2
Beloe Rd BS7 .....18 E5
Belroyal Ave BS4 .....9 F3
Belsher Dr BS15 .....11 A6
Belstone Wlk BS4 .....2 C8
Belton Rd BS5 .....19 A2
Belvedere Mews GL6 ...148 C5
Belvedere Rd BS6 .....18 B3
Belvoir Rd BS6 .....18 E2
Belworth Cl GL51 .....129 F7
Belworth Dr GL51 .....130 A7
Bence Ct [3] BS15 .....10 B5
Bences Cl SN14 .....14 F8
Bendall Ho [4] GL52 ...193 C4
Bendy Bow SN16 .....141 F4
Benford Cl BS16 .....20 C6
Benhall Ave GL51 .....129 E8
Benhall Gdns GL51 .....132 E1
Benhall Ho GL51 .....129 F8
Benhall Inf Sch GL51 ...129 D7
Bennett Rd BS5 .....9 E7
Bennett Way BS1,BS8 ....7 F5
Bennett's Ct GL7 .....44 A1
Bennington St GL50 ....193 B4
Bensaunt Gr BS10 .....28 D4
Benson Cl [3] GL4 .....119 E6
Bentley Cl BS14 .....2 F3
Quedgeley GL2 .....117 F2
Bentley La GL52 .....134 D7
Benton Cl GL10 .....89 E6
Benville Ave BS9 .....17 C8
Berchel Ho [4] BS4 .....8 D4
Bereton Dr BS30 .....11 B3
Beresford Cl BS31 .....5 E2
Beresford Ho GL7 .....190 C6
Berkeley Ave
Bristol,Bishopston BS7 ...18 D3
Bristol,Brandon Hill BS1 ..194 C3
Berkeley Castle & Butterfly
Ho* GL13 .....85 F2
Berkeley Cl Bristol BS16 ..21 A8
Charfield GL12 .....67 A5
Gloucester GL3 .....120 C6
South Cerney GL7 .....142 F7
Stroud GL7 .....98 D7
Berkeley Cres BS8 .....194 B3
Lydney GL15 .....92 B5
Berkeley Ct
Bristol,Bishopston BS7 ...18 D3
Cheltenham GL52 .....193 C3
Slimbridge GL2 .....95 D3
Berkeley Cts Bsns Pk BS5 ..9 B7
Berkeley Gdns BS16 .....30 B1
Berkeley Gn BS16 .....10 F5
Berkeley Gn Rd BS5 .....19 D2
Berkeley Grange GL2 ....19 C2
Berkeley Ho
Bristol,Brandon Hill BS1 ..194 C3
[7] Bristol,Staple Hill BS16 ..20 D5
[7] Cheltenham GL52 ...133 F2
Bristol,Hester's Way
GL51 .....132 E3
Berkeley Hospl GL13 ....85 E3
Berkeley Mews GL52 ...193 C3
Berkeley Pl Bristol BS8 ..194 B3
Berkeley Prim Sch GL13 ..85 E3
Berkeley Rd
Bristol,Bishopston BS7 ...18 D3
Bristol,Kingswood BS15 ..10 D7
Bristol,Mayfield Park BS16 ..20 B2
Bristol,Staple Hill BS16 ..20 D5
Bristol,Westbury Park BS6 ..17 E8
Cirencester GL7 .....190 C1
Berkeley Sq BS8 .....194 C3
Cheltenham GL52 .....193 C3
Gloucester GL1 .....196 A3
Berkeley Sta GL13 .....85 F5
Berkeley Vale Com Sch
GL13 .....85 E7
Berkeley Vale Pk GL13 ...85 F7
Berkeley Way Bristol BS16 ..21 B7
[7] Tetbury GL8 .....140 C5
Berkeleys Mead BS34 ....30 A6
Berkhampstead Sch
GL52 .....134 A2
Berkley Pl BS3 .....8 D2
Berkshire Rd BS7 .....18 D3
Berlington Ct BS1 .....195 B1
Berners Cl BS4 .....2 E2
Berrells Rd GL8 .....140 B3
Berrells The GL8 .....140 B3
Berrington Rd GL51 .....129 F6
Berrow Wlk BS3 .....8 E2
Berrows Mead BS37 .....43 A8
Berry Cl GL6 .....103 F8
Berry Croft [5] BS3 .....8 C2
Berry Hill Cl BS10 .....28 D1
Berry Hill Cres GL7 .....190 C7
Berry Hill Prim Sch
GL16 .....155 A4
Berry La BS7 .....18 F6
Berry La Rd GL7 .....190 D7
Berrycroft GL13 .....85 E4
Berryfield GL5 .....98 F2

Berryfield Glade GL3 ....128 A6
Berrymore Rd GL5 .....98 F2
Bertha's Field GL9 .....57 B4
Berton Cl SN26 .....144 E1
Berwick Cl BS10 .....27 E8
Berwick Ct BS10 .....27 B5
Berwick Dr BS10 .....27 E5
Berwick La BS10 .....27 D7
Berwick Rd
Bishop's Cleeve GL52 ...137 F5
Bristol BS5 .....19 B2
Beryl Gr BS14 .....3 C8
Beryl Rd BS3 .....8 B3
Besbury Pk GL6 .....148 A4
Besford Rd GL52 .....138 E3
Besom La BS37 .....32 D5
Bessemer Cl [2] GL16 ...155 A5
Beta Cl GL20 .....182 B4
Bethel Rd BS5 .....9 F8
Bethesda St GL50 .....193 B1
Betjeman Cl GL2 .....118 C4
Betjeman Ct [2] BS3 .....8 E2
Bettenson Rise [1] GL54 ..168 A1
Bettertons Cl GL7 .....152 D3
Bettridge Cl GL52 .....134 B3
Bettridge Sch GL52 ....130 A6
Betts Gn BS16 .....21 C7
Betworthy Est GL11 .....88 E8
Bevan Ct BS34 .....28 F2
Bevan Gdns GL20 .....182 C5
Bevans Hill GL13 .....85 D4
Beverley Ave BS10 .....30 F1
Beverley Cl BS5 .....10 B6
Beverley Croft GL51 ....132 C2
Beverley Gdns Bristol BS9 ..17 D7
Woodmancote GL52 ...138 C3
Beverley Rd BS7 .....18 F8
Beverly Cl [3] BS16 .....20 D3
Beverston Gdns BS11 ....27 B2
Beverstone BS15 .....10 D8
Beverstone Ct GL7 .....142 F7
Beverstone Rd GL7 .....142 F7
Bevington Cl BS34 .....39 E1
Bevington La GL13 .....76 F7
Bevington Wlk BS34 .....39 E1
Bewicks The GL2 .....95 D3
Bewley Way GL3 .....128 A6
Bexley Rd BS16 .....207 B3
Beyon Cl GL11 .....87 F6
Beyon Dr GL11 .....87 F6
Bibstone BS15 .....11 A8
Bibsworth Ave [4] WR12 ..185 C8
Bibsworth La
Broadway WR12 .....185 D8
Broadway WR12 .....188 B1
Bibury Ave BS34 .....29 B8
Bibury CE Prim Sch
GL7 .....160 A1
Bibury Cl BS19 .....18 D7
Bibury Cres
Bristol,Hanham BS15 ...10 C5
Bristol,Henleaze BS9 ....18 D7
Bibury Farm Cotts GL7 ..160 B2
Bibury Rd
Cheltenham GL51 .....129 E8
Gloucester GL4 .....119 A6
Bickerton Cl BS10 .....27 F3
Bickford Cl BS30 .....11 A6
Bickley Cl BS15 .....10 C2
Bickleywood Dr BS16 ....11 C3
Bicks La [3] GL54 .....174 A7
Biddel Springs SN6 ....145 D3
Biddestone Rd BS7 .....28 E1
Biddulph Way HR8 .....178 E7
Bideford Cres BS4 .....2 D8
Bidwell Cl BS10 .....28 B3
Bifield Cl BS14 .....3 F5
Bifield Gdns BS14 .....3 F5
Bifield Rd BS14 .....3 F5
Bigstone Cl NP16 .....73 A2
Bigstone Gr NP16 .....73 A2
Bigstone Mdw NP16 ....73 A2
Bigwood La BS1 .....194 C2
Bijou Ct GL1 .....126 F4
Bilberry Cl Bristol BS9 ...17 C8
[3] Gloucester GL4 .....119 F5
Bilbie Cl BS10 .....18 E7
Biland Cl BS13 .....1 A1
Billbrook Rd GL3 .....120 A7
Billingham Cl GL4 .....119 B6
Billings Way GL50 .....130 B6
Bilsham La BS35 .....48 F2
Bilson GL14 .....191 C5
Bindon Dr BS10 .....28 D4
Binley Gr BS14 .....3 E6
Binmead Gdns BS13 .....2 B4
Binyon Rd GL54 .....139 F5
Birbeck Rd BS9 .....17 E5
Birch Ave GL4 .....119 C6
Birch Cl
Bishop's Cleeve GL52 ...138 B4
Bristol BS34 .....28 E7
Charlton Kings GL53 ...131 C4
Ledbury HR8 .....178 E8
Birch Croft BS14 .....3 A4
Birch Dr Alveston BS35 ..50 F4
Pucklechurch BS16 .....22 B5
Birch Glade [4] SN6 ....142 F4
Birch Ho BS16 .....21 C6
Birch Rd
Bristol,Kingswood BS15 ..20 A3
Bristol,Southville BS3 ...8 B4
Dursley GL11 .....88 A4

Birch Rd continued
Mile End GL16 .....155 C6
Woodchester GL5 .....99 A3
Yate BS37 .....43 D2
Birchall Ave GL4 .....119 C3
Birchall Rd BS6 .....18 C4
Birchdale Rd BS14 .....3 A8
Birches Cl GL5 .....99 C8
Birches La BS15 .....10 C8
Birches Gr GL5 .....99 C8
Birches La GL18 .....170 F7
Birches Rd NP25 .....154 B5
Birches The GL5 .....99 C8
Birchfield Rd GL2 .....138 A4
Birchills Trad Est BS4 ....9 F1
Birchley Rd GL52 .....131 B8
Birchmore Rd GL1 .....119 A8
Birchwood Cl GL4 .....191 B5
Birchwood Ct BS4 .....9 F6
Birchwood Fields GL4 ..118 E3
Birchwood Rd Bristol BS4 ..9 F4
Woolaston GL15 .....147 C3
Bird Rd GL3 .....120 B6
Birdale Cl BS10 .....27 E3
Birdcombe Cl GL54 ....168 F7
Birdlip Pin GL4 .....121 F1
Birdlip Ho GL1 .....127 A2
Birdlip Rd GL4 .....121 F1
Birds Bush La GL6 .....106 B5
Birdwell Prim Sch BS41 ..1 A8
Birdwood BS15 .....10 D6
Birdwood Cl GL4 .....119 E4
Birdwood Gdns NP16 ...60 C4
Birgage Rd GL9 .....55 F2
Birkdale Bristol BS30 ...11 D6
Yate BS37 .....32 E8
Birkin St [5] BS2 .....8 E8
Bishop Cl GL51 .....133 A2
Bishop La BS7 .....18 E4
Bishop Manor Rd BS10 ..18 D7
Bishop Mews BS2 .....195 B4
Bishop Rd
Bristol,Bishopston BS7 ...18 D4
Bristol,Emerson's Green
BS16 .....21 C6
Shurdington GL51 .....129 E2
Bishop Road Prim Sch
BS7 .....18 D4
Bishop Terr BS2 .....195 C4
Bishop's Castle Way
GL1 .....119 A8
Bishop's Cl GL5 .....99 D6
Bishop's Cleeve Prim Sch
GL52 .....137 F3
Bishop's Wlk GL19 .....181 C3
Bishop's Wood BS32 ...40 C6
Bishops Cl
Bishop's Cleeve GL52 ...138 A3
Bristol BS9 .....17 C3
Chepstow/Cas-Gwent NP16 ..60 F4
Bishops Cove BS13 .....1 F5
Bishops Cl BS9 .....17 C3
Bishops Dr GL52 .....137 F3
Bishops Gate GL15 .....92 A2
Bishops Knoll BS9 .....17 C3
Bishops Mdw GL52 .....137 F3
Bishops Mead NP16 .....60 B4
Bishops Rd GL4 .....119 E6
Bishops Wlk
Cirencester GL7 .....190 C4
Tewkesbury GL20 .....180 C3
Whiteshill GL6 .....102 F3
Bishopsfield [8] SN6 ...143 F4
Bishopstone Cl GL51 ...132 C1
Bishopstone Rd GL4 ....119 A6
Bishopsworth CE Jun Sch
BS13 .....1 F6
Bishopsworth Rd BS13 ..2 A7
Bishopthorpe Rd BS10 ..18 E7
Bishport Ave BS13 .....2 C3
Bishport Cl BS13 .....2 B4
Bishport Gn BS13 .....2 B3
Bishton La NP16 .....73 B3
Bisley BS37 .....32 C7
Bisley Bluecoat CE Prim Sch
GL6 .....148 D8
Bisley Old Rd GL5 .....104 E2
Bisley Rd Bisley GL6 ...129 E8
Cheltenham GL53 .....129 E8
Gloucester GL4 .....119 E1
Stroud GL5 .....99 E6
Bisley St GL6 .....103 F8
Bissex Mead BS16 .....21 B5
Bittern Ave GL4 .....119 D6
Bitterwell Cl BS36 .....31 D3
Bitton Rd GL4 .....137 F3
Bitton Sta* BS30 .....11 B1
Bixhead Wlk GL16 .....155 C5
Blaby Cl GL4 .....119 F5
Black Berry Rd GL53 ...134 C3
Black Dog Way GL1 ....196 B3
Black Horse Hill GL8 ...40 B2
Black Jack Mews GL7 ..190 C5
Black Jack St GL7 .....190 C5
Black Stone Kilns La
HR9 .....162 D3
Black Wells GL11 .....80 B7
Blackacre BS14 .....3 C4
Blackberry Ave [5] BS16 ..119 E4
Blackberry Dr BS36 .....31 C6
Blackberry Hill BS16 ....19 F4
Blackberry Ho BS16 .....21 C6
Blackberry Hill Hospl
BS16 .....19 F5
Blackbird Ave GL53 ....127 D6
Blackbird Cl GL10 .....97 F8
Blackboy [18] GL5 .....99 C7

Blackboys GL11 .....88 A3
Blackburn Rd GL12 .....137 E1
Blackdown Ct BS14 .....3 B5
Blackford La GL7 .....144 E6
Blackfriars BS1 .....195 A3
Blackfriars Church*
GL1 .....196 A2
Blackhorse Ct BS15 .....10 C8
Blackhorse Hill BS35,
BS10 .....28 B8
Blackhorse La BS16 .....21 A8
Blackhorse Pl BS16 .....21 A8
Blackhorse Prim Sch
BS16 .....21 A8
Blackhorse Rd
Bristol,Mangotsfield BS16 ..21 A7
Bristol,Mangotsfield BS16 ..21 A7
Blacklow Cl GL5 .....98 F2
Blackmans Cl GL18 .....170 F4
Blackmoor Rd BS8 .....16 E2
Blackmoors La BS3 .....7 E4
Blackquarries Hill GL12 ..68 E7
Blackrock La BS14 .....2 D5
Blacksmith's Cl GL20 ...183 B5
Blacksmith Hill GL12 ....69 C7
Blacksmith La
Churchdown GL3 .....128 D4
The Leigh GL19 .....173 D5
Blacksmith's La BA1 .....6 B3
Blacksmiths Ground
GL2 .....125 D5
Blacksmiths La
Beckford GL20 .....183 B5
Cheltenham GL52 .....134 C4
Dumbleton WR11 .....183 F7
Highnam GL2 .....125 F7
Blacksmiths Rd GL20 ...183 E4
Blackswarth Ho [6] BS5 ..9 D7
Blackswarth Rd BS5 .....9 C7
Blackthorn Cl BS13 .....2 D5
Blackthorn Dr BS32 .....29 D7
Blackthorn End GL3 ....130 A4
Blackthorn Gdns GL2 ..117 F1
Blackthorn Rd BS13 .....2 D5
Blackthorn Wlk BS15 ...10 E3
Blackwater Way GL2 ...127 E5
Blackworth SN6 .....145 D6
Blackworth Ct SN6 .....145 D4
Blackworth Ind Est SN6 ..145 D4
Bladon Mews GL51 .....129 B7
Blagdon Cl BS3 .....8 B4
Blagrove Cl BS13 .....2 C3
Blagrove Cres BS13 .....2 C3
Blaisdon BS37 .....32 D7
Blaisdon Cl Avonmouth BS11 ..27 C2
Bristol BS11 .....27 C2
Blaisdon La GL17 .....165 B4
Blaisdon Way GL14 .....165 C1
Blaise Castle Mus* BS10 ..27 E2
Blaise Hamlet BS11 .....27 F2
Blaise Prim Sch BS10 ...27 F2
Blake Croft GL51 .....132 E6
Blake Hill Way GL4 ....119 D7
Blake Rd Bristol BS7 .....19 B6
Cirencester GL7 .....190 C5
Blake St [13] NP25 .....154 A7
Blakeley Ct GL3 .....127 F6
Blakeney Cl GL4 .....118 D3
Blakeney Hill Rd GL15 ..156 D2
Blakeney Mills BS37 .....43 D1
Blakey Prim Sch
GL15 .....156 D3
Blakeney Rd Bristol BS34 ..39 F1
Bristol,Horfield BS7 .....19 A8
Blakes Rd BS35 .....64 B3
Blakewell Mead GL6 ...103 E8
Blanchards Cotts BS37 ...33 D6
Blandford Alley SN6 ...145 D3
Blandford Cl [2] BS9 ....17 F5
Blands Row GL5 .....48 B3
Bleasby Gdns GL50 .....130 B5
Bledington Prim Sch
OX7 .....177 E7
Blenheim Cl
Alderton GL20 .....183 D4
Upper Rissington GL54 ..168 F7
Blenheim Ct Bristol BS32 ..40 D3
[14] Cheltenham GL54 ...174 A7
Blenheim Dr
Bredon GL20 .....182 C2
Ledbury HR8 .....178 F7
[2] Newent GL18 .....161 C2
Yate BS37 .....43 D3
Blenheim Ho GL1 .....120 D2
Blenheim Orch GL53 ...129 E2
Blenheim Rd Bristol BS6 ..18 D3
Gloucester GL1 .....196 C1
Blenheim Sq GL54 .....132 E6
Blenheim St BS5 .....19 A1
Blenheim Way GL56 ....186 D6
Blenman Cl BS16 .....20 B4
Bleriot Rd GL4 .....169 D6
Blethwin Cl BS10 .....18 B1
Blimeshire GL15 .....155 F1
Blind La
Chipping Campden GL55 ..188 F7
Tetbury GL8 .....140 D4
Blinkhorns Bridge La
GL2 .....127 B3
Block 2 Government Bldgs
BS10 .....28 B1
Blockley CE Prim Sch
GL56 .....186 C6
Blockley Ct GL56 .....186 C6

oomfield Rd Bristol BS4 .....9 D4
loucester GL1 ....118 D7
oomfield Road Link BS4 ...9 C4
oomfield Terr GL1 ....118 D6
oxmasbury St GL51 ......193 A4
oxham Rd WR12 ....188 A1
oxhams Orch GL19 ......172 D4
oy Sq BS5 ....19 C1
oy St BS5 ....19 C1
oe Boys' Pk GL6 ....148 A4
oe Coat CE Prim Sch GL12 ...68 B6
oe Falcon Rd BS15 ......20 E1
oe Ga GL18 ....170 D4
oe Quarry Rd GL7 ......190 E5
oe Rock Cres 5 GL15 ..155 D1
oebell Chase GL6 ......148 C6
oebell Cl Bristol BS9 ....37 B6
 loucester GL4 ....119 D5
 likwall GL16 ....155 B4
 hornbury BS35 ....64 D2
oebell Dr
 hepstow/Cas-Gwent NP16 .60 F5
 ircencester GL7 ....190 E2
oebell Gr GL51 ....130 A5
oebell Rise GL6 ....148 C6
oebells The BS32 ....29 F7
onsdon Hill SN26 ......144 C2
unts Hay GL7 ....153 C8
oakes Dr GL10 ....97 E6
oat Ho The HR9 ....162 E4
oat Rd GL4 ....169 C6
ackenem Cl BS35 ....51 D7
andenham Field GL4 ..119 F6
edey GL3 GL30 ....11 A5
oldman Ave GL4 ....118 B1
omin Wlk BS4 ....2 F8
omin Rd GL51 ....132 E4
odyce Rd 4 BS35 ....51 A5
oiling Wells La BS2 ....19 A3
oleyn Ho GL54 ....139 F5
oleyn Cotts GL51 ......133 B7
oleyn Ho GL54 ....139 F5
olton Rd BS7 ....198 E1
ond St BS1 ....195 B3
ond's La SN14 ....24 E1
ondend Rd GL4 ....119 F2
onds Mill Est GL10 ......97 C7
onnington Wlk BS7 ....19 B7
onville Bsns Ctr BS4 ....9 F2
onville Rd BS4 ....9 F2
ook End GL7 ....164 F5
oot La BS3 ....17 B6
ootenhay Rd GL52 ....138 A4
ordesley Rd BS14 ....3 A3
arleyton Wlk BS13 ......1 F4
orn Ct 6 HR8 ....178 F8
orough Cl GL10 ....98 A3
orver Gr BS13 ....2 B4
oscombe Cres BS16 ....20 F7
oscombe La GL6 ....90 E1
oseway Way GL14 ....191 C4
ospin La GL5 ....98 F1
oston Rd BS7 ....19 B5
oswell St 4 BS5 ....19 C2
otany SN6 ....145 C3
otham Dr BS4 ....9 E1
oucher Pl 2 BS2 ......19 A2
oulevard The GL5 ......99 B5
oulton Rd BS13 ....2 C4
oulton La GL11 ....88 B1
oulton Rd GL51 ....133 D5
oulton's La 6 BS15 ..10 D8
oulton's Rd 5 BS15 ..10 D8
ouncer's La GL52 ....134 B3
oundary Cotts GL3 ..121 A4
oundary Pl GL19 ......172 A7
oundary Rd
 vonmouth BS11 ....26 D3
 oalpit Heath BS36 ......31 D7
ourchier Gdns BS13 ....2 B3
ourne Cl Bristol BS15 ..10 B8
ourne La GL11 ....88 B1
ourne Rd BS36 ....30 E7
ourne La
 brimscombe GL5,GL6 ..148 A6
 ourne BS5 ....18 A1
ourne Lake Pk SN6 ..143 C3
ourne Rd BS15 ....10 A8
ourne Rd GL2 ....153 D8
ourneville Rd BS5 ......9 D8
ournside Cl GL51 ......130 A7
ournside Dr GL51 ......130 A7
ournside Rd GL51 ......130 B7
oursland Cl BS32 ......40 D2
ournside Rd BS34 ......29 C8
ovone La GL2 ....124 D8
ow Cots BS20 ....16 C4
ow La
 5 Bourton on-t-W GL54 .168 F7
 Ripple GL20 ....181 D8

Bow Mead GL7 ....143 A8
Bowbridge La
 Cheltenham GL52 ......134 B5
 Stroud GL5 ....99 D6
Bowbridge Lock GL5 ....99 D5
Bowden Cl BS9 ....17 C8
Bowden Pl BS16 ....20 F7
Bowden Rd BS5 ....19 E1
Bowen Cl GL52 ....134 A3
Bowen's Hill 10 GL16 ..155 A5
Bowen's Hill Rd 15 GL16 .155 A5
Bower Ashton Terr BS3 ..7 F4
Bower Ct BS3 ....8 A2
Bower Rd BS3 ....8 A3
Bower Wlk BS3 ....8 E3
Bowerleaze BS9 ....17 C5
Bowes Lyon Cl 4 GL56 .187 A2
Bowl Hill GL5 ....99 A3
Bowland Ct BS32 ....40 D1
Bowldown Cotts GL8 ....71 A5
Bowldown Rd GL8 ......71 C3
Bowler Rd GL20 ....182 C5
Bowlers Lea GL11 ....87 F5
Bowling Green Ave GL7 .190 C6
Bowling Green Cres GL7 .190 C6
Bowling Green Ct GL56 .187 A3
Bowling Green La GL7 .190 C6
Bowling Green Rd GL7 .190 C6
Bowling Hill BS37 ....44 A1
Bowling Hill Bsns Pk BS37 .40 E2
Bowly Rd BS4 ....33 B8
Bowly Cres GL7 ....150 E2
Bowly Rd Cirencester GL7 190 B2
 Gloucester GL1 ....118 D6
Bowmead 7 BS4 ....9 D1
Bownham Mead GL5 ....99 D2
Bownham Pk GL5 ....99 D1
Bowood BS16 ....30 C1
Bowring Cl BS13 ....2 C3
Bowsland BS32 ....40 E2
Bowsland Green Prim Sch BS32 .40 E2
Bowsland Way BS32 ....40 E2
Bowson Rd GL15 ......155 D1
Bowson Sq GL15 ......155 D1
Bowstreet La BS35 ......28 A8
Box Cres GL6 ....91 F6
Box Gdns GL6 ....91 F6
Box La GL6 ....91 F5
Box Rd GL11 ....88 A8
Box Road Ave GL11 ....88 A8
Box Tree Cl GL17 ......163 F4
Box Wlk BS31 ....4 C1
Boxbush Cl GL17 ......143 A8
Boxbush Rd
 Coleford GL16 ....155 A5
 South Cerney GL7 ....152 A1
Boxhedge Farm La BS36 .31 E3
Boxwell Rd GL8 ....70 B4
Boxwood Cl GL8 ....82 B5
Boyce Cl GL4 ....119 E3
Boyce Dr BS2 ....19 A2
Boyce's Ave BS8 ......194 A3
Boyd Cl BS30 ....12 B7
Boyd Rd BS31 ....5 D3
Bozard La GL20 ....136 B8
Brabazon Rd BS34 ......29 B2
Bracelands GL16 ......148 C7
Bracelands Dr 1 GL16 .155 A7
Bracewell Gdns BS10 ..28 C3
Bracey Dr BS16 ....20 C6
Bracken Cl GL13 ....92 C3
Bracken Dr GL15 ....92 B3
Brackenbury Dr BS34 ..29 F5
Brackendene BS32 ......40 C1
Bracton Dr BS14 ....3 A5
Bradestone Gr BS16 ....20 A7
Bradford Rd 8 GL52 ..127 B2
Bradfords Cl GL18 ....170 F4
Bradfords Ct GL18 ....170 F4
Bradfords La GL18 ....170 F4
Bradhurst St 8 BS5 ....19 C1
Bradley Ave Bristol BS11 .16 E6
 Winterbourne BS36 ....30 E5
Bradley Cl GL2 ....127 C4
Bradley Court Rd GL17 .164 D6
Bradley Cres BS11 ......16 E6
Bradley Ct BS16 ....20 C5
Bradley Pavilions GL2 ..40 C2
Bradley Rd Bristol BS34 .39 F1
 Charlton Kings GL52 ..131 A4
 Wotton-u-E GL12 ......68 A8
Bradley Rise GL17 ....164 D6
Bradley St GL12 ....68 A7
Bradley Stoke Way BS32 .29 E7
Bradshaw Cl GL2 ......127 E5
Bradstone Rd BS36 ....30 D5
Bradwell Gr BS10 ......18 C4
Brae Wlk GL4 ....119 D4
Braeburn Cl
 Cheltenham GL51 ......132 E2
 Gloucester GL2 ....127 C2
Braemar Ave BS7 ......28 F1
Braemar Cres BS7 ......28 F1
Braemor Ct BS9 ....18 A4
Bragg's La BS2 ....195 C3
Braikenridge Rd BS4 ....9 B8
Brainsfield BS9 ....17 F6
Brake Cl
 Bristol,Bradley Stoke BS32 .29 E7
 Bristol,Warmley Hill BS15 ..10 F7
Brake The
 Coalpit Heath BS36 ....31 C5
 Yate BS37 ....43 E5
Brakewell Gdns BS14 ....3 A4

Bramble Chase GL52 ..137 F4
Bramble Dr Bristol BS9 .17 D3
 Dursley GL11 ....88 A3
Bramble La Bristol BS9 .17 C3
 Stonehouse GL10 ....97 F8
Bramble Lawn GL4 ....119 D3
Bramble Rd GL16 ......155 B4
Bramble Rise GL52 ....134 C3
Brambles The
 Berkeley GL13 ....85 E4
 Bristol BS13 ....2 C4
 Keynsham BS31 ....4 D3
 Lea HR9 ....164 C8
Brambling Wlk BS16 ....19 F6
Bramery The GL51 ....133 B2
Branch Hill Rise GL53 .131 A4
Branch Rd
 Bamfurlong GL51 ......129 A7
 Cheltenham GL51 ......129 B7
Branche The GL17 ......164 B3
Brandash Rd GL17 ......44 C1
Branders GL7 SN6 ......143 E4
Brandon Cl GL3 ....128 A8
Brandon Ho BS8 ......194 B2
Brandon Pl GL50 ......193 A1
Brandon St BS1 ....194 C2
Brandon Steep BS1 ....194 C2
Brangwyn Gr BS7 ......19 B6
Branksome Cres BS34 ..29 B3
Branksome Dr
 Bristol BS34 ....29 B3
 Winterbourne BS36 ....30 E6
Branksome Rd BS6 ....18 B3
Brannigan Ct GL20 ....182 C5
Brans La SL56 ....177 C4
Branscombe Ct BS3 ....8 D2
Branscombe Rd BS9 ..17 C4
Bransdown Hill SN16 ..59 A3
Brantwood Rd GL4 ....148 C6
Branwhite Cl BS7 ......19 B7
Brasenose Rd GL20 ..182 C7
Brassington Gdns GL54 .166 E2
Bratches The GL55 ....189 A3
Bratton Rd BS4 ....9 B8
Braunton Rd BS3 ....8 C3
Bravender Ho GL7 ....190 D4
Bray Ave HR8 ....178 F8
Braybrooke Cl GL8 ....140 C4
Braydon Ave BS32 ......29 D7
Braydon La SN6 ......143 D3
Braydon Rd SN6 ......143 A1
Brayne Ct BS30 ....10 F3
Breach Rd BS3 ....8 A2
Breaches Gate BS32 ....29 F6
Breaches The BS20 ....16 B5
Bread St BS5 ....155 B1
Bream CE Prim Sch GL15 .155 D1
Bream Rd Bream GL15 .147 D1
 St Briavels GL15 ......147 B7
Bream Down Ave BS9 .18 B5
Bream Gdns BS3 ....8 E2
Brecknock Rd BS4 ......9 B3
Brecon Cl Bristol BS9 ..18 B6
 Quedgeley GL2 ....109 E8
Brecon Rd BS9 ....18 B6
Brecon Way GL16 ....155 C8
Bredon BS37 ....32 D7
Bredon Cl BS15 ....10 F7
Bredon Hancock's Endowed
 Fst Sch The GL20 ....182 C8
Bredon Lodge GL20 ..182 C7
Bredon Nook Rd BS10 ..18 C7
Bredon Rd GL20 ......192 D6
Bredon Sch GL20 ......181 C7
Bredon Tythe Barn* GL20 .182 A8
Bredon View WR12 ..185 D8
Bregawn Cl GL52 ......137 E2
Breinton Way GL2 ....127 D5
Brendon Cl BS30 ....11 C4
Brendon Rd BS3 ....8 D3
Brendon Wlk GL52 ....134 B3
Brenner St BS5 ....19 B2
Brensham Cl GL3 ......120 A7
Brent Rd BS7 ....18 F5
Brentry Ave 5 BS5 ......9 B7
Brentry La BS10 ....28 A3
Brentry Lo BS10 ....28 A3
Brentry Prim Sch BS10 .28 A4
Brentry Rd BS16 ....19 F3
Bretforton Fst Sch WR11 .188 A6
Bretforton Rd WR11 ..188 B7
Brevel Terr BS37 ......131 B5
Brewerton Cl BS10 ......28 A4
Brewery Cotts NP25 ..154 C5
Brewery Ct BS3 ....8 A1
Brewery Hill BS30 ....5 F7
Brewery La
 Nailsworth GL6 ....91 B3
 Thrupp GL5 ....99 D2
Brewery Row SN6 ....187 F1
Brewery St SN6 ....145 D3

Brewery Yd 25 GL54 ..176 F4
Brewhouse The BS1 ..195 B2
Briar Cl GL5 ....103 D1
Briar Ct BS20 ....16 C4
Briar Lawn GL4 ....119 D3
Briar Way BS16 ....20 C3
Briar Wlk Bristol BS16 ..20 C3
 Cheltenham GL52 ......134 C3
Briarbank Rise GL52 ..131 C7
Briarfield Ave BS15 ....10 C5
Briarleaze BS35 ....50 F2
Briars Cl GL3 ....128 A6
Briarside Ho BS10 ......28 D3
Briarside Rd BS10 ......28 D3
Briarwood BS9 ....17 F6
Briarwood Sch BS16 ..20 B3
Briary Rd GL7 ....153 E2
Briavels Gr BS6 ....18 F2
Brick Cotts BS35 ....62 E1
Brick St BS2 ....195 C3
Brick Wlk WR11 ......188 C6
Brickfield Terr GL51 ....99 A6
Brickfields GL12 ....68 B6
Brickhill Ave GL20 ....182 C7
Brickrow GL5 ....99 C7
Brickworks Trad Est WR11 .188 C8
Bridewell St BS1 ......195 A3
Bridge Access Rd BS35 .49 A7
Bridge Cl
 Cirencester GL7 ......190 D2
 Gloucester GL2 ....118 B6
 Lechlade on t GL7 ....153 F2
 Whitchurch SN14 ....3 C4
Bridge End
 Cirencester GL7 ......190 D3
 Staunton GL19 ....180 C2
Bridge Farm GL2 ......126 B7
Bridge Farm Cl BS14 ....3 A4
Bridge Farm Inf Sch BS14 .3 A4
Bridge Farm Jun Sch BS14 .3 A4
Bridge Ho Alveston BS35 .50 F5
 Bristol BS1 ....195 A2
Bridge Rd
 Bristol,Eastville BS5 ....19 B3
 Bristol,Lower Soundwell BS15 .21 A3
 Bristol,Shortwood BS16 ..21 C4
 Cirencester GL7 ......190 D2
 Frampton on Severn GL2 .157 F3
 Harrow Hill GL17 ......164 B3
 Leigh Woods BS8 ......7 E6
 Sharpness SL13 ....93 C1
 Stroud GL5 ....98 D6
 Yate BS37 ....43 A2
Bridge Valley Rd BS8 ..7 B4
Bridge Way BS36 ......31 B8
Bridge Wlk BS7 ....19 A8
Bridge-Side GL5 ....98 F6
Bridgeleap Rd BS16 ....20 F8
Bridgemans Cl WR12 .188 B1
Bridgend Cl GL10 ......97 E6
Bridgend Rd GL11 ....129 C7
Bridges Ct 8 BS16 ......20 B4
Bridges Dr 3 BS16 ......20 C6
Bridgeside GL54 ......168 F8
Bridget Dr GL51 ....61 A7
Bridgman Gr BS34 ....29 B3
Bridgwater Rd BS41,BS13,
 BS48 ....1 D6
Bridle The GL5 ....98 D7
Bridle Way BS35 ....50 F4
Briercliffe Rd BS9 ......17 D7
Brierley Banks GL17 ..163 F2
Brierley Cl GL4 ....119 E5
Brierley Council Hos GL17 .163 F2
Brierley Rd GL17 ......163 F3
Brierley Way GL15 ....156 B1
Briery Furlong BS34 ..29 D3
Briery Leaze Rd BS14 ..3 A4
Bright St
 Bristol,Kingswood BS15 ..10 D8
 Bristol,Russell Town BS5 ..9 F7
Brightlands GL14 ......157 A6
Brighton Cres BS3 ......8 D2
Brighton Mews BS8 ..194 B4
Brighton Pk 18 BS5 ....9 B8
Brighton Pl BS15 ......10 C8
Brighton Rd
 Bristol,Patchway BS34 ..28 F8
 Bristol,Redland BS6 ....18 C1
 Chepstow/Cas-Gwent NP16 .72 F7
 Fairford GL7 ....152 E4
 Ledbury HR8 ....178 E8
 Nailsworth GL6 ....91 C4
Brighton St 18 BS2 ....19 B4
Brighton Terr 9 BS3 ....8 B2
Brigstocke Rd BS2 ....195 B4
Brimbles The BS7 ......29 B2
Brimley GL10 ....97 F6
Brimscombe CE Prim Sch GL5 .99 F1
Brimscombe Hill GL5 ..91 B8
Brimscombe La GL5 ....99 F2
Brimscombe Port Bsns Ctr
 BS37 ....43 F4

Brimsome Mdw GL2 ..125 D5
Brindle Cl GL4 ....119 C4
Brinkmarsh La GL12 ....65 D2
Brinkworthy Rd BS16 ..19 E6
Brinmead Wlk BS13 ....1 F3
Brins Cl BS34 ....29 C6
Brinsham La BS37 ......44 A6
Brinsmead Cres BS20 ..16 D4
Brionne Way GL2 ......127 B5
Brisbane GL10 ....101 F1
Briscoes Ave BS13 ......2 D4
Brislington Enterprise Coll
 BS4 ....3 F8
Brislington Hill BS4 ....9 E2
Brislington Ret Pk BS4 ..9 E1
Brislington Trad Est BS4 .9 E1
Bristol & Anchor Ho BS5 .9 D8
Bristol & Exeter Mews
 BS1 ....195 C1
Bristol Bsns Pk BS16 ..29 E1
Bristol Cathedral * BS1 .194 C2
Bristol Cathedral Sch BS1 .194 C2
Bristol Dental Hospl BS1 .195 A3
Bristol Eye Hospl BS1 .195 A3
Bristol Gate 8 BS8 ......7 F5
Bristol Gateway Sch The
 BS2 ....19 A3
Bristol General Hospl BS1 .195 A1
Bristol Gram Sch BS8 .194 C3
Bristol Harbour Rly* BS1 .195 A1
Bristol Hill BS4 ....9 D2
Bristol Homeopathic Hospl
 BS6 ....194 C4
Bristol Ind Mus * BS1 .195 A1
Bristol Old Vic Theatre Sch
 BS8 ....18 A1
Bristol Parkway N BS34 .29 E4
Bristol Parkway Sta BS34 .29 E4
Bristol Rd Bristol BS16 ..30 C2
 Cambridge GL2 ....95 F3
 Cirencester GL7 ......190 D3
 Cromhall GL12 ....53 B7
 Frampton Cotterell BS36 ..42 B3
 Gloucester GL1,GL2 ..118 C6
 Keynsham BS31 ....4 E6
 Luckington SN14 ....47 E3
 Stonehouse GL10 ......97 E7
 Thornbury BS35 ....51 B8
 Upper Rissington GL54 .169 D7
 Whitchurch BS14 ....3 D3
 Winterbourne BS16 ....30 D4
Bristol Royal Hospital for
 Children BS1 ....195 A4
Bristol Royal Infmy BS2 .195 A4
Bristol South End BS3 ..8 D2
Bristol Steiner Waldorf Sch
 BS6 ....18 B2
Bristol Vale Ctr For Ind BS3 .8 B1
Bristol Zoo Gdns* BS8 .17 F1
Bristow Broadway BS11 .26 C1
Bristow Rd GL20 ......192 E1
Bristowe Ho BS16 ......20 B5
Bristowe Lodge BS16 ..20 C4
Britannia Cl 4 BS16 ....30 F1
Britannia Cres BS34 ....29 D5
Britannia Ct 1 BS16 ....20 D5
Britannia Ho BS34 ....29 C6
Britannia Rd
 Bristol,Kingswood BS15 ..10 C8
 Bristol,Lower Easton BS5 ..19 C1
 Bristol,Patchway BS34 ..28 E7
Britannia Way GL52 ..138 B3
British Empire &
 Commonwealth Mus*
 BS1 ....195 C1
British Rd BS3 ....8 C3
British Sch The GL12 ..68 C6
British The BS37 ....43 B4
Briton Cl NP16 ....61 A4
Brittania Bldgs BS8 ..194 A1
Britten Ct 11 BS30 ....11 F4
Britten Pl GL51 ....132 E2
Britton Bottom GL54 ..56 B1
Britton Cl GL55 ....20 C1
Britton Ho BS15 ....11 B8
Brittons Pas SN14 ......14 F8
Brixham Rd BS3 ....8 C1
Brixton Rd BS5 ....9 B8
Brixton Road Mews 22
 BS5 ....9 B8
Brizen La GL53 ....130 B4
Broad Croft BS32 ......40 C2
Broad La
 Coalpit Heath BS36 ....31 D5
 Westerleigh BS37 ......32 A4
 Yate BS37 ....43 C4
Broad Leys Rd GL4 ....119 F7
Broad Marston Rd BS35 .189 A7
Broad Oak Rd BS13 ....1 F4
Broad Oak Way GL51 .129 F6
Broad Oaks BS8 ....7 E6
Broad Plain BS2 ....195 C2
Broad Quay BS1 ......195 A2
Broad Rd BS15 ....10 D5
Broad St Bristol BS1 ..195 A3
 Bristol,Staple Hill BS16 ..20 F4
 Chipping Sodbury BS37 ..44 B1
 Hartpury GL19 ....172 C4
 King's Stanley GL10 ....98 A3
 Littledean GL14 ......191 F4

Broad St continued
18 Newent GL18 ....171 A4
Stroud GL5 ....98 D3
Broad Wer BS1 ....195 B3
Broad Wlk BS4 ....9 A2
Broad Wlk The GL50 ...193 B2
Broadacre CI GL20 ....182 C7
Broadbury Rd A2 ....2 E8
Broadclose Rd GL2 ....173 B2
Broadfield Ave BS15 ...20 C1
Broadfield Cotts GL54 ...160 C6
Broadfield Rd Bristol BS4 ...9 B1
  Eastington GL10 ......96 F8
Broadlands Ave BS31 ...4 D6
Broadlands Ct BS14 ...168 F7
Broadlands Dr BS11 ...27 A1
Broadlands St BS31 ....4 D6
Broadleas BS13 ....2 C7
Broadleaze Bristol BS11 ...16 E7
  Down Ampney GL7 ...143 F8
Broadleys Ave BS9 ....18 C7
Broadmead BS1 ....195 B3
Broadmead La BS31 ....5 A6
Broadmead Lane Ind Est
BS31 ....5 B7
Broadmere GL11 ....87 E4
Broadmere Ct GL11 ....87 E3
Broadmoor La La 6 F4
Broadmoor Pk GL14 ...191 B7
Broadmoor Rd GL14 ...191 B7
Broadoak Hill BS41 .....1 F2
Broadoak Wlk BS16 ...20 B4
Broadstone CI GL4 ...119 E8
Broadstone Wlk BS13 ...2 D5
Broadwalk Sh Ctr BS4 ...9 B2
Broadway Gloucester GL4 ...118 F5
  Saltford BS31 ....5 D3
  Yate BS37 ....43 F2
Broadway Ave BS9 ....18 D6
Broadway Bears & Dolls
Mus* WR12 ....185 C8
Broadway CI
  Cheltenham GL52 ...134 A5
  Kempsford GL7 .....144 E8
Broadway Ct GL7 .....142 F7
Broadway Fst Sch
WR12 ....188 B1
Broadway Inf Sch BS37 ...43 F2
Broadway La
  Minsterworth GL2 ...116 A2
  South Cerney GL7 ...143 A6
Broadway Rd
  Bristol,Bishopston BS7 ...18 D3
  Bristol,Bishopsworth BS13 ...1 F5
  Mickleton GL55 ....189 A6
  Toddington GL54 ...184 C3
  Willersey WR12 ....188 B2
  Winchcombe GL54 ...174 A7
Broadway The
  Chalford GL6 ....148 E6
  Dursley GL11 ....80 A8
  North Nibley GL11 ...79 F8
Broadway Tower Cntry Pk*
WR12 ....185 D4
Broadway,St Mary's RC Prim
Sch WR12 ....185 B8
Broadwell Bridge 7
GL16 ....155 B6
Broadwell CI GL4 ....119 E5
Broadwell Rd GL56 ...177 C5
Broadwell Terr GL11 ...88 B1
Brock CI GL51 ....129 B6
Brockeridge Inf Sch
BS36 ....31 C7
Brockeridge Rd GL20 ...181 F7
Brockhampton La GL51 ...133 B7
Brockhampton Pk GL54 ...174 B1
Brockhollands GL15 ...147 E8
Brockhollands Rd GL15 ...147 D8
Brockhurst Gdns BS15 ...10 A8
Brockhurst Rd BS15 ...10 A8
Brockley Acres GL6 ...148 C7
Brockley CI BS34 .....29 C7
Brockley Rd
  Leonard Stanley GL10 ...97 F4
  Saltford BS31 ....5 D3
Brockley Wlk BS13 .....2 A8
Brockmoor La HR9 ...170 C4
Brockridge La BS36 ...31 C7
Brocks 4 BS8 ....9 D1
Brocks Rd BS13 ......2 C3
Brockworth BS37 .....32 C6
Brockworth Cotts GL3 ...120 F4
Brockworth Cres BS16 ...19 F6
Brockworth Enterprise Sch
GL3 ....120 F6
Brockworth Prim Sch
GL3 ....120 E5
Brockworth Rd GL2 ...128 E2
Brome Rd GL4 ....119 F5
Bromesberrow Heath Bsns
Pk HR8 ....179 B3
Bromfield Wlk BS16 ...21 B7
Bromley Dr BS16 ......20 D8
Bromley Heath Ave BS16 ...20 D8
Bromley Heath Jun & Inf
Schs BS16 ....20 D8
Bromley Heath Rd BS16 ...20 D8
Bromley Rd Bristol BS7 ...18 F8
  Ellwood GL16 ......155 C3
Brompton CI BS15 ....11 A8
Broncksea Rd BS7 ....28 F1
Bronte 2 GL51 ....129 F7

Bronte Dr 2 HR8 .....178 E8
Bronte Wlk BS7 ......19 A8
18 Northleach GL54 ...168 A1
  Winchcombe GL54 ...139 F4
Brook Ct
  Cheltenham GL50 ...130 B6
  Tewkesbury GL20 ...192 E5
Brook End SN14 ......47 F5
Brook Gate BS3 ....7 E1
Brook Hill BS6 ....18 F1
Brook Ho Bristol BS34 ...29 C8
  8 Cheltenham GL51 ...129 F7
  8 Thornbury BS35 ...51 C8
Brook La
  1 Blockley GL56 ...186 C5
  Bristol,Montpelier BS6 ...18 F1
  Bristol,Stapleton BS16 ...19 E6
  Down Hatherley GL2 ...173 B1
Brook Lintons BS4 ....10 B6
Brook Office Pk BS16 ...31 B2
Brook Rd
  Bristol,Hillfields BS16 ...20 B4
  Bristol,Mangotsfield BS16 ...20 F6
  Bristol,Montpelier BS6 ...18 F1
  Bristol,Southville BS3 ...8 A3
  Bristol,Speedwell BS5 ...19 F1
  Bristol,Warmley BS15 ...11 B8
  Cheltenham GL51 ...133 A4
Brook St Bristol BS5 ...9 C7
  Chipping Sodbury BS37 ...33 A8
  Gloucester GL1 ....196 B1
  Mitcheldean GL17 ...164 D5
Brook Vale GL52 .....131 A7
Brook Way BS32 ......29 D8
Brookbank CI GL50 ...193 A4
Brookcote Dr BS34 ...29 D6
Brookdale Rd BS13 .....2 B6
Brooke Rd GL7 ....190 B2
Brookfield Ave BS7 ...18 D3
Brookfield CI BS37 ....44 C2
Brookfield La
  2 Bristol BS6 ....18 D2
  2 Churchdown GL3 ...128 A7
Brookfield Rd
  3 Bristol,Montpelier BS6 ...18 D2
  Bristol,Patchway BS34 ...29 B8
  Churchdown GL3 ...128 D5
  Gloucester GL3 ....119 F7
Brookfield Wlk BS30 ...11 C3
Brookhouse Mill GL6 ...104 A7
Brookland Rd BS6 ....18 D5
Brooklands Pk GL22 ...127 D5
Brooklea BS30 ....10 D3
Brookleaze BS9 ......17 C5
Brooklet Rd GL15 ...147 B4
Brooklyn CI 4 GL51 ...132 F3
Brooklyn Ct GL51 ...133 A4
Brooklyn Gdns GL51 ...133 A3
Brooklyn Rd Bristol BS13 ...2 B8
  Cheltenham GL51 ...132 F3
Brookmead BS35 .....51 D7
Brookridge Ct 5 BS16 ...20 D4
Brookridge Ho BS16 ...27 F3
Brooksdale La GL53 ...130 C6
Brookside Alderton GL20 ...183 E4
  Crudwell SN16 ....141 C3
  4 Newent GL18 ....171 A4
  Paxford GL55 ....186 E8
  Pill BS20 ....16 D3
  Tewkesbury GL20 ...192 E6
  Tintern Parva NP16 ...146 B3
Brookside Cotts GL5 ...91 B5
Brookside Dr BS36 ...31 B8
Brookside Rd Bristol BS4 ...9 F2
  Gloucester GL4 ....191 B5
Brookside Villas GL2 ...187 A7
Brookthorpe BS37 ...32 D8
Brookthorpe Ave BS11 ...27 A1
Brookthorpe CI GL4 ...118 D3
Brookthorpe Ct BS37 ...32 D8
Brookview Wlk BS13 ...2 B7
Brookway Dr GL53 ...131 A6
Brookway Rd GL53 ...131 A6
Broom CI GL51 ......132 E3
Broom Hill Bristol BS16 ...179 C5
Brown's End Cotts HR8 ...179 C5
Brown's La GL10 .....98 A6
Brown's Piece GL12 ...68 B7
Browne Ct 5 BS8 ......7 F6
Browning Ct BS7 .....19 B8
Browning Mews GL51 ...129 F7
Browns Hill GL6 .....148 B5
Brownshill Rd GL6 ...148 B5
Broxholme Wlk BS11 ...16 F8
Bruce Ave BS5 ....19 C1
Bruce Rd BS5 ....19 C1
Brummels Dr GL16 ...155 A7
Brunel CI BS30 ......11 C7
Brunel Ct BS37 ......43 C2
Brunel Lock Rd BS1 ...7 F5
Brunel Rd Bristol BS13 ...2 A8
  Chepstow/Cas-Gwent NP16 ...60 E6
Brunel Way Bristol BS1,BS3 ...7 F4
  Honeybourne WR11 ...188 C7

Brunel Way continued
  Stonehouse GL10 ...101 C1
  Thornbury BS35 .....51 B7
Brunswest Ct GL1 ...196 B2
Brunswick Pl 10 BS1 ...7 F5
Brunswick Rd GL1 ...196 B2
Brunswick Sq
  Bristol BS2 ....195 B4
  Gloucester GL1 ...196 B2
Brunswick St
  Bristol,Redfield BS5 ...9 C7
  Bristol,St Pauls BS2 ...195 B4
  Cheltenham GL50 ...133 D3
Brush The GL5 ......91 F8
Bruton CI BS5 ....9 F8
Bruton La GL12 ......67 F5
Bruton Pl BS8 ......194 B3
Bruton Way GL1 ....196 C3
Bryansons CI BS16 ...19 D6
Bryant's Hill BS5 ....10 B6
Bryants CI BS16 ......30 C1
Bryaston Cl GL51 ...133 A2
Bryerland Rd GL3 ...121 A4
Brymore Ave GL52 ...134 A5
Brymore CI GL52 ...134 A5
Brynland Ave BS7 ...18 E4
Bryony Bank GL53 ...130 B4
Bryworth La GL7 ...153 C3
Buchan Ho 6 GL56 ...186 C5
Buchan La GL52 ...134 A2
Buchanan CI 2 GL16 ...155 A6
Buckholt Rd GL4 ...112 E8
Buckholt Way GL3 ...120 E5
Buckholt Wood Nature
  Reserve* GL4 ....112 F7
Buckingham Ave GL51 ...132 F2
Buckingham
  Eastington GL10 ......96 E8
  Tewkesbury GL20 ...192 E2
Buckingham Ct
  Bristol BS32 ....40 D3
  Cheltenham GL50 ...193 B3
Buckingham Dr
  Bristol BS34 ....29 D5
  Churchdown GL3 ...128 A7
Buckingham Gdns BS16 ...20 E6
Buckingham Ho BS16 ...20 E6
Buckingham Lodge BS31 ...4 F5
Buckingham Par GL51 ...64 B1
Buckingham Pl
  Bristol,Mangotsfield BS16 ...20 E6
  Bristol,Victoria Park BS8 ...194 A3
Buckingham Rd BS4 ...9 D5
Buckingham The GL51 ...64 B1
Buckingham Vale BS8 ...194 A4
Buckland CI GL52 ...137 F3
Buckle St
  Broadway WR12,GL54,
  GL56 ....185 D5
  Honeybourne WR11 ...188 C8
  Weston-s-E GL55 ...188 D4
Buckle Wood NP16 ...60 D8
Buckle's Way GL53 ...131 B5
Buckleaven GL53 ...130 F5
Buckles CI GL53 ...131 B5
Bucklewell CI BS11 ...16 F6
Buckshaft Rd GL14 ...191 C1
Buckstone CI GL16 ...155 B7
Budding Rd GL10 ...96 E8
Budding The GL5 ...103 E1
Buddleia CI GL4 ...119 F4
Buddleia Ct 7 GL3 ...128 A7
Bude Ave BS5 ....10 A8
Buildings The GL6 ...87 D3
Bull La Bristol BS5 ...9 F6
  Gloucester GL1 ...196 B3
  Pill BS20 ....16 C3
  7 Winchcombe GL54 ...174 A7
Bull Pitch GL11 .....88 B1
Bull Ring The GL17 ...164 D5
Bullens CI BS32 .....40 D2
Buller Rd BS4 ....9 C2
Bulley La Birdwood GL2 ...165 F6
  Churcham GL2 .....124 C3
Bullfinch Rd GL4 ...119 A5
Bullfinch Way GL3 ...127 D7
Bullingham Ct GL51 ...133 C3
Bulls Cross GL6 ...104 B6
Bully La BS37 ....53 D1
Bulwark Ave NP16 ...60 F7
Bulwark Bsns Pk NP16 ...60 E6
Bulwark Rd NP16 ...60 E7
Bulwarks The GL6 ...148 A3
Bungalows The
  Coleford GL16 ....155 B5
  Lydney GL15 ......92 C2
Bunting Hill GL6 ....91 A4
Bunting Way GL3 ...90 F4
Burbank CI BS30 ....11 A3
Burchells Ave BS15 ...20 B1
Burchells Green CI BS15 ...20 B1
Burchells Green Rd BS15 ...20 B1
Burcombe GL7 .....158 B4
Burcombe CI BS36 ...31 D6
Burcombe La GL7 ...158 A3
Burcott CI BS11 .....26 D5
Burden CI BS32 .....29 F6
Burdett CI GL10 .....99 F7
Burdett Ho 10 GL10 ...97 F7
Burdett Rd GL10 ...97 F7
Burdock CI Bristol BS16 ...9 E5
Burford Ave BS34 ...29 C8
Burford Dr GL5 ....99 A7
Burford Gr BS11 ...16 F5

Burford Mews GL1 ...119 A8
Burford St GL7 ....153 E2
Burgage 4 NP25 ...154 A8
Burgage Ct BS37 ....33 B8
Burgage The GL52 ...134 B5
Burge Ct GL7 .....190 D3
Burgess Green CI BS4 ...9 E7
Burghill Rd BS10 ...28 A1
Burghley Ct BS36 ...30 E5
Burghley Rd BS6 ...18 E2
Burgis Rd GL54 ......3 D6
Burleigh Croft GL3 ...119 F8
Burleigh La GL5 ....91 F8
Burleigh Tor GL5 ...91 F7
Burleigh View 7 GL6 ...148 B6
Burleigh Way GL12 ...54 B5
Burley Ave BS16 ....20 F5
Burley Crest BS16 ...20 F5
Burley Gr BS16 ....20 F5
Burlington Ct 9 BS6 ...18 B2
Burlington Rd BS6 ...18 B2
Burltons The GL12 ...66 B2
Burma Ave GL2 ....134 B2
Burma Rd GL6 .....91 A4
Burnbush CI BS14 ...3 E6
Burnbush Prim Sch BS14 ...3 D5
Burnell Dr BS2 ....195 C4
Burneside CI BS10 ...28 C2
Burnet CI GL4 ....119 A4
Burnett Bsns Pk BS31 ...5 B1
Burney Way BS30 ...11 A3
Burnham CI BS15 ...20 F1
Burnham Dr BS15 ...20 F1
Burnham Rd BS11 ...16 D6
Burns Ave GL2 ....118 C4
Burnt Barn Rd NP16 ...60 F4
Burnt Oak GL11 ....88 A2
Burrington Wlk BS13 ...2 A8
Burrough Way BS36 ...30 E6
Burrups La HR9 ...170 B5
Burton CI BS1 ....195 B1
Burton Ct
  2 Bristol,Upper Eastville
  BS16 ....19 E3
  Bristol,Victoria Park BS8 ...194 B3
Burton Farm CI SN14 ...26 B3
Burton Rd GL9 .....35 F6
Burton St GL50 ...193 A4
Burtons Bank OX7 ...169 F7
Burwalls Rd BS8 .....7 E6
Bury Bar La GL18 ...124 A4
Bury Court Rd GL14 ...157 F6
Bury Hill BS36 ......30 F3
Bury Hill View GL16 ...30 E1
Bury La Doynton BS30 ...12 F7
  Minsterworth GL2 ...116 E7
Burycourt CI BS11 ...27 A1
Burytown La SN26 ...144 E1
Buscombe Gdns GL53 ...120 B7
Bush Ave BS34 .....29 D5
Bush CI GL10 ......96 F8
Bush Ct Alveston BS32 ...50 F5
  10 Bristol BS4 ......8 F4
  Cheltenham GL52 ...134 B3
Bush Hay GL51 ....128 B5
Bushcombe CI GL52 ...138 C3
Bushcombe La GL52 ...138 C3
Bushes La BS37 .....45 A6
Bushy Beeches GL6 ...105 D7
Bushy Ho BS2 ......8 F3
Bushy Pk BS2 ......8 F3
Bushy Way GL51 ...132 D5
Business Park The BS13 ...2 E3
Bussage CE Prim Sch
GL6 ....148 B6
Bussage Hill GL6 ...148 B6
Butcher Hill's La GL6 ...91 F1
Butcher Row Folk Mus*
HR8 ....178 F8
Butcombe Wlk BS14 ...3 B5
Bute CI SN6 ......145 C4
Butler Ho BS5 ......9 F8
Butler's Field GL7 ...153 E3
Butlers CI Bristol BS5 ...9 F7
  Sherston SN16 .....58 C1
Butlers Mead GL15 ...156 E1
Butlers Wlk 3 BS5 ...9 F6
Butt Gn GL6 ......111 F1
Butt La BS35 ......64 C3
Butt St GL6 ....148 A3
Butt's La Dyrham SN14 ...24 B4
  Woodmancote GL52 ...138 C4
Butt's Wlk GL51 ...129 C7
Buttercross La GL52 ...134 D3
Buttercup Lawn GL4 ...119 D2
Butterfield CI Bristol BS10 ...18 E7
  Frampton Cotterell BS36 ...31 B6
Butterfield Rd BS10 ...18 E7
Buttermere CI GL51 ...129 F6
Buttermilk La GL53 ...128 C6
Butterow W GL5 ....99 B5
Butterow Hill GL5 ...99 C4
Butterrow La GL5 ...99 D4
Buttersend La GL19 ...171 A4
Butterworth Ct BS4 ...9 D4
Buttington GL14 ...119 F5
Buttington Hill NP16 ...61 B7
Buttington Rd NP16 ...61 A7
Buttington Terr NP16 ...61 B6
Button CI BS14 .....3 A6
Butts Farm The* GL7 ...151 B1
Butts La GL15 ....156 E2
Butts The Crudwell SN16 ...141 C3

Butts The continued
  Gloucester GL4 ....119 A4
  Newent GL18 ......171 A4
  Poulton GL7 ......151 D4
Buxton Wlk BS7 .....19 A8
Byard Rd GL2 .....118 E4
Bybrook Gdns GL4 ...118 C3
Bybrook Rd GL4 ...118 C3
Bydemill Gdns SN6 ...145 C4
Bye Mead BS16 ......21 A5
Bye St HR8 ....178 E8
Byfield CI GL52 ...138 C8
Byfords CI GL19 ...165 D5
Byfords Rd GL19 ...165 C5
Byrc CI SN6 ....143 A5
Byres The GL56 ...187 D5
Byron Ave GL2 ....118 C4
Byron CI GL20 ....192 E4
Byron Ct 17 GL52 ...133 F4
Byron Pl
  Bristol,Brandon Hill BS8 ...194 B3
  Bristol,Staple Hill BS16 ...20 D8
Byron Rd
  Cheltenham GL51 ...132 F4
  Dursley GL11 ......80 C7
  Stroud GL5 ....99 A7
Byron St
  Bristol,Moorfields BS5 ...9 C8
  5 Bristol,St Pauls BS2 ...19 A1
Byzantine CI BS1 ...195 A2

C

Cabot CI Bristol BS15 ...10 C6
  Saltford BS31 ....5 D1
  Yate BS37 ....43 E3
Cabot Ct BS37 .....43 D5
Cabot Gn BS5 .....9 C6
Cabot Ho 6 BS35 ...51 C8
Cabot Pk BS11 ......26 B6
Cabot Prim Sch BS2 ...195 C4
Cabot Twr* BS1 ....194 B2
Cabot Way Bristol BS8 ...7 F5
  Pill BS20 ....16 D7
Cadbury Cl GL3 ...120 E5
Cadbury Heath Prim Sch
BS30 ....11 E5
Cadbury Heath Rd BS30 ...11 E5
Cadbury Rd BS31 .....5 A4
Caddick CI BS15 ...20 F2
Cade CI
  Bristol,Kingswood BS15 ...10 F5
  Bristol,Stoke Gifford BS34 ...29 E5
Cadmium Rd BS11 ...26 C7
Cadogan Ho 10 BS2 ...132 A3
Cadogan Rd BS14 .....3 A7
Caen Rd BS3 ......8 A3
Caernarvon CI GL51 ...129 C1
Caernarvon Ct GL51 ...129 C1
Caernarvon Rd
  Cheltenham GL51 ...129 F1
  Keynsham BS31 .....4 C4
Caerwent La NP16 ...60 F7
Caesar Rd GL2 ....118 C4
Caesars CI GL15 ...92 C2
Caine Rd BS7 ......18 A4
Caine Sq GL51 ....132 C1
Cains CI BS15 ......10 E5
Cainscross Rd GL5 ...90 F1
Cainscross Rdbt GL5 ...98 F8
Caird St NP16 .....60 F4
Cairn Gdns BS36 ...30 E1
Cairns CI BS6 .....18 C3
Cairns Rd BS6 .....18 C2
Cairns' Cres 12 BS2 ...18 F1
Caitlin Ct BS14 ......3 D5
Cakebridge Pl GL52 ...133 F4
Cakebridge Rd GL52 ...133 F4
Cala Trad Est BS3 ....7 F2
Calcott Rd BS4 ......9 F4
Calcutt St SN6 ....143 F3
Caldbeck CI BS10 ...28 C2
Calder CI BS31 ......5 A5
Calderdale GL4 ...119 F5
Calderwood CI GL50 ...193 B4
Caldicot CI
  Bristol,Lawrence Weston
  BS11 ....27 C2
  Bristol,Willsbridge BS30 ...11 F1
Caledonia Mews BS8 ...7 F6
Caledonia Pl BS8 .....7 F6
Caledonian Rd
  Bristol BS1 ....194 B1
  Gloucester GL1 ...119 C1
Calf Way GL6 .....105 C5
Calf's La GL55 ...189 A4
California Rd BS30 ...11 B2
Callicroft Inf Sch BS34 ...29 A8
Callicroft Jun Sch BS34 ...28 F8
Callicroft Rd BS34 ...29 A8
Callington Rd BS4 ...9 C1
Callowell CI GL6 ...103 A6
Callowell Prim Sch GL5 ...103 A6
Callowhill CI BS11 ...195 B4
Calspick Way GL2 ...127 D5
Calton Jun & Inf Schs
  GL1 ....118 E6
Calton Rd GL1 ....118 E6
Calverley Mews 1
  GL51 ....129 B6
Cam & Dursley Sta GL10 ...96 F5
Cam Everlands Prim Sch
GL11 ....88 A5
Cam Gn GL11 ......88 C3
Cam Hopton CE Prim Sch
GL11 ....88 B6
Cam House Cotts GL11 ...88 C3

Cam House Sch GL11 ....88 C2
Cam Pitch GL11 ....87 F5
Cam Rd GL52 ....134 B3
Cam Woodfield Inf Sch
GL11 ....87 E5
Cam Woodford Jun Sch
GL11 ....87 E5
Camberley Cl GL3 ......120 A8
Camberley Dr BS36 ......30 F8
Camberley Rd BS4 ....2 D8
Camberwell Rd GL1 ....132 D2
Camborne Rd BS7 ....19 A7
Cambourne Pl GL15 .....92 B2
Cambray Ct
Cheltenham GL50 ......193 B3
Cirencester GL7 ....190 D4
Cambray Mews GL50 ....193 C3
Cambray Pl GL50 ....193 C3
Cambrian Dr BS37 ....43 E3
Cambrian Rd GL20 .....192 E2
Cambridge Ave
Cheltenham GL51 ......132 F1
Dursley GL11 ....80 B7
Cambridge Cres BS9 .....18 A7
Cambridge Pk BS6 ......18 B3
Cambridge Rd BS7 ......18 E4
Cambridge Sq GL20 ....183 E4
Cambridge St
8 Bristol,Redfield BS5 ....9 C7
Bristol,Windmill Hill BS3 ....8 F4
Gloucester GL1 ....196 C2
Cambridge Way GL51 ....91 F6
Camden Cl GL56 ....187 F3
Camden Rd BS3 ....194 B1
Campbell Cl GL3 ....194 B1
Campbell Ct BS11 ....26 F1
Campbell Farm Dr BS11 ...26 F1
Campbell Farm Dr BS11 ...26 F1
Campbell Rd GL16 .....155 B6
Campbell St BS2 ....18 E1
Camden Ave VC36 ......189 E5
Camden Hill VC36 ......189 F6
Camden La
Hawking GL54 ....174 D5
Willersey WR12 ....188 C2
Camden Pitch CV36 .....189 F6
Campden Rd
Cheltenham GL51 ......129 E8
Chipping Campden GL55 ..189 A4
Ebrington GL55 ....189 C3
Gloucester GL4 ....118 E3
Mickleton GL55 ....189 B8
Campian Wlk BS4 ....2 D6
Campion Cl
Gloucester GL4 ....119 B4
Thornbury BS35 ....64 D2
Campion Dr BS32 ....40 D2
Campion Pk GL51 ......130 A4
Cams Ground GL2 ......125 D6
Camwal Ind Est BS2 .....9 A5
Camwal Rd BS2 ....9 A5
Canada Way BS1 ....194 B1
Canal Ironworks GL1 ....99 E2
Canal Row GL2 ....108 A1
Canal Way GL2 ....126 B4
Canal Wlk HR8 ....178 E8
Canberra Cl GL51 ......101 E1
Canberra Gr BS34 ......29 B4
Canberra Ho
Cheltenham GL51 ......132 C1
11 Coleford GL16 .....155 B5
Candy Ct BS4 ....9 D5
Canford La BS9 ....17 E8
Canford Rd BS9 ....17 F8
Cann La BS30 ....11 E6
Cannans Cl BS36 ....30 E7
Canning Rd GL2 ....127 E5
Cannon St
Bristol,Kingsdown BS1 ..195 A4
Bristol,Southville BS3 ....8 C4
Cannop Cotts GL16 ....155 D6
Cannop Rd GL11 ....155 E3
Cannop Valley Trail*
GL16 ....155 E5
Cannop Villas GL16 ....155 D7
Canon Pk GL13 ....85 F4
Canon St BS5 ....9 C8
Canon's Rd BS1 ....194 C1
Canon's Wlk BS15 ......20 F2
Canonbury St GL13 .....85 F3
Canons Ct GL52 ....153 F9
Canons Rd BS1 ....194 C2
Canowie Rd BS6 ....18 B3
Cantell Gr BS14 ....3 F5
Canterbury Cl BS37 .....43 E3
Canterbury St BS16 .....19 E6
Canterbury Leys GL52 ..192 E5
Canterbury St 5 BS5 ....9 B6
Canterbury Wlk GL51 ...130 A4

Canters Leaze GL12 .....54 B4
Cantock's Cl BS8 ......194 C3
Canton Acre GL6 ......111 F1
Cantors Ct GL52 ....137 F2
Cantors Dr GL52 ......137 E2
Cantors Way SN16 .....142 E1
Canvey Cl BS10 ....18 E7
Canynge Ho 2 BS1 ....195 B1
Canynge Rd BS8 ....7 F8
Canynge Sq BS8 ....7 F8
Canynge St BS1 ....195 B2
Capel Cl BS15 ....11 B8
Capel Ct GL5 ....99 D8
Capel Rd Bristol BS11 ...27 B1
Gloucester GL4 ....119 C2
Capgrave Cl BS4 ....10 A3
Capgrave Cres BS4 .....10 A3
Capital Edge BS8 ......194 B2
Capital Pk GL2 ....118 B4
Capricorn Pl BS1 ......194 B2
Captain Barton Cl GL5 ..99 E8
Captains Green Rd
GL15 ....156 A2
Caraway Gdns BS5 ......19 C2
Cardigan Mews BS9 .....18 B5
Cardigan Rd BS9 ....18 B6
Cardill Cl BS13 ....2 A8
Carers Cl GL52 ....138 A4
Carfax Ct BS9 ....18 A3
Carisbrook Rd GL17 ...164 D6
Carisbrooke Dr GL52 ..131 C6
Carisbrooke Lodge BS6 ..18 A3
Carisbrooke Rd BS4 ....2 D7
Gloucester GL4 ....120 A7
Carlow Rd BS4 ....2 E8
Carlton Ct
3 Bristol,Ashley Down BS7 ..18 F4
3 Bristol,Eastfield BS9 ...18 A7
Carlton Gdns GL5 ......99 C6
Carlton Ho 2 BS8 ......18 A7
Carlton Pk BS5 ....9 C8
Carlton Pl GL50,GL51 ..133 C3
Carlton St GL52 ....133 F1
Carlyle Gr GL51 ....132 D4
Carlyle Rd BS5 ....9 C1
Carmarthen Ct BS37 ....43 F4
Carmarthen Gr BS30 ....11 B1
Carmarthen Rd
Bristol BS9 ....18 A5
Cheltenham GL51 ......129 E6
Carmarthen St 2 BS1 ...18 D2
Carnarvon Rd BS6 .....18 D2
Carne Pl GL4 ....127 C1
Carolina Ho 20 BS1 ...195 A4
Caroline Cl
Chipping Sodbury BS37 ..44 B2
Keynsham BS31 ....4 C4
Carpenter Cotts GL16 ..154 F3
Carpenter's Shop La
BS16 ....20 E6
Carpenters Cl SN16 .....58 D1
Carpenters La
Cirencester GL7 ....190 D4
Keynsham BS31 ....4 E5
Carr Ho 3 BS2 ....18 F1
Carrant Brook Jun Sch
GL20 ....182 C5
Carrant Rd GL20 ......192 D5
Carriage Dr BS10 ......28 B2
Carrick Ho 8 BS8 ......7 F6
Carrington Rd BS3 ......8 A3
Carrol Gr GL51 ....132 D4
Carroll Ct BS16 ....29 E1
Carsons Rd BS16 ....21 B2
Cart La BS1 ....195 B2
Carter Rd GL51 ....132 F4
Carter Wlk BS32 ....29 D8
Carter's Bldgs 18 BS8 ...7 F7
Carters Leaze CV36 ...187 E5
Carters Orch GL2 .....117 F2
Carters Way GL6 ....90 F5
Cartledge Rd 6 BS5 ....19 C1
Cartway Gn GL2 ....119 A6
Carwardine Field GL4 ..119 E6
Cary Ct 2 BS2 ....18 F1
Casey Cl GL1 ....127 B1
Cash Hill GL17 ....163 E4
Cashes Green Prim Sch
GL5 ....98 D8
Cashes Green Rd GL5 ...98 E7
Cashmore Ho 9 BS5 ....9 B7
Casino Pl GL50 ....193 A1
Caslon Ct BS1 ....195 B1
Cassell Rd BS16 ....20 C5
Cassey Bottom La BS5 ..10 A7
Cassey Compton GL54 ..166 F2
Cassin Dr GL51 ....132 E2
Cassin Rd BS16 ....19 E8
Castle Cl Bristol BS10 ...27 E2
Painswick GL6 ....103 F7
Castle Coombe BS35 ....64 C1
Castle Cotts
Gloucester GL1 ....119 F8
Marshfield SN14 ....24 E2
Castle Cres GL15 .....146 F7
Castle Ct Bristol BS34 ...30 A4
Bristol,Arno's Vale BS4 ...9 C4
20 Stroud GL5 ....9 C7
Stroud GL5 ....98 D6
Castle End GL16 ......111 E5
Castle Farm Cl GL8 ....70 C3
Castle Farm La BS41 ....4 E1
Castle Farm Rd BS15 ...10 C2
Castle Gdns
Chepstow/Cas-Gwent NP16 ..72 D1
Chipping Sodbury BS37 ..189 B2
Castle Hill GL3 ....120 F4
Keynsham BS31 ....4 D4

Castle Hill Prim Sch
GL3 ....120 E4
Marshfield SN14 ....24 E2
Moreton Valence GL2 ..108 E2
Castle Mead GL10 .....197 F3
Castle Nurseries GL55 ..189 B2
Castle Pitch GL5 ....99 C6
Castle Prim Sch BS31 ....4 D4
Castle Rd
Bristol,Kingswood BS15 ..20 D2
Bristol,Oldland Common
BS30 ....11 D3
Pucklechurch BS16 .....22 C6
Castle Rise GL5 ....99 C6
Castle Sch Sixth Form Ctr
The BS35 ....64 B1
Castle Sch The BS35 ....64 B2
Castle St Bristol BS1 ...195 B3
Cirencester GL7 ......190 C4
Dursley GL11 ....80 A3
King's Stanley GL10 ....98 A3
Stroud GL5 ....99 C6
Thornbury BS35 ....64 B1
Winchcombe GL54 .....174 A7
Castle The GL5 ....99 C6
Castle View NP16 ......73 A1
Castle Villas 18 GL5 ....99 C7
Castle Wood/Coed Castell
NP16 ....60 C8
Castlefields Ave GL52 ..131 C6
Castlefields Dr GL52 ..131 C6
Castlefields Rd GL52 ..131 C6
Castleford Gdns NP16 ...72 F2
Castleford Hill NP16 ....72 E2
Castlegate Ho BS4 ......9 E3
Castlemaine Dr GL51 ..129 C8
Castlemead Rd GL1 ....99 B6
Castlemeads Ct GL1 ...196 A4
Castleton Rd GL4 .....119 D8
Castlett St GL54 ......175 B3
Caswell Ct GL11 ....80 D8
Caswell La BS20 ....28 A6
Catbrain Hill BS10 ......28 B6
Catbrain La BS10 ......28 B6
Catbrook Cl BS15 .....189 A1
Catbrook Gdns GL55 ..189 A1
Catchmays Ct NP25,
NP25 ....146 C5
Catchpot La BS37 ....34 A6
Cater Rd BS13 ....2 B6
Cathedral Church of St Peter
& the Holy Family*
GL1 ....196 B3
Catherine Ct 14 BS6 ...18 E8
Catherine Ct BS16 .....49 F2
Catherine Mead St BS3 ..8 D4
Catherine St BS11 .....16 C8
Catholic Sch of St Gregory
the Great The GL50 ...193 A4
Catkin Cl GL2 ....109 E7
Catley Gr BS41 ....7 B2
Cato St BS5 ....19 B1
Catswood Cl GL5 .....103 E1
Catswood La GL6 .....100 D3
Cattle Market Rd BS1 ..195 C1
Cattybrook Rd N BS16 ..21 D5
Cattybrook Rd
7 Bristol BS5 ....9 B7
28 Bristol BS5 ....9 B8
Caudle Ct GL17 ......163 E4
Caudle La GL17 ......163 E4
Causeway Rd GL14 ....191 E5
Causeway The
Coalpit Heath BS36 .....31 D7
3 Quedgeley GL2 .....117 D1
Redmarley D'Abitot GL19 ..179 D2
Causley Dr BS30 ....11 A5
Cavan Wlk BS4 ....8 D1
Cavendish Ave GL3 ...128 D5
Cavendish Bldgs 3 GL55 ..92 A3
Cavendish Cl Saltford BS31 ..5 D2
Tormarton GL9 ....34 C2
Cavendish Gdns BS9 ...17 C4
Cavendish Rd
Bristol,Henleaze BS9 ....18 A5
Bristol,Patchway BS34 ...28 F7
Charlton Kings GL53 ...131 B5
Chepstow/Cas-Gwent NP16 ..60 E5
Down Ampney GL7 ....143 E8
Stroud GL5 ....98 D6
Cedar Court Rd GL53 ..193 B2
Cedar Ct
Bristol,Oldland BS30 ....11 B4
Bristol,Patchway BS34 ...28 F7
Chepstow/Cas-Gwent NP16 ..60 E5
Stroud GL5 ....98 D6
Bristol,Sneyd Park BS9 ...17 F8
Bristol,Westbury on Trym
BS9 ....17 F8
Ledbury HR8 ....178 F8
Cedar Dr Dursley GL11 ..88 A1
Keynsham BS31 ....4 D4

Cedar Gdns GL10 ......97 F8
Cedar Gr Bristol BS9 ...17 D5
Walford HR9 ....163 C8
4 Winchcombe GL54 ..174 A7
Cedar Hall BS16 ....20 C8
Cedar Pk BS9 ....17 D5
Cedar Rd
Brockworth GL3 ......120 C1
Mickleton GL55 ....189 B6
Northway GL20 ....182 C4
Cedar Row BS11 ....16 F6
Cedar Way Mile End GL16 ..155 B6
Pucklechurch BS16 .....22 C5
Winterbourne BS36 .....30 D5
Cedardean GL14 ......191 C5
Cedars The
Gloucester GL4 ....120 A8
Wotton-u-E GL12 ....68 C8
Cedarwood Dr GL4 ....118 E3
Celandine Bank GL52 ..138 B4
Celandine Cl BS35 ......64 D2
Celandine Cl NP16 .....60 F5
Celestine Rd BS37 ......43 C3
Celia Terr BS4 ....9 F4
Cemetery La Bibury GL7 ..160 A1
Bourton-on-t-W GL54 ..169 A7
Cennick Ave BS15 ......20 E1
Centaurus Rd BS34 .....28 D7
Central Ave Bristol BS10 ..10 C5
Mitcheldean GL17 ....164 D5
Severn Beach BS35 .....38 A3
Central Cross Dr GL50,
GL52 ....133 C3
Central Pk BS14 ....3 B7
Central Rd
Gloucester GL1 ....118 E7
Stroud GL5 ....9 B8
Central Tech Coll GL4 ..119 B5
Central Trad Est BS4 ....9 B4
Central Way Bristol BS10 ..16 C5
Centre for Science & Art*
GL5 ....99 C7
Centre The BS31 ....4 F5
Centurion Cl 1 GL4 ...119 E6
Centurion Rd GL15 .....92 B4
Centurions Wlk GL16 ..155 A5
Century Cl GL7 ....190 F5
Century Ct GL50 ......133 C3
Ceres Cl BS30 ....10 E2
Cerimon Gate GL54 .....29 E5
Cerney House Gdns*
GL7 ....158 C2
Cerney La BS11 ....16 E5
Cerney Wick La GL7 ...143 C7
Cesson Cl BS37 ....33 C8
Ceylon Rd GL51 ......132 F4
Chaceley Cl
Gloucester GL4 ....119 C5
Quedgeley GL2 ....116 C8
Chad Rd GL51 ....132 F1
Chadbournes GL3 ......28 B6
Chadleigh Gr BS4 ......3 B1
Chadwick Cl GL4 .....118 D2
Chaffinch Cl GL3 .....127 D7
Chaffinch Ct 8 GL10 ...97 F8
Chaingate La BS37 .....43 A6
Chakeshill Cl BS10 ....28 B1
Chakeshill Dr BS10 ....28 B2
Chalcombe GL54 ....29 C8
Chalcroft Ho 2 BS5 .....8 A4
Chalcroft Wlk BS13 .....1 A4
Chalfield Cl BS31 ......27 F3
Chalfield Cl BS31 ....5 A2
Chalford Ave GL51 ....129 B7
Chalford Cl BS37 ....32 D8
Chalford Hill Prim Sch
GL6 ....148 C5
Chalford Ind Est GL6 ..148 C5
Chalford Rd GL4 .....118 E1
Chalks Rd BS5 ....9 D8
Challender Ave BS10 ...27 F2
Challoner Ct BS1 .....195 A1
Chamberlayne Cl 29
GL54 ....176 F4
Chamberlayne Ho 28
GL54 ....176 F4
Chambon Cl SN14 .....142 D1
Champ Ho BS15 ....21 A2
Champions Ct GL11 ....80 B8
Champneys Ave BS10 ...27 F3
Champs Sur Marne BS32 ..29 E7
Chamwells Ave GL2 ...127 B4
Chamwells Wlk GL2 ...127 B4
Chance St GL20 ......192 D4
Chancel Cl Bristol BS9 ..17 B7
Chancel Ct GL2 ....127 C1
Chancel Pk GL53 .....148 A3
Chancel Way GL16 ....155 B7
Chandag Inf Sch BS31 ...5 A4
Chandag Jun Sch BS31 ...5 A4
Chandag Rd BS31 ....5 A4
Chandler Rd GL52 ....137 F2
Chandos BS6 ....18 F5
Chandos Almshouses 22
GL54 ....174 A7
Chandos Dr GL13 ....8 B1
Chandos Rd Bristol BS6 ..18 C1
Keynsham BS31 ....4 E4
Chandos St GL54 .....174 A7
Chandos Trad Est BS2 ...9 A5
Change The GL6 ......102 D1

Channel View NP16 .....60 E5
Channell's Hill BS9 .....18 A8
Channon's Hill BS16 ....19 F5
Chantry Cl
Cirencester GL7 ....190 C5
Lydney GL15 ....92 A1
Chantry Ct Bristol BS1 ..194 C2
Ilethury GL8 ....140 C4
Chantry Gate GL52 ....137 E2
Chantry Gdns GL56 ...186 D3
Chantry Gr BS11 ....27 C2
Chantry La BS16 ....30 F1
Chantry Rd Bristol BS8 ..18 B1
Thornbury BS35 ....64 B2

Chapel Apartments 13
GL16 ....55 A5
Chapel Barton 7 BS3 ....8 B2
Chapel Bglws HR9 ....170 B4
Chapel Cl Bristol BS15 ..11 B8
Chepstow/Cas-Gwent NP16 ..60 B5
Kempsford GL7 ....144 E8
Monmouth/Trefynwy
NP25 ....154 A7
Tarlton GL7 ....149 C2
Chapel Cotts GL54 ....174 B1
Chapel Ct
Bristol,Brentry BS10 ....28 D3
Bristol,St Philip's Marsh BS2 ..9 A5
Dursley GL11 ....87 D4
Chapel Gdns BS31 ......28 A1
Hardwicke GL2 ....120 F8
Chapel Green La BS6 ...18 B2
Chapel Hay La GL3 ....128 D4
Chapel Hay La GL3 ....128 D4
Chapel Hill
Aylburton GL15 ....147 E4
Broad Blunsdon SN26 ..144 D1
English Bicknor GL16 ..163 A1
Newport GL13 ....78 B7
Chapel Ho 11 GL20 ...192 C4
Chapel La
Acton Turville GL9 ......36 A6
Birdwood GL2 ....165 F5
Blockley GL56 ....186 C5
Bristol,Clay Hill BS5 ....19 E2
Bristol,Fishponds BS16 ..20 A4
Bristol,Frenchay BS16 ..20 F3
Bristol,Lawrence Weston
BS11 ....27 C2
Bristol,Warmley BS15 ..10 F3
Cheltenham BS50 .....193 B1
Chepstow/Cas-Gwent NP16 ..60 B5
Chipping Sodbury BS37 ..34 A7
Cold Aston GL54 ......168 B6
Guarlay HR9 ....170 B4
Hankerton SN16 ....141 E1
Hillesley GL12 ....55 E8
Hinton SN14 ....23 C5
Kinsham GL20 ....182 D6
Longhope GL17 ....165 B5
Mickleton GL55 ....189 A6
Minchinhampton GL6 ..148 A3
Nanny SN16 ....112 F7
North Cerney GL7 ....158 D3
Staunton GL19 ....171 E8
Stroud GL5 ....98 D6
Thornbury BS35 ....65 D6
Westmancote GL20 ...182 D8
Weston-s-E GL52 .....188 D3
Woodmancote GL52 ..138 C3
Chapel Orch BS37 .....43 C2
Chapel Pill La BS20 ....26 D5
Chapel Pitch GL18 ....170 D2
Chapel Rd
Berry Hill GL16 ....155 A7
Bristol,Bishopsworth BS13 ..2 A6
Bristol,Hanham BS15 ...10 C5
2 Bristol,Lower Easton
BS5 ....19 B1
Kempsford GL7 ....144 E8
Oldbury-on-S BS35 .....63 C5
Viney Hill GL15 ....156 C1
Chapel Row
4 Blockley GL56 ......186 C5
Little Compton GL56 ..187 F1
Luckington SN14 ....47 E4
Marshfield SN14 ....24 C4
4 Stonehouse GL10 ....97 F7
Chapel St
Bledington OX7 ......177 E1
Bristol BS2 ....9 A3
Broadwell GL56 ......177 A6
Cheltenham GL50 .....193 B4
Dursley GL11 ....88 A5
8 Stow-on-t-W GL54 ..176 F4
Stroud GL5 ....99 D7
Thornbury BS35 ....51 B8
Chapel Way 8 GL6 ......9 F6
Chapel Wlk
Cheltenham GL50 .....193 B3
Didmarton GL9 ....57 B3
Edge End GL16 ....155 C8
ChapelFields HR9 ....162 B6
Chaplin Rd BS5 ....19 B1
Chapman Way GL11 ...147 F3
Chapman's Cross GL6 ..149 A4
Chapter St BS2 ....195 B4
Charbon Gate GL54 ...29 E5
Charborough Ct
Bristol BS34 ....28 F2
Bristol BS34 ....28 F2
Charborough Rd BS34 ..28 F2
Charborough Road Prim Sch
BS34 ....28 F2

Charbury Wlk BS11 .....16 E5
Chard Ct BS14 ....3 B6
Chardstock Ave BS9 ...17 D8
Chardwar Gdns ⑦ GL54 .168 F7
Charfield ④ BS15 .....11 A8
Charfield Prim Sch GL12 .66 F5
Charfield Rd Bristol BS10 .28 D1
 Kingswood GL12 ....67 E5
Chargrove ② Bristol BS30 .11 C6
 Yate BS37 ....32 D7
Chargrove La GL51 ...129 E4
Charis Ave BS10 ......18 C7
Charlecombe Ct BS9 ...17 F6
Charlecombe Rd BS9 ...17 F6
Charlecote La GL4 ...110 C8
Charlecote Cnr GL52 ..137 E3
Charles Ave BS34 .....29 E4
Charles Cl
 Tewkesbury GL20 ....192 E2
 Thornbury BS35 ......64 C3
Charles Ct BS8 ....194 A2
Charles England Ho
 BS34 ....28 F7
Charles Pl BS8 ......194 A2
Charles Rd BS34 ......29 B3
Charles St Bristol BS1 .195 A4
 Cheltenham GL51 ....133 C3
 Gloucester GL1 ......196 C2
Charles Wesley Cl BS5 .10 A6
Charlesway GL56 .....176 E8
Charleswood Rd GL15 .155 F1
Charleton Ho ⑧ BS2 .195 C3
Charlham La GL7 .....143 E8
Charlham Way GL7 ...143 E8
Charlock Cl GL4 .....119 A4
Charlotte Rose Ho ③
 GL50 ....133 B1
Charlotte St
 Bristol,Brandon Hill BS1 .194 C2
 Bristol,St Pauls BS2 ..195 C4
Charlotte St S BS1 ...194 C2
Charlton Ave BS34 ....28 F2
Charlton Cl GL53 ....131 A5
Charlton Ct Bristol BS34 .39 F1
 Gloucester GL1 ......196 C3
Charlton Down Cotts
 GL8 ....71 E4
Charlton Dr GL53 ....130 F7
Charlton Gdns BS10 ..28 D4
Charlton Kings Inf Sch
 GL52 ....131 B6
Charlton La Bristol BS10 .28 A3
 Cheltenham GL53 ....130 D5
Charlton Lane Ctr Hospl
 GL53 ....130 E5
Charlton Lawn GL53 ..131 A4
Charlton Mead Cl BS10 .28 D4
Charlton Mead Dr BS10 .28 D3
Charlton Park Dr GL53 .130 F7
Charlton Park Gate
 GL53 ....130 F6
Charlton Pk BS10 ....28 D4
Charlton Pl BS10 ....28 D4
Charlton Rd
 Bristol,Brentry BS10 ..28 D2
 Bristol,Kingswood BS15 .20 B1
 Keynsham BS31 ......4 C3
 Tetbury GL8 ....140 B4
Charlton St ⑰ BS5 ...9 B7
Charlton Terr ⑪ GL6 .187 B3
Charlton Way GL7 ...127 C5
Charminster Rd BS10 .20 B3
Charmouth Ct BS3 ....8 D1
Charnell Rd BS16 ....20 E4
Charnhill Brow BS16 .21 A4
Charnhill Cres BS16 .20 F4
Charnhill Dr BS16 ...20 F4
Charnhill Ridge BS16 .21 A4
Charnhill Vale BS16 .20 F4
Charnwood BS16 .....21 A4
Charnwood Cl GL53 ..130 D5
Charnwood Rd GL15 ..92 B5
Charnwood Rd BS14 ..3 B4
 Cheltenham GL53 ....130 D5
Charter Cl GL1 ......196 C1
Charter Ho BS1 .....194 B2
Charter Wlk BS14 ....3 A6
Charterhouse Rd BS9 .9 D8
Chartford Ho BS8 ....7 F8
Chartist La GL19 ....179 F2
Chartist Piece GL19 .172 B8
Chartist Way GL19 ..172 A8
Chartists Way NP16 .60 E5
 Chepstow BS9 ....17 D2
Chartwell Cl GL2 ....118 A6
Chase Ave GL52 .....131 C6
Chase La Gloucester GL4 .119 B7
 Wickwar GL12 ....54 C6
Chase Rd BS15 ......20 D2
Chase The Bristol BS16 .20 C2
 Churchdown GL3 ....128 D4
 Gloucester GL4 ......119 D5
 Stroud GL5 ....98 E2
Chasefield La ① BS16 .20 B4
Chasely Cres ⑥ GL51 .129 E5
Chasewood Cnr ③ GL6 .148 B6
Chatcombe GL54 .....32 E7
Chatcombe Ho GL4 ..118 C4
Chatcombe La GL4 ..119 B5
Chatcombe Rd GL4 ..119 B5
Chatsworth Ave GL4 .118 C1
Chatsworth Dr GL53 .130 D4

Chatsworth Pk BS35 ..64 C3
Chatsworth Rd
 Bristol,Arno's Vale BS4 ..9 C4
 Bristol,Hillfields BS16 ..20 B3
Chattenden Ho BS9 ..17 E3
Chatterton Gn BS14 ..2 F3
Chatterton Ho ⑤ BS1 .195 B1
Chatterton Rd BS37 ..43 D1
Chatterton Sq BS1 ..195 C1
Chatterton St BS1 ...195 C1
Chaucer Cl GL1 .....118 D5
Chaucer Rd GL4 .....80 C7
Chaundey Gr BS13 ...2 B5
Chavenage BS15 ....21 A1
Chavenage Ho* GL8 .140 A6
Chavenage La GL8 ..140 B4
Cheap St GL54 ......159 A6
Cheapside Bristol BS2 .195 C4
 Stroud GL5 ....99 B7
Cheapside St ⑧ BS3 .8 F4
Cheddar Gr BS13 ....2 A8
Cheddar Grove Prim Sch
 BS13 ....2 A8
Chedworth Bristol BS15 .20 F3
 ⑩ Newent GL18 ....171 A4
Chedworth Rd BS37 ..32 B7
Chedworth Rd Bristol BS7 .19 A6
 Gloucester GL4 ......118 E3
Chedworth Roman Villas
 (rems of)* GL54 ....159 A8
Chedworth Way GL54 .129 E8
Cheese La BS2 ......195 B2
Chelbury Mews ① GL52 .134 A3
Chelford Gr BS34 ....29 B8
Chelmer Gr BS31 ....5 A4
Chelmsford Ave GL51 .130 A5
Chelmsford Wlk BS4 ..9 F5
Chelsea Cl
 Cheltenham GL53 ...130 F7
 Keynsham BS31 .....5 A5
Chelsea Pk BS5 .....9 C8
Chelsea Rd BS5 .....19 B1
Chelston Rd BS4 ....2 D2
Chelt Rd GL52 ......134 B3
Cheltenham & Gloucester
 Nuffield Hospl The
 GL51 ....129 C7
Cheltenham Bournside Sch &
 Sixth Form Ctr GL51 .130 A6
Cheltenham Coll Jun Sch
 GL51 & GL53 ....193 B1
Cheltenham Coll Jun Sch
 GL53 ....193 B1
Cheltenham Cres ② BS6 .18 D1
Cheltenham General Hospl
 GL53 ....193 C2
Cheltenham Kingsmead
 GL51 ....132 F4
Cheltenham La BS6 ..18 D2
Cheltenham Ladies' Coll The
 GL50 ....193 B3
Cheltenham Mus & Art Gal*
 GL50 ....193 B4
Cheltenham Race Course*
 GL50,GL52 ....134 A6
Cheltenham Racecourse Hall
 of Fame* GL50 ......133 F6
Cheltenham Racecourse
 Sta* GL50 ....133 E7
Cheltenham Rd
 Beckford GL20 ......183 B6
 Bishop's Cleeve GL52 .137 F3
 Bisley GL6 ....105 A1
 Bredon GL20 ....182 D7
 Bristol BS6 ....18 E1
 Broadway WR12 .....185 A8
 Gloucester GL2 ......127 D3
 Painswick GL6 ......112 A2
 Pitchcombe GL6 .....103 C4
 Stratton GL7 ....150 D7
 Winchcombe GL54 ...139 F4
Cheltenham Rd E GL3 .128 A7
Cheltenham Spa Sta
 GL51 ....133 A1
Cheltenham Trade Pk
 GL51 ....133 B3
Chelvy Cl BS13 .....2 D3
Chelwood Rd Bristol BS11 .16 F7
 Saltford BS31 ....5 E4
Chelworth Ind Est SN6 .143 D3
Chelworth Rd SN6 ..143 E3
Chepstow Bulwark*
 NP16 ....60 D8
Chepstow Castle* NP16 .72 E1
Chepstow Com Hospl
 NP16 ....60 D8
Chepstow Comp Sch
 NP16 ....72 D2
Chepstow Ho ⑯ GL51 .132 E2
Chepstow Mus* NP16 .72 F1
Chepstow Pk BS16 ..30 F1
Chepstow Race Course*
 NP16 ....72 C3
Chepstow Rd BS4 ...2 D8
Chepstow Wlk BS31 .4 D5
Chequers Cl BS30 ...11 C3
Chequers Ct BS34 ..30 A6
Chequers Rd GL4 ...119 B7
Cherington Bristol BS16 .10 B5
 Yate BS37 ....32 D6
Cherington Rd BS10 .18 D7
Cheriton Cl GL51 ...129 F5
Cheriton Pl
 Bristol,Eastfield BS9 .18 B7
 Bristol,Warmley BS30 .11 C6
Cherrington Gr GL4 ..119 E5
Cherry Ave GL53 ....131 C4
Cherry Bank GL18 ..171 A4

Cherry Blossom Cl GL52 .137 F5
Cherry Cl GL22 .....109 E7
Cherry Ct BS11 .....195 A4
Cherry Garden La BS30 .11 B2
Cherry Garden Prim Sch
 BS30 ....11 C2
Cherry Garden Rd BS30 .11 C1
Cherry Gdns Bristol BS30 .11 C1
 Gloucester GL1 ......120 A8
Cherry Gr BS16 .....21 A6
Cherry La ⑪ BS1 ...195 B4
Cherry Orch
 Bredon GL20 ....182 C7
 Highworth SN6 ......145 D3
 Wotton-u-E GL12 ....68 C7
Cherry Orch The GL51 .173 F2
Cherry Orchard Cl GL55 .189 A1
Cherry Orchard La
 ④ Bristol BS5 ....9 F8
 Luckington SN14 ....47 C5
 Twyning GL20 ....181 F7
Cherry Orchard Rd ⑥
 GL8 ....140 C4
Cherry Rd BS37 .....44 A1
Cherry Tree Cl
 Bristol 20 C2
 Churchdown GL3 ....128 A7
 Keynsham BS31 .....4 C4
 Nailsworth GL6 .....91 A4
Cherry Tree ⑭ GL4 ..119 C4
Cherry Tree La GL16 .155 C6
Cherry Tree Rd ⑫ SN6 .143 E4
Cherry Wlk GL15 ....92 A4
Cherry Wood BS30 ..11 B2
Cherrytree Cres BS16 .20 C2
Cherrytree Ct BS16 .22 C5
Cherrytree La GL7 ..150 F5
Cherrytree Rd BS16 .20 C2
Cherrywood Gdns GL4 .118 E3
Cherston Ct GL4 ...119 E8
Chertsey Rd BS6 ...18 B1
Chervil Cl GL4 .....119 B4
Cherwell Cl BS35 ...51 C7
Cherwell Rd BS31 ..5 A4
Chesford Dr GL3 ...128 C6
Chesham Way BS15 .20 D1
Cheshire Cl BS37 ..43 E3
Cheshire Rd GL3 ...127 E6
Chesils The GL54 ..174 A8
Chesley Hill BS30 ..11 F7
Chessmann Ct GL1 .126 F4
Chessel Cl BS32 ...40 C2
Chessel Ct ⑥ BS3 .8 B2
Chessel St BS3 ....8 B3
Chessell Ave BS35 .64 A3
Chessgrove La GL17 .164 F6
Chessington Ave BS14 .3 B5
Chester Cl GL11 ...88 B1
Chester Cl GL19 ...173 C7
Chester Cres GL7 ..190 D4
Chester Ct ④ BS5 .9 C7
Chester Ho BS10 ...193 B3
Chester Park Jun & Inf Schs
 BS16 ....20 A3
Chester Park Rd BS16 .20 B2
Chester Pk BS5 ....19 E1
Chester Rd Bristol BS5 .19 E1
 Gloucester GL4 .....119 C8
Chester St Bristol BS5 .19 E1
 Cirencester GL7 ....190 D4
Chester Wlk BS16 ..193 B4
Chesterfield Ave BS6 .18 E2
Chesterfield Bldgs BS6 .194 B3
Chesterfield Ho BS10 .27 F1
Chesterfield Hospl BS6 .194 A2
Chesterfield Rd
 Bristol,Mangotsfield BS16 .20 E5
 Bristol,Montpelier BS6 .18 E2
Chestermaster Cl BS32 .40 A5
Chesters BS30 .....11 A4
Chesterton Cl GL2 .126 F6
Chesterton Gr GL7 .190 C3
Chesterton Ho
 ⑧ Bristol BS2 ......195 B4
 Cirencester GL7 ....190 C3
Chesterton La GL7 .190 C3
Chesterton Link GL7 .190 D3
Chesterton Pk GL7 .190 B4
Chesterton Prim Sch
 GL7 ....190 C2
Chestnut Ave GL10 .97 F8
Chestnut Cl
 Acton Turville GL9 ..36 A6
 Bristol BS14 ....3 F5
 Down Ampney GL7 ..143 E8
 Hardwicke GL2 .....109 E7
 ⑮ Ledbury HR8 ....178 E8
 ② Mile End GL16 ...155 B6
 Nailsworth GL6 .....91 B4
 ④ Tetbury GL8 .....140 B4
Chestnut Cnr WR12 .124 C5
Chestnut Cotts GL7 .125 D5
Chestnut Ct
 Bristol,Bishopsworth BS13 .2 A7
 Bristol,Hillhouse BS16 .18 E2
 ⑩ Monmouth/Trefynwy
 NP25 ....154 A7
Chestnut Dr
 Chipping Sodbury BS37 .44 A1
 Thornbury BS35 ....64 C1
Chestnut Hill GL6 ..91 B4
Chestnut Ho
 Bristol,Hartcliffe BS13 .2 D3
 ⑦ Bristol,Staple Hill BS16 .20 D4
Chestnut La GL51 ..129 B2
Chestnut Park Est GL12 .67 F4
Chestnut Pl GL53 ..130 B4

Chestnut Rd
 Bristol,Lower Soundwell
 BS15 ....20 F3
 Bristol,Mangotsfield BS16 .20 D6
 Gloucester GL4 .....119 E5
 Long Ashton BS41 ..7 B2
Chestnut Terr
 Charlton Kings GL53 .131 A5
 ⑦ Monmouth/Trefynwy
 NP25 ....154 A7
Chestnut Way BS15 .20 F3
Chestnut Wlk Bristol BS13 .2 A6
 Saltford BS31 ......5 E3
Chestnuts The
 Bussage GL6 ....148 B6
 Gloucester GL1 .....196 A1
Chetwode Cl BS10 ..28 D3
Chetwood Ho BS5 ..9 C6
Chevening Cl BS34 .29 D4
Cheviot Cl Quedgeley GL2 .109 E8
 ① Tetbury GL8 ....140 C5
Cheviot Dr BS35 ...51 E8
Cheviot Rd GL52 ..134 B4
Cheviot Way BS30 .11 C5
Chew Cotts BS31 ..4 F5
Chewton Cl BS16 ..20 B3
Chewton Rd BS31 ..4 F2
Cheyne Rd BS9 ....17 E4
Cheyney Cl GL4 ...119 B6
Chichester Ho BS4 .9 F6
Chichester Way GL51 .43 D3
Chicknalls La GL15 .156 F3
Childer Rd HR8 ...178 D8
Chidswickham Rd
 WR12 ....185 A8
Chillingworth Mews
 GL1 ....196 B2
Chillwood Cl BS37 .42 E3
Chiltern Ave GL52 .137 E4
Chiltern Cl
 Bristol,Warmley BS30 .11 C5
 Bristol,Whitchurch BS14 .3 A8
 Chiltern Pk BS35 ...51 E8
Chiltern Rd
 Cheltenham GL52 ..134 B3
 Quedgeley GL2 .....109 E8
Chilton Rd BS4 ....3 A8
Chilwood Cl BS37 .42 E3
China Cnr WR11 ..188 C6
Chine The BS16 ...19 D5
Chine View BS16 ..20 F8
Chiphouse Rd BS15 .20 F3
Chipmans Platt GL10 .101 A3
Chippenham Rd SN14 .15 A8
Chipperfield Dr BS15 .20 F1
Chipping Campden Bsns Pk
 GL55 ....189 B2
Chipping Campden Sch
 GL55 ....189 A2
Chipping Cl GL12 ..68 C7
Chipping Ct ⑫ GL18 .140 C4
Chipping Edge Est BS37 .44 C1
Chipping Gdns ⑥ GL12 .68 B7
Chipping Sodbury Sch
 BS37 ....33 B8
Chipping St GL18 ..140 C4
Chipping The GL12 .67 F4
Chippings The BS16 .19 C5
Chisbury St BS5 ...19 C3
Chislet Way GL4 ..118 D1
Chittening Ind Est BS11 .26 E8
Chittening Rd BS11 .26 E7
Chock La BS9 .....18 A7
Choirs Cl GL4 ....119 E6
Chosen Ho GL3 ...128 E5
Chosen Hill Sch GL3 .128 E5
Chosen View Rd GL51 .133 B5
Chosen Way GL3 ..119 F8
Christ Church CE Inf Sch
 BS16 ....20 D5
Christ Church CE Prim Sch
 Bristol,Victoria Park BS8 .194 A3
 Gloucester GL4 .....148 C5
 Cheltenham GL50 ..193 B3
Christ Church Hanham CE
 Prim Sch BS15 .....10 B4
Christ Church Jun Sch
 BS16 ....20 D5
Christ Church Rd BS8 .194 A3
Christ Church Terr ⑧
 GL50 ....133 B1
Christ Church Villas ⑦
 GL50 ....133 B1
Christ the King RC Prim Sch
 Bristol BS8 ....2 E8
 Thornbury BS35 ....64 C1
Christchurch Ave BS16 .20 D5
Christchurch Ct ④
 GL50 ....133 B1
Christchurch La BS16 .20 D5
Christchurch Rd BS8 .194 A3
Christina Terr BS8 .194 A1
Christmas St BS1 ..195 A3
Christmas Stps BS1 .195 A3
Christmas Tree BS34 .28 D6
Christowe La GL53 .193 C1
Chubb Cl BS30 ...11 F6
Church Ave
 Bristol,Sneyd Park BS9 .17 C4
 ③ Bristol,Upper Easton
 BS5 ....11 D7
 Bristol,Warmley BS30 .11 D7
 Falfield GL12 ....65 E7
 Siddington GL7 ....190 E1
Church Cl Bristol BS10 .27 F2
 Broadway WR12 ....185 B8
 Cranham GL4 ......112 E5

Church Cl *continued*
 Ebrington GL55 ....189 D3
 Frampton Cotterell BS36 .31 B8
 Longborough GL56 .176 D8
Church Cotts ⑱ GL55 .189 A2
Church Ct ⑨ BS16 .20 D3
Church Dr Bristol BS5 .9 E8
 Parkend GL15 ......155 C2
 Quedgeley GL2 .....127 A3
Church Farm ② NP25 .154 A7
Church Farm Bsns Ctr
 GL53 ....130 C3
Church Farm La GL54 .187 A6
Church Farm Rd BS16 .21 C6
Church Furlong GL4 .176 C1
Church Gdns GL15 .92 A2
Church Hill Bisley GL6 .148 D8
 Bristol BS4 ....9 E2
 Burton SN14 ....36 B3
 Oldbury-on-S BS35 .63 B5
 Olveston BS35 .....49 F3
 Upper Lydbrook GL17 .163 D2
Church Hill Cl GL16 .163 B2
Church Hill Ho BS4 .9 E2
Church Ho BS7 ....18 F8
Church La
 Ashton Keynes SN6 .142 F5
 Badminton GL9 ....46 E5
 Berkeley GL13 .....85 D3
 Bitton BS30 ....5 E7
 Bledington OX7 ....177 E1
 Bristol BS1 ....195 B2
 Bristol,Bromley Heath BS16 .30 F1
 Bristol,Clifton Wood BS8 .194 B2
 Bristol,Henbury BS10 .27 E2
 Bristol,Southville BS3 .8 D3
 Chipping Sodbury BS37 .34 B8
 Churcham GL2 .....124 D1
 Coalpit Heath BS36 .31 C6
 Corse GL19 ....172 B5
 ⑤ Cricklade SN6 ..143 E4
 Cromhall GL12 .....66 A1
 Evenlode GL56 ....177 C7
 Forthampton GL19 .181 C3
 Gloucester GL4 ....119 D8
 Hambrook BS16 ...30 E2
 Hankerton SN16 ..141 E1
 Hardwicke GL2 ...109 D6
 Harnhill GL7 ......151 B3
 ⑰ Ledbury HR8 ...178 F8
 Long Ashton BS41 .7 C2
 Marshfield SN14 ..13 A8
 Minsterworth GL2 .116 F7
 Moreton Valence GL2 .101 A8
 Northwood Green GL14 .165 C2
 Rangeworthy BS37 .52 F1
 Saggarton GL7 ....149 B6
 Saul GL2 ....100 A4
 Sevenhampton GL54 .166 E8
 Sharpness GL13 ...84 B6
 Shurdington GL51 .129 E2
 Sopworth SN14 ...57 D1
 South Cerney GL7 .142 F8
 St Arvans NP16 ...72 B6
 Stanton WR12 ....184 B5
 Stonehouse GL10 .97 E7
 The Leigh GL19 ..173 C4
 Toddington GL54 .183 B4
 Whaddon GL4 ....110 E8
 Whitchurch BS14 .3 B3
 Wickwar GL12 ....54 A6
 Windrush OX18 ...161 C7
 Winterbourne BS36 .30 C6
 Woolaston,Alvington GL15 .147 D3
 Woolaston,Plusterwine
 GL15 ....147 B2
Church Leaze BS11 .16 D6
Church Mdws
 Toddington GL54 .184 B3
 Whitchurch BS14 .3 C4
Church Par BS4 ...9 E2
Church Path Rd BS20 .16 C4
Church Piece GL53 .131 B5
Church Pl
 Lower Oddington GL56 .177 D4
 Pill BS20 ....16 C4
Church Rd Abbots Leigh BS8 .7 A8
 Alderton GL20 .....183 E4
 Almondsbury BS32 .40 A5
 Alveston BS35 .....51 A1
 Arlingham GL2 ....157 B5
 Aylburton GL15 ...147 E5
 Bibury GL7 ....160 A1
 Bishop's Cleeve GL52 .137 F4
 Bitton BS30 ....5 E7
 Bristol,Bedminster BS3 .8 C3
 Bristol,Bishopsworth BS13 .2 A6
 Bristol,Filton BS34 .29 A3
 Bristol,Frenchay BS16 .20 C7
 Bristol,Hanham BS15 .10 B5
 Bristol,Horfield BS7 ..18 E5
 Bristol,Kingswood BS15 .10 E8
 Bristol,Moorfields BS5 .9 D8
 Bristol,Sneyd Park BS9 .17 D3
 Bristol,Stoke Gifford BS34 .29 E4
 Bristol,Upper Soundwell
 BS9 ....18 A7
 Bristol,Westbury on Trym
 BS9 ....18 A7
 Cheltenham,Leckhampton
 GL53 ....130 C3
 Cheltenham,St Mark's
 GL51 ....129 F8
 Chepstow/Cas-Gwent NP16 .72 F1
 Churchdown GL3 ..128 C4
 Cinderford GL14 ..191 C3
 Doynton BS30 ....23 A1
 Dundry BS41 ......1 B1

urch Rd continued
ursley GL11 . . . . .88 B3
aster Compton BS35 . . . . .39 A1
anson-in-G BS20 . . . . .16 A4
ampton Cotterell BS36 . . . . . . .31 C8
oucester GL2 . . . . .127 C4
uting Power GL54 . . . . .175 B3
ewelsfield GL15 . . . . .146 F5
amble GL7 . . . . .141 F8
1 Ledbury HR8 . . . . .178 F8
eigh Woods BS8 . . . . .7 D6
eonard Stanley GL10 . . . . .97 E3
onghope GL17 . . . . .164 F6
ower Oddington GL56 . . . . . . .177 D4
uckington SN14 . . . . .47 F4
ydney GL15 . . . . .92 A2
aisemore GL2 . . . . .126 A7
ailsworth GL6 . . . . .91 A6
1 Newnham GL14 . . . . .157 A6
idbury-on-S BS35 . . . . .63 B5
ilning BS35 . . . . .38 B7
uemington GL7 . . . . .152 D7
evern Beach BS35 . . . . .38 A6
tanton WR12 . . . . .184 C8
troud GL5 . . . . .98 E6
windon GL51 . . . . .133 B6
hornbury BS35 . . . . .64 B2
ormarton GL9 . . . . .34 D2
pper Lydbrook GL17 . . . . .163 D2
pper Soudley GL14 . . . . .156 C5
Whitchurch BS14 . . . . .3 C4
Vick BS30 . . . . .12 B6
Vinterbourne BS36 . . . . .30 E4
Voodchester GL5 . . . . .98 F2
tke BS37 . . . . .43 E3
BS37 .43 F2
hurch Rise GL2 . . . . .126 A7
hurch Road PI GL14 . . . . . . .191 D4
hurch Row
hedworth GL54 . . . . .159 A7
ketton GL54 . . . . .183 E1
Vailsworth GL6 . . . . .91 A6
Dverbury GL20 . . . . .182 F8
Poole Keynes GL7 . . . . .142 A6
thipton GL54 . . . . .166 E5
hurch Sq GL15 . . . . .156 E2
hurch St Avening GL8 . . . . .148 A1
Bledington OX7 . . . . .177 E1
Bredon GL20 . . . . .182 C7
BS1 . . . . .195 B2
Bristol,Lower Easton BS5 . . . . . .9 B1
Bristol,Russell Town BS5 . . . . . . .9 B6
Broadway WR12 . . . . .185 B8
Charlton Kings GL53 . . . . .131 B5
Cirencester GL7 . . . . .190 D3
Clearwell GL16 . . . . .155 A2
Gloucester GL2 . . . . .196 A2
Kings's Stanley GL10 . . . . .98 A4
Kingham OX7 . . . . .177 F2
5 Ledbury HR8 . . . . .178 F8
ittledean GL14 . . . . .156 E8
Meysey Hampton GL7 . . . . . . .152 A2
Moreton-in-M GL56 . . . . .187 A3
Nailsworth GL6 . . . . .91 C4
Newent GL18 . . . . .171 A4
Nympsfield GL10 . . . . .89 E5
Thornbury SN16 . . . . .58 C1
St Briavels GL15 . . . . .146 E7
9 Stow-on-t-W GL54 . . . . .176 F4
Stroud GL5 . . . . .99 C7
Tetbury GL8 . . . . .140 B3
Tewkesbury GL20 . . . . .192 C4
Willersey WR12 . . . . .188 B2
Wotton-u-E GL12 . . . . .68 B7
hurch View
Almondsbury BS32 . . . . .39 F4
Aston Magna GL56 . . . . .187 A6
Bristol,Filton BS34 . . . . .29 A3
Bristol,Staple Hill BS16 . . . . . . .20 D5
Castle Eaton SN6 . . . . .144 D6
Churchdown GL3 . . . . .128 C4
Coleford GL16 . . . . .163 C4
Gorsley HR9 . . . . .170 A4
Highworth SN6 . . . . .145 C3
Hillesley GL12 . . . . .55 D8
Leonard Stanley GL10 . . . . .97 E3
Newport GL13 . . . . .78 C8
Thornbury GL13 . . . . .64 E7
hurch Way
Blakeney GL15 . . . . .156 E2
Gloucester GL4 . . . . .119 C7
6 Newent GL18 . . . . .171 A4
hurch Wlk
Ashton Keynes SN6 . . . . .142 F5
Charlton Kings GL52 . . . . .131 B6
6 Coleford GL16 . . . . .155 B6
Littledean GL14 . . . . .156 E8
Parkend GL15 . . . . .162 A1
BS20 .16 C4
8 Stow-on-t-W GL54 . . . . .176 F4
Viney Hill GL15 . . . . .156 C1
hurcham Prim Sch
GL2 . . . . .124 C2
Churchdown La GL3 . . . . . .120 C8
Churchdown Parton Manor
Jun Sch GL3 . . . . .128 B5
Churchdown Sch GL3 . . . . .128 B5
Churchdown Village Inf Sch
GL3 . . . . .128 C5
Churchdown Village Jun Sch
GL3 . . . . .128 C4
Churchdown Wlk BS11 . . . . .16 F7
Churchend GL2 . . . . .95 D4
Churchend Cotts GL2 . . . . . .95 D4
Churchend La GL12 . . . . .66 F3
Churches Mill GL5 . . . . .99 A1

Churchfarm Cl BS37 . . . . . . .43 F3
Churchfield Rd
Stroud GL5 . . . . .99 D6
Upton St Leonards GL4 . . . . . . .119 E3
Churchfields GL2 . . . . .145 B2
Churchill Rd GL5 . . . . .148 A5
Churchill Ave SN26 . . . . .144 E1
1 Nailsworth GL6 . . . . .91 B4
Churchill Dr Bristol BS9 . . . . .17 D7
Cheltenham GL52 . . . . .131 A7
Churchill Gdns GL52 . . . . . .131 A7
Churchill Gr GL20 . . . . .192 F4
Churchill Ind Est GL53 . . . . . .130 D6
Churchill Mdw HR8 . . . . .178 E8
Churchill PI 9 GL7 . . . . .152 E4
Churchill Rd Bristol BS4 . . . . .9 C4
Cheltenham GL53 . . . . .130 E6
Cirencester GL7 . . . . .190 E5
Gloucester GL1 . . . . .118 E7
Nailsworth GL6 . . . . .91 B4
Churchill Sq GL5 . . . . .186 C7
Churchill Way
Mitcheldean GL17 . . . . .164 D5
Painswick GL6 . . . . .103 F8
Churchlands Flats GL54 . . . .174 A4
Churchlands Lawns
GL54 .139 F5
Churchlands 8 BS3 . . . . .8 B2
Churchside BS16 . . . . .20 D7
Churchview Dr GL4 . . . . .119 D8
Churchward Cl
Bristol BS15 . . . . .10 B5
Honeybourne WR11 . . . . .188 C7
Churchward Rd BS37 . . . . . . .43 B3
Churchway SN26 . . . . .144 E1
Churchways BS14 . . . . .3 C4
Churchways Ave BS7 . . . . . . .18 E6
Churchways Cres BS7 . . . . . .18 E6
Churn Ave BS34 . . . . .134 A2
Churn Cl GL7 . . . . .142 F8
Churn Hill GL7 . . . . .158 D3
Churn The GL6 . . . . .103 F8
Churnside GL7 . . . . .158 D2
Churston Cl BS14 . . . . .3 A3
Cicely Way GL4 . . . . .119 F5
Cicester Terr 16 GL56 . . . . . .187 A3
Cicil Rd 1 BS15 . . . . .10 D8
Cidermill Cl NP16 . . . . .60 F4
Cidermill La GL7 . . . . .189 A2
Cidermill Orch GL7 . . . . .189 A2
Cilgant Defiw/Oak Cres 8
NP25 .154 A7
Cinder Hill Coleford GL16 . . . .155 A5
St Briavels GL15 . . . . .146 E7
Cinder La GL7 . . . . .152 F4
Cinderford Ent Ctr
GL14 .191 C5
Cinderford Rd GL15 . . . . . . .163 C5
Cinderhill Way GL17 . . . . . . .163 E4
Circle The GL5 . . . . .99 C8
Circuit 32 BS5 . . . . .9 F7
Circular Rd BS9 . . . . .17 E2
Cirencester Bsns Ctr
GL7 . . . . .190 D2
Cirencester Deer Park Sch
GL7 . . . . .190 B4
Cirencester Hospl GL7 . . . . .190 B4
Cirencester Jun & Inf Sch
GL7 . . . . .190 D3
Cirencester Kingshill Sch
GL7 . . . . .190 F5
Cirencester Rd
Charlton Kings GL53 . . . . .131 A4
Fairford GL7 . . . . .152 C3
Latton SN6 . . . . .143 D7
Little Witcombe GL3 . . . . .121 A4
Minchinhampton,Burleigh
GL5,GL6 . . . . .91 E7
Minchinhampton,Hyde GL6 . . . .148 C4
South Cerney GL7 . . . . .151 A2
Tetbury GL8 . . . . .140 C4
Cirencester Tertiary Coll
GL7 . . . . .190 A4
City Academy Bristol The
BS5 . . . . .9 C8
City Bank Rd GL7 . . . . .190 D3
City Bsns Pk BS5 . . . . .9 A8
City Mus & Art Gal*
BS8 . . . . .194 C3
City of Bristol Coll (Folly La
Ctr) BS2 . . . . .9 A6
City of Bristol Coll
(Kingswood Ctr) GL16 . . . . .10 E8
City of Bristol Coll Hartcliffe
Ctr BS13 . . . . .2 D4
City of Bristol Coll,
Bedminster Ctr BS3 . . . . .8 D7
City of Bristol Coll, College
Green Ctr BS1 . . . . .194 C2
City of Bristol Coll Downend
Ctr BS16 . . . . .21 A8
City of Bristol Coll,Ashley
Down Ctr BS7 . . . . .18 F4
City of Bristol Coll,Soundwell
Ctr BS16 . . . . .20 E2
City of Bristol College
Lawrence Weston Ctr
BS11 .27 B1
City of Bristol Parkway
Transport Tech Cty
BS34 .29 D3
City Rd BS2 . . . . .195 B4
City View BS4 . . . . .9 A3
Claire's Cl GL5 . . . . .148 A5
Clamp The BS30 . . . . .11 C3
Clanage Rd BS3 . . . . .7 E4
Clanna Cty Pk GL15 . . . . . . .147 C5

Clanna La GL15 . . . . .147 C4
Clanna Rd GL15 . . . . .147 D4
Clapham Ct GL1 . . . . .196 C3
Clapton Row 8 GL54 . . . . . . .168 F7
Clapton Wlk BS9 . . . . .17 C5
Clare Ave BS7 . . . . .18 C3
Clare Ct Cheltenham GL53 . . .193 B1
Stroud GL5 . . . . .99 E7
Clare Mews GL53 . . . . .193 B1
Clare Pl GL53 . . . . .193 B1
Clare Rd
Bristol,Cotham BS6 . . . . .18 D1
Bristol,Kingswood BS15 . . . . . . .20 C2
Bristol,Lower Easton BS5 . . . . . .19 B2
Clare St Bristol BS1 . . . . .195 A2
Gloucester GL1 . . . . .196 A3
Cheltenham GL53 . . . . .193 B1
Gloucester GL1 . . . . .196 A3
Clare Wlk BS35 . . . . .63 F2
Claremont 1 GL52 . . . . .133 F2
Claremont Ave BS7 . . . . .18 C3
Claremont Ct Bristol BS9 . . . . .18 C5
Gloucester GL1 . . . . .196 C3
Claremont Rd Bristol BS7 . . . .18 D3
Gloucester GL1 . . . . .196 C3
Claremont Specl Sch
BS9 . . . . .18 C5
Claremont St BS5 . . . . .19 A1
Claremont Terr 10 BS5 . . . . . . .9 D7
Clarence Ave BS16 . . . . .20 E5
Clarence Ct Bristol BS15 . . . . .20 B1
Clarence Ho BS15 . . . . .20 B1
Clarence Par GL50 . . . . .193 B3
Clarence Pl BS2 . . . . .194 C4
Clarence Rd Bristol BS1 . . . .195 B1
Bristol,Kingswood BS15 . . . . . . .20 B1
Bristol,Newton BS2 . . . . .9 A7
Cheltenham GL52 . . . . .193 C4
Cheltenham GL50 . . . . .192 C2
Wotton-u-E GL12 . . . . .68 B7
Clarence Sq GL50 . . . . .193 C4
Clarence St
Cheltenham GL50 . . . . .193 B4
Gloucester GL1 . . . . .196 B2
Clarence Wlk
Cheltenham GL50 . . . . .193 B3
Gloucester GL1 . . . . .196 B2
Clarendon Cl NP16 . . . . .61 A4
Clarendon Ct 6 GL51 . . . . . . .99 C7
Clarendon Rd Bristol BS6 . . . .18 C2
Winchcombe GL54 . . . . .174 A8
Claridge Cl GL4 . . . . .119 D4
Clarington Mews GL50 . . . . .133 E3
Clark Dr BS16 . . . . .19 F8
Clark St BS5 . . . . .9 A8
Clark's Alley GL20 . . . . .192 C5
Clark's Hay GL7 . . . . .142 F8
Clark's La Blakeney GL15 . . . .156 E2
Siddington GL7 . . . . .150 D2
Clarke Ave GL56 . . . . .187 A3
Clarke St BS3 . . . . .8 C4
Clarke Way GL50 . . . . .133 D3
Clarken Coombe BS41 . . . . . . .7 B3
Clarkes Field SN6 . . . . .142 D1
Clarkia Cl GL3 . . . . .127 F7
Clarrie Rd 1 GL8 . . . . .140 C4
Clattergrove GL6 . . . . .112 A2
Clatworthy Dr BS14 . . . . .3 A7
Claudians Cl GL4 . . . . .119 E7
Claudius Way GL15 . . . . .92 B4
Clavell Rd BS10 . . . . .27 E7
Claverham Rd BS16 . . . . .20 A5
Claverton Rd BS31 . . . . .5 E4
Claverton Rd W BS31 . . . . .5 D3
Clay Bottom BS5 . . . . .19 E2
Clay Hill BS5 . . . . .9 E3
Clay La Bitton BS30 . . . . .5 D8
Bristol,Little Stoke BS34 . . . . . . .29 C7
Bristol,Willsbridge BS30 . . . . . .11 D1
Thornbury BS35 . . . . .64 E1
Clay Pit Rd BS6 . . . . .18 B5
Clay Pitch BS37 . . . . .45 E3
Clay Rd GL16 . . . . .155 B7
Clayburn Cl GL2 . . . . .125 E5
Claydon Gn BS14 . . . . .2 F3
Clayfield BS37 . . . . .43 E5
Clayfield Rd BS4 . . . . .9 E5
Clayfurlong Gr GL7 . . . . .141 F8
Claymore Cres BS16 . . . . .20 B1
Claypatch Rd 5 NP25 . . . . . .154 A7
Claypiece Rd BS13 . . . . .1 F4
Claypit Hill BS37 . . . . .33 B7
Claypits Hill GL2,GL10 . . . . .100 C1
Claypits La GL6 . . . . .91 F5
Claypool Rd BS15 . . . . .10 E7
Clays Rd GL16 . . . . .155 B2
Clayton St
Avonmouth BS11 . . . . .26 A1
21 Bristol BS5 . . . . .9 B8
Clearview NP25 . . . . .154 B1
Clearwater Dr GL2 . . . . .117 B8
Clearwell Caves* GL16 . . . . . .155 A3
Clearwell CE Prim Sch
GL16 .155 A2
Cleave St BS2 . . . . .19 A2
Clee Ho GL20 . . . . .192 C3
Cleeve Ave BS16 . . . . .20 E7
Cleeve Cloud La GL52 . . . . . .134 D3
Cleeve Ct
Bishop's Cleeve GL52 . . . . .137 F3
Bristol BS16 . . . . .20 D7
Cleeve Gdns BS16 . . . . .20 D7
Cleeve Gr BS31 . . . . .4 D5
Cleeve Hill BS16 . . . . .20 D7

Cleeve Hill Extension
BS16 . . . . .20 E6
Cleeve Ho GL5 . . . . .99 F1
Cleeve La BS30 . . . . .22 D1
Cleeve Lake Ct GL52 . . . . . . .137 E4
Cleeve Lawns BS16 . . . . .20 D7
Cleeve Lodge Cl BS16 . . . . . . .20 E6
Cleeve Lodge Rd BS16 . . . . . .20 E6
Cleeve Mill Bsns Pk
GL18 .171 A5
Cleeve Mill La GL18 . . . . .171 A5
Cleeve Park Rd BS16 . . . . .20 E7
Cleeve Rd Bristol BS4 . . . . .9 B3
Bristol,Frenchay BS16 . . . . .20 E6
Bristol,Mangotsfield BS16 . . . . . .20 E6
Gloucester GL4 . . . . .119 B4
Gotherington GL52 . . . . .138 A7
Yate BS37 . . . . .43 E1
Cleeve Rise GL18 . . . . .171 A4
Cleeve View GL52 . . . . .136 E5
Cleeve View Rd GL52 . . . . . .134 A2
Cleeve Wood Pk BS16 . . . . . . .20 C8
Cleeve Wood Rd BS16 . . . . . . .20 D7
Cleevecroft Ave GL52 . . . . . .138 A5
Cleeveland St GL51 . . . . .133 C3
Cleevelands Ave GL50 . . . . . .133 E4
Cleevelands Cl GL50 . . . . . . .133 E5
Cleevelands Dr GL50 . . . . . . .133 E5
Cleevemont Cl GL52 . . . . . . .133 F3
Cleevemont Rd GL52 . . . . . . .133 F4
Clegram Rd GL1 . . . . .118 D7
Clematis Ct GL52 . . . . .137 E3
Clement St Bristol BS2 . . . . . .195 C4
Gloucester GL1 . . . . .119 A8
Clementine Ho GL56 . . . . . . .186 C6
Clements End Rd GL16 . . . . . .155 B2
Clencher's Mill La HR8 . . . . .179 B7
Clent Ct GL1 . . . . .133 F1
Cleve Ct
Bristol,Clifton Wood BS8 . . . . . . .7 F4
Bristol,Filton BS34 . . . . .29 B4
Cleve House Sch BS4 . . . . .9 B3
Cleve Rd BS34 . . . . .29 A4
Clevedale BS16 . . . . .20 D7
Clevedale Ct Bristol BS7 . . . . .18 D4
Gloucester GL1 . . . . .118 C7
Clevedon Sq GL51 . . . . .133 A2
Clevedon Terr BS6 . . . . .195 A4
Cleveland Ct BS35 . . . . .51 E8
Cleevewood BS16 . . . . .20 C7
Cliff Court Dr BS16 . . . . .20 B7
Cliff View NP16 . . . . .61 B7
Clifford Ave GL20 . . . . .192 E2
Clifford Gdns BS11 . . . . .16 E6
Clifford Rd BS16 . . . . .20 D2
Cliffords 8 SN6 . . . . .143 E4
Clift House Rd BS3 . . . . .8 A4
Clift House Spur BS3 . . . . .7 F4
Clift Pl BS1 . . . . .195 A1
Clift Rd BS3 . . . . .8 A4
Clifton Arc BS8 . . . . .194 A3
Clifton C BS8 . . . . .194 A4
Clifton Cl 8 Bristol BS8 . . . . . .7 F7
14 Stow-on-t-W GL54 . . . . . . .176 F4
Clifton Coll BS8 . . . . .194 A4
Clifton College Prep Sch
BS8 . . . . .17 F1
Clifton Down BS8 . . . . .7 F7
Clifton Down Rd BS8 . . . . .7 F6
Clifton Down Sh Ctr 11
BS8 . . . . .18 B1
Clifton Down Sta BS8 . . . . . . .18 A1
Clifton High Gr BS9 . . . . .17 E5
Clifton High Sch BS8 . . . . . . .194 A4
Clifton Hill BS8 . . . . .194 A3
Clifton Metro 10 BS8 . . . . .7 E7
Clifton Park Rd BS8 . . . . .194 A3
Clifton Pk BS8 . . . . .194 A4
Clifton Pl BS5 . . . . .9 C8
Clifton Rd Bristol BS8 . . . . . .194 A2
Gloucester GL1 . . . . .196 A1
Clifton St
Bristol,Bedminster BS3 . . . . .8 C3
Bristol,Upper Easton BS5 . . . . . . .9 A8
*Clifton Suspension Bridge**
. . . . .7 E7
Clifton Vale BS8 . . . . .194 A2
Clifton Vale Cl BS8 . . . . .194 A2
Clifton View 1 BS3 . . . . .8 B3
Clifton Wood Ct BS8 . . . . . . .194 B2
Clifton Wood Rd BS8 . . . . . .194 B2
Clifton Wood Cres BS8 . . . . .194 B2
Cliftonwood Terr BS8 . . . . . .194 A2
Clinger Ho GL7 . . . . .190 D5
Clingre Down GL11 . . . . .87 C4
Clingre La GL11 . . . . .87 C4
Clinton Rd BS3 . . . . .8 C2
Clissold Ct GL6 . . . . .91 B3
Clive Rd BS14 . . . . .3 C8
Cloatley Rd SN16 . . . . .141 E1
Clock House Sq GL54 . . . . . .166 C6
Cloisters BS5 . . . . .7 F8
Cloisters Rd BS36 . . . . .30 F6
Cloisters The
Bishop's Cleeve GL52 . . . . .137 E4
Chepstow,Cas-Gwent NP16 . . . .72 D2
Clomoney Way GL20 . . . . . . .127 D5
Clonmel Rd BS4 . . . . .8 E1
Close Field GL54 . . . . .183 F1
Close Gdns
Condicote GL54 . . . . .176 B7
14 Tetbury GL8 . . . . .140 B4
Close The
Bristol,Henbury BS10 . . . . .28 A5

Close The continued
Bristol,Little Stoke BS34 . . . . . . .29 C6
Bristol,Patchway BS32 . . . . .40 C1
Bristol,Upper Soundwell
BS16 . . . . .20 D3
Cheltenham GL53 . . . . .130 D4
Coalley GL11 . . . . .88 E7
Coalpit Heath BS36 . . . . .31 C6
Coleford GL16 . . . . .155 C5
Dursley GL11 . . . . .87 E4
Lechlade on T GL7 . . . . .153 E3
Siddington GL7 . . . . .150 E2
Slimbridge GL2 . . . . .95 E3
South Cerney GL7 . . . . .143 A8
Southam GL52 . . . . .134 C8
Thornbury BS35 . . . . .51 B8
Whiteshill GL6 . . . . .102 F3
Whitminster GL2 . . . . .100 F5
Clothier Rd BS4 . . . . .9 F2
Cloud The GL12 . . . . .68 B7
Clouds Hill Ave BS5 . . . . .9 E8
Clouds Hill Rd BS5 . . . . .9 F8
Clovelly Cl BS5 . . . . .9 F8
Clovelly Rd BS5 . . . . .9 F8
Clover Cl
Cinderford GL14 . . . . .156 C6
Milkwall GL16 . . . . .155 B4
Clover Dr GL2 . . . . .109 C4
Clover Ground BS9 . . . . .18 B7
Clover Leaze BS32 . . . . .29 D6
Clover Piece GL4 . . . . .119 D6
Cloverdale Dr BS30 . . . . .11 A3
Cloverlea Bsns Ctr BS36 . . . . .31 C3
Cloverlea Rd BS30 . . . . .11 C5
Clyde Ave BS31 . . . . .4 F4
Clyde Cres GL52 . . . . .134 A2
Clyde Ct 2 BS3 . . . . .8 C3
Clyde Gdns BS5 . . . . .19 B8
Clyde Gr BS34 . . . . .28 F2
Clyde Ho 7 BS35 . . . . .51 C8
Clyde La BS6 . . . . .18 C2
Clyde Mews 3 BS6 . . . . .18 C2
Clyde Rd
Bristol,Redland BS6 . . . . .18 B2
Bristol,Totterdown BS4 . . . . .9 A3
Brockworth GL3 . . . . .120 C5
Frampton Cotterell BS36 . . . . . . .31 B8
Clyde Terr
3 Bristol,Bedminster BS3 . . . . . .8 C3
Bristol,Totterdown BS4 . . . . .9 A3
Clydesdale Cl BS14 . . . . .3 A6
Co-operation Rd BS5 . . . . .19 C1
Coach Cl GL13 . . . . .85 E3
Coach Ho The
Blockley GL56 . . . . .186 C7
Tewkesbury GL20 . . . . .192 D4
Coach House Mews
GL7 . . . . .190 D4
Coach Rd HR9 . . . . .164 D8
Coachworks The BS30 . . . . . . .10 F4
Coaley CE Prim Sch
GL11 . . . . .88 E8
Coalbrook Rd BS11 . . . . .16 D5
Coalsack La BS36 . . . . .31 B3
Coalville Rd BS36 . . . . .31 D7
Coalway Jun Sch GL16 . . . . .155 B5
Coalway Rd GL16 . . . . .155 B5
Coape Rd BS14 . . . . .3 F5
Coates Gdns GL10 . . . . .97 F8
Coates Ho 8 BS1 . . . . .132 E2
Coates La GL7 . . . . .149 F4
Coates Mill Cotts GL54 . . . . .139 F4
Coates The GL54 . . . . .139 F4
Coates Wlk BS4 . . . . .2 D6
Cobbler's Cl The GL52 . . . . . .138 A7
Cobblestone Mews BS8 . . . . .194 A4
Cobden Ctr The BS16 . . . . . . .31 B2
Cobden St BS5 . . . . .9 C6
Coberley BS15 . . . . .10 C6
Coberley CE Prim Sch
GL53 .123 A5
Coberley Rd
Cheltenham GL51 . . . . .129 D8
Gloucester GL4 . . . . .118 C2
Cobham Ct GL51 . . . . .133 B3
Cobham Dr BS11 . . . . .133 B3
Cobharn Rd GL51 . . . . .1 F4
Cobourg Rd BS6 . . . . .18 F2
Coburn Gdns GL51 . . . . .132 C1
Cochran Cl GL3 . . . . .128 C5
Cock La SN14 . . . . .23 D5
Cock Rd BS15 . . . . .10 F6
Cockadilly GL10 . . . . .89 D5
Cockatoos La HR9 . . . . .170 C5
Cockshoot Hill GL15 . . . . . . .146 E7
Codrington Pl BS8 . . . . .194 A3
Codrington Rd BS7 . . . . .18 D3
Cody Ct 2 BS15 . . . . .10 B5
Coed Barnet/Barnets Wood
NP16 . . . . .60 C8
Coed Castell/Castle Wood
NP16 . . . . .60 C8
Coed Gilfach/Alcove Wood
NP16 . . . . .60 C8
Coed Fedw/ Fedw Wood
NP16 . . . . .60 C8
Coed Ffwyth/Fryth Wood
NP16 . . . . .60 C8
Coed Hale/Hale Wood
NP16 . . . . .60 C8
Coed Maenor/Manor Wood
NP16 . . . . .60 C8
Coed Wallwern/Wallwern
Wood NP16 . . . . .72 C1

Coed Woolpitch/Woolpitch
 Wood NP16 ....60 B8
Cogan Rd BS16 ....20 E3
Cogsall Rd BS14 ....3 F6
Colburn Ct BS7 ....18 F7
Colchester Cl
 Mitcheldean GL17 ....164 D5
 Westbury-on-S GL14 .....165 C1
Colchester Cres BS4 .....2 D7
Cold Pool La
 Cheltenham,Up Hatherley
 GL51 ....129 D6
 Cheltenham Badgeworth
 GL51 ....129 B5
Coldharbour La
 Bristol BS16 ....19 E8
 Newent GL18 ....170 F6
Coldharbour Rd
 Bristol BS6 ....18 B4
 St Briavels GL15 ....146 E6
Coldicott Leys GL55 .....189 D2
Coldicotts Cl 7 GL55 ...189 A2
Coldpark Gdns BS13 ....1 E5
Coldpark Rd BS13 ....1 E5
Coldray Cl GL1 ....127 B1
Coldrick Ct BS14 ....2 F3
Coldwell GL10 ....98 B3
Coldwell Cl GL10 ....98 B3
Coldwell La GL10 ....98 B3
Cole Ave GL2 ....118 C3
Cole Rd BS2 ....9 B6
Colebridge Ave GL2 .....127 C3
Colebrook Rd BS15 .....10 C8
Coleford Rd Bream GL15 .147 C8
 Bristol BS10 ....28 D1
 Tutshill NP16 ....72 F2
Colemead BS13 ....2 B5
Coleridge Ho BS34 ....40 A1
Coleridge Rd BS5 ....19 C3
Colerne Dr GL3 ....32 E8
Colesborne Rd BS7 .....32 E8
Colesbourne Rd GL51 ...129 D8
Coleshill Dr BS13 ....2 B5
Colin Cl BS35 ....64 C1
Colin Rd GL4 ....127 D1
Collard Ho 2 BS16 ....19 F4
College Ave BS16 ....20 A5
College Baths Rd GL53 ..193 C2
College Ct
 Bristol,Clifton BS8 .....194 A4
 Bristol,Fishponds BS16 ..20 A5
 Gloucester GL1 ....196 B3
College Farm Wkshps
 GL7 ....150 B3
College Fields Bristol BS8 ..7 F8
 Gloucester GL2 ....127 D4
College Gate GL53 ......193 C2
College Gn Bristol BS1 ..194 C2
 Gloucester GL1 ....196 B3
College Lawn GL53 ......193 C1
College Mews BS4 ....18 A7
College Park Dr BS10 ...27 F1
College Rd Bredon GL20 ..182 B7
 Bristol,Clifton BS8 .....7 F8
 Bristol,Fishponds BS16 ..20 A5
 Bristol,Westbury on Trym
 BS9 ....18 A7
 Cheltenham GL53 ....193 C2
 Cinderford GL14 ....191 C4
 Stroud GL5 ....99 A8
College Sq BS1 ....194 C2
College St Bristol BS1 ..194 C2
 Gloucester GL1 ....196 B3
College View
 Cirencester GL7 ....190 B1
 3 Stonehouse GL10 ....97 F7
College Way BS34 ....29 A4
College Yd GL1 ....196 A3
Collett Cl BS15 ....10 B5
Collett Ho BS36 ....30 C4
Collett Pl SN6 ....143 E6
Collett Way BS37 ....43 C3
Colletts Ct 2 GL54 .....168 F7
Colletts Dr GL51 ....133 B3
Colletts Fields WR12 ...185 C8
Colletts Gdns 6 WR12 ..185 C8
Colliers Break BS16 .....21 B5
Colliers Pitch GL15 .....147 C5
Colliers Wood GL1 ....91 A5
Collin Cl WR12 ....188 B2
Collin La WR12 ....188 A2
Collin Rd BS4 ....9 D4
Collingbourne Rd GL4 ..119 A7
Collingwood Ave BS15 ..20 E1
Collingwood Cl
 Chepstow NP16 ....61 A5
 Saltford BS31 ....3 E2
Collingwood Rd 4 BS6 ..18 B1
Collins Ave BS34 ....29 C6
Collins Cl GL19 ....172 A8
Collins Dr BS35 ....38 C3
Collins St BS11 ....16 B8
Collinson Rd BS13 ....2 B5
Colliter Cres BS3 ....8 A2
Collum End Rise GL53 ...138 D4
Collyberry Rd GL52 .....138 B4
Coln House Sch GL7 ....152 D3
Coln Pk GL54 ....166 D6
Coln Rise GL54 ....166 D6
Coln Sq BS35 ....51 C8
Colne Ave GL52 ....134 A3
Colne Gn BS31 ....5 A4
Colston Ave BS1 ....194 C2
Colston Cl Bristol BS16 ..20 D3
 Winterbourne BS36 .....30 E4

Colston Ct BS7 ....18 D3
Colston Dale BS16 ....19 E4
Colston Fort 2 BS2 .....195 A4
Colston Hall* BS1 ....195 A3
Colston Hill BS16 ....19 D4
Colston Mews BS6 ....18 E1
Colston Par BS1 ....195 B1
Colston Rd BS5 ....19 C1
Colston St
 Bristol,Kingsdown BS1 ..195 A3
 Bristol,Upper Soundwell
 BS16 ....20 D3
Colston Yd BS1 ....195 A3
Colston's Almshouses
 BS2 ....195 A3
Colston's Lower Sch
 BS16 ....19 D5
Colston's Prim Sch BS6 ..18 D1
Colston's Sch BS16 .....19 C4
Colstone Ct 3 BS16 .....19 E3
Colstons Girls' Sch BS6 ..18 E1
Colsty Mdw GL15 ....156 D1
Coltham Cl 7 GL52 .....130 F8
Coltham Fields GL52 ...130 F8
Coltham Rd GL52 ....130 F8
Colthurst Dr BS15 ....10 E5
Coltman Cl GL1 ....127 B1
Colts Gn BS37 ....33 E8
Columbia Cl GL1 ....196 C3
Columbia St GL12 ....193 C4
Columbine Rd GL20 .....192 E1
Colville Ho GL7 ....190 D5
Colwell Ave GL3 ....128 A1
Colwell School Cl GL1 ..127 A1
Colwyn Dr BS11 ....129 E6
Colwyn Rd 8 BS5 ....19 C1
Colyton Ct BS3 ....8 D1
Comb Paddock BS9 ....18 B7
Combe Ho GL8 ....140 B4
Combermere BS35 ....51 D8
Combfactory La 10 BS5 ..9 B8
Combrook Cl GL4 ....119 E4
Commerce Rd GL12 ......173 E1
Commercial Rd
 Bristol BS1 ....195 A1
 Chalford GL6 ....148 C5
 Gloucester GL1 ....196 A2
Commercial St
 Cheltenham GL50 ....193 B1
 Cinderford GL14 ....191 D4
Common (East) The
 GS32 ....40 C1
Common Hill SN6 ....143 E4
Common La BS31 ....16 B2
Common Mead La BS16 ..30 A1
Common Rd Bristol BS15 ..10 B3
 Minchinhampton GL6 ....91 E6
 Winterbourne BS36 ....30 F7
Common The
 Berkeley Heath GL13 ...96 E3
 Bristol,Frenchay BS16 ..20 B7
 Bristol,Patchway BS32 ..40 C1
 Minety SN16 ....142 E1
 Olveston BS35 ....49 F3
 Siddington GL7 ....150 E2
Commonfield Rd BS11 ...27 B1
Commonmead La BS37 ...33 F8
Compton Cl
 Churchdown GL3 ....128 A8
 Corse GL19 ....172 A7
Compton Dr GL7 ....17 C7
Compton Gn BS31 ....4 E4
Compton Lodge 3 BS6 ..18 B1
Compton Rise GL54 .....166 E2
Compton St BS5 ....9 C7
Compton's Alley GL20 ..192 C4
Comyn Wlk BS16 ....20 A5
Concord GL6 ....91 A3
Concorde Dr BS10 ....28 B1
Concorde Ho BS34 ....28 F2
Concorde Way GL4 ....119 B7
Condell Cl GL20 ....183 A8
Condicote La GL54 .....176 B5
Condor Ho BS7 ....19 C7
Condover Rd BS4 ....10 A3
Conduit Hill GL55 ....188 F1
Conduit Pl 2 BS2 ....19 A1
Conduit Rd BS2 ....19 A1
Conduit St GL1 ....196 C1
Coney Hill Par BS15 .....10 E5
Coney Hill Par GL4 .....119 C7
Coney Hill Rd GL4 .....119 C7
Coneygar Rd GL7 ....152 C7
Coneygree BS13 ....1 F6
Coneygree La WR12 ....185 B7
Congleton Rd BS5 ....9 D8
Conham Hill BS15 ....10 A5
Conham Rd BS4,BS5,BS15 ..9 F5
Conifer Cl Bristol BS16 ..20 D6
 Frampton Cotterell BS36 ..42 A1
Conifers The
 2 Cheltenham GL52 ...134 A3
 Gloucester GL1 ....119 A7
 Minety SN16 ....142 D1
Conigree La GL20 ......192 C2
Coniston Ave GL4 ....127 D2
Coniston Cl BS30 ....11 D6
Coniston Prim Sch BS34 ..39 F1
Coniston Rd Bristol BS34 ..39 F1
 Cheltenham GL51 ....129 E2
 Gloucester GL2 ....127 C4
Connaught Prim Sch BS4 ..2 E8

Connaught Rd BS4 ....2 E8
Consell Gn GL54 ....184 C3
Constable Cl BS31 ....4 F6
Constable Rd BS7 ....19 B6
Constance Cl GL5 ....98 F5
Constantine Ave BS34 ..29 E5
Constitution Hill BS8 ..194 B2
Contemporis BS8 ....194 A3
Convent Cl BS10 ....27 D3
Convent La GL5 ....90 F7
Convent The OX7 ....169 E7
Conway Ct 4 GL16 .....155 A7
Conway Gn BS31 ....5 A3
Conway Rd Bristol BS4 ..9 C4
 Gloucester GL3 ....120 A8
Conygar Rd GL8 ....140 C4
Conygre Gr BS34 ....29 C3
Conygre Rd BS34 ....29 B3
Cook Cl BS30 ....11 C4
Cook St BS11 ....16 C8
Cook's Folly Rd BS9 ...17 D3
Cook's Hill GL19 ....172 C4
Cook's La GL19 ....179 F4
Cooke's Dr BS35 ....39 A1
Cooks Cl BS32 ....40 D3
Cooks La BS36 ....31 D3
Cooks Orch GL1 ....127 A3
Cooksley Rd BS5 ....9 C8
Cookson Terr GL15 .....84 E8
Cookspool 2 GL8 ......140 C4
Cookworthy Cl 2 BS5 ....9 B6
Coomb Dr GL14 ....191 C1
Coomb Rocke BS9 ....17 D6
Coombe Ave BS35 ....64 B2
Coombe Bridge Ave BS9 ..17 D6
Coombe Cl BS10 ....27 D3
Coombe Dale BS9 ....17 E6
Coombe Gdns Bristol BS9 ..17 E6
 Stinchcombe GL11 ....87 C3
Coombe Glen La GL51 ...129 D6
Coombe Ho BS15 ....10 E8
Coombe La Bristol BS9 ..17 E6
 Easton-in-G BS8 ....16 A1
 King's Stanley GL10 ....98 C2
Coombe Lea NP16 ....146 A5
Coombe Mead GL7 ......138 B3
Coombe Rd Bristol BS5 ..19 C2
Coombe Terr GL12 ....68 C8
Coombe Way BS10 ....27 F1
Coombes Way BS30 .....11 D4
Coombs Rd GL14 ......155 A6
Cooper Rd Bristol BS9 ..17 F7
 Thornbury BS35 ....51 B7
Cooper's Ct
 Brockworth GL3 ....120 E5
 Charlton Kings GL53 ..131 B5
Cooper's Hill* GL3 ...120 C2
Cooper's View GL3 .....120 E5
Cooperage Rd BS5 .....194 B1
Coopers Dr BS37 ....43 F5
Coopers Elm GL2 ....117 F2
Coopers Mill GL6 ....91 A6
Coopers Rd GL18 ......155 A8
Coopers Way GL18 .....171 A4
Coots The BS14 ....3 E6
Copeland Dr BS14 ....3 A5
Copenacre SN16 ....142 B1
Copford La BS41 ....7 B1
Copley Ct BS15 ....10 C5
Copley Gdns BS7 ....19 B6
Copper Beech Gr GL2 ..117 E1
Copper Beeches SN6 ...145 C3
Copperfield Ct GL14 ...119 B4
Coppice Daw Pitch
 GL19 ....165 D5
Coppice Gdns 8 GL51 ..132 F5
Coppice Hill GL16 .....148 D5
Coppice La SN16 ....141 F4
Coppice The
 Bristol,Bradley Stoke BS32 ..29 E7
 Bristol,Highridge BS13 ....1 E4
Copse Rd Bristol BS21 ..18 C1
Copse The
 Broad Blunsdon SN26 ..144 D1
 Gloucester GL4 ....119 E7
 Thornbury BS35 ....51 A5
Copseclose La GL7 .....150 C3
Copt Elm Cl GL53 .....131 C4
Copt Elm Rd GL53 .....131 A6
Coral Cl GL4 ....118 B3
Corbett Cl BS37 ....43 F4
Corbett Ho BS5 ....9 C8
Corbiere Cl GL4 ....118 B3
Corders Cl 3 GL56 .....187 A3
Cordingley Cl GL3 ....128 C5
Cordwell Wlk BS10 .....18 D7
Corey Cl 6 BS2 ....19 A1
Corfe Cl GL52 ....134 C4
Corfe Cres BS31 ....4 E5
Corfe Pl BS30 ....11 B1
Coriander Dr Bristol BS34 ..40 A7
 Innsworth GL2 ....127 F7
Corinium Ave GL4 ....127 D2
Corinium Cntr GL7 .....190 D1
Corinium Gate GL7 .....190 D5
Corinium Ho GL7 ....190 D1
Corinium Mus* GL7 ....190 C5

Corinthian Ct 9 BS1 ...195 B1
Cotswold Cl BS16 ....21 C6
Corker's Hill 9 BS5 ....9 F6
Cormorant Ave GL20 ...192 E2
Corn St BS1 ....195 A3
Corncroft La GL4 ....119 D2
Corndean La GL54 .....174 A5
Corner Farm Dr WR11 ..188 C6
Corner Rd GL15 ....155 F1
Cornfield Cl BS32 ....40 C1
Cornfield Dr
 Bishop's Cleeve GL52 ..137 E4
 Hardwicke GL2 ....109 E7
Cornfields The GL52 ...137 E4
Cornflower Cl GL20 ....192 E1
Cornflower Rd GL4 .....119 E5
Cornhill GL5 ....99 C7
Cornhill Dr BS14 ....3 A7
Cornish Cl BS14 ....3 E6
Cornish Hos
 Cinderford GL14 ....156 C6
 Moreton-in-M GL56 ...187 B3
Cornish Rd BS14 ....3 E6
Cornish Wlk BS14 ....3 E6
Cornmeadow Dr GL51 ..132 D5
Cornwall Ave GL51 ....133 A2
Cornwall Cres BS37 .....43 F3
Cornwall Rd BS7 ....18 D4
Cornwallis Ave BS8 ...194 B2
Cornwallis Cres BS8 .....7 F6
Cornwallis Ho BS8 ....194 A2
Corolin Rd GL2 ....118 B4
Coronation Ave
 Bristol BS16 ....20 A4
 Keynsham BS31 ....4 D4
Coronation Cl
 Bristol BS30 ....11 A5
 Chipping Campden GL55 ..188 F2
Coronation Flats GL52 ..131 A7
Coronation Gr GL2 .....127 B2
Coronation Pl BS1 .....195 A2
Coronation Rd
 Bristol,Cadbury Heath BS30 ..11 B5
 Bristol,Mangotsfield BS16 ..20 E5
 Bristol,Southville BS3 ...194 C1
 Bristol,Warmley BS15 ...11 A7
 Cheltenham GL52 ....134 B4
 Cinderford GL14 ....191 D3
 Stroud GL5 ....99 B6
 Tetbury GL8 ....140 B5
Coronation Sq GL51 ...132 C2
Coronation St GL7 ....192 D4
Corpus St GL52 ....193 C2
Corriett The GL11 ....88 A5
Corsby Rd GL19 ......172 B4
Corsley Wlk BS4 ....2 F8
Cossham Cl BS35 ....64 C2
Cossham Meml Hospl
 BS16 ....20 C2
Cossham Rd BS5 ....9 D7
Cossham St BS16 ....21 B5
Cossham Wlk BS5 ....20 A1
Cossington Rd BS4 ....2 F8
Cossins Rd BS6 ....18 B3
Costers Cl BS35 ....51 A5
Costiland Dr BS13 ....1 F6
Cote Bank Ho BS9 ....28 A8
Cote Dr BS9 ....18 A4
Cote House La BS9 .....18 A5
Cote La BS9 ....18 A4
Cote Lea Pk BS9 ....18 B7
Cote Pk BS9 ....17 E6
Cote Rd BS9 ....18 A4
Cotham Brow BS6 ....18 C1
Cotham Gdns 8 BS6 ....18 B1
Cotham Gr BS6 ....18 C1
Cotham Hill BS6 ....18 C1
Cotham Lawn Ho BS6 ..194 C4
Cotham Lawn Rd BS6 ..18 C1
Cotham Pk BS6 ....18 C1
Cotham Pk N BS6 ....18 C1
Cotham Pl 8 BS6 ....18 C1
Cotham Rd BS6 ....18 C1
Cotham Rd S BS6 ....195 A4
Cotham Sch BS6 ....18 C1
Cotham Side BS6 ....18 D1
Cotham Vale BS6 ....18 C1
Cothar's Pitch HR9 .....170 A5
Cothers Ct GL56 ......186 C6
Cotman Wlk BS7 ....19 C6
Cotmore Ho GL19 .....180 A8
Cotrith Gr BS10 ....27 C3
Cotshill Gdns GL56 ....187 A4
Cotswold Ave GL51 ....133 B3
Cotswold Chine Home Specl
 Sch GL6 ....126 D1
Cotswold Cl
 Bredon GL20 ....182 C7
 Brimscombe GL5 ....118 B1
 Wotton-u-E GL12 ....68 B4

Cotswold Ct BS37 44
Cotswold Ed Ctr The
 BS34 28
Cotswold Edge GL55 189
Cotswold Edge Bsns Pk
 GL2 118
Cotswold Falconry Ctr*
 GL56 186
Cotswold Farm Pk*
 GL54 175
Cotswold Gdns
 Gloucester GL2 127
 25 Moreton-in-M GL56 ..187
 Tewkesbury GL20 192
 Wotton-u-E GL12 68
Cotswold Gn GL10 98
Cotswold La BS37 254
Cotswold Lo 3 GL52 ...133
Cotswold Mdws GL54 ...169
Cotswold Mead GL6 103
Cotswold Mill GL7 190
Cotswold Pl GL20 182
Cotswold Rd Bristol BS3 ..8
 Cheltenham GL52 134
 Chipping Sodbury BS37 ..33
 Stroud GL5 98
Cotswold Sch The GL54 ..168
Cotswold Terr GL14 89
Cotswold View
 Bristol,Filton BS34 29
 Bristol,Kingswood BS15 ..20
 Charfield GL12 72
 Tirley GL19 172
 Wickwar GL12 52
 Woodmancote GL52 138
Cotswold Water Pk*
 GL7 142
Cotswold Wildlife Pk &
 Gardens* OX18 168
 Cold Ashton SN14 114
 Highworth SN6 145
Cotswolds Countryside Mus*
 GL54 167
Cotswolds Motoring Mus &
 Toy Collection The*
 GL54 168
Cotswold Water Pk*
 GL7 153
Cottage Field GL2 125
Cottage Pitch GL18 ...171
Cottage Rd BS2 195
Cottage Rake Ave GL50 ..133
Cottage The GL5 98
Cotteswold Rd
 Gloucester GL4 119
 Tewkesbury GL20 192
Cottington Ct BS15 10
Cottisford Rd BS5 19
Cottle Gdns BS14 3
Cottle Rd BS14 3
Cotton Cl GL14 119
Cotton Mead GL51 133
Cottonwood Dr BS30 ...11
Cottrell Ave BS15 20
Cottrell Rd BS5 19
Cotts The GL56 186
Coughton Pl HR9 163
Coulson Ho 2 BS7 19
Coulson Wlk BS15 20
Coulson's Cl BS14 3
Coulson's Rd BS14 3
Council Hos
 Cold Ashton GL54 168
 Eastnor HR8 179
 Ledbury HR8 179
 Stow-on-t-W GL54 168
Council Villas
 Clearwell GL16 154
 Edge End GL16 163
 English Bicknor GL16 ..163
 Sling GL16 170
Counterpool Rd GL55 ...10
Countership BS11 16
Countership Gdns GL4 ..119
Countess Wlk BS16 190
Country Choice Cvn Pk
 GL20 180
County Court Rd GL14 ..191
County Cres 5 GL1 127
County Way BS34 30
County Rd GL19 180
Court Farm Oaksey SN16 ..142
Court Farm Rd
 Bristol,Longwell Green
 BS30 10
Court Farm La
 Beckford GL20 183
 Mitcheldean GL17 164
Court Farm Mews GL10 ..97
Court Gdns
 Bristol,Whitchurch BS14 ..3
Court Field 11 GL18 ...140
Court Gdn Cl GL11 89
Court Gdns
 St Arvans NP16 72
 Westbury-on-S GL14 ..157
 Yate BS37 27
Court Gdns The GL2 ...157
Court Hay BS20 15
Court La 8 Newent GL18 ..171
 Wick BS30 11

ourt La continued
Woolaston GL15 . . . 147 D3
ourt Mdw Stone GL13 . . . 77 E3
Wotton-u-E GL12 . . . 68 C7
ourt Mead GL13 . . . 77 E3
dney GL15 . . . 92 B5
ourt Mews GL52 . . . 131 A7
ourt Orch Gretton GL54 . . . 183 E1
Wotton-u-E GL12 . . . 68 C7
ourt Pl GL14 . . . 119 D7
ourt St
Bristol,Horfield BS7 . . . 18 F6
Bristol,Kingswood BS15 . . . 10 D7
S30 . . . 11 C3
Brockworth GL3 . . . 120 E6
Cheltenham GL52 . . . 134 C4
Brampton Cotterell BS36 . . . 30 F8
Worcester GL10 . . . 97 B3
dney GL15 . . . 92 B5
Newent GL18 . . . 171 A5
Upper Strensham WR8 . . . 180 A10
ourt St SN16 . . . 58 C1
ourt View Chalford GL6 . . . 148 D6
Stonehouse GL10 . . . 97 D7
Vick BS30 . . . 12 D6
ourt View Cl BS32 . . . 40 A5
ourt Way GL5 . . . 99 A5
ourtbrook GL7 . . . 152 E3
ourtenay Cres BS4 . . . 2 D7
ourtenay Rd BS31 . . . 5 B2
ourtenay St GL50 . . . 133 D3
ourtfield Dr GL52 . . . 131 B6
ourtfield Gr BS16 . . . 20 A4
ourtfield Rd GL2 . . . 109 F8
ourthouse Gdns GL11 . . . 87 F6
ourtiers Dr GL52 . . . 138 A3
ourtlands Bristol BS32 . . . 40 C1
Keynsham BS31 . . . 4 E5
ourtlands La BS3 . . . 7 E4
ourtlands Unit BS4 . . . 2 D8
ourtney Cl GL2 . . . 192 D1
ourtney Prim Sch BS55 . . . 10 F7
ourtney Rd BS16 . . . 10 E7
ourtney Way BS15 . . . 11 A7
ourtridge Mews BS6 . . . 18 C1
ourtyard The
Bourton-on-t-W GL54 . . . 168 F8
Cheltenham GL50 . . . 193 A2
Gloucester GL1 . . . 127 A2
low-on-t-W GL54 . . . 176 F5
wkesbury GL20 . . . 182 B5
ourville Cl BS35 . . . 51 A4
ousins Cl BS10 . . . 27 D3
ousins La BS5 . . . 9 F8
ousins Mews BS4 . . . 9 F6
ousins Way BS16 . . . 21 B8
ousley Cl GL3 . . . 120 A7
ouzens Cl BS37 . . . 44 B2
ouzens Pl BS34 . . . 29 F5
ove House Gdns **3**
SN6 . . . 142 F5
oventry Cl GL2 . . . 192 D1
oventry Wlk BS4 . . . 9 F6
overham Cl GL10 **10** . . . 155 A7
overham Rd GL16 . . . 155 A7
ow La GL5 . . . 91 A6
ow St SN6 . . . 143 D1
wcombe Hill GL6 . . . 148 C5
owdray Rd BS4 . . . 9 E7
owhorn Hill BS30 . . . 11 C4
owl La GL54 . . . 174 A7
owler Wlk BS13 . . . 1 F4
owley Cl GL51 . . . 129 E7
owley La HR9 . . . 170 C2
owley Rd BS14 . . . 118 E3
owling Dr BS14 . . . 3 C5
owling Rd BS14 . . . 3 D5
owlsmead GL51 . . . 129 E2
owper Rd Bristol BS6 . . . 18 C1
Cheltenham GL51 . . . 132 E1
owper St BS5 . . . 9 C7
owship La GL12 . . . 53 D6
owslip Mdw GL52 . . . 138 B3
owswell La GL6 . . . 148 B6
ox Ct BS30 . . . 10 F4
ox's Hill SN6 . . . 142 F5
ox's Way Bream GL15 . . . 155 D1
Gloucester GL2 . . . 120 A6
oxbury & Wyegate La
GL15 . . . 154 D2
oxgrove Hill BS16 . . . 21 F7
oxmoor Cl OX7 . . . 177 F2
oxmore Cl GL2 . . . 120 A7
oxwell Ct GL7 . . . 190 C5
oxwell St GL7 . . . 190 C5
ozens La GL7 . . . 190 C4
rab Tree Pl GL50 . . . 133 C3
ozens La BS41 . . . 1 D1
rabtree La
Cirencester GL7 . . . 190 F3
Dundry BS41 . . . 1 D2
Duntisbourne Abbots GL7 . . . 107 B3
rabtree Rd GL7 . . . 107 B4
rabtree Rd GL14 . . . 191 B5
rabtree Wlk BS5 . . . 19 D2
raddock Ct GL6 . . . 90 F5
raddock Ct **7** GL18 . . . 171 A4
radock Ct BS30 . . . 11 A6
ranbourne Cl GL7 . . . 68 C7
ranbourne Rd BS34 . . . 28 F7
ranbrook Rd BS6 . . . 18 C3
randell Cl BS10 . . . 27 F4
rane Cl BS15 . . . 11 B8
rane Furlong SN6 . . . 145 D4

Cranford Cl GL52 . . . 138 C3
Cranford Ct **1** BS9 . . . 18 B6
Cranham BS37 . . . 32 C7
Cranham CE Prim Sch
GL4 . . . 112 C6
Cranham Cl Bristol BS15 . . . 20 F2
6 Gloucester GL4 . . . 119 E5
Cranham Dr BS34 . . . 40 C1
Cranham La GL3 . . . 128 D3
Cranham Rd Bristol BS10 . . . 18 C8
Cheltenham GL52 . . . 133 F1
Cranhams La GL7 . . . 190 B2
Cranleigh Court Inf Sch
BS37 . . . 43 D2
Cranleigh Gdns BS9 . . . 17 E4
Cranleigh Rd BS14 . . . 3 B5
Cranley GL50 . . . 133 E3
Cranmoor Gn BS35 . . . 38 D6
Cranmore Ave BS31 . . . 4 E6
Cranmore Cres BS10 . . . 28 D1
Cranside Ave BS6 . . . 18 C4
Cransley Cres BS9 . . . 18 C2
Crantock Ave BS13 . . . 18 C4
Crantock Dr BS32 . . . 40 B5
Crantock Rd BS37 . . . 43 D1
Cranwell Cl GL4 . . . 119 C4
Cranwell Gr BS14 . . . 3 A5
Crapen The GL11 . . . 87 E4
Crashmore La GL12 . . . 182 F7
Crates Cl BS15 . . . 10 E8
Craven Cl BS30 . . . 10 F5
Craven Dr GL3 . . . 128 B6
Craven Way BS30 . . . 10 F5
Crawley Hill GL11 . . . 89 B3
Crawley La GL11 . . . 89 B3
Crawshay Pl GL14 . . . 191 C4
Craydon Gr BS14 . . . 3 D4
Craydon Rd BS14 . . . 3 D4
Craydon Wlk BS14 . . . 3 D5
Crease The **16** GL18 . . . 171 A4
Crediton Cres BS14 . . . 3 B4
Credon Rd GL3 . . . 127 E1
Crescent Cl
Coleford GL16 . . . 155 A6
Stonehouse GL10 . . . 97 E6
Crescent Pl GL50 . . . 193 B3
Crescent Rd Bristol BS16 . . . 20 C6
Stonehouse GL10 . . . 97 E6
Crescent Terr GL50 . . . 193 B3
Crescent The
5 Berry Hill GL16 . . . 155 A7
Bristol BS16 . . . 29 F1
Bristol,Frenchay BS16 . . . 29 F1
Bristol,Henleaze BS9 . . . 18 C6
Bristol,Sea Mills BS9 . . . 17 C6
Bristol,Upper Soundwell
BS16 . . . 20 D6
Brockworth GL3 . . . 148 E6
Coleford GL16 . . . 155 A5
Coleford,Baker's Hill
GL16 . . . 155 A6
Dursley GL11 . . . 87 D4
Mitcheldean GL17 . . . 164 D6
Newton GL13 . . . 85 D8
Northwood Green GL14 . . . 165 D3
Olveston BS35 . . . 50 D4
Wick BS30 . . . 12 C7
Crescentdale GL2 . . . 127 A5
Crest The Bristol BS4 . . . 9 C2
West Kington SN14 . . . 25 F3
Crest Way GL4 . . . 119 F2
Creswicke Ave BS15 . . . 10 C5
Creswicke Rd BS4 . . . 2 E7
Crew's Hole Rd BS5 . . . 9 E7
Cribbs Causeway Ctr
BS34 . . . 28 A6
Cribbs Cswy BS10 . . . 28 A6
Cricket La BS10 . . . 18 A8
Cricklade Mus* SN6 . . . 143 F4
Cricklade Rd Bristol BS7 . . . 18 E8
Cirencester GL7 . . . 190 E2
Highworth SN6 . . . 145 C3
Purton Stoke SN5 . . . 143 E1
Cricklade St
Cirencester GL7 . . . 190 C4
Poulton GL7 . . . 151 E3
Crickley Hill Ctry Pk*
GL4 . . . 122 A5
Crickley Hill Ctry Pk Visitor
Ctr* GL4 . . . 121 F5
Criftycraft La GL3 . . . 128 C3
Crippetts La GL51 . . . 130 B3
Cripps Rd BS13 . . . 18 C5
Crispin Ct GL7 . . . 190 C4
Crispin Cl Gloucester GL2 . . . 127 C5
1 Winchcombe GL54 . . . 174 A7
Crispin Cl **4** BS35 . . . 64 B1
Crispin Rd GL54 . . . 174 A7
Crispin Way GL15 . . . 78 A1
Critchford La GL54 . . . 175 A5
Crock Mead GL4 . . . 119 E4
Crockerne CE Prim Sch
BS20 . . . 16 C4
Crockerne Dr BS20 . . . 16 C4
Crockerne Ho BS20 . . . 16 C4
Croft Ave Bristol BS16 . . . 19 C4
Charlton Kings GL53 . . . 131 B5
Croft Cl Bitton BS30 . . . 5 D8
Churchdown GL3 . . . 128 B8
Newent GL18 . . . 171 A5
Croft Cotts GL7 . . . 142 C6
Croft Dr GL53 . . . 13 B5
Croft Farm Leisure & Water
Pk* GL20 . . . 182 A6

Croft Gdns
8 Broadway WR12 . . . 185 B8
Charlton Kings GL53 . . . 131 B4
Croft Holm GL56 . . . 187 B3
Croft La **12** Fairford GL7 . . . 152 E4
Latton SN6 . . . 143 E6
Winstone GL7 . . . 107 A7
Croft Par GL53 . . . 131 B5
Croft Rd
Charlton Kings GL53 . . . 131 A5
Newent GL18 . . . 171 A5
Croft Sch The GL6 . . . 103 E8
Croft St GL53 . . . 130 D6
Croft The
Bristol,Mangotsfield BS16 . . . 20 C5
Bristol,Oldland Common
BS30 . . . 11 C3
Cirencester GL7 . . . 190 D4
Dursley GL11 . . . 88 A4
14 Fairford GL7 . . . 152 E4
Painswick GL6 . . . 111 F1
Croft Thorne Cl GL51 . . . 129 F5
Croft View BS9 . . . 18 C6
Crofters Wlk GL7 . . . 29 D8
Croftlands The GL20 . . . 182 C7
Crofton Ave BS7 . . . 18 E8
Crofton Fields BS36 . . . 30 E6
Crofton Mews BS15 . . . 10 C6
Crofts End Ind Est BS5 . . . 19 E1
Crofts End Rd BS5 . . . 19 E1
Crofts Field GL20 . . . 181 D5
Crofts The GL18 . . . 171 A5
Crokeswood Wlk BS11 . . . 27 A1
Crome Rd BS7 . . . 19 A8
Cromer Rd BS5 . . . 19 C2
Cromers Cl GL20 . . . 182 C5
Cromhall La GL12 . . . 65 D1
Cromwell Ct BS15 . . . 10 E5
Cromwell Rd
Bristol,Montpelier BS6 . . . 18 C2
Bristol,St George BS5 . . . 10 A8
Cheltenham GL52 . . . 134 A3
Chepstow/Cas-Gwent NP16 . . . 140 F1
Cromwell St Bristol BS3 . . . 8 C3
Gloucester GL1 . . . 196 B2
Cromwell View BS6 . . . 18 C2
Cromwells Hide BS16 . . . 19 E5
Crookes Rd End Pl GL17 . . . 163 F4
Crookes Ind Est GL53 . . . 130 D6
Croomes Hill BS16 . . . 20 C5
Cropthorne Rd BS7 . . . 29 A1
Cropthorne Road S BS7 . . . 19 A8
Crosby Cl GL3 . . . 120 B6
Crosby Row BS8 . . . 194 A2
Cross Barn GL16 . . . 163 B2
Cross Chambers GL15 . . . 147 F5
Cross Combe Dr BS13 . . . 2 B3
Cross Combe Wlk BS13 . . . 2 B3
Cross Cotts GL13 . . . 76 C3
Cross Elms La BS9 . . . 17 E5
Cross Farm Cl GL15 . . . 147 E4
Cross Hands GL15 . . . 92 C4
Cross Hands Rd BS35 . . . 38 D7
Cross Keys GL14 . . . 166 B3
Cross Keys La BS13 . . . 14 A5
Cross Keys Rd Bd **1** GL2 . . . 109 E4
Cross Lanes BS20 . . . 16 C4
Cross St Bristol BS15 . . . 20 D1
Keynsham BS31 . . . 4 E4
Cross The
Bromesberrow Heath HR8 . . . 179 B4
Horsley GL6 . . . 90 F1
Nympsfield GL10 . . . 89 E6
Ripple GL20 . . . 181 D8
Cross Tree Cres GL7 . . . 144 E8
Cross Tree Flats GL7 . . . 144 E7
Cross Tree Gr BS32 . . . 29 D8
Cross Vane NP25 . . . 154 B3
Cross Wlk BS14 . . . 3 A6
Crossfield Rd BS16 . . . 20 C3
Crossfields GL54 . . . 166 D6
Crossing La SN16 . . . 142 C2
Crossleaze Rd GL54 . . . 166 A2
Crossley Cl BS36 . . . 30 F7
Crossman Ave BS36 . . . 30 E7
Crossways Coleford GL16 . . . 154 F6
Lower Wick GL11 . . . 78 F8
Crossways Jun & Inf Schs
BS35 . . . 64 D1
Crossways La BS35 . . . 64 D1
Crossways Rd Bristol BS4 . . . 9 A1
Thornbury BS35 . . . 64 D1
Crouch Cl GL20 . . . 192 C3
Crow Ash **9** GL16 . . . 155 A7
Crow Ash Rd GL16 . . . 155 A7
Crow La E Bristol BS1 . . . 195 A2
Henbury BS10 . . . 27 F4
Crow Mdw GL12 . . . 67 F4
Crowfield GL52 . . . 138 B4
Crowfield La GL54 . . . 178 E2
Crowgate La GL4 . . . 157 F8
Crowley Way BS11 . . . 26 B1
Crown Cl
Bishop's Cleeve GL52 . . . 137 F3
Dymock GL18 . . . 178 D2
Crown Cotts GL53 . . . 98 F8
Crown Ct GL10 . . . 98 A3
Crown Dr GL52 . . . 137 F2
Crown Gdns BS30 . . . 11 B7
Crown Hill BS5 . . . 19 C1
Crown Hill Wlk BS5 . . . 19 C2
Crown Ind Est BS30 . . . 11 C7
Crown La Bristol BS16 . . . 20 D1
Parkend GL15 . . . 155 C2
St Briavels GL15 . . . 146 E7
Yorkley GL15 . . . 156 A1
Crown Mdw **13** GL16 . . . 155 B5

Crown Rd
Bristol,Upper Soundwell
BS15 . . . 20 D2
Bristol,Warmley BS30 . . . 11 C6
Crown Way BS30 . . . 11 C7
Crowndale Rd BS4 . . . 9 A3
Crownleaze BS16 . . . 20 D3
Crows Gr BS32 . . . 40 D3
Crowther Pk BS7 . . . 19 A4
Crowther Rd BS7 . . . 19 A4
Crowther St **4** BS3 . . . 8 B3
Croydon Ho **1** BS5 . . . 9 B8
Croydon St BS5 . . . 9 B8
Crucible Cl GL16 . . . 155 A5
Crucible Cl GL16 . . . 155 A5
Crudwell CE Prim Sch
SN16 . . . 141 C3
Crudwell La GL8 . . . 140 F3
Crump Pl GL15 . . . 92 C2
Crumps Cotts GL20 . . . 183 B6
Crunnis The BS32 . . . 29 E6
Crusty La BS20 . . . 16 C5
Crypt Ct GL4 . . . 118 C3
Crypt Sch The GL2 . . . 118 D4
Crypt The GL18 . . . 178 D2
Crystal Way BS32 . . . 29 E8
Crythan Wlk **4** GL51 . . . 129 F5
Cuckoo Cl **4** GL6 . . . 148 C6
Cuckoo La BS36 . . . 30 F3
Cuckoo Row GL6 . . . 91 F6
Cud La GL16 . . . 103 B8
Cudnall St GL53 . . . 131 A7
Cuffington Ave BS4 . . . 9 D4
Culkerton GL8 . . . 140 F6
Cullens The SN6 . . . 145 D3
Culleysgate La BS30 . . . 12 F6
Cullimore View GL14 . . . 191 C1
Cullinghamn Cl GL19 . . . 172 A8
Culls La GL16 . . . 155 B6
Culls Mdw GL16 . . . 184 A4
Culross Cl GL50 . . . 133 E4
Culver Hill GL5 . . . 91 A8
Culver St BS1 . . . 194 C2
Newent GL18 . . . 171 A4
Culverhay
1 Cricklade SN6 . . . 143 E4
Wotton-u-E GL12 . . . 68 B7
Culverhill Rd BS37 . . . 44 A1
Culverhill Sch GL2 . . . 32 D7
Culvers Cl BS31 . . . 4 E6
Culvers Rd BS31 . . . 4 E6
Culvert The BS32 . . . 29 D8
Culverwell Rd BS13 . . . 1 F4
Cumberland Basin Rd BS8 . . . 7 F5
Cumberland Cl BS1 . . . 194 A1
Cumberland Cres GL51 . . . 133 A2
Cumberland Gr **5** BS6 . . . 18 F2
Cumberland Pl **7** BS8 . . . 7 A6
Cumberland St BS2 . . . 195 B4
Cumbria Cl BS35 . . . 64 E1
Cumming Ct GL52 . . . 134 A4
Cunningham Gdns BS16 . . . 20 B5
Cunnington Cl BS30 . . . 11 B1
Cupola Cl GL16 . . . 155 A5
Curland Gr BS14 . . . 3 B5
Curlew Cl Bristol BS16 . . . 19 F6
Northway GL20 . . . 182 B5
Curlew Rd GL4 . . . 119 C6
Cursey La GL51 . . . 136 B5
Cursey Lane Cvn Site
GL51 . . . 173 F7
Cursus The GL7 . . . 153 E3
Curtis Hayward Dr GL2 . . . 117 E1
Curtis La BS34 . . . 30 A4
Custom Cl BS14 . . . 3 A7
Custom Ho The BS1 . . . 195 A1
Cut & Fry Rd GL15 . . . 156 A1
Cut Throat La HR9 . . . 170 A2
Cutham La GL4 . . . 158 C1
Cuthline Pl GL7 . . . 153 E3
Cutler Rd Bristol BS13 . . . 1 F6
Stroud GL5 . . . 99 D8
Cutsdean Cl GL52 . . . 137 D4
Cutsheath Rd GL12 . . . 52 C8
Cutters Row BS3 . . . 8 E4
Cutwell GL8 . . . 140 B3
Cylde Pk BS6 . . . 18 B2
Cynder Way BS16 . . . 31 A1
Cypress Ct BS9 . . . 17 D3
Cypress Gdns Bristol BS8 . . . 7 E6
Gloucester GL2 . . . 127 D5
Cypress Gr BS9 . . . 18 C6
Cypress Rd GL20 . . . 192 E2
Cypress Wlk SN14 . . . 15 F6
Cyrus Ct BS16 . . . 31 B7

D

Daffodil Cl GL4 . . . 119 E5
Daffodil Leaze GL10 . . . 98 B3
Daffodil St GL50 . . . 193 B2
Daffodils The GL10 . . . 98 B3
Daglingworth Path GL7 . . . 149 E6
Dagmar Rd BS3 . . . 193 A1
Daines Ct **4** BS16 . . . 19 E3
Dainty St GL1 . . . 118 F7
Dairy Farm SN6 . . . 142 F4
Dairy La WR11 . . . 183 E6
Dairycroft BS2 . . . 195 B4
Daisy Bank GL5 . . . 99 C6
Daisy Green La GL12 . . . 79 D2
Daisy Rd BS5 . . . 19 C1
Daisybank Rd GL53 . . . 130 E2
Dakin Cl BS4 . . . 8 E1

Dakota Dr BS14 . . . 3 A4
Dalby Ave BS3 . . . 8 D4
Daldry Gdns BS35 . . . 50 A3
Dale Cl GL4 . . . 118 F5
Dale St Bristol,St George BS5 . . . 9 F8
Bristol,St Pauls BS2 . . . 195 C4
Temple Gating GL54 . . . 175 D2
Dale Wlk GL52 . . . 138 A3
Dalebrook HR9 . . . 170 B4
Dalkeith Ave BS15 . . . 20 C1
Dallaway GL5 . . . 99 E2
Dalrymple Rd **10** BS2 . . . 18 E1
Dalston Rd BS3 . . . 8 B3
Dalton Sq BS2 . . . 195 B4
Damery La Stone GL13 . . . 77 F3
Woodford GL13 . . . 78 A4
Damery Works GL13 . . . 78 B3
Dampier Rd BS3 . . . 8 A3
Damsells The **9** GL8 . . . 140 C4
Damson Cl GL4 . . . 119 E4
Danbury Cres BS10 . . . 28 C1
Danbury Wlk BS10 . . . 28 C1
Danby Cl Cinderford GL14 . . . 191 E4
Yorkley GL15 . . . 156 B2
Danby Ho BS7 . . . 19 A5
Danby Wlk GL15 . . . 156 B2
Dancers Hill GL4 . . . 119 E6
Dancey Mead BS13 . . . 1 F6
Dancey Rd GL3 . . . 127 F6
Dancing Gn HR9 . . . 164 A7
Dane Cl GL2 . . . 127 C5
Dane La GL7 . . . 149 B6
Danes Cl BS31 . . . 5 A2
Danes Hill NP16 . . . 61 B7
Danford La GL19 . . . 172 B3
Danford Villas GL19 . . . 172 B3
Dangerfield Ave BS13 . . . 1 F6
Daniels Ind Est GL6 . . . 98 F5
Daniels Mdw GL14 . . . 118 A2
Daniels Rd GL5 . . . 99 F7
Danwood Cl GL14 . . . 118 D7
Dapps Hill BS31 . . . 4 F5
Dapwell La BS14,BS31 . . . 4 A1
Darell Cl GL2 . . . 109 F7
Darell Gdns GL12 . . . 127 D6
Dark La Chalford GL6 . . . 148 C5
Nailsworth GL6 . . . 91 A4
North Cerney GL7 . . . 158 E3
Stroud GL5 . . . 99 B5
Swindon GL51 . . . 133 A7
Dark Ride GL7 . . . 149 C8
Darken La GL15 . . . 147 E4
Darks Rd GL18 . . . 170 C2
Darley Cl BS10 . . . 27 D3
Darleydale Cl GL2 . . . 109 D8
Darnell's La HR9 . . . 170 B4
Darnley Ave BS7 . . . 18 F6
Darren Rd **13** GL16 . . . 155 A7
Dart Cl Quedgeley GL2 . . . 117 F2
Thornbury BS35 . . . 51 B8
Dart Rd GL2 . . . 125 A5
Dartford Ave GL51 . . . 92 A2
Dartmoor St BS3 . . . 8 B3
Dartmouth Wlk BS31 . . . 4 D4
Darwin Cl GL51 . . . 129 C8
Darwin Rd GL4 . . . 119 A5
Daston Ct **2** WR12 . . . 185 C8
Daubeny Cl BS16 . . . 20 B5
Daubeny Ct BS1 . . . 194 B1
Davallia Dr GL51 . . . 129 F5
Daventry Rd BS4 . . . 8 F1
Daventry Terr GL51 . . . 196 C1
Davey Cl GL2 . . . 120 D8
Davey Rd GL20 . . . 182 C4
Davey St BS2 . . . 18 F1
David French Ct GL51 . . . 130 A5
David St BS2 . . . 195 C3
David Thomas Ho BS6 . . . 18 E2
David's La BS35 . . . 51 A4
Davids Ct BS35 . . . 51 A4
Davies Dr BS4 . . . 9 F5
Davies Rd **1** GL56 . . . 187 B3
Davillian Ct GL2 . . . 50 B5
Davin Cres BS20 . . . 16 C3
Davis Cl BS30 . . . 10 F5
Davis Ct BS35 . . . 64 C2
Davis St BS11 . . . 16 B8
Davron Ct BS3 . . . 8 E4
Dawes Cl
Meysey Hampton GL7 . . . 152 A3
Southrop GL7 . . . 153 C6
Dawes Ct **3** BS8 . . . 7 F6
Dawes The GL2 . . . 109 F8
Dawley Cl BS36 . . . 30 E7
Dawlish Rd BS3 . . . 8 D2
Dawn Rise BS15 . . . 11 A3
Dawneys The SN16 . . . 141 C3
Daws Ct BS16 . . . 20 A4
Day House La GL2 . . . 55 C8
Day's Gdns GL16 . . . 186 C5
Day's Rd BS2 . . . 195 C2
Daylesford Cl GL51 . . . 129 D8
Days Ct SN16 . . . 141 A4
Days Road Commercial Ctr
BS2 . . . 9 A7
De Clifford Rd BS11 . . . 27 C2
De Ferrieres Wlk **12**
GL51 . . . 132 D2
De Havilland Rd GL54 . . . 169 D7
De La Warre Ct **11** BS4 . . . 9 F5
De Verose Ct GL14 . . . 10 E4
Deacon Cl
Cheltenham GL51 . . . 129 F7

Deacon Cl *continued*
 Winterbourne BS36 . . . . .30 E5
Deacons Pl GL52 . . . . . . .137 E2
Deakin Cl GL51 . . . . .133 B7
Deakin's Ho GL15 . . . . . . .155 E2
Dean Ave BS35 . . . . .64 C2
Dean Cl BS15 . . . . .10 B4
Dean Close Prep Sch
 GL51 . . . . .130 A8
Dean Close Sch GL51 . . . .129 F8
Dean Cres **8** Bristol BS3 . . .8 C4
 1 Bristol BS3 . . . . .8 D4
 Littledean GL14 . . . . .156 E8
Dean Ct Lydney GL15 . . . . .92 B5
 Yate BS37 . . . . .43 C3
Dean Farm Cotts GL7 . . . .160 F2
Dean Forest Railway Mus*
 GL15 . . . . .147 F7
Dean Forest Rly* GL15 . . . .92 A2
Dean Hall Sch GL16 . . . . .155 F6
Dean Heritage Mus*
 GL14 . . . . .156 D5
Dean La Bristol BS3 . . . . . . .8 C4
 Stoke Orchard GL52 . . . . .136 E5
Dean Mdws GL17 . . . . . . .164 D5
Dean Rd Avonmouth BS11 . .26 C5
 Newnham GL14 . . . . .156 F6
 Yate BS37 . . . . .43 C3
Dean Rise GL14 . . . . .156 F6
Dean St
 Bristol,Southville BS3 . . . . .8 C4
 Bristol,St Pauls BS2 . . . . .195 B4
Dean Swift Cl HR9 . . . . . .162 F6
Dean The HR9 . . . . .163 E6
Dean View GL14 . . . . .191 C1
Dean's Ct BS11 . . . . .194 C2
Dean's Dr BS5 . . . . .20 A2
Dean's Quarry GL5 . . . . . . .91 F7
Dean's Terr GL1 . . . . .196 B4
Dean's Way GL1 . . . . .196 B4
Dean's Wlk GL1 . . . . .196 B4
Dean's Wlk GL17 . . . . . . .164 B4
Deanery Cl BS15 . . . . .11 B8
Deanery Rd
 Bristol,Warmley BS15 . . . . .11 B8
 Bristol,Brandon Hill BS1 . .194 C2
Deanery Rd Rdbt BS15 . . . .11 B8
Deanhill La GL1 . . . . .6 F2
Deanna Ct BS16 . . . . .20 E6
Deans Ct **3** GL51 . . . . . .129 F7
Deans Hill NP16 . . . . .60 D8
Deans Mead BS11 . . . . .17 A8
Deans Row GL1 . . . . .126 E4
Deans Way GL52 . . . . .137 F3
Deansfield SN6 . . . . .143 E4
Debecca's La BS20 . . . . . . .16 B4
Deep Coombe Rd BS3 . . . . .8 A2
Deep Pit Rd BS5 . . . . .19 F2
Deep St GL52 . . . . .134 B4
Deer Park Rd GL3 . . . . . . .128 A1
Deer Pk GL15 . . . . .156 A2
Deer's Wood Sch BS15 . . . .12 A2
Deerhurst Bristol BS15 . . . .20 E3
 Yate BS37 . . . . .32 C8
Deerhurst & Apperley CE
 Prim Sch GL19 . . . . .173 C7
Deerhurst Cl
 Gloucester GL4 . . . . .119 E4
 Little Compton GL56 . . . . .187 F1
Deerhurst Pl GL2 . . . . .117 E1
Deering Cl BS11 . . . . .27 B1
Deerswood BS15 . . . . .21 A2
Dehaviland Rd GL52 . . . . .137 E1
Delabere Ave BS16 . . . . . . .20 B5
Delabere Rd GL52 . . . . . . .138 A2
Delancey Hospl GL53 . . . .130 D4
Delavale Rd GL54 . . . . . . .174 A7
Deleware Rd GL7 . . . . .152 E2
Delius Gr BS4 . . . . .2 D7
Delkin Rd GL11 . . . . .87 F4
Delkin The GL11 . . . . .87 F4
Dell Prim Sch The NP16 . . .72 E1
Dell The Blockley GL56 . . . .186 C6
 Bredon GL20 . . . . .182 C8
 Bristol,Bradley Stoke BS32 . .29 E7
 Bristol,Oldland Common
 BS30 . . . . .11 C5
 Bristol,Westbury on Trym
 BS9 . . . . .17 F5
 Gloucester GL4 . . . . .119 E7
Dell View NP16 . . . . .60 E8
Delmont Gr GL5 . . . . .99 C8
Delphinium Dr GL52 . . . . .137 E3
Delta Dr GL20 . . . . .136 A3
Delta Way GL3 . . . . .120 C6
Delvin Rd BS10 . . . . .18 C8
Denbigh Dr NP16 . . . . .61 A5
Denbigh Rd GL51 . . . . . . .129 E6
Denbigh St BS2 . . . . .18 F1
Dene Cl BS31 . . . . .4 F3
Dene Magna Sch GL17 . .164 D4
Dene Rd BS14 . . . . .3 C4
Denehurst GL17 . . . . .163 F3
Denfurlong Farm Trail*
 GL54 . . . . .159 B5
Denham Cl
 Gloucester GL4 . . . . .118 C1
 Woodmancote GL52 . . . . .138 C3
Denleigh Cl BS14 . . . . .3 A4
Denley Cl GL52 . . . . .137 F2
Denmark Ave BS1 . . . . . . .194 C2
Denmark Ct GL1 . . . . .127 A3
Denmark Dr NP16 . . . . .61 B7
Denmark Pl BS7 . . . . .18 E3

Denmark Rd GL1 . . . . .196 C4
Denmark St BS1 . . . . .194 C2
Denmark Villas GL14 . . . .165 F1
Deming Ct GL50 . . . . .193 A1
Dennisworth BS16 . . . . .22 B5
Dennor Pk BS14 . . . . .3 B7
Denny Isle Dr BS35 . . . . . . .38 A6
Denston Wlk BS13 . . . . .2 A7
Dent's La GL19 . . . . .172 B2
Dent's Terr **3** GL54 . . . . .174 A7
Denton Patch BS16 . . . . . .21 B7
Dentwood Gr BS9 . . . . .17 B8
Denvale Trad Pk BS4 . . . . . .2 E7
Denys Ct BS35 . . . . .50 A3
Derby Ct GL1 . . . . .127 A1
Derby Rd Bristol BS7 . . . . .18 E3
 Gloucester GL1 . . . . .127 A1
Derby St BS5 . . . . .9 D7
Derham Rd BS13 . . . . .2 A5
Dermot St **1** BS2 . . . . . . .18 F1
Derrick Rd BS15 . . . . .10 D8
Derricke Rd BS14 . . . . .3 F6
Derry Pk SN16 . . . . .142 E1
Derry Rd BS3 . . . . .8 B2
Derry The SN6 . . . . .143 D4
Derwent Cl Bristol BS34 . . .29 A8
 Brockworth GL3 . . . . .120 E5
Derwent Ct BS35 . . . . .51 D8
Derwent Dr GL20 . . . . . . .192 E6
Derwent Gr BS31 . . . . .5 A5
Derwent Rd BS5 . . . . .19 F1
Derwent Wlk **1** GL51 . . .129 F7
Desford Cl GL4 . . . . .119 F5
Despenser Rd GL20 . . . . .192 C2
Detmore Cl GL53 . . . . .131 D5
Devaney Cl BS4 . . . . .9 F5
Devauden Rd NP16 . . . . . . .72 B7
Devereaux Cres GL5 . . . . . .98 C7
Devereaux Rd GL5 . . . . . . .98 C7
Deveron Gr BS31 . . . . .5 A4
Devil's Chy* GL53 . . . . . . .130 D1
Devil's Elbow The GL6 . . . . .91 E4
Devil's La GL12 . . . . .67 A2
Devon Ave GL51 . . . . .133 A2
Devon Gr BS5 . . . . .9 C8
Devon Rd BS5 . . . . .19 C1
Devon Road Trad Est **1**
 BS5 . . . . .19 C1
Devonshire Bldgs BS3 . . . . .8 E4
Devonshire Pl GL20 . . . . . .192 C2
Devonshire Rd BS6 . . . . . . .18 B4
Devonshire St GL50 . . . . .193 A4
Devonshire Terr **2**
 GL56 . . . . .187 A3
Dewey Cl GL52 . . . . .138 B3
Dewfalls Dr BS32 . . . . .40 D1
Dial La BS16 . . . . .20 D6
Diamond Rd BS5 . . . . .9 F7
Diamond St BS3 . . . . .8 C3
Diamonite Ind Pk BS16 . . .20 A3
Diana Gdns GL3 . . . . .29 E8
Dianas Cl GL4 . . . . .119 F6
Dibden Cl BS16 . . . . .21 A8
Dibden La Alderton GL24 . .183 E4
 Bristol BS16 . . . . .21 B7
Dibden Rd BS16 . . . . .21 A7
Dickens Cl Bristol BS7 . . . .19 A8
 Gloucester GL4 . . . . .118 F5
Dickens Mews GL4 . . . . . .119 E4
Didbrook Mews GL4 . . . . .119 E4
Didbrook Prim Sch
 GL54 . . . . .184 D2
Didsbury Cl BS10 . . . . .27 F1
Digbeth St **10** GL54 . . . .176 F4
Digby Dr GL20 . . . . .192 E6
Dighton Ct **3** BS2 . . . . . .195 A4
Dighton Gate BS34 . . . . . .29 E5
Dighton St BS2 . . . . .195 A4
Dikler Cl GL54 . . . . .169 A6
Dikler Cl BS13 . . . . .2 B3
Dill Ave GL51 . . . . .132 E4
Dillon Cl **3** GL54 . . . . .9 D7
Dimore Cl GL2 . . . . .109 E7
Dinas Cl GL51 . . . . .129 F6
Dinas Rd GL51 . . . . .129 F6
Dinely St GL1 . . . . .196 C1
Dingle Bglws GL53 . . . . . .158 A8
Dingle Cl BS9 . . . . .17 C6
Dinglewell GL3 . . . . .119 E7
Dinglewell Inf Sch GL3 . . .119 F7
Dinglewell Jun Sch GL3 . . .119 F7
Dinglewood Cl BS9 . . . . . .17 D7
Dings Wlk **4** BS2 . . . . .9 A6
Discovery Rd GL4 . . . . . . .118 C1
Distel Cl GL50 . . . . .133 C5
District Ctr BS32 . . . . .29 E8
Ditch La GL7 . . . . .159 E3
Dixon Bsns Ctr BS4 . . . . . . .9 F2
Dixon Rd BS4 . . . . .9 F2
Dixton Cl NP25 . . . . .154 A8
Dixton Rd NP25 . . . . .154 A8
Dock Gate La BS8 . . . . . . .194 A1
Dock La GL20 . . . . .182 C8
Dock Rd GL13 . . . . .93 B1
Dockham Rd GL14 . . . . . . .191 D4
Docks Hill Way GL17 . . . . .164 D4
Doctors La **3** GL54 . . . . .168 A1
Dodding Ash BS37 . . . . . . .33 B7
Dodington Ct GL4 . . . . . . .119 D7
Dodington La BS37 . . . . . . .33 C1
Dodington Rd BS37 . . . . . . .33 B7

Dodisham Wlk BS16 . . . . . .20 B6
Dog La GL3 . . . . .121 D5
Dog Trap La SN16 . . . . . . .142 C1
Dollar St GL7 . . . . .190 C5
Dolman Cl BS10 . . . . .27 F3
Domby Cl **18** GL16 . . . . . .155 A5
Domestic Fowl Trust*
 WR11 . . . . .188 C7
Dominion Rd BS16 . . . . . . .19 F3
Donald Rd BS13 . . . . .1 F7
Doncaster Rd BS10 . . . . . . .18 C8
Doncombe Hill SN14 . . . . .15 F7
Doncombe La SN14 . . . . . .15 F7
Donegal Rd BS4 . . . . .8 D1
Dongola Ave BS7 . . . . .18 E4
Dongola Rd BS7 . . . . .18 E4
Donkey Field The GL7 . . . .151 C5
Donkey La GL56 . . . . .186 C5
Donnington Wlk BS31 . . . . .4 D4
Donside GL7 . . . . .190 A7
Doone Rd BS7 . . . . .18 F8
Dora Wlk **6** GL1 . . . . . . .118 F7
Dorcas Ave BS34 . . . . .29 F5
Dorchester Ct GL50 . . . . .130 C6
Dorchester Rd BS7 . . . . . . .19 A7
Dorian Cl BS7 . . . . .28 C4
Dorian Ct BS7 . . . . .18 E8
Dorian Rd BS7 . . . . .18 E8
Dorian Way BS7 . . . . .18 E8
Dorington Ct **6** GL6 . . . . .148 B6
Dorington Wlk **13** GL51 . .132 D2
Dormer Cl BS36 . . . . .31 D6
Dormer Rd Bristol BS5 . . . .19 F1
 Gloucester GL51 . . . . . . .132 F4
Dormers The SN6 . . . . . . .145 D3
Dorn GL56 . . . . .187 A5
Dorney Rd GL1 . . . . .118 E7
Dorrit Cl GL1 . . . . .118 F6
Dorset Ave GL51 . . . . .133 A2
Dorset Gr **9** BS2 . . . . .19 A2
Dorset Rd **2** GL50 . . . . . .193 A4
Dorset Rd
 Bristol,Kingswood BS15 . . .20 D1
 Bristol,Westbury on Trym
 BS9 . . . . .18 B6
Dorset St **3** BS3 . . . . .8 B3
Dorset Way BS37 . . . . .44 A3
Double View GL14 . . . . . . .191 D3
Doubledays **7** SN6 . . . . . .143 E4
Doudney Ct BS3 . . . . .8 F4
 Salford BS31 . . . . .4 E4
Doughmeadow Cotts
 WR12 . . . . .184 F6
Douglas Rd
 Bristol,Horfield BS7 . . . . . .18 F7
 Bristol,Kingswood BS15 . . .10 D7
Douglas Road Ind Pk
 BS15 . . . . .10 D7
Doulton Way BS14 . . . . .3 B5
Douro Lo GL50 . . . . .193 A2
Douro Rd GL50 . . . . .133 B1
Dove La
 Bristol,Russell Town BS5 . . .9 C7
 Bristol,St Pauls BS2 . . . . .195 C4
Dove St BS2 . . . . .195 A4
Dove St S BS2 . . . . .195 A4
Dovecote BS37 . . . . .27 D8
Dovedale BS35 . . . . .51 D8
Dovedale Cl GL2 . . . . .109 D8
Dovel Way BS13 . . . . .2 A4
Dover Hay GL55 . . . . .129 F5
Dover Pl BS8 . . . . .194 B3
Dover's View GL55 . . . . . .188 D4
Dovercourt Rd BS7 . . . . . . .19 A6
Doverdale Dr GL2 . . . . . . .127 D4
Doveswell Gr BS13 . . . . .2 A4
Dovey Ct BS30 . . . . .11 A5
Dowdeswell Cl BS10 . . . . . .27 F3
Dowding Cl BS37 . . . . .44 C2
Dowding Way GL3 . . . . . .128 C5
Dowers' La GL7 . . . . .150 A8
Dowland Gr BS4 . . . . .2 D7
Dowling Rd BS13 . . . . .2 D3
Down Ampney CE Prim Sch
 GL7 . . . . .143 F8
Down Ampney Rd GL7 . . .143 D7
Down Farm Ho BS36 . . . . .30 D6
Down Hatherley La GL2 . .173 C1
Down Leaze **2** BS35 . . . . .51 A5
 Marshfield SN14 . . . . .18 B2
 Winterbourne BS36 . . . . . .30 F4
Down The Alveston BS35 . .50 D3
 Tockington BS32 . . . . .50 D3
Down View West Rd GL2 . .26 E3
Chalford GL6 . . . . .148 C6
Downend Park Rd BS16 . . .20 D5
Downend Rd BS7 . . . . .18 F5
Downend Rd
 Bristol,Fishponds BS16 . . .20 C5
 Bristol,Horfield BS7 . . . . . .18 F5
 Bristol,Kingswood BS15 . . .20 F7
Downend Sch BS16 . . . . . .20 F7
Downfield Bristol BS9 . . . . .17 C7
 Keynsham BS31 . . . . .5 A3
Downfield Cl BS35 . . . . . . .51 A5
Downfield Dr BS36 . . . . . . .31 B8
Downfield Ho GL51 . . . . . .132 D2
Downfield La GL20 . . . . . .182 A8
Downfield Lodge BS8 . . . . .18 A1
Downfield Rd
 Bristol,Clifton BS8 . . . . . . .18 A1
 Keynsham BS31 . . . . .5 A3
Downham View GL11 . . . . .80 D8
Downham Way GL11 . . . . .80 D8
Downhams The **14**
 NP25 . . . . .154 A7

Downleaze
 Bristol,Downend BS16 . . . .20 D8
 Bristol,Stoke Bishop BS9 . .17 F3
Downleaze Dr BS37 . . . . . .33 B8
Downman Rd BS7 . . . . .19 A5
Downs Cl BS35 . . . . .51 A5
Downs Cote Ave BS9 . . . . .17 F6
Downs Cote Dr BS9 . . . . . .17 F6
Downs Cote Gdns BS9 . . . .18 A6
Downs Cote Pk BS9 . . . . . .18 A6
Downs Cote View BS9 . . . .18 A6
Downs Gr BS9 . . . . .18 B6
Downs Mill GL6 . . . . .148 E4
Downs Pk E BS6 . . . . .18 A4
Downs Pk W BS6 . . . . .18 A4
Downs Rd Bristol BS9 . . . . .18 A6
 Dundry BS41 . . . . .1 D2
Downs Sch The GL12 . . . . .53 F7
Downs View SN6 . . . . .145 D3
Downs Way GL7 . . . . .150 D7
Downside BS8 . . . . .10 F5
Downside Cl BS30 . . . . . . .11 D6
Downside Rd BS8 . . . . .18 A1
Downsview Ct BS8 . . . . . . .18 A1
Downton Rd Bristol BS4 . . . .8 D1
 Stonehouse GL10 . . . . .97 E6
Downy Cl GL12 . . . . .117 E2
Dowry Mews BS8 . . . . . . .194 A2
Dowry Pl **3** BS8 . . . . .7 F5
Dowry Rd BS8 . . . . .194 A2
Dowry Sq BS8 . . . . .194 A2
Dowty Rd GL51 . . . . .132 E2
Doynton La SN14,BS30 . . .23 B3
Dozule Cl GL10 . . . . .97 F3
Dr Brown's Cl GL6 . . . . . . .91 F6
Dr Brown's Rd GL6 . . . . . . .91 F7
Dr Crawfords Way GL6 . . . .91 F6
Dr Crouch's Rd GL6 . . . . .148 B7
Dr Middletons Rd GL6 . . .148 C5
Dr Newton's Way GL5 . . . . .99 C6
Dr White's Cl BS1 . . . . . . .195 B1
Drag Rd HR9 . . . . .162 E3
Dragon Ct BS5 . . . . .19 E1
Dragon Rd BS36 . . . . .29 D5
Dragon Wlk BS5 . . . . .19 F1
Dragons Hill Cl BS31 . . . . . .4 F5
Dragons Hill Ct BS31 . . . . . .4 F5
Dragons Hill Gdns BS31 . . . .4 F5
Dragonswell Rd BS10 . . . . .28 A2
Drake Cl Innsworth GL3 . . .127 F7
 Saltford BS31 . . . . .4 E3
Drake Ho BS1 . . . . .195 A3
Drake La GL11 . . . . .88 C2
Drake Rd GL51 . . . . .132 E4
Drakes Pl GL50 . . . . .193 A3
Dram La BS5 . . . . .10 A6
Dramway Rdbt BS16 . . . . . .21 D6
Draper Cl **3** BS55 . . . . .9 C7
Drapers Ct GL19 . . . . .172 D6
Drapers Ct GL52 . . . . .138 B3
Draycot Pl BS1 . . . . .195 A1
Draycott Cl GL51 . . . . .87 F7
Draycott Rd BS4 . . . . .28 C6
Draycott Rd Bristol BS14 . . .3 B8
 Cheltenham GL51 . . . . . . .133 B6
Drayton Rd Bristol BS9 . . . .17 C8
 Cheltenham GL51 . . . . . . .129 E8
Drayton Way GL4 . . . . . . .119 C5
Drews Cl GL3 . . . . .128 C4
Driffield Cross Rds GL7 . . .151 B1
Drift Cl GL7 . . . . .190 A2
Drift Hill BS9 . . . . .17 D7
Drift La GL7 . . . . .190 A2
Drifton Hill SN14 . . . . .25 F7
Drive The
 Bristol,Henleaze BS14 . . . . .3 C6
 Bristol,Henleaze BS9 . . . . .18 B5
 Gloucester GL11 . . . . .80 A7
 Tetbury GL8 . . . . .140 D2
Drivemoor GL4 . . . . .119 D3
Druetts Cl BS10 . . . . .18 E6
Drugger's End La WR13 . .180 C8
Druid Cl BS9 . . . . .17 F3
Druid Hill BS9 . . . . .17 F3
Druid Rd BS9 . . . . .17 D4
Druid Stoke Ave BS9 . . . . .17 D5
Druid Woods BS9 . . . . . . .17 D5
Druids La GL4 . . . . .119 C7
Druids Oak GL2 . . . . .100 F8
Druidstone View GL2 . . . . .26 E4
Drummond Rd
 Bristol,Fishponds BS16 . . .19 F3
 Bristol,St Pauls BS2 . . . . .195 C4
Drury La GL17 . . . . .164 B4
Dry Meadow La GL3 . . . . .127 E6
Drybrook Prim Sch
 GL17 . . . . .164 B6
Drybrook Cl BS13 . . . . .2 A4
Drybrook Rd GL17 . . . . . . .164 B8
Dryleaze BS31 . . . . .4 E4
Dryleaze Ct BS35 . . . . .51 A5
Dryleaze Gdns GL12 . . . . . .80 A7
Dryleaze Ho GL12 . . . . .80 A7
Dryleaze Rd BS16 . . . . .20 D8
Dublin Cres BS9 . . . . .18 B6
Duchess Way BS16 . . . . . . .19 D6
Ducie Cl GL12 . . . . .66 B2
Ducie Ct BS16 . . . . .20 E4

Ducie Rd
 Bristol,Russell Town BS5 9
 Bristol,Staple Hill BS16 . . .20
Ducie Rd Bsns Pk **6** BS5 . . .9
Ducie St GL1 118
Duck St GL12 118
Duckmoor Rd BS3 8
Duckmoor Road Ind Est
 BS3 8
Duckworth Cl GL53 130
Dudbridge Hill GL5 98
Dudbridge Mdw GL5 98
Dudbridge Rd GL5 98
Duderstadt Cl GL5 98
Dudley Cnr GL7 151
Dudley Ct **3** BS30 10
Dudley Farm GL7 151
Dudley Gr BS7 19
Dudley Rd WR11 188
Duffield's La NP25 154
Dugar Wlk BS6 18
Dugdale Rd GL7 151
Duglynch La GL54 183
Duke of Beaufort Ct
 GL4 118
Duke of York Rd GL16 154
Duke St GL12 118
Dukeries The GL1 196
Dukes Field GL7 143
Dukes Way GL20 192
Dulverton Cl GL51 132
Dulverton Pl GL54 168
Dulverton Rd BS7 18
Dumaine Ave BS34 29
Dumbleton Gr GL51 129
Dunalley Par GL51 133
Dunalley Prim Sch
 GL50 193
Dunalley St GL50 193
Dunbar Cl GL51 132
Duncombe La BS15 20
Duncombe Rd BS15 20
Duncroft Rd GL3 127
Dundas Cl BS10 27
Dundonald Rd BS6 18
Dundridge Gdns BS5 10
Dundridge La BS5 10
Dundry CE Prim Sch BS41 . . .1
Dundry Cl BS15 10
Dundry La BS41 1
Dunford Rd BS3 8
Dunkeld Ave BS34 28
Dunkerry Rd BS3 8
Dunkirk Cotts GL9 56
Dunlin Cl GL2 117
Dunmail Prim Sch GL10 . . .28
Dunmore St **3** BS2 19
Dunmurry BS9 17
Dunns Copse **15** HR8 178
Dunsdown La SN14 24
Dunsmore Gn GL14 181
Dunstall Ho **1** GL56 187
Dunstan Glen GL3 128
Dunster Cl
 Cheltenham GL51 132
 Gloucester GL4 118
Dunster Gdns Bristol BS30 . .11
 Cheltenham GL51 132
Dunster Gr GL51 132
Dunster Ho GL51 132
 Cheltenham GL51 132
Dunstone Pl GL17 164
Durand Ct GL12 67
Durand Cl GL2 127
Durban Ho **4** GL50 132
Durban Rd BS34 28
Durbin Wlk BS5 9
Durbridge Rd GL10 179
Durdham Ct BS6 18
Durdham Pk BS6 18
Durham Ct GL51 130
Durham Gr BS31 5
Durham Rd **10** Bristol BS2 . .19
 Gloucester GL4 119
Durleigh Cl BS13 2
Durley Hill BS31 4
Durley La BS31 4
Durncourt Cotts GL7 151
Durnford Ave BS3 8
Durnford St BS3 8
Dursley CE Prim Sch
 GL11 80
Dursley Cl BS37 43
 Slimbridge GL2 80
Dursley Rd Bristol BS11 . . .18
 Dursley GL11 80
Dutton Cl BS14 3
Dutton Leys GL54 168
Dutton Rd BS14 3
Dutton Wlk BS14 3
Duttons La GL17 163
Dye House Rd GL12 67
Dyer St GL7 190
Dyer's La
 Chipping Campden GL55 . .188
 Yate BS37 27
Dyers Cl BS13 2
Dyersbrook GL12 53

Dyke House La GL18 ....179 B4
Dylan Thomas Ct 🔼
BS30 ....11 A5
Dymock Rd Ledbury HR8 ..178 E7
Much Marcle HR8 ....178 A3
Dynevor St GL1 ....118 F7
Dynevor Terr GL7 ....152 D4
Dyrham BS16 ....30 C1
Dyrham Cl
Bristol,Henleaze BS9 ....18 D6
Bristol,Kingswood BS15 ....10 F8
Pucklechurch BS16 ....22 C4
Thornbury BS35 ....64 C3
Dyrham Par BS34 ....29 C8
Dyrham Park* SN14 .....23 F5
Dyrham Rd BS15 ....10 F8

E

Eagar Ho GL53 ....131 B4
Eagle CI GL6 ....148 B6
Eagle Cres BS16 ....22 C5
Eagle Dr BS34 ....28 E8
Eagle Mill CI GL5 ......99 D5
Eagle Rd BS4 ....19 A4
Eagle Way GL4 ....119 C5
Eagles Wood BS32 .....40 D3
Eagles Wood Bsns Pk
BS32 ....40 C3
Ealy Hill GL7 ....107 C5
Eardisland Rd GL4 .....118 E2
Earl Russell Way BS5 ....9 B7
Earl St SS1 ....195 A4
Earls Cor SN16 ....141 F4
Earlsmead BS16 ....17 E4
Earlstone CI BS30 .....11 A4
Earlstone Cres BS30 ...11 A4
Early Way GL7 ....18 E8
Earthcott Rd BS35 .....51 F1
Easedale CI BS10 .....28 D2
East Allcourt GL7 .....153 E2
East Approach Dr GL52 ..133 F4
East Ave GL54 ....168 A1
East Croft BS9 ....18 C7
East St GL3 ....7 F3
East Dr GL5 ....98 C7
East Dundry La BS41 ...2 A1
East Dundry Rd BS13,BS14 .2 F2
East End GL54 ....168 A1
East End Flats GL53 ...131 C5
East End Rd GL52,GL53 ..131 C5
East Gable GL52 ....138 B3
East Gr BS6 ....18 F1
East Hill BS9 ....18 B7
East Link GL17 ....164 D5
East Par BS9 ....17 C6
East Park Dr BS5 ......19 C2
East Pk BS5 ....19 C2
East Priory CI GL9 .....18 A7
East Ridge Dr BS13 .....1 F5
East Shrubbery **3** BS6 ..18 B2
East St Avonmouth BS11 ...26 A1
Bristol,Southville BS3 ....8 D4
Bristol,St Pauls BS2 ....195 C4
Moreton-in-M GL56 .....187 A3
St Briavels GL15 ....146 F7
Tewkesbury GL20 ....192 C4
East View Bristol BS16 ...20 F6
Newnham GL14 ....156 F7
East Wlk BS34 ....43 E1
Eastbourne Rd **9** BS5 ..9 B8
Eastbourne Terr GL7 ...152 E3
Eastbrook Rd GL4 ......119 C8
Eastbury CI BS35 ....64 C1
Eastbury Rd Bristol BS16 ..20 A4
Thornbury BS35 ....64 C1
Eastcote Rd BS4 ....3 B5
Eastcott Way GL3 .....128 A6
Easter Ct BS37 ....43 B1
Eastern Ave
Gloucester GL4 ....119 B8
Mitcheldean GL17 ......164 D5
Eastern Way GL14 .....156 C6
Eastfield
Ashton Keynes SN6 ....142 F5
Bristol BS9 ....18 B7
Eastfield Dr BS37 ......43 E4
Eastfield Mews GL4 ....118 F5
Eastfield Rd
Bristol,Eastfield BS9 ....18 B7
Bristol,Montpelier BS6 ...18 D2
Bristol,Westbury on Trym
BS9 ....18 A7
Minchinhampton GL6 ...148 A3
Eastfield Terr BS9 .....18 B6
Eastgate Office Ctr BS5 ..19 B3
Eastgate Sh Ctr GL1 ...196 B2
Eastgate St GL1 ....196 B2
Eastholm Lawns GL3 ..128 C5
Eastington Prim Sch
GL10 ....97 A8
Eastington Rd GL54 ...168 A1
Eastington Trad Est
GL10 ....100 F1
Eastlake CI BS37 ....19 B7
Eastland Ave BS35 .....64 C2
Eastland Rd BS35 .....64 C2
Eastleigh CI BS16 ......20 E4
Eastleigh Rd
Bristol,Brentry BS10 ....28 D1
Bristol,Staple Hill BS16 ..20 E3
Eastley CI GL12 ....65 E7
Eastlyn Rd BS13 ....2 B8
Eastmead Ct BS9 ......17 E4
Eastmead La BS9 ......17 E4

Eastnor Castle* HR8 ...179 B7
Eastnor CE Prim Sch
HR8 ....179 B7
Eastnor Ho **14** GL12 ..132 E2
Eastnor Rd BS14 ....3 A3
Easton Bsns Ctr BS5 ....9 B8
Easton CE Prim Sch BS5 ..9 A8
Easton Hill Rd BS35 ...64 D1
Easton Rd
Bristol,Newton BS5 .....9 A7
Bristol,Upper Easton BS5 ..9 B8
Pill BS20 ....16 C4
Easton Sq SN16 ....58 D1
Easton Town SN16 ....58 D1
Easton Way BS5 ....9 A8
Eastover CI BS9 ....18 A5
Eastpark Trad Est BS5 ..19 D1
Eastrip SN6 ....145 D3
Eastrop Inf Sch SN6 ...145 D3
Eastview Terr SN6 .....145 D3
Eastville CI GL4 ......119 B8
Eastwood Cres BS4 .....9 F3
Eastwood Rd Bristol BS4 ..9 F4
Harrow Hill GL17 ......164 B3
Eaton CI
Bristol,Fishponds BS16 ...20 B4
Bristol,Stockwood BS14 ...3 E5
Eaton Cres BS8 ....194 A4
Eaton PI GL53 ....193 B2
Eaton St **15** BS3 ......8 C3
Ebenezer La BS9 ......17 E5
Ebenezer St BS5 ....9 D7
Ebley Ind Pk GL5 ......98 D6
Ebley Rd GL10 ....98 B6
Ebor Rd GL2 ....127 C1
Ebrington GL55 ....189 D3
Ebrington CE Prim Sch
GL55 ....189 D3
Ebrington CI GL4 .....119 D8
Eccles St **11** GL8 ....140 C4
Eccleston Ho **1** BS5 ....9 B6
Echo La GL15 ....87 B2
Eclipse Ct **11** BS16 ...20 C4
Eclipse Office Pk **2**
BS16 ....20 C4
Eddys La GL17 ....163 E3
Eden Gr BS7 ....29 A1
Eden Office Pk BS20 ...16 E4
Eden's Hill GL14 ......171 D6
Edencroft SN6 ....145 D4
Edendale App GL51 ...129 C8
Edendale Rd GL51 ....132 C1
Edenwall GL16 ....155 B5
Edenwall Rd GL16 ....155 B4
Edge End Rd **1** GL16 ..155 B6
Edge Hills Rd GL14 ...191 D5
Edge La GL6 ....103 C8
Edge Rd GL6 ....103 E8
Edgecombe CI BS15 ...20 F1
Edgecorner La SN14 ...36 A3
Edgefield CI BS14 ......2 F3
Edgefield Rd BS14 .....2 F3
Edgeware Rd
Bristol,Southville BS3 ....8 C4
Bristol,Staple Hill BS16 ..20 D4
Edgewood CI
Bristol,Hengrove Bristol ...3 B8
Bristol,Longwell Green
BS30 ....11 F6
Edgeworth BS37 ......32 C6
Edgeworth CI
Cirencester GL7 ....190 B2
3 Gloucester GL4 ....119 E5
Edinburgh PI
Cheltenham GL51 .....132 E2
3 Coleford GL16 ....155 B5
Edinburgh Rd BS31 .....4 E4
Edington Gr BS10 .....28 A2
Edmond Rd NP16 ......61 A8
Edmund Cl GL16 ......20 D6
Edmund Ct BS16 ......22 B6
Edna Ave BS4 ....9 E3
Edward Bird Ho BS7 ...19 B6
Edward CI BS31 ....4 F4
Edward Jenner Mus*
GL13 ....85 E3
Edward Massey Gdns
GL4 ....119 C3
Edward PI GL20 ......192 D1
Edward Rd
Bristol,Kingswood BS15 ..10 E8
Bristol,Totterdown BS4 ...9 B4
Edward St
Bristol,Eastville BS5 ....19 D2
Bristol,Moorfields BS5 ....9 C7
Cheltenham GL50 ......193 B1
Edward Wilson Ho **2**
GL51 ....132 E3
Edward Wilson Villas **3**
GL50 ....130 B6
Edwards CI
Joy's Green GL17 ......163 D3
Poulton GL7 ....151 E3
Edwards Ct **11** BS7 ....9 D7
Edwards' Coll GL7 ....142 F8
Edwin Short CI BS30 ...5 E8
Edwy Par GL1 ....196 B4
Effingham Rd BS6 ....18 E2
Egerton Brow BS7 .....18 D4
Egerton La BS7 ....18 D4
Egerton Rd BS7 ......43 D1
Eggshill La BS37 ....27 E1
Eglin CI BS35 ....8 B3
Eglin Croft BS13 ....2 B4
Egypt Ho GL6 ....91 B4
Eighth Ave
Bristol,Filton BS7 ......29 B1
Bristol,Hengrove BS14 ...3 A7

Eirene Terr BS20 ......16 D4
Elberton BS35 ....11 A8
Elberton Rd Bristol BS9 ..17 B7
Elberton BS35 ....49 F5
Elbridge Ho **4** BS2 ..195 C3
Elbury Ave BS15 ......20 C2
Elbury View GL12 ......67 B5
Elcombe GL11 ....81 A7
Elderberry Mews GL3 ..127 F6
Elderberry Wlk BS10 ..28 C3
Eldersfield CI
Quedgeley GL2 ....117 E2
Winchcombe GL54 ....174 A8
Eldersfield Lawn CE Prim Sch
GL19 ....180 F1
Elderwood Dr BS30 ....11 A3
Elderwood Rd BS14 ....3 B7
Elderwood Way GL4 ..118 C2
Eldon Ave GL52 ......134 A1
Eldon Rd GL12 ....133 F1
Eldon St BS5 ....9 C5
Eldon Way BS4 ....9 C5
Eldonwall Trad Est BS4 ..9 C5
Eldorado Cres GL50 ...133 B1
Eldorado Rd GL50 ....133 B1
Eleanor CI BS9 ....17 D5
Eleventh Ave BS7 .....29 B1
Elf Mdw GL7 ....151 F4
Elfin Rd BS16 ....20 A5
Elgar CI Bristol BS4 .....2 D6
Ledbury HR8 ....178 E8
Elgar Ho GL51 ....132 E2
Elgin Ave BS7 ....28 F1
Elgin Hall GL10 ....97 F7
Elgin Pk BS6 ....18 B2
Elgin Rd BS16 ....20 B2
Eliot CI BS7 ....28 F1
Gloucester GL2 ....118 C4
Elizabeth CI BS35 .....51 D8
Elizabeth Cres BS34 ...29 E4
Elizabeth Gdns
Meysey Hampton GL7 ..152 B3
Northway GL20 ....140 B4
Elizabeth Way
Bristol BS16 ....21 B3
Siddington GL7 ....190 E2
Elkstone Wlk BS30 ....11 C2
Ellacombe Rd BS30 ...10 E5
Ellan Hay Rd BS34 ....30 A6
Ellbridge CI BS9 ......17 D5
Ellenborough Ho BS8 ..194 A2
Ellenborough Rd GL52 .138 A4
Ellendene Dr BS20 ...182 E4
Ellenor Dr GL20 ......183 E4
Ellercroft Rd
Kingswood GL12 ....67 F8
Wotton-u-E GL12 ......68 A8
Highworth SN6 ....145 C3
Tockington BS32 ....50 B2
Ellesmere CI BS15 ....20 F1
Ellesmere Gr **5** GL50 .130 B6
Ellesmere Rd BS4 ......9 D1
Ellfield CI BS13 ....1 F6
Ellicks CI BS32 ....40 E2
Ellicott Rd BS7 ....18 F5
Ellingham CI GL52 ...133 F8
Ellinghurst CI BS10 ...28 A2
Elliott Ave BS16 ....20 C1
Elliott CI **5** GL20 ....192 C4
Elliott Ho BS7 ....19 A8
Elliott PI GL51 ....129 F7
Elliott Rd BS7 ....190 E1
Ellis Ave BS13 ....1 E8
Ellison CI GL4 ....120 A6
Ellison Rd GL51 ......132 C2
Elliston La BS6 ....18 C2
Elliston Rd BS6 ....18 C2
Ellsbridge Ho Norton
Radstock Coll BS31 .....5 B5
Ellsbridge Ho BS31 ....27 F2
Ellwood Prim Sch GL16 .155 B3
Ellwood Rd GL16 .....155 B3
Ellyott CI **5** BS16 .....19 E3
Elm CI Avonmouth BS11 .26 F1
Bristol BS34 ....29 D7
Cheltenham,Prestbury
GL52 ....134 A3
Cheltenham,St Peter's
GL51 ....133 B3
Chipping Sodbury BS37 ..40 A1
King's Stanley GL10 ....98 A8
Tutshill NP16 ....73 A2
Elm Ct
Bristol,Hengrove BS14 ...3 A6
Bristol,Redland BS6 ....18 C2
Cheltenham GL53 .....131 F4
Keynsham BS31 ....4 C4
Woolaston GL15 ......192 D1
Elm Dr GL3 ....120 D7
Elm Farm CI SN16 ....142 E1
Elm Garden Dr GL51 ..129 A7
Elm Gr Dursley GL11 ...80 E4
Ebrington GL55 ......189 D3
Elm Hayes BS13 ....1 B6
Elm Hayes BS13 ....1 B6
Elm La BS6 ....18 C2
Elm Lodge GL11 ....88 B4
Elm Park Prim Sch BS36 .30 E6
Elm Pk BS34 ....29 D7
Elm Rd Bristol,Horfield BS7 .29 F2
Bristol,Kingswood BS15 ...10 D8
Bristol,Tyndall's Park
BS8 ....194 C3
Littledean GL14 ......156 E8
Elton St BS2 ....195 C4
Elvard CI BS13 ....2 A4
Elvard Rd BS13 ....2 A4
Elvaston Rd BS3 ....8 E3
Elwell La BS40,BS41 ....1 A1
Ely Gr BS9 ....17 B7
Embassy Rd BS5 ......19 E1
Embassy Wlk BS5 .....19 E1
Embleton Prim Sch BS10 .28 C2
Embleton Rd BS10 .....28 C2
Embrook GL56 ....177 C4
Emerald CI GL4 ......118 C3
Emerson Sq BS7 ......19 A8
Emerson Way BS16 ...21 C7
Emersons Green La BS16 .21 C8
Emersons Green Prim Sch
BS16 ....21 B7
Emery Rd BS4 ....9 E4
Emet Gr BS16 ....21 B6
Emet La BS16 ....21 B6
Emlyn Rd BS5 ....19 C1
Emma-Chris Way BS34 .29 C2
Emmanuel CI BS34 ....29 B4
Emmanuel Gdns GL51 .130 D6
Emmerson La GL6 ....149 A4
Emmett Wood BS14 ....3 C3
Emperor **7** GL51 ....132 D2
Emperor Ct **5** GL50 ..196 B3
Empire Cres BS15 .....10 E8
Empire Way GL2 ......118 C5
Empress Rd GL4 .....119 C8
Emra CI BS5 ....19 F8
Enborne CI GL4 ......118 A5
Enfield Rd BS16 ....20 A3
Enfield Villas GL54 ...139 C5
Engine Common La BS37 .43 C5

England's Cres BS36 ...30 E7
English Bicknor CE Prim Sch
GL16 ....163 B2
Englishcombe Rd BS13 ..2 C3
Ennerdale Ave GL2 ...127 D5
Ennerdale Rd Bristol BS10 .28 D2
Cheltenham GL51 ....129 E7
Enoch's Row GL14 .....54 E6
Enstone Cvn Pk GL51 ..129 C7
Enterprise Way GL51 ..133 B3
Epney CI BS34 ....39 F1
Epney Rd GL4 ....118 C3
Epsom CI BS16 ....30 F1
Epworth Rd BS10 .....28 A3
Equinox BS32 ....40 C3
Erin Pk GL5 ....99 B2
Erin Wlk BS4 ....2 D8
Ermin Rd GL3 ....120 D6
Ermin PI GL7 ....190 E2
Ermin St
Broad Blunsdon SN26 ..144 D1
Brockworth GL3 ......120 E5
Ermine Par GL3 ......120 E6
Ermine Way BS16 .....16 C7
Ermine Way GL3 .....120 A7
Ermleet Rd **1** BS6 ...18 C2
Ernest Barker CI **13** BS5 .9 B7
Ernestville Rd BS16 ....19 F3
Eros CI GL5 ....99 A5
Errington **2** GL56 ...187 B3
Ervine Terr BS2 ......195 C4
Eskdale BS35 ....51 D7
Esland PI GL7 ....190 D2
Essery Rd BS5 ....19 C2
Essex Ave GL51 ....133 A2
Essex CI GL3 ....128 A8
Essex PI GL54 ....168 F8
Esson Rd BS15 ....20 B1
Estate Rd GL14 ......191 B6
Estcote Rd GL7 ......190 C5
Estcourt Cl GL12 .....127 A4
Estcourt Gdns BS16 ...19 D5
Estcourt Rd GL12 ....127 A3
Estoril BS37 ....43 F1
Estune Wlk BS41 ....7 A2
Etheldene Rd GL5 .....98 D8
Etheridge PI GL1 ....127 B1
Etloe Rd BS6 ....18 A4
Eton Rd BS4 ....9 D3
Ettington CI GL12 ....132 C3
Ettricke Dr BS16 ......20 B5
Eugene Flats **7** BS2 ..195 A4
Eugene St
Bristol,Kingsdown BS2 ..195 A4
Bristol,St Pauls BS2,BS5 .195 C4
Eunice Saunders Way
HR9 ....164 A7
Evans CI BS4 ....9 F5
Evans Rd BS6 ....18 B2
Eve Rd BS5 ....19 B1
Evelyn CI GL53 ......130 F5
Evelyn CI GL53 ......193 A3
Evelyn Rd BS10 ....18 C2
Evelyn Terr BS6 ......18 C2
Evenlode Gdns
Bristol BS11 ....16 F5
Moreton-in-M GL56 ...187 B3
Evenlode Rd
Gloucester GL4 ......118 D1
Moreton-in-M GL56 ...187 B3
Evenlode Way BS31 ....5 A3
Evercreech Rd BS14 ....3 B4
Everest CI BS16 ....19 E4
Everest Rd BS16 ......19 E4
Cheltenham GL53 ....130 E4
Evergreen Ind Pk GL2 ..142 F7
Evergreen Wlk GL2 ...127 D5
Everlands GL11 ....80 E4
Everside CI GL11 ......87 F6
Everside La GL11 ......87 F6
Everyman Theatre The*
GL50 ....193 B3
Evesham Rd
Bishop's Cleeve GL52 ..137 F5
Cheltenham GL50,GL52 ..133 E5
Greet GL54 ....184 A1
Stow-on-t-W GL54 ....176 E5
Evington Ct **7** GL51 ..132 E2
Evington Rd **8** GL51 ..132 E2
Ewell Rd BS14 ....3 A4
Ewens Rd GL52 ......131 A8
Ewlyn Rd GL53 ......130 D6
Ewlyn Terr GL53 .....130 D6
Exchange Ave **6** BS1 .195 A2
Exchange The **11** GL50 .10 D8
Exmoor St BS3 ....8 E3
Exmouth Cl GL53 ....193 B1
Exmouth Rd BS4 ......9 C3
Exmouth St GL53 ....193 B1
Exon St BS4 ....9 C4
Eyer's La BS2 ....195 C3
Eyford Cotts GL54 ....176 A3
Eynon CI GL52 ......130 C5

F

Faber Gr BS13 ....2 C4
Fabian Dr BS34 ....29 E5
Factory Rd BS36 ......30 F7

Failand Cres BS9 ....17 C5
Failand La BS20 ....16 A1
Failand Wlk BS9 ....17 C6
Fair Furlong BS13 ....2 A4
Fair Furlong Prim Sch
BS13 ....2 B4
Fair Lawn BS30 ....11 B4
Fair View
Chepstow/Cas-Gwent NP16 .60 D6
Highworth SN6 ....145 C3
Fair View Cl GL6 ....91 B5
Fair View Cvn Pk GL1 ..126 C3
Fair View Dr BS6 ....18 C2
Fairacre Cl BS7 ....19 B5
Fairacres Cl BS31 ....4 F5
Fairfax Cl GL7 ....190 D3
Fairfax Rd GL7 ....190 D3
Fairfax St BS1 ....195 B3
Fairfield 14 SN6 ....143 E4
Fairfield Ave GL53 ......130 D6
Fairfield Cl
21 Coleford GL16 ....155 A5
Marshfield SN14 ....15 A8
Fairfield Ct 13 GL4 ......119 C4
Fairfield High Sch BS6 ...18 F2
Fairfield Par GL53 ....130 D6
Fairfield Park Rd GL53 ..130 D6
Fairfield Pl BS3 ....8 B4
Fairfield Rd
Bristol,Montpelier BS6 ....18 F2
Bristol,Southville BS3 .....8 B4
Cheltenham GL53 ....130 D6
Chepstow/Cas-Gwent NP16 .60 E6
Lydney GL15 ....92 B3
Fairfield St GL53 ....130 D6
Fairfield Wlk GL53 ......130 D6
Fairfields GL14 ....191 C4
Fairfields Rd 18 HR8 ....178 E8
Fairfoot Rd BS4 ....9 A3
Fairford CE Prim Sch
GL7 ....152 E4
Fairford Cl BS15 ....20 F2
Fairford Cres BS34 ....29 C8
Fairford Hospl GL7 ......152 E4
Fairford Rd Bristol BS11 ..16 D7
Quenington GL7 ....152 D7
Fairford Way GL4 ....119 B7
Fairhaven BS37 ....43 F1
Fairhaven Ave GL3 .....120 E6
Fairhaven Park Cvn Pk
GL51 ....129 B6
Fairhaven Rd Bristol BS6 .18 C4
Cheltenham GL51 ....130 D6
Fairhaven St GL53 ......130 D6
Fairhavens Ct 9 GL52 ..133 F2
Fairhaven BS16 ....20 D4
Fairlawn Ave BS34 ....29 A3
Fairlawn Rd BS6 ....18 F2
Fairlyn Dr BS15 ....20 F3
Fairmead GL11 ....87 F5
Fairmile Gdns GL2 ......126 F5
Fairmoor Cl GL15 ....155 E2
Fairmount Rd GL51 .....132 F1
Fairoaks BS30 ....11 A3
Fairview SN6 ....143 F4
Fairview Cl
Cheltenham GL52 ....193 C3
Monmouth/Trefynwy
NP25 ....154 A7
Fairview Ct BS15 ....10 D6
Fairview Ho BS9 ....17 F8
Fairview Rd Bristol BS15 ..10 F8
Cheltenham GL52 ....193 C4
Fairview St GL52 ....193 C4
Fairwater Pk GL4 ....127 D1
Fairway Bristol BS4 ....9 D1
Northway GL20 ....182 C4
Fairway Cl BS30 ....11 B4
Fairway Ind Ctr BS34 ....28 F3
Fairways BS31 ....5 E2
Fairways Ave GL16 .....155 A5
Falcon Cl
Bristol,Patchway BS34 ....28 E8
Bristol,Westbury on Trym
BS9 ....17 F8
Innsworth GL3 ....127 C6
Quedgeley GL2 ....117 F3
Falcon Ct BS9 ....18 A7
Falcon Dr BS34 ....28 E8
Falcon La HR8 ....178 C8
Falkner St GL1 ....196 C1
Fallodon Ct BS9 ....18 B5
Fallodon Way BS9 ....18 B5
Fallowfield BS30 ....11 D5
Fallows Rd GL54 ....168 A1
Falmouth Rd BS7 ....18 E4
Fancy Rd GL15 ....155 E3
Fane Ct BS30 ....28 A3
Fanshawe Rd BS14 ......3 A7
Far Handstones BS30 ....11 A4
Far Leazes GL5 ....99 D7
Far Sandfield GL3 ....28 C5

Far View Cotts 7 GL10 ...97 F7
Far Wells Rd GL6 ......148 D8
Far Westrip GL6 ....98 C8
Faraday Cl 4 GL1 ....18 F7
Faraday Rd 2 BS8 ....7 F5
Farendell Rd BS16 ......31 B1
Farfield La SN6 ....143 F2
Faringdon Rd GL51 .....129 D7
Farington Rd BS10 ......18 D7
Farlands BS16 ....22 B6
Farleigh Cl GL52 ....131 C6
Farleigh La GL12 ....66 C2
Farleigh Rd BS31 ....4 D4
Farleigh Wlk BS13 ....2 A8
Farley Cl BS34 ....29 C7
Farm Cl Bristol BS16 ....21 B6
Cheltenham GL51 ....132 E3
Northway GL20 ....182 C5
Farm Ct Bristol BS16 ....20 C7
Willersey WR12 ....188 B2
Woodchester GL5 ....90 F8
Farm Hill GL8 ....140 A8
Farm La Bredon GL20 ..182 C7
Cheltenham GL51,GL53 ..130 B4
Easter Compton BS35 ....38 E2
Leighterton GL8 ....70 C3
Llangrove HR9 ....162 B5
Shurdington GL51 ......129 E1
Westmancote GL20 .....182 E8
Farm Lees GL12 ....67 A6
Farm Mews GL1 ....196 B1
Farm Rd Bristol BS16 ...20 E7
Edgeworth GL6 ....106 C1
Ruardean Woodside GL17 .63 B6
Farm St GL1 ....196 B1
Farman Cres GL4 ....169 D6
Farmcote GL12 ....55 D8
Farmcote Cl GL2 ....148 B6
Farmcote Gdns GL54 ...139 F5
Farmer Rd BS13 ....1 E4
Farmfield Rd GL51 .....130 A5
Farmhill Cres GL5 ....98 F8
Farmhill La GL5 ....102 F1
Farmhouse Mews NP25 .146 B7
Farmington Cl 4 GL4 ...119 E5
Farmington Rd
Cheltenham GL51 ....129 E8
Northleach GL54 ....168 A1
Farmington Rise 13
GL54 ....168 A1
Farmer's Sch GL7 ......152 E4
Farmwell Cl BS13 ....2 B5
Farnaby Cl BS4 ....2 C7
Farndale BS5 ....10 A6
Farr St BS11 ....16 B8
Farr's La Bristol BS1 ...195 A2
Stroud GL5 ....99 C7
Farrell Cl GL7 ....190 C4
Farriers Croft 9 GL6 ...148 C6
Farriers End GL52 .....155 A6
Farriers End GL2 ....117 F1
Farriers Reach GL52 ...137 D4
Farriers The GL7 ....153 F5
Farringford Ho BS5 .....19 D2
Farthing Croft GL2 .....125 D4
Farthings WR13 ....180 C5
Farthings The GL54 ....166 E2
Fauconberg Rd GL50 ...193 A3
Faulkner's Cl GL7 ......152 E3
Fawkes Cl BS15 ....11 B8
Fawkes Pl 7 GL15 ......199 C7
Fawley Dr GL52 ....134 C4
Featherbed La BS35 ......9 E1
Featherstone Rd 4 BS16 .19 F4
Fedw Wood/Coed Fedw
NP16 ....60 C8
Feeder Rd BS2 ....9 A5
Felix Rd BS5 ....9 B8
Felstead Rd BS10 ....18 D3
Feltham Cl BS34 ....28 F2
Feltham Rd BS16 ....22 C6
Fen Gr BS13 ....2 A8
Fenbrook Cl BS16 ....30 B1
Fenhill Cl GL56 ....186 D3
Fennel Cl GL4 ....119 D4
Fennel Dr BS34 ....30 A7
Fennel Rd BS10 ....28 A2
Fennell's View GL5 .....103 E1
Fenshurst Gdns BS41 ....1 A8
Fenton Cl BS31 ....5 D3
Fenton Ct BS7 ....18 D4
Fenton Rd BS7 ....18 D4
Fern Cl BS10 ....18 C4
Fern Gr BS32 ....29 D8
Fern Lawn GL4 ....119 D2
Fern Rd Bristol BS16 ....20 D5
Ellwood GL16 ....155 C3

Ferndown Rd 7 HR8 ...178 E7
Ferney GL11 ....80 C8
Fernhill BS32 ....40 C7
Fernhill Ct Bristol BS11 ..27 B1
Tockington BS32 ....40 C7
Fernhill La BS11 ....27 B1
Fernhurst Rd BS5 ....19 F1
Fernihough Ave WR11 ..188 C7
Fernlea Gdns BS20 ......16 B4
Fernleaze BS36 ....31 C6
Fernleigh Cres GL51 ...129 E6
Fernleigh La 1 BS6 ......18 B2
Ferns The GL8 ....140 B4
Fernsteed Rd BS13 ....1 F6
Ferrie La HR9 ....162 E3
Ferris Court View 9
GL6 ....148 B6
Ferry Gdns GL2 ....117 D1
Ferry La GL20 ....181 C8
Ferry Rd BS15 ....10 D1
Ferry St BS1 ....195 B2
Ferry Steps Ind Est BS2 ..9 A4
Ferry Way NP16 ....61 B4
Ferryman's Ct BS2 .....195 B2
Festival Ho GL52 ....193 C3
Festival Rd GL10 ....97 B7
Fewster Rd GL4 ....91 B4
Fewster Sq GL6 ....91 B4
Fiddes Rd BS6 ....18 C4
Fiddle The SN6 ....143 E4
Fiddler's Green La GL51 .132 C2
Fiddlers Wood La BS32 ..29 E8
Fidges La GL6 ....148 C7
Field Cl GL7 ....143 A8
Field Court CE Inf Sch
GL2 ....109 F8
Field Court Dr GL2 .....109 E7
Field Court Gdns GL2 ..109 E7
Field Court Jun Sch
GL2 ....109 F8
Field Farm Cl BS34 .....29 F4
Field La Bristol BS30 ....10 F3
Coaley GL11 ....88 E7
Dursley GL11 ....87 D5
Dyrham SN14 ....23 F6
Littleton-u-S BS35 ....50 A8
Tytherington BS35 ......51 E3
Field Marshal Slim Ct 1
BS2 ....9 C8
Field Pl GL5 ....98 F8
Field Rd Bristol BS15 ...20 C1
Kingham OX7 ....177 F2
Stroud,Bowbridge GL5 ...99 D6
Stroud,Rodborough GL5 ..99 B6
Whiteshill GL6 ....103 A3
Field View BS5 ....9 A8
Field View Dr BS16 .....20 C6
Fieldcote Dr GL3 ....120 A7
Fieldcourt Farmhouse
GL20 ....182 A7
Fielden Cl GL4 ....119 D5
Fieldfare GL4 ....119 D5
Fieldgate Rd GL2 ......138 A4
Fields La WR12 ....188 B2
Fields Rd GL54 ....159 B5
Fieldview GL13 ....85 E4
Fieldways GL2 ....91 A4
Fiennes Cl BS16 ....20 A4
Fiery La GL11 ....89 C2
Fifth Ave Bristol,Filton BS7 .29 A1
Bristol,Hengrove BS14 .....3 B7
Fifth Way BS11 ....26 E2
Filbert Cl GL4 ....119 D3
Filby Dr BS34 ....29 F6
Filton Abbey Wood Sta
BS34 ....29 B1
Filton Ave
Bristol,Filton BS34,BS7 ..29 A7
Bristol,Horfield BS7 ......19 A7
Filton Avenue Jun & Inf Schs
BS7 ....29 A1
Filton Coll S BS34 ......29 A4
Filton Coll S BS34 ......29 A4
Filton Gr BS7 ....18 F6
Filton High Sch BS34 ....29 B5
Filton Hill Prim Sch
BS34 ....29 B4
Filton Rd
Bristol,Frenchay BS16 ....29 F2
Bristol,Harry Stoke BS34 ..28 F3
Bristol,Horfield BS7 ......18 F4
Filton Rdbt BS34 ....29 D2
Filton Way GL4 ....119 B7
Filwood Broadway BS4 ..9 E8
Filwood Ct BS16 ....20 B3
Filwood Dr BS15 ....20 B3
Filwood Ho BS15 ....10 A2
Filwood Rd BS16 ....20 A3
Finch Rd
Chipping Sodbury BS37 ...33 A8
Innsworth GL3 ....127 D7
Finchcroft Ct GL52 .....134 C6
Finchcroft La GL52 .....134 C4
Finchmoor Mews GL2 ..126 F6
Finlay Com Sch GL4 ...119 A6
Finlay Pl GL4 ....119 A6
Finlay Rd GL4 ....119 A5
Finstock Cl GL51 ....129 B8
Fir Rd SN14 ....15 F6
Fir Tree Cl Bristol BS34 ..28 E7
Firbank Ave SN14 ......13 F2
Fircombe Hill GL13 ......71 D4
Fircroft Cl GL20 ....119 F8
Fircroft Rd GL2 ....126 F5

Fire Engine La BS36 .....31 D7
Fire Service Coll The
GL56 ....187 C3
Fire Station La GL51 ....26 B2
Firethorne Cl GL2 ......127 B5
Firework Cl BS15 ....11 B8
Firfield St BS4 ....9 A4
Firgrove Cres BS37 ......44 A2
Firgrove Wlk GL51 .....129 C7
Firs Ct OX7 ....177 E1
Firs Ct BS31 ....4 C4
Firs Rd GL5 ....91 C5
Firs The Bristol GL16 ...20 E6
Gloucester GL1 ....196 C4
Kemble GL7 ....141 D6
Swindon GL51 ....133 B7
First Ave
Bristol,Hengrove BS14 .....3 A7
Bristol,St Anne's BS4 ......9 E5
Dursley GL11 ....80 C8
First Way BS11 ....26 D3
Firth Ave GL56 ....187 C3
Firwood Dr GL4 ....118 E3
Fish Alley 18 GL20 .....192 C4
Fish Hill WR12 ....185 D8
Fisher Ave BS15 ....21 A1
Fisher Cl 10 GL54 ......176 F4
Fisher Rd BS15 ....21 A1
Fisherman's Wlk NP16 ..60 F5
Fishers La GL52 ....193 C4
Fishers Rd GL13 ....85 E4
Fishers Way GL5 ....99 A4
Fishponds BS BS5 ....19 D3
Fishponds Trad Est BS5 ..12 A8
Fishpool Mill BS10 ......28 B4
Fitchett Wlk BS10 ......27 F3
Fitzgerald Rd BS3 ....8 F3
Fitzhamon Pk GL20 ....182 C4
Fitzharding Rd BS20 ....16 E3
Fitzhardinge Way GL13 ..85 E4
Fitzosborn Cl NP16 ....60 D7
Fitzroy Rd BS16 ....20 B2
Fitzroy St BS4 ....9 A4
Fitzroy Terr 7 BS6 ......18 B2
Five Acre Dr BS16 ......20 A7
Five Acres GL11 ....80 A8
Five Lanes SN16 ....141 B1
Five Mile Dr GL56 .....186 C5
Five Trees Cl 8 GL4 ...140 B4
Flaxley Rd GL3 ....127 A2
Flaxley Rd GL4 ....118 E3
Flaxley St GL14 ....191 D4
Flaxman Cl BS7 ....19 B8
Flaxpits La BS36 ....31 A7
Flecker's Dr GL51 ......129 F7
Fleece Alley 24 GL54 ..176 F4
Fleece Inn* WR11 .....188 A6
Fleece La BS31 ....4 A1
Fleet Close Cvn Site
GL20 ....182 A7
Fleet La GL20 ....182 A7
Fleet Rd GL20 ....182 A7
Fleming Cl GL2 ....127 C6
Fletchers Alley 17 GL20 192 C4
Flint Rd GL15 ....191 B4
Flisteridge Rd SN16 ....141 B1
Florence Brown Com Sch
The BS4 ....2 D8
Florence Pk
Almondsbury BS32 ......40 C5
Bristol BS6 ....18 B2
Florence Rd BS16 ......20 E7
Florence Terr GL15 ....142 E1
Florida Ave GL7 ....152 E3
Florida Dr GL52 ....134 B1
Flower Way GL2 ....127 A4
Flowers Hill BS4 ....9 E1
Flowers Hill Cl BS4 .....9 E1
Flowers Hill Trad Est BS4 .9 E1
Flowerwell Rd BS13 .....2 B5
Folders The GL15 ....92 B3
Foley Cl GL4 ....118 D3
Foley Rd GL18 ....171 A4
Foley Rise GL19 ....172 C2
Folk Mus* GL1 ....196 A3
Folland Ave GL3 ....120 B6
Folleigh Cl BS41 ....7 B2
Folleigh Dr BS41 ....7 B2
Folleigh La BS41 ....7 B2
Folliot Cl BS16 ....20 A7
Folly Brook Rd BS16 ....31 A1
Folly Cl SN6 ....145 D4
Folly Cres SN6 ....145 D4
Folly Field SN6 ....145 D4
Folly Gdns GL50 ....169 A8
Folly La Bristol BS2 ......9 A6
Cheltenham GL50 ......133 D3
English Bicknor GL16 ....64 C2
Huntley GL17 ....165 B7
Stroud GL5,GL6 ....103 A3
Folly Rd BS37 ....43 D2
Folly Vw GL13 ....111 E5
Folly View Rd BS16 .....31 B7
Fonthill Prim Sch BS10 ..28 E2
Fonthill Rd BS10 ....28 B1
Fonthill Way BS30 ......11 D6
Fontmell Cl GL4 ....3 D7
Fontwell Dr BS16 ....30 F1
Footes La BS36 ....31 B7

Footshill Cl BS15 ....10 C6
Footshill Dr BS15 ....10 C7
Footshill Rd BS15 ......10 C7
Fop St GL11 ....89 A1
Forbes Cl GL4 ....119 F6
Ford House Rd GL18 ...171 B6
Ford La Bristol BS16 ....21 B6
Gorsley GL18 ....170 D4
Ford St BS5 ....9 C6
Forde Cl BS30 ....10 F5
Fordell Pl BS4 ....9 A3
Fordwich Cl NP16 ......72 B5
Fore St SN6 ....142 F5
Forest Ave BS16 ....20 B3
Forest Cl GL16 ....154 E2
Forest Dr BS10 ....28 C3
Forest Edge BS15 ......10 C4
Forest Hills BS32 ......40 B5
Forest of Dean Sculpture
Trail* GL16 ....155 C7
Forest Par 2 GL15 .....92 A3
Forest Park Camping Site
GL16 ....154 F6
Forest Patch 6 GL16 ...155 A7
Forest Rd Bream GL15 ..142 D8
Bristol,Fishponds BS16 ...20 B4
Bristol,Kingswood BS15 ..10 C8
Cinderford GL14 ......191 D4
Lydney GL15 ....92 A3
Mile End GL16 ....155 B7
Milkwall GL16 ....155 B6
Ruardean Woodside GL17 .63 F4
Forest Rise
Cinderford GL14 ......191 E5
Nailsworth GL6 ....90 F4
Upper Lydbrook GL17 ..163 D2
Forest Vale Ind Est
GL14 ....191 B5
Forest Vale Rd GL14 ...191 A5
Forest View
Cinderford GL14 ......191 C1
North The NP25 ....154 B1
Forest View Cots Site
GL14 ....191 C3
Forest View Prim Sch
GL14 ....191 C4
Forest View Rd
Berkeley GL13 ....85 E4
Gloucester GL4 ....118 E1
Forest Wlk
Bristol,Fishponds BS16 ...20 B2
Bristol,Kingswood BS15 ..10 C8
Foresters Rd GL20 .....192 C2
Forge Cotts GL18 ......171 B6
Forge Gdns NP16 ....72 B6
Forge Hill GL17 ....163 C3
Forge La GL18 ....171 D6
Forge The GL17 ....163 C3
Forsdene Wlk GL16 ....155 B5
Forsyte Way GL4 ......118 A2
Forsythia Cl 8 GL3 ....128 A7
Fort La GL11 ....88 E8
Fort View Terr 98 E6
Fortey Rd GL54 ....168 A1
Fortfield Rd BS14 ....3 B6
Forthampton GL19 ......80 B8
Fortina Cl GL50 ....133 C5
Fortress The GL11 ......80 B8
Forty Acre La
Alveston BS35 ....51 B3
Stroud GL6 ....148 A8
Forty The SN6 ....143 E4
Fortys Pitch HR9 ......178 C7
Forum The GL1 ....196 C2
Foscombe La GL19 ....172 C5
Foss Ct 8 BS35 ....9 E2
Foss Field GL7 ....107 A8
Foss La BS35 ....13 E5
Fosscross La GL54,GL7 ..159 C3
Fosse Cl Cirencester GL7 .190 E5
Gloucester GL4 ....119 E6
Fosse La GL14 ....176 F5
Fossedale Ave BS14 .....3 C6
Fosseway Ave GL54 ....187 A2
Fosseway 7 GL56 ......187 A2
Fosseway Ct Bristol BS8 .194 A2
Lechlade on T GL7 .....153 E3
Fosseway La GL56 .....187 A2
Fosseway The BS8 .....194 A3
Foster Cl GL52 ....134 A3
Foster Ct GL52 ....134 A3
Foster St 3 GL52 ......134 A4
Foster St BS5 ....9 E6
Foster's Almshouses
BS1 ....195 A2
Foundry La BS5 ....19 F2
Foundry Rd GL14 .....191 D5
Foundry Wood Forest
Trails* GL14 ....156 D5
Foundry Yd BS5 ....9 F7
Fountain Cl GL12 ......108 F8
Fountain Ct Bristol BS32 .40 C3
3 Yate BS37 ....27 F2
Fountain Sq GL1 ....196 A3
Fountain St GL6 ....91 C4
Fountain Way NP16 .....60 F4
Fountaine Ct 3 BS35 ....9 E2
Four Acre Cl SN6 ......146 A6
Four Acre Cres BS16 ...19 F4
Four Acre Rd BS16 .....20 A4
Four Acres BS13 ....1 E4
Four Acres Cl BS13 ......1 F4
Four Acres Prim Sch BS13 .1 E4
Four Acres View GL7 ..190 B3

our Seasons Sq BS37 . . .43 E1
ourth Ave
 Bristol,Filton BS7 . . . . .29 A1
 Bristol,Hengrove BS14 . . . .3 B7
Oursley GL11 . . . . .80 C8
ourth Way BS11 . . . . .26 E1
owbridge Gdns HR9 . .163 C8
owler's Hill GL7 . . . . . .152 D7
ox & Hounds La BS31 . . . .4 F5
ox Ave BS37 . . . . .43 D2
ox Cl Bristol BS4 . . . . .9 F5
Gloucester GL4 . . . . .119 F5
Hawkesbury Upton GL9 . . . .5S F3
Stroud GL5 . . . . .98 C7
ox Ct BS30 . . . . .10 F3
ox Den Rd BS34 . . . . .29 D3
ox Dr GL54 . . . . .176 D4
ox Elms Rd GL4 . . . . . . .118 E2
ox Hill GL8 . . . . .140 C3
ox Ho BS4 . . . . .9 E3
ox La 11 GL54 . . . . .176 F4
ox Rd BS5 . . . . .19 B1
ox Run GL2 . . . . .118 A2
'ox's La GL16 . . . . .155 B5
oxborough Gdns BS32 . .40 D2
oxcombe Rd BS14 . . . . . . .3 B4
oxcote Bristol BS15 . . . . . .10 F7
Gloucester GL2 . . . . .185 B5
oxcote Hill GY36 . . . . . .189 F5
oxcote Rd BS3 . . . . .8 A3
oxcott SN6 . . . . .143 E6
oxcroft Cl BS32 . . . . . . .29 F6
oxcroft Rd BS5 . . . . .9 D8
oxe Rd BS36 . . . . .31 B8
oxes Bank Dr GL7 . . . . .190 B2
oxes Bridge Rd GL14 . .191 B5
oxes Cl
 8 Bourton-on-t-W GL54 . .168 F7
 Chalford GL6 . . . . .148 C6
oxes Dell GL6 . . . . .91 A5
oxes Row GL56 . . . . .177 A6
oxfield Ave BS32 . . . . . . .40 D3
oxglove Cl Bristol BS16 . .19 E5
 Cirencester GL7 . . . . . . .190 E2
 Gloucester GL4 . . . . .119 E5
 Thornbury BS35 . . . . .64 D2
oxglove Way GL5 . . . . .155 B4
oxgrove Dr GL52 . . . . . .134 A1
oxholes La BS32 . . . . . . .50 C4
oxleaze SN6 . . . . .143 E5
oxleigh Cres GL2 . . . . . .127 E5
oxmoor GL2 . . . . .54 C6
oxmoor La GL5 . . . . .98 C7
oxmoor Prim Sch GL5 . . .98 D7
oxtail Cl GL4 . . . . .119 A5
oxwell Dr GL3 . . . . .120 A8
oye Ho BS8 . . . . .7 E6
Fraley Rd BS9 . . . . .18 A7
Framlington Ct GL51 . . .133 A1
Frampton Cotterell CE Prim
 Sch BS36 . . . . .31 A8
Frampton Cotts GL20 . .183 E3
Frampton Cres BS16 . . .20 C4
Frampton Ct
 8 Bristol,Longwell Green
 BS30 . . . . .10 F4
 18 Bristol,Pile Marsh BS5 . . .9 D7
Frampton Dr WR12 . . . . .188 E2
Frampton End Rd BS37 . . .42 D2
Frampton Mews GL51 . .129 B7
Frampton Rd GL11 . . . . .118 D7
France La GL9 . . . . .56 B2
Frances Ct GL52 . . . . . . .133 F1
Frances Greeves Ct BS10 .27 F1
Francis Ct BS5 . . . . .9 E7
Francis Ho BS2 . . . . .195 A4
Francis Pl BS30 . . . . .10 F4
Francis Rd
 Bristol,Bedminster BS3 . . . .8 C2
 Bristol,Westbury on Trym
 BS10 . . . . .18 C8
Francis St GL53 . . . . . . .193 B1
Francis Way BS30 . . . . . .11 D6
Francis Woodcock Trad Est
 5 GL1 . . . . .119 A8
Francombe Gd BS10 . . . .18 E6
Francombe Ho BS1 . . . . .195 A1
Frank Brookes Rd GL51 . .133 A4
Franklin Ct BS1 . . . . .195 B1
Franklyn Ct
 6 Bristol BS16 . . . . .19 E3
 Cheltenham GL51 . . . . . .132 E2
Franklyn La 10 BS2 . . . . . .18 F1
Franklyn St BS2 . . . . .18 F1
Fraser St BS3 . . . . .8 D3
Frayne Rd BS3 . . . . .8 A4
Frazier's Folly GL7 . . . . .150 E2
Freame Cl GL54 . . . . . . .148 B6
Frederick Pl BS8 . . . . . . .194 B3
Frederick Thomas Rd
 GL11 . . . . .87 E4
Fredericks Way SN14 . . . .36 B3
Fredrick St BS4 . . . . .9 A4
Free Tank BS2 . . . . .195 C2
Freeland Bldgs 11 BS5 . .19 C2
Freeland Pl BS8 . . . . .7 F6
Freeling Ho BS1 . . . . . . .195 B1
Freemans Cl GL20 . . . . .181 F8
Freemans Orch 2 GL18 . .171 A4
Freemantle Gdns BS6 . . .19 C3
Freemantle Ho BS2 . . . .195 A4
Freemantle Rd BS5 . . . . .19 C3
Freeminers Way GL14 . .191 D5
Freestone Rd BS2 . . . . .9 A6
Freezinghill La BS30 . . . .13 B4
Fremantle La 8 BS6 . . . . .18 D1
Fremantle Rd BS6 . . . . . . .18 D1
Fremantle Sq BS6 . . . . . .18 D1

French La
 Lower Redbrook NP25 . . . .154 C4
 Newland GL16 . . . . .154 D4
Frenchay CE Prim Sch
 BS16 . . . . .20 B7
Frenchay La BS16 . . . . . .20 B7
Frenchay Hill BS16 . . . . . .20 C7
Frenchay Hospl BS16 . . . .20 B8
Frenchay Park Rd BS16 . . .19 F6
Frenchay Rd BS16 . . . . . .20 C6
Freshland Way BS15 . . . .10 B8
Fretherne Rd GL4 . . . . . .132 D3
Frewin Cl GL51 . . . . .132 D2
Frewins La GL14 . . . . . . .165 D3
Friar's Wlk BS18 . . . . . . .171 A5
Friars Cl GL51 . . . . .130 B5
Friars Ho 4 BS37 . . . . . . .32 D7
Friary BS1 . . . . .195 C2
Friary Grange Pk BS36 . . .30 E4
Friary Rd Bristol BS7 . . . .18 D4
 Gloucester GL4 . . . . .119 E6
Friday St Arlingham GL2 . .157 C6
 Minchinhampton GL6 . . . .148 A3
 Painswick GL6 . . . . .98 B5
Fridays Ham La SN6 . . . .143 A5
Friendly Row BS20 . . . . . .16 C5
Friendship Rd BS4 . . . . . . .9 A2
Friezewood Rd BS3 . . . . . .8 A4
Fripp Cl BS5 . . . . .9 B6
Frith La GL12 . . . . .53 F3
Frith The GL6 . . . . .148 B6
Frithwood GL6 . . . . .148 B6
Frithwood Cl GL6 . . . . . .148 B6
Frithwood Pk GL6 . . . . . .148 B6
Frobisher Mews GL3 . . . .127 F8
Frobisher Rd BS3 . . . . .8 A3
Frocester Hill GL10 . . . . . .89 C8
Frog Furlong La GL2,
 GL3 . . . . .127 E8
Frog La Bristol BS1 . . . . .194 C2
 Coalpit Heath BS36 . . . . . .31 E7
 Frocester GL10 . . . . .97 A3
 Huntley GL19 . . . . .165 D6
 Ilmington CV36 . . . . . . .189 F6
 North Nibley GL11 . . . . . .79 C5
Frogmarsh La GL5 . . . . . .91 A8
Frogmore Rd GL19 . . . . .165 D6
Frogmore St BS1 . . . . . .194 C2
Frome Ave GL5 . . . . .99 A6
Frome Ct BS35 . . . . .51 C8
Frome Gdns BS5 . . . . . . .99 B8
Frome Glen BS36 . . . . . . .30 E4
Frome Park Rd BS16 . . . .99 A6
Frome Pl 11 BS16 . . . . .19 E5
Frome Rd Bristol BS2 . . .195 C4
 Chipping Sodbury BS37 . . .44 C1
Frome Terr BS16 . . . . .19 E5
Frome Valley Rd BS16 . . .19 F6
Frome View BS36 . . . . . . .31 B7
Frome Villas BS16 . . . . . .20 C7
Frome Way BS36 . . . . . . .30 E5
Fromebank Jun Sch
 BS37 . . . . .43 D3
Fromeside GL5 . . . . .99 C6
Fromeside Dr GL5 . . . . . .98 D6
Fromeside Ind Est GL5 . . .99 C6
Fromeside Pk BS16 . . . . . .20 C4
Fromeside Rd BS16 . . . . . .20 D3
Front La SN26 . . . . .144 D2
Front St Ilmington CV36 . .189 F6
 Nympsfield GL10 . . . . .89 E5
Froomshaw Rd BS16 . . . . .20 A7
Frost & Reed Ho 3 BS5 . . .9 B7
Frowens La HR9 . . . . .170 B4
Fry Ct 2 BS3 . . . . .8 C4
Fry's Cl BS16 . . . . .19 D4
Frys Hill BS4 . . . . .9 D2
Frys Hill BS15 . . . . .20 E2
Frys House of Mercy
 BS1 . . . . .195 B1
Fryth Wood/Coed Fferwth
 NP16 . . . . .60 C8
Fulbrook Cl GL51 . . . . . .132 D5
Fulford Ctr BS13 . . . . .2 C4
Fulford Rd BS13 . . . . .2 B5
Fulford Wlk BS13 . . . . .2 B5
Fullers Ave 10 SN6 . . . . .143 E4
Fullers Ct BS35 . . . . .64 D2
Fulmar Cl BS35 . . . . .64 D2
Fulmar Rd BS20 . . . . .1 F4
Furber Ct BS5 . . . . .10 B6
Furber Rd BS5 . . . . .10 B6
Furber Ridge BS5 . . . . . . .10 B6
Furber Vale BS5 . . . . .10 B6
Furlong Cl 3 BS37 . . . . . .178 E7
Furlong La GL52 . . . . . . .137 F3
Furlong Rd GL11 . . . . . . .118 E2
Furlong The GL6 . . . . . . .148 B6
Furlongs The GL12 . . . . . .69 C3
Furnace La GL14 . . . . . . .171 A5
Furnace Valley GL14 . . . .171 A5
Furnace Valley GL15 . . . .156 D1
Furze Croft GL2 . . . . .109 F7
Furze Rd BS16 . . . . .5 F2
Furze Rd BS16 . . . . .20 C3
Furzewood Rd BS15 . . . . .10 F8
Fussell Ct BS15 . . . . .10 F6
Fylton Croft BS14 . . . . .3 B3

G
Gabb La GL19 . . . . .173 B7
Gable Cl BS35 . . . . .39 A2
Gable Cotts GL7 . . . . . . .152 E3
Gable Point GL2 . . . . . . .138 B3
Gable Rd 7 BS5 . . . . .19 A1

Gable Row GL20 . . . . . . .182 F8
Gadshill Dr BS34 . . . . .29 E5
Gadshill Rd Bristol BS5 . . .19 C2
 Charlton Kings GL53 . . . .131 B3
Gadwell Rd GL20 . . . . . .192 E3
Gages Cl BS15 . . . . .10 F7
Gages Rd BS15 . . . . .10 F7
Gaineys Well GL5 . . . . . . .99 D7
Gainsborough Dr GL4 . .118 C2
Gainsborough Ho GL55 .189 B2
Gainsborough Mews
 BS10 . . . . .28 B2
Gainsborough Rd BS31 . . .4 F5
Gainsborough Sq BS7 . . .19 B7
Gainsborough Terr
 GL55 . . . . .189 A1
Gales Ct GL7 . . . . .153 E2
Galileo Gdns GL51 . . . . .132 C5
Gallagher Ret Pk
 Bristol BS30 . . . . .10 E4
 Cheltenham GL51 . . . . . .132 F5
Galleries The BS1 . . . . . .195 B3
Galley Orch SN6 . . . . . . .143 F4
Gallivan Cl BS34 . . . . .29 B8
Gallops La GL52 . . . . . . .134 D4
Gallops The GL2 . . . . . . .118 B6
Gallows Pound La GL7 . .190 B8
Gallows Rd 6 GL14 . . . . .158 E2
Gambier Parry Gdns
 GL2 . . . . .126 F4
Gambles La GL12 . . . . . . .53 A4
Gambril La GL12 . . . . .65 F5
Ganborough Rd GL56 . .176 D8
Gander Cl BS13 . . . . .2 B5
Gander La
 Teddington GL20 . . . . . . .181 E4
 Tewkesbury GL20 . . . . . .192 C3
Gannaway La GL20 . . . . .192 F4
Gannet Cl GL33 . . . . .120 E5
Gannicox Rd GL5 . . . . . . .98 D7
Ganzell La GL11 . . . . .80 C7
Gara Cl BS13 . . . . .132 F5
Garamond Ct BS1 . . . . . .195 B1
Garden City Way 12
 NP16 . . . . .60 E8
Garden Cl Bristol BS9 . . . .17 C5
 Cirencester GL7 . . . . . . .190 D4
 Dumbleton WR11 . . . . . .183 F7
 Mickleton GL55 . . . . .189 B4
Garden Cotts GL19 . . . . .172 A2
Garden Ct BS8 . . . . .194 A4
Garden Rd GL53 . . . . . . .131 B4
Garden Suburb GL11 . . . .88 A1
Garden The GL5 . . . . .99 A3
Garden Way GL7 . . . . . . .127 B4
Gardeners Way
 King's Stanley GL10 . . . . .98 A4
 Newent GL18 . . . . .170 F4
Gardeners Wlk BS41 . . . . .7 B1
Gardenia Gr GL51 . . . . . .129 F5
Gardens The
 Bristol,Frenchay BS16 . . . .19 F7
 4 Bristol,Upper Soundwell
 BS16 . . . . .20 D3
 Cheltenham GL50 . . . . . .133 E4
 Monmouth/Trefynwy
 NP25 . . . . .154 A8
Gardner Cl GL16 . . . . . . .148 C6
Gardiners Cl GL3 . . . . . . .128 A6
Gardner Ave GL3 . . . . . . .128 A6
Gardner Ct GL7 . . . . .190 D3
Gardner's La GL15 . . . . . .138 A2
Gardners Lane Prim Sch
 GL51 . . . . .133 C4
Garfield Ct BS5 . . . . .9 F8
Garfield Rd BS5 . . . . .10 C8
Garland Ct GL7 . . . . .190 C3
Garlands Rd GL15 . . . . . .147 D3
Garlandstone Wlk GL2 . .118 C6
Garnalls Rd GL4 . . . . . . .119 C4
Garnet St BS3 . . . . .8 B3
Garnett Pl BS16 . . . . .20 F7
Garnett Rd GL51 . . . . . . .129 E2
Garren View HR9 . . . . . . .162 C7
Garrett Dr BS32 . . . . .29 D7
Garretts The GL7 . . . . . . .152 D4
Garth Rd BS13 . . . . .2 A7
Garton Ho 3 BS16 . . . . . . .20 F7
Garvey Ho 14 BS5 . . . . .9 C7
Gas La Bristol BS2 . . . . . . .9 B6
 Cricklade SN6 . . . . .143 F4
Gasferry Rd BS1 . . . . . . .194 B1
Gaskins The BS7 . . . . .19 A5
Gassons Rd GL7 . . . . . . .153 E2
Gassons Way GL7 . . . . . .153 E2
Gaston Ave BS18 . . . . .4 F6
Gaston La SN16 . . . . .58 D1
Gastons The GL11 . . . . . . .17 A8
Gastrells Com Prim Sch
 GL5 . . . . .99 A4
Gasworks La GL54 . . . . . .168 F7
Gasworks Villas GL5 . . . . .99 C6
Gatcombe Cl GL17 . . . . . .18 C6
Gatcombe Dr BS34 . . . . . .37 E3
Gatcombe Rd BS13 . . . . . . .2 A5
Gatehouse Ave BS13 . . . . .2 A5
Gatehouse Cl BS13 . . . . . . .2 A5
Gatehouse Ctr BS13 . . . . . .2 B5
Gatehouse Way BS13 . . . . .2 A5
Gatesby Mead BS34 . . . . .29 E5
Gathorne Cres BS37 . . . . .43 D2
Gathorne Rd BS3 . . . . .8 C3
Gatton Ave GL17 . . . . . . .119 C3
Gatton Rd BS2 . . . . .19 B8
Gatton Way GL13 . . . . . . .127 F1
Gatwick Cl BS37 . . . . . . .157 C4

Gaunt's La BS1 . . . . .194 C2
Gaunts Earthcott La
 BS32 . . . . .41 B5
Gaunts Rd BS37 . . . . .33 B8
Gay Elms Prim Sch BS13 . .2 A4
Gay Elms Rd BS13 . . . . . . .2 A4
Gayner Rd BS7 . . . . .29 A1
Gays Rd BS15 . . . . .10 B4
Gaywood Ho 7 BS3 . . . . . .8 B3
Gazelle Cl GL2 . . . . .117 F2
Gazzard Cl BS36 . . . . .30 E7
Gazzard Rd BS36 . . . . . . .30 E7
Gee Moors BS15 . . . . .10 F7
Gefle Cl BS1 . . . . .194 B1
Genista Way 3 GL51 . . . .129 F5
Geoffrey Cl BS13 . . . . .1 E6
George & Dragon La 11
 BS5 . . . . .9 D7
George Ct 6 Bristol BS6 . .18 B1
 Painswick GL6 . . . . .103 F8
George Dowty Dr GL52 . .155 C8
George Jones Rd BS2 . . . . .9 A6
George La
 Chipping Campden GL55 . .189 A1
 Cinderford GL14 . . . . . . .164 E1
 Littledean GL14 . . . . .191 F4
 Marshfield SN14 . . . . .24 E1
George Naisey Ho 6
 GL52 . . . . .134 A3
George Pl GL10 . . . . .155 A7
George Pl GL10 . . . . .155 A2
George Pl SN6 . . . . .145 D3
George Rd Bristol BS5 . . . .9 E8
 Cheltenham GL52 . . . . . .134 B4
 Kingswood BS41 . . . . .7 C2
 Minchinhampton GL6 . . . .148 A3
 Newent GL18 . . . . .170 F4
George St Bisley GL6 . . . .105 A1
 Bristol BS5 . . . . .9 E8
 Gloucester GL1 . . . . .196 C3
 Nailsworth GL6 . . . . .91 C4
 5 Stroud GL5 . . . . .99 C7
George The GL54 . . . . . .174 A7
George Whitefield Cl 5
 GL4 . . . . .119 C4
George Whitefield Ct
 BS1 . . . . .195 B3
Georgia Rd GL7 . . . . .152 E2
Georgian Cl GL4 . . . . . . .119 E3
Georgian House Mus*
 BS1 . . . . .194 C2
Gerald Rd BS3 . . . . .8 A3
Geralds Way GL6 . . . . . . .148 C6
Gere Cl GL4 . . . . .118 D2
Gerrish Ave
 Bristol,Moorfields BS5 . . . .9 C8
 Bristol,St George BS5 . . . .10 A8
Gervase Rd GL54 . . . . . . .174 A8
Gibbs Ct BS14 . . . . .3 D7
Gibbsfold Rd BS13 . . . . . . .2 C4
Gibraltar Way NP16 . . . . . .61 B4
Gibson Ave GL51 . . . . . . .129 C3
Gibson Cl GL17 . . . . .99 F7
Gibson Rd Bristol BS6 . . .18 D1
 Innsworth GL3 . . . . .127 F8
Giffard Ho BS34 . . . . .29 D6
Giffard Way GL53 . . . . . .130 D4
Gifford Cl Gloucester GL2 .127 C5
 Rangeworthy BS37 . . . . . . .43 A8
Gifford Cres BS34 . . . . . . .29 D2
Gifford Rd GL54 . . . . .174 B8
Giffords Pl BS13 . . . . .2 B6
Gilbert Hill GL13 . . . . .85 E4
Gilbert Rd
 Bristol,Moorfields BS5 . . . .9 C8
 Bristol,Staple Hill BS16 . . .20 A8
Gilberts La GL14 . . . . . . .110 F6
Gilda Cl BS14 . . . . .3 D5
Gilda Cres BS14 . . . . .3 C6
Gilda Par BS14 . . . . .3 D5
Gilda Sq W BS14 . . . . .3 C5
Gilder Rd GL52 . . . . .138 A2
Gilders Paddock GL52 . . . .7 F8
Giles Ave BS14 . . . . .143 E3
Giles Cox GL2 . . . . .109 F8
Gill Ave BS16 . . . . .19 D4
Gillard Cl BS15 . . . . .10 B5
Gillard Rd BS15 . . . . .10 B5
Gilled Cl BS14 . . . . .3 D5
Gillett Cl GL54 . . . . .176 A7
Gillingham Hill 17 BS15 . .10 B5
Gillingstool BS35 . . . . . . .51 B8
Gillingstool Prim Sch
 BS35 . . . . .51 B8
Gilpin Cl BS15 . . . . .10 B6
Gilpin Ave GL4 . . . . .127 F1
Gilroy Cl BS30 . . . . .10 B6
Gilslake Ave BS10 . . . . . . .18 C3
Gilton Ho BS4 . . . . .9 E4
Gimson Cl BS13 . . . . .1 F6
Gingell's Gn 4 BS5 . . . . . .10 A8
Gipsy La Chalford GL6 . . .148 A6
 Leonard Stanley GL10 . . . . .97 E2
Gipsy Patch La BS34 . . . . .29 C6
Gladbeck Way BS6 . . . . . .18 E6
Glades The BS5 . . . . .19 C1
Gladfield Gdns GL53 . . . .131 C1
Gladfield St GL1 . . . . .119 D7
Gladiator Cl GL2 . . . . . . .120 D6
Gladstone Ct
 Bristol BS16 . . . . .20 E8
 Bristol,Downend BS16 . . . .20 E8
Gladstone La BS5 . . . . .9 C6
Gladstone Rd
 Bristol,Hanham BS15 . . . .10 B4
 Bristol,Redland BS6 . . . . . .18 C1
 Yate BS37 . . . . .43 E2
Glena Ave BS4 . . . . .9 E2
Glenarm Rd BS4 . . . . .9 E2
Glenarm Wlk BS4 . . . . .9 E2
Glenavon Pk BS9 . . . . . . .17 C4
Glenburn Rd GL20 . . . . . .20 B1
Glencairn Cl GL30 . . . . . .130 A8
Glencairn Park Rd GL50 .130 A8
Glencarn Pl 15 GL16 . . . .155 A7
Glencoe GL17 . . . . .164 D4
Glencoyne Sq BS10 . . . . .28 C2
Glendale 17 Bristol BS6 . . .7 F6
 Bristol,Downend BS16 . . . .20 E8
Glendare St BS5 . . . . .9 C6
Glendevon Rd BS14 . . . . . .3 B3
Glendower Cl GL3 . . . . . .127 E3
Glendower Ho 5 BS8 . . .194 A2
Gleneagles BS37 . . . . .43 E1
Gleneagles Cl BS30 . . . . .11 B6
Gleneagles Dr BS10 . . . . .28 D2
Gleneagles Rd GL51 . . . . .30 D7
Glenfall GL52 . . . . .32 D7
Glenfall Com Prim Sch
 GL52 . . . . .131 C5
Glenfall St GL52 . . . . . . .131 B6
Glenfall Way GL52 . . . . . .131 B6
Glenfrome Prim Sch BS5 . .19 B4
Glenfrome Rd BS2 . . . . . . .19 B3
Glenlea Gr GL51 . . . . .132 E5
Glenlea Rd BS9 . . . . .20 C7
Glenroy Ave BS15 . . . . . . .10 B5
Glensanda Ct GL50 . . . . .193 B2
Glenside Hospl Mus*
 BS35 . . . . .19 E5
Glenside Pk 8 BS16 . . . . .19 E5
Glenthorne Cl GL17 . . . . .101 F1
Glentworth Rd
 Bristol,Clifton Wood BS8 . .194 B2
 Bristol,Redland BS6 . . . . . .18 C1
Glenview Rd BS4 . . . . .9 D2
Glenville Par GL17 . . . . . .20 B1
Glenwood BS16 . . . . .20 D3
Glenwood Dr GL11 . . . . . .41 D8
Glenwood Rd BS10 . . . . . .18 E7
Glevum Cl Bristol BS16 . . .20 D6
 Gloucester GL2 . . . . .127 B4
Glevum Ct Bristol BS11 . . .17 D7
Glevum Sh Ctr GL4 . . . . .119 E4
Glevum Way GL4 . . . . . . .119 E4
Glevum Works (Trad Est)
 GL1 . . . . .119 A7
Glevum Works Trad Est
 GL1 . . . . .118 F7
Gloster Ades Rd WR11 . .188 B6
Gloster Ave BS5 . . . . .19 D3
Gloster Bsns Pk GL20 . . .120 B6
Gloucester Cl BS34 . . . . . .29 D5

Fou – Glo 215

Gladstone Rd continued
 Gloucester GL1 . . . . .118 D6
Gladstone St
 Bristol,Bedminster BS3 . . . .8 B3
 Bristol,Kingswood BS16 . . .20 D3
 15 Bristol,Pile Marsh BS5 . . .9 D7
Glaisdale Rd BS16 . . . . . . .20 A5
Glamorgan Rd GL51 . . . .129 D6
Glanville Gdns BS15 . . . . .20 E7
Glass House Ltd BS2 . . . . .9 B5
Glasshouse The GL50 . . .193 A3
Glastonbury Cl BS30 . . . . .10 F5
Glebe Cl
 Frampton on Severn GL2 . .157 F1
 Long Ashton BS41 . . . . . . .7 C2
Mitcheldean GL17 . . . . . .164 B5
Newent GL18 . . . . .170 F5
11 Stow-on-t-W GL54 . . .176 F4
 Stratton GL7 . . . . .190 B8
Glebe Ct GL18 . . . . .170 F5
Glebe Farm Ct GL51 . . . .129 F5
Glebe Fold 10 GL55 . . . . .189 A2
Glebe La GL54 . . . . .141 F8
Glebe Rd Bristol BS6 . . . . .18 C1
Glebe Pl SN6 . . . . .145 D3
Glebe Rd Bristol BS5 . . . . .9 E8
 Cheltenham GL52 . . . . . .134 B4
 Long Ashton BS41 . . . . . . .7 C2
 Minchinhampton GL6 . . . .148 A3
 Newent GL18 . . . . .170 F4
Glebe The Pilning BS35 . . .38 C7
 Sapperton GL7 . . . . .149 B6
Glebe View GL17 . . . . . . .158 C4
Glebe Way GL18 . . . . . . .170 F5
Glebe Wlk BS31 . . . . .4 D3
Glebeland Dr GL20 . . . . .182 C7
Glebelands GL11 . . . . .87 F5
Glebelands Rd BS34 . . . . .29 A3
Glebes The BS5 . . . . .9 E8
Gledemoor Dr BS36 . . . . .31 D7
Glen Cl GL10 . . . . .97 F8
Glen Dr BS9 . . . . .17 C5
Glen Hospl The BS8 . . . . . .18 A2
Glen La BS4 . . . . .9 E4
Glen Park Cres BS5 . . . . . .99 A4
Glen Park Rd BS5 . . . . . . .10 A8
Glen The
 Bristol,Eastville BS5 . . . . . .19 C2
 Bristol,St George BS5 . . . .10 A8
 Bristol,Hanham BS15 . . . .10 B4
 Bristol,Redland BS6 . . . . . .18 C1
 Saltford BS31 . . . . .5 F1
 Yate BS37 . . . . .43 E2

Gloucester Coll of Arts &
Tech GL1 . . . . .196 B2
Gloucester Cotts 5
GL50 . . . . .133 B2
Gloucester Ho 12 BS2 . .195 C3
Gloucester House Mews
GL12 . . . . .68 A8
Gloucester La
20 Bristol BS2 . . . . .195 C3
Mickleton GL55 . . . . .189 A6
Gloucester Mus & Art Gal*
GL1 . . . . .196 B2
Gloucester Pl GL52 . . . .193 C4
Gloucester Prison Mus*
GL1 . . . . .196 A3
Gloucester Rd
Almondsbury BS32,BS35 . .40 C6
Andoversford GL54 . . . . .166 D6
Avonmouth BS11 . . . . . . .26 A1
Bristol,Bishopston BS7 . . .18 E4
Bristol,Patchway BS34 . . . .29 B7
Bristol,Staple Hill BS16 . . .20 E3
Cheltenham GL51 . . . . . .132 D1
Cirencester GL7 . . . . . . .190 B6
Coleford GL16 . . . . .155 A5
Corse GL19 . . . . .172 B8
Mitcheldean GL17 . . . . . .164 D5
Newton GL13 . . . . .85 C8
Painswick GL6 . . . . .111 F1
Stone GL13 . . . . .77 F3
Stonehouse GL10 . . . . . .101 F1
Tadwick BA1 . . . . .13 F2
Tewkesbury GL20 . . . . . .181 F1
Thornbury BS35 . . . . .64 C3
Tutshill NP16 . . . . .73 A2
Upleadon GL18 . . . . .171 D5
Gloucester Rd N BS7,
BS34 . . . . .29 A4
Gloucester Retail Pk
GL4 . . . . .119 C8
Gloucester Road Prim Sch
GL51 . . . . .133 B2
Gloucester Row
7 Bristol BS8 . . . . .7 F7
Kingswood GL12 . . . . .67 F8
Gloucester Royal Hospl
GL1 . . . . .196 C3
Gloucester Rugby Football
Gd GL1 . . . . .196 B4
Gloucester Ski Ctr*
GL4 . . . . .119 B3
Gloucester St
12 Bristol,Clifton BS8 . . . . . .7 F7
Bristol,Eastville BS5 . . . . .19 D3
5 Bristol,St Pauls BS2 . . .195 B4
Cirencester GL7 . . . . . . .190 B6
Newent GL18 . . . . .171 A4
Painswick GL6 . . . . .103 F8
2 Stroud GL5 . . . . .99 C7
Winchcombe GL54 . . . . . .174 A7
Wotton-u-E GL12 . . . . . . .68 A7
Gloucester Sta GL1 . . . .196 C3
Gloucestershire &
Warwickshire Rly*
Bishop's Cleeve GL52 . . .138 B5
* Toddington GL54 . . . . .184 C1
* Winchcombe GL54 . . . .174 B8
Gloucestershire Airport
GL51 . . . . .128 D8
Gloucestershire Coll of Art &
Tech GL51 . . . . .132 D2
Gloucestershire Cty Cricket
Club* BS7 . . . . .18 F4
Gloucestershire Royal Hospl
GL1 . . . . .127 A2
Gloucestershire
Warwickshire Rly*
GL54 . . . . .183 D1
Glyn Terr GL5 . . . . .99 E3
Glyn Vale BS3 . . . . .8 E1
Glynbridge Ct 3 GL1 . . .118 F7
Glynbridge Gdns GL51 . .132 D2
Glyndthorpe Gr 12 GL51 .129 E5
Glynfield Rise GL5 . . . . . .98 C7
Glynrosa Rd GL53 . . . . . .131 B5
Goddard Way Bristol BS10 .28 A1
Gloucester GL4 . . . . .118 D2
Godfrey Cl GL51 . . . . . . .130 A7
Godfrey Ct 7 BS30 . . . . . .10 F4
Godwin Cl 15 GL52 . . . . .133 F2
Godwin Rd GL54 . . . . . . .174 A8
Goffenton Dr BS16 . . . . . .20 B6
Goldcrest Ct 8 GL10 . . . . .97 F8
Goldcrest Rd BS37 . . . . . .52 F7
Golden Cl GL4 . . . . .118 C2
Golden Farm Rd GL7 . . . .190 E4
Golden Hay WR11 . . . . . .183 F7
Golden Hill BS6 . . . . .18 A4
Golden Jubilee Way GL5 . .98 E6
Golden La GL12 . . . . .67 F4
Golden Lion Ct BS1 . . . . .195 B2
Golden Miller Rd GL50 . .133 C5
Golden Vale GL3 . . . . . . .128 B6
Golden Valley
Brimscombe GL5 . . . . . . .148 A5
Newent GL18 . . . . .171 D4
Golden Valley La BS30 . . .11 F2
Goldfinch Way BS16 . . . . .22 C4
Goldfoot Ho GL41 . . . . . .132 F1
Goldney Ave
Bristol,Clifton Wood BS8 . .194 A2
Bristol,Warmley BS30 . . . .11 C7
Goldney Ct 7 BS16 . . . . . .19 E3
Goldney Rd BS8 . . . . .194 A2
Goldsborough Cl GL4 . . . .119 B6

Goldsbury Wlk BS11 . . . . .27 A1
Goldsmith Cl GL51 . . . . .132 E2
Goldsmith Rd GL51 . . . . .132 E2
Goldsmiths Ho BS2 . . . . .195 C2
Golf Club La Saltford BS31 . .5 E2
Watermead GL1 . . . . .120 C5
Golf Course La BS34 . . . .28 F3
Golf Course Rd GL6 . . . . .111 F2
Gooch Cl WR11 . . . . .188 C7
Gooch Ct BS30 . . . . .11 C3
Good Neighbours La
NP25 . . . . .154 B7
Good Shepherd Cl BS7 . . .18 C4
Goode Ct 2 GL15 . . . . . . .92 A3
Goodeve Pk BS9 . . . . .17 D3
Goodeve Rd BS9 . . . . .17 D3
Goodhind St BS5 . . . . .9 A8
Goodier's La GL20 . . . . . .182 A7
Goodmans Terr 6 GL47 . .152 E4
Goodmoor Cres GL1 . . . .128 A6
Goodneston Rd BS16 . . . . .20 A8
Goodrich Castle* HR9 . . .163 A6
Goodrich CE Prim Sch
HR9 . . . . .163 A6
Goodrich Cl BS37 . . . . . . .43 B1
Goodrich Mill GL19 . . . . .172 D4
Goodridge Ave GL2 . . . . .118 A3
Goodridge Trad Est
GL2 . . . . .118 A4
Gooding Hill BS11 . . . . . . .27 A1
Goodwin Ct GL1 . . . . .118 E7
Goodwin Dr BS14 . . . . . . .2 F4
Goodwood Gdns BS16 . . . .30 F1
Goodyere St GL1 . . . . . . .196 C1
Golden St BS4 . . . . .9 A3
Goose Acre BS32 . . . . . . .29 F6
Goose Gn Bristol BS30 . . . .21 C1
Frampton Cotterell BS36 . . .31 C8
Yate BS37 . . . . .43 E3
Goose Green Way BS37 . . .43 E4
Goose La GL14 . . . . .157 F8
Gooseacre Ct GL7 . . . . . .190 C6
Gooseacre La GL7 . . . . . .190 C6
Gooseland Cl BS14 . . . . . . .2 F3
Gooselands SN16 . . . . . . .141 B3
Gopshill La GL54 . . . . . . .183 E1
Gordano Gdns BS20 . . . . .16 B4
Gordon Ave BS5 . . . . .19 C8
Gordon Cl Bristol BS5 . . . .19 E1
Broadway WR12 . . . . .185 B8
Highnam GL2 . . . . .125 E5
Gordon Rd
14 Bristol,St Pauls BS2 . . .18 F1
Bristol,Victoria Park BS8 . .194 B3
Bristol,Whitehall BS5 . . . .19 D1
Cheltenham GL53 . . . . . .130 C5
Gordon Terr
Brimscombe GL5 . . . . .99 F1
Stroud GL5 . . . . .99 D7
Gore Rd BS3 . . . . .8 A3
Gore's Marsh Rd BS3 . . . .8 A1
Gorham Cl BS11 . . . . .27 C2
Gorlands Rd BS37 . . . . . . .44 C1
Gorlangton Cl BS14 . . . . . .3 A7
Gorse Bglws GL16 . . . . . .155 A6
Gorse Cl
Bourton-on-t-W GL54 . . . .169 A7
Gloucester GL4 . . . . .119 F4
Gorse Cover Rd BS35 . . . .38 A7
Gorse Hill BS16 . . . . .20 C3
Gorse La Bristol BS8 . . . . .194 B2
Cold Ashton BS30,SN14 .13 D7
Sling GL16 . . . . .155 B3
Gorse Mdw GL14 . . . . . . .169 A6
Gorse The GL54 . . . . .169 A7
Gorsley Gdns HR9 . . . . . .170 B4
Gorsley Goff's Prim Sch
HR9 . . . . .170 B5
Gosditch
Ashton Keynes SN6 . . . . . .142 F4
Cirencester GL7 . . . . .143 E6
Gosditch St GL7 . . . . .190 C5
Gosforth Cl BS10 . . . . . . .28 B1
Gosforth Rd BS10 . . . . . . .28 B1
Goshawk Rd GL2 . . . . . . .117 F3
Goslet Rd BS14 . . . . .3 E5
Goss Wood Cnr GL2 . . . .109 E8
Gotherington Fields
GL52 . . . . .137 E8
Gotherington La GL52 . . .138 A5
Gotherington Prim Sch
GL52 . . . . .138 B7
Gotherington Sta*
GL52 . . . . .138 D8
Gothic Cotts GL1 . . . . . . .196 C2
Gotley Rd BS4 . . . . .9 D2
Gouda Way GL1 . . . . .196 B4
Gould Dr GL20 . . . . .182 C5
Goulston Rd BS13 . . . . . . .2 A5
Goulston Wlk BS13 . . . . . .2 A5
Goulter St BS5 . . . . .9 B6
Gover Rd BS15 . . . . .21 D7
Govier Way BS35 . . . . . . .38 C4
Gowle Rd GL5 . . . . .99 D6
Gowan Ct BS37 . . . . .44 A6
Grace Cl BS37 . . . . .20 C6
Grace Dr Bristol BS15 . . . .11 A8
1 Northleach GL54 . . . . . .168 A1
Grace Gdns GL51 . . . . . . .129 D7
Grace Park Rd BS4 . . . . . . .9 D1
Grace Ct BS16 . . . . .20 C5
Graces Pitch 16 GL18 . . . .171 A4
Graeme Cl GL50 . . . . .193 B1
Grafton La GL19 . . . . .180 B3

Grafton Rd
Cheltenham GL50 . . . . . . .193 A1
Gloucester GL2 . . . . .127 B3
Graham Ct GL20 . . . . .192 D5
Graham Gdns GL2 . . . . . .127 B3
Graham Pl GL51 . . . . .132 D3
Graham Rd
4 Bristol,Bedminster BS3 . . .8 C3
Bristol,Downend BS16 . . . .20 F6
21 Bristol,Upper Easton
BS5 . . . . .19 B1
Grahamstown Gr NP16 . . .61 B8
Grahamstown Rd NP16 . . .61 B8
Grainger Ct BS11 . . . . . . .16 E7
Grampian Cl BS30 . . . . . . .11 C4
Granary The
Blockley GL56 . . . . .186 C7
Bristol BS1 . . . . .195 A2
Granby La GL55 . . . . .189 B7
Granby Hill BS8 . . . . .7 F6
Grandmother's Rock La
BS30 . . . . .12 D2
Grange Ave
Bristol,Hanham BS15 . . . . .10 D5
Bristol,Little Stoke BS34 . . .29 C6
Grange Cl
Bristol,Patchway BS32 . . . .40 C2
Bristol,Stoke Gifford BS34 . .30 A4
Highworth SN6 . . . . .145 D3
Minchinhampton GL6 . . . . .91 F6
Grange Cl N BS9 . . . . .18 B6
Grange Ct Bristol BS15 . . . .10 C3
Grange Court La GL19 . . .165 D6
Grange Court Rd
Bristol,Henleaze BS9 . . . . .18 B6
Bristol,Westbury on Trym
BS9 . . . . .18 A8
Northway GL20 . . . . .182 C5
Grange Dr
Bishop's Cleeve GL52 . . . .137 F3
Bristol BS16 . . . . .20 C6
Grange Inf Sch GL4 . . . . .118 C2
Grange Jun Sch GL4 . . . .118 C3
Grange Pk
Bristol,Frenchay BS16 . . . .20 C8
Bristol,Westbury on Trym
BS9 . . . . .18 B6
St Arvans NP16 . . . . .72 A6
Grange Rd
Bristol,Bishopsworth BS13 . .2 A5
Bristol,Victoria Park BS8 . .194 A3
Gloucester GL4 . . . . .118 D1
Northway GL20 . . . . .182 C5
Saltford BS31 . . . . .5 C3
St Arvans NP16 . . . . .72 A6
Grange Sch & Sports Coll
The BS30 . . . . .11 B7
Grange The
Bristol,Coombe Dingle BS9 . .17 D7
Bristol,Sneyd Park BS9 . . . .17 F3
Cheltenham GL53 . . . . . .129 B6
Gloucester GL2 . . . . .127 B2
8 Moreton-in-M GL56 . . .187 A3
Grange Wlk GL53 . . . . . . .131 B5
Grangefield Prim Sch
GL52 . . . . .137 E3
Grangeville Cl BS30 . . . . .11 B3
Grangewood Cl 4 BS16 . . .20 D6
Granley Cl GL51 . . . . .129 F8
Granley Dr GL51 . . . . .129 F8
Granley Gdns GL51 . . . . .129 F8
Granley Rd GL51 . . . . . . .129 F8
Granna La GL52 . . . . .138 D8
Granny's La BS15 . . . . . . .10 E6
Gransmoor Grange GL3 . .120 B7
Grantham Ho BS15 . . . . . .20 C1
Grantham La BS15 . . . . . .20 C1
Grantham Rd BS15 . . . . . .20 C1
Grantley Cres GL7 . . . . . .190 E2
Granton Cl BS4 . . . . .9 F2
Granville Cl BS15 . . . . .10 B3
Granville St BS5 . . . . .9 C6
Grasby Cl GL14 . . . . .119 E7
Grasmere Cl BS10 . . . . . . .18 A8
Grasmere Rd
Cheltenham GL51 . . . . . . .129 F7
Gloucester GL2 . . . . .127 C4
Grass Meers Dr BS14 . . . . .3 A5
Grassington Dr BS37 . . . . .33 A8
Grasscroft Gdns BS30 . . . .11 D6
Gratitude Rd BS5 . . . . .19 C1
Gratton Rd GL50 . . . . . . .193 A1
Gratton St GL50 . . . . .193 B1
Gravel Hill Rd N BS37 . . . .44 A5
Gravel Pit Cotts GL52 . . .131 C6
Gravel Pit La GL52 . . . . . .134 C5
Gravel Pit Rd GL52 . . . . . .182 C7
Gravel Wlk
Bristol GL52 . . . . .134 C8
Cirencester GL7 . . . . .190 D5
Graveney Cl BS4 . . . . .9 D1
Graveney Rd GL54 . . . . . .168 A1
Gravney Cl GL51 . . . . .132 E4
Gray Cl BS10 . . . . .27 E2
Grayling Ct 7 BS10 . . . . . .27 E2
Innsworth GL3 . . . . .127 E7

Gray Rd GL7 . . . . .151 A2
Gray's La 20 GL56 . . . . . .187 A3
Grayle Rd BS10 . . . . .28 A2
Grayling Cl 7 GL4 . . . . . .119 E5
Grayling Ho BS9 . . . . .17 F7
Grayson Cl GL20 . . . . .192 E6
Great Ann St BS2 . . . . . . .195 C3
Great Brockeridge BS9 . . .17 F6
Great Dowles BS30 . . . . . .11 A4
Great George St
Bristol,Brandon Hill BS1 . .194 C2
Bristol,St Pauls BS2 . . . . .195 C3
Great Gr GL4 . . . . .119 D7
Great Hayles Rd BS14 . . . .3 A6
Great Leaze BS30 . . . . . . .11 A4
Great Mdw BS34 . . . . .30 A6
Great Meadow Rd BS32 . .29 F6
Great Norwood St GL50 . .193 B1
Great Orch GL5 . . . . .99 E3
Great Park Rd BS32 . . . . . .40 C3
Great Rissington Prim Sch
GL54 . . . . .169 D4
Great Rose La SN26 . . . . .144 D3
Great Stoke BS34 . . . . . . .30 A5
Great Stoke Way
Bristol,Great Stoke BS34 . . .30 A5
Bristol,Harry Stoke BS34 . . .29 D3
Great Western Bsns Pk
BS37 . . . . .43 B3
Great Western Ct
Bristol BS34 . . . . .29 F4
Gloucester GL1 . . . . .127 A1
Great Western La BS5 . . . . .9 C6
Great Western Railway Mus*
GL50 . . . . .155 A5
Great Western Rd
Cheltenham GL50 . . . . . . .193 B4
Gloucester GL1 . . . . .196 C3
Sharpness GL13 . . . . .93 B1
Great Western Terr
GL50 . . . . .193 A4
Great Witcombe Roman
Villa* GL3 . . . . .120 F1
Great Wood Cl BS13 . . . . . .2 C4
Greatfield Dr GL53 . . . . . .130 F5
Greatfield La
Cheltenham,Hatherley
GL51 . . . . .129 E5
Cheltenham,Warden Hill
GL51 . . . . .129 E5
Greatfield Park Prim Sch
GL51 . . . . .129 F5
Grebe Cl GL4 . . . . .119 E5
Grebe Sq GL54 . . . . .169 D6
Green Acre Bream GL15 . .147 D8
Bristol,Stoke Gifford BS34 . . .3 A3
Green Acre Rd BS14 . . . . .120 E4
Green Bank GL3 . . . . .120 E4
Green Cl
Honeybourne WR11 . . . . .188 C6
Uley GL11 . . . . .89 C2
Watermead GL1 . . . . .120 D4
Green Colley Cl HR9 . . . . .163 B6
Green Croft BS5 . . . . .20 A1
Green Dell Cl BS10 . . . . . .27 D3
Green Dragon Rd BS36 . . .30 D5
Green Gdns GL2 . . . . .120 E4
Green Hayes BS37 . . . . . . .33 C8
Green Hill BS35 . . . . .51 A4
Green La Avonmouth BS11 . .26 B1
Chedworth GL54 . . . . .159 B6
Churchdown GL3 . . . . .128 C4
Evenlode GL56 . . . . .177 C7
Gloucester GL3 . . . . .128 B8
Hardwicke GL2 . . . . .109 E6
Little Witcombe GL3 . . . . .121 C3
Marshfield SN14 . . . . .14 E8
Moreton Valence GL2 . . . .101 A6
Naunton WR8 . . . . .180 D10
Rangeworthy BS37,GL12 . . .53 B2
Severn Beach BS35 . . . . . .38 B8
Sherston SN16 . . . . .58 C1
Tewkesbury GL20 . . . . . . .182 B4
Tytherington GL12 . . . . . . .52 B8
Upper Rissington GL54 . . .168 D3
West Littleton SN14 . . . . . .29 E7
Green Lake Cl GL54 . . . . .168 F8
Green Meadow Bank
GL52 . . . . .134 E3
Green Pastures NP25 . . . .154 A3
Green Pippin Cl GL2 . . . .127 D7
Green Pk GL2 . . . . .109 E6
Green Side BS5 . . . . .21 A6
Green St Bristol BS3 . . . . . .8 F4
Bushley GL19,GL20 . . . . . .181 B5
Chepstow/Cas-Gwent NP16 .60 E8
Dursley GL11 . . . . .38 C6
Watermead GL1 . . . . .120 D3
Green The
Bishop's Cleeve GL52 . . . .138 B4
Bledington OX7 . . . . .177 E1
Bristol,Filton BS34 . . . . . . .29 E4
6 Bristol,Stoke Gifford BS34 . .29 E4
6 Broadway WR12 . . . . . .185 C6
Chepstow/Cas-Gwent NP16 . .60 B5
Chipping Campden GL55 . .189 A1
Chipping Sodbury BS37 . . .34 A8
Churchdown GL3 . . . . .128 C3
Cromhall GL12 . . . . .53 F6
Fairford GL7 . . . . .152 D4
Frampton on Severn GL2 . .157 F2
Great Wolford CV36 . . . . .187 E5

Green The continued
Highworth SN6 . . . . .145 E4
Honeybourne WR11 . . . . .188 C6
Iron Acton BS37 . . . . .42 C1
Luckington SN14 . . . . .47 F2
10 Moreton-in-M GL56 . . .187 A3
Newnham GL14 . . . . .156 H
11 Northleach GL54 . . . . .168 A
Olveston BS35 . . . . .141 F
Olveston BS35 . . . . .50 F
Pill BS20 . . . . .16 D
Tetbury GL8 . . . . .140 C
Uckington GL51 . . . . .132 C
Uley GL11 . . . . .89 C
Woodmancote GL52 . . . . .138 C
Green Way GL54 . . . . .9 A
Green Wlk BS4 . . . . .9 A
Green's Cl GL54 . . . . .169 C
Greenacres Bristol BS9 . . .17 F
Twyning GL20 . . . . .181 H
Greenacres Park Homes
BS36 . . . . .31 E
Greenacres Pk GL7 . . . . . .152 A
Greenaways GL18 . . . . . . .170 H
Greenbank Avenue E
BS5 . . . . .19 C
Greenbank Avenue W
BS5 . . . . .19 C
Greenbank Cl GL17 . . . . . .164 E
Greenbank Rd
Bristol,Hanham BS15 . . . . .10 D
Bristol,Lower Easton BS5 . .19 C
Bristol,Southville BS3 . . . . . .8 C
Greenbank View BS5 . . . . .19 E
Greenbanks NP25 . . . . . . .146 E
Greendale Rd
Bristol,Lower Knowle BS3 . . .8 E
Bristol,Redland BS6 . . . . . .18 E
Greendicth Ave BS13 . . . . .2 C
Greendicth BS35 . . . . .49 C
Greendown BS5 . . . . .10 D
Greenfield Ave BS10 . . . . .18 C
Greenfield Cl GL17 . . . . . .163 C
Greenfield Ct BS10 . . . . . .28 C
Greenfield Rd
Bristol BS10 . . . . .28 D
Coleford GL16 . . . . .163 D
Joy's Green GL17 . . . . . . .163 D
Greenhaven BS3 . . . . .51 A
Greenhill BS15 . . . . .51 A
Greenhill Cl GL4 . . . . .191 E
Greenhill Ct GL4 . . . . .118 E
Greenhill Down BS35 . . . . .51 A
Greenhill Flats GL5 . . . . . .99 E
Greenhill Gdns BS35 . . . . .51 A
Greenhill Ho GL52 . . . . . .137 F
Greenhill La
Alveston BS35 . . . . .50 F
Bristol BS11 . . . . .27 A
Greenhill Par 5 BS35 . . . . .51 A
Greenhill Rd BS35 . . . . . . .51 A
Greenhills Rd GL53 . . . . . .130 F
Greenhouse La GL6 . . . . . .92 A
Greenings The GL51 . . . . .129 F
Greenlands Cl 16 NP25 . .154 A
Greenlands Rd GL51 . . . . .27 F
Green Mdw GL53 . . . . . . .130 D
Marston Meysey SN6 . . . .144 A
Greenleaze Ave BS16 . . . . .30 D
Greenleaze Cl BS16 . . . . . .30 D
Greenmead Park Cvn Site
GL51 . . . . .129 D
Greenmeadows Pk
GL51 . . . . .129 D
Greenmore Rd BS4 . . . . . . .9 B
Greenore BS15 . . . . .21 E
Greenpark Rd GL52 . . . . . .28 E
Greenridge Cl BS13 . . . . . . .1 E
Greenside GL50 . . . . .193 B
Greensplot Rd BS11 . . . . . .26 E
Greenstreet GL10 . . . . . . .191 D
Greenview Bristol BS30 . . .11 C
Great Wolford QL . . . . . . .152 D
Greenway Bush La BS3 . . . .8 B
Greenway Cl GL52 . . . . . .138 B
Greenway Dr BS10 . . . . . .129 D
Greenway Ho 10 BS6 . . . . .19 B
Greenway La
Charlton Kings GL52 . . . . .131 C
Cheltenham GL53 . . . . . . .122 B
Cold Ashton SN14 . . . . .13 A
Gretton GL54 . . . . .183 F
Little Shurdington GL51,
GL53 . . . . .121 E
Llandogo NP25 . . . . .146 A
Shurdington GL51 . . . . . . .121 E
Greenway Pk BS10 . . . . . .18 D
Greenways
Blockley GL56 . . . . .186 C
Bristol BS6 . . . . .18 B
Cinderford GL14 . . . . .191 C
Greenways The
Gloucester GL2 . . . . .118 D
Greenways Bristol BS15 . . .21 E
Lydney GL15 . . . . .147 E
Greenways La GL54 . . . . .173 D
Greenways Dr GL16 . . . . .153 C
Greenways Rd BS37 . . . . . .43 E
Greenwich Apartments
BS6 . . . . .18 C
Greenwood Cl Bristol BS7 . .18 C
Gloucester GL3 . . . . .120 B

reenwood Dr BS35 . . . . . .50 F4
reenwood Rd BS4 . . . . .9 A1
reet Rd BS14 . . . . .174 A8
regory Ct BS30 . . . . .11 A6
renadier Cl GL4 . . . . . . .119 F6
renadier Rd GL51 . . . . . .132 E4
renville Chapel **5** BS8 . . . .7 F5
renville Cl Bristol BS5 . . . . .9 F8
Tnnsworth GL3 . . . . .127 F8
renville Pl **7** BS1 . . . . . . .7 F5
renville Rd BS6 . . . . .18 E3
iresham Ct **5** GL51 . . . . .132 E2
retton Prim Sch GL54 . .183 E1
retton Rd
Gotherington GL52 . . . . . . .138 C8
Winchcombe GL54 . . . . . .174 A8
rentham Rd GL54 . . . . . .183 E4
reve Ct **5** BS30 . . . . .10 F4
revil Rd GL51 . . . . .189 A2
revil Rd **3** GL51 . . . . . .132 F4
reville Ct GL4 . . . . .126 E4
reville Ct GL51 . . . . .129 F8
reville Rd BS3 . . . . .8 A3
reville St BS3 . . . . .8 C4
rey Gables BS35 . . . . . . .50 A3
reyfriars GL1 . . . . .196 B2
reyfriars Church *
GL1 . . . . .196 B3
reyfriars Wlk GL7 . . . . . .190 B2
reyhound Gdns GL2 . . . .127 D5
reylag Cres GL20 . . . . . .192 E3
reylands Rd BS13 . . . . . . .1 F7
reyrick Ct GL51 . . . . . . .189 A6
reys Cl **5** GL6 . . . . .148 B6
reystoke Ave BS10 . . . . .28 C1
reystoke Gdns BS10 . . . . .18 A8
reystone Lodge GL3 . . . .120 B7
reystones BS16 . . . . .30 E1
reystones La GL54 . . . . .169 A7
rierson Cl GL3 . . . . .120 B6
riffin Cl GL54 . . . . .177 A4
riffin Ct GL54 . . . . .177 A4
riffin Mill Est GL5 . . . . . . .99 D4
riffiths Ave GL51 . . . . . .132 F1
riffon Cl GL2 . . . . .117 F3
riggfield Wlk BS14 . . . . . . .3 A7
riggs Cl **3** GL55 . . . . . .189 A2
rimsbury Rd BS15 . . . . . . .11 A7
rimwade Cl GL51 . . . . . .132 F1
rindell Rd BS5 . . . . .9 D7
rinfield Ave BS13 . . . . .2 C4
rinfield Ct BS13 . . . . .2 C4
risdale Cl GL2 . . . . .127 D5
rist Mill Cl GL51 . . . . . . .132 D5
rittleton Rd BS7 . . . . .18 E8
rosten The WR11 . . . . . .183 D8
rosvenor Ct **2** BS6 . . . . .18 B1
rosvenor Ho GL1 . . . . . .196 B3
rosvenor Pl S GL52 . . . .193 C3
rosvenor Rd Bristol BS2 . . .18 F1
Gloucester GL2 . . . . .127 B2
Stonehouse GL10 . . . . . . .101 F1
rosvenor St GL52 . . . . . .193 C3
rosvenor Terr GL52 . . . .193 C3
rove Ave Bristol BS1 . . . . .195 A1
Bristol,Coombe Dingle BS9 . .17 C7
3 Bristol,Fishponds BS16 . .19 F4
Honeybourne WR11 . . . . . .188 C7
rove Bank BS16 . . . . .30 C1
rove Cotts GL5 . . . . .98 F8
rove Cres
Cheltenham GL50 . . . . . . .193 A4
Gloucester GL1 . . . . .196 C1
7 Coleford GL16 . . . . . .155 A6
Gloucester GL4 . . . . .127 D1
rove Ct BS9 . . . . .17 E5
rove Gdns GL8 . . . . .140 B5
rove Hall BS4 . . . . .9 D2
rove Hill SN6 . . . . .145 C4
rove Ind Est The BS34 . . . .29 B8
rove La Cirencester GL7 . .190 D5
Hinton SN14 . . . . .23 C6
Lydney GL15 . . . . .92 B6
Whitminster GL2 . . . . . . .100 F4
rove Leaze BS11 . . . . . . .16 D6
rove Orch SN6 . . . . .145 C4
rove Park Ave BS4 . . . . . . .9 D2
rove Park Rd Bristol BS4 . . .9 D2
Stroud GL5 . . . . .99 C8
rove Park Terr BS16 . . . . .19 F4
rove Pk
Bristol,Brislington BS4 . . . . .9 D2
Bristol,Redland BS6 . . . . . .18 C2
Whitecroft GL15 . . . . .155 F1
rove St
Cheltenham GL50 . . . . . . .193 A4
Gloucester GL1 . . . . .196 C1
Bristol,Canon's Marsh
BS1 . . . . .195 A1
Bristol,Oldland BS30 . . . . . .11 A4
Cheltenham,Battledown
GL52 . . . . .134 A1
Cheltenham,Lansdown
GL50 . . . . .130 B8
Chelworth SN16 . . . . .141 E5
5 Moreton-in-M GL56 . .187 B3
Rangeworthy BS37 . . . . . . .43 A8
Selsley GL5 . . . . .98 E4
Stonehouse GL10 . . . . .98 A6
Stroud GL5 . . . . .98 A6
Grove View BS16 . . . . .19 E6

Grove View continued
Greet GL54 . . . . .184 A1
Grovefield Cl BS36 . . . . . . .37 E5
Grovefield Way GL51 . . . .129 B7
Grovelands GL4 . . . . .127 E1
Grovelands Cl **1** GL53 . .131 B6
Groves Pl GL7 . . . . .152 E3
Groves The BS13 . . . . .2 D4
Grovesend Rd BS35 . . . . . .51 D8
Grump St CV36 . . . . .189 F6
Gryphons The **16** GL52 . .133 F2
Guardian Ct **10** Bristol BS8 . .7 F7
Cheltenham GL53 . . . . . . .130 F6
Guernsey Ave BS4 . . . . .9 F4
Guest Ave BS16 . . . . .21 B7
Guestriss Cotts GL50 . . . .133 C5
Guggle La **7** GL54 . . . . .168 A1
Guild Ct BS1 . . . . .195 B2
Guildford Rd GL4 . . . . . . .127 E1
Guildings Way GL10 . . . . . .98 A4
Guinea La Bristol BS16 . . . .20 A4
Bristol BS16 . . . . .20 A5
Guinea St Bristol BS1 . . . .195 A1
Gloucester GL1 . . . . .5 F6
Guise Ave GL3 . . . . .120 F4
Guise Cl GL2 . . . . .109 F8
Gullimores Gdns BS13 . . . . .2 B4
Gullivers Pl BS37 . . . . .33 A8
Gullon Wlk BS13 . . . . .1 F5
Gullons Cl BS13 . . . . .1 F5
Gully La BS35 . . . . .64 E7
Gully The BS36 . . . . .30 F7
Gullybrook La **3** BS5 . . . .9 B6
Gumstool Hill **18** GL8 . .140 C4
Gunhouse La GL5 . . . . . . .99 D5
Gunning Cl BS15 . . . . .10 D6
Gunter's Hill BS5 . . . . .10 A6
Gupshill Cl GL20 . . . . . . .192 C2
Gurney Ave GL4 . . . . .118 C3
Gustav Holst Birthplace
Mus * GL52 . . . . .193 C4
Guthrie Rd BS8 . . . . .7 A4
Gwentlands Cl NP16 . . . . . .60 E7
Gwernant Rd GL51 . . . . . .129 F6
Gwilliam St BS3 . . . . .8 D3
Gwinnett Ct GL51 . . . . . .129 F2
Gwy Ct NP16 . . . . .72 F1
Gwyn St BS2 . . . . .18 E1
Gyde Ho GL6 . . . . .111 F1
Gyde Rd GL6 . . . . .111 F1
Gydynap La GL5 . . . . .91 A7
Gypsy La Gorsley GL18 . . .170 C3
Marshfield SN14 . . . . .14 F7

H
Haberdashers Sch for Girls
NP25 . . . . .154 A8
Haberdashers' Agincourt
Sch NP25 . . . . .154 A8
Haberfield Hill BS8 . . . . . . .16 E2
Haberfield Ho BS8 . . . . .7 F6
Hacket Hill BS35 . . . . .51 F8
Hacket La BS35 . . . . .51 F8
Haddrell Ct BS35 . . . . .50 F5
Hadfield Cl GL19 . . . . .172 A8
Hadley Ct BS30 . . . . .11 B6
Hadley Rd GL11 . . . . .87 E4
Hadnock Rd NP25 . . . . . . .154 A8
Hadnock Road Ind Est **3**
NP25 . . . . .154 A8
Hadow Way GL2 . . . . .109 F8
Hadrian Ct Bristol BS9 . . . .17 C4
Lydney GL15 . . . . .92 B4
Hadrians Way GL4 . . . . . .119 F7
Hadrians Wlk BS16 . . . . . .21 C6
Hague Ave GL11 . . . . .87 F4
Haig Cl BS9 . . . . .17 B7
Hailes Abbey & Mus *
GL54 . . . . .184 D1
Hailes Green Barns
GL54 . . . . .174 C8
Hailes Rd GL4 . . . . .119 D7
Hailes St **22** GL54 . . . . .174 A1
Hakeburn Rd GL7 . . . . . . .190 C5
Halbrow Cres BS16 . . . . . .20 C5
Haldon Cl BS3 . . . . .8 D1
Hale Cl BS15 . . . . .10 D4
Hale La GL6 . . . . .103 F8
Hale Wood/Coed Hale
NP16 . . . . .60 C8
Hale's Rd GL52 . . . . .134 A1
Hales Cl GL52 . . . . .134 A1
Hales Horn Cl BS32 . . . . . .29 D6
Halface Cl BS14 . . . . .3 A3
Halface La BS14 . . . . .3 B4
Halford Ho GL2 . . . . .118 C4
Halfpenny Pitch GL6 . . . . .103 B4
Halifax Rd BS37 . . . . .43 D4
Hall End La BS37 . . . . .53 D2
Hall La
Cold Ashton BA1,SN14 . . . . .13 E2
Horton BS37 . . . . .45 E5
Lower Hamswell BA1 . . . . . .13 B3
Hall Rd GL53 . . . . .130 D4
Hall St BS3 . . . . .8 C2
Halland Rd GL53 . . . . .130 D5
Hallards Cl BS11 . . . . .16 F8
Hallen Cl
Bristol,Emerson's Green
BS16 . . . . .21 C6
Bristol,Henbury BS10 . . . . . .27 D3
Hallen Dr BS9 . . . . .17 C7
Hallen Est BS10 . . . . .27 A7
Hallen Rd BS10 . . . . .27 D4
Hallmead Cl GL51 . . . . . .132 D5
Halls Gdns BS34 . . . . .30 A4

Halls Rd BS15 . . . . .10 D8
Hallsfield SN6 . . . . .143 E5
Hallwood Dr HR8 . . . . . . .178 D8
Halmore La GL13 . . . . .86 A8
Halsbury Rd BS6 . . . . .18 B4
Halstock Ave BS16 . . . . . . .19 F3
Halston Dr BS2 . . . . .195 C4
Halswell Gdns BS13 . . . . . . .2 B4
Halt End BS14 . . . . .3 C3
Halwyn Cl BS9 . . . . .17 D5
Ham Cl GL52 . . . . .131 C7
Ham Farm La BS16 . . . . . . .21 B6
Ham Gn BS20 . . . . .16 D3
Ham Green Hospl BS20 . . . .16 E4
Ham La Bristol BS16 . . . . . .19 E6
Charlton Kings GL52 . . . . .131 D7
Doynton BS30 . . . . .22 E1
Dundry BS41 . . . . .1 D3
Kempsford GL7 . . . . .144 F7
Oldbury-on-S BS35 . . . . . . .63 C7
South Cerney GL7 . . . . . . .142 F7
Ham Mill La GL5 . . . . .99 E3
Ham Rd
Andoversford GL54 . . . . . .166 A8
Ashleworth GL19 . . . . .172 E5
Charlton Kings GL52,GL54 . .131 D7
Ham Sq GL52 . . . . .131 C7
Ham The GL11 . . . . .89 A6
Hambidge La GL7 . . . . . . .153 E3
Hamble Cl GL4 . . . . .119 F5
Hambledon Cl GL7 . . . . . .150 F7
Hamblins Cotts GL53 . . . . .123 A5
Hambrook La BS34 . . . . . . .30 A3
Hambrook Prim Sch
BS16 . . . . .30 D3
Hambrook St GL52 . . . . . .131 B7
Hambutts Dr GL6 . . . . . . .103 E8
Hambutts Mead GL6 . . . . .103 E8
Hamer St GL1 . . . . .127 B5
Hamfallow La GL13 . . . . . . .85 D3
Hamfield La GL13 . . . . .85 D3
Hamilton Croft GL7 . . . . . . .62 A4
Hamilton Ct GL51 . . . . . . .132 D3
Hamilton Rd
Bristol,Southville BS3 . . . . . .8 B4
Bristol,Upper Easton BS5 . . . .9 B8
Hamilton St GL53 . . . . . . .131 A6
Hamlen Cl GL19 . . . . .165 D6
Hamlet The GL53 . . . . . . .132 E2
Hammersmith Bottom
GL7 . . . . .153 B7
Hammersmith Rd BS5 . . . . .9 D8
Hammett Ct NP25 . . . . . . .154 B7
Hammond Ct GL7 . . . . .9 E1
Hammond Cl GL53 . . . . . .193 C1
Hammond Dr **3** GL61 . . .64 F1
Hammond Gdns BS9 . . . . . .17 E7
Hammond Way
Cirencester GL7 . . . . .190 C4
Gloucester GL7 . . . . .127 D1
Hammonds SN6 . . . . .143 F4
Hampden Cl BS37 . . . . .43 D4
Hampden Rd BS4 . . . . .9 D4
Hampden Way GL51 . . . . .196 B2
Hampen Cotts GL54 . . . . .167 A3
Hampshire Gdns GL16 . . . .155 A5
Hampshire Way BS37 . . . . .43 F4
Hampstead Rd BS4 . . . . .9 C3
Hampton Cl Bristol BS30 . . .11 A6
Cheltenham GL52 . . . . .2 B4
Gloucester GL2 . . . . .120 B7
Hampton Cnr BS16 . . . . . . .18 E1
Hampton Ct BS6 . . . . .18 E1
Hampton Fields GL6 . . . . .107 A8
Hampton Gr GL52 . . . . . . .152 A3
Hampton Hill GL6,GL8 . . . .148 B1
Hampton La **17** BS6 . . . .18 E1
Hampton Pk BS6 . . . . .18 E1
Hampton Pl GL53 . . . . . . .128 A8
Hampton Rd BS6 . . . . .18 E1
Hampton St Bristol BS15 . . .20 D1
Tetbury GL8 . . . . .140 B4
Hamshill Ditches * GL7 . . . . . .
Hamworthy Rd BS34 . . . . . .4 F7
Hanbury Cl BS15 . . . . .10 D6
Hanbury Ct BS15 . . . . .10 D6
Hanbury Ho NP16 . . . . .60 C8
Hanbury Rd BS8 . . . . .7 A8
Handel Ave **2** BS5 . . . . . .9 D7
Handel Cossham Ct **3**
BS15 . . . . .20 C1
Handel Rd BS31 . . . . .4 E5
Handley La BS37 . . . . .2 B4
Handley's La HR9 . . . . . . .164 A8
Hanford Ct BS14 . . . . .3 D8
Hang Hill BA15 . . . . .155 D1
Hangerberry New Rd
GL17 . . . . .163 D1
Hanham Abbots Jun Sch
BS15 . . . . .10 C4
Hanham Bsns Pk BS15 . . . .10 D5
Hanham High Sch BS15 . . . .10 D4
Hanham Mills BS15 . . . . . .10 E3
Hanham Rd BS15 . . . . .10 D6
Hanley Ct NP16 . . . . .60 C8
Hanman Cl GL4 . . . . .118 F7
Hanman Rd GL4 . . . . .118 F7
Hanman Villas GL4 . . . . . .124 C8
Hanna Ct GL50 . . . . .193 B4
Hannah Boote Ho **8**
GL52 . . . . .150 F2
Hannah Cres
Siddington GL7 . . . . .150 F2
South Cerney GL7 . . . . . . .151 A2

Hannah More Prim Sch
BS1 . . . . .195 C2
Hannah Pl GL3 . . . . .127 E7
Hannam Cl GL53 . . . . .130 E4
Hanover Cl NP16 . . . . .72 D1
Hanover Ct
Bristol,Filton BS34 . . . . . . .29 A3
Bristol,St Pauls BS1 . . . . . .195 B3
14 Cheltenham GL51 . . .130 B8
Cirencester GL7 . . . . .190 D4
2 Tewkesbury GL20 . . .192 C4
Hanover Gdns **2** GL6 . . .91 B4
Hanover Ho Bristol BS2 . . . .9 A7
Highworth SN6 . . . . .145 C3
Hanover Lodge GL5 . . . . . .98 D7
Hanover Pl BS1 . . . . .194 B1
Hanover St
2 Bristol BS1 . . . . .195 A2
Bristol,Russell Town BS5 . . . .9 C7
Hanover Way GL **3** 128 A7
Hanson Gdns GL52 . . . . . .137 D4
Hanstone Cl GL7 . . . . .190 B2
Happy Land SN6 . . . . .142 F4
Harbour Rd GL15 . . . . .84 B8
Harbour View GL20 . . . . . .192 D5
Harbour Wall BS9 . . . . .17 D5
Harbour Way BS1 . . . . . . .194 C1
Harbour Wlk BS1 . . . . . . .194 C1
Harbourside GL20 . . . . . . .192 D5
Harbury Mews GL1 . . . . . .119 A8
Harbury Rd BS9 . . . . .18 C7
Harcombe Hill BS36 . . . . . .30 E4
Harcombe Rd BS36 . . . . . . .30 D5
Harcourt Ave BS5 . . . . .10 A6
Harcourt Cl BS31 . . . . .5 E2
Harcourt Hill BS6 . . . . .18 C3
Harcourt Rd BS6 . . . . .18 C4
Harden Rd BS14 . . . . .3 E5
Hardenhuish Rd BS4 . . . . . . .9 D5
Harding's Dr GL11 . . . . . . .88 A1
Harding's La GL11 . . . . . . .88 A1
Hardington Dr BS31 . . . . . . .5 A2
Hardwick Ave NP16 . . . . . .60 E7
Hardwick Bank Rd GL20 . .182 B5
Hardwicke BS37 . . . . .32 C7
Hardwick Cl
Bristol,Broom Hill BS4 . . . . . .9 E3
Bristol,North Common BS30 . .11 D5
Hardwick Hill La NP16 . . . .60 E8
Hardwick Rd BS20 . . . . . . .16 D2
Hardy Ave BS3 . . . . .8 A3
Hardy Ct BS30 . . . . .10 F5
Hardy La GL52 . . . . .10 F5
Hardy Rd
Bishop's Cleeve GL52 . . . . .138 A4
Bristol BS3 . . . . .8 A2
Hare La GL1 . . . . .196 B3
Harebell Cl GL4 . . . . .119 E5
Hareclive Prim Sch BS13 . . . .2 C4
Harefield Cl BS15 . . . . .10 C2
Harefield Gr GL50 . . . . . . .193 A4
Harescombe BS37 . . . . .32 E7
Haresdown Hill GL7 . . . . . .141 C8
Haresfield CE Prim Sch
GL10 . . . . .113 B1
Haresfield La GL2,GL10 . . .113 B1
Haresfield Lodge GL4 . . . .118 C1
Harewood Cl GL4 . . . . . . .118 C1
Harewood Ho BS6 . . . . . . .18 D4
Harewood Rd BS5 . . . . . . .20 A1
Harford Cl BS9 . . . . .17 A7
Harford Dr BS16 . . . . .31 C2
Harington Pl BS1 . . . . .195 A2
Harleston St **4** BS5 . . . . .9 A8
Harley Ct **3** BS8 . . . . . . .7 F7
Harley La GL52 . . . . .149 C7
Harley Mews **1** Bristol BS7 . .18 E4
Harley Pl **4** BS8 . . . . .7 F7
Cheltenham GL51 . . . . . . .130 B7
Gloucester GL51 . . . . .130 B7
Harley St **1** GL50 . . . . . .130 B7
Harmer Cl BS10 . . . . .27 D6
Harness Cl GL7 . . . . .118 B6
Harnham La GL54 . . . . . . .166 E2
Harold St BS5 . . . . .9 D6
Harolds Way BS15 . . . . . . .10 B4
Harp Hill GL52 . . . . .134 B1
Harper Rd GL5 . . . . .99 B8
Harpfield Cl GL52 . . . . . . .137 F2
Harptree Ct BS30 . . . . .11 A4
Harptree Gr BS3 . . . . .8 A1
Harptree **5** BS30 . . . . . . .11 A4
Harptree Way GL17 . . . . . .164 D6
Harrier Cl GL7 . . . . .150 F7
Harrington Ave BS14 . . . . . .3 E6
Harrington Gr BS14 . . . . . . .3 E6
Harrington Rd BS14 . . . . . . .3 E6
Harrington Wlk BS14 . . . . . .3 E6
Harris Barton BS36 . . . . . . .31 B7
Harris Ct BS30 . . . . .10 F4
Harris Gdns GL54 . . . . . . .169 D6
Harris La BS8 . . . . .16 C5
Harris Rd SN6 . . . . .143 A5
Harrison Cl Bristol BS16 . . .21 B6

Harrison Cl continued
Newnham GL14 . . . . .156 F6
Harrison Rd GL51 . . . . . . .129 D2
Harrison Way GL15 . . . . . . .92 C2
Harrow Rd BS4 . . . . .9 D3
Harrowdene Rd BS4 . . . . . . .9 B3
Harry Stoke Rd BS34 . . . . .29 E2
Harry Yates Way GL51 . . . .132 D4
Hart Cl BS20 . . . . .15 F4
Hart Gn GL14 . . . . .191 C2
Hart La GL17 . . . . .163 F4
Hartbury Cl GL51 . . . . . . .132 C3
Hartcliffe Engineering Com
Coll BS13 . . . . .2 E4
Hartcliffe Rd BS4 . . . . .2 E8
Hartcliffe Way BS3,BS4,
BS13 . . . . .2 C7
Hartcliffe Wlk BS4 . . . . .2 E8
Hartcliffe Wlk BS6 . . . . . . .194 C4
Hartgill Cl BS13 . . . . .2 B3
Harthurstfield Pk GL51 . . .132 B1
Hartland Ho BS5 . . . . .9 C6
Hartland Rd GL1 . . . . .118 C6
Hartlands **22** GL18 . . . . .171 A4
Hartlebury Way GL51 . . . .131 C6
Hartley Cl
Cheltenham GL53 . . . . . . .130 F4
Chipping Sodbury BS37 . . . .44 C1
Hartley La GL3 . . . . .122 E8
Hartpury CE Prim Sch
GL19 . . . . .172 C3
Hartpury Coll
Blaisdon GL17 . . . . .165 A4
Hartpury GL19 . . . . .172 A1
Harts Barn Flower & Craft
Ctr * GL17 . . . . .164 E5
Harts Cotts GL7 . . . . .157 F2
Harts Croft BS37 . . . . .42 A4
Harvard Ave WR11 . . . . . .188 C7
Harvard Cl **3** BS32 . . . . .187 B3
Harvest Cl BS32 . . . . .40 D1
Harvest Gr GL51 . . . . .132 D5
Harvest Way BS22 . . . . . . .109 F7
Harvesters View GL52 . . . .137 D4
Harvey's La **8** Bristol BS5 . .9 F8
Winchcombe GL54 . . . . . . .139 F5
Harveys La GL13 . . . . .156 A2
Harwell Cl GL4 . . . . .118 D1
Harwood Ho **14** BS5 . . . . .9 B7
Haselbury Gr BS31 . . . . . . .5 B2
Hasfield Cl GL19 . . . . .117 E1
Hasfield Rd GL19 . . . . . . .172 C6
Haskins Ct **4** BS30 . . . . .11 A4
Haslemere Ct GL51 . . . . . .120 F5
Haslemere Ind Est BS11 . . .26 C2
Haslette Way GL51 . . . . . .129 E5
Hassell Dr BS2 . . . . .9 C7
Hastings Cl BS3 . . . . .8 C1
Hastings Pl GL20 . . . . . . .192 C2
Hastings Rd BS3 . . . . .8 C1
Hatchford GL14 . . . . .191 C4
Hatchet's Cres SN26 . . . . .144 A8
Hatchet La BS34 . . . . .29 E4
Hatchmere BS35 . . . . .51 D8
Hathaway Cl GL14 . . . . . . .118 C4
Hathaway Ho BS2 . . . . . . .195 B4
Hatherley GL51 . . . . .32 E7
Hatherley Brake GL51 . . . .129 E7
Hatherley Court Rd
GL51 . . . . .130 B2
Hatherley Ct GL51 . . . . . . .130 B2
Hatherley Gate GL51 . . . . .130 B2
Hatherley La GL51 . . . . . . .130 A7
Hatherley Rd Bristol BS4 . . . .9 C4
Cheltenham GL51 . . . . . . .129 D7
Hatherley Mews GL51 . . . .129 D7
Hatherley Rd Bristol BS7 . .18 E4
Cheltenham GL51 . . . . . . .130 B2
Hatherop Castle Sch
GL7 . . . . .152 E8
Hatherop Rd GL7 . . . . . . .152 E8
Hatherop Castle Sch
GL7 . . . . .152 E8
Hathway Wlk BS5 . . . . .9 A8
Hatters' La BS37 . . . . .44 C1
Havelock Rd GL2 . . . . .120 A8
Haven Cl GL10 . . . . .14 C1
Haven Gr GL20 . . . . .127 C3
Haven Park Mobile Home
Site GL15 . . . . .129 C5
Haven The BS15 . . . . .20 C8
Haverstock Rd BS4 . . . . .9 A3
Haviland Ho **10** BS2 . . . . .9 C7
Haw La GL19 . . . . .171 F6
Haw Rd GL16 . . . . .155 C8
Hawcombe Mews **11**
GL51 . . . . .129 F5
Hawesdowns BS32 . . . . . . .29 E7
Haweswater Cl BS30 . . . . . .11 D6
Haweswater Rd GL51 . . . .129 F6

Hawk Cl **5** Chalford GL6 . .148 C6
Gloucester GL4 . . . . .119 D5
Hawker Hill GL17 . . . . . . .164 D5
Hawker Rd GL51 . . . . . . .133 E8
Hawker Sq GL54 . . . . . . .169 D6
Hawkers Hill GL7 . . . . . . .160 A1
Hawkesbury CE Prim Sch
GL9 . . . . .55 F3
Hawkesbury Rd
Bristol BS16 . . . . .19 E3
Hillesley GL12 . . . . .55 D6
Hawkesley Dr BS34 . . . . . .29 D6
Hawkesworth Rd BS37 . .43 C3
Hawkfield Bsns Pk BS14 . .2 D5
Hawkfield Cl BS14 . . . . . . .2 D5
Hawkfield Rd BS13 . . . . . . .2 D5
Hawkfield Way BS14 . . . . .2 D5
Hawkins Cl BS30 . . . . . . .11 C5
Hawkins Cres BS32 . . . . . .29 E8
Hawkins La GL14 . . . . . .157 A7
Hawkins St BS2 . . . . . . .195 C3
Hawkley Dr BS22 . . . . . . .40 D3
Hawkridge Cl GL20 . . . . .192 E2
Hawkridge Dr BS16 . . . . .22 C5
Hawksmoor Cl BS14 . . . . . .3 A6
Hawksmoor La BS16 . . . . .19 E8
Hawkswood Rd GL51 . . . .130 B5
Hawksworth Dr BS15 . . . .10 B5
Hawkwell Cotts GL17 . . . .164 B3
Haworth Cl GL2 . . . . . . .117 F2
Haworth Rd Ave BS15 . . . .10 B5
Hawthorn Cl Bristol BS34 . .28 E7
Charfield GL12 . . . . .67 A4
Chepstow/Cas-Gwent NP16 . .60 E4
Hawthorn Cres BS35 . . . . .64 C2
Hawthorn Ct GL15 . . . . . .92 B3
Hawthorn Dr
Innsworth GL3 . . . . .127 F6
Sling GL16 . . . . .155 B2
Woodmancote GL52 . . . . .138 B3
Hawthorn Rd GL51 . . . . .132 E3
Hawthorn Ridge GL6 . . . . .90 F5
Hawthorn Rise GL5 . . . . . .98 D8
Hawthorn Way
Bristol BS34 . . . . .29 E5
Northway GL20 . . . . .182 C5
Hawthorne Ave GL54 . . .119 C6
Hawthorne Cl BS16 . . . . . .22 C5
Hawthorne Gdns BS16 . . .20 F4
Hawthorne Hill GL18 . . . .170 D5
Hawthorne Rise BS10 . . . .28 C3
Hawthorne St BS4 . . . . . . .9 A3
Hawthornes The
Bristol BS16 . . . . .20 F4
Cheltenham GL51 . . . . . .129 D6
Hawthorns La BS31 . . . . . .4 E5
Hawthorns Rd GL17 . . . . .164 B5
Hawthorns The
Bishop's Cleeve GL52 . . . .137 E4
Bussage GL6 . . . . .148 B6
Dursley GL11 . . . . .87 F5
Lydney GL15 . . . . .92 B3
Hay La Ablington GL7 . . . .159 E1
Horsley GL6 . . . . .83 A7
Hay Leaze BS37 . . . . .43 D4
Hay St SN14 . . . . .15 A8
Hay's Cotts GL53 . . . . . .130 E6
Haycombe BS14 . . . . .2 F6
Haycroft Cl GL52 . . . . . .137 E4
Haycroft Dr GL4 . . . . . . .119 A7
Haycroft La GL13 . . . . . . .78 C6
Haycroft Rd BS34 . . . . . .29 A3
Northleach GL54 . . . . . . .168 F2
Haydale Gdns GL2 . . . . .127 C5
Hayden Court Cvn Pk
GL51 . . . . .132 A1
Hayden Gn GL51 . . . . . .132 A3
Hayden La GL51 . . . . . . .132 A3
Hayden Rd GL51 . . . . . . .132 F5
Haydock Cl BS16 . . . . . . .30 F1
Haydon Cl **12** BS8 . . . . . .18 A2
Haydon Gdns BS7 . . . . . .19 B5
Haydons Ct GL55 . . . . . .189 A2
Haye's La GL6 . . . . .46 F2
Hayeley Dr BS32 . . . . . . .29 E6
Hayes Cl BS2 . . . . .9 B7
Hayes Ct Bristol BS34 . . . .29 A7
Cheltenham GL52 . . . . . .134 A2
Gloucester GL2 . . . . . . .126 F6
Hayes Knoll Sta* SN5 . . .143 F1
Hayes La GL7 . . . . .158 B4
Hayes Rd
Cheltenham GL52 . . . . . .134 A2
Nailsworth GL6 . . . . .91 A5
Hayes The NP16 . . . . .61 B8
Hayfield SN14 . . . . .15 A8
Hayfield Way GL52 . . . . .137 E5
Haygarth Cl GL7 . . . . . . .190 B2
Hayhedge La GL6 . . . . . .148 D8
Haylea Rd GL52 . . . . . . .137 D4
Hayleigh Ho BS13 . . . . . . .2 C4
Haymarket The BS1 . . . . .195 A3
Haymarket Wlk **1** BS1 . .195 A4
Haymead La GL8 . . . . . . .70 C5
Haymes Dr GL52 . . . . . . .138 C1
Haymes Rd GL52 . . . . . . .138 C1
Haynes Ho **2** BS16 . . . . . .20 D6
Haynes La BS16 . . . . .20 D5
Hays Cl WR12 . . . . .188 B2
Haysum's Cl GL55 . . . . . .189 A1
Hayter Cl BS10 . . . . .28 D3
Haythorn Ct BS16 . . . . . .20 F5
Haythorne Ct **8** BS16 . . . .19 E3
Haytor Pk BS9 . . . . .17 D6
Hayward Cl GL4 . . . . . . .119 D7

Hayward Ind Est **1** BS16 . .20 D3
Hayward Rd
Bristol,Russell Town BS5 . . .9 C7
Bristol,Staple Hill BS16 . . . .20 D3
Hayward's Rd GL52 . . . . .131 A8
Haywards GL7 . . . . .144 F7
Haywards La GL52 . . . . . .131 A8
Haywood Pitch HR9 . . . . .170 C5
Hazebrouck Cl GL51 . . . .129 E7
Hazel Ave BS6 . . . . .18 B2
Hazel Cl GL2 . . . . .127 B5
Hazel Cote Rd BS14 . . . . . .3 B4
Hazel Cres BS35 . . . . .64 D1
Hazel Cl GL4 . . . . .127 D1
Hazel Field GL17 . . . . . . .164 B5
Hazel Gdns BS35 . . . . . . .51 A4
Hazel Gr BS7 . . . . .19 A8
Hazel La Alveston BS35 . . . .50 F2
Tockington BS32 . . . . .50 E3
Hazel Rd GL17 . . . . .164 B4
Hazelbury Dr BS30 . . . . . .11 C6
Hazelbury Rd BS14 . . . . . . .3 C7
Hazelcroft GL3 . . . . .128 B6
Hazeldean GL14 . . . . . . .191 C5
Hazeldene GL7 . . . . .153 E3
Hazeldene Rd BS34 . . . . . .29 A7
Hazelgrove BS36 . . . . . . .30 E5
Hazelhurst Bglws HR9 . . .163 B5
Hazels The GL4 . . . . .119 E7
Hazelton Cl GL4 . . . . . . .118 F6
Hazelton Rd BS7 . . . . . . .18 D3
Hazelwood **1** GL10 . . . . . .97 F7
Hazelwood Cl BS9 . . . . . .17 D3
Hazelwood Ct BS9 . . . . . .17 D3
Hazelwood Rd BS9 . . . . . .17 D3
Hazle Cl HR8 . . . . .178 E7
Hazlecote La GL6,GL8 . . . .82 F6
Hazledean Rd GL51 . . . . .132 D4
Hazlewood Cl GL51 . . . . .130 B5
Hazlitt Croft GL51 . . . . . .132 D4
Headford Ave BS5 . . . . . .10 B7
Headford Rd BS4 . . . . .8 D1
Headington Cl BS15 . . . . . .10 D4
Headlam Cl GL4 . . . . . . .118 D1
Headland The NP16 . . . . . .61 A4
Headlands The GL5 . . . . . .98 F2
Headley Cl BS13 . . . . .2 B6
Headley La BS13 . . . . .2 B7
Headley Park Ave BS13 . . . .2 B7
Headley Park Prim Sch
BS13 . . . . .2 B6
Headley Park Rd BS13 . . . .2 A7
Headley Rd BS13 . . . . .2 A6
Headley Wlk BS13 . . . . . . .2 B7
Healey Dr SN14 . . . . .23 C6
Healey Mews GL1 . . . . . .127 A2
Heapey Cl **8** GL51 . . . . . .132 D2
Hearne Cl GL53 . . . . .131 B6
Hearne Rd GL53 . . . . . . .131 B6
Heart Meers BS14 . . . . . . .3 B5
Heath Cl BS36 . . . . .30 E6
Heath Ct Bristol BS16 . . . .20 D7
Dursley GL11 . . . . .80 C8
Heath Gdns Bristol BS16 . .20 D8
Coalpit Heath BS36 . . . . . .38 C7
Heath House La BS7,BS16 . .19 C5
Heath House Priory Hospl
BS16 . . . . .19 B4
Heath Lo **6** BS37 . . . . . . .133 F2
Heath Rd
Bristol,Downend BS16 . . . .20 D8
Bristol,Eastville BS5 . . . . . .19 B1
Bristol,Hanham BS15 . . . . .10 B4
Heath Ridge BS41 . . . . . . .7 A2
Heath Rise BS30 . . . . . . .11 B5
Heath St Bristol BS5 . . . . .19 C3
3 Monmouth/Trefynwy
NP25 . . . . .154 A7
Heath The BS9 . . . . .17 E3
Heath Wlk BS16 . . . . . . .20 D7
Heathcote Dr BS36 . . . . . .31 D7
Heathcote La BS36 . . . . . .31 D7
Heathcote Rd
Bristol,Chester Park BS16 . .20 B2
Bristol,Staple Hill BS16 . . . .20 E5
Heathcote Wlk BS16 . . . . .20 C2
Heathdean Rd GL3 . . . . . .127 F6
Heather Ave
Frampton Cotterell BS36 . . .31 B6
Gloucester GL4 . . . . .119 D5
Heather Cl Bristol BS15 . . .10 B8
Chepstow/Cas-Gwent NP16 . .60 F5
Stroud GL5 . . . . .99 A4
Heatherdene BS14 . . . . . . .2 F7
Heathfield Cl BS31 . . . . . . .4 C5
Heathfield Cres BS14 . . . . .3 B4
Heathfield Rd GL5 . . . . . .103 A1
Heathfields BS16 . . . . . . .20 D8
Heathville Rd GL1 . . . . . .127 A3
Heazle Pl GL5 . . . . .99 C8
Hebden Cl GL2 . . . . .120 F5
Heber St BS5 . . . . .9 F7
Heberden La **6** SN6 . . . . .143 E4
Hebron Cl BS3 . . . . .8 C3
Hebron Rd **10** BS3 . . . . . . .8 C3
Hedgeditch La GL8 . . . . . .59 D7
Hedgemead Cl BS16 . . . . .19 D5
Hedgemead View BS16 . . .19 E5
Hedgerow The GL2 . . . . . .127 B4
Hedwick Ave BS5 . . . . .9 E7
Hedwick St BS5 . . . . .9 E7
Heggard Cl BS13 . . . . .2 A5
Helens Cl GL51 . . . . .132 D3
Hellens* HR8 . . . . .178 A4
Hellier Wlk BS13 . . . . .2 C2
Hembury Cl GL2 . . . . . . .109 D7
Hemming Way GL52 . . . . .137 F3
Hemmings Par GL5 . . . . . .9 B7
Hemmingsdale Rd GL2 . .126 C1

Hemplands The GL54 . . . .159 B5
Hemplow Cl BS14 . . . . .3 D7
Hempsted CE Prim Sch
GL2 . . . . .118 A7
Hempsted La GL2 . . . . . .118 B7
Hempton La BS32 . . . . . . .40 B2
Henacre Rd BS11 . . . . . . .16 F8
Henbury Court Prim Sch
BS10 . . . . .27 F3
Henbury Ct BS10 . . . . . . .27 E3
Henbury Gdns BS10 . . . . .27 E2
Henbury Hill BS9 . . . . . . .27 F1
Henbury Rd
Bristol,Hanham BS15 . . . . .10 B5
Bristol,Henbury BS10 . . . . .27 F2
Bristol,Westbury on Trym
BS9 . . . . .18 A8
Henbury Road Henbury Hill
BS9 . . . . .18 A8
Henbury Sch BS10 . . . . . .27 E3
Pill BS20 . . . . .16 F7
Hencliffe Rd BS14 . . . . . . .3 D7
Hencliffe Way BS15 . . . . . .10 B3
Henderson Ho **1** BS2 . . .195 B4
Henderson Rd BS15 . . . . . .10 B5
Hendingham Cl GL4 . . . . .118 B2
Hendre Mews GL50 . . . . .193 A3
Hendre Rd BS3 . . . . .8 B3
Hendrick Dr NP16 . . . . . . .61 A8
Heneage La GL12 . . . . . . .65 F8
Henfield Cres BS30 . . . . . .11 B3
Henfield Rd BS36 . . . . . . .31 C4
Hengaston St BS3 . . . . . . .8 B2
Hengrove Ave BS14 . . . . . .3 B8
Hengrove Com Arts Coll
BS14 . . . . .3 B8
Hengrove La BS14 . . . . . . .3 B8
Hengrove Rd BS4 . . . . .9 A2
Hengrove Way BS14 . . . . . .2 E6
Henleaze Ave BS9 . . . . . . .18 A5
Henleaze Gdns BS9 . . . . . .18 A5
Henleaze Jun & Inf Schs
BS9 . . . . .18 C6
Henleaze Park BS9 . . . . . .18 C6
Henleaze Pk BS9 . . . . . . .18 C5
Henleaze Rd BS9 . . . . . . .18 B6
Henleaze Terr BS9 . . . . . . .18 B7
Henley Dr SN6 . . . . .145 D4
Henley Gr BS9 . . . . .18 B5
Henley Grove Ct BS9 . . . . .18 B5
Henley Pl GL1 . . . . .118 D5
Henley Rd Bream GL15 . . .145 D5
Cheltenham GL51 . . . . . .132 C3
Henley Villas GL5 . . . . . . .99 C8
Henlow Dr GL11 . . . . .80 B8
Hennessy Cl BS14 . . . . . . .2 F3
Henrietta St
Bristol,Kingsdown BS2 . . .195 A4
5 Bristol,Lower Easton
BS5 . . . . .19 B1
Henry Rd GL1 . . . . .196 C4
Henry Ryder Cl GL4 . . . . .119 F6
Henry St Bristol BS3 . . . . . .8 F4
Gloucester GL1 . . . . .196 C4
Henry Williamson Ct **1**
BS30 . . . . .11 A5
Henry Withers Pl GL2 . . . .100 F5
Henshaw Cl BS15 . . . . . . .20 C2
Henshaw Rd BS15 . . . . . . .20 C2
Henshaw Wlk BS15 . . . . . .20 C2
Hensman's Hill BS8 . . . . .194 A2
Hentley Tor GL2 . . . . .68 C6
Heol Merthyr
Tewdrig/Mathern Rd
NP16 . . . . .60 D5
Hepburn Rd BS2 . . . . . . .195 B4
Herald Cl BS9 . . . . .17 D5
Herapath St BS5 . . . . .9 C6
Herbert Cl **1** GL50 . . . . .193 A4
Hereford Pl GL50 . . . . . . .193 A4
Hereford Rd GL52 . . . . . . .19 A2
Hereford St BS3 . . . . .8 D3
Herkomer Cl GL3 . . . . . . .128 B7
Hermitage Cl BS11 . . . . . .16 E7
Hermitage Dr GL11 . . . . . .80 B7
Hermitage Rd BS16 . . . . . .20 E5
Hermitage St GL53 . . . . . .193 B1
Heron Cl GL5 . . . . .129 E7
Heron Prim Sch GL4 . . . . .119 D5
Heron Rd BS5 . . . . .9 C8
Heron Way
Chipping Sodbury BS37 . . . .33 A8
Gloucester GL4 . . . . .119 C5
Herrick Cl GL51 . . . . .173 F1
Herrick Rd BS5 . . . . .173 F1
Herridge Cl BS13 . . . . .2 B4
Herridge Rd BS13 . . . . . . .2 B4
Hersey Gdns BS13 . . . . . . .1 E3
Hersta Cl GL7 . . . . .190 E4
Hertford Rd GL52 . . . . . .138 A4
Hertford St BS5 . . . . .19 B8
Hesters Way La GL51 . . . .132 D4
Hester's Way Prim Sch
GL51 . . . . .132 E4

Hester's Way Rd GL51 . . .132 E3
Hestercombe Rd BS13 . . . .2 B6
Hethersett Rd GL1 . . . . . .119 A8
Hetton Gdns BS33 . . . . . .131 A7
Hever Cl GL20 . . . . .192 E2
Hewelsfield La GL15 . . . . .146 F7
Hewelsfield Rd GL15 . . . .147 A4
Hewland Ct BS11 . . . . . . .27 C2
Hewlett Pl GL52 . . . . . . .193 C3
Hewlett Rd GL52 . . . . . . .133 F1
Hewlett Way GL14 . . . . . .156 C6
Hewlins La HR9 . . . . .162 D3
Heyford Ave BS5 . . . . .19 B4
Heyron Wlk BS13 . . . . .2 B4
Heywood Com Sch
GL14 . . . . .191 E6
Heywood Rd
Cinderford GL14 . . . . . . .191 D5
Pill BS20 . . . . .16 F6
Heywood Terr BS20 . . . . . .16 C4
Ham's La GL19 . . . . .172 C2
Hiatt Rd GL6 . . . . .91 F7
Hibbs Cl SN14 . . . . .14 F8
Hicking Ct **8** BS15 . . . . . .20 D1
Hickley Gdns GL3 . . . . . .120 E6
Hicks Ave Bristol BS16 . . . .21 B8
Hicks Beach Rd GL51 . . . .132 D2
Hicks Common Rd BS36 . .30 E5
Hicks Ct BS30 . . . . .11 A6
Hidcote Ave GL51 . . . . . .130 A5
Hidcote Boyce GL55 . . . . .189 C4
Hidcote Cl GL6 . . . . .148 B6
Hidcote Manor Gdns*
GL55 . . . . .189 C5
Hidcote Rd GL55 . . . . . . .189 C3
Hide Mkt BS2 . . . . .195 C3
High Beech Ave GL16 . . . .155 C7
High Beech La/Lon
Ffawyden Uchel NP16 . . .60 D6
High Cnr BS10 . . . . .27 F1
High Cross GL53 . . . . . . .115 B7
High Delf Cl **4** GL16 . . . .155 B5
High Delf Way GL16 . . . . .155 F1
High Elm BS15 . . . . .10 E6
High Furlong GL11 . . . . . . .87 F5
High Gr BS9 . . . . .17 B7
High Nash GL16 . . . . .155 A5
High Orchard St GL2 . . . . .196 A1
High Pk BS14 . . . . .9 B1
High Point GL50 . . . . .193 A3
High Point Ho **1** BS15 . . .20 C1
High Rd
Ashton Keynes SN6 . . . . .142 F4
Midsomer Norton BA3 . . . .9 B8
High Row GL17 . . . . .163 C3
High Sch for Girls GL1 . . .196 C4
High St Arlingham GL2 . . .157 B6
Avening GL8 . . . . .148 A3
Aylburton GL15 . . . . .147 E4
Badminton GL9 . . . . .46 E2
Berkeley GL13 . . . . .85 E3
Bisley GL6 . . . . .88 F4
Bitton BS30 . . . . .5 E8
Blakeney GL15 . . . . .156 E1
Blockley GL56 . . . . .46 F6
Bourton-on-t-W GL54 . . . .168 F7
Bream GL15 . . . . .147 D8
Bredon GL20 . . . . .182 C7
Brierley GL17 . . . . .163 F2
Bristol BS31 . . . . .195 A2
Bristol,Clifton BS8 . . . . . . .18 A2
Bristol,Jefferies Hill BS15 . .10 C5
Bristol,Kingswood BS15 . . .10 E8
Bristol,Lower Easton BS5 . .19 B1
Bristol,Oldland Common
BS30 . . . . .11 D4
Bristol,Shirehampton BS11 . .16 E6
Bristol,Staple Hill BS16 . . . .20 D4
Bristol,Warmley BS15 . . . . .11 B8
Bristol,Westbury on Trym
BS9 . . . . .18 A7
Broad Blunsdon SN26 . . .144 D1
Broadway WR12 . . . . . . .185 B8
Chalford GL6 . . . . .148 C5
Cheltenham,Prestbury
GL52 . . . . .134 C4
Cheltenham,St Paul's
GL50,GL52 . . . . .193 B4
Chepstow/Cas-Gwent NP16 . .60 E8
Chipping Campden GL55 . .189 A2
Chipping Sodbury BS37 . . . .44 B1
Cinderford GL14 . . . . . . .191 D5
Clearwell GL16 . . . . .155 A3
Cricklade SN6 . . . . .143 F4
Doynton BS30 . . . . .22 F1
Drybrook GL17 . . . . .164 B8
Dursley GL11 . . . . .87 F6
Fairford GL7 . . . . .152 E4
Gloucester GL1 . . . . .118 F7
Hawkesbury Upton GL9 . . . .55 F3
Highworth SN6 . . . . .155 D8
Hillesley GL12 . . . . .55 D6
Honeybourne WR11 . . . . .188 C6
Huntley GL19 . . . . .142 D4
Iron Acton BS37 . . . . .42 D5
Kempsford GL7 . . . . .144 E7
Keynsham BS31 . . . . .4 E6
King's Stanley GL10 . . . . . .98 A3
Kingswood GL12 . . . . . . .67 F4
Lechlade on t-T GL7 . . . . .153 C1
Ledbury HR8 . . . . .178 F6
Littledean GL14 . . . . .191 B8
Longhope GL17 . . . . .176 D8
Lydney GL15 . . . . .92 A3
Marshfield SN14 . . . . .14 F8
Mickleton GL55 . . . . .189 . .
Minchinhampton GL6 . . . .148 . .
Mitcheldean GL17 . . . . . .164 . .
Moreton-in-M GL56 . . . . .187 . .
Newent GL18 . . . . .171 . .
Newnham GL14 . . . . .157 . .
Northleach GL54 . . . . . . .168 . .
Ruardean GL17 . . . . .163 . .
Saltford BS31 . . . . .5 . .
Saul GL2 . . . . .157 . .
South Cerney GL7 . . . . . .142 . .
St Briavels GL15 . . . . . . .146 . .
Stanton WR12 . . . . .184 . .
Stonehouse GL10 . . . . . . .97 . .
Stow-on-t-W GL54 . . . . . .176 . .
Stroud GL5 . . . . .99 . .
Tewkesbury GL20 . . . . . .192 . .
Thornbury BS35 . . . . .51 . .
Upper Lydbrook GL17 . . . .163 . .
Upton St Leonards GL4 . . .119 . .
Westbury-on-S GL14 . . . .165 . .
Wick BS30 . . . . .12 . .
Wickwar GL12 . . . . .54 . .
Winchcombe GL54 . . . . . .174 . .
Winterbourne BS36 . . . . . .30 . .
Withington GL54 . . . . .55 . .
Woodchester GL5 . . . . . . .98 . .
Wotton-u-E GL12 . . . . . . .68 . .
High View Lodge **14** GL5 . .99 . .
High View
Chepstow/Cas-Gwent NP16 . .60 . .
Gloucester GL2 . . . . .118 . .
Highbank St **2** BS2 . . . . . .8 . .
Highbank Pk GL2 . . . . . . .126 . .
Highbeech Rd
Bream GL15 . . . . .147 . .
Upper Lydbrook GL17 . . . .163 . .
Highbury La GL52 . . . . . .193 . .
Highbury Rd
Bream GL15 . . . . .147 . .
Bristol BS3 . . . . .8 . .
Bristol,Horfield BS7 . . . . . .18 . .
Lower Redbrook NP25 . . . .154 . .
Highbury Terr NP25 . . . . .154 . .
Highbury Villas BS2 . . . . .194 . .
Highclere Rd GL2 . . . . .9 . .
Highcroft **3** Bristol BS30 . .11 . .
Minchinhampton GL6 . . . .148 . .
Highcroft Jun Sch BS36 . . .31 . .
Highdale Cl BS14 . . . . .3 . .
Higher Newmarket Rd
GL6 . . . . .90 . .
Higgett Dr BS55 . . . . .19 . .
Highfield Blakeney GL15 . .156 . .
Whiteshill GL6 . . . . .19 . .
Highfield Ave BS15 . . . . . .10 . .
Highfield Bsns Pk GL19 . .172 . .
Highfield Cl **4** GL55 . . . . .11 . .
Highfield Gdns BS30 . . . . .11 . .
Highfield Gr BS7 . . . . . . .18 . .
Highfield La
Cirencester GL7 . . . . .190 . .
Horton BS37 . . . . .45 . .
Lydney GL15 . . . . .92 . .
Highfield Pl
4 Coleford GL16 . . . . . .155 . .
Gloucester GL4 . . . . .119 . .
Highfield Rd
Bream GL15 . . . . .147 . .
Chipping Sodbury BS37 . . . .44 . .
Gloucester GL4 . . . . .119 . .
Keynsham BS31 . . . . .4 . .
Ruardean GL17 . . . . .163 . .
Stroud GL5 . . . . .99 . .
Tetbury GL8 . . . . .140 . .
Whiteshill GL6 . . . . .103 . .
Highfield Rise GL15 . . . . .156 . .
Highfield Villas GL14 . . . .156 . .
Highfield Way GL14 . . . . .156 . .
Highfields
Frampton Mansell GL6 . . .148 . .
Hawkesbury Upton GL9 . . . .55 . .
Highfields App GL11 . . . . .80 . .
Highgate Ct WR12 . . . . . .185 . .
Highgrove Cotts GL8 . . . .140 . .
Highgrove St BS4 . . . . .9 . .
Highgrove Way GL2 . . . . .127 . .
Highland Cres **3** BS8 . . . . .18 . .
Highland Pl **13** BS8 . . . . . .18 . .
Highland Rd BS8 . . . . .18 . .
Highland Sq **4** BS8 . . . . . .18 . .
Highland St GL51 . . . . . . .130 . .
Highlands La BS37 . . . . . . .11 . .
Highleaze Rd BS30 . . . . . .11 . .
Highliffe Dr GL2 . . . . .118 . .
Highmead Gdns BS13 . . . . .1 . .
Highmeadow NP25 . . . . . .19 . .
Highmore Ct BS9 . . . . .18 . .
Highnam Bsns Ctr GL2 . . .125 . .
Highnam CE Prim Sch
GL2 . . . . .125 . .
Highnam Cl BS34 . . . . . . .40 . .
Highnam Woods (Nature
Reserve)* GL2 . . . . . . .124 . .
Highridge Cres BS13 . . . . . .1 . .
Highridge Gn BS13 . . . . . . .1 . .
Highridge Inf Sch BS13 . . . .1 . .
Highridge Pk BS13 . . . . . . .1 . .
Highridge Rd
Bristol,Bedminster BS3 . . . .8 . .

ighridge Rd continued
Bristol,Withywood BS13,BS41 .1 E4
ighridge Wlk BS13 . . . . . . .1 E7
ighridge Rd Bristol BS15 . . .20 F2
Cinderford GL14 . . . . .191 E4
Ruardean Hill GL17 . . . . . .64 A3
Yorkley GL15 . . . . .156 A2
ighview Way GL15 . . . . . .147 D8
ighwall La BS14,BS31 . . . .3 F1
ighway BS37 . . . . .43 F2
ighwood Ave GL53 . . . . . .130 C5
ighwood Bsns Pk BS34 . . .28 E7
ighwood Cl GL6 . . . . .90 F5
ighwood La BS10,BS34 . . .28 D7
ighwood Pk Cvn Site
BS34 . . . . .28 E6
ighwood Rd BS34 . . . . . . .28 E7
ighworth Cres BS37 . . . . . .32 D8
ighworth Rd Bristol BS4 . . .9 D6
Gloucester GL1 . . . . .118 F6
ighworth SN6 . . . . .145 F1
Stanton Fitzwarren SN6 . . .145 B1
ighworth Warneford Sch
SN6 . . . . .145 D3
ilcote Ct GL54 . . . . .169 A6
ildyard Ct GL2 . . . . .109 E7
ilhouse BS9 . . . . .1 E7
ill Ash Mdw GL18 . . . . . .178 E3
ill Ave BS3 . . . . .8 E3
ill Burn BS9 . . . . .18 C6
ill Cl BS16 . . . . .21 B8
Dursley GL11 . . . . .87 F4
Westmancote GL20 . . . . . .182 D8
ill Court Rd GL52 . . . . . .133 E4
ill Crest Bristol BS4 . . . . .9 E6
Highnam GL2 . . . . .125 E5
ill Ct GL52 . . . . .133 E4
ill End Cl GL20 . . . . .181 F7
ill End Dr BS10 . . . . .27 D3
ill End Rd GL20 . . . . . . .181 F8
ill Gr BS9 . . . . .18 C6
ill Hay Rd GL4 . . . . .119 C3
ill Ho GL7 . . . . .190 D5
ill House Rd BS16 . . . . . .20 F5
ill La
Chipping Sodbury BS37 . . . .34 B7
Thornbury BS35 . . . . .76 A2
ill Lawn BS4 . . . . .9 D3
ill Mead GL4 . . . . .110 F5
ill Paul GL15 . . . . .99 B7
ill Pk GL15 . . . . .156 A2
ill Rd Bundry BS41 . . . . .1 D2
Dursley GL11 . . . . .88 A1
Gloucester GL4 . . . . .118 F4
Wotton-u-E GL12 . . . . . . .68 C6
ill Sq GL11 . . . . .88 A3
ill St
Bristol,Brandon Hill BS1 . .194 C2
Bristol,Kingswood BS15 . . .10 F8
Bristol,St George BS5 . . . .9 F8
Bristol,Windmill Hill BS3 . .8 F4
Lydney GL15 . . . . .92 A3
ill The Almondsbury BS32 . .40 B4
Randwick GL6 . . . . .102 E2
Stroud GL5 . . . . .99 B7
Westwell OX18 . . . . .161 F5
ill Top NP16 . . . . .60 D7
ill Top GL5 . . . . .99 F7
ill Top La GL18 . . . . . . .171 B5
ill Top Rd GL50 . . . . . . .133 D5
ill Top View GL6 . . . . . . .148 B6
ill View
Bristol,Blackhorse BS16 . . .21 A8
Bristol,Clifton Wood BS8 . .194 B2
Bristol,Filton BS34 . . . . . .29 A3
Bristol,Henleaze BS9 . . . .18 C6
Bristol,Upper Soundwell
BS16 . . . . .20 D2
Elkstone GL53 . . . . .115 B6
Lydney GL15 . . . . .92 A3
Naunton GL54 . . . . .175 E2
Sandhurst GL2 . . . . .172 E1
ill View Cl BS30 . . . . . . .11 C4
ill View Cotts GL4 . . . . . .118 E2
ill View Ct BS16 . . . . . . .20 C5
ill View Ho ? BS15 . . . . .20 C1
ill View Rd Bristol BS13 . . .2 A8
Upper Stresnham WR8 . . .180 A10
ill View Villas GL5 . . . . . .98 D6
ill's Barton BS13 . . . . . . .8 A1
illands Dr GL53 . . . . . . .130 D4
illary Rd GL53 . . . . .130 E4
illborough Rd GL4 . . . . .118 E3
illbrook Rd ? BS35 . . . . .51 D8
illburn Rd BS35 . . . . . . .10 A8
illclose Est GL5 . . . . .99 A4
illcot Cl GL2 . . . . .117 E1
illcrest Berkeley GL13 . . .85 F4
Thornbury BS35 . . . . .64 B1
illcrest Cl ? NP25 . . . . .154 A7
illcrest La GL14 . . . . . . .155 B6
illcrest Prim Sch BS4 . . . .9 A3
illcrest Rd
Berry Hill GL16 . . . . .155 A7
Monmouth/Trefynwy
NP25 . . . . .154 A7
Stroud GL5 . . . . .98 E8
illcroft Cl BS15 . . . . .10 C4
illersland La GL16 . . . . .155 A8
illesley CE Prim Sch
GL12 . . . . .55 E8
illesley Rd GL12 . . . . . . .67 F4
illfield Cheltenham GL51 . .132 F1
Stroud GL5 . . . . .98 F7
illfield Court Rd GL11 . . .127 A3
illfield Ct GL2 . . . . .127 A3
illfields Ave BS16 . . . . . .20 C3

Hillfields Prim Sch BS16 . . .20 C2
Hillgrove St BS2 . . . . .195 B4
Hillier Cl GL5 . . . . .103 D1
Hillier Dr ? GL51 . . . . . . .129 F5
Hillmill La GL12 . . . . .69 B5
Hillrise GL15 . . . . .155 D1
Hills Cl BS31 . . . . .5 F6
Hills View ? GL18 . . . . . .171 A4
Hillsborough BS8 . . . . . . .194 A2
Hillsborough Rd BS4 . . . . .9 C4
Hollow La GL5 . . . . .99 D7
Hillside
Bristol,Mangotsfield BS16 . .21 A5
Bristol,Tyndall's Park
BS6 . . . . .194 C4
Burton SN14 . . . . .36 A4
Chalford GL6 . . . . .148 D6
Leigh SN6 . . . . .143 B3
Hillside Ave BS15 . . . . . .10 C8
Hillside Cl
? Bream GL15 . . . . .155 D1
Cheltenham GL51 . . . . . .130 A7
Frampton Cotterell BS36 . . .31 C7
Woodmancote GL52 . . . . .138 C3
Hillside Ct Bristol BS5 . . . .10 B7
Dursley GL11 . . . . .80 B8
Hillside Est ? GL51 . . . . .155 D1
Hillside Gdns GL52 . . . . .138 C3
Hillside Ho ? BS6 . . . . . .18 D1
Hillside La BS36 . . . . . . .31 C7
Hillside Rd Bristol BS5 . . . .10 A7
Drybrook GL17 . . . . .164 B5
Long Ashton BS41 . . . . . .7 B2
Mitcheldean GL17 . . . . . .164 D5
Hillside St ? BS4 . . . . . . .9 A4
Hillside Terr GL17 . . . . . .163 D3
Hillside Villas GL5 . . . . . .99 D5
Hilltop ? GL15 . . . . .147 D8
Hilltop Gdns
Bristol,St George BS5 . . . .10 A8
Bristol,Upper Soundwell
GL11 . . . . .20 D2
Hilltop Rd BS16 . . . . .20 D2
Hilltop View Bristol BS5 . . .10 A7
Hillview GL7 . . . . .158 D3
Hillview Ave GL3 . . . . . . .120 A6
Hillview Dr GL3 . . . . .120 A8
Hillview House Pk (Mobile
Home Pk) ? GL3 . . . . . .120 A8
Hillview La GL20 . . . . . . .181 F8
Hillview Prim Sch GL3 . . .120 A8
Hillview Rd
Cheltenham GL52 . . . . . .134 B2
Gloucester GL3 . . . . .120 A8
Pucklechurch BS16 . . . . . .22 C5
Hillview Rise GL16 . . . . . .155 A7
Hillwell SN16 . . . . .141 E1
Hilly Orch GL5 . . . . .98 E6
Hillyfield Rd BS13 . . . . . .2 A6
Hilton Cl GL2 . . . . .118 B6
Hilton Ct ? BS5 . . . . .9 B8
Hinders La GL17,GL19 . . .165 B5
Hine Gdns GL5 . . . . .133 F3
Hinton Cl BS31 . . . . .5 E3
Hinton Ct GL13 . . . . .85 C8
Hinton Dr BS30 . . . . .11 C6
Hinton La ? BS8 . . . . . . .7 F6
Hinton Rd
Bristol,Fishponds BS16 . . .20 A4
Bristol,Lower Easton BS5 . .19 C1
Gloucester GL1 . . . . .126 B4
Hisnams Field GL52 . . . . .137 F3
Historic Gloucester Docks*
GL1 . . . . .196 A2
Hitchen Cl SN14 . . . . . . .14 F8
Hitchen Hollow NP16 . . . .61 B4
Hitchings GL15 . . . . .156 D3
Hithe The GL5 . . . . .99 C3
Hither Bath Bridge BS4 . . .9 C1
Hither Mead BS36 . . . . . .31 B6
Hive The GL54 . . . . .166 E5
Hobart Ho GL51 . . . . . . .132 E2
Hobb's La BS1 . . . . .194 C2
Hobbs La Bristol BS30 . . . .21 B1
Longhope GL17 . . . . .165 A6
Woodmancote GL7 . . . . .158 B4
Hobby Cl GL53 . . . . .130 C5
Hobhouse Cl BS9 . . . . . . .18 C7
Hobwell La BS41 . . . . . . .7 C2
Hocker Hill St ? NP16 . . .60 E8
Hockeys La BS16 . . . . . . .20 A4
Hoddon La BS16 . . . . . . .22 D5
Hodges Way GL14 . . . . . .191 C3
Hodses Yd ? HR8 . . . . . .178 E8
Hogarth Wlk GL7 . . . . . . .19 C7
Hogues Wlk BS13 . . . . . .2 B4
Holbeach Way BS14 . . . . .3 A2
Holbein Cl ? GL3 . . . . . .163 D2
Holbrook Cres BS13 . . . . .2 D4
Holbrook La BS30 . . . . . .12 B7
Holbury Cres GL52 . . . . .100 E5
Holcombe BS14 . . . . .3 A5
Holcombe Gr BS31 . . . . . .4 D5
Holcot Cl ? GL16 . . . . . .155 B5
Holcot Rd GL16 . . . . .155 B5
Holdcroft Cl SN26 . . . . . .144 E1
Holdenhurst Rd BS15 . . . .20 C1
Holder Cl ? GL14 . . . . . .191 C3
Holder Rd GL52 . . . . . . .137 F2
Holders La GL18 . . . . . . .170 E6
Holford Cres GL7 . . . . . . .144 F2
Holford Ct BS14 . . . . .3 B5
Hollams Rd GL20 . . . . . . .192 D5
Holland Ct GL11 . . . . . . .127 A3
Hollidge Gdns ? BS3 . . . .8 D4
Hollies Hill GL6 . . . . .91 C4

Hollies The BS15 . . . . . . .10 E6
Hollingham La GL6 . . . . . .90 E1
Hollis Cl NP16 . . . . .72 F1
Hollis Cl Long Ashton BS41 . .1 A8
Long Ashton BS41 . . . . . .7 A1
Hollis Gdns
Cheltenham GL51 . . . . . .129 D6
Luckington SN14 . . . . . . .47 E4
Hollis Rd GL51 . . . . .129 D6
Hollister's Dr BS13 . . . . . .2 D4
Hollow Rd
Almondsbury BS32 . . . . . .40 A4
Bristol BS15 . . . . .10 E8
Hollow The GL17 . . . . . . .164 A4
Holloway Hill GL14 . . . . . .25 F7
Holloway Rd Bisley GL6 . .148 D8
Severn Beach BS35 . . . . .38 C4
Hollows The BS36 . . . . . .31 D2
Holloway Cl BS14 . . . . . . .3 E5
Hollway Rd BS14 . . . . . . .3 D5
Holly Cl Alveston BS35 . . .50 F4
Bretforton WR11 . . . . . . .188 A7
Bristol BS5 . . . . .20 A2
Chepstow/Cas-Gwent NP16 .60 E5
Pucklechurch BS16 . . . . . .22 C5
Holly Cr BS2 . . . . .20 E1
Holly Ct BS2 . . . . .194 C4
Holly Dr SN14 . . . . .15 F6
Holly End GL2 . . . . .109 F8
Holly Gn BS15 . . . . .21 A1
Holly Gr BS16 . . . . .20 D2
Holly Gr The GL2 . . . . . . .109 F8
Holly Hill BS37 . . . . .42 E3
Holly Hill Rd BS15 . . . . . .20 F1
Holly Ho BS31 . . . . .27 C2
Holly La GL15 . . . . .155 C3
Holly Lodge Cl BS5 . . . . .20 A2
Holly Lodge Rd BS5 . . . . .19 F2
Holly Tree Gdn GL5 . . . . .98 D6
Holly Tree Pl GL15 . . . . . .156 B1
Holly Wlk BS31 . . . . .4 D4
Hollybush Cl GL9 . . . . . . .36 A6
Hollybush La Bristol BS9 . .17 E5
Bristol BS9 . . . . .17 F4
Hollydean GL14 . . . . .191 C5
Hollyguest Rd BS15 . . . . .10 E6
Hollyhill Pk GL14 . . . . . . .191 B5
Hollyhill La GL14 . . . . . . .191 B5
Hollyhock La GL6 . . . . . . .103 F8
Hollyleigh Ave BS34 . . . . .28 F2
Hollymead La BS9 . . . . . .17 E4
Hollyridge BS13 . . . . .3 C6
Hollywell Rd GL17 . . . . . .164 D6
Hollywood La BS10,BS35 . .28 A7
Hollywood Rd BS4 . . . . . .9 D2
Holm La BS35 . . . . .49 B2
Holm-Mead La BS36 . . . . .5 C7
Holmdale Rd BS34 . . . . . .29 C3
Holme Rd GL20 . . . . .192 D1
Holmer Cres GL51 . . . . . .129 D6
Holmes Ct BS9 . . . . .18 E5
Holmes Gr BS9 . . . . .18 E5
Holmes Hill Rd BS5 . . . . .9 F6
Holmes St BS5 . . . . .9 B6
Holmesdale Rd BS3 . . . . .8 F2
Holmfield Dr NP25 . . . . . .146 B7
Holmleigh Par GL4 . . . . . .118 D2
Holmleigh Rd GL4 . . . . . .118 C3
Holmoak Cl GL20 . . . . . . .192 E2
Holmoak Rd BS13 . . . . . .2 A3
Holmwood BS15 . . . . .10 C5
Holmwood Cl
Gloucester GL4 . . . . .118 D2
Winterbourne BS36 . . . . . .30 D6
Holmwood Gdns BS9 . . . .18 B8
Holroyd Ho BS3 . . . . .8 D3
Holsom Rd BS14 . . . . . . .3 F6
Holsom Rd BS14 . . . . . . .3 F6
Holst Gdns GL4 . . . . .118 C3
Holst Way GL4 . . . . .118 C3
Holt La
Bishop's Cleeve GL52 . . . .137 E2
Gloucester GL4 . . . . .119 E7
Holtham Ave GL3 . . . . . . .128 B7
Holton Rd BS7 . . . . .19 A6
Holts Rd GL18 . . . . .170 F4
Holy Apostles CE Prim Sch
GL52 . . . . .131 A8
Holy Cross RC Prim Sch
BS5 . . . . .8 C4
Holy Family RC Prim Sch
BS34 . . . . .29 B8
Holy Trinity CE Prim Sch
GL52 . . . . .193 C4
Holy Trinity Prim Sch
BS32 . . . . .40 C2
Holy Well Inf Sch WR11 . . . .9 E6
Holymead Inf Sch BS4 . . . .9 D2
Holymead Jun Sch BS4 . . .9 D3
Holyrood Ct BS34 . . . . . . .29 D1
Holywell Rd Dursley GL11 . .88 A1
Wotton-u-E GL12 . . . . . . .68 C8
Home Cl Bristol BS10 . . . .28 F2
Cheltenham GL51 . . . . . .132 E3
Lower Oddington GL56 . . .177 C5
Home Farm Ct GL52 . . . . .131 A7
Home Farm Rd BS16 . . . .7 B8
Home Farm Way BS35 . . .39 F1
Home Field Cl BS16 . . . . .21 B6
Home Ground
Bristol,Eastfield BS9 . . . . .18 B7
Bristol,Shirehampton BS11 . .16 D2
Cricklade SN6 . . . . .143 E4
Home Mead Bristol BS4 . . .9 A4
Home Orch Stroud GL5 . . .98 D6
Yate BS37 . . . . .43 D2

Home Piece GL7 . . . . . . .149 B6
Homeabbey Ho GL20 . . . .192 C5
Homeapple Hill BS30 . . . .11 F6
Homeavon Ho BS31 . . . . .4 F5
Homeclose Rd GL7 . . . . . .190 C4
Homecroft Dr GL51 . . . . . .132 E6
Homefarm SN6 . . . . .145 C3
Homefield Nailsworth GL6 . .91 A3
Thornbury BS35 . . . . .51 D8
Yate BS37 . . . . .43 E3
Homefield Cl BS31 . . . . . .5 E3
Homefield Dr BS16 . . . . . .20 A5
Homefield Rd
Pucklechurch BS16 . . . . . .22 B5
Saltford BS31 . . . . .5 F3
Homeground BS16 . . . . . .21 B6
Homeground La GL7 . . . . .152 F4
Homelea Rd BS10 . . . . . . .28 D3
Homeland BS30 . . . . .11 A4
Homemead Dr BS4 . . . . . .9 D1
Homend Cres ? BS37 . . . .178 F8
Homend The ? HR8 . . . . .178 F8
Homepiece WR12 . . . . . . .185 B4
Homesfield ? GL2 . . . . . .133 B1
Homespring Ho GL52 . . . .134 A2
Homestead Cl
Bredon GL20 . . . . .182 C7
Frampton Cotterell GL4 . . .31 D7
Homestead Ct GL4 . . . . . .119 F5
Homestead Gdns BS16 . . .20 A3
Homestead Rd BS34 . . . . .29 A3
Homestead The BS31 . . . .4 F2
Hone ? GL20 . . . . .192 C4
Honey Garston Cl BS13 . . .2 B4
Honey Garston Rd BS13 . . .2 B4
Honey Hill Rd BS15 . . . . .10 F8
Honey Suckle La BS16 . . .20 A3
Honey Way BS15 . . . . . . .10 F8
Honeybourne Airfield Ind Est
WR11 . . . . .188 C5
Honeybourne Dr GL51 . . .132 D4
Honeybourne Fst Sch
WR11 . . . . .188 C6
Honeybourne Pottery*
WR11 . . . . .188 C6
Honeybourne Rd WR11 . . .188 B6
Honeybourne Sta WR11 . . .188 C6
Honeybourne Way GL50 . .193 A4
Honeymead BS14 . . . . . . .3 C6
Honeysuckle Cl
Bristol BS32 . . . . .40 E2
Cheltenham GL52 . . . . . .134 C3
Honeysuckle Dr GL4 . . . . .119 E5
Honeysuckle Way GL52 . .137 F5
Honeythorn Cl GL2 . . . . . .118 B7
Honeywick Cl BS3 . . . . . .8 C2
Honister Ho BS34 . . . . . . .29 A8
Honiton Rd BS16 . . . . . . .20 A3
Honyland Cl GL4 . . . . . . .196 C4
Hoo La
Chipping Campden GL55 . .188 F2
Tewkesbury GL20 . . . . . .173 E8
Hook's La GL18 . . . . .171 D5
Hookshouse La
Doughton GL8 . . . . .71 C4
Tetbury GL8 . . . . .140 A3
Hooper Cl GL14 . . . . .119 B6
Hooper Rd BS14 . . . . .3 D5
Hoovers La HR9 . . . . .164 B8
Hop Gdn The NP16 . . . . . .60 F4
Hope Brook CE Prim Sch
GL17 . . . . .164 F6
Hope Cotts GL17 . . . . . . .99 D6
Hope Ct BS1 . . . . .194 B1
Hope Mill La GL5 . . . . . . .99 E2
Hope Mills Bsns Ctr GL5 . .99 E2
Hope Orch BS37 . . . . .132 D4
Hope Rd Bristol BS3 . . . . .8 C2
Yate BS37 . . . . .43 A2
Hope Sq BS8 . . . . .7 F6
Hope St GL51 . . . . .133 B3
Hope Villas GL5 . . . . .99 C8
Hopechapel Hill ? BS8 . . .7 A6
Hopes Cl GL15 . . . . .92 C2
Hopetoun Rd BS2 . . . . . . .18 F3
Hopewell Cl NP16 . . . . . .61 A4
Hopewell Colliery Mus*
GL16 . . . . .155 D6
Hopewell Gdns BS11 . . . .16 F7
Hopewell St BS5 . . . . . . .9 D7
Hopkin Cl BS35 . . . . .51 D7
Hopkins Ct ? BS6 . . . . . .18 D2
Hopkins Orch ? SN6 . . . .143 E4
Hopkins St BS30 . . . . . . .11 A5
Hopp's Rd BS15 . . . . .10 D7
Hopton Rd GL11 . . . . .88 B4
Hopwood Gr ? GL52 . . . .134 A1
Hopyard La GL18 . . . . . . .181 E5
Hopyard The GL20 . . . . . .182 B5
Horcott Ind Est GL7 . . . . .152 D3
Horcott Rd GL7 . . . . .152 D3
Horefield Gr BS13 . . . . . .2 A5
Horfield CE Prim Sch
BS10 . . . . .18 D7
Horfield Rd BS2 . . . . .195 A4
Horn La GL55 . . . . .188 B7
Hornbeam Ho ? BS16 . . .20 C7
Hornbeam Mews GL2 . . . .127 B5
Hornbeam Wlk BS31 . . . . .4 C3
Hornbeams The BS16 . . . .30 B1
Hornbury CP SN16 . . . . . .142 D1
Hornbury Hill SN16 . . . . .142 D1
Horns Rd GL5 . . . . .99 D6
Horsbere Rd GL3 . . . . . . .120 B8

Horse Fair La SN6 . . . . . .143 F4
Horse La BS35 . . . . .64 D5
Horse Lane Orch HR8 . . . .178 F8
Horse Pool La HR9 . . . . . .162 E2
Horse St BS37 . . . . .44 C1
Horsecroft Gdns BS30 . . . .11 A6
Horsefair Cl GL13 . . . . . . .85 C8
Horsefair La GL18 . . . . . .170 F5
Horsefair St GL53 . . . . . . .131 A5
Horsefair The ? BS1 . . . . .195 B3
Horsemarling La GL10 . . . .101 F1
Horsepool La
Doynton BS30 . . . . .12 F8
St Briavels GL15 . . . . . . .146 E6
Horsepool Rd BS13 . . . . . .1 C3
Horseshoe Cl BS37 . . . . . .155 A7
Horseshoe Dr BS36 . . . . .31 D7
Horseshoe Dr Bristol BS9 . .17 C4
Over GL2 . . . . .126 B4
Horseshoe La BS37 . . . . . .44 B1
Horseshoe Way GL11 . . . .118 B6
Horstrough Rdbt GL10 . . . .97 F6
Horsford Rd GL2 . . . . .67 B5
Horslea GL17 . . . . .162 A3
Horsley CE Prim Sch GL6 . .90 F1
Horsley Cl GL4 . . . . .119 E5
Horsley Hill GL6 . . . . .91 A1
Horsley Rd GL6 . . . . .91 A2
Hortham La BS32 . . . . . . .40 E5
Horton CE Prim Sch
Horton BS37 . . . . .45 C5
Horton Ct* BS37 . . . . .45 D7
Horton Hill BS37 . . . . . . .45 D7
Horton Rd
Chipping Sodbury BS37 . . .44 C2
Chipping Sodbury,Little
Sodbury End BS37 . . . . .44 D4
Gloucester GL1 . . . . .127 A2
Horton St ? BS2 . . . . . . .195 C3
Horwood La BS37 . . . . . . .54 B4
Hosey Wlk BS13 . . . . . . .2 A5
Hospital Rd (West St)
GL56 . . . . .187 A3
Hossil La SN6 . . . . .145 A1
Host La BS1 . . . . .195 A3
Hot Water La BS15 . . . . . .21 A3
Hottom Gdns BS7 . . . . . .19 A2
Hotwell Rd BS8 . . . . .194 B1
Hotwells Ho BS8 . . . . . . .194 A2
Hotwells Prim Sch BS8 . . .7 F6
Houlton St BS2 . . . . .195 C4
Hounds Cl BS37 . . . . .44 B1
Hounds Rd BS37 . . . . . . .44 B1
Howard Ave BS5 . . . . . . .9 E8
Howard Cl
Northway GL20 . . . . .182 C4
Saltford BS31 . . . . .5 D3
Howard Rd
Bristol,Southville BS3 . . . .8 C4
Bristol,Staple Hill BS16 . .20 D4
? Coleford GL16 . . . . . .155 B6
Bristol,Westbury Park BS6 . .18 C1
Northway GL20 . . . . .182 C4
Thornbury BS35 . . . . .64 C2
Howard St BS5 . . . . .19 E1
Gloucester GL1 . . . . .118 F7
Howard Wlk BS30 . . . . . . .11 D7
Howcroft Ct GL3 . . . . . . .128 C4
Howcroft GL53 . . . . .17 E4
Howecroft Gdns BS9 . . . . .17 E4
Howell Rd
Bristol,Clifton BS8 . . . . . .18 A2
Bristol,Horfield BS7 . . . . .18 E5
Hughes Cl NP16 . . . . .60 E7
Hughes Cres NP16 . . . . . .60 E7
Hughes Gdn GL7 . . . . . . .19 A8
Hughes Terr GL15 . . . . . .155 E3
Hulbert Cl Bristol BS4 . . . .10 A2
Swindon GL51 . . . . .133 A7

Hulbert Cres GL51 ....129 F5
Hulse Rd BS4 ....9 D1
Humber Pl GL3 ....120 F5
Humber Rd GL52 ....134 A2
Humber Way BS11 ....26 D5
Humberstam Wlk BS11 ..16 E8
Humphreys Cl GL5 ....98 E8
Humphry Davy Way 6
BS8 ....7 F5
Humphrys Barton BS4 ....9 F5
Hung Rd BS11 ....16 E5
Hunger Hill GL11 ....80 A8
Hungerford Cl BS4 ....3 E8
Hungerford Cres BS4 ......9 E1
Hungerford Gdns BS4 .....3 E8
Hungerford Rd BS4 ....3 E8
Hungerford St GL50 .....133 D3
Hungerford Wlk BS4 ....9 E1
Hunter's Way
Andoversford GL54 .....166 C6
Bristol BS34 ....29 B3
Hunters Cl Bristol BS15 ..10 C5
Stroud GL5 ....98 D7
Hunters Dr BS35 ....20 F1
Hunters Gate GL4 ....119 D4
Hunters Mead GL9 ....56 A2
Hunters Rd
Bishop's Cleeve GL52 ...137 E4
Bristol BS15 ....10 C4
Hunters Rd E BS15 ....10 C4
Hunters Way GL5 ....98 D7
Huntfield Rd NP16 ....60 D8
Hunthill GL14 ....165 E1
Huntingdon Cl GL5 ....98 D6
Huntingham Rd BS11 .....1 F4
Huntings The 7 WR12 .185 B8
Huntley CE Prim Sch
GL19 ....165 C6
Huntley Cl GL14 ....119 E5
Hunts Ground Rd BS34 ..29 F4
Hunts Grove View GL2 ..110 B7
Hunts Hill SN26 ....144 D1
Hunts La BS7 ....18 E6
Huntscote Rd GL51 .....133 A5
Huntsfield Cl GL50 ......133 E4
Huntsmans Cl GL52 .....138 A4
Huntsmans Meet GL54 ..166 D6
Hurcombe Way GL3 .....120 E6
Hurle Cres BS8 ....18 B1
Hurle Rd BS8 ....18 B1
Hurlingham Rd BS7 ......18 F2
Hurn La BS31 ....5 A3
Hurricane Rd GL3 ....120 C5
Hursley Hill BS14 ....3 D1
Hursley La BS14 ....3 E1
Hurst Cl GL2 ....127 D5
Hurst Rd BS4 ....2 F8
Hurst Wlk BS4 ....2 F8
Hurston Rd BS4 ....2 D7
Hurstwood Rd BS16 .....20 D5
Hutton Cl Bristol BS9 ....17 E7
Keynsham BS31 ....5 A2
Hutton Raufe GL51 ......132 F1
Huxley Cl GL7 ....143 A8
Huxley Rd GL11 ....118 F7
Huxley Way GL52 ....137 D4
Huyton Rd BS5 ....19 E3
Hyatts Way GL52 ....138 A3
Hyde Apartments BS6 ..18 C3
Hyde Ave BS35 ....64 B3
Hyde Bank GL14 ....156 F7
Hyde Cl GL1 ....127 A2
Hyde Cotts GL54 ....139 F4
Hyde La Gloucester GL1 ..127 A2
Newnham GL14 ....156 F7
Hyde Park Cnr GL19 .....179 D2
Hyde The GL54 ....139 F5
Hyde View GL16 ....154 F3
Hyde's La SN14 ....14 A6
Hydes The BS31 ....4 F5
Hyett Cl GL6 ....103 F8
Hyett Orch GL6 ....103 F8
Hyett Rd GL5 ....98 E7
Hygrove La GL2 ....125 B1
Hyland Gr BS9 ....17 F8

I

Ibis Wlk GL2 ....117 D1
Icehouse La GL56 ....186 D1
Icombe Cl GL7 ....137 F3
Ida Rd 2 BS5 ....9 C8
Idaho St GL7 ....152 E2
Iddesleigh Rd BS6 ....18 B3
Idsall Dr GL52 ....134 C4
Idstone Rd BS16 ....20 B4
Ilford Cl BS31 ....5 E3
Ilchester Cres BS13 ......18 A1
Ilchester Rd BS13 ....2 B8
Iles Cl BS15 ....10 D4
Ile 1 Cl BS15 ....1 F6
Ilmington CE Prim Sch
CV36 ....189 F6
Ilminster Ave BS4 ....2 F8
Ilminster Avenue Prim Sch
BS4 ....3 A8
Ilsom Cotts GL8 ....140 D5
Ilsyn Gr BS14 ....3 D7
Imber Court GL14 ....3 B8
Imjin Rd GL52 ....134 B2
Imperial Arc 11 BS3 .....9 B8
Imperial Cir GL50 ....193 B3

Imperial Ct GL50 ....193 B3
Imperial Gate GL50 ......193 B3
Imperial Gate Bsns Pk
GL4 ....127 D2
Imperial La GL50 ....193 B3
Imperial Pl BS13 ....2 C6
Imperial Rd
8 Bristol,Clifton BS6 ....18 B1
Bristol,Knowle BS14 ......3 C8
Imperial Sq GL50 ....193 B2
Imperial Wlk BS14 ....9 B1
Ince Castle Way GL1 ...119 A8
Inchbrook Ct GL5 ....90 F6
Inchbrook Hill GL5,GL6 ..91 A6
Inchbrook Trad Est GL5 ..91 A7
Inchbrook Way GL6 ......90 F6
India Ho 2 GL51 ....132 E2
India Rd GL1 ....119 A8
Inglecote Cl GL52 ....131 B6
Ingleside Rd BS15 ....20 C1
Ingleside Sch GL7 ....190 D4
Inglestone Rd GL12 .....154 B5
Ingmire Rd BS5 ....19 B3
Ingram Cl CV36 ....187 E5
Ingst Hill BS35 ....49 B3
Ingst Rd BS35 ....49 D4
Inkerman Cl BS7 ....18 E7
Inkerman La 16 GL50 ...130 B8
Inn Cotts BS11 ....17 A7
Inner Ctyd GL7 ....190 D7
Inner Down The BS12 ...50 D3
Inner Loop Rd NP16 .....61 B6
Innerstone La GL19 .....171 D8
Innocks Est GL11 ....79 D4
Innox Gdns BS13 ....2 A5
Inns Court Ave BS4 ....2 D7
Inns Court Dr BS4 ....2 D6
Inns Court Gn BS4 ....2 D7
Innsworth Jun Sch GL3 ..127 D6
Innsworth La GL3 ....127 D7
Innsworth Tech Pk GL3 .127 C6
Insley Gdns GL3 ....119 F8
Instow Rd BS4 ....2 E8
Instow Wlk BS4 ....2 E8
International Sch of
Choueifat SN14 ....15 C4
International Trad Est
BS11 ....26 B2
Interplex 16 BS32 ....40 C3
Inverlea Cl GL55 ....189 A6
IO Ctr BS11 ....26 F5
Ipswich Dr BS4 ....9 E6
Irby Rd BS3 ....8 A3
Irena Rd BS16 ....19 F3
Ireton Rd BS3 ....8 B3
Iron Acton CE Prim Sch
BS37 ....42 E4
Iron Acton Way BS37 ....43 B3
Iron Hogg La GL12 ....65 C3
Iron Mills GL6 ....91 E3
Ironchurch Rd BS11 .....26 C5
Ironmonger's La GL13 ...86 B4
Ironmould La BS4 ....10 A1
Ironstone Ct 2 GL15 ...147 D8
Irving Cl BS16 ....20 E4
Irving Ct GL52 ....193 C3
Irving Ho Bristol BS1 ...194 C3
14 Cheltenham GL52 ...133 F2
Isambard Wlk BS1 ....195 C2
Isbourne Rd GL52 ....134 B2
Isbourne Way GL54 .....174 B8
ISF Rd BS11 ....26 C3
Islamic Sec Sch for Girls
GL1 ....196 C2
Island Gdns BS16 ....19 C4
Island Trad Pk BS11 .....26 C1
Islay Cres SN6 ....145 C4
Isle Of Rhé GL11 ....79 C5
Isleys Ct BS30 ....10 F3
Islington Rd BS3 ....8 C4
Ismay Rd GL51 ....132 F4
Ison Hill Rd BS10 ....27 D3
Itchington Rd
Alveston BS35 ....51 F4
Tytherington GL12 ......52 B4
Itlay GL7 ....150 A8
Itton Rd NP16 ....72 B2
Ivanhoe Rd GL2 ....118 C4
Ivor Rd BS5 ....9 C8
Ivory Cl GL4 ....118 C2
Ivy Bank GL14 ....134 C3
Ivy Cotts NP16 ....73 B1
Ivy House Est HR9 ....170 B5
Ivy House La HR9 ....170 B5
Ivy La Bristol BS16 ....20 A3
Broad Blunsdon SN26 ..144 D1
Ivy Lodge 4 BS9 ....18 A7
Ivy Lodge Barns GL4 ...121 F1
Ivy Mews GL1 ....118 F5
Ivy Terr BS37 ....32 B4
Ivywell Rd BS9 ....17 E3
Izod's Cl GL55 ....188 F1

J

Jack Knight Ho BS7 .....18 F5
Jack Price Cl BS13 ....2 C3
Jackbarrow Rd GL7 .....107 A8
Jackson Cl BS35 ....38 D7
Jackson Cres GL4 ....127 E6
Jackson Rd
Bledington OX7 ....177 E1
Siddington GL7 ....150 F2
Jacob St BS2 ....195 C3
Jacob's Ct BS1 ....194 B2
Jacob's Wells Rd BS8 ...194 B2

Jacobs Cl 4 GL8 ....140 C5
Jamaica St BS2 ....195 B4
James Ave 10 GL2 ....117 D1
James Cl Bristol BS16 ...20 E4
12 Quedgeley GL2 ......117 D1
James Ct
Cheltenham GL51 ....132 F1
Yorkley GL15 ....156 B1
James Donovan Ct
GL52 ....134 A2
James Dr 9 GL2 ....117 D1
James Grieve Rd GL4 ...119 F6
James Orch GL13 ....85 E3
James Pl 8 GL2 ....117 D1
James Rd BS16 ....20 E3
James Row 10 GL2 ......117 D1
James St
Bristol,Baptist Mills BS2 ..19 A2
Bristol,St Pauls BS5 ....195 C4
James Way
Gloucester GL3 ....120 C6
Quedgeley GL2 ....117 E1
James Wlk Pillowell GL15 ..155 E1
11 Quedgeley GL2 ......117 D1
Jameson Cl 24 GL56 ....187 A3
Jane St BS5 ....9 B7
Japonica Cl 5 GL3 ......128 A7
Japonica Dr GL51 ....130 A5
Jardine Dr GL52 ....137 E4
Jarvis St BS5 ....9 B6
Jasmin Way GL51 ....130 A5
Jasmine Cl GL4 ....119 D4
Jasmine Gr BS11 ....27 C2
Jasper St BS3 ....8 B3
Javelin Pk GL10 ....109 E1
Javelin Way GL3 ....120 F5
Jay's Gn HR9 ....170 A5
Jay's Mead GL12 ....68 C7
Jays The GL12 ....92 B6
Jaythorpe GL4 ....119 D3
Jean Rd BS4 ....9 E2
Jefferies Cl 7 GL7 ....152 E4
Jefferies Hill Bottom
BS15 ....10 B5
Jeffery Ct BS30 ....11 B6
Jeffreys Ct 9 BS16 ....19 E3
Jeffries Cl GL7 ....190 D4
Jellicoe Ave BS16 ....19 E8
Jena Ct BS31 ....5 E3
Jenkin's La GL6 ....103 C7
Jenner Cl
Chipping Sodbury BS37 ..33 D8
Gloucester GL3 ....119 F8
Jenner Ct GL13 ....85 E3
Jenner Wlk GL50 ....193 B4
Jennings Ct 4 BS3 ....8 A4
Jersey Ave Bristol BS4 ...9 F4
Cheltenham GL51 ....133 F2
Jersey Rd GL1 ....119 A8
Jersey St GL52 ....193 C4
Jesse Mary Chambers
Almshouses GL51 ....132 F1
Jesson Rd GL52 ....138 A3
Jessop Cl GL52 ....193 A3
Jessop Cres BS10 ....28 A1
Jessop Ct BS1 ....195 B2
Jessop Dr 2 BS35 ....168 A1
Jessop Underpass BS3 ..7 F4
Jet Age Air Mus* GL2 ..128 C8
Jewson Cl GL4 ....118 D2
Jeynes Bldgs GL20 ......192 D5
Jeynes Row GL20 ....192 D5
Jim O'Neil Ho BS11 .....16 D7
Joan Hawley Mews
GL52 ....131 A7
Job's La GL20 ....182 E8
Jobbins Ct GL7 ....190 C4
Jocelyn Rd BS7 ....18 F7
Jockey La BS5 ....10 A7
Jockey Stable Cotts
GL56 ....186 A4
John Bevan Cl GL5 ....99 D8
John Buck Ho 8 GL52 ..193 C4
John Cabot City Tech Coll
BS15 ....10 C7
John Cabot Ct BS1 ......194 A1
John Carr's Terr BS8 ....194 B2
John Cozens Ho BS37 ..195 C3
John Daniels Way GL3 ..128 B4
John James Ct BS1 ....19 B7
John Lamb Ho GL51 ....129 D2
John Masefield High Sch
HR8 ....178 F8
John Moore Countryside
Mus* GL20 ....192 C4
John Moore Gdns 4
GL50 ....130 B6
John Moore Prim Sch The
GL20 ....192 E1
John of Gaunt Rd GL7 ..144 E8
John Repton Gdns BS10 ..28 B2
John Rushout Ct GL56 ..186 A4
John St Bristol BS1 ......195 A3
Bristol,Baptist Mills BS2 ..19 A2
Bristol,Two Mile Hill BS15 ..10 C8
Stroud GL5 ....99 C7
John Tame Cl 4 GL7 ....152 E4
John Wesley Ct 9 BS5 ..20 D5
John Wesley Rd BS5 ....10 A6
John Wesleys Chapel*
BS1 ....195 B3
John Woolfe Ct GL56 ...186 C7
Johnson Dr BS30 ....10 F5
Johnson Rd BS16 ....21 C5
Johnsons La BS16 ....19 D1
11 Bristol,Moorfields BS5 ..9 C8
Johnsons Way GL15 .....156 B2

Johnstone Cl GL19 ......172 A7
Johnstone Rd 3 GL18 ..171 A4
Joiners La GL6 ....148 B8
Jones Ho 3 NP25 ....154 A8
Jordan Wlk BS32 ....29 D8
Jordans Cl GL12 ....188 B2
Jordans Way GL2 ....126 F5
Jorrocks Ind Est BS37 ...32 C4
Josend Cres GL19 ....172 F7
Joy Hill BS8 ....7 F6
Joyce Cl BS7 ....19 A8
Joyford Hill GL16 ....155 A8
Joyner Rd GL11 ....133 A4
Joys Green Prim Sch
GL17 ....163 D3
Joys Green Rd GL17 .....163 D2
Jubilee Ave GL11 ....87 F6
Jubilee Cl
Chipping Campden GL55 ..188 F2
Dursley GL11 ....87 F6
Ledbury HR8 ....178 F7
12 Stow-on-t-W GL54 ..176 F4
Jubilee Cotts GL6 ....148 B5
Jubilee Cres BS16 ....21 A6
Jubilee Ct Bristol BS4 ....9 D4
Cheltenham GL50 ....193 B3
Jubilee Dr Bredon GL20 ..182 C7
Thornbury BS35 ....64 D1
Jubilee Flats GL7 ....150 F2
Jubilee Gdns
South Cerney GL7 ....142 F7
Yate BS37 ....44 A2
Jubilee Gn GL7 ....190 D3
Jubilee Ho BS34 ....29 C4
Jubilee La Bream GL15 ..147 D8
Cromhall GL12 ....53 B7
Jubilee Pk* HR9 ....162 E4
Jubilee Pl Bristol BS1 ...195 A1
Bristol,Woodstock BS15 ..10 F7
Corse GL19 ....172 A7
Jubilee Rd
Bristol,Baptist Mills BS2 ..19 A1
Bristol,Crew's Hole BS5 ...9 F7
Bristol,Staple Hill BS15 ..20 E3
Bristol,Upper Knowle BS4 ..9 C2
Dursley GL11 ....88 A2
Lydney GL15 ....92 C3
Mitcheldean GL17 ......164 D3
Nailsworth GL6 ....91 A5
Jubilee St BS2 ....195 C3
Jubilee Way
Avonmouth BS11 ....26 A7
Newton GL13 ....85 D8
Judge's La
Longhope GL18 ....170 F1
Taynton GL18 ....171 A1
Julian Cl Bristol BS9 ....17 E3
Gloucester GL4 ....119 D8
Julian Ct BS9 ....17 E3
Julian Rd BS9 ....17 E3
Julius Cl BS16 ....21 C6
Julius Rd BS7 ....18 E3
Julius Way GL15 ....92 B8
Jumpers La GL13 ....85 E3
Junction Rd BS4 ....9 C4
Juniper Ave GL4 ....119 B4
Juniper Cotts GL6 ....103 F5
Juniper Ct 2 Bristol BS5 ..19 C2
Cheltenham GL51 ....132 C2
Juniper Way Bristol BS34 ..30 A7
Stonehouse GL10 ....97 F8
Juno Dr GL15 ....92 B5
Jupiter Rd BS34 ....28 F7
Jupiter Way GL4 ....119 F6
Justice Ave BS31 ....5 E3
Justice Rd BS16 ....20 A3
Justicia Way GL51 ......129 F5
Justin's Hill NP25 ....154 A7
Jutland Rd BS11 ....26 B1

K

Kansas Dr GL7 ....152 E2
Karelean Ct BS10 ....28 D3
Kaskelot Way GL7 ....118 C6
Katharine Cl GL51 ......130 A5
Katharine Lady Berkeley
Mews GL12 ....68 B7
Kathdene Gdns GL3 ....119 F8
Katherine Cl
Charfield GL12 ....67 A5
Innsworth GL3 ....127 F8
Katherine Lady Berkeley's
Sch GL12 ....67 F6
Katherine's Wlk
Lechlade on T GL7 ......153 E2
5 Ledbury HR8 ....178 E7
Kaybourne Cres GL3 ...128 D5
Kayte Cl GL52 ....137 F2
Kayte La GL52 ....138 A2
Keable Rd BS4 ....118 C4
Keats Ct BS7 ....19 A8
Keats Gdns GL15 ....103 A1
Keble Ave BS13 ....1 F5
Keble Cl Cirencester GL7 ..190 D1
Keble Lawns GL52 ....152 E3
Keble Rd Chalford GL6 ..148 D6
Moreton-in-M GL56 .....187 A2
Keck's La BS35 ....34 F8
Keedings The GL14 .....159 C5
Keels SN6 ....143 E5
Keen's Gr BS35 ....30 C4
Keep The BS30 ....11 D5
Keepers La BS7 ....18 E5
Keepers Mill GL52 ....138 B3
Keg Store The BS1 ......195 B2

Keil Cl 5 WR12 ....185 B8
Keinton Wlk BS10 ....28 A2
Keirle Wlk GL51 ....133 A4
Kelbra Cres BS36 ....31 B6
Kellaway Ave GL51 ......18 D5
Kellaway Cres BS9 ......18 E5
Kellaway Ct BS6 ....18 D5
Kells Meend GL16 ....155 A3
Kells Rd GL16 ....155 A4
Kellys La NP16 ....146 F1
Kelston Cl Saltford BS31 ..5 D4
Yate BS37 ....32 D7
Kelston Gdns BS10 ......18 D8
Kelston Gr BS15 ....10 E6
Kelston Rd Bristol BS10 ..18 D8
Kelston BA1 ....6 B8
Keynsham BS31 ....4 D5
Kelston Wlk BS16 ....20 C4
Kemble Bsns Pk SN16 ..141 D6
Kemble Cl Bristol BS15 ..10 E6
Gloucester GL4 ....118 D2
Kemble Dr GL7 ....190 B2
Kemble Gdns BS11 ......16 E5
Kemble Gr GL53 ....129 B3
Kemble Ho BS34 ....39 F1
Kemble Pk GL7 ....141 F7
Kemble Prim Sch GL7 ..141 F7
Kemble Rd GL4 ....118 E2
Kemble St GL7 ....141 F6
Kemerton Rd
Bredon GL20 ....182 C7
Cheltenham GL50 ....130 B6
Westmancote GL20 .....182 D8
Kempe's Cl BS41 ....7 A2
Kemperleye Way BS32 ..29 D7
Kempley Rd GL18 ....178 C3
Kemps La GL18 ....103 F8
Kempsford Acre GL52 ..138 B3
Kempsford CE Prim Sch
GL7 ....144 E8
Kempton Cl
2 Bristol BS16 ....30 F1
Thornbury BS35 ....64 B3
Kempton Gr GL51 ......132 D2
Kencot Wlk BS13 ....2 B3
Kencourt Cl 2 GL12 ....127 B2
Kendal Rd Bristol BS7 ...19 A4
Gloucester GL2 ....127 C4
Kendall Gdns BS16 ......20 D4
Kendall Rd BS16 ....20 D4
Kendon Dr BS10 ....18 D7
Kendon Way BS10 ....18 D8
Kendrick La 11 GL5 ......99 C7
Kendrick St 9 GL5 ....99 C7
Kenelm Cl GL53 ....130 C6
Kenelm Gdns GL53 .....130 B6
Kenelm Rise GL54 ......174 A8
Kenilworth BS37 ....32 F6
Kenilworth Ave GL2 ....127 B3
Kenilworth Cl BS31 ....4 D4
Kenilworth Dr BS30 .....11 D5
Kenilworth Ho 3 GL51 ..132 E3
Kenilworth Rd BS6 ....18 C1
Kenmare Rd BS4 ....8 E1
Kenmore Cres BS7 ....28 E1
Kenmore Dr BS7 ....28 E1
Kenmore Gr BS7 ....28 E1
Kenn Court Bsns Pk BS4 ..2 E7
Kenn Rd BS5 ....10 A7
Kennard Rd BS15 ....10 C7
Kennard Way BS15 ......10 C8
Kennard Rise BS15 ......10 C8
Kennedy Cl GL3 ....127 F1
Kennedy Ho BS37 ....43 F1
Kennedy Way BS37 ......43 F1
Kennel Dr GL9 ....46 E2
Kennel La
Broadwell GL56 ....177 A6
Waterhead GL3 ....120 E4
Wotton-u-E WR12 ....185 B8
Kennel Lodge Rd BS3 ....7 F4
Kennerwell La GL12 .....68 C3
Kennet Cl GL20 ....182 B4
Kennet Rd BS31 ....5 E4
Kennet Way 4 BS35 .....51 E8
Kenneth Cl GL53 ....130 E4
Kennett Ave GL54 ....9 D2
Kennett Gdns GL4 ......119 F4
Kennington Ave
Bristol,Bishopston BS7 ..18 F4
3 Bristol,Two Mile Hill
BS15 ....20 D1
Kennion Rd BS5 ....10 A7
Kennmoor Cl BS30 ......11 A6
Kensal Ave BS3 ....8 E3
Kensal Rd BS3 ....8 E3
Kensington Apartments
BS6 ....18 C3
Kensington Ave GL50 ..130 A8
Kensington Cl BS35 .....64 B2
Kensington Ct BS8 ......194 A3
Kensington Pk 18 BS5 ...9 A8
Kensington Park Rd BS4 ..9 C2
Kensington Pk BS5 ......19 A3
Kensington Pl BS8 ......194 A3
Kensington Rd
Bristol,Redland BS6 .....18 C1
3 Bristol,St George BS5 ..10 A8
6 Bristol,Staple Hill BS16 ..20 D4
Kensley Vale GL14 ....159 C5
Kent Ave BS37 ....43 F3
Kent Cl Bristol BS34 .....29 D4
Churchdown GL3 ....128 D5
Kent End GL54 ....143 A5
Kent End Cl SN6 ....143 A5
Kent Mews BS16 ....19 F2
Kent Rd BS7 ....18 E4
Kent St BS3 ....8 B4

entmere Cl GL51 . . . . .129 E7
enton Dr GL22 . . . . .127 C5
enton Ho BS34 . . . . .39 F1
enton Mews BS9 . . . . .18 C5
ents Gn BS15 . . . . .20 E2
enulf Rd 20 GL54 . . . . . . .174 A7
eppel Cl BS31 . . . . .5 D2
eriston Ave GL22 . . . . .128 A6
err Way GL56 . . . . .187 C3
errin La GL15 . . . . .147 C2
erris Ct 9 GL3 . . . . .128 A7
erry Rd BS4 . . . . .8 E1
erstman Rd BS6 . . . . .18 C3
erstin Cl GL50 . . . . .133 C5
estrel Cl Bristol BS34 . . . . .28 E8
Chipping Sodbury BS37 . . . . .32 F8
Thornbury BS35 . . . . .64 D2
estrel Ct 8 GL10 . . . . .97 F8
estrel Dr BS16 . . . . .22 C4
estrel Gdns GL22 . . . . .117 C3
estrel Par BS16 . . . . .127 D6
estrel Way GL20 . . . . .182 B5
eswick Cl GL2 . . . . .127 B3
eswick Rd GL51 . . . . .129 E7
eswick Wlk BS10 . . . . .28 C2
eswick Rd BS3 . . . . .8 F3
evin Cl GL4 . . . . .127 D1
ew Pl GL53 . . . . .193 B1
ew Wlk BS4 . . . . .9 A8
ews La GL18 . . . . .170 D4
ewstoke Rd BS9 . . . . .17 E4
eynes Acre GL55 . . . . .189 D3
ibble's La GL14 . . . . .191 C1
idnalls Rd GL15 . . . . .155 F1
idnams Wlk GL2 . . . . .100 F5
idnappers La GL53 . . . . . . .130 B4
igney Hill BS37 . . . . .32 A3
iftsgate Court Gdns*
GL55 . . . . .189 C6
ilburnie Rd GL14 . . . . .3 A3
ilburn Ct 7 BS5 . . . . .9 B8
ilburn St 10 BS5 . . . . .9 B8
ilda Rd SN6 . . . . .145 C4
ildare Rd BS4 . . . . .8 D1
iilham La GL54 . . . . .166 E5
ilkenny St BS2 . . . . .195 C2
illcott Rd GL12 . . . . .55 E8
ilmersdon Rd BS13 . . . . . . .2 B4
ilminster Cl BS34 . . . . .29 D7
ilminster Cl 10 GL3 . . . . . .128 A7
ilminster Rd BS11 . . . . .16 D7
ilmore La GL20 . . . . .181 F7
iln Cl BS15 . . . . .20 B2
iln Ct BS5 . . . . .9 B8
ilnhurst Cl BS30 . . . . .10 F2
ilvert Ct BS4 . . . . .9 D5
imberland Way GL4 . . . . .119 E6
imberley Ave GL4 . . . . . . .20 C5
imberley Cl Bristol BS16 . . .20 F7
Gloucester GL2 . . . . .127 D4
Lydney GL15 . . . . .92 B3
imberley Cres BS16 . . . . . .20 C5
imberley Dr GL15 . . . . .92 B3
imberley Rd
Bristol,Fishponds BS16 . . . . .20 C5
Bristol,Kingswood BS15 . . . .20 C5
imberley Wlk GL52 . . . . . .134 C2
imbrose Cl GL1 . . . . .196 A2
imbrose Way GL1 . . . . . . .196 A2
immins Rd GL10 . . . . .98 A8
imber Ho GL52 . . . . .134 B4
inema Ho BS7 . . . . .9 C4
ing Alfred Way GL52 . . . . .130 F8
ing Alfreds Rd NP16 . . . . . .61 A8
ing Arthur Cl GL53 . . . . . .130 F7
ing Dick's La 7 BS5 . . . . . .9 F8
ing Edmund Com Sch
BS37 . . . . .43 E1
ing Edward 7 BS14 . . . . . .80 A6
ing Edward's Ave GL1 . . . .118 E7
ing George Cl GL53 . . . . . .130 F6
ing George V Pl 6
BS1 . . . . .195 A2
ing George's Rd BS13 . . . . .1 F5
ing Georges Field
GL54 . . . . .176 F4
ing Henry Cl GL53 . . . . . . .130 F6
ing John's Cotts GL20 . . . .192 C5
ing John's Rd BS15 . . . . . . .20 B2
ing Johns Ct GL20 . . . . . . .192 C5
ing La BS37 . . . . .45 A7
ing Rd BS4 . . . . .9 C1
ing Road Ave BS11 . . . . . . .26 B2
ing Sq BS2 . . . . .195 A4
ing Square Ave BS2 . . . . . .195 A4
ing St Avonmouth BS11 . . . .26 A1
Bristol BS1 . . . . .195 A2
Bristol,Lower Easton BS5 . . .19 C1
Bristol,St George BS15 . . . . .10 B8
Cheltenham GL50 . . . . .193 B4
Cirencester GL7 . . . . .190 D3
Minchinhampton GL6 . . . . .148 A3
Stroud GL5 . . . . .99 C7
King Street Par 4 GL5 . . . . .99 C7

King William Ave BS1 . . . . .195 A2
King William Dr GL53 . . . . .130 F6
King William St BS3 . . . . . . .8 B4
King's Ave BS6,BS7 . . . . . . .18 C4
King's Barton St GL1 . . . . .196 C2
King's Dr BS7 . . . . .18 C4
King's Head La BS13 . . . . . . .1 F7
King's Mill La GL6 . . . . . . .103 E7
King's Parade Ave 1
BS8 . . . . .18 B1
King's Parade Mews BS8 . .18 A1
King's Rd
Bristol,Kensington Park BS4 . .9 C3
Bristol,Victoria Park BS8 . . .194 A3
Cheltenham GL52 . . . . .133 F1
Stonehouse GL10 . . . . .101 F1
Stroud GL5 . . . . .99 B6
King's Sch The GL1 . . . . . .196 B3
King's Sq GL1 . . . . .196 B3
King's Stanley CE Jun Sch
GL10 . . . . .98 A4
King's Stanley Inf Sch
GL10 . . . . .98 A3
Kingcomb La GL55 . . . . . . .188 F2
Kingfisher Bsns Pk GL5 . . . .99 E2
Kingfisher Cl Bristol BS32 . .40 E2
Thornbury BS35 . . . . .64 D2
Kingfisher Ct GL51 . . . . . .132 E5
Kingfisher Dr Bristol BS16 . .19 E6
Cheltenham GL51 . . . . .132 E5
Kingfisher Pl GL7 . . . . .143 A8
Kingfisher Rd BS37 . . . . . . .33 A8
Kingfisher Rise 6 GL2 . . . .117 D1
Kingham Sta OX7 . . . . .177 F7
Kingley Rd GL5 . . . . .98 E7
Kingrove Cres BS37 . . . . . . .33 C8
Kingrove La BS37 . . . . .5 C2
Kings Ave Bristol BS15 . . . . .10 B4
Highworth SN6 . . . . .145 D3
Kings Chase BS15 . . . . .10 D8
Kings Court Prim Sch
BS37 . . . . .32 E8
Kings Ct Bristol BS13 . . . . . . .1 F4
Bristol,Canon's Marsh
BS1 . . . . .195 A2
Bristol,Kingsdown BS34 . . .195 B4
Bristol,Little Stoke BS34 . . . .29 C6
Kings Dr
Bristol,Hanham BS15 . . . . . .10 B4
Bristol,Stoke Gifford BS34 . .30 A4
Dursley GL11 . . . . .88 A2
Kings Elm GL2 . . . . .173 B3
Kings Gate GL22 . . . . .192 F4
Kings Head La GL54 . . . . . .166 F2
Kings Ho 8 GL50 . . . . .193 A4
Kings Mdw
Bourton-on-the-W GL54 . . .168 F8
Crudwell SN16 . . . . .141 B3
Kings Mead GL14 . . . . .156 F6
Kings Meade GL16 . . . . . . .155 A5
Kings Park Ave BS2 . . . . . . .9 C6
Kings Sq BS30 . . . . .5 D8
Kings Walk Sh Ctr GL1 . . . .196 B2
Kings Well La GL54 . . . . . .176 C1
Kings Weston Ave BS11 . . . .16 E8
Kings Weston La
Avonmouth BS11 . . . . .26 E3
Bristol BS11 . . . . .17 A8
Kings Weston Rd BS11,
BS10 . . . . .27 C1
Kings Wlk Bristol BS13 . . . . . .1 E7
Gloucester GL1 . . . . .196 B3
Kingsbridge Mews
GL51 . . . . .132 D3
Kingsclere Dr GL52 . . . . . .137 E3
Kingscote BS37 . . . . .32 D6
Kingscote Ave GL51 . . . . . .129 D7
Kingscote Cl
Cheltenham GL51 . . . . .129 D7
Churchdown GL3 . . . . .128 D4
Kingscote Dr GL4 . . . . .119 E5
Kingscote Gr GL51 . . . . . . .129 D7
Kingscote Pk BS5 . . . . .10 B6
Kingscote Rd GL51 . . . . . . .129 D7
Kingscote Rd W GL51 . . . . .129 D7
Kingscourt Cl BS14 . . . . .3 A4
Kingscourt La GL5 . . . . .99 A4
Kingscroft Rd GL3 . . . . .120 A7
Kingsdale Ct WR12 . . . . . . .185 C8
Kingsditch La GL51 . . . . . .133 A5
Kingsditch Ret Pk GL51 . . .133 A5
Kingsdown GL11 . . . . .88 A3
Kingsdown Par BS6 . . . . . .195 A4
Kingsfield La
Bristol,Longwell Green
BS15 . . . . .10 E5
Bristol,Mount Hill BS30 . . . .10 E4
Kingsfield Rdbt BS15 . . . . . .10 E5
Kingsfield Sch BS15 . . . . . .11 A8
Kingsgate Ct BS37 . . . . .32 E8
Kingshill GL7 . . . . .190 F4
Kingshill Ho 9 BS1 . . . . .9 B1
Kingshill La
Cirencester GL7 . . . . .150 F4
Dursley GL11 . . . . .88 A2
Kingshill Pk GL11 . . . . .88 A3
Kingshill Rd Bristol BS4 . . . . .9 A2
Dursley GL11 . . . . .88 A2
Kingsholm CE Prim Sch
GL1 . . . . .196 C4
Kingsholm Cl GL1 . . . . . . .126 E4
Kingsholm Rd
Bristol BS10 . . . . .18 D8
Gloucester GL1 . . . . .196 B4
Kingsholm Sq GL1 . . . . . . .196 B4
Kingsholme Rd BS15 . . . . . .20 D1
Kingsland Cl 1 BS2 . . . . .9 A6
Kingsland Rd BS2 . . . . .9 A6

Kingsland Road Bridge 3
BS2 .9 A6
Kingsland Trad Est BS2 . . . . .9 A7
Kingsleigh Cl BS15 . . . . .10 F7
Kingsleigh Gdns BS15 . . . . .10 F7
Kingsleigh Pk BS15 . . . . . . .10 F7
Kingsley Gdns GL51 . . . . . .129 E8
Kingsley Ho Bristol BS2 . . .195 C2
Bristol,Westbury on Trym
BS9 . . . . .18 A8
Kingsley Pl 1 BS3 . . . . .8 C4
Kingsley Rd
Bristol,Lower Easton BS5 . . .19 C1
Bristol,Montpelier BS6 . . . . .18 D2
Gloucester GL1 . . . . .119 A5
Kingsmark La/Lon Cyn Farch
NP16 . . . . .72 D1
Kingsmarsh Ho 3 BS5 . . . . .9 B2
Kingsmead
Cirencester GL7 . . . . .190 E2
Gloucester GL4 . . . . .119 E8
Lechlade on T GL7 . . . . . . .153 E3
Painswick GL6 . . . . .103 E8
Kingsmead Ave GL51 . . . . .132 F4
Kingsmead Cl GL51 . . . . . .132 F4
Kingsmead Ind Est
GL51 . . . . .133 A4
Kingsmead Rd Bristol BS5 . .20 A1
Cheltenham GL51 . . . . .132 F4
Kingsmead Wlk BS5 . . . . . .20 A1
Kingsmill BS9 . . . . .17 D5
Kingston Ave Bristol BS4 . . . .5 C3
Kingston Cl BS16 . . . . .21 A7
Kingston Dr Bristol BS16 . . .21 A7
Cheltenham GL51 . . . . .132 C1
Kingston Rd Bristol BS3 . . . . .8 C4
Northway GL20 . . . . .182 C4
Slimbridge GL2 . . . . .95 C4
Kingstone Ave GL3 . . . . . . .127 A6
Kingstree St BS4 . . . . .9 A4
Kingsville Rd GL15 . . . . . . .155 D8
Kingsway
Bristol,Little Stoke BS34 . . . .29 C6
Bristol,St George BS5 . . . . . .10 B8
Coleford GL16 . . . . .155 B6
Dursley GL11 . . . . .88 A3
Preston GL7 . . . . .150 F3
Kingsway Ave BS15 . . . . . . .10 B8
Kingsway Cres GL6 . . . . . . .102 F2
Kingsway La GL17 . . . . . . .163 F4
Kingsway Pk BS30 . . . . .11 B6
Kingsway Sh Prec BS5 . . . . .10 B7
Kingswear Rd BS3 . . . . .8 D2
Kingsweston Down Nature
Res* BS9,BS11 . . . . .27 A3
Kingswood Sch BS11 . . . . . .17 A8
Kingswood Abbey
Gatehouse* GL12 . . . . .67 F5
Kingswood Cl GL52 . . . . . .137 F3
Kingswood Foundation Est
BS15 . . . . .10 C7
Kingswood Heritage Mus*
BS30 . . . . .11 B6
Kingswood Hts GL52 . . . . . .20 D1
Kingswood Prim Sch
GL12 . . . . .67 F5
Kingswood Rd GL12 . . . . . . .55 D8
Kingswood Trad Est
GL15 . . . . .53 D1
Kington La BS35 . . . . .63 E1
Kington Rd BS35 . . . . .63 E1
Kinmoor GL4 . . . . .119 D3
Kinsale Rd BS14 . . . . .3 C2
Kinsale Wlk BS4 . . . . .8 E1
Kinsham La GL20 . . . . .182 E7
Kinvara Rd BS4 . . . . .2 E8
Kipling Cl GL2 . . . . .118 C4
Kipling Rd Bristol BS7 . . . . .29 B1
Cheltenham GL52 . . . . .132 E1
Dursley GL11 . . . . .80 C7
Kirby Rd GL15 . . . . .169 E6
Kirkby Rd BS11 . . . . .16 C7
Kirkstone Gdns BS10 . . . . . .28 C2
Kirkstone Ho BS34 . . . . .29 A8
Kirtlington Rd BS5 . . . . .19 B3
Kitchener Ave GL1 . . . . . . .118 E5
Kite Hay Cl BS16 . . . . .19 B6
Kitefield 15 SN6 . . . . .143 E4
Kites Cl BS32 . . . . .40 C2
Kitesnest La GL5 . . . . .99 A4
Klondyke Ave GL15 . . . . . . .92 B3
Knap La GL6 . . . . .120 F7
Knap Cl HR9 . . . . .163 A6
Knapp Cotts GL18 . . . . . . .179 B3
Knapp La
Brimscombe GL5 . . . . .148 A4
Cheltenham GL50 . . . . .193 A4
Coaley GL11 . . . . .87 F6
Cromhall GL12 . . . . .66 B3
Dursley GL11 . . . . .87 F6
Stroud GL6 . . . . .104 B2
Woolaston GL15 . . . . .147 D3
Knapp Rd
Cheltenham GL50 . . . . .193 A4
Thornbury BS35 . . . . .64 D1
Wotton-u-E GL12 . . . . .68 C7
Knapp The Dursley GL11 . . .88 B1
Yate BS37 . . . . .43 F5
Knapps Cres GL52 . . . . . . .138 B4
Knapps La BS5 . . . . .19 E2
Kneller Cl BS11 . . . . .16 E7
Knighton Rd BS10 . . . . .28 E1
Knights Cl BS9 . . . . .17 F5
Knights Cres GL18 . . . . . . .170 F4
Knights Way
Newent GL18 . . . . .170 F4
Tewkesbury GL20 . . . . .192 E4

Knightsbridge Bsns Ctr
GL51 . . . . .173 F5
Knightsbridge Cres
GL53 . . . . .130 F7
Knightsbridge Gn GL51 . . .173 F5
Knightsbridge Pk BS13 . . . . .2 E4
Knightshill HR9 . . . . .164 D8
Knightstone Cl BS5 . . . . . . .19 D2
Knightstone Gdns BS4 . . . . . .9 B2
Knightstone Ho 1 BS5 . . . .195 A4
Knightstone Lodge BS6 . . . .18 D1
Knightstone Mount BS5 . . . .10 A6
Knightstone Rise 5 BS5 . . . . .9 F8
Knightstone Sq BS14 . . . . . . .3 C5
Knightstone Wlk BS4 . . . . .194 C4
Knightwood Rd BS34 . . . . . .29 F5
Knockdown Rd SN16 . . . . . .58 C1
Knockley Patch GL15 . . . . .155 D1
Knole Cl BS32 . . . . .39 F4
Knole La BS10 . . . . .28 B3
Knole Pk BS32 . . . . .39 F3
Knoll Ct BS9 . . . . .17 D3
Knoll Hill BS9 . . . . .17 D3
Knoll The Kempsford GL7 . .144 E8
Stroud GL5 . . . . .99 D7
Uley GL11 . . . . .89 C1
Knollys End GL2 . . . . .109 F8
Knovill Cl BS11 . . . . .27 B2
Knowland's SN6 . . . . .145 D4
Knowle Park Jun & Inf Sch
BS4 .9 A1
Knowle Rd BS2 . . . . .8 F3
Knowles Rd GL1 . . . . .118 F7
Knowsley Rd BS16 . . . . .19 E3
Knox Rd GL15 . . . . .147 E8
Kyberworster Rd GL54 . . . .174 A8
Kyght Cl BS15 . . . . .11 A8
Kylross Ave BS14 . . . . .3 B5
Kymin Lea NP25 . . . . .154 A7
Kymin Rd NP25 . . . . .154 B7
Kynges Mill Cl BS16 . . . . . . .20 A2
Kyngstone 10 BS5 . . . . .19 E3

L

La Maison BS5 . . . . .20 A2
Labbott The BS31 . . . . .4 E5
Laburnum Cres GL6 . . . . . .102 F2
Laburnum Ct GL11 . . . . . . .132 C2
Laburnum Gdns GL2 . . . . .117 F2
Laburnum Gr BS16 . . . . .20 A4
Laburnum Mews GL10 . . . . .97 E7
Laburnum Rd Bristol BS15 . .10 C5
Gloucester GL1 . . . . .118 D5
Laburnum Way NP16 . . . . . .60 E9
Laburnum Wlk
Keynsham BS31 . . . . .4 C3
Stonehouse GL10 . . . . .97 E7
Lacca Cl GL2 . . . . .117 B4
Lacey Rd BS14 . . . . .3 F6
Lacock Dr BS30 . . . . .11 D8
Lacy Cl GL2 . . . . .127 C6
Ladbarrow Cotts GL54 . . . .161 A4
Ladd Cl BS15 . . . . .11 A8
Ladden Ct BS35 . . . . .51 C8
Ladder The GL6 . . . . .91 C4
Ladies Mile BS8 . . . . .17 F1
Ladman Gr BS14 . . . . .3 E5
Ladman Rd BS14 . . . . .3 E5
Lady Chapel Rd GL4 . . . . . .119 E6
Lady Downe Cl GL4 . . . . . .119 E3
Lady La SN25 . . . . .144 F5
Lady Margaret Ct NP16 . . . .60 F4
Lady Mead SN6 . . . . .143 E4
Ladybellegate St GL1 . . . . .196 A2
Ladygrove Bsns Pk
GL7 . . . . .164 E5
Ladysmith Rd Bristol BS6 . .18 B4
Cheltenham GL52 . . . . .134 B2
Gloucester GL1 . . . . .118 E6
Ladywell Cl GL2 . . . . .118 B7
Laggar La GL5 . . . . .99 A4
Laines Est The GL54 . . . . . .158 F6
Laira Ct BS3 . . . . .8 A3
Lake Cl GL2 . . . . .124 B3
Lake La Churcham GL2 . . . .124 B3
Frampton on Severn GL2 . . .157 F3
Lake Louise SN6 . . . . .143 E6
Lake Rd BS10 . . . . .28 D8
Lake Side BS8 . . . . .171 A5
Lake St Cheltenham GL52 . .134 B5
Quedgeley GL2 . . . . .116 D4
Lake View BS16 . . . . .19 F3
Lake View Rd BS5 . . . . .9 F6
Lakefield CE Prim Sch
GL2 . . . . .100 A6
Lakemead Gdns GL51 . . . . . .1 F4
Lakemead Gr BS13 . . . . .1 F6
Lakers Rd GL16 . . . . .155 A7
Lakeside Bristol BS16 . . . . .155 B7
Lakeside Cl GL15 . . . . .92 D2
Lakeside Dr GL15 . . . . .92 C2
Lakeside Prim Sch
GL51 . . . . .129 E7
Lakewood Cres BS10 . . . . . .18 B8
Lakewood Rd BS10 . . . . .18 B8
Lamb Hill BS5 . . . . .10 A6
Lamb La GL14 . . . . .191 D4
Lamb St BS2 . . . . .195 C3
Lambert Ave GL51 . . . . . . .129 D1
Lambert Cl GL51 . . . . .129 D1
Lambert Dr GL51 . . . . .129 D1
Lambert Gdns GL51 . . . . . .129 D1

Lambert Pl BS4 . . . . .2 D6
Lambert Terr GL51 . . . . . . .129 D2
Lamberts Field GL54 . . . . . .169 A7
Lambley Rd BS5 . . . . .9 E8
Lambourn Cl Bristol BS3 . . . .8 D3
Gloucester GL2 . . . . .127 E3
Lambourn Rd BS31 . . . . .5 A4
Lambourne Ave GL19 . . . . .145 D6
Lamborne Cl 10 HR8 . . . . .178 F8
Lambrook Rd BS16 . . . . .20 A4
Lambs Barn Pitch GL18 . . .171 A5
Lambs Cross HR9 . . . . .170 B4
Lambsdowne GL11 . . . . .87 F3
Lambsquay Rd GL16 . . . . . .155 A3
Lamington Cl BS13 . . . . .1 F6
Lamord Gate BS34 . . . . .29 E5
Lampen Ave GL11 . . . . .89 B1
Lampeter Rd BS9 . . . . .18 A7
Lampreys The GL4 . . . . . . .119 B6
Lampton Ave BS13 . . . . .2 E3
Lampton Gr BS13 . . . . .2 E3
Lampton Rd BS41 . . . . .7 A1
Lanaway Rd BS16 . . . . .20 B6
Lancashire Rd BS7 . . . . .18 E3
Lancaster Cl BS34 . . . . .29 D4
Lancaster Ct
2 Cheltenham GL50 . . . . .130 B8
Lydney GL15 . . . . .92 B5
Lancaster Dr Lydney GL15 . .92 B5
Upper Rissington GL54 . . . .169 D6
Lancaster Rd Bristol BS2 . . .18 F2
Kempsford GL7 . . . . .144 E7
Tewkesbury GL20 . . . . .192 D2
Yate BS37 . . . . .43 E3
Lancaster St 10 BS5 . . . . . . .9 C7
Lancaster Terr GL11 . . . . . .171 A5
Lancaut La NP16 . . . . .72 F6
Lancelot Cl GL2 . . . . .95 D4
Lancelot Rd BS16 . . . . .19 C5
Land The BS36 . . . . .31 C7
Landgate Yd 2 GL54 . . . . .176 F4
Landmark Ct BS1 . . . . .194 C1
Landor Gdns 20 GL52 . . . .133 F2
Landseer Ave BS7 . . . . .19 B7
Lane End Fairford GL7 . . . .152 F2
Great Rissington GL54 . . . .169 C4
Lane The
Broadway WR12 . . . . .184 F7
Chaddleton BS36 . . . . .177 E8
Easter Compton BS35 . . . . .38 F2
Randwick GL6 . . . . .102 D2
Lanercost Rd BS10 . . . . .28 C2
Lanes Ct GL20 . . . . .192 C3
Lanes Dairy BS34 . . . . .29 A3
Lanes End BS4 . . . . .9 C1
Lanes The
Cheltenham GL53 . . . . .130 B4
Gorsley HR9 . . . . .170 D4
Lanesborough Rise BS14 . . . .3 D7
Lanescourt Cl GL20 . . . . . .192 D3
Langdale Ct BS34 . . . . .29 A8
Langdale Gdns GL2 . . . . . .127 C5
Langdale Rd Bristol BS16 . . .20 F5
Langdon Rd GL53 . . . . .130 D6
Langdown BS14 . . . . .3 E5
Langet GL7 . . . . .142 F7
Langetts Rd 4 GL16 . . . . . .155 A5
Langfield Cl BS10 . . . . .27 E3
Langford Cl BS13 . . . . .1 F8
Langford Way BS15 . . . . . . .10 F7
Langham Ho NP16 . . . . .60 F5
Langham Rd BS4 . . . . .9 B2
Langhill Ave BS4 . . . . .2 D7
Langley Cl GL54 . . . . .139 F5
Langley Cres BS3 . . . . .7 E1
Langley Mow BS16 . . . . .21 B7
Langley Rd
Gloucester GL4 . . . . .119 B5
Winchcombe GL54 . . . . . . .139 D5
Langsdown Ho 7 BS2 . . . . .18 F1
Langston Priory Workshops
OX7 . . . . .177 F1
Langthorn Cl BS36 . . . . .31 C7
Langtoft Rd GL5 . . . . .99 E2
Langton Cl GL4 . . . . .119 E8
Langton Court Rd BS4 . . . . . .9 F5
Langton Ct 18 BS16 . . . . . . .19 E3
Langton Grove Rd GL52 . . .131 A7
Langton Ho 10 BS2 . . . . . . .195 C3
Langton Pk BS3 . . . . .8 C4
Langton Pl GL53 . . . . .131 A7
Langton Rd BS4 . . . . .9 D5
Langton Way BS4 . . . . .9 F6
Lanham Gdns GL2 . . . . . . .109 F7
Lannett Rd GL51 . . . . .118 E6
Lansdown Stroud GL5 . . . . . .99 C7
Yate BS37 . . . . .32 E8
Lansdown Castle Dr
GL51 . . . . .129 F8
Lansdown Cl Bristol BS15 . . .20 D2
Cheltenham GL51 . . . . .130 A8
Lansdown Cotts GL54 . . . . .168 B4
Lansdown Cres GL54 . . . . .193 A2
Lansdown Ct
GL51 . . . . .193 A2
Lansdown Ind Est GL51 . . .133 A1
Lansdown Lodge Dr
GL51 . . . . .130 A8
Lansdown Par GL50 . . . . . .130 B8
Lansdown Pl Bristol BS8 . . .194 A3

Landsown Pl continued
Cheltenham GL50 ....193 A2
Landsown Place La
GL50 ....193 A2
Landsown Rd
Bristol,Kingswood BS15 ....20 D2
Bristol,Redland BS6 ....18 C1
6 Bristol,Upper Easton BS5 ..9 B8
Bristol,Victoria Park BS8 ..194 A3
Cheltenham GL51 ....130 A8
Gloucester GL1 ....127 A3
Pucklechurch BS16 ....22 C6
Saltford BS31 ....5 E3
Landsown Terr
Bristol BS6 ....18 D5
Cheltenham GL50 ....193 A2
Landsown Terrace La
GL50 ....193 A2
Landsown View BS15 ....10 F8
Landsown Wlk
11 Bream GL15 ....147 D8
Cheltenham GL50 ....193 A2
Landsowne BS16 ....30 C1
Landsowne Ct **2** BS5 .....9 B8
Lantern Cl Berkeley GL13 ...85 E3
Cinderford GL14 ....191 C4
Lapdown La GL9 ....34 D1
Laphams Ct **11** BS30 .....10 F4
Lapwing Cl Bristol BS32 ...40 D2
Northway GL20 ....182 B5
Lapwing Ct **10** GL6 .....148 C6
Lapwing Gdns BS16 ....19 F6
Larch Cl GL53 ....131 C5
Coerne SN14 ....15 F6
Larch Rise GL53 ....130 B4
Larch Way BS34 ....28 E7
Larches The GL4 ....119 E6
Larchmere Gr **2** GL51 ..129 E5
Larchwood Dr GL4 ....118 E3
Lark Rise Chalford GL6 ...148 C6
Coleford GL16 ....155 A6
Yate BS37 ....43 F4
Lark's La BS37 ....42 B7
Larkfield BS36 ....31 D7
Larkfield Ave NP16 ....60 E7
Larkfield Gr NP16 ....60 D7
Larkfield Ho NP16 ....60 D7
Larkfield Inf Sch GL3 ....127 E6
Larkfield Pk NP16 ....60 D7
Larkham Cl GL4 ....119 B3
Larkham Pl GL4 ....119 B3
Larkhall Cl NP16 ....60 D7
Larkrise GL11 ....87 F5
Larks Field BS16 ....19 E5
Larksfield Rd
Harrow Mill GL17 ....164 B4
Stroud GL5 ....99 A4
Larksleaze Rd BS30 ....10 F2
Larkspear Cl GL11 ....118 E5
Larkspur Cl BS35 ....64 D1
Larput Pl GL50 ....133 D3
Lasbury Gr BS13 ....2 C5
Lasne Cres GL2 ....120 F4
Lassington Gr GL2 ....125 C5
Lassington La GL2 ....125 D6
Lassington Wood (Nature
Reserve)* GL2 ....125 E6
Latchen Cl GL2 ....164 F5
Latchen Orch GL17 ......164 F5
Latchmoor Ho BS13 ....2 A8
Latimer Cl Bristol BS4 ....9 E4
Minchinhampton GL6 ....148 A3
Latimer Ct GL54 ....175 B3
Latimer Rd
Cinderford GL14 ....191 E5
Stonehouse GL10 ....101 D1
Latteridge La
Latteridge BS37 ....42 A7
Tytherington BS35 ....51 F1
Latteridge Rd BS37 ....42 D4
Latton Rd BS7 ....18 F8
Latymer Croft GL3 ......128 B5
Launceston Ave BS15 ....11 B5
Launceston Rd BS15 ......20 B1
Laundry Cotts GL56 .....177 E5
Laundry Rd GL16 ....154 C4
Laura Cl GL2 ....127 B4
Laurel Ave GL20 ....192 E2
Laurel Cotts GL20 ....192 E2
Laurel Dr
Cheltenham GL52 ....134 B4
Coerne SN14 ....15 F6
Laurel Farm Cl GL4 .....118 F4
Laurel Gate GL4 ....119 F5
Laurel Pk NP16 ....72 B6
Laurel St BS15 ....10 D8
Laureldene GL16 ....155 B3
Laurels The
Bristol,Catbrain BS10 .....28 A6
Bristol,Mangotsfield BS16 ..21 A6
Castle Eaton SN6 ....144 D6
Gloucester GL1 ....118 F7
South Cerney GL7 ....142 F8
Laurence Cl GL12 ....129 D2
Laurie Cres BS9 ....18 D6
Laurie Lee Ct **3** BS30 ..11 A6
Lauriston Pk GL50 ......130 C5
Lavender Cl BS31 ....64 D1
Lavender Ct Bristol BS5 ...19 F1
Cirencester GL7 ....190 C3
Lavender La GL7 ....190 C3
Lavender Mews GL52 ....137 E3
Lavender Rd GL51 ......129 F5

Lavender View GL4 ......119 F4
Lavender Way BS32 ....29 F7
Lavenham Rd BS37 ....43 B2
Lavers Cl BS15 ....10 E6
Lavington Dr GL2 ....127 E4
Lavington Rd BS5 ....10 B6
Lawford Ave BS34 ....29 C6
Lawford St BS2 ....195 C3
Lawfords Gate BS2 .....195 C3
Lawfords Gate Ho **16**
BS2 ....195 C3
Lawn Ave BS16 ....20 B5
Lawn Cres GL51 ....129 E2
Lawn Rd
Ashleworth GL19 ....172 D4
Bristol BS16 ....20 B5
Lawns Pk GL5 ....98 F2
Lawns Rd BS37 ....43 F2
Lawns The Bristol BS11 ...16 E7
Gloucester GL4 ....119 D3
Gotherington GL52 ......138 B7
Stonehouse GL10 ....97 E8
Lawnside GL6 ....91 A4
Lawnside Rd **6** HR8 ....178 E8
Lawnwood Ind Units **14**
BS5 ....9 B8
Lawnwood Rd **15** BS5 ....9 B8
Lawrence Ave BS5 ....19 B1
Lawrence Cl Bristol BS15 ..21 A2
Charlton Kings GL52 .....131 B6
Lawrence Dr BS37 ....43 B2
Lawrence Gr Bristol BS9 ...18 B5
Dursley GL11 ....88 A2
Lawrence Hill BS5 ....9 C8
Lawrence Hill Ind Pk BS5 ..9 B8
Lawrence Hill Rd BS5 .....9 A7
Lawrence Hill Sta BS5 .....9 B7
Lawrence Rd
Avening GL8 ....148 B1
Cirencester GL7 ....190 B3
Lawrence Way N GL1 ....126 E4
Lawrence Weston Rd
Avonmouth BS11 ....26 F4
Bristol BS11 ....27 A2
Lawrence's Mdw GL52 ...138 A8
Lawrenceman Way N GL1 ..12 D4
Lawson Cl BS31 ....5 C2
Lawson Glade GL53 ......131 A4
Laxey Rd BS7 ....18 F7
Laxton Cl BS35 ....50 A3
Laxton Dr GL12 ....67 F4
Laxton Rd
Cheltenham GL51 ....132 E2
Gloucester GL4 ....120 A6
Laymore Rd GL14 ....191 B5
Laynes Rd GL3 ....120 A7
Lays Dr BS31 ....4 C5
Lays Farm Bsns Ctr BS31 ..4 C4
Lays Farm Trad Est BS31 ..4 C4
Lazenby Ct GL51 ....132 C1
Lea CE Prim Sch HR9 ....164 C8
Lea Cres GL2 ....127 C5
Lea Croft BS13 ....2 A4
Lea Rd GL3 ....120 F5
Leacey Ct GL3 ....120 A6
Leacey Mews GL3 ....128 A7
Leading Edge The BS8 ...194 B2
Leadon Cl GL3 ....120 F5
Leadon Pl **9** HR8 ......178 E7
Leadon Way HR8 ....178 E7
Leafield Rd GL7 ....152 E4
Leaholes Cl GL7 ....190 D4
Leaholme Gdns BS14 .....3 A3
Leap Vale BS16 ....21 A8
Leap Valley Cres BS16 ....21 A8
Leaping Stocks Rd HR9 ..162 D3
Lear Cl BS30 ....11 B5
Lears Dr GL52 ....138 A3
Leaze CE/Lon Leadwork Reserve*
NP25 ....154 A8
Leaside Cl GL11 ....88 A4
Leasow La GL54 ....169 B5
Leasows The
Broadwell GL56 ....177 A6
Chipping Campden GL55 ..188 F1
Mickleton GL55 ....189 B6
Leaze Cl GL13 ....85 E3
Leaze Ct GL15 ....102 F2
Leaze The
2 Ashton Keynes SN6 ..142 F5
South Cerney GL7 ......142 F7
Yate BS37 ....43 D2
Lechlade Rd
Highworth SN6 ....145 D4
Lechlade GL7 ....153 F1
Southrop GL7 ....153 C6
Upper Inglesham SN6 ...145 D7
Lechmere Rd **1** GL51 ...132 E3
Leckhampton CE Prim Sch
GL53 ....130 D4
Leckhampton Farm Ct
GL51 ....130 A4
Leckhampton Gate
GL51 ....130 A4
Leckhampton Hill GL53 ..130 D2
Leckhampton La GL51,
GL53 ....130 A1
Leckhampton Pl GL53 ...130 D5
Leckhampton Rd GL53 ...130 D5
Leckhampton View
GL51 ....129 F2
Leda Ave BS14 ....3 A7
Ledbury Heritage Ctr*
HR8 ....178 F8
Ledbury Pk **9** HR8 ....178 F8
Ledbury Prim Sch HR8 ..178 E8

Ledbury Rd Bristol BS16 ...20 C4
Dymock GL18 ....178 E3
Eastnor HR8 ....179 B8
Ledbury Road Cres
GL19 ....172 A8
Leddington Ct HR8 ......178 D7
Ledmore Rd GL53 ....131 B6
Lee Cl Bristol BS34 ....28 F8
Cheltenham GL51 ....132 F3
Lee Rd GL20 ....182 C4
Lee Villa Cvn Pk HR9 ....164 D8
Leechpool Way BS37 .....43 E5
Leeming Way BS11 ....16 C8
Lees Ct BS15 ....20 E1
Lees Hall BS30 ....20 E2
Lees La BS30 ....11 D5
Lefroy Ct GL51 ....130 C6
Leicester Sq BS16 ....20 D3
Leicester St **6** BS3 .....8 D4
Leicester Wlk BS4 ....195 A2
Leigh CE Prim Sch SN6 ..143 B3
Leigh Court Bsns Ctr
BS8 ....17 A2
Leigh Ct BS9 ....17 D3
Leigh La Cold Ashton BA1 ..14 B3
Westerleigh BS37 ....32 B1
Leigh Rd BS8 ....194 B4
Leigh St BS3 ....8 A4
Leigh Woods Forest Walks*
BS8 ....17 A1
Leighterton Prim Sch
GL8 ....70 C3
Leighton Rd
Bristol,Southville BS3 .....8 B4
Bristol,Upper Knowle BS4 ..9 B2
Cheltenham GL52 ....133 F1
Leinster Ave BS4 ....2 D8
Leisure Rd BS15 ....10 E5
Lemon La BS2 ....195 C4
Lena Ave **8** BS5 ....19 C1
Lena St BS5 ....19 C1
Lennards The GL7 ....143 A8
Lennox Ho BS11 ....26 B1
Lenover Gdns BS13 ....2 B4
Lensbrook GL15 ....93 A8
Leonard La BS1 ....195 A3
Leonard Rd Bristol BS5 ....9 D7
Leonard Stanley CE Prim Sch
GL10 ....97 F4
Leonards Ave BS5 ....19 C1
Leopold Rd BS6 ....18 E2
Lesanne Ct GL1 ....196 B2
Lescren Way BS11 ....26 D1
Letch Hill Dr GL54 ......168 F7
Letch La GL2 ....33 D2
Leven Cl GL2 ....127 D4
Lever's Hill GL11 ....89 B7
Lewin St **9** BS5 ....9 D7
Lewington Rd BS16 ......20 C4
Lewins Mead BS1 ....195 A3
Lewis Ave GL2 ....126 F6
Lewis Cl
Bristol,Emerson's Green
BS16 ....21 C5
Bristol,North Common BS30 ..11 D5
Lewis Glade **2** GL16 ...155 B5
Lewis La GL7 ....190 D4
Lewis Rd Bristol BS13 .....2 A8
Cheltenham GL51 ....132 D2
Lewis St BS2 ....9 D7
Lewis Way NP16 ....60 E4
Lewisham Rd GL1 ......118 E5
Lewisham Terr GL13 .....85 C8
Lewiston Cl GL5 ....148 A5
Lewiston Cl GL54 ....148 A5
Lewton La BS36 ....30 E7
Lexington Cl GL20 ......192 E2
Lexington Sq GL52 ......133 E5
Ley La BS35 ....49 F3
Ley Mary Farm OX18 ....161 C8
Ley Orch WR12 ....188 B2
Ley Rd GL2 ....116 A5
Leyland Wlk BS13 ....1 F4
Leys The GL3 ....85 E4
Leysbourne GL55 ....189 A2
Leyson Rd GL51 ....129 C6
Leyton Villas BS6 ....18 B2
Libby's Dr GL5 ....99 D8
Libertus Ct GL51 ....133 A1
Libertus Rd GL51 ....133 A1
Liberty Gdns BS1 ....194 C1
Liberty Ind Pk BS3 ....8 A1
Library Pl **2** NP16 .....60 E8
Lichfield Dr GL51 ....130 E6
Lichfield Rd Bristol BS4 ....9 E8
Gloucester GL4 ....119 D8
Lidderdale Rd GL54 .....169 D6
Liddiation Rd GL53 .....130 E8
Liddington Rd
Cheltenham GL52 ....130 E8
Gloucester GL2 ....127 E3
Liddington Trad Est
GL53 ....130 D5
Lifford Gdns WR12 .....185 B8
Lightenbrook La GL2 .....95 C3
Lightfoot **2** GL18 ......171 A4
Lightpill Trad Est GL5 ....99 A6
Lightwood La GL6 ......102 E3
Lilac Cl Bristol BS10 .....130 C6
Cheltenham GL51 ....130 A5
Lilac Ct BS31 ....4 C4
Lilac Way Gloucester GL4 ..118 F3
Quedgeley GL2 ....117 F1
Lilley's Alley **8** GL20 ..192 C4
Lillian St **5** BS5 ....9 C8
Lilliesfield Ave GL3 .....119 F8

Lilliput Ave BS37 ....33 A8
Lilliput Ct BS37 ....33 B8
Lilly Hall La HR8 ....178 C7
Lilstock Ave BS7 ....18 F4
Lilton Wlk BS13 ....8 A1
Lilymead Ave BS4 ....9 A3
Limber Hill GL50 ....133 C5
Limbury Hostels GL19 ...172 A8
Lime Ave GL1 ....35 B8
Lime Cl Brentry BS10 ....28 B3
Cheltenham GL52 ....134 A5
Lime Croft BS37 ....43 F4
Lime Ct Innsworth GL3 ..127 F6
Keynsham BS31 ....4 C4
Lime Gr Alveston BS35 ....50 F4
Stroud GL5 ....99 F7
Lime Kiln La BS34 ....29 D3
Lime Kiln Gdns BS32 .....40 D2
Lime Kiln Rd BS1 ......194 B2
Lime Rd
Bristol,Hanham BS15 ....10 A5
Bristol,Southville BS3 .....8 B4
Tewkesbury GL20 ....192 E1
Lime Terr GL15 ....18 D3
Lime Tree Ave **3** WR12 ..185 C8
Lime Tree Cotts GL7 ....152 D7
Lime Tree Ct GL1 ......118 E5
Lime Tree Gr BS20 ......16 D3
Lime Trees Rd BS9 ......18 D6
Lime Way GL15 ....92 B4
Limekiln Gr GL2 ....125 B8
Limekiln La GL6 ....148 E8
Limekiln Rd BS37,GL12 ..53 C2
Limekilns Cl BS31 ....4 F5
Limerick Rd BS6 ....18 C2
Limes Cl GL7 ....190 C3
Limes Pl SN6 ....143 E6
Limes Rd GL7 ....141 F8
Limes The Badminton GL9 ..46 E2
Bristol BS16 ....20 D3
Gloucester,Brockworth GL4 ..127 C1
Gloucester,Kingsholm GL2 ..126 E5
South Cerney GL7 ......142 F7
Limetree Ave **9** NP25 ..154 A7
Linacre Cres GL7 ....190 B2
Lincoln Ave GL51 ....130 A5
Lincoln Cl Keynsham BS31 ..4 C4
Tewkesbury GL20 ....193 C6
Upper Rissington GL54 ..168 F7
Lincoln Ct BS16 ....19 D6
Lincoln Green La GL20 ..192 B2
Lincoln Rd BS16 ....19 B7
Lincombe Ave BS16 .....20 D6
Lincombe Rd BS16 ......20 C6
Linden Ave GL52 ....134 A5
Linden Cl
Bristol,Mayfield Park BS16 ..20 A2
Bristol,Warmley BS14 .....3 E6
Cheltenham GL52 ....134 A5
Chepstow/Cas-Gwent NP16 ..60 E5
Colerne SN14 ....15 F6
Winterbourne BS36 ....30 F6
Linden Dr BS32 ....29 E8
Linden Grange GL52 ....134 A5
Linden Ho **4** BS5 ....19 F8
Linden Lea GL7 ....143 F8
Linden Prim Sch GL1 ...118 D6
Linden Rd Bristol BS6 ....18 B4
Gloucester GL1 ....118 D6
Lindores St **3** BS3 ....8 E3
Lindrea St BS3 ....8 A3
Lindsay Rd BS7 ....19 A4
Line The HR9 ....170 A3
Linegar Wood Rd GL14 ..191 C1
Lines Way BS14 ....3 C3
Linfoot Rd GL3 ....140 B4
Lingfield Pk BS16 ....20 F2
Link Rd Bristol BS34 .....29 B3
Pillowell GL15 ....155 F1
Tewkesbury GL20 ....192 D4
Yate BS37 ....43 F1
Linkend Rd GL19 ....180 F2
Links The GL16 ....155 D5
Links View GL7 ....150 C7
Linley Rd BS16 ....144 E1
Linnell St BS5 ....18 F7
Linnet Cl BS34 ....118 A2
Linsley Way GL4 ....118 D1
Lintern Cres BS30 ....11 B6
Lintham Dr BS15 ....10 F6
Linton Pl GL51 ....129 C6
Linton Rd HR9 ....170 B4
Linton's Wlk BS14 ....3 A7
Linwell Cl GL50 ....133 B5
Lion Cl Bristol BS34 ......2 A8
Lion Cl GL2 ....117 F2
Lipson Rd GL51 ....132 E2
Lipson Villas GL51 .....132 E1
Lisburn Rd BS4 ....8 E1
Lisle Pl GL20 ....80 E4
Lismore Rd SN6 ....145 C4
Listers Pl GL14 ....191 C4
Litfield Pl BS8 ....194 B3
Litfield Rd BS8 ....194 B3
Lithgow Rd GL54 ......168 F8
Little Acorns GL52 ......137 E5
Little Acre GL12 ....68 B8
Little Ann St BS2,BS5 ...195 C4
Little Bayshill Terr
GL50 ....193 B3
Little Birch Croft BS14 ....3 A3
Little Bishop St BS2 ....195 B4
Little Bristol Cl GL12 ....67 B4
Little Bristol La GL12 ....67 B4
Little Caroline Pl **4** BS8 ..7 F5

Little Cleevemount
GL52 ....133 F1
Little Compton Jun & Inf Sch
GL56 ....177 F6
Little Dowles BS30 ......11 A4
Little Elmbridge GL2 ....127 E5
Little Field GL4 ....119 D2
Little Gn GL19 ....179 D2
Little Green La BS35 .....38 A1
Little George St BS2 ...195 C4
Little Gn GL19 ....179 D2
Little Green La BS35 .....38 A1
Little Hayes BS16 ....20 B6
Little Headley Cl BS13 ....2 B2
Little Herbert's Cl GL53 ..131 B5
Little Herbert's Rd GL53 ..131 B4
Little Holbury GL2 .....100 E8
Little Horcott La GL7 ...152 E8
Little King St BS1 ....195 A2
Little Lancarridge GL2 ..125 D4
Little Marcle Court Rd
HR8 ....178 A4
Little Marcle Rd HR8 ...178 E4
Little Mdw BS34 ....30 A6
Little Mead BS11 ....27 B8
Little Normans GL2 .....127 C5
Little Oaks GL18 ....179 B4
Little Orch GL52 ....137 E4
Little Paradise BS3 ....8 E4
Little Parr Cl BS16 ......19 C7
Little Paul St BS2 ......194 C4
Little Pheasants GL53 ...131 A8
Little Quillet Ct GL11 ....87 F3
Little Rd WR11 ....88 E8
Little Rose La SN16 .....144 C2
Little Stoke La BS34 .....29 D6
Little Stoke Prim Sch
BS34 ....29 D6
Little Stoke Rd BS9 .....17 F4
Little Trewen La HR9 ...162 C5
Little Witcombe Ct GL3 ..121 C2
Little Withey Mead BS9 ..17 F4
Little Wlk GL2 ....192 D4
Littlecote Cl GL52 ......137 E5
Littlecross Ho BS3 ....8 B4
Littledean BS37 ....39 D3
Littledean CE Prim Sch
GL14 ....156 E8
Littledean Hall* GL14 ...156 E8
Littledean Hill Rd GL14 ..191 E4
Littledown Rd GL53 ....130 D4
Littlefield GL2 ....117 E2
Littleton St BS34 ....29 F7
Littleton Drew La GL9 ....36 A6
Littleton La BS41 ....1 C1
Littlewood Gr BS14 ....3 A2
Littleworth GL55 ....188 F2
Livia Way GL13 ....92 B4
Livingstone Mews GL1 ....8 A2
Llanarth Villas **3** BS6 ..18 D2
Llandilo St **1** GL1 .....118 F7
Llandogo Prim Sch
NP25 ....146 B3
Llanganton Bsns Ctr
HR9 ....162 B2
Llangrove CE Prim Sch
HR9 ....161 D6
Llanthony Cotts GL20 ...136 B7
Llanthony Ind Est GL2 ..126 C2
Llanthony Rd GL2 ......126 C2
Llanthony Secunda Priory*
GL1 ....126 C2
Llanwrtthy Hill GL17 ....163 D8
Llewellyn Ct BS9 ....17 E8
Lloyd Baker Ct GL2 ....109 E2
Lloyd Cl GL51 ....132 A2
Lobb Ct **4** GL2 ....120 A4
Lobleys Dr GL4 ....120 A8
Lock Gdns BS13 ....1 F8
Lockeridge Rd GL13 ......5 A4
Lockemor Rd BS13 ....2 C4
Locking Hill **3** GL5 .....99 C2
Lockingwell Rd BS31 .....4 D4
Lockleaze Rd BS7 ....19 A6
Locombe Hill GL17 ....19 A6
Locombe Pl GL12 ....68 C6
Lodersfield GL7 ....152 D6
Lodge Causeway Trdr Ctr
BS16 ....19 F5
Lodge Cswy BS16 ....20 A5
Lodge Ct BS9 ....17 A7
Lodge Ct Bristol BS30 ....11 F2
Long Ashton BS41 ....1 F1
Lodge Gdns GL15 ......146 C2
Lodge Hill GL15 ....146 F3
Lodge Hill Rd GL16 .....106 A1
Lodge Park & Sherborne
Est* GL54 ....160 D2
Lodge Pl BS1 ....194 C2
Lodge Rd Bristol BS15 ...20 D6
Wick BS30 ....11 B2
Yate BS37 ....43 A2
Lodgemore Cl **4** GL5 ....99 C2
Lodgemore La GL5 ....99 A2
Lodgeside Ave BS15 .....20 D6
Lodgeside Gdns BS15 ....20 D6
Lodore Rd BS16 ....20 C4
Lodway BS20 ....16 C5
Lodway Cl BS20 ....16 D6
Lodway Gdns BS20 ......16 C5
Lodway Rd BS4 ....9 A1
Logan Rd BS7 ....18 E3
Logus Ct **14** BS30 ......11 F5
Loiterpin GL15 ....156 D2
Lombard St BS3 ....8 C4

Lomond Rd BS7 . . . . .28 F1
Lon Cyn Farch/Kingsmark La
NP16 .72 D1
Lon Ffawyoden Uchel/High
Beech La NP16 . . . . .60 D6
Lon Leasbrook/Leasbrook La
NP25 . . . . .154 A8
London La SN16 . . . . .142 E1
London Pl GL7 . . . . .190 D4
London Rd
Brimscombe GL5,GL6 . . . . . .148 B5
Bristol,St Pauls BS2 . . . . .18 F1
Bristol,Warmley BS30 . . . . . . .11 D7
Charlton Kings GL52,GL53 . . .131 C5
Cheltenham GL52 . . . . .130 F8
Fairford GL7 . . . . .152 F4
Gloucester GL1,GL2 . . . . .127 A2
Moreton-in-M GL56 . . . . .187 B3
Stroud GL5 . . . . .99 C6
10 Tetbury GL8 . . . . .140 C4
Thrupp GL5 . . . . .99 E3
Wick BS30 . . . . .12 L6
London Road Terr 6
GL56 . . . . .187 B3
London St Bristol BS15 . . . . . .10 D8
Fairford GL7 . . . . .152 E3
Londonderry Farm BS30 . . . . .5 A8
Lone La NP25 . . . . .154 C4
Long Acre Rd BS14 . . . . .3 A3
Long Acres 5 HR8 . . . . .178 E8
Long Acres Cl BS9 . . . . .17 D7
Long Ashton Rd BS41 . . . . . . .7 B2
Long Beach Rd BS30 . . . . .11 B3
Long Cl
Bristol,Fishponds BS16 . . . . . .20 C6
Bristol,Little Stoke BS32 . . . . .29 E6
Long Croft BS37 . . . . .43 D4
Long Cross BS11 . . . . .27 B2
Long Dr GL16 . . . . .155 B6
Long Eaton Dr BS14 . . . . .3 B7
Long Eights GL20 . . . . .182 C5
Long Field GL2 . . . . .125 D6
Long Fox Manor BS4 . . . . .10 A1
Long Furlong GL52 . . . . .137 F7
Long Furlong La GL8 . . . . . . .140 B3
Long Handstones BS30 . . . . . .11 A4
Long Lease SN14 . . . . .36 C1
Long Marston Rd CV37,
GL55 . . . . .189 A8
Long Mdw BS16 . . . . .19 D6
Long Mead BS37 . . . . .43 E5
Long Mynd Ave GL51 . . . . . . .129 E6
Long Rd BS16 . . . . .21 A5
Long Row Bristol BS1 . . . . . .195 B2
Castle Eaton SN6 . . . . .144 D6
Long St Dursley GL11 . . . . .38 B1
Tetbury GL8 . . . . .140 B4
Wotton-u-E GL12 . . . . .68 B7
Longaston Cl GL2 . . . . .95 D4
Longaston La GL2 . . . . .95 D5
Longborough CE Prim Sch
GL56 . . . . .176 D8
Longborough Dr GL4 . . . . . . .119 E4
Longcross GL12 . . . . .66 B1
Longden Rd BS16 . . . . .20 F6
Longdon St Mary's CE Prim
Sch GL20 . . . . .180 F7
Longfield GL12 . . . . .117 E2
Longfield Rd BS7 . . . . .18 E3
Longford BS37 . . . . .32 C8
Longford Ave BS10 . . . . .18 D8
Longford Ct GL50 . . . . .193 A1
Longford La GL2 . . . . .127 A5
Longford Mews GL2 . . . . .126 F6
Longhill Rd GL7 . . . . .149 E8
Longhope GL3 3 GL4 . . . . . . .119 E5
Longhope Rd GL19 . . . . .165 C6
Longland Ct GL2 . . . . .127 B4
Longland Gdns GL2 . . . . .127 B4
Longlands Cl GL2 . . . . .127 B4
Longlands Ho 18 BS5 . . . . .9 C7
Longlands Rd GL52 . . . . .138 B4
Longleat GL53 . . . . .131 A5
Longleat Ave GL4 . . . . .118 C1
Longleat Cl BS9 . . . . .18 C5
Longlength La GL6 . . . . .83 C8
Longlevens Inf Sch GL2 . . . . .127 D4
Longlevens Jun Sch
GL2 .127 C4
Longmead Ave BS7 . . . . .18 D5
Longmead Croft BS13 . . . . .1 F4
Longmead Rd BS16 . . . . .31 B1
Longmeadow Rd BS31 . . . . .4 C4
Longmoor Ct BS3 . . . . .8 A2
Longmoor Rd BS3 . . . . .8 A2
Longmore Ave GL54 . . . . .169 D6
Longney CE Prim Sch
GL2 .108 C5
Longney Pl BS34 . . . . .39 F1
Longney Rd GL4 . . . . .118 D3
Longreach Gr BS14 . . . . .3 D6
Longridge La GL19 . . . . .172 C3
Longs Dr BS37 . . . . .43 C2
Longs View GL12 . . . . .67 A5
Longsmith St GL1 . . . . .196 B3
Longtown Rd GL20 . . . . .192 E2
Longtree Cl GL8 . . . . .140 B5
Longville Cl GL4 . . . . .119 F5
Longway Ave
Bristol BS13,BS14 . . . . .2 F4
Charlton Kings GL52 . . . . .131 A4
Longwell Green Prim Sch
BS30 .10 F3
Longwell Ho BS30 . . . . .10 A2
Longwood GL4 . . . . .10 A2
Lonk The GL16 . . . . .155 A4
Lons Ct BS30 . . . . .11 C1
Lonsdale Bsns Ctr BS15 . . . . .20 C2

Lonsdale Cl SN26 . . . . .144 E1
Lonsdale Rd GL2 . . . . .127 C2
Loop Rd NP16 . . . . .61 B5
Lorain Wlk BS10 . . . . .27 F2
Lord Eldon Dr NP16 . . . . .60 F4
Lord's Hill GL16 . . . . .155 A5
Lord's Hill Cl 5 GL16 . . . . . . .155 A5
Lords Gate GL16 . . . . .155 A5
Lords Gn GL52 . . . . .138 C3
Loriners Cl GL2 . . . . .117 F2
Lorton Cl BS10 . . . . .28 B1
Lorton Rd BS10 . . . . .28 B1
Lotts The 6 SN6 . . . . .142 F5
Loughman Cl BS15 . . . . .108 F8
Louisa St BS2 . . . . .195 C2
Louise Ave BS16 . . . . .21 A5
Lovage Cl GL3 . . . . .127 F6
Love La
Chipping Sodbury BS37 . . . . . .33 A8
Cirencester GL7 . . . . .190 D2
Yate BS37 . . . . .44 A4
Love Lane Ind Est GL7 . . . . . .190 D2
Lovedays Mead GL5 . . . . .99 C8
Lovell Ave BS30 . . . . .11 D4
Lovell's Hill BS15 . . . . .10 B5
Lovells The BS20 . . . . .16 B4
Loveridge Ct BS36 . . . . .31 B7
Loveringe Cl BS10 . . . . .27 F4
Lovers Wlk HR9 . . . . .170 B4
Lovett Cl GL19 . . . . .172 A8
Lowbourne BS14 . . . . .2 F6
Lowdilow La GL51 . . . . .136 E1
Lower Ashley Rd
Bristol,Baptist Mills BS2,
BS5 . . . . .19 A1
18 Bristol,St Pauls BS2 . . . . .18 F1
Lower Berrycroft GL13 . . . . . .85 E3
Lower Castle St BS1 . . . . .195 B3
Lower Chapel La BS36 . . . . . .31 C7
Lower Chapel Rd BS15 . . . . . .10 C5
Lower Cheltenham Pl
BS6 . . . . .18 F1
Lower Church La BS2 . . . . . . .195 A3
Lower Church St NP16 . . . . . . .72 F1
Lower Churchfield Rd
GL5 . . . . .99 D6
Lower Clifton Hill BS8 . . . . . .194 B2
Lower Cock Rd BS15 . . . . .10 F7
Lower College St BS1 . . . . . . .194 C2
Lower Comm GL15 . . . . .147 D5
Lower Conham Vale
BS15 .10 A5
Lower Court Rd BS32 . . . . .40 A5
Lower Croft GL7 . . . . .152 E4
Lower Cross GL16 . . . . .154 F3
Lower Fallow Cl BS14 . . . . .2 F3
Lower Farm Cotts GL7 . . . . . .151 C3
Lower Gay St BS2 . . . . .195 A4
Lower Grove Rd BS16 . . . . . . .19 F4
Lower Guinea St BS1 . . . . . . .195 A1
Lower Hanham Rd BS15 . . . . .10 C6
Lower High St
Bristol BS11 . . . . .16 D7
Chipping Campden GL55 . . . . .189 A2
Lower House Cres BS34 . . . . . .29 B4
Lower Kitesnest La GL6 . . . . .103 A3
Lower Knole La BS10 . . . . .28 A3
Lower Lamb St BS1 . . . . .194 C2
Lower Lode La GL20 . . . . .192 A2
Lower Maudlin St BS1 . . . . . .195 A3
Lower Mdw GL2 . . . . .109 F7
Lower Mill St GL11 . . . . .133 B3
Lower Moor Rd BS37 . . . . .43 E4
Lower Newmarket Rd
GL6 . . . . .90 F4
Lower Park Row BS1 . . . . . . .195 A3
Lower Park St 2 GL54 . . . . . .170 F4
Lower Poole Rd GL12 . . . . .80 B8
Lower Quay St GL1 . . . . .196 A3
Lower Rd Berry Hill GL16 . . . .155 A7
Ledbury HR8 . . . . .178 E8
St Briavels GL15 . . . . .146 E7
Upper Soudley GL14 . . . . .156 C5
Yorkley GL15 . . . . .156 A2
Lower Redland Mews 2
BS6 . . . . .18 B2
Lower Redland Rd BS6 . . . . . .18 B2
Lower Road Trad Est
HR8 .178 E8
Lower Sidney St BS3 . . . . .8 A4
Lower Spillman's GL5 . . . . . . .99 A6
Lower St Blockley GL56 . . . . .186 C5
Dyrham SN14 . . . . .23 D4
Stroud GL5 . . . . .99 D6
Whitehill GL6 . . . . .102 F3
Lower Station Rd
6 Bristol,Ridgeway BS16 . . . .20 A4
Bristol,Staple Hill BS16 . . . . . .20 C4
Lower Stone Cl BS36 . . . . .31 C7
Lower Terr 7 GL56 . . . . .186 C5
Lower Thirlmere Rd
BS34 .29 A8
Lower Tockington Rd
BS32 .50 B1
Lower Tuffley La GL2 . . . . . . .118 B4
Lower Washwell La
GL6 .104 A8
Lower Wharf Ind Est GL5 . . . .99 B7
Lower Wyndcliff Nature
Trail* NP16 . . . . .72 D7
Lowesmoor La GL11 . . . . .79 D5
Loweswater Cl GL51 . . . . .129 F7
Loweswater Rd GL51 . . . . . . .129 F7
Lowfield Rd GL8 . . . . .140 B5
Lowlis Cl BS10 . . . . .27 F3
Lowther Rd BS10 . . . . .28 C2
Loxton Sq BS14 . . . . .3 A6

Lucas Cl BS4 . . . . .9 D1
Luccombe Hill BS6 . . . . .18 B2
Lucinia Mews GL51 . . . . .132 F3
Luckington Com Sch
SN14 .47 E5
Luckington Court Gdns*
SN14 .47 F5
Luckington Rd BS7 . . . . .18 E8
Luckley Ave BS13 . . . . .2 C5
Luckwell Prim Sch BS3 . . . . . .8 A3
Luckwell Rd BS3 . . . . .8 B3
Lucky La BS3 . . . . .8 D4
Lucy Ct GL16 . . . . .163 B2
Ludgate Hill GL12 . . . . .68 B7
Ludlow Cl
Bristol,St Pauls BS2 . . . . .18 F1
Bristol,Willsbridge BS30 . . . . .11 B2
Keynsham BS31 . . . . .4 D5
Ludlow Ct BS30 . . . . .11 B1
Ludlow Gn GL6 . . . . .102 F3
Ludlow Rd BS7 . . . . .19 A7
Ludwell Cl BS36 . . . . .30 D5
Luggs The GL10 . . . . .98 A3
Luke La GL3 . . . . .127 E6
Lullington Rd BS4 . . . . .9 B2
Lulsgate Rd BS13 . . . . .2 A8
Lulworth Cres BS16 . . . . .20 F8
Lulworth Rd BS31 . . . . .4 E4
Lurgan Wlk BS4 . . . . .8 D2
Lurks La GL6 . . . . .103 B4
Lushill Cotts SN6 . . . . .144 E5
Luther Challis Bsns Ctr The
GL4 .127 D2
Lutyens Cl BS16 . . . . .19 F8
Lux Furlong BS9 . . . . .17 B7
Luxton St BS5 . . . . .9 B8
Lych Gate Mews GL51 . . . . . .92 A2
Lych Vale Cwn Pk GL13 . . . . .85 D4
Lydbrook Cl BS37 . . . . .32 D8
Lydbrook Prim Sch
GL17 .163 D2
Lyddington Rd BS16 . . . . .18 F8
Lyde Green Rdbt BS16 . . . . . .21 A8
Lydfield Rd GL15 . . . . .92 B3
Lydford Wlk BS3 . . . . .8 B2
Lydiard Croft BS15 . . . . .10 C4
Lydney & District Hospl
GL15 .147 F6
Lydney CE Com Sch
GL15 .147 F8
Lydney Ind Est GL15 . . . . .84 C8
Lydney Jnc Sta* GL15 . . . . . . .92 A1
Lydney Park Gdns*
GL15 .147 E5
Lydney Rd Bream GL15 . . . . . .147 D8
Bristol,Southmead BS10 . . . . .28 D1
Bristol,Staple Hill BS16 . . . . . .20 E4
Lydney Sta GL15 . . . . .84 C8
Lydney Town Sta* GL15 . . . . . .92 A3
Lydstep Terr BS3 . . . . .8 C4
Lye La GL52 . . . . .138 D1
Lyefield Cl GL52 . . . . .131 B6
Lyefield Rd E GL53 . . . . .131 B6
Lyefield Rd W GL53 . . . . .131 A6
Lygon Ct GL7 . . . . .152 E3
Lygon Wlk 3 GL12 . . . . .132 F3
Lyley Ho GL51 . . . . .68 A7
Lynch Ct BS30 . . . . .11 B1
Lynch Rd Berkeley GL13 . . . . .85 D3
Chalford GL6 . . . . .104 D2
Lynch Road Ind Est GL13 . . . .85 C3
Luncombe Wlk BS16 . . . . .20 B2
Lyncroft Farm Wkshps
GL7 .150 C8
Lyndale Ave BS9 . . . . .17 D5
Lyndale Rd Bristol BS5 . . . . . . .9 D8
Yate BS37 . . . . .43 D1
Lyndale Terr
Cheltenham GL51 . . . . .133 A2
Norton GL2 . . . . .173 B3
Lynde Cl BS13 . . . . .2 B4
Lyndhurst GL52 . . . . .138 B3
Lyndhurst Gdns GL51 . . . . . . .129 E2
Lyndhurst Rd Bristol BS9 . . . . .17 F7
Keynsham BS31 . . . . .4 F3
Lyndley Chase GL52 . . . . .137 D4
Lyng Cl GL4 . . . . .119 E5
Lynmouth Rd
3 Bristol BS2 . . . . .19 A2
Gloucester GL2 . . . . .128 A5
Lynn Rd BS16 . . . . .19 D5
Lynt Farm Cotts SN6 . . . . . . .145 D7
Lynt Rd SN6 . . . . .145 D7
Lynton 5 BS15 . . . . .11 A8
Lynton Pl 3 BS5 . . . . .9 C8
Lynton Rd Bristol BS3 . . . . .8 D2
Lynton Way BS16 . . . . .30 B1
Lynwood Rd Bristol BS3 . . . . . .8 B2
Lydney GL15 . . . . .92 A5
Lynworth Ct 8 GL52 . . . . . . .134 A3
Lynworth Exchange 9
GL52 .134 A3
Lynworth La GL52 . . . . .134 A3
Lynworth Orch GL52 . . . . . . .181 F8
Lynworth Pl GL52 . . . . .134 A3
Lynworth Prim Sch
GL52 .134 A3
Lynworth Terr GL52 . . . . .134 B4
Lyons Court Rd BS14 . . . . .3 D7
Lypiatt Dr GL50 . . . . .193 A3
Lypiatt La GL50 . . . . .193 A3
Lypiatt Mews GL50 . . . . .193 A3
Lypiatt Rd GL50 . . . . .193 A3
Lypiatt St GL50 . . . . .193 A3
Lypiatt View GL6 . . . . .148 B6
Lyppiatt Rd BS5 . . . . .9 D8

Lyppincourt Rd BS10 . . . . . . .28 A3
Lysander Ct GL3 . . . . .128 C5
Lysander Rd BS10,BS34 . . . . .28 C6
Lysander Wlk BS34 . . . . .29 E5
Lysons Ave GL1 . . . . .118 D7
Lytchet Dr BS16 . . . . .20 F8
Lytes Cary Rd BS31 . . . . .5 A3
Lytham Ho BS4 . . . . .9 D1
Lytton Gr Bristol BS7 . . . . .19 A8
Keynsham BS31 . . . . .5 A5
Lyveden Gdns BS13 . . . . .2 B5
Lyvedon Way BS41 . . . . .7 B1

M

Mabberley Cl BS16 . . . . .21 C5
Mabel's Furlong 12 HR8 . . . .178 F8
Macaroni Wood GL7 . . . . .153 A7
Macarthur Rd GL54 . . . . .168 A1
Macauley Rd BS7 . . . . .19 A8
Macdonald Wlk 3 BS15 . . . . .10 D8
Macey's Rd BS13 . . . . .2 D3
Machen Rd GL16 . . . . .155 B6
Machin Cl BS10 . . . . .27 F3
Machin Gdns BS10 . . . . .28 A3
Machin Rd BS10 . . . . .28 A3
Machine Ct 1 GL20 . . . . .192 C4
MacKenzie Way GL51 . . . . . .133 A5
Mackie Ave BS34 . . . . .29 B2
Mackie Gr BS34 . . . . .29 B2
Mackie Rd BS34 . . . . .29 B2
Macrae Ct BS15 . . . . .10 E8
Macrae Rd BS20 . . . . .16 E4
Madeline Rd BS16 . . . . .19 F2
Madison Cl BS37 . . . . .43 D2
Madleaze Ind Est GL1 . . . . . .196 A1
Madleaze Rd GL1 . . . . .196 A1
Madocke Rd NP16 . . . . .61 A7
Maesbury BS15 . . . . .10 E6
Maesbury Rd BS31 . . . . .5 A2
Maesknoll La BS14 . . . . .3 E5
Maesknoll Rd BS4 . . . . .9 B2
Magdala Rd 1 GL1 . . . . .127 A1
Magdalana GL51 . . . . .195 B1
Magdalen Rd GL8 . . . . .140 B4
Magdalene Pl BS2 . . . . .18 F1
Maggs Cl BS10 . . . . .28 C3
Maggs La Bristol BS5 . . . . .19 E2
Bristol BS14 . . . . .3 E5
Magnolia Cl NP16 . . . . .60 F5
Magnolia Ct 1 GL51 . . . . . . .132 D2
Magnolia Wlk GL2 . . . . .117 E1
Magpie Bottom La
Bristol BS15 . . . . .10 B6
Bristol BS5 . . . . .10 B6
Magpie Ct GL10 . . . . .97 F8
Maida Vale Rd GL53 . . . . .130 D6
Maiden Way BS11 . . . . .27 C2
Maidencroft 144 F7
Maidenhall GL2 . . . . .25 B4
Maidenhead Rd BS13 . . . . .1 F4
Maidenhill Sch GL10 . . . . .101 F1
Maidstone St BS3 . . . . .8 E4
Main Rd Bristol BS16 . . . . .21 D5
Mile End GL16 . . . . .155 F1
Tintern Parva NP16 . . . . .146 B3
Whiteshill GL6 . . . . .99 D4
Woolaston GL15 . . . . .147 D3
Woolaston,Brookend GL15 . . .147 C2
Main St Adlestrop GL56 . . . . .177 E6
Beckford GL20 . . . . .179 F1
Bledington OX7 . . . . .177 E1
Willersey WR12 . . . . .188 B2
Main View BS36 . . . . .31 D7
Maisemore BS37 . . . . .39 C8
Maisemore Ave BS34 . . . . .40 B1
Maitlands GL14 . . . . .156 B6
Makin Cl GL3 . . . . .110 C5
Malago Rd BS3 . . . . .8 C3
Malago Vale Est BS3 . . . . .8 C3
Maldon Gdns GL51 . . . . .133 A3
Maldowers La 2 BS5 . . . . .10 B8
Malet Cl GL2 . . . . .117 C4
Mall The Bristol,Clifton BS8 . . . .7 F7
Bristol,Cribbs Causeway
BS10 .28 C5
Bristol,Crofts End BS5 . . . . . . .19 E6
Cheltenham GL53 . . . . .132 C5
Chipping Sodbury BS37 . . . . .117 D1
1 Quedgeley GL2 . . . . .117 D1
Malleson Rd GL52 . . . . .137 F8
Mallow Cl BS15 . . . . .64 D2
Malmains Dr BS16 . . . . .18 D2
Malmesbury Cl
Bristol,Bishopston BS6 . . . . . . .18 C4
Bristol,Longwell Green
BS30 .11 A4
Malmesbury Rd
Cheltenham GL51 . . . . .133 A5
Gloucester GL4 . . . . .143 C3
Malton Sq GL5 . . . . .181 B7
Malvern Cl BS5 . . . . .9 F7
Malvern Court GL51 . . . . .133 A5
Malvern Ct BS5 . . . . .9 F7
Malvern Dr Bristol BS30 . . . . . .11 C5
Thornbury BS35 . . . . .51 D8
Malvern Gdns GL5 . . . . .98 E7
Malvern Pl GL50 . . . . .193 A3
Malvern Rd
Bristol,Crew's Hole BS5 . . . . . . .9 F7
Bristol,Kensington Park BS4 . . .9 D3
Cheltenham GL50 . . . . .133 B1
Corse GL19 . . . . .172 B8
Gloucester GL1 . . . . .126 F4
Malvern St GL51 . . . . .133 B4
Malvern View Bsns Pk
GL52 .137 C2
Malvern Way GL16 . . . . .155 C8
Malverns The GL14 . . . . .119 D6
Manchester Ct 4 GL56 . . . . .187 A3
Manchester Way GL1 . . . . . . .133 B4
Manchester Way 1
GL50 .193 A4
Mancroft Ave BS11 . . . . .16 F7
Mandalay Dr GL2 . . . . .173 B3
Mandara Gr GL4 . . . . .119 D4
Mandarin Way GL50 . . . . .133 C5
Mandeville Cl GL2 . . . . .127 C6
Mangotsfield CE Prim Sch
BS16 .21 B6
Mangotsfield Sch BS16 . . . . . .21 B4
Manilla Rd BS8 . . . . .194 A3
Mankley Rd GL10 . . . . .97 F4
Manley Gdns BS37 . . . . .127 C5
Mannings Rd GL17 . . . . .164 B4
Manor Ave Dursley GL11 . . . . .38 B5
Lechlade on T GL7 . . . . .153 F2
Manor Barn GL53 . . . . .122 C6
Manor Cl
Broad Blunsdon SN26 . . . . . . .144 E1
Coalpit Heath BS36 . . . . .31 C6
Dursley GL11 . . . . .87 F6
Easton-in-G BS20 . . . . .16 A4
6 Fairford GL7 . . . . .152 E4
Honeybourne WR11 . . . . .188 C6
Minchinhampton GL6 . . . . .91 F6
Sherston SN16 . . . . .58 C1
Stratton GL7 . . . . .150 C7
Teddington GL20 . . . . .183 A3
Tockington BS32 . . . . .50 C1
Manor Cl The BS8 . . . . .7 A8
Manor Coalpit Heath Prim
Sch The BS36 . . . . .31 D6
Manor Cotts BS10 . . . . .141 B4
Manor Cotts Pct Ct GL11 . . . .79 F5
Sopworth SN14 . . . . .57 F1
Manor Court Dr BS7 . . . . .18 E7
Manor Ct
Bristol,Fishponds BS16 . . . . . .19 B1
5 Bristol,Upper Easton
BS5 . . . . .19 B1
18 Fairford GL7 . . . . .152 E4
Gloucester GL4 . . . . .119 D6
Lydney GL15 . . . . .92 C3
Swindon GL51 . . . . .133 A6
Whitminster GL2 . . . . .100 F5
Manor Dr GL5 . . . . .99 A1
Manor Farm Abbots Leigh BS8 . .7 A8
Manor Farm Barns
GL54 .166 D6
Manor Farm Cl OX7 . . . . .177 F3
Manor Farm Cotts GL8 . . . . . .141 A4
Manor Farm Cres GL2 . . . . . . .40 D1
Manor Fields
Gloucester GL4 . . . . .119 E8
Haresfield GL54 . . . . .183 F1
Manor Gardens Ho BS16 . . . . .19 B1
Manor Gdns
Gloucester GL4 . . . . .119 E8
Lechlade on T GL7 . . . . .153 E2
Newnham GL14 . . . . .156 F6
Woodchester GL5 . . . . .99 A2
Manor Gr BS34 . . . . .40 B8
Manor La
Bretforton WR11 . . . . .188 A6
Charfield GL12 . . . . .67 A4
Gotherington GL52 . . . . .138 B7
Winterbourne BS36 . . . . .30 F7
Wotton-u-E GL12 . . . . .68 C7
Manor Orch SN6 . . . . .143 F4
Manor Park Bsns Ctr
GL54 .166 D6
Manor Pk Bristol BS6 . . . . .18 B3
Cheltenham GL51 . . . . .129 D6
Gloucester GL4 . . . . .127 E4
Tewkesbury GL20 . . . . .192 E6
Tockington BS32 . . . . .50 C1
Manor Rd Abbots Leigh BS8 . . . .7 A8
Bristol,Bishopston BS7 . . . . . . .18 B4
Bristol,Bishopsworth BS13 . . . .18 A4
Bristol,Fishponds BS16 . . . . . .20 A4
Bristol,Mangotsfield BS16 . . . . .21 A4
Bristol,Redland BS6 . . . . .18 B3
Bristol,Stoke Gifford BS34 . . . .30 A4
Cheltenham GL51 . . . . .129 D6
Manor The
Churchdown GL3 . . . . .128 C4

Manor The continued
4 Newnham GL14 ......157 A6
Manor View
St Arvans NP16 ....72 B5
Stroud GL5 ....98 E4
Manor Way BS37 ......44 C2
Manor Wlk BS35 ......64 B3
Manor Wood Forest Trail*
NP25 ....146 B8
Manor Wood/Coed Maenor
NP16 ....60 C8
Manorbrook Prim Sch
BS35 ....64 C2
Manse Gdns 4 GL51 ...129 F7
Manse La The HR9 .....170 B5
Manse Rd GL17 ....164 B4
Mansel Cl BS31 ....5 C3
Mansell Cl GL2 ....118 C5
Manser St GL50 ....133 D3
Mansfield Mews GL2 ...109 F7
Mansfield St BS3 ....8 C2
Manson's La NP25 .....162 A1
Manston Cl BS14 ....3 C7
Manworthy Rd BS4 ......9 D3
Manx Rd BS7 ....18 F8
Maple Ave Bristol BS16 ..20 C3
  Chepstow/Cas-Gwent NP16 .60 E5
  Thornbury BS35 ....64 C1
Maple Cl
  Bristol,Little Stoke BS34 ..29 C7
  Bristol,Oldland BS30 .....11 B4
  Bristol,Stockwood BS14 ...3 D5
  Dursley GL11 ....88 A3
  Hardwicke GL2 ....109 E8
Maple Ct Bristol BS9 ....17 F8
  Gloucester GL2 ....127 E4
  5 Bristol BS15 ....20 D1
Maple Dr
  Brockworth GL3 ....120 D7
  Charlton Kings GL53 ...131 B5
  Stroud GL5 ....103 A1
Maple Ho BS2 ....195 A4
Maple Leaf Ct BS8 .....194 A3
Maple Rd
  Bristol,Horfield BS7 .....18 E5
  Bristol,St Anne's BS4 .....9 D5
Maple Wlk Keynsham BS31 ..4 D4
  Pucklechurch BS16 ......22 C5
Mapledean GL14 ....191 C5
Maplefield GL15 ....147 E5
Mapleleaze BS4 ....9 D2
Maplemeade BS7 ....18 C4
Mapleridge La BS37 ....44 D7
Maples The
  Cirencester GL7 ....190 B1
  Gloucester GL4 ....119 E6
Maplestone Rd BS14 .....3 A3
Mapstone/Cas-Gwent GL5 ...30 B3
Marbeck Rd BS10 ....28 B1
Marchant Cl GL51 ......132 F3
Mardale Cl BS10 ....28 C2
Marden Rd BS31 ....5 A4
Mardon Rd BS4 ....9 D6
Mardyke Ferry Rd BS1 .194 B1
Marefield Cl GL4 ......119 E7
Marfells Way GL17 ....163 F3
Margaret Rd Bristol BS13 ..1 F4
  3 Ledbury HR8 ....178 E8
  Tewkesbury GL20 ......192 D3
Margate St BS3 ....8 F3
Margery La GL15 ....154 F2
Margrett Rd GL50 .....133 D3
Marguerite Rd BS13 .....1 F7
Marham Rd GL15 ....116 A3
Marian La GL16 ....155 A7
Marians Wlk GL16 .....155 A7
Marigold Wlk BS3 ....8 A2
Marina Gdns BS16 ......19 E3
Marina The GL15 ....84 B8
Marine Gdns GL16 ....155 A5
Marne Par BS20 ....16 C5
Mariner's Way BS20 ...16 C5
Mariners Dr BS9 ....17 D4
Mariners Reach NP16 ..61 A4
Mariners' Path BS9 ....17 E3
Marion Rd BS15 ....10 B3
Marion Wlk BS5 ....10 A7
Marissal Cl BS10 ......27 E3
Marissal Rd BS10 .....27 E3
Maristow Way BS30 ....11 C6
Marjoram Cl 8 GL4 ...119 F5
Marjoram Pl BS32 .....29 F7
Mark La BS1 ....194 C2
Market Cl GL54 ....168 F8
Market Gate BS1 ......195 C3
Market La GL54 ....184 A1
Market Par GL1 ....196 B3
Market Pl Berkeley GL13 ..85 E3
  Cirencester GL7 ....190 C5
  Coleford GL16 ....155 A5
  Dursley GL11 ....88 B1
  11 Fairford GL7 ......152 E4
  Lechlade ot GL7 ......153 E2
  Marshfield SN14 ....15 A8
  14 Tetbury GL8 ....140 C4
Market Sq Bristol BS16 ..20 C3
  Minchinhampton GL6 ..148 A3
  14 Newent GL18 ......171 A4
  Stow-on-t-W GL54 ....176 F4
Market St
  Cheltenham GL50 .....193 A4
  Cinderford GL14 ......191 D5
  Ledbury HR8 ....178 E8
  Nailsworth GL6 ....91 B3
  Wotton-u-E GL12 ......68 B7

Market Way GL1 ....196 B2
Marketside BS2 ....9 B4
Marklands BS9 ....17 E3
Marksbury Rd BS3 ......8 D2
Marlborough Ave 13
  BS16 ....19 E3
Marlborough Cl
  Bishop's Cleeve GL52 ..137 E3
  Cheltenham GL53 .....130 F6
Marlborough Cres GL4 .119 A7
Marlborough Dr BS16 ...30 B1
Marlborough Flats 8
  BS2 ....195 A4
Marlborough Hill BS2 ..195 A4
Marlborough Hill Pl
  BS2 ....195 A4
Marlborough Ho BS2 ...195 A4
Marlborough Pl GL52 ..133 F1
Marlborough Rd GL4 ...119 A7
Marlborough St
  Bristol,Eastville BS5 ....19 E3
  Bristol,Kingsdown BS2 ..195 A4
  Bristol,St Paul's BS1 ...195 B4
Marle Hill Gl6 ....148 C5
Marle Hill Par GL50 ....133 D3
Marle Hill Rd GL50 ....133 D3
Marle Rise GL52 ......133 E4
Marlepit Gr BS13 ....1 F6
Marley La GL6 ....148 D5
Marleyfield Cl 8 GL3 ..128 A7
Marleyfield Way GL3 ..128 A7
Marlfield Wlk BS13 .....1 E7
Marling Cl GL5 ....91 C8
Marling Cres GL5 ......98 F7
Marling Rd BS5 ....9 F8
Marling Sch GL5 ....98 F7
Marlstone Rd GL11 ....88 A4
Marlwood Dr BS10 ....28 B3
Marlwood Sch BS32 ....50 F5
Marmaduke St BS3 ......8 F3
Marment Rd GL11 ......87 E4
Marmion Cres BS10 ....27 F3
Marne Cl BS14 ....3 D5
Marram Cl GL4 ....119 F5
Marsh Cl
  Cheltenham GL51 .....133 C3
  Winterbourne BS36 ....30 E5
Marsh Common Rd BS35 .38 E3
Marsh Dr 1 GL56 .....187 A3
Marsh Dr GL1 ....133 C4
Marsh Gdns GL51 .....133 C3
Marsh La
  Bristol,Ashton Vale BS3 ..8 B2
  Bristol,Barton Hill BS5 ...9 D6
  Burton SN14,GL9 ....36 C4
  Cheltenham GL51 .....133 C3
  Easton-in-G BS20 ....16 A4
  Frampton on Severn GL2 .157 F1
  Leonard Stanley GL10 ...97 F3
Marsh Mews GL10 .....97 F4
Marsh Rd Bristol BS3 ....F3
  Chapstow/Cas-Gwent GL5 .30 B3
  Leonard Stanley GL10 ...97 E4
Marsh St Avonmouth BS11 ..16 C8
  Bristol BS1 ....195 A2
Marsh Terr GL51 ......129 D2
Marsh Way GL16 ......155 B2
Marsharce La BS35 .....49 F6
Marshall Ho 1 BS16 ....19 F4
Marshall Wlk BS4 ....2 C3
Marshall's La GL14 ....191 D5
Marshall's Rd BS5 ......9 C7
Marshfield CE Prim Sch
  SN14 ....15 B8
Marshfield La BS30 ....12 D1
Marshfield Pk BS16 ....20 C8
Marshfield Rd
  Bristol,Frenchay BS16 ...20 C8
  Bristol,Hillfields BS16 ...20 C4
  Tormarton GL9 ....34 E1
Marshmouth La GL54 ..169 A6
Marshland La BS32 .....39 E6
Marsland Rd GL11 .....132 D2
Marston Hill GL7 ......152 C2
Marston Rd Bristol BS4 ..9 B3
  Cheltenham GL52 .....133 F4
Martcombe Rd BS20 ...16 C2
Marten Cl GL4 ....120 A5
Marten Rd NP16 ....60 E6
Martha's Orch BS13 .....1 E7
Martin Cl Bristol BS34 ..28 E8
  Cirencester GL7 ....190 C3
Martin Ct 12 BS16 .....19 E3
Martin's Rd BS5 ....10 C5
Martindale Rd GL3 ....128 B6
Martins Cl BS15 ....10 C5
Martins The Stroud GL5 ..98 D8
  Tutshill NP16 ....73 A1
Martins Way HR8 ......178 E7
Martlock Cres BS3 ......8 C1
Martock Cres BS3 ......8 C1
Martock Rd Bristol BS3 ..8 C2
  Keynsham BS31 ....5 A3
Martor Ind Est SN14 ...25 A2
Marwood Rd BS4 ....2 E8
Mary Carpenter Pl 15
  BS2 ....195 B4
Mary Godwin Ct GL51 .132 F4
Mary Gr GL2 ....125 D5
Mary Rose Ave GL3 ...127 F7
Mary St BS5 ....9 D8
Mary St GL16 ....154 F6
Marybrook St GL13 .....85 E3
Marybush La BS2 ......195 B3
Marygold Leaze BS30 ..11 A4
Mascot Rd BS3 ....8 D3

Masefield Ave GL2 .....118 C4
Masefield Cl 8 HR8 ....178 E8
Masefield Rd GL7 ......190 B2
Masefield Way BS7 .....19 A6
Maskelyne Ave BS10 ...18 D7
Mason Cl GL13 ....85 E3
Mason Rd BS5 ....99 F7
Masons View BS36 ......30 F7
Massey Par 5 GL1 ....118 F7
Massey Rd GL1 ....119 A7
Massey Sham Ave GL56 .187 C3
Matchells Cl BS4 ....9 E6
Materman Rd BS14 ......3 E5
Matford Cl Bristol BS10 ..28 D4
  Winterbourne BS36 .....30 E5
Matford La GL13 ....77 F4
Mathern Cres NP16 .....60 B4
Mathern Rd/Heol Merthyr
  Tewdrig NP16 ....60 D5
Mathern Way NP16 .....60 D5
Mathews Way GL5 ......99 A8
Matson Ave GL4 ....119 C3
Matson La GL4 ....119 B3
Matson Lodge 13 GL4 .119 C4
Matson Pl GL1 ....119 A4
Matthew Ho BS1 ......195 A3
Matthew's Rd 17 BS5 ...9 C7
Matthews Cl BS34 .....19 C5
Maud's Elm Ho GL51 ..133 B4
Maugersbury La GL54 ..176 F4
Maugersbury Pk GL54 ..176 F4
Maules La BS16 ....29 F2
Maunsell Rd BS11 ......27 B2
Maurice Rd BS6 ....18 E2
Mautravers Cl BS32 ....29 D7
Maverdine Ct GL1 ......196 A3
Mawdeley Ho BS3 ......8 E4
Mawley Rd GL7 ....152 D7
Maxse Rd BS4 ....9 B2
Maxstone Cl GL20 .....192 E2
May Bush La HR9 .....162 E2
May Evans Cl BS11 .....87 F5
May Gr GL12 ....67 B5
May La Dursley GL11 ...88 A1
  Ebrington GL55 ....189 D2
May Meadow La GL7 ...164 D5
May Park Prim Sch BS5 ..19 C2
May St BS15 ....20 C1
May Tree Cl GL7 ......149 E3
May Tree Sq GL4 ......119 C7
May Tree Wlk BS31 .....4 C3
May Trees GL50 ....193 A2
May's Cres 6 GL54 ...184 C5
Mayall Ct GL4 ....119 C3
Mayalls Cl GL19 ......172 F7
Mayalls The GL20 .....182 A7
Maybank Rd BS37 ......43 D1
Maybec Gdns BS5 ......10 A7
Maycliffe Pk BS6 ....18 F2
Mayfair Cl GL2 ....118 C8
Mayfield Ave BS16 .....20 A2
Mayfield Cl GL52 .....137 F2
Mayfield Dr GL3 ......119 F8
Mayfield Ho 8 GL50 ...130 B8
Mayfield Pk BS16 ......20 A2
Mayfield Pk (Mobile Home
  Cty) GL7 ....150 C8
Mayfield Pk N BS16 ....20 A2
Mayfield Pk S BS16 ....20 A2
Mayfields 4 E5
Mayhill Ind Est 22 NP25 .154 A7
Mayhill Way GL1 ......127 A2
Maynard Cl BS13 ....2 C5
Maynard Rd BS13 ....2 C5
Mayors Bldgs BS16 .....20 B5
Maypole Cl GL9 ....56 A2
Maypole Rd BS15 ......10 B5
Maypole Gn 8 GL15 ...147 D8
Maypole Terr GL5 ......98 F8
Mays Cl BS36 ....31 D7
Mays La GL8 ....140 B8
Maythorn Dr GL1 .....124 B6
Maytree Ave BS13 ......2 B7
Maytrees GL19 ....19 C2
Mayville Ave BS34 .....29 A3
Maywood Ave 8 BS16 ..20 B4
Maywood Cres BS16 ...20 B4
Maywood Rd BS16 .....20 C4
Maze St BS5 ....9 B6
Maze Wlk BS16 ....155 A7
McAdam Way BS1 ....7 F5
McLaren Rd BS11 ......16 E6
Mead Cl Bristol BS11 ..16 E6
  Cheltenham GL53 .....130 E5
  22 Moreton-in-M GL56 .187 A3
Mead Ct Bsns Pk BS35 ..51 B8
Mead La Ayburton GL15 ..147 F4
  Inglst BS35 ....49 D2
  Lydney GL15 ....84 A8
  Saltford BS31 ....5 F4
Mead Lane Ind Est GL15 .147 F4
Mead Rd Bristol BS34 ...29 F5
  Chipping Sodbury BS37 ..44 C1
  Stonehouse GL10 .....101 E1
Mead St BS3 ....195 C1
Mead Vale GL10 ......101 E1
Mead Way BS35 ....51 B7
Meade-King Gr GL52 ..138 B3

Meadgate BS16 ....21 B7
Meadow Cl Bristol BS16 ..20 F7
  Cheltenham GL51 .....132 C1
  Cirencester GL7 ......190 C3
  Tewkesbury GL20 .....192 E6
  Viney Hill GL15 ....156 C1
Meadow Cotts WR12 ..184 F6
Meadow Court Dr BS30 ..11 C3
Meadow Gr BS11 ....16 D7
Meadow La 9 GL51 ....129 E5
Meadow La W GL5 ......98 E6
Meadow Lea GL52 .....137 E2
Meadow Mead
  Frampton Cotterell BS36 ..31 B8
  Yate BS37 ....43 E5
Meadow Orch 4 WR12 .185 B8
Meadow Rd
  Chipping Sodbury BS37 ..44 A1
  Cinderford GL14 ......191 E5
  Cirencester GL7 ......190 C3
  Honeybourne WR11 ...188 A8
  Leyhill GL12 ....66 B4
  Stonehouse GL10 ......97 F8
Meadow Rise GL17 ....164 F6
Meadow St
  Avonmouth BS11 ....26 A1
  Bristol BS2 ....195 C4
Meadow Vale Bristol BS5 ..20 A1
  Dursley GL11 ....87 F4
Meadow View
  Baunton GL7 ....150 D7
  Frampton Cotterell BS36 ..31 D2
  Kempsford GL7 ....144 E8
Meadow Way Bristol BS32 .29 E7
  Churchdown GL3 .....128 B7
  Kingham OX7 ....177 F2
  South Cerney GL7 ....142 F8
  Stroud GL5 ....98 E6
Meadow Wlk
  Chepstow/Cas-Gwent NP16 .60 D8
  Sling GL16 ....155 B2
  Stroud GL5 ....98 C6
Meadoway GL52 ....137 E2
Meadowbank GL15 .....92 C3
Meadowbrook Prim Sch
  BS32 ....29 E8
Meadowcroft Bristol BS16 .21 A8
  Gloucester GL4 ....119 E5
Meadowland Rd BS10 ..27 E4
Meadowleaze GL2 .....127 E4
Meadows End GL17 ...164 F6
Meadows Prim Sch The
  BS30 ....5 D8
Meadows The
  Bristol BS15 ....10 D4
  Luckington SN14 .....142 D1
  Minety SN16 ....142 D1
Meadowside 2 BS35 ...51 A8
Meadowside Prim Sch
  GL2 ....117 F2
Meadowsweet Ave BS34 .29 B3
Meadowview Cotts GL6 .148 C5
Meads Cl
  Bishop's Cleeve GL52 ..138 A3
  4 Coleford GL16 ......155 A5
Meads Ct NP16 ....60 E6
Meads The Bristol BS16 ..36 B3
  Burton SN14 ....36 B3
  Leighterton GL8 ....70 C3
Meadvale Cl GL4 ......119 A7
Meadway BS9 ....17 C6
Meadway Rd GL10 .....97 E6
Meardon Rd BS14 ....3 E6
Mechanical Organ Mus*
  GL17 ....84 B5
Medad Rd BS5 ....19 C5
Media Ho BS8 ....194 B3
Medical Ave BS2,BS8 ..194 C3
Medina Cl BS35 ....51 C7
Medoc Cl BS15 ....133 C5
Medway Cl BS31 ....5 D4
Medway Cres GL3 .....120 F5
Medway Ct
  Cheltenham GL52 .....134 A2
  Keynsham BS31 ....5 D4
Medway Dr
  Frampton Cotterell BS36 ..31 B7
  Keynsham BS31 ....5 D4
Meekshill Rd GL52 ....134 A3
Meeks Hill NP25 ......154 B1
Meeks Well La HR9 ...162 E2
Meend Gardens Terr
  GL15 ....91 D3
Meend La GL17 ....163 F4
Meendhurst Rd GL14 ..191 C4
Meere Bank BS11 ......27 B2
Meerstone Way GL4 ..119 D3
Meg Thatcher's Gdns
  BS5 ....10 A6
Meg Thatcher's Gn BS5 .10 C1
Melbourne Ct
  Cheltenham GL52 .....134 A2
  Stonehouse GL10 .....101 F1
Melbourne Dr
  Chipping Sodbury BS37 ..44 C1
  Keynsham BS31 ....5 D4
Melbourne Rd BS7 .....18 C3
Melbourne Rd E GL20 ..192 C4
Melbourne St W GL11 ..119 F3
Melbury Rd BS4 ....9 A2
Meldon Terr GL51 .....129 E5
Melick Cl GL4 ....119 A5
Melita Rd BS6 ....18 E3
Mellent Ave BS13 ....2 C3
Mellersh Ho GL50 .....193 A1

Mells Cl BS31 ....5 A2
Melmore Gdns GL7 ...190 E2
Melody Way GL2 .....127 E5
Melrose Ave Bristol BS8 .194 B4
  Yate BS37 ....44 A2
Melrose Cl BS37 ....44 A2
Melrose Pl BS8 ....194 B4
Melton Cres BS7 ....19 A7
Melville GL54 ....168 F8
Melville Rd Bristol BS6 ..18 B1
  Churchdown GL3 .....128 B5
Melville Terr BS3 ....8 C1
Melvin Sq BS4 ....8 E1
Memorial Cl BS15 ......10 B4
Memorial Cotts
  Coln St Aldwyns GL7 ..152 DE
  Tetbury GL8 ....140 A2
Memorial Rd BS15 .....10 B4
Memorial Stadium (Bristol
  Rovers FC)* BS7 ......18 Fe
Mendip Cl
  Gloucester GL14 ......134 A3
  Keynsham BS31 ....4 D5
  Quedgeley GL2 ....109 E8
Mendip Cres BS16 ......21 A8
Mendip Ho 7 GL52 ...134 A3
Mendip Rd Bristol BS3 ...8 D2
  Cheltenham GL52 .....134 A3
Mendip View Bristol GL2 ..12 C2
Mendip View Ave BS16 ..20 A3
Menhir Gr BS10 ....27 F3
Meon Rd GL55 ....189 B7
Mercer Ct BS14 ....3 B8
Merchant St BS1 ......195 B3
Merchants Almshouses 5
  BS1 ....194 A3
Merchants Ct BS8 .....194 A1
Merchants Mead 5
  GL2 ....117 D1
Merchants Quay BS1 ..195 A1
Merchants Rd
  Bristol,Hotwells BS8 ...194 A1
  Bristol,Victoria Park BS8 ..194 A2
Merchants Row BS1 ...194 C1
Merchants Trad Pk BS2 ...9 C4
Merchants' Rd GL2 ...196 A2
Mercia Dr BS2 ....19 A2
Mercia Rd
  Gloucester GL1 ....196 B4
  Winchcombe GL54 ....139 F6
Mercian Cl GL7 ....190 D3
Mercian Way GL15 .....84 A8
Mercier Ct BS1 ....194 A1
Mercier Ct BS37 ....43 F2
Mercury Way GL4 ....119 F6
Meredith Ct BS1 ......194 A1
Merefield Ind Est GL17 ..163 C3
Merestones Cl GL50 ..130 B6
Merestones Dr GL50 ..130 B6
Merestones Rd GL52 ..127 C2
Merfield Rd BS4 ....9 A2
Meridian Pl BS8 ......194 B3
Meridian Vale BS8 ....194 B3
Meriet Ave BS13 ....2 B4
Merioneth St BS3 ....8 F3
Meriton St GL52 ....17 F8
Merkland Cl 1 Bristol BS9 .17 F8
  Cheltenham GL53 .....130 C5
Merlin Cl BS10 ....18 B7
Merlin Dr GL2 ....117 F2
Merlin Haven GL12 ....68 A7
Merlin Pk BS10,BS34 ..27 C4
Merlin Ridge BS16 .....22 C4
Merlin Way
  Chepstow/Cas-Gwent GL53 ..130 C5
  Chipping Sodbury BS37 ..32 F8
Merret Cl GL2 ....182 C5
Merrett Ct BS7 ....19 B6
Merretts Orch GL2 .....95 D3
Merrick Cl BS11 ....195 A1
Merricks La SN14 .....146 D4
Merrimans Rd BS11 ...16 D6
Merrivale Ct GL7 .....164 D5
Merriville Rd GL51 ...133 A3
Merryfields GL4 ....110 B1
Merrywalks GL5 ....99 B7
Merrywalks Sh Ctr 1
  GL5 ....99 C7
Merryweathers GL7 ...190 E2
Merryweathers Ct BS2 ...9 E2
Merrywood Cl 5 BS3 ...8 C4
Merrywood Rd BS3 .....8 C4
Mersey Rd BS37 ....39 D8
Mersham Rd 12 BS2 ...19 A2
Merthyr Terr GL17 ....168 F6
Merton Cl GL10 ....98 B6
Merton Rd BS7 ....18 C3
Mervyn Rd BS7 ....18 F6
Mertons The BS16 ....156 F6
Meryl Ct BS6 ....18 B1
Meteor Way GL3 ......128 B8
Metford Gr BS6 ....18 C3
Metford Pl BS6 ....18 C4
Metford Rd BS6 ....18 C4
Metropolitan The BS1 .195 B1
Metz Way GL1,GL4 ...196 C2
Mews Enterprise Workshops
  GL17 ....164 D5
Mews The
  Highworth SN6 ....145 D3
  6 Tewkesbury GL20 ...192 C4
Meysey Cl GL7 ....152 B1

Meysey Hampton CE Prim
Sch GL7 . . . . 152 A3
Michaelmas Ct GL1 . . . . . 127 A3
Michaels Mead GL7 . . . . . 190 B2
Michaels Way GL16 . . . . . 155 B2
Mickle Mead
Gloucester GL4 . . . . 119 E6
Highnam GL2 . . . . 125 D5
Mickleton Rd
Honeybourne WR11 . . . . . . 188 D7
Ilmington CV36 . . . . 189 F7
Middi Haines Ct SN6 . . . . 145 D3
Middle Ave BS1 . . . . 195 A2
Middle Croft GL4 . . . . 119 D7
Middle Farm Ct GL7 . . . . . 144 E8
Middle Ground SN6 . . . . . 143 E4
Middle Hill Chalford GL6 . 148 C6
Stroud GL5 . . . . 99 E7
Middle Hill Cres GL6 . . . . 148 C6
Middle Leazes GL5 . . . . 99 D7
Middle Orch OX7 . . . . 177 E1
Middle Rd Bristol BS15 . . . 20 F3
Little Barrington OX18 . . . 161 D7
Thrupp GL5 . . . . 99 E3
Middle Spilman's GL5 . . . . 99 A6
Middle Spring GL5 . . . . . . 102 F3
Middle St
[7] Chepstow/Cas-Gwent
NP16 . . . . 60 E8
Stroud,Bowbridge GL5 . . . . 99 D7
Stroud,Uplands GL5 . . . . . . 99 C8
Middle Tynings GL6 . . . . . . 91 A4
Middle Way NP16 . . . . 60 F5
Middlecroft GL10 . . . . 96 F7
Middledown Rd SN14 . . . . 24 C1
Middleford Ho BS13 . . . . . . 2 C4
Middlehay Ct GL52 . . . . . 137 E3
Middlemoor Mill GL5 . . . . 91 A6
Middleton Lawn GL3 . . . . 126 F6
Middleton Rd BS11 . . . . . . 16 F8
Midland Ct GL7 . . . . 190 D3
Midland Mews [14] BS2 . . . 195 C3
Midland Rd
Bristol,Newton BS2 . . . . . 195 C3
Bristol,Staple Hill BS16 . . . 20 D4
Cirencester GL7 . . . . 190 D2
Gloucester GL1 . . . . 196 B1
Stonehouse GL10 . . . . 97 E8
Midland Road Bsns Pk
BS16 . . . . 20 D4
Midland St GL1 . . . . 195 C2
Midland Terr BS16 . . . . 19 F3
Midland Way BS35 . . . . . . 51 C7
Midsummer Wlk GL2 . . . . 118 C6
Midwinter Ave GL51 . . . . 133 C3
Midwinter Gdns GL50 . . . 133 C5
Midwinter Rd [4] GL54 . . . 168 A1
Mildred St BS5 . . . . 9 C7
Mildred's Farm Barns
GL7 . . . . 150 F3
Mile End Rd GL16 . . . . . . 155 B6
Mile Wlk BS14 . . . . 3 A6
Miles Cl BS20 . . . . 16 E3
Miles Cotts GL51 . . . . . . 155 A3
Miles Ct
Bristol,Cadbury Heath BS30 . 10 F4
Bristol,Clifton BS8 . . . . 18 A1
Miles Rd
Bishop's Cleeve GL52 . . . . 137 E1
Bristol BS8 . . . . 18 A1
Milestone Sch The GL2 . . 127 B5
Milestone Wlk GL16 . . . . 155 B2
Milford Ave BS30 . . . . 12 B7
Milford Cl GL2 . . . . 127 B5
Milford St BS3 . . . . 8 C4
Mill Ave Bristol BS1 . . . . 195 A2
Broadway WR12 . . . . 185 A8
Mill Bank GL20 . . . . 192 B4
Mill Cl [3] Blockley GL56 . . 186 C5
Brimscombe GL5 . . . . 99 F2
Frampton Cotterell BS36 . . 31 C7
South Cerney GL7 . . . . . . 143 A8
Wotton-u-E GL12 . . . . 68 C6
Mill Cotts Saltford BS31 . . . 5 F2
Upper Redbrook NP25 . . . 154 C5
Mill Cres BS37 . . . . 32 B4
Mill Ct [1] GL18 . . . . 171 A4
Mill Dene Gdn* GL56 . . . 186 C5
Mill End GL7 . . . . 164 D5
Mill Farm Dr GL5 . . . . 98 E8
Mill Gr GL2 . . . . 117 D1
Mill Ho NP16 . . . . 146 D4
Mill Ho Bristol BS1 . . . . . 195 A2
[1] Bristol,Baptist Mills BS5 . 19 A1
Mill La Avening GL8 . . . . . 140 B8
Mill La
Bitton BS30 . . . . 5 E8
Bristol,Southville BS3 . . . . . 8 D4
Bristol,Warmley BS30 . . . . 11 C5
Brockworth GL3 . . . . 120 F6
Castle Eaton SN6 . . . . . . 144 D6
Charlton Kings GL54 . . . . 131 D8
Cheltenham GL52 . . . . 87 C4
Chipping Sodbury BS37 . . . 33 E6
Cranham GL4 . . . . 112 D6
Doynton BS30 . . . . 22 F1
Fairford GL7 . . . . 152 D4
Falfield GL12 . . . . 65 F7
Frampton Cotterell BS36 . . 42 B1
Gorsley GL18 . . . . 170 C3
Great GL54 . . . . 168 A8
Lechlade on T GL7 . . . . . 153 F2
Longhope GL17 . . . . 165 A5
Lower Slaughter GL54 . . . 176 C1
Lower Swell GL54 . . . . . . 176 D4
Mickleton GL55 . . . . 189 A6
Redmarley D'Abitot GL19 . 179 F2
Stanton Fitzwarren SN6 . . 145 A1

Mill La continued
Staunton GL19 . . . . 179 F1
Stoke Orchard GL52 . . . . 136 D5
Tockington BS32 . . . . 50 B1
Upper Strensham WR8 . . 180 B10
Upton Cheyney BS30 . . . . 11 F1
Winchcombe GL54 . . . . . 174 A7
Mill Pl Cirencester GL7 . . 190 B5
Gloucester GL1 . . . . 119 A7
Mill Place Trad Est GL1 . 118 D7
Mill Rd BS36 . . . . 38 A6
Mill Row Blockley GL56 . . 186 D6
King's Stanley GL10 . . . . . 98 A5
Lower Lydbrook GL17 . . . 163 C3
Mill St Cheltenham GL52 . 134 C5
Gloucester GL1 . . . . 119 A7
Tewkesbury GL20 . . . . . . 192 B4
Mill Stps BS36 . . . . 30 E4
Mill View Baunton GL7 . . 150 D7
Northleach GL54 . . . . 168 A1
Mill Way GL11 . . . . 87 F4
Millar Ho BS8 . . . . 194 A2
Millard Cl BS10 . . . . 28 D2
Millbank GL11 . . . . 88 A4
Millbank Ct BS4 . . . . 9 E3
Millbook Cl [3] BS6 . . . . . 18 E1
Millbridge Rd GL12 . . . . . 120 A7
Millbrook GL5 . . . . 148 A5
Millbrook Ave BS4 . . . . 9 F3
Millbrook Cl Bristol BS30 . 11 C6
[6] Gloucester GL1 . . . . . . 127 A1
Millbrook Ct GL50 . . . . . . 193 A4
Millbrook Gdns
Cheltenham GL50 . . . . . . 133 B2
Lea HR9 . . . . 164 D8
Millbrook Gn GL15 . . . . . 147 C5
Millbrook Ley GL6 . . . . . . 177 A6
Millbrook Pl GL5 . . . . 99 D7
Millbrook Rd BS37 . . . . . . 43 B2
Millbrook Rdbt GL50 . . . 193 A4
Millbrook St
Cheltenham GL50 . . . . . . 193 A4
Gloucester GL1 . . . . 193 A4
Millbrook Wlk GL5 . . . . . . 90 F6
Millend GL15 . . . . 156 E1
Millend La GL10 . . . . 97 A7
Millend Row GL10 . . . . . . 97 A7
Millennium
Frampton Cotterell BS36 . . 31 D7
Tewkesbury GL20 . . . . . . 192 A7
Millennium Cotts GL19 . . 172 A7
Millennium Park Ctr*
GL7 . . . . 142 D6
Millennium Sq BS1 . . . . . 194 C1
Millennium Way GL7 . . . . 190 F5
Miller Cl
Ashleworth GL19 . . . . 172 D4
Gloucester GL1 . . . . 127 D5
Miller Craddock Way [1]
HR8 . . . . 178 E7
Millers Cl BS20 . . . . 16 C4
Millers Dr BS30 . . . . 11 D5
Millers Dyke GL2 . . . . 117 B1
Millers Gn
Drybrook GL17 . . . . 164 A4
Gloucester GL1 . . . . 196 B3
Millers Way GL14 . . . . . . 191 C4
Millfield BS35 . . . . 64 C2
Millfield Dr BS30 . . . . 11 C6
Millfields GL3 . . . . 120 A8
Millground Rd BS13 . . . . . . 1 F5
Milligan Rd [8] BS2 . . . . . 195 B4
Millgrove St N BS2 . . . . . 195 A4
Millham Rd GL52 . . . . 138 A4
Millhill La GL16 . . . . 154 F3
Millhouse Dr GL50 . . . . . 133 C5
Milliman Cl BS13 . . . . 2 C5
Millin Ave GL4 . . . . 118 D2
Milling Cl SN6 . . . . 143 A5
Milling Cres GL15 . . . . . . 147 E5
Millmead Ho BS13 . . . . 2 C4
Millpill Cl BS9 . . . . 17 D5
Millpond End GL5 . . . . 99 A2
Millpond Prim Sch BS5 . . 19 A1
Millpool St [9] BS5 . . . . . . 19 A1
Millpool Ct BS9 . . . . 18 B8
Mills Cl [2] WR12 . . . . . . 185 B8
Mills Way GL54 . . . . 186 C6
Millward Gr BS16 . . . . 20 C4
Milne Pastures GL20 . . . . 182 B4
Milne Wlk GL51 . . . . 132 E4
Milner Gn BS30 . . . . 11 A5
Milner Rd BS7 . . . . 18 F5
Milo Pl GL1 . . . . 118 E6
Milsom St Bristol BS5 . . . . 9 A8
Cheltenham GL50 . . . . . . 193 A4
Milton Ave
Cheltenham GL51 . . . . . . 129 F8
Gloucester GL1 . . . . 118 C5
Milton Cl BS37 . . . . 43 D2
Milton Gr GL5 . . . . 99 E7
Milton Pk [1] BS5 . . . . 9 C7
Milton Pl GL1 . . . . 118 D3
Milton Rd Bristol BS7 . . . . 18 E6
Cheltenham GL51 . . . . . . 132 F1
Yate BS37 . . . . 27 A3
Milton St GL7 . . . . 152 D3
Miltons Cl BS13 . . . . 2 D4
Milverton Gdns BS6 . . . . . 18 F2
Milward Rd BS7 . . . . 18 E5
Mimosa Ave GL51 . . . . . . 130 A4
Mimosa Cl BS31 . . . . 128 A7
Mina Rd BS2 . . . . 19 A2
Minchinhampton Sch
GL6 . . . . 148 A3
Mine Pitts La HR9 . . . . . . 162 E3
Minehead Rd BS4 . . . . 9 E5
Miners Wlk GL14 . . . . . . 191 C4
Minerva Cl GL4 . . . . 119 D6

Minerva Ct GL7 . . . . 190 D4
Minerva Wlk GL15 . . . . . . 92 B5
Minetts Ave GL52 . . . . . . 138 A3
Minety CE Prim Sch
SN16 . . . . 142 D1
Minety La SN16 . . . . 142 A3
Minnow La OX18 . . . . . . 161 D7
Minor's La BS10 . . . . 27 A8
Minsmere Rd BS31 . . . . 5 A4
Minster Cl GL52 . . . . 137 E4
Minster Ct [1] BS37 . . . . . 32 D7
Minster Gdns GL4 . . . . . . 119 F6
Minsterworth CE Prim Sch
GL2 . . . . 116 F7
Minstrel Way GL3 . . . . . . 127 F8
Minto Rd BS2 . . . . 19 A2
Minto Road Ind Ctr [8]
BS2 . . . . 19 A2
Minton Cl BS14 . . . . 3 B5
Misarden Park Gdns*
GL6 . . . . 106 B6
Misarden Park Woodland
Trail* GL6 . . . . 106 B6
Miserden CE Prim Sch
GL6 . . . . 106 A6
Miserden Rd GL51 . . . . . . 132 D1
Miss Grace's La NP16 . . . 146 D7
Mission Rd BS37 . . . . 43 A5
Mistletoe Mews GL3 . . . . 127 F6
Mitcheldean Endowed Prim
Sch GL17 . . . . 164 D5
Mitchell Cl BS1 . . . . 195 B2
Mitchell La BS1 . . . . 195 B2
Mitchell Wlk BS30 . . . . . . 11 D7
Mitford Cotts OX18 . . . . . 161 F5
Mitford Villas GL50 . . . . . 133 A4
Mitre Pitch GL12 . . . . 68 C7
Mitre St GL53 . . . . 193 C2
Mitton Ct GL20 . . . . 192 E6
Mitton Manor Prim Sch
GL20 . . . . 192 E6
Mitton Way GL20 . . . . . . 192 E6
Mivart St BS5 . . . . 19 A1
Moat Bank GL20 . . . . 180 F7
Moat Ho GL4 . . . . 119 B4
Moat La Corse GL19 . . . . 172 A8
Huntley GL19 . . . . 165 E8
Uckington GL51 . . . . 132 B8
Moat Prim Sch GL4 . . . . . 119 B4
Moat The Kingham OX7 . . 179 F7
Quedgeley GL2 . . . . 117 F1
Mobley GL13 . . . . 66 D3
Modecombe Gr BS10 . . . . 27 F3
Model Village The*
GL54 . . . . 169 A7
Moffatt Rd GL6 . . . . 91 A4
Mogg St BS2 . . . . 195 A4
Mogridge Cl GL2 . . . . 120 A7
Mohair Countryside Ctr*
GL6 . . . . 165 A5
Molescroft Cl BS23 . . . . . . 3 A4
Molesworth Dr BS13 . . . . . 2 A4
Monarch Cl GL4 . . . . 119 E4
Monarch Ct BS16 . . . . 31 A1
Monica Dr GL50 . . . . 133 E4
Monk Meadow Trad Est
GL2 . . . . 118 C7
Monk Rd BS2 . . . . 18 D8
Monk's Park Ave BS7 . . . . 18 E8
Monkey Mdw GL20 . . . . . 182 C5
Monkey Puzzle Cl GL51 . . 98 E6
Monks Ave BS15 . . . . 10 B8
Monks Croft GL51 . . . . . . 132 C5
Monks Ho BS37 . . . . 32 D7
Monks La GL20 . . . . 182 C2
Monks Park Ave BS7 . . . . 18 E8
Monks Wlk GL7 . . . . 153 F2
Monkscroft Com Prim Sch
GL51 . . . . 132 D3
Monkswell Cl [2] NP25 . . 154 A8
Monkswell Rd [1] NP25 . . 154 A8
Monkton Rd BS15 . . . . . . 10 B5
Monmouth Comp Sch
NP25 . . . . 154 D6
Monmouth Ho BS20 . . . . 16 C5
Monmouth Hill BS32 . . . . 39 E4
Monmouth Rd Bristol BS7 . 18 E2
Edge End GL16 . . . . 155 C8
Keynsham BS31 . . . . 24 D5
Pill BS20 . . . . 16 C5
Monmouth St BS3 . . . . 8 F3
Monsdale Cl BS10 . . . . 28 A3
Monsdale Dr BS10 . . . . . . 28 A2
Monson Ave GL4 . . . . 193 B4
Mont The [2] BS6 . . . . 18 F1
Montague Cl BS34 . . . . . . 29 C5
Montague Ct BS2 . . . . . . 195 A4
Montague Flats [8] BS2 . . 195 A4
Montague Hill BS2 . . . . . 195 A4
Montague Hill S [5] BS2 . 195 A4
Montague Pl BS6 . . . . 195 A4
Montague Rd BS31 . . . . 5 A4
Montague Terr GL7 . . . . . 142 F7
Monterey Rd GL51 . . . . . 132 A7
Montfort Rd GL52 . . . . . . 127 B5
Montgomery Cl GL4 . . . . 119 E4
Montgomery Rd GL51 . . . 129 D6
Montgomery St [1] BS3 . . . 8 D3
Montpelier Central [1]
BS6 . . . . 18 E1
Montpelier Sta BS6 . . . . . 18 E1
Montpellier GL50 . . . . . . 193 B1
Montpellier Arc GL50 . . . 193 B2
Montpellier Ave GL50 . . . 193 B2

Montpellier Ct GL50 . . . . 193 A2
Montpellier St GL50 . . . . 193 B2
Montpellier Gr GL50 . . . . 193 B2
Montpellier Ho GL50 . . . 193 A2
Montpellier Mews GL1 . . 196 B2
Montpellier Par GL50 . . . 193 B2
Montpellier Rd GL15 . . . . 155 E1
Montpellier Retreat
GL50 . . . . 193 B2
Montpellier Spa Rd
GL50 . . . . 193 B2
Montpellier St GL50 . . . . 193 B3
Montpellier Terr GL50 . . . 193 B2
Montpellier Villa GL50 . . 193 B2
Montpellier Wlk GL50 . . . 193 A2
Montreal Ave BS7 . . . . 19 A8
Montreal Dr GL51 . . . . . . 132 E3
Montreaux Ho [2] BS5 . . . 10 A7
Montrose Ave BS6 . . . . . . 18 C1
Montrose Dr BS30 . . . . . . 11 B6
Montrose Pk BS4 . . . . 9 A2
Montroy Cl BS9 . . . . 18 C6
Montserrat GL5 . . . . 99 D3
Moon St BS2 . . . . 195 A4
Moon's La GL6 . . . . 148 E7
Moor Court Dr GL52 . . . . 133 F2
Moor Croft BS30 . . . . 10 F3
Moor Gr BS11 . . . . 17 A8
Moor Hall Pl GL5 . . . . 98 E8
Moor Cvn Pk BS5
BS5 . . . . 27 A4
Moor La
Bourton-on-the-W GL54 . . 169 A8
Fairford GL7 . . . . 152 E3
Tockington BS32 . . . . 40 A8
Moor Lane Ct GL7 . . . . . . 152 E3
Moor St
Chepstow/Cas-Gwent NP16 . 60 E8
Gloucester GL1 . . . . 118 F7
Saul GL2 . . . . 157 F4
Moor The SN16 . . . . 142 D2
Moor Wood Cotts GL7 . . 158 B3
Moordell Cl BS37 . . . . 43 D1
Moore Cottage Hospl
GL54 . . . . 168 F8
Moore Rd GL54 . . . . 168 F7
Moorend Cres GL53 . . . . 130 C6
Moorend Gdns BS11 . . . . . 16 F7
Moorend Glade GL53 . . . 130 C6
Moorend Gr GL53 . . . . . . 130 C5
Moorend La GL2 . . . . 78 E6
Moorend Park Rd GL53 . . 130 C5
Moorend Rd
Cheltenham,Charlton Park
GL53 . . . . 130 F6
Cheltenham,Leckhampton
GL53 . . . . 130 C6
Hambrook BS16 . . . . 30 D3
Staunton GL19 . . . . 180 C1
Moorend St GL53 . . . . . . 130 C6
Moores Ground GL17 . . . 173 C6
Moorfield Ave GL15 . . . . 156 D1
Moorfield Rd GL53 . . . . . 120 F5
Moorfields Ho BS5 . . . . 9 C7
Moorgate GL7 . . . . 153 D2
Moorgrove Ho BS9 . . . . . . 17 C2
Moorhen Ct GL2 . . . . 117 D1
Moorhouse Cl BS10 . . . . . 19 B1
Moorhouse La BS10 . . . . . 27 B4
Moorings The BS20 . . . . . . 16 C4
Moorland Cl GL14 . . . . . . 191 D5
Moorland Rd BS37 . . . . . . 43 D1
Moorlands Rd
Bristol,Mayfield Park BS16 . 20 A3
Bristol,Ridgeway BS16 . . . 19 F3
Moorpark Ave BS37 . . . . . 39 C4
Moors La GL4 . . . . 133 A4
Moorslade La GL13 . . . . . . 67 D1
Mop Hale GL56 . . . . 186 C6
Mopla Rd GL56 . . . . 186 C6
Moravian Ct [4] BS15 . . . 10 D8
Moravian Rd BS15 . . . . . . 10 D8
Morcroft Pl GL15 . . . . 155 F1
Morden Wlk BS14 . . . . 3 D8
More Hall Pk GL5 . . . . . . 102 D1
Morelands Gr GL1 . . . . . . 118 E5
Morelands Trad Est
GL1 . . . . 196 A1
Morestall Dr GL7 . . . . 190 B2
Moreton Cl
Bishop's Cleeve GL52 . . . . 138 A2
Cheltenham GL53 . . . . . . 130 C6
Moreton La GL20 . . . . . . 182 C8
Moreton-in-Marsh District
Hospl GL56 . . . . 187 A3
Moreton-in-Marsh Sta
GL56 . . . . 187 A3
Morgan Cl BS31 . . . . 5 A4
Morgan St BS2 . . . . 195 B4
Morgan's Way GL14 . . . . 156 C6
Morgans Dr GL50 . . . . . . 129 C6
Morgans La GL17 . . . . . . 164 A3
Morgans Terr GL7 . . . . . . 142 F7
Mork La GL15 . . . . 146 E4
Mork Rd GL15 . . . . 146 E4
Morlands Dr GL53 . . . . . . 131 B4
Morley Ave Bristol BS16 . . 20 C5
Morley Cl
Bristol,Little Stoke BS34 . . 29 C7
Bristol,Staple Hill BS16 . . . 20 C4
Morley Rd
Bristol,Southville BS3 . . . . . 8 C4
Bristol,Staple Hill BS16 . . . 20 C4
Morley Sq BS7 . . . . 18 E4

Morley St
Bristol,Baptist Mills BS5 . . . 18 F1
Bristol,Russell Town BS5 . . . 9 B7
Morley Terr [1] BS15 . . . . 20 D1
Morman Cl GL2 . . . . 164 B4
Morningside Cl GL52 . . . 134 C4
Morningside Ctyd GL52 . 134 C4
Mornington Dr GL53 . . . . 130 D6
Mornington Rd [14] BS8 . . 18 A2
Mornington Terr [7]
GL14 . . . . 157 A6
Morpeth Rd BS4 . . . . 2 D8
Morpeth St GL1 . . . . 118 F7
Morris Cl GL15 . . . . 156 B2
Morris St [7] GL51 . . . . . 129 F7
Morris Rd BS5 . . . . 9 A5
Morris Orch GL11 . . . . 87 F6
Morris Rd Bristol BS7 . . . . 18 E5
Broadway WR12 . . . . 185 B8
Morse La GL17 . . . . 164 A4
Morse Rd Bristol BS5 . . . . . 9 C7
Drybrook GL17 . . . . 164 B4
Mortimer House Hospl
BS8 . . . . 194 A3
Mortimer Rd
Bristol,Filton BS34 . . . . . . 29 B2
Bristol,Victoria Park BS8 . 194 A3
Gloucester GL2 . . . . 127 C5
Morton Mill BS35 . . . . 64 C3
Morton Cl Bristol BS5 . . . . . 9 B7
Gloucester GL1 . . . . 118 F7
Thornbury BS35 . . . . 64 C4
Morton Way BS35 . . . . 64 D1
Morwent Cl GL4 . . . . 119 E4
Mosedale GL56 . . . . 187 B3
Moselle Dr GL3 . . . . 128 A6
Mosley Cres GL4 . . . . 98 E7
Mosley Cl GL3 . . . . 98 E7
Mostham Pl GL3 . . . . 120 D6
Motor Mus (The Bugatti
Trust)* GL52 . . . . 138 E8
Motorway Distribution Ctr
BS11 . . . . 26 C2
Mottershead Dr GL3 . . . . 127 E6
Mottershead Rd GL7 . . . . 150 F2
Moulder Rd GL20 . . . . . . 192 E4
Mount Cl Cirencester GL7 . 190 C3
Frampton Cotterell BS36 . . 30 F8
Harrow Hill GL17 . . . . . . 164 B4
Mount Craig Hall HR9 . . . 152 F4
Mount Cres BS36 . . . . 30 E5
Mount Gdns BS15 . . . . . . 10 D6
Mount Hill Rd BS15 . . . . . 10 D6
Mount Pleasant
Bisley GL6 . . . . 148 D8
Blockley GL56 . . . . 186 C6
Chepstow/Cas-Gwent NP16 . 60 E8
Fairford GL7 . . . . 152 E4
Hallen BS10 . . . . 27 C4
Lechlade on T GL7 . . . . . 153 E2
Lydney GL15 . . . . 92 C2
Parkend GL15 . . . . 155 E3
Pill BS20 . . . . 16 D4
Stroud GL5 . . . . 99 E7
Tirley GL19 . . . . 172 F7
Wotton-u-E GL12 . . . . 68 C7
Mount Pleasant Cl
Lydney GL15 . . . . 92 C2
[1] Stow-on-t-W GL54 . . . 176 F4
Mount Pleasant Rd
Cinderford GL14 . . . . 191 D3
Tewkesbury GL20 . . . . . . 192 D4
Mount Pleasant Terr BS3 . . 8 C4
Mount St Cirencester GL7 . 190 C3
Gloucester GL1 . . . . 196 A3
Mount Way
Chepstow/Cas-Gwent NP16 . 60 F6
Chepstow/Cas-Gwent NP16 . 72 D1
Mountain Mews [5] BS5 . . 10 A7
Mountain View GL17 . . . . 163 F4
Mountbatten Cl BS37 . . . . 43 D3
Monteney's La GL12 . . . . . 54 D7
Mountjoy's La GL14 . . . . 191 D5
Mounton Chambers
GL14 . . . . 191 D5
Mounton Chambers
NP16 . . . . 60 D8
Mounton Cl NP16 . . . . 60 D7
Mounton Dr NP16 . . . . 60 D7
Mounton House Sch
NP16 . . . . 60 B7
Mounton Rd NP16 . . . . 60 C8
Mousell La GL14 . . . . 191 D4
Mousetrap La GL54 . . . . . 168 F8
Mow Barton Bristol BS13 . . . 1 F6
Yate BS37 . . . . 43 D2
Mowberry Cl GL2 . . . . . . 127 C5
Mowbray Rd BS14 . . . . . . 20 D1
Mowbray Rd BS14 . . . . 3 C7
Moxham Dr BS13 . . . . 2 C4
Moyle Old School La
BS37 . . . . 73 A4
Muirfield Bristol BS30 . . . . 11 A6
Yate BS37 . . . . 32 E8
Mulberry Cl Bristol BS15 . . 11 A6
Hardwicke GL2 . . . . 109 E8
Mulberry Ct [2] GL51 . . . 132 D2
Mulberry Dr BS15 . . . . . . 20 F1
Mulberry Gdns [11] BS16 . 20 D1
Mulberry Rd GL15 . . . . . . 177 C4
Mulberry Wlk BS9 . . . . . . 17 C8
Mulberry Rd GL53 . . . . . . 18 F3
Mule St GL13 . . . . 78 B3
Muller Ave BS7 . . . . 18 F4
Muller Rd BS5,BS7 . . . . . . 19 B3

Mullings Ct GL7 . . . . .190 C0
Mulready Cl BS7 . . . . .19 C6
Mumbleys Hill BS35 . . . . .50 E7
Mumbleys La
  Thornbury,Alveston Down
  BS35 . . . . .50 E6
  Thornbury,Kington BS35 . . .50 E8
Munday Cl **8** GL6 . . . . . .148 B6
Munsley Gr GL4 . . . . .119 C3
Murdoch Sq BS7 . . . . .18 F8
Murford Ave BS13 . . . . .2 B4
Murford Wlk BS13 . . . . .2 B4
Murray Cl GL52 . . . . .137 F5
Murray St **9** BS3 . . . . .8 C4
Murrells Rd GL16 . . . . .163 A2
Murvagh GL53 . . . . .193 C1
Murvagh Cl GL53 . . . . .193 C1
Muscroft Rd GL4 . . . . .134 D2
Musgrove Cl BS11 . . . . .27 C2
Mushat Ind Pk GL16 . . . .155 B5
Mushet Pl GL16 . . . . .155 A5
Musket Cl GL20 . . . . .192 E2
Mutsilver Mews GL2 . . . .127 E5
Muzzle Patch GL2 . . . . . .124 C8
Myers Rd GL4 . . . . .127 A1
Myrtle Cl GL4 . . . . .119 A5
Myrtle Dr BS11 . . . . .16 E5
Myrtle Hill BS20 . . . . .16 C5
Myrtle Pl NP16 . . . . .72 F1
Myrtle Rd BS2 . . . . .194 C4
Myrtle St BS3 . . . . .8 B3
Myrtles The NP16 . . . . .73 A2
Mythe Rd GL20 . . . . .192 C5
Mythe Terr **3** GL14 . . . . .157 A6

N

Naas La Lydney GL15 . . . . . .92 D2
  Quedgeley GL2,GL4 . . . . . .110 C6
Naas La Rdbt GL2 . . . . . . .109 F7
Nags Head Hill BS5 . . . . . .10 A7
Nagshead Nature Reserve*
  GL15 . . . . .155 D4
Nagshead Nature Trails*
  GL15 . . . . .155 D3
Nailers La GL18 . . . . .170 D3
Nailsea Cl BS13 . . . . .2 A7
Nailsworth Ave BS37 . . . . .43 E1
Nailsworth CE Prim Sch
  GL6 .90 F5
Nailsworth Mills Est GL6 .91 C4
Nailsworth Terr **2**
  GL50 . . . . .193 A4
Naishcombe Hill BS30 . . .12 C7
Naite The BS35 . . . . .193 A6
Nanfan & Dobyn Pl
  GL18 . . . . .171 A5
Napier Ct BS1 . . . . .194 B1
Napier Ho BS6 . . . . .18 B2
Napier Miles Rd BS11 . . . .17 A8
Napier Rd
  Avonmouth BS11 . . . . .26 B1
  Bristol,Baptist Mills BS5 . .19 B2
  Bristol,Redland BS6 . . . . . . .18 B2
Napier Sq BS11 . . . . .9 B6
  Gloucester GL1 . . . . .196 C2
Napping La GL17 . . . . .164 F6
Napping The GL17 . . . . . . .164 F6
Narles Rd GL2 . . . . .96 A3
Narrow La BS16 . . . . .20 E4
Narrow Plain BS2 . . . . . . .195 B2
Narrow Quay BS1 . . . . . . .195 A2
Narroways Rd BS2 . . . . . . .19 A3
Narrow La GL6 . . . . .90 F1
Narrows The GL55 . . . . . . .188 E1
North La NP25 . . . . .154 B1
Naseby Ho **4** GL52 . . . .134 A3
Naseby Wlk BS5 . . . . .19 F1
Nash Cl BS31 . . . . .5 A5
Nash Dr BS7 . . . . .19 C7
Nash Way **1** GL16 . . . . .155 A5
Nash's La GL55 . . . . .189 D3
Nasse Ct GL11 . . . . .87 F5
Nastend La GL10 . . . . .101 C1
National Birds of Prey Ctr*
  GL18 . . . . .170 E2
National Star Coll The
  GL53 . . . . .122 C6
National Waterways Mus*
  GL1 . . . . .196 A2
Nature Cl GL3 . . . . .120 E5
Naunton Cres GL53 . . . . . .130 D6
Naunton La GL53 . . . . .130 D6
Naunton Par GL53 . . . . . .193 B1
Naunton Park Cl GL53 . . .130 D6
Naunton Park Ind Est
  GL53 . . . . .130 E6
Naunton Park Prim Sch
  GL53 . . . . .130 E6
Naunton Park Rd GL53 . .130 D6
Naunton Rd GL4 . . . . .119 D7
Naunton Terr GL53 . . . . . .193 B1
Naunton Way GL53 . . . . . .130 D6
Naval Temple* NP25 . . . .154 B7
Neads Dr BS30 . . . . .11 C5
Neale Way BS11 . . . . .26 C1
Neata Farm GL54 . . . . . . .184 A1
Neate Ct BS34 . . . . .29 C8
Neath Rd BS5 . . . . .10 A6
Nebraska Circ GL7 . . . . . .152 E1
Nebsworth La CV36 . . . . . .189 E5
Needham Ave GL2 . . . . . . .110 B6

Neigh Bridge Ctry Pk*
  GL7 . . . . .142 C5
Nell Hill SN6 . . . . .145 A4
Nelmes Row GL53 . . . . . . .131 C5
Nelson Ho Bristol BS1 . . .195 A3
  3 Bristol,Staple Hill BS16 . .20 D6
Nelson Par **1** BS3 . . . . . .8 D4
Nelson Rd **3** Bristol BS16 .20 D4
  Bristol BS16 . . . . .20 D5
Nelson St Bristol BS1 . . . .195 A3
  Bristol,Ashton Vale BS3 . . . .8 A2
  Chepstow/Cas-Gwent NP16 .60 F8
  Gloucester GL1 . . . . .118 F6
  Stroud GL5 . . . . .99 C7
  Tewkesbury GL20 . . . . .192 C4
Nelsons Cl HR9 . . . . .163 B7
Nene Cl GL2 . . . . .117 E2
Neptune Cl GL4 . . . . .119 F6
Nero Cl GL15 . . . . .92 C4
Neston Wlk BS4 . . . . .2 F8
Netham Gdns BS5 . . . . .9 D7
Netham Park Ind Est BS5 .9 D6
Netham Rd BS5 . . . . .9 D7
Netham View Ind Pk BS5 .9 D7
Nether-Swell Manor
  GL54 . . . . .176 E3
Nethercote CV36 . . . . .187 F5
Nethercote Dr GL54 . . . . .169 A7
Nethercote Farm Dr
  GL54 . . . . .169 A6
Netherend GL15 . . . . .147 C3
Netherend Cres GL15 . . . .147 C3
Netherhope La NP16 . . . . .73 B5
Netheridge Cl GL2 . . . . . .118 A4
Netherley La GL19 . . . . . . .180 A4
Netherwood Cl GL11 . . . .133 A3
Netherwood Gdns GL51 .133 A3
Netting La GL2 . . . . .157 B6
Nettlestone Cl BS10 . . . . . .27 E4
Nettleton Rd Burton SN14 .36 B2
  Cheltenham GL51 . . . . . . .129 E7
Nevalan Dr BS5 . . . . .10 A6
Nevil Rd BS7 . . . . .18 E4
Neville Rd Bristol BS15 . . .20 E2
  Tewkesbury GL20 . . . . .192 D3
New Barn Ave GL52 . . . . .134 A4
New Barn Cl GL52 . . . . . . .134 A4
New Barn La GL52 . . . . . . .134 A4
New Bldgs BS16 . . . . .1 B4
New Brunswick Ave BS5 .10 B7
New Charlotte St BS3 . . . . .8 D4
New Cheltenham Rd
  BS15 . . . . .20 E1
New Church St GL8 . . . . .140 B4
New Cut GL11 . . . . .89 B1
New Fancy View* GL15 . .155 F4
New Fosseway Rd BS14 . . . .3 B6
New Fosseway Sch BS14 . .3 B6
New Inn La Avening GL8 . .140 B8
  Gloucester GL51 . . . . .196 B3
New John St **1** BS3 . . . . .8 C3
New Kings Ct BS7 . . . . .18 C4
New Kingsley Rd BS2 . . . .195 C2
New La BS35 . . . . .51 C5
New Leaze BS32 . . . . .40 C3
New Mdws BS14 . . . . .3 B6
New Mills GL15 . . . . .92 A6
New mills Ind Est HR8 . .178 E8
New Mills La GL12 . . . . . . .192 A6
New Mills Trad Est GL5 . . .99 D8
New Mills Way **1** HR8 . .178 E8
New Queen St
  Bristol,St George BS15 . . . .10 B8
  Bristol,Windmill Hill BS3 . . .8 E4
New Rd Aylburton GL15 . .147 D5
  Blakeney GL15 . . . . .156 D1
  Bledington OX7 . . . . .177 E7
  Bream GL15 . . . . .147 D8
  Bristol,Filton BS34 . . . . . . .28 F3
  Bristol,Harry Stoke BS34 . .29 D3
  Coleford GL16 . . . . .155 B5
  Coleford,Cannop GL15,
  GL16 . . . . .155 D6
  Dursley GL11 . . . . .87 E4
  Erdington GL55 . . . . .189 D8
  Kingham OX7 . . . . .177 F2
  Kingswood GL12 . . . . .67 F6
  Lydney GL15 . . . . .147 F7
  Minchinhampton GL6 . . . . . .91 F5
  Mitcheldean GL17 . . . . . . .164 D5
  9 Moreton-in-M GL56 . . .187 A3
  Newton GL13 . . . . .85 C8
  Painswick GL6 . . . . .103 F8

New Stadium Rd BS5 . . . . .19 B2
New Station Rd BS16 . . . . .20 A4
New Station Way BS16 . . .20 A4
New Street Flats **5**
  BS2 . . . . .195 C3
New Thomas St BS2 . . . . .195 C2
New Town
  Cinderford GL14 . . . . .191 B7
  New Town GL54 . . . . .184 C3
  Toddington GL54 . . . . .184 C3
New Tyning La BS37 . . . . . .45 C4
New Villa SN14 . . . . .57 D1
New Walls BS41 . . . . .8 F4
New Wlk BS15 . . . . .10 B5
New Zealand Ho **2**
  GL51 . . . . .132 F3
Newark Ho GL2 . . . . .118 B7
Newark Pk* GL12 . . . . .69 A7
Newark Rd GL1 . . . . .118 C6
Newbrick Rd BS34 . . . . . . .30 A5
Newbridge Cl BS4 . . . . .9 D5
Newbridge Farm Pk*
  HR8 . . . . .178 A8
Newbridge Ho BS9 . . . . . . .17 C4
Newbridge Rd BS4 . . . . .9 E6
Newbridge Trad Est BS4 . . .9 D5
Newburgh Ho SN6 . . . . . .145 C3
Newburgh Pl SN6 . . . . . . .145 C3
Newbury Rd BS7 . . . . .19 A7
Newcombe Cl GL4 . . . . . . .134 B8
Newcombe Ct GL7 . . . . . . .190 D4
Newcombe Dr BS9 . . . . . . .17 C4
Newcombe Rd BS9 . . . . . . .17 F7
Newcourt Pk GL53 . . . . . . .131 A6
Newcourt Rd GL53 . . . . . . .131 A5
Newent Ave BS15 . . . . .10 B7
Newent Bsns Pk GL18 . . .171 B4
Newent Comm Sch
  GL18 . . . . .170 F4
Newent La GL19 . . . . .165 C6
Newerne St GL15 . . . . .92 B3
Newfoundland Ct BS2 . . .195 C4
Newfoundland Way
  BS2 . . . . .195 C4
Newgate BS1 . . . . .195 B3
Newgrounds La GL12 . . . . .95 B6
Newhouse Farm Ind Est
  NP16 . . . . .60 F3
Newland Dr BS32 . . . . .2 A4
Newland Pl GL20 . . . . .192 D4
Newland Rd BS13 . . . . .2 A3
Newland St
  Coleford GL16 . . . . .155 A5
  Gloucester GL1 . . . . .196 C3
Newland View GL51 . . . . .132 F5
Newland Way **1** NP25 . .154 A7
Newlands Ave BS36 . . . . . .31 C7
Newlands Cr
  20 Newent GL18 . . . . .171 A4
  Stow-on-t-W GL54 . . . . . . .176 E5
Newlands Rd BS31 . . . . .4 D4
Newlands The BS16 . . . . . . .20 B7
Newleaze BS34 . . . . .29 A2
Newleaze Gdns GL8 . . . . .140 B4
Newleaze Ho BS34 . . . . . . .29 B2
Newlyn Ave BS9 . . . . .17 D5
Newlyn Way BS37 . . . . .43 F2
Newlyn Wlk BS4 . . . . .9 B1
Newman Cl BS37 . . . . .32 B4
Newmarket Ave BS1 . . . . .195 A3
Newmarket Rd GL6 . . . . . . .91 A4
Newmills Hill HR9 . . . . . . .162 F5
Newnham Cl BS14 . . . . .3 D7
Newnham Pl BS34 . . . . .39 F1
Newnham St Peter's CE Prim
  Sch GL14 . . . . .157 A7
Newnton Hill GL14 . . . . . .140 D5
Newnton Rd GL8 . . . . .140 C3
Newpit La BS30 . . . . .11 F2
Newport Rd
  Chepstow/Cas-Gwent NP16 .60 D7
  Pill BS20 . . . . .16 C5
Newport St BS3 . . . . .8 E3
Newquay Rd BS4 . . . . .9 F1
Newry Wlk BS4 . . . . .8 E1
Newsome Ave BS20 . . . . . .16 C4
Newstead Rd GL4 . . . . . . .134 C8
Newth's La SN5 . . . . .143 E1
Newton Ave GL4 . . . . .117 C1
Newton Cl BS37 . . . . .23 A1
  Cheltenham GL51 . . . . . . .132 E2
  Huntley GL19 . . . . .165 D6
  2 Ledbury HR8 . . . . .178 F7
Newton Court La NP25 . .162 B1
Newton Dr BS30 . . . . .11 A5
Newton Rd Bristol BS30 . .11 A5
  Cheltenham GL51 . . . . . . .132 E2
  Newton SN13 . . . . .9 A8
  Twerton BS13 . . . . .67 A5
Newtown GL14 . . . . .192 F5
Newtown Rd GL14 . . . . . . .191 B7
Niblett Cl BS15 . . . . .10 F6
Niblett's Hill BS5 . . . . .10 A6
Nibley Cl BS11 . . . . .27 A6
Nibley La BS37 . . . . .42 F3
Nibley Rd BS11 . . . . .26 E5
Nicholas La BS5 . . . . .10 A6
Nicholas Rd BS5 . . . . .19 B1
Nicholas St BS3 . . . . .8 E4
Nicholls Ct BS36 . . . . .30 E7
Nicholls La BS36 . . . . .30 E7
Nicholson Cl GL3 . . . . .127 C6
Nigel Pk BS11 . . . . .16 E7

Nightingale Cl Bristol BS4 . .9 E6
  Frampton Cotterell BS36 . .31 A6
  Thornbury BS35 . . . . .64 D2
Nightingale Croft GL2 . . .127 D6
Nightingale Ct BS4 . . . . .9 D3
Nightingale Ho GL4 . . . . . .119 D4
Nightingale La BS36 . . . . . .31 A8
Nind La GL12 . . . . .68 B4
Nine Elms Rd GL2 . . . . . . .127 E4
Nine Tree Hill **10** BS1 . . .18 E1
Nine Wells Cl **11** GL16 . .155 A7
Nine Wells Rd GL16 . . . . .155 B7
Ninewells Forest Wlk*
  NP25 . . . . .146 B6
Ninth Ave BS7 . . . . .29 B1
Niven Ctyd GL51 . . . . .132 C1
Noake Rd GL3 . . . . .120 A8
Noble Ave BS30 . . . . .11 C4
Noden Dr HR9 . . . . .164 C8
Nodens Way GL15 . . . . .92 C4
Noel Cl **8** GL55 . . . . .189 A2
Noel Lee Way GL11 . . . . . . .87 F5
Norbury Ave GL4 . . . . .119 B4
Norchard Sta* GL15 . . . . .147 F7
Nordown Cl GL11 . . . . .87 F4
Nordown Rd GL11 . . . . .87 F4
Norfolk Ave
  Bristol,Montpelier BS6 . . . .18 E2
  Bristol,St Pauls BS2 . . . . . .195 B4
Norfolk Cl GL51 . . . . .132 F2
Norfolk Gr BS31 . . . . .4 C4
Norfolk Ho BS1 . . . . .195 B4
Norfolk Mews GL51 . . . . .132 F2
Norfolk Pl BS3 . . . . .8 C3
Norfolk St GL1 . . . . .196 A2
Norland Rd BS8 . . . . .7 F8
Norley La GL19 . . . . .179 F2
Norman Ave BS37 . . . . .27 D2
Norman Ball Way GL11 . . .127 B1
Norman Cl GL20 . . . . .181 F7
Norman Gr BS15 . . . . .20 D2
Norman Hill GL11 . . . . .87 F4
Norman Rd
  Bristol,Baptist Mills BS2 . .19 A2
  Bristol,Warmley BS30 . . . . .11 B8
  Saltford BS31 . . . . .5 E3
Norman Way GL17 . . . . . .163 F4
Norman's Cotts BS36 . . . . .30 D7
Normanby Rd **20** BS5 . . . .19 B1
Normandy Way NP16 . . . . .72 D1
Normanton Rd **16** BS8 . . .18 A2
Norrisville Rd **8** BS6 . . . .18 E1
Norrmal Pl HR9 . . . . .163 C8
Norse Way NP16 . . . . .61 B7
Nortenham Cl GL52 . . . . .137 D4
North Ave
  Ashchurch GL20 . . . . .182 D4
  Drybrook GL17 . . . . .165 A5
North Cerney CE Prim Sch
  GL7 . . . . .158 D3
North Circular Rd GL4 . .187 C4
North Croft BS30 . . . . .11 C4
North Devon Rd BS16 . . . .20 A5
North East Rd BS35 . . . . . .64 C4
North East Terr GL20 . . . .192 D4
North End SN14 . . . . .47 E5
North End Gdns SN16 . . . .58 C7
North Farm Cotts GL8 . . .141 A6
North Gate BS2 . . . . .16 C4
North Green St **12** BS8 . . .7 F6
North Hall Mews GL52 . . .133 F2
North Hill Rd GL7 . . . . . . .190 E2
North Home Rd GL7 . . . . .190 F3
North Leaze BS41 . . . . .7 B2
North Meadow (Nature
  Reserve)* SN6 . . . . .143 E5
North Meadow Rd SN6 . .143 F5
North Nibley CE Prim Sch
  GL11 . . . . .79 D5
North Par GL51 . . . . .43 E2
North Pk BS15 . . . . .20 E1
North Pl GL50 . . . . .193 C4
North Pole La HR9 . . . . . . .170 C5
North Rd Bristol BS37 . . . . .24 C8
  Bristol,Bishopston BS6 . . . .18 E2
  Bristol,Stoke Gifford BS34 . .29 E4
  Coleford GL16 . . . . .155 B5
  Engine Common BS37 . . . . .33 B6
  Gloucester GL1 . . . . .196 B4
  Huntley GL19 . . . . .165 D6
  Leigh Woods BS8 . . . . .7 E3
  Thornbury BS35 . . . . .64 C2
  Winterbourne BS36 . . . . . . .30 F7
  Yate BS37 . . . . .27 D1
North Rd E GL51 . . . . .129 C6
North Rd W GL51 . . . . . . .129 B6
North Road Com Prim Sch
  BS37 . . . . .27 D1
North Somerset Junc BS5 . .9 B6
North St
  Bristol,Dowand Common
  BS30 . . . . .11 C4
  Bristol,Southville BS3 . . . . . .8 B3
  Bristol,St Pauls BS5 . . . . . .195 B4
  Cheltenham GL50 . . . . . . .193 B4
  Wickwar GL12 . . . . .54 A6
  Winchcombe GL54 . . . . . . .184 F2
North Stoke La BS30 . . . . .25 D7
North Upton La GL4 . . . . .119 E8
North View Bristol BS6 . . .18 A4
  Bristol,Upper Soundwell
  BS16 . . . . .20 E5
  Highworth SN6 . . . . .145 C3
North View Bglws GL7 . . .151 F3

North Wall SN6 . . . . .143 F4
North Way Bristol BS34 . . .29 B4
  Cirencester GL7 . . . . .190 C4
North Wlk BS37 . . . . .43 E1
Northavon Bsns Ctr BS37 .43 C3
Northbank Cl GL51 . . . . . .129 B7
Northbrook Rd GL4 . . . . . .127 C8
Northcot La GL56 . . . . .186 D6
Northcote Ho **2** BS8 . . . .194 A3
Northcote Rd
  Bristol,Clifton BS8 . . . . .17 F1
  Bristol,Crew's Hole BS5 . . . .9 E7
  Bristol,Staple Hill BS16 . . .20 F6
Northcote St **18** BS5 . . . . .9 F1
Northcroft GL50 . . . . .130 B7
Northen Cl GL7 . . . . .144 F7
Northend Ave BS15 . . . . . . .20 D2
Northend Gdns BS15 . . . . .20 D2
Northend Rd BS15 . . . . .20 E1
Northern Way GL17 . . . . . .164 D5
Northfield BS37 . . . . .32 D8
Northfield Ave BS15 . . . . . .10 D5
Northfield Cl GL8 . . . . .140 C4
Northfield Ho **10** BS3 . . . . .8 C4
Northfield La SN14 . . . . . . .21 F1
Northfield Pas GL50 . . . . .193 C4
Northfield Rd Bristol BS5 . .19 C8
  Gloucester GL4 . . . . .118 F5
  Tetbury GL8 . . . . .140 C4
Northfield Terr GL50 . . . . .193 C4
Northfields GL5 . . . . .99 D8
Northgate St GL1 . . . . .196 B3
Northington La GL14 . . . . .157 B3
Northlands Way GL4 . . . . .127 C6
Northleach CE Prim Sch
  GL54 . . . . .168 A1
Northleach Wlk BS11 . . . . .16 C7
Northleaze GL8 . . . . .140 C4
Northleaze Prim Sch BS41 .7 B2
Northmead La BS37 . . . . . .42 D2
Northmoor La GL7 . . . . . . .151 A1
Northover Ct BS35 . . . . .38 C6
Northover Rd BS9 . . . . .28 A1
Northridge Bsns Ctr
  BS37 . . . . .43 C2
Northumberland Rd BS6 . .18 D2
Northumbria Dr BS9 . . . . . .18 D4
Northview Prim Sch
  SN6 . . . . .145 B4
Northville Rd BS7 . . . . .29 A1
Northway Inf Sch GL20 . .182 C4
Northway La GL20 . . . . . . .182 B4
Northway Trad Est
  GL20 . . . . .182 C4
Northwick Bsns Ctr
  GL56 . . . . .186 C6
Northwick Rd Bristol BS7 . .18 F8
  Northwick BS35 . . . . .48 E1
Northwick Terr GL56 . . . .186 C5
Northwood Cl GL14 . . . . . .191 D5
Northwoods Wlk BS10 . . . .28 D3
Norton CE Prim Sch
  GL2 . . . . .173 B2
Norton Cl Bristol BS15 . . . .10 F7
  Whitchurch HR9 . . . . .162 D4
  Winchcombe GL54 . . . . . . .174 A8
Norton Ct GL6 . . . . .90 F5
Norton Ho **10** Bristol BS1 .195 B1
  Bristol,Patchway BS34 . . . .39 F1
  Cheltenham GL51 . . . . . . .133 A2
Norton La BS14 . . . . .3 A1
Norton Rd BS4 . . . . .9 A3
Norton Ridge GL6 . . . . .90 F4
Norton View 189 A6
Nortonwood GL16 . . . . . . .155 C3
Norwell Wlk BS10 . . . . .27 F1
Norwich Dr BS4 . . . . .9 E5
Norwood Rd GL50 . . . . . . .193 B1
Nostle Rd GL14 . . . . .168 A1
Notch Rd GL7,GL53 . . . . .107 C8
Notgrove Cl
  Cheltenham GL51 . . . . . . .129 B8
  Gloucester GL4 . . . . .118 C2
Notgrove Long Barrow*
  GL54 . . . . .167 E8
Notley Pl GL3 . . . . .120 A7
Nottingham Rd
  Bishop's Cleeve GL52 . . . . .137 F5
  Bristol BS7 . . . . .18 F3
Nottingham St **3** BS3 . . . . .8 E4
Nouncells Cross GL5 . . . . . .99 D7
Nouncells Dr GL5 . . . . .130 B4
Nourse Cl GL52 . . . . .130 B4
Nourse Pl GL17 . . . . .164 D5
Nova Distribution Ctr
  BS11 . . . . .26 B1
Nova Scotia Pl BS1 . . . . . .194 A1
Nova Way BS11 . . . . .26 B1
Novers Cres BS4 . . . . .8 C1
Novers Hill BS3 . . . . .8 D1
Novers Hill Trad Est BS3 . .8 C2
Novers La BS4 . . . . .8 C1
Novers Lane Jun Sch BS4 . .8 C1
Novers Park Dr BS4 . . . . . . .8 C1
Novers Park Rd BS4 . . . . . . .8 C1
Novers Rd BS4 . . . . .8 C1
Noverton Ave GL52 . . . . . .134 D4
Noverton La GL52 . . . . . . .134 D4
Nugent Hill BS6 . . . . .18 D1
Nunnery La GL11 . . . . .80 B7
Nunney Cl BS31 . . . . .5 C2
Nunney Cl GL51 . . . . .132 C1
Nup End Cl GL19 . . . . .172 D4
Nup End La GL19 . . . . .172 D4
Nupdown Rd BS35 . . . . .75 A5

Nupend Gdns GL17 ......164 F5
Nupend La GL17 ....164 F5
Nurseries The
Bishop's Cleeve GL52 .....137 E2
Tytherington GL12 ....52 B5
Nursery Cl
Cirencester GL7 ....190 E2
Mickleton GL55 ....189 B7
Moreton-in-M GL56 ....187 A4
Stroud GL5 ....99 D6
Nursery Cott GL7 ....190 D3
Nursery Dr GL5 ....148 A5
Nursery Gdns BS10 ......28 A3
Nursery Rd GL7 ....190 E2
Nursery The Bristol BS3 .....8 B3
King's Stanley GL10 ....98 A4
Nursery View GL7 ....150 E2
Nut Croft GL4 ....119 B7
Nut Orchard La GL20 .....181 F8
Nutbridge Cotts GL52 ...138 C3
Nutfield Gr BS34 ....29 B2
Nutfield Ho BS34 ....29 B1
Nutgrove Ave BS3 ....8 E3
Nuthatch Dr BS16 ....19 F6
Nuthatch Gdns BS16 .....20 A6
Nuthill GL4 ....120 B2
Nutley Ave GL4 ....118 C2
Nutmeg Cl GL4 ....119 D4
Nympsfield BS15 ....20 E2
Nympsfield Long Barrow*
GL11 ....89 C7
Nympsfield Rd
Gloucester GL4 ....118 D3
Nailsworth GL6 ....90 E5

O

O'Brien Rd GL51 ....133 A4
Oak Ave GL52 ....131 A7
Oak Cl Bristol BS34 ....29 D7
Chepstow/Cas-Gwent NP16 .60 E5
Yate BS37 ....43 D3
Oak Cres GL15 ....147 C3
Oak Cres/Cilgant Defiw 8
NP25 ....154 A7
Oak Ct Bristol BS14 ....3 A5
Cheltenham GL52 ....134 A1
Oak Dr Brockworth GL3 ...120 D6
Dursley GL11 ....88 A3
Highworth SN6 ....145 C3
Northway GL20 ....182 B4
Stroud GL5 ....99 B6
Oak Field The GL14 .....191 E5
Oak Gdns GL20 ....182 C7
Oak Gr BS20 ....16 C5
Oak Hill CE Prim Sch (Inf)
WR11 ....183 F7
Oak Hill CE Prim Sch (Jun)
GL20 ....183 E4
Oak Ho Bristol BS13 ....2 D4
Brockworth GL3 ....120 D6
Oak Inn GL1 ....119 A7
Oak La Bredon GL20 .....182 C7
Bristol BS5 ....19 F2
Oak Lodge BS37 ....32 D8
Oak Manor 3 GL52 ......134 A1
Oak Manor Dr GL52 .....134 A1
Oak Mdw GL15 ....92 B6
Oak Rd Bristol BS7 ....18 E5
Colerne SN14 ....15 F5
Down Ampney GL7 ....143 F7
Marston Meysey SN6 .....144 A6
Oak St GL7 ....153 E2
Oak The BS9 ....17 D3
Oak Tree Ave BS16 ....22 B4
Oak Tree Cl Bristol BS15 ...10 C3
Hardwicke GL2 ....109 E7
Oak Tree View GL4 ......119 C3
Oak Tree Wlk BS31 ....4 D3
Oak Way Huntley GL19 ...165 D6
Littledean GL14 ....156 E8
South Cerney GL7 ....142 F7
Stonehouse GL10 ....97 F7
Oakbank GL4 ....118 F4
Oakbrook Dr GL51 ......129 C7
Oakcroft Cl GL4 ....119 D3
Oakdale Ave BS16 ....20 D8
Oakdale Cl BS16 ....20 E8
Oakdale Ct BS16 ....20 D7
Oakdale Rd
Bristol,Downend BS16 .....20 E8
Bristol,Hengrove BS14 ......3 A8
Oakdean GL14 ....191 C5
Oakdene
11 Cheltenham,Lansdown
GL51 ....130 B8
2 Cheltenham,Whaddon
GL52 ....134 A1
Oakdene Ave BS5 ....19 D3
Oakenhill Rd BS4 ....9 E2
Oakenhill Wlk BS4 ....9 E2
Oakes La GL9 ....35 B5
Oakeys Cl 20 GL54 ......176 F4
Oakfield Ave NP16 ....72 D1
Oakfield Bsns Pk BS15 ...10 D7
Oakfield Gr BS8 ....194 B4
Oakfield Pl BS8 ....194 B4
Oakfield Rd
Bishop's Cleeve GL52 .....138 A4
Bristol,Kingswood BS15 ....10 D7
Bristol,Victoria Park BS8 ..194 B4
Keynsham BS31 ....4 F2
Oakfield St GL50 ....130 B7
Oakfield Way GL13 ....93 D1
Oakfields GL16 ....155 A6
Oakford La SN14 ....15 B2
Oakhanger Dr BS11 ......27 B1
Oakhill Ave BS30 ....11 C2
Oakhill La BS10 ....27 C4
Oakhill Pitch GL15 ......146 F3
Oakhill Rd GL17 ....164 D5
Oakhunger La GL13 ......85 C4
Oakhurst Cl GL3 ....128 A5
Oakhurst Rd BS9 ....17 F5
Oakhurst Rise GL52 .....131 A8
Oakland Ave GL52 ....133 F3
Oakland Bsns Pk BS37 ...43 A3
Oakland Dr HR8 ....178 E8
Oakland Rd
Bristol,Crew's Hole BS5 ......9 E8
6 Bristol,Redland BS6 .....18 B1
Harrow Hill GL17 ....164 B3
Oakland St GL53 ....131 A7
Oaklands Cirencester GL7 .190 C2
Sling GL16 ....155 B2
Oaklands Cl BS16 ....21 B5
Oaklands Dr
Almondsbury BS32 ....40 A4
Bristol,Frenchay BS16 .....20 A7
Bristol,Oldland Common
BS30 ....11 C2
Oaklands Pk GL15 ......155 E1
Oaklands Rd BS16 ....21 A5
Oaklea Rd GL15 ....156 B2
Oakleaze
Coalpit Heath BS36 ....31 D7
Gloucester GL2 ....127 D3
Minety SN16 ....142 D1
Oakleaze Rd BS35 ....64 C1
Oakleigh Ave BS5 ....19 D1
Oakleigh Gdns BS30 .....11 C2
Oakley Flats GL7 ....144 E7
Oakley Rd Bristol BS7 .....18 F7
Cheltenham GL52 ....134 B1
Cirencester GL7 ....190 C2
Oakley Way 1 GL15 .....147 D8
Oakmeade Pk BS4 ....9 B2
Oakridge GL2 ....125 E5
Oakridge Cl Bristol BS15 ...11 A7
Gloucester GL4 ....119 E5
Oakridge Parochial Sch
GL6 ....148 E6
Oaks La GL18 ....170 D2
Oaks The Berry Hill GL16 ..155 A8
Bristol BS7 ....18 E4
Cheltenham GL51 ....129 D6
Cinderford GL14 ....191 C5
Gloucester GL4 ....119 E7
Kemble GL7 ....141 F8
Oaksey CE Prim Sch
SN16 ....141 F4
Oaksey Rd SN16 ....142 B2
Oaktree Cres BS32 ....40 C2
Oaktree Ct BS11 ....16 E7
Oaktree Gdn GL4 ....119 C3
Oaktree Gdns BS13 ....1 E5
Oakwood Ave BS9 ....18 C6
Oakwood Cl Bream GL15 .155 D1
Cinderford GL14 ....191 D5
Oakwood Dr GL3 ....119 F6
Oakwood Gdns BS36 .....31 E7
Oakwood Pk BS16 ....20 A3
Oakwood Rd
Bream GL15 ....155 D1
Bristol BS9 ....18 B6
Sling GL16 ....155 B3
Oatfield GL2 ....117 E2
Oatfield Rd GL2 ....100 A6
Oatground GL12 ....68 C7
Oathill La GL7 ....141 A8
Oatlands Ave BS14 ....3 A6
Oatley Ho BS9 ....18 A5
Oatley Trad Est 6 BS15 ...20 D1
Oatleys Cres 11 HR8 .....178 E8
Oatleys Rd HR8 ....178 E8
Oatleys Terr 10 HR8 .....178 E8
Oberon Ave BS5 ....19 E2
Ocker Hill GL6 ....102 E2
Octagon The NP16 ....60 F5
Octavia Pl GL15 ....92 B4
Odda's Chapel* GL19 ...173 C8
Oddfellows Row 3
GL54 ....176 F4
Oddfellows Terr 18
GL54 ....174 A7
Oddfellows' Terr 14
GL56 ....187 A3
Oddington Rd GL54 .....176 F4
Odessa Pk GL20 ....173 F8
Offa's Mead Prim Sch
NP16 ....61 A8
Offas Cl NP16 ....61 A7
Office Rd GL14 ....191 C3
Ogbourne Cl GL2 ....127 E3
Ohio Ave GL7 ....152 E2
Okebourne Cl BS10 ......28 B4
Okebourne Rd BS10 ......28 B4
Okus Rd GL53 ....131 A5
Old Acre Rd BS14 ....3 A3
Old All Saints Sch 12
GL50 ....193 C4
Old Ashley Hill BS6 ....18 F2
Old Aust Rd BS32 ....40 C6
Old Barns The WR8 ....180 A10
Old Barrow Hill BS11 .....16 D7
Old Bath Rd GL53 ....130 E5
Old Bell Chambers 3
NP16 ....60 E8
Old Bread St BS2 ....195 C2
Old Brewery La 16 GL8 ...140 B4
Old Bristol Rd GL6 ....91 B3
Old Bulwark Rd NP16 .....60 E7
Old Burford Rd OX7 .....177 E1
Old Cheltenham Rd
GL2 ....127 D4
Old Co-op The GL15 .....156 A2
Old Coach Cl NP16 ....61 C2
Old Coach Rd NP16 ....61 C3
Old Coach The WR12 ....185 C8
Old Comm GL6 ....148 A4
Old Comm The GL6 ......148 C6
Old Common The GL6 ...148 B6
Old Court Dr GL19 ......171 D1
Old Dam Rd GL15 ....92 D7
Old Dean Rd GL17 ......164 D6
Old Dixton Rd NP25 .....154 A8
Old Down Hill BS32 ......50 B2
Old Down Rd GL9 ....35 C8
Old Elmore La GL2 ......117 F2
Old Farm Cl SN16 ....141 E1
Old Farm La BS5 ....10 B6
Old Forge Cl OX7 ....177 E1
Old Forge Cotts
Didbrook GL54 ....184 D2
Stoke Orchard GL52 ......136 E5
Old Forge The GL15 .....147 D3
Old Furnace Cl GL15 ....147 F5
Old George The GL6 ......91 C4
Old Gloucester Rd
Alveston BS35 ....51 B5
Bourton-on-t-W GL54 .....168 E7
Bristol,Hambrook BS16 .....30 B2
Bristol,Stoke Gifford BS16 ..30 B4
North Corner BS36 ....41 D3
Staverton GL51 ....173 F1
Thornbury BS35 ....65 B2
Uckington GL51 ....132 B5
Old Gram School Mews The
9 GL55 ....189 A2
Old Hill Avening GL8 ....148 B1
Longhope GL17 ....165 A5
Old Horsley Rd GL6 ......91 B3
Old Hospital La GL20 ...192 D5
Old Hundred La GL9 .....34 D2
Old King Street Ct BS1 ..195 B3
Old La BS16 ....21 C6
Old La (Simmonds La)
HR9,GL18 ....170 C4
Old Lodge Ct GL50 .....133 E3
Old London Rd GL12 .....80 C1
Old Malt Ho BS2 ....195 C4
Old Manor Cl GL12 ....67 A5
Old Manor Gdns GL55 ...189 B6
Old Manor La GL20 .....192 E6
Old Mansion The GL52 ..134 C4
Old Market GL6 ....91 B4
Old Market Rdbt BS2 ...195 C3
Old Market St BS2 ......195 C3
Old Market Way 12
GL56 ....187 A3
Old Mill Cl BS37 ....32 B4
Old Mill Mus The*
GL54 ....176 C1
Old Mill The WR12 ......185 B8
Old Millbrook Terr 4
GL50 ....133 B2
Old Moat Ctyd GL2 ......172 F1
Old Monmouth Rd GL17 .165 A5
Old Neighbourhood
GL6 ....148 C6
Old Oak Cl NP16 ....60 F5
Old Orchard Ct GL7 .....152 D7
Old Orchard The GL55 ..189 D3
Old Painswick Cl GL4 ...119 B6
Old Painswick Rd GL4 ...119 B6
Old Park Hill BS2 ....194 C3
Old Park Rd BS11 ....16 D7
Old Pk BS2 ....194 C3
Old Police Sta The BS4 ....9 A3
Old Pooles Yd BS4 ....9 E2
Old Post Office Alley 15
GL20 ....192 C4
Old Priory Rd BS20 ......16 B4
Old Quarry Ind Units The
GL8 ....140 C3
Old Quarry Rd BS11 ......16 E7
Old Quarry Rise BS11 .....16 E7
Old Rd Coleford GL16 ...155 B5
Maisemore GL2 ....126 A8
Southam GL52 ....134 C8
Old Rd The/Yr Hen Heol 22
NP25 ....154 A7
Old Rectory Cl GL5 ......99 A5
Old Rectory Gdns GL56 .176 D8
Old Rectory Rd GL12 .....67 F4
Old Rectory The
Longborough GL56 ....176 D8
Staunton GL16 ....154 E7
Old Reddings Cl GL51 ...129 C7
Old Reddings Rd GL51 ..129 C7
Old Row GL1 ....196 C1
Old School Cl
Bristol BS30 ....11 D7
Nailsworth GL6 ....91 B4
Old School Ct The 18
GL8 ....140 B4
Old School Ho Bristol BS4 ..9 B2
3 Cheltenham GL50 .....193 A4
Old School Mews The 4
GL53 ....131 B6
Old Silk Mill The GL6 ...148 B5
Old Sneed Ave BS9 ......17 D4
Old Sneed Cotts BS9 .....17 E4
Old Sneed Pk BS9 ....17 D4
Old Sneed Rd BS9 ....17 D4
Old Sodbury CE Prim Sch
BS37 ....34 B8
Old Station Dr GL53 .....130 D5
Old Station Rd GL18 .....171 A5
Old Station Way GL16 ...155 A5
Old Tannery The BS2 ...195 C3
Old Town
26 Moreton-in-M GL56 ....187 A3
Old Town *continued*
Wotton-u-E GL12 ....68 B7
Old Town Mews GL15 ...147 F5
Old Tram Rd GL1 ....196 A2
Old Vicarage Ct
6 Coleford GL16 ....155 A5
Whitchurch BS14 ....3 C4
Old Vicarage Gn BS31 .....4 E6
Old Vicarage La GL7 ....141 F7
Old Vicarage Pl BS8 .....18 A1
Old Vicarage The
Bristol,Highridge BS13 ......1 F6
Bristol,Montpelier BS6 .....18 E1
Old Wesleyan Chapel The
BS30 ....11 B5
Old Wharf Ind Est HR8 ..178 E7
Old Wharf La HR9 ......162 E4
Old White Hart GL13 .....85 E3
Old Winding Wheel The
GL15 ....147 C8
Oldacre Dr GL52 ....138 A4
Oldbridge Rd BS14 ....3 C3
Oldbury Chase BS30 .....11 A2
Oldbury Cl GL51 ....132 D3
Oldbury Court Dr BS16 ...20 B6
Oldbury Court Prim Sch
BS16 ....20 C7
Oldbury Court Rd BS16 ...20 A5
Oldbury Ho GL20 ....192 D5
Oldbury La
Thornbury BS35 ....64 B4
Wick BS30 ....12 D5
Oldbury Orch GL3 ......128 D4
Oldbury Power Station
Visitor Ctr* BS35 ....75 B1
Oldbury Rd
Cheltenham GL51 ....132 E3
Tewkesbury GL20 ....192 C5
Oldbury-on-Severn Prim Sch
BS35 ....63 B5
Oldcroft Rd GL15 ....156 B1
Olde La GL54 ....184 B3
Oldends La GL10 ....97 D8
Oldfield GL20 ....192 D4
Oldfield Cres GL51 .....129 F8
Oldfield Girls Sch BA1 .....6 F1
Oldfield Pl BS8 ....7 F5
Oldfield Rd BS8 ....194 A1
Oldfields La BS35 ....41 D7
Oldhill GL5 ....98 D8
Oldland Common Sta*
BS30 ....11 C3
Oldlands Ave BS36 ....31 C6
Oldmead Wlk BS13 ....1 E7
Oldminster Rd GL13 .....93 D1
Oldown Cty Pk* BS32 ....50 C4
Oldwood La BS37 ....43 B8
Olio La GL53 ....193 C2
Olive Gdns BS35 ....50 F4
Olive Gr GL11 ....88 A2
Oliver Cl GL4 ....118 D2
Ollney Rd GL6 ....91 F6
Olveston CE Prim Sch
BS35 ....50 A3
Olveston Rd BS7 ....18 E5
Olympus Cl BS34 ....29 D6
Olympus Pk GL2 ....118 A2
Olympus Rd BS34 ....28 D7
Onslow Rd GL18 ....171 A4
Oram Ct BS30 ....10 F4
Orange Cl SN6 ....145 D3
Orange St BS2 ....195 C4
Orangery The GL4 ......119 E7
Orchard Ave Bristol BS1 ..194 C2
Broadway WR12 ....185 C8
Cheltenham GL51 ....132 F2
Chepstow/Cas-Gwent NP16 .60 E5
Thornbury BS35 ....64 D1
Orchard Bank
2 Blockley GL56 ....186 C5
Great Rissington GL54 ....169 C4
Orchard Bvd BS30 ....11 B4
Orchard Cl
Aylburton GL15 ....147 E4
Bredon GL20 ....182 D7
Bretforton WR11 ....188 A6
Bristol,Kingswood BS15 ....10 E8
Bristol,Westbury on Trym
BS9 ....17 F5
Charfield GL12 ....67 A5
Clearwell GL16 ....154 F3
Dursley GL11 ....87 F5
English Bicknor GL16 .....163 A2
Gloucester GL2 ....126 E5
Hardwicke GL2 ....109 D7
Kemble GL7 ....141 F8
Keynsham BS31 ....4 D6
King's Stanley GL10 ....98 B3
Lea HR9 ....164 C8
Lechlade on T GL7 ....153 D2
Leonard Stanley GL10 .....97 F4
Mickleton GL55 ....189 B7
Mitcheldean GL17 ....164 D5
Winterbourne BS36 ....30 E5
Woodcroft NP16 ....73 A4
Yate BS37 ....43 F2
Orchard Cotts
10 Bristol BS16 ....20 D5
Chipping Campden GL55 ..189 C2
Orchard Cres BS11 ....16 D7
Orchard Ct Bristol BS9 ....17 C3
Bristol,Filton BS34 ....29 A2
19 Bristol,Pile Marsh BS5 ...9 D7
3 Monmouth/Trefynwy
NP25 ....154 A7
Painswick GL6 ....103 F8
Stonehouse GL10 ....97 E7
Tewkesbury GL20 ....192 D4
Orchard Ct *continued*
Yate BS37 ....43 B3
Orchard Dr Aust BS35 .....49 A7
Bristol BS13 ....2 A6
Churchdown GL3 ....128 D4
Twyning GL20 ....182 A7
Orchard End
Apperley GL19 ....173 C7
Monmouth/Trefynwy
NP25 ....154 A7
Orchard Farm Cl NP16 ...61 B7
Orchard Field GL8 ......140 B8
Orchard Gate
Blakeney GL15 ....156 D2
Bristol BS32 ....40 C2
Orchard Gdns BS15 ......10 F8
Orchard Gr The GL51 ...129 D1
Orchard Grange BS35 ....64 B2
Orchard Ho 2 Bristol BS5 ...9 F8
Cirencester GL7 ....190 D5
Orchard Ind Est GL54 ...184 A3
Orchard La
Brimscombe GL5 ....99 F1
Bristol BS1 ....194 C2
Ledbury HR8 ....178 E8
Orchard Lea
6 Alveston BS35 ....51 A5
Pill BS20 ....16 D4
Orchard Leaze GL11 .....87 D4
Orchard Mead
Nailsworth GL6 ....91 B4
Painswick GL6 ....103 F7
Orchard Pk
Cheltenham GL51 ....132 F5
Gloucester GL3 ....120 A6
Twigworth GL2 ....173 A1
Orchard Pk The GL19 ...173 C6
Orchard Pl
4 Ledbury HR8 ....178 F7
Stonehouse GL10 ....97 E7
Orchard Rd
Alderton GL20 ....183 E4
Bishop's Cleeve GL52 .....137 F3
Bishop's Cleeve,Brockhampton
GL52 ....137 E1
Bristol,Ashley Down BS7 ...18 E4
Bristol,Crew's Hole BS5 .....9 F8
Bristol,Kingswood BS15 ....10 E8
Coalpit Heath BS36 ....31 D7
Coleford GL16 ....155 A6
Gloucester GL2 ....127 E4
Joy's Green GL17 ....163 D3
Lydney GL15 ....92 B2
Newent GL18 ....171 A7
Pucklechurch BS16 ....22 B5
Stroud GL5 ....98 C6
Winchcombe GL54 ....139 F6
Orchard Ridge GL20 ....180 F7
Orchard Rise
Chepstow/Cas-Gwent NP16 .60 B5
Dursley GL11 ....87 F3
Longborough GL56 ....176 D8
Newnham GL14 ....156 F6
Olveston BS35 ....50 A3
Tibberton GL19 ....171 E1
Orchard Springs GL6 .....91 A4
Orchard Sq BS5 ....9 D7
Orchard St Bristol BS1 ...194 C2
Wotton-u-E GL12 ....68 B7
Orchard The Bristol BS34 ..29 F5
Clapton-on-t-H GL54 .....168 F4
13 Fairford GL7 ....152 E4
Frampton Cotterell BS36 ....31 C8
North Cerney GL7 ....158 D3
Oaksey SN16 ....141 F4
Pill BS20 ....16 C4
Tewkesbury GL20 ....192 D5
Tytherington GL12 ....52 B5
Uckington GL51 ....132 D7
Uley GL11 ....89 B1
Woolaston GL15 ....147 C3
Orchard Vale BS15 ....10 F7
Orchard View
Draycott GL56 ....186 E6
Stroud GL5 ....99 A4
Orchard Villas GL10 .....98 C3
Orchard Way
17 Berry Hill GL16 ....155 A7
Cheltenham GL51 ....132 F3
Churchdown GL3 ....128 B7
Huntley GL19 ....165 D6
Kingham OX7 ....177 F2
Maisemore GL2 ....126 A7
Orchard Wlk GL12 ....67 F4
Orchards The
Bristol,Kingswood BS15 ....10 F7
Bristol,Shirehampton BS11 ..16 E6
Charlton Kings GL52 ......131 C6
Gloucester GL3 ....120 A6
Longhope GL17 ....164 F6
Lydney GL15 ....92 A3
Orchid Mdw NP16 ....60 B5
Organ's Alley GL1 ......196 B2
Oridge St GL19 ....172 A6
Oriel Gr GL56 ....187 A2
Oriel Rd GL50 ....193 B3
Oriole Way GL4 ....119 D6
Orion Dr BS34 ....29 D6
Orland Way BS30 ....11 A3
Orlebar Gdns BS11 ......27 B2
Orlham La HR8 ....178 D6
Ormerod Rd Bristol BS9 ...17 E5
Sedbury NP16 ....61 B7
Ormond Pl GL50 ....193 B3
Ormond Terr GL50 ......193 B3

Ormonds Cl BS32 ... 40 E1
Ormsley Cl BS34 ... 29 C8
Orpen Gdns BS7 ... 19 B5
Orpen Pk BS32 ... 40 B3
Orpheus Ave BS34 ... 29 D6
Orrisdale Terr GL53 ... 193 C2
Orwell Dr BS31 ... 5 A4
Orwell St BS3 ... 8 E3
Osborne Ave Bristol BS7 ... 18 F3
Gloucester GL4 ... 118 C1
Osborne Cl BS34 ... 29 D4
Osborne Gdns GL20 ... 192 D4
Osborne Rd
Bristol,Clifton BS8 ... 18 A1
Bristol,Southville BS3 ... 8 C4
Severn Beach BS35 ... 38 A7
Osborne Terr
10 Bristol BS3 ... 8 B2
Thrupp GL5 ... 99 E3
Osborne Villas BS2 ... 194 C4
Osborne Wallis Ho BS8 ... 194 A1
Osbourne Ho 6 GL50 ... 130 B8
Osier Cl GL4 ... 119 A4
Osprey Cl GL4 ... 119 D5
Osprey Ct BS14 ... 2 D5
Osprey Dr GL10 ... 97 F8
Osprey Pk BS35 ... 64 D3
Osprey Rd 15 Bristol BS5 ... 9 C7
Cheltenham GL53 ... 130 C5
Osric Rd GL1 ... 118 F6
Ossage GL54 ... 166 C6
Othello Cl GL51 ... 132 E2
Otter Rd GL4 ... 120 A5
Otterburn Ho GL2 ... 118 C4
Otterford Cl BS14 ... 3 B5
Otters Field GL54 ... 174 A8
Ottery Cl BS11 ... 27 A1
Ottrells Mead BS32 ... 40 C3
Our Lady of Lourdes RC Prim Sch BS15 ... 10 E7
Our Lady of the Rosary CR Prim Sch BS11 ... 17 A8
Our Lady of the Rosary Prim Sch BS11 ... 27 A1
Oval App GL2 ... 157 F3
Oval The
Frampton on Severn GL2 ... 100 A5
Gloucester GL1 ... 118 D6
Over Bridge* GL2 ... 126 B4
Over Cswy GL1 ... 126 C3
Over La BS35 ... 39 D2
Over Old Rd GL19,GL2 ... 172 C3
Overbrook Cl GL4 ... 127 C1
Overbrook Dr GL52 ... 133 F3
Overbrook Rd GL2 ... 109 E7
Overbury CE Fst Sch GL20 ... 182 F8
Overbury Rd GL1 ... 119 A8
Overbury St GL53 ... 131 A7
Overhill BS20 ... 16 D4
Overhill Rd GL7 ... 190 B8
Overley Rd GL7 ... 149 E7
Overndale Rd BS16 ... 20 C6
Overndale Sch BS37 ... 34 A7
Overnhill Ct BS16 ... 20 D5
Overnhill Rd BS16 ... 20 D5
Overnhurst Ct 2 BS16 ... 20 D5
Overton 5 BS4 ... 9 D1
Overton Ct GL50 ... 193 A3
Overton La GL2 ... 157 E5
Overton Park Rd GL50 ... 193 A3
Overton Rd Bristol BS6 ... 18 E2
Cheltenham GL50 ... 193 A3
Owen Gdns 1 GL16 ... 155 A6
Owen Gr BS9 ... 18 B5
Owen Henry Ho BS2 ... 19 A1
Owen St 18 BS5 ... 9 B8
Owl Cl GL4 ... 119 D5
Owlpen Manor & Gdns* GL11 ... 89 E1
Owls End Rd GL52 ... 138 A4
Owls Eye Cl 4 GL16 ... 155 B6
Owls Head Rd BS15 ... 10 E6
Ox Yd GL7 ... 149 B1
Oxbarton BS34 ... 29 F5
Oxbutts Cvn Pk GL52 ... 138 B4
Oxbutts Ind Est GL52 ... 138 B4
Oxebode The GL1 ... 196 B3
Oxen Leaze BS32 ... 40 E2
Oxford Cl 1 GL52 ... 130 F8
Oxford Ho GL7 ... 190 D4
Oxford Pas GL50 ... 193 B4
Oxford Pl
19 Bristol,Clifton BS8 ... 7 F6
14 Bristol,Upper Easton BS5 ... 19 B1
Oxford Rd GL1 ... 196 C4
Oxford St Bristol BS2 ... 195 C2
7 Bristol,Redfield BS5 ... 9 C7
Bristol,The Dings BS2 ... 9 A6
Bristol,Tyndall's Park BS2 ... 194 C4
Bristol,Windmill Hill BS3 ... 8 F4
Cheltenham GL52 ... 130 F8
10 Chepstow/Cas-Gwent NP16 ... 60 E8
Gloucester GL1 ... 196 C3
Lydney GL15 ... 92 A2
Moreton-in-M GL56 ... 187 A3
Oxford Terr
Gloucester GL1 ... 196 C3
Stroud GL5 ... 99 C8
Oxford Way GL51 ... 130 A6
Oxford Wlk 2 GL52 ... 130 F8
Oxhouse Gdns BS10 ... 27 E3
Oxleaze BS13 ... 2 D4
Oxleaze Cl 4 GL8 ... 140 B4
Oxleaze La BS41 ... 1 E3
Oxleaze Rd Culkerton GL8 ... 140 F6
7 Tetbury GL8 ... 140 B4
Oxmead Cl GL52 ... 138 B4
Oxmoor GL4 ... 119 E3
Oxpens GL54 ... 167 D1
Oxstalls Com Sch GL1 ... 127 A4
Oxstalls Dr GL2 ... 127 A5
Oxstalls La GL2 ... 127 B4
Oxstalls Way GL2 ... 127 B4
Ozleworth BS15 ... 11 A8

P

Packer's Rd GL14 ... 191 D4
Packhorse La GL7 ... 160 A1
Pacquet Ho BS20 ... 16 D5
Paddock Cl Bristol BS32 ... 40 E2
Bristol,Emerson's Green BS16 ... 21 C6
Paddock Gdn BS14 ... 2 F4
Paddock Gdns
Alveston BS35 ... 51 A5
Gloucester GL2 ... 127 D5
Paddock Rise GL10 ... 97 F8
Paddock The
Chepstow/Cas-Gwent NP16 ... 60 D6
Cirencester GL7 ... 190 E4
Coleford GL16 ... 155 B6
Highworth SN6 ... 145 D3
17 Ledbury HR8 ... 178 E8
South Cerney GL7 ... 142 F7
Paddocks La GL50 ... 133 D5
Paddocks The
Baunton GL7 ... 150 D7
Bristol BS16 ... 31 A1
Highnam GL2 ... 125 D5
Thornbury BS35 ... 64 D1
Paddocks The/Y Padggau 6 NP25 ... 154 A7
Padin Cl 3 GL6 ... 148 C6
Padmore Ct 7 BS5 ... 9 D7
Padstow Rd BS4 ... 2 F8
Pady Ct GL7 ... 190 C3
Paganhill Est GL5 ... 98 F8
Paganhill La GL5 ... 98 F7
Page Ct BS16 ... 20 F4
Page Rd BS16 ... 20 D4
Page's La GL20 ... 181 F7
Pages Mead BS11 ... 16 C8
Paget Ho GL7 ... 190 D5
Pagets Rd GL52 ... 138 A2
Painswick Ave BS34 ... 29 B8
Painswick Dr BS37 ... 43 E1
Painswick Hts GL6 ... 104 A6
Painswick Lodge 2 GL4 ... 119 C4
Painswick Old Rd GL6 ... 103 C1
Painswick Rd
Cheltenham GL50 ... 193 A1
Gloucester GL4 ... 119 C4
Stroud GL6 ... 103 B2
Watermead GL3 ... 120 D3
Painswick Rococo Gdn* GL6 ... 111 E2
Pakistan Ho 1 GL51 ... 132 E2
Palestra Lo GL7 ... 190 C5
Palm Rd GL20 ... 192 E2
Palmdale Cl BS30 ... 11 A3
Palmer Ave
Gloucester GL4 ... 119 F5
Severn Beach BS35 ... 38 C3
Palmers Cl BS30 ... 11 A6
Palmers Leaze BS34 ... 30 A6
Palmerston Rd BS6 ... 18 C4
Palmerston St 6 BS3 ... 8 C3
Palmyra Rd BS3 ... 8 B2
Pancake La GL19 ... 173 E5
Panoramic The BS1 ... 194 C3
Pantile The 8 BS3 ... 8 C3
Paper Mill Cotts OX18 ... 161 E7
Parabola Cl GL50 ... 193 A3
Parabola La GL50 ... 193 A3
Parabola Rd GL50 ... 193 A3
Parade Ct BS5 ... 19 F2
Parade The Bristol BS34 ... 39 F1
Bristol,Bishopsworth BS13 ... 2 A6
Bristol,Shirehampton BS11 ... 16 E6
Brockworth GL3 ... 120 E5
Chipping Sodbury BS37 ... 44 A1
Gloucester GL2 ... 127 E4
Paradise Row GL54 ... 167 E2
Paragon Terr GL53 ... 193 B2
Paragon The BS8 ... 7 F6
Parawell La GL15 ... 147 C8
Parbrook Ct BS14 ... 3 B5
Parfitt's Hill 8 BS5 ... 9 F6
Parish The BS3 ... 194 B1
Park Ave Bristol BS32 ... 40 A2
Bristol,Eastville BS5 ... 19 D3
Bristol,Rose Green BS5 ... 9 E8
Bristol,Windmill Hill BS3 ... 8 E3
Frampton Cotterell BS36 ... 31 B6
Gloucester GL2 ... 127 C5
Highworth SN6 ... 145 D3
Winterbourne BS36 ... 30 E7
Park Brake GL2 ... 125 D4
Park Cl
Bristol,Cadbury Heath BS30 ... 11 B5
Bristol,Kingswood BS15 ... 10 E7
Fairford GL7 ... 152 E4
Keynsham BS31 ... 4 D5
Northway GL20 ... 182 B5
St Briavels GL15 ... 146 F7
8 Tetbury GL8 ... 140 C4
Park Cres
Bristol,Cadbury Heath BS30 ... 11 B5
Bristol,Frenchay BS16 ... 30 C1
Bristol,Rose Green BS5 ... 9 E8
Park Ct Lydney GL15 ... 92 A3
Stroud GL5 ... 99 D6
Park Dr GL2 ... 117 F1
Park End 1 SN6 ... 142 F4
Park End Rd GL1 ... 196 B1
Park Farm GL54 ... 168 F8
Park Farm Ct 13 BS30 ... 10 F4
Park Farm Village Gn BS36 ... 31 B6
Park Gate
Cheltenham GL50 ... 193 A1
Redmarley D'Abitot GL19 ... 179 E2
Park Glade NP16 ... 146 B4
Park Gr Bristol BS9 ... 18 C5
Whitecroft GL15 ... 155 E1
Park Hill Bristol BS11 ... 16 F6
Whitecroft GL15 ... 155 E1
Park Hill Comm GL15 ... 147 A2
Park Hill La NP16,GL15 ... 146 E2
Park Hill Rd
Tidenham Chase GL15 ... 146 F2
Woolaston GL15 ... 147 A2
Park Ho GL50 ... 193 A1
Park Inf Sch The GL10 ... 97 E7
Park Jun Sch GL10 ... 97 E7
Park La Bristol BS2 ... 194 C3
Brockhampton GL54 ... 174 A1
Cheltenham GL52 ... 134 B6
Cirencester GL7 ... 190 C4
Frampton Cotterell BS36 ... 31 B6
Ilmington CV36 ... 189 E7
North Nibley GL11 ... 79 E7
Woodchester GL5 ... 90 F6
Wotton-u-E GL12 ... 69 A8
Park Leaze BS34 ... 39 E1
Park Mews GL50 ... 130 C6
Park Par GL10 ... 97 E8
Park Pl
5 Ashton Keynes SN6 ... 142 F5
Bristol,Tyndall's Park BS2 ... 194 C3
Bristol,Upper Eastville BS5 ... 19 E3
Bristol,Victoria Park BS8 ... 194 B3
Cheltenham GL50 ... 193 A1
Park Prim Sch The BS15 ... 10 E8
Park Rd Berry Hill GL16 ... 155 A7
Blockley GL56 ... 186 C6
Bristol,Brandon Hill BS3 ... 194 B1
Bristol,Cadbury Heath BS30 ... 11 B5
Bristol,Kingswood BS15 ... 10 D8
Bristol,Northville BS7 ... 29 A1
Bristol,Shirehampton BS11 ... 16 F6
Bristol,Staple Hill BS16 ... 20 E5
Bristol,Stapleton BS16 ... 19 D5
Chipping Campden GL55 ... 188 F1
6 Coleford GL16 ... 155 A6
Gloucester GL1 ... 196 B2
Highleadon GL19 ... 171 F2
Keynsham BS31 ... 4 E4
Leyhill GL12 ... 66 B4
Nailsworth GL6 ... 91 C3
Stonehouse GL10 ... 97 E8
Stroud GL5 ... 99 D6
Thornbury BS35 ... 64 B2
Park Road Cres GL6 ... 91 C3
Park Row Aylburton GL15 ... 147 D4
Bristol BS1 ... 194 C3
Frampton Cotterell BS36 ... 31 A8
Park St
Bristol,Brandon Hill BS1 ... 194 C3
Bristol,Crew's Hole BS5 ... 9 F8
Bristol,Totterdown BS4 ... 9 A3
Cheltenham GL50 ... 193 A4
Cirencester GL7 ... 190 C5
Fairford GL7 ... 152 E4
Gloucester GL1 ... 196 B3
Hawkesbury Upton GL9 ... 56 A2
Iron Acton BS37 ... 42 D4
Stow-on-t-W GL54 ... 176 F4
Park Street Ave BS1 ... 194 C3
Park Terr GL6 ... 91 F6
Park The Bristol BS32 ... 40 C3
Bristol,Frenchay BS16 ... 30 B1
Bristol,Kingswood BS15 ... 10 E8
Bristol,Willsbridge BS30 ... 11 B1
Cheltenham GL50 ... 130 B6
Keynsham BS31 ... 4 E6
Northway GL20 ... 182 B5
Stow-on-t-W GL54 ... 176 F4
Park View
Bristol,Kingswood BS15 ... 10 E7
Bristol,Southville BS3 ... 8 C4
Cheltenham GL51 ... 132 E4
Chepstow/Cas-Gwent NP16 ... 72 C1
4 Gloucester GL4 ... 119 C4
Ruardean GL17 ... 163 F4
Saul GL2 ... 157 F4
Sedbury NP16 ... 61 B8
Stratton GL7 ... 190 B8
Yate BS37 ... 32 E8
Park View Ave BS35 ... 64 C2
Park View Ct BS16 ... 20 E5
Park View Dr GL5 ... 98 E8
Park View Rd GL13 ... 85 D3
Park View Terr BS5 ... 9 E8
Park Way BS30 ... 11 B5
Park Wood Cl BS14 ... 2 F4
Parkbury Cl GL51 ... 133 A2
Parkend Prim Sch GL15 ... 155 F2
Parkend Rd Bream GL15 ... 155 D1
Coleford GL16 ... 155 B5
Yorkley GL15 ... 156 A2
Parkend Sta* GL15 ... 155 E3
Parkend Wlk
Coleford GL16 ... 155 B5
Sling GL16 ... 155 B3
Parker Pl 1 WR12 ... 185 B8
Parker St 5 BS3 ... 8 B3
Parkers Ave BS30 ... 12 C7
Parkers Barton BS5 ... 9 B6
Parkers Cl BS10 ... 28 E4
Parkers La GL56 ... 187 A3
Parkfield Ave 3 BS5 ... 9 D7
Parkfield Cotts GL6 ... 112 A2
Parkfield Rank BS16 ... 22 A7
Parkfield Rd BS16 ... 22 A6
Parkhouse La BS31 ... 4 C2
Parkhurst Ave 4 BS16 ... 20 B4
Parkland Mews 26 GL54 ... 176 F4
Parkland Rd
Cheltenham GL53 ... 130 F4
Dursley GL11 ... 87 F4
Parkland Sq GL7 ... 190 B2
Parkland Way BS35 ... 64 C3
Parklands
Bristol,High Kingsdown BS8 ... 194 C4
Bristol,Kingswood BS15 ... 10 E8
Churchdown GL3 ... 128 A6
Quedgeley GL2 ... 117 F1
Wotton-u-E GL12 ... 68 B8
Quedgeley GL2 ... 109 E8
Parklands Cl NP16 ... 60 B4
Parklands Rd BS3 ... 7 E4
Parkmill HR9 ... 162 C7
Parks Rd GL17 ... 164 D5
Parkside GL16 ... 155 A5
Parkside Ave BS36 ... 30 E6
Parkside Cl GL3 ... 127 F6
Parkside Dr GL3 ... 127 F6
Parkside Gdns BS5 ... 19 B4
Parkstone Ave BS7 ... 18 F6
Parkwall Cres BS30 ... 10 F4
Parkwall Prim Sch BS30 ... 11 A4
Parkwall Rd BS30 ... 11 A4
Parkway Bristol BS34 ... 30 A4
Siddington GL7 ... 150 D2
Parkway N BS34 ... 30 A4
Parkway Trad Est 10 BS2 ... 18 F2
Parkwood Cres GL3 ... 119 F6
Parkwood Gr GL53 ... 131 A4
Parliament Cl GL5 ... 99 C7
Parliament Prim Sch GL5 ... 99 F7
Parliament St Bristol BS4 ... 9 A4
Gloucester GL1 ... 196 B2
Stroud GL5 ... 99 D7
Parnall Cres BS37 ... 43 C2
Parnall Rd BS16 ... 20 A3
Parnall Road Ind Est BS16 ... 20 A3
Parnell Rd BS16 ... 19 E7
Parr Cl GL3 ... 127 F7
Parr Ho GL54 ... 139 F5
Parragate GL14 ... 191 D5
Parragate Rd GL14 ... 191 C5
Parry Rd GL1 ... 118 F6
Parry's Cl BS9 ... 17 E5
Parry's La BS9 ... 17 F5
Parrys Gr BS9 ... 17 E5
Parslow Barton 4 BS5 ... 10 A7
Parson St BS3 ... 8 B2
Parson Street Prim Sch BS3 ... 8 C2
Parson Street Sta BS3 ... 8 B2
Parson's Cnr GL54 ... 176 F5
Parsonage Farm 3 SN6 ... 143 E4
Parsonage Rd BS41 ... 7 C2
Parsonage St GL11 ... 88 A1
Parsons Ave BS34 ... 29 F5
Parsons Ct GL6 ... 148 A3
Parsons La
Redmarley D'Abitot GL19 ... 179 F2
Weston-s-E GL55 ... 188 D3
Parsons Paddock BS14 ... 3 A7
Parsons Wlk BS30 ... 11 D7
Partition St BS1 ... 194 C2
Parton Dr GL3 ... 128 C5
Parton Manor Inf Sch GL3 ... 128 B6
Parton Mews GL3 ... 128 B6
Parton Rd GL3 ... 128 C6
Partridge Cl
Gloucester GL2 ... 118 C5
Stonehouse GL10 ... 97 F8
Yate BS37 ... 43 F4
Partridge Dr BS16 ... 20 C6
Partridge Rd BS16 ... 22 C4
Partridge Way GL7 ... 190 E4
Parva Springs NP16 ... 146 B4
Passage Leaze BS11 ... 16 D6
Passage Rd
Arlingham GL2 ... 157 B6
Aust BS35 ... 48 F7
Bristol,Brentry BS10 ... 27 F3
Bristol,Westbury on Trym BS9 ... 18 A8
Saul GL2 ... 157 F4
Passage Road Brentry Hill BS9,BS10 ... 28 A2
Passage St BS2 ... 195 B2
Pastor's Hill GL15 ... 147 D8
Pasture La GL56 ... 186 C5
Patch Ct BS16 ... 21 A8
Patch Elm La BS37 ... 42 F7
Patch La BS37 ... 43 A8
Patches The GL17 ... 163 F3
Patchway BS34 ... 29 B8
Patchway Brook BS32 ... 40 C2
Patchway CE Prim Sch BS34 ... 40 C1
Patchway High Sch BS32 ... 40 B1
Patchway Sta BS34 ... 29 C
Patchway Trad Est BS34 ... 28 E
Paternoster Sch GL7 ... 190 D
Paterson Rd GL7 ... 190 E
Pates Ave GL51 ... 133 B
Pates Gram Sch GL51 ... 132 E
Patseamur Mews GL2 ... 127 E
Patterdale Cl GL51 ... 132 F
Patterson Ho 8 BS1 ... 195 B
Paul Mead GL6 ... 111 B
Paul St Bristol BS2 ... 194 C
Gloucester GL1 ... 118 F
Paul's Rise GL5 ... 99 A
Pauls Croft SN6 ... 143 F
Pauls Wlk GL19 ... 165 D
Paulton Dr BS7 ... 18 C
Paultow Ave BS3 ... 8 E
Paultow Rd BS3 ... 8 E
Pauntley CE Prim Sch GL18 ... 171 B
Pauntley Court Dr GL19 ... 171 C
Pavey Cl BS13 ... 2 C
Pavey Rd BS13 ... 2 C
Pavilion Bsns Pk GL14 ... 191 B
Pavilion Gdns GL50 ... 130 C
Pavilion Rd NP16 ... 61 C
Pavilions The Bristol BS4 ... 9 C
Cheltenham GL53 ... 193 B
Pawlett Rd BS13 ... 2 C
Pawlett Wlk BS13 ... 2 C
Paxford Rd GL55 ... 189 B
Paxhill La GL20 ... 182 A
Paxton BS16 ... 19 E
Paybridge Rd BS13 ... 1 F
Paygrove La GL2 ... 127 D
Payne Dr BS5 ... 9 B
Paynes Mdw GL2 ... 100 F
Paynes Orchard Pk BS10 ... 28 D
Paynes Pitch GL3 ... 128 D
Peach Cl GL20 ... 192 E
Peach Cotts GL20 ... 192 E
Peache Ct BS16 ... 20 E
Peache Rd BS16 ... 20 F
Peacock Cl
5 Cheltenham GL51 ... 132 D
Gloucester GL4 ... 119 E
5 Newent GL18 ... 171 A
Peacock Gdns 6 GL18 ... 171 A
Peacock La GL14 ... 191 C
Peacocks La BS15 ... 10 C
Peak La GL11 ... 89 A
Peakstile Piece GL52 ... 138 B
Pear Orch The GL20 ... 182 C
Pear Tree Cl
Chipping Campden GL55 ... 189 A
Hardwicke GL2 ... 109 E
Lower Swell GL54 ... 176 D
32 Winchcombe GL54 ... 174 A
Woodmancote GL52 ... 138 C
Pear Tree Hey BS37 ... 43 E
Pear Tree Rd BS32 ... 40 C
Pearce Way GL2 ... 118 B
Pearces Hill BS16 ... 20 B
Pearcroft Rd GL10 ... 98 A
Pearl St BS3 ... 8 B
Pearsall Rd BS30 ... 10 E
Peart Cl Bristol BS13 ... 1 E
Gloucester GL1 ... 127 B
Peart Dr BS13 ... 1 E
Peartree Cl BS13 ... 2 B
Peartree La
Bristol,Lower Soundwell BS15 ... 20 F
Bristol,St George BS5 ... 10 B
Pearwood Way GL4 ... 118 C
Peashill Cnr GL54 ... 176 B
Pecked La GL52 ... 138 A
Peel Cl GL53 ... 131 C
Peel Ctr The GL1 ... 196 A
Peel St BS5 ... 195 C
Peg Hill BS37 ... 43 F
Pegasus Bldg GL2 ... 118 A
Pegasus Ct
Bourton-on-t-W GL54 ... 169 A
12 Broadway WR12 ... 185 B
Cheltenham GL51 ... 130 B
Gloucester GL4 ... 127 E
Pegasus Gdns GL2 ... 117 F
Pegasus Pk BS34 ... 29 C
Pegasus Rd BS34 ... 28 D
Peggotty Bglws GL4 ... 119 C
Peghouse Cl GL5 ... 103 D
Peghouse Rise GL5 ... 103 D
Pelham Cres GL3 ... 128 A
Pemberton Ct BS16 ... 20 C
Pembery Rd BS3 ... 8 B
Pembridge Cl GL52 ... 131 C
Pembridge Ct GL50 ... 193 A
Pembroke Ave BS11 ... 16 E
Pembroke Gate BS8 ... 18 A
Pembroke Gr BS8 ... 194 A
Pembroke Mans BS8 ... 194 A
Pembroke Pl
Bristol,Hotwells BS8 ... 194 A
Bristol,St Pauls BS1 ... 195 B
Pembroke Prim Sch NP16 ... 60 E
Pembroke Rd
Bristol,Clifton BS8 ... 194 A
Bristol,Kingswood BS15 ... 20 E
Bristol,Shirehampton BS11 ... 16 E
Bristol,Southville BS3 ... 8 C
Cheltenham GL51 ... 129 E
Chepstow/Cas-Gwent NP16 ... 60 E
Pembroke St Bristol BS2 ... 195 B
Cinderford GL14 ... 191 D
Gloucester GL1 ... 196 C
Pembroke Vale BS8 ... 194 A

embury GL50 ....193 A2
embury Rd GL4 ......118 E4
en Park Rd BS10 .....28 D2
en-Moel Cotts NP16 ..73 A4
enard Way BS15 ......10 F7
enby Lawn GL14 ....156 F6
enda Pl NP16 ....61 A8
endennis Ave BS16 ..20 D4
endennis Ho 5 BS16 ..20 D5
endennis Pk BS4 .....9 D2
endennis Rd BS16 ...20 D5
endill Cl GL50 ......133 B6
endock CE Prim Sch
  GL19 ....180 A4
endock Cl Bristol BS30 ..11 C1
  Quedgeley GL2 ....117 E1
endock Cross GL19 ..180 A3
endock Ct BS16 .....21 B7
endock Rd Bristol BS16 ..20 C6
  Winterbourne BS36 ..30 E5
enfield Cl BS2 ......19 A2
enfield Rd BS2 .....19 A2
enhall Cl GL51 .....133 A3
enhill Ho GL4 ......119 B5
enhill Rd GL4 .....119 B5
enlea Cl BS11 ......16 D7
enlea Ho BS11 .....16 D7
enmoel La NP16 ....73 A3
enmoyle Gdns NP16 ..73 A4
enn Dr BS16 ....30 C1
enn La GL10 ....98 B2
enn St BS1 ....195 B3
ennard Ct BS14 .....3 B5
enngrove BS30 .....11 A3
ennine Cl GL2 .....109 E8
ennine Rd Bristol BS30 ..11 C4
  Cheltenham GL52 ..134 B3
ennington Ct GL51 ..132 E4
enlea BS13 ....2 C7
ennon Rise BS1 ....194 C1
ennsylvania Ave GL51 ..132 F3
ennsylvania Mews
  GL51 ....132 F3
enny Cl GL2 ....127 D4
enny La GL2 ....95 B2
ennyroyal Gr BS16 ..19 E4
ennywell Ct 3 BS5 ..9 A8
ennywell Rd BS5 ...9 A8
enpole Ave BS11 ...16 E6
enpole Cl BS11 ....16 D7
enpole La BS11 ....16 E7
enpole Pk BS11 ...16 E7
enpole Pl BS11 ....16 E6
enrith Cl GL51 .....129 F7
enrith Gdns BS10 ..18 D8
enrith Rd BS10 ....16 A4
enrose BS14 ....2 F7
enrose Cl GL2 .....102 E3
enrose Dr BS32 ....29 D7
enrose Rd BS13 ...127 D6
ensford Ct BS14 ....3 D5
enside Rd GL6 .....91 D4
entagon The BS9 ...17 B5
entathlon Way GL50 ..133 D5
enterry La NP16 ...72 B7
enterry Pk NP16 ...60 D8
entire Ave BS13 ...2 A6
entland Ave BS35 ..51 E8
entwyn Cl NP16 ...60 B6
entwyns Cl SN6 ...145 C4
eppercorn Alley GL20 ..182 E8
epys Cl BS31 ....5 D2
erch Dr GL10 .....155 C6
ercival Rd
  Bishop's Cleeve GL52 ..137 E1
  Bristol BS8 ....7 F8
ercy St 8 Bristol BS3 ..8 D4
  Gloucester GL1 ...118 F7
ercy Walker Ct BS16 ..20 C6
eregrine Cl GL2 ...117 F3
eregrine Rd GL53 ..130 C5
errett Ho BS32 ...195 C3
errett Way BS20 ..16 E4
erretts Ct BS1 ....194 C1
erricks Cl GL4 ....165 D3
errinar Dr WR11 ..188 C2
errinpit Rd BS36 ..41 E2
errinsfield GL7 ...153 E3
errott Rd BS15 ....21 A1
erry Cl
  Charlton Kings GL53 ..131 B5
  28 Newent GL18 ..171 A4
  Winterbourne BS36 ..30 D4
erry Court Inf Sch BS14 ..3 A6
erry Court Jun Sch BS14 ..3 A6
erry Ctr The GL2 ..109 F6
erry Field GL15 ...147 C3
erry Hill GL20 ...192 C3
erry Orch Stroud GL5 ..98 D8
  Upton St Leonards GL4 ..119 E2
erry St BS5 ....9 A8
erry Way GL2 ....100 B3
erry's Court La GL17 ..163 E4
errycroft Ave BS13 ..2 A6
errycroft Rd BS13 ..2 A6
erryfield Cl 1 GL54 ..168 F7
errygrove Rd GL16 ..155 A4
errygrove Rly* GL16 ..155 B5
erryman La BS16 ...20 A6
erry's Lea BS32 ...40 D2
ersh La GL2 ......125 F6
ersh Way GL2 ....126 A7
erth GL10 ....101 E1
erwell Cl GL20 ...182 C8
esley Cl BS13 ......2 A4
ester Pennell Cl GL15 ..132 E4

Peter's St GL10 ......96 E3
Peter's Terr BS5 .....9 B7
Petercole Dr BS13 ...2 A6
Peters Field GL2 ...125 E5
Peterson Sq BS13 ...2 C3
Petersway Gdns BS5 ..10 A6
Petherbridge Way BS7 ..19 A5
Petherton Cl BS15 ..10 E7
Petherton Gdns BS14 ..3 B7
Petherton Rd BS14 ..3 B7
Petherton Road Inf Sch
  BS14 ....3 B7
Pethick Ho BS4 .....2 F8
Pettigrew Gdns BS15 ..10 E7
Pettigrove Rd BS15 ..10 E6
Petty La GL52 .....138 F3
Petty Marsh GL15 ..146 E6
Pettycroft GL17 ...163 F4
Petworth Cl GL4 ...110 C8
Pevelands GL11 ....87 F5
Pevensey Wlk BS4 ..2 D7
Peveril Cl BS10 ....27 F3
Peverell Dr BS10 ..27 F3
Peveril Ho GL2 ...118 C4
Peymans Terr GL7 ..142 F7
Pheasant La GL51 ..132 B1
Pheasant Mead GL10 ..97 F8
Pheasant Rise HR9 ..162 F7
Pheasant Way GL7 ..143 F8
Pheasantry The GL7 ..143 F8
Phelps Way GL19 ..171 E1
Philadelphia Ct BS1 ..195 B3
Philip St
  Bristol,St Philip's Marsh BS2 ..9 B5
  Bristol,Windmill Hill BS3 ..8 D4
  Gloucester GL1 ...118 D7
Philip's Cl GL15 ..156 B1
Philippa Cl BS14 ..3 A7
Philips Ho 2 BS2 ..195 B4
Phillimore Gdns GL2 ..100 A5
Phillimore Rd GL11 ..87 E4
Phillips La GL19 ..179 F2
Phillips Rd WR12 ..188 A1
Phippen St 1 BS1 ..195 B1
Phipps Barton BS15 ..10 B8
Phipps St BS3 ......8 A3
Phoenix Bsns Pk BS3 ..8 A2
Phoenix Ct GL18 ..155 A5
Phoenix Dr NP16 ..61 A4
Phoenix Gr BS6 ...18 C5
Phoenix Ho BS5 ...9 B6
Phoenix Trad Est GL5 ..199 E3
Phoenix Way GL7 ..190 C4
Piccadilly
  Guiting Power GL54 ..175 B3
  Stroud GL5 ....99 D7
Piccadilly Way GL52 ..134 D4
Picked Acre GL4 ..124 C2
Pickedmoor La BS35 ..63 E5
Pickering Cl GL53 ..130 C6
Pickering Rd GL53 ..130 C6
Picklenash Jun Sch
  GL18 ....170 F5
Pickwick Cl GL2 ..127 D3
Picton Ho GL7 ...190 D5
Picton La BS6 .....18 E1
Picton Mews 6 BS6 ..18 E1
Picton St BS6 ....18 E1
Piece Hedge GL54 ..168 F8
Piece The
  Churchdown GL3 ..128 D4
  Hatherop GL7 ....152 E7
Piercefield Ho GL2 ..72 C1
Piercefield Terr NP16 ..72 B5
Piermont Dr NP16 ..73 A2
Pigeon House Dr BS13 ..2 D4
Pigeon La GL20 ...183 A8
Pigott Ave BS13 ...2 A4
Pigs Cross GL18 ..170 C3
Pike Cnr WR12 ...188 B2
Pike Hill Rise GL54 ..167 B3
Pike House Cl 13 SN6 ..143 E4
Pike La GL6 ....91 B3
Pike Rd 9 Coleford GL16 ..155 A4
  Winstone GL7,GL53 ..115 A1
Pilemarsh BS5 .....9 D7
Pilford Ave GL53 ..130 E3
Pilford Ct GL53 ...130 E3
Pilford Rd GL53 ..130 E3
Pilgrim Ct 4 GL4 ..119 F6
Pilgrims Way
  Avonmouth BS11 ..16 C7
  Bristol BS10 ......20 D8
Pilgrims Wharf BS4 ..9 E7
Pilgrove Cl GL51 ..132 E5
Pilgrove Way GL51 ..132 E5
Pilkington Cl BS34 ..29 C3
Pill La GL56 ......187 F1
Pill Rd Abbots Leigh BS8 ..16 F1
  Abbots Leigh BS8 ..7 A8
Pill St BS20 ....16 D4
Pillcroft Cl GL3 ..121 A4
Pillcroft Rd GL3 ..121 A4
Pilley Cres GL53 ..130 D4
Pilley La GL53 ...130 D4
Pillingers Gdns BS6 ..18 B2
Pillingers Rd BS15 ..10 C7
Pillowell Com Prim Sch
  GL15 ....155 F1
Pillowell Dr GL12 ..117 E4
Pillowell Rd GL15 ..155 F1
Pillows Green Rd GL19 ..172 B8
Pilning Prim Sch BS35 ..38 E6
Pilning St BS35 ...39 C8
Pilning Sta BS35 ..38 F5

Pimpernel Mead BS32 ..29 E7
Pincoate GL2 .....125 D6
Pincot La GL6 ....103 D5
Pincots La GL12 ..54 B3
Pine Bank GL2 ...138 B4
Pine Cl
  Bishop's Cleeve GL52 ..138 B4
  Cheltenham GL52 ..131 A8
  Thornbury BS35 ...64 C1
Pine Crest Way 5 GL15 ..147 D8
Pine Ct BS31 ....4 C4
Pine Gr BS7 ....29 A1
Pine Grove Pl BS7 ..18 D3
Pine Halt GL54 ...166 C6
Pine Rd BS10 .....28 B3
Pine Ridge GL59 ..17 C4
Pine Tree Dr GL4 ..119 E8
Pine Tree Way GL15 ..156 C1
Pinecroft BS14 ....2 F7
Pinedale GL15 ...147 B3
Pinefield BS9 .....18 B7
Pineholt Gate GL3 ..120 B7
Pinemount Rd GL3 ..120 A7
Pinery Rd GL4 ...119 E7
Pines La BS35 .....50 D3
Ponting's Cl SN26 ..144 E1
Pines The
  Brimscombe GL6 ..148 B5
  Cheltenham GL50 ..193 A3
  Greet GL54 ....174 A8
Pinetrees GL53 ..130 D7
Pinetum Dr GL2 ..125 A3
Pineway GL4 .....119 B6
Pinewood Cl Bristol BS9 ..18 B7
  Cinderford GL14 ..191 C5
Pinewood Rd GL2 ..109 E8
Pinewood Way SN14 ..15 F7
Pinhay Rd BS13 ...2 B6
Pinkers Mead BS16 ..21 C6
Pinkhams Twist BS14 ..3 A5
Pinlocks GL4 ....119 E3
Pinnell Gr BS16 ..21 C7
Pinnells End La GL11 ..88 D8
Pintail Cl GL2 ...117 D1
Pioneer Pk BS4 ...9 C5
Pipe La BS1 ......194 C2
Piper Rd BS37 ....43 E3
Pipers Gr GL2 ...125 D5
Pippin Cl Gloucester GL4 ..120 A6
  Newent GL18 .....171 A4
Pippin Ct 8 BS30 ..10 F4
Pippins Rd GL20 ..182 C7
Pirton Cres GL3 ..128 B5
Pirton La GL3 ...128 B5
Pirton Mdw GL3 ..128 B5
Pitch & Pay La BS9 ..17 F3
Pitch & Pay Pk BS9 ..17 E3
Pitch La BS6 ......18 D1
Pitch The GL6 ...148 B5
Pitchcombe BS37 ..32 C7
Pitchcombe Gdns BS9 ..17 F7
Pitching Gn GL51 ..156 C2
Pithay Ct BS1 ...195 A3
Pithay The BS1 ..195 A3
Pitlochry GL53 ..133 F3
Pitman Pl GL12 ...68 C6
Pitman Rd GL51 ..132 E1
Pitt Ho GL52 ....133 F1
Pitt Mill Gdns GL3 ..120 A8
Pitt Rd BS7 ......18 E5
Pitt St GL1 ......196 B3
Pittsfield SN6 ...143 E4
Pittville Cir GL52 ..133 F2
Pittville Circus Rd GL52 ..133 F2
Pittville Cl BS35 ..64 C3
Pittville Cres GL52 ..133 F3
Pittville Crescent La
  GL52 ....133 F3
Pittville Ct GL52 ..133 F3
Pittville Lawn GL52 ..133 F3
Pittville Mews GL52 ..133 F2
Pittville Pump Room & Mus*
  GL52 ....133 F2
Pittville St GL52 ..193 C4
Pittville Terr GL52 ..133 F2
Pixash Bsns Ctr BS31 ..5 B5
Pixash La BS31 ...5 C5
Place Hill GL18 ..170 C4
Plain The Stroud GL6 ..103 A2
  Thornbury BS35 ...64 B1
Plantation Cres GL20 ..182 C7
Plantation The
  Gloucester GL4 ...119 C6
  Hardwicke GL2 ...119 C6
Platts Row GL17 ..164 D5
Players Ct BS16 ...30 B3
Playford Gdns BS11 ..16 C7
Playhouse Ct GL15 ..147 D8
Playhouse The* GL50 ..193 B3
Pleasant Ho GL3 ..120 A8
Pleasant Rd BS16 ..20 D3
Pleasant Stile GL14 ..156 F7
Pleydells 16 SN6 ..143 E4
Pleydells The GL7 ..151 B5
Plies The GL7 ...143 F8
Plimsoll Ho
  3 Bristol BS1 ....195 B1
  Bristol,Woolcott Park BS6 ..18 B1
Plock Ct GL2 .....18 B1
Ploughmans Way GL20 ..109 C6
Plover Cl BS37 ...43 C2
Plowright Ho 8 BS15 ..10 F8
Pludds Court Rd GL17 ..163 B3
Plum Tree GL4 ..119 E4

Plummer's Hill BS5 ..9 E8
Plumpton Ct BS16 ..30 F1
Pochard Cl GL2 ..117 D1
Pockhill La GL54 ..168 F7
Poden La GL55 ...188 E4
Podsmead Pl GL1 ..118 D5
Podsmead Rd GL1 ..118 D5
Poets' Cl BS5 ......9 D8
Point Rd GL8 ....140 B8
Polar Gdns SN14 ..47 E4
Polden Ho BS3 ....8 D3
Polefield Gdns GL51 ..130 B8
Polefield Ho 18 GL51 ..130 B8
Pollards La GL1 ..156 D1
Polly Barnes Cl 6 BS15 ..10 B5
Polly Barnes Hill BS15 ..10 B5
Polygon Rd BS8 ..194 A2
Polygon The
  Avonmouth BS11 ..26 D1
  18 Bristol BS8 ...7 F6
Pomfrett Gdns BS14 ..3 E5
Pomphrey Hill BS16 ..21 C4
Pond La SN6 .....143 D1
Ponsford Rd BS4 ..9 B1
Ponting Cl BS5 ...20 A1
Ponting's Cl SN26 ..144 E1
Pool Cl GL56 ....187 F1
Pool Cnr BS32 ...50 B2
Pool Ho BS34 ....29 A8
Pool La NP25 ...175 D6
Pool Meadow Cvn Pk
  GL1 ....126 C3
Pool Rd BS15 ....20 E3
Poole Court Dr BS37 ..43 E2
Poole Ground GL2 ..125 D6
Poole St BS11 ...16 B8
Poole Way GL50 ..193 A4
Pooles La GL5 ...98 E4
Pooles Wharf BS8 ..194 A1
Pooles Wharf Ct BS8 ..194 A1
Poolhay Cl GL19 ..180 E1
Poolway Ct 1 GL16 ..155 A5
Poolway Ho GL16 ..155 A6
Poolway Rd GL16 ..155 B6
Poolway Rise 8 GL16 ..155 A6
Pope's Cl GL7 ...190 A8
Pope's Ct GL7 ...153 A1
Pope's Cl GL50 ..133 D3
Poplar Ave BS9 ..17 D6
Poplar Cl Bristol BS30 ..118 D5
Gloucester GL1 ..118 D5
Poplar Cres GL2 ..138 B4
Poplar Dr
  Pucklechurch BS16 ..22 B5
  Woodmancote GL52 ..138 C3
Poplar Fields BS30 ..11 B6
Poplar Gardens Ho BS15 ..10 B5
Poplar La GL12 ...54 B4
Poplar Pl BS16 ...20 A3
Poplar Rd
  Bristol,Hanham BS15 ..10 A5
  Bristol,Highridge BS13 ..1 F7
  Bristol,North Common BS30 ..11 D6
  Bristol,Speedwell BS5 ..19 F7
Poplar Rdbt BS15 ..26 E5
Poplar Terr BS15 ..10 A5
Poplar Way Colerne SN14 ..15 F5
  Hardwicke GL2 ...109 E2
Poplar Way E BS11 ..26 F5
Poplar Way W BS11 ..26 F6
Poplars Cl GL55 ..156 F1
Poplars Pk BS37 ..95 F3
Poplars The
  Cheltenham GL51 ..129 C5
  Easton-in-G BS20 ..16 D7
Poppy Field GL54 ..125 E6
Poppy Mead BS32 ..29 E7
Porchester Rd GL3 ..119 F7
Porlock Rd BS3 ...8 D2
Port Elizabeth Ho BS10 ..28 B3
Port Ind Est GL1 ..99 F1
Port La GL1 .....99 F1
Port Side Cl 5 BS5 ..9 F6
Port Terr GL1 ...99 F1
Port View BS20 ..16 C5
Port Wall* NP16 ..160 B8
Portbury Gr BS11 ..16 D6
Portbury Wlk BS11 ..16 D6
Portishead Way BS3 ..7 F2
Portland Cl Bristol BS21 ..194 B1
  Bristol,Upper Soundwell
  BS16 ....20 D3
Portland Lofts BS2 ..195 A4
Portland Mans BS2 ..195 B4
Portland Pl Bristol BS16 ..20 D3
  18 Cheltenham GL52 ..193 C4
Portland Sq Bristol BS2 ..195 B4
Portland St Bristol BS2 ..195 A4
Portman Terr GL52 ..193 B1
Portmeirion Cl BS14 ..3 B5
Portview Rd BS11 ..16 B8
Portway 2 BS11 ..131 B6
Portview Rd BS11 ..16 B8
Portwall La BS1 ..195 B1
Portwall La E 10 BS1 ..195 B1
Portway
  Bristol,Shirehampton BS11 ..16 C6
  Bristol,Sneyd Park BS8 ..17 C4
  Upton St Leonards GL4 ..112 B7
Portway Com Sch BS11 ..16 B8
Portway La BS37 ..44 F2
Portway Rdbt BS11 ..16 C8
Portwell 4 SN6 ..143 E4

Post Office Cotts GL2 ..108 C6
Post Office La
  Cheltenham GL50 ..193 B3
  Cleeve Hill GL52 ..138 C3
  Draycott GL56 ...196 C6
  Tewkesbury GL20 ..192 C4
Post Office Row GL2 ..101 B2
Post Office Sq GL7 ..150 E2
Post Paddocks The
  GL15 ....147 C3
Postlip Way GL51 ..129 D8
Potticker's La
  Ablington GL7 ...159 F2
  Coln Rogers GL54,GL7 ..159 E4
Potters Croft NP16 ..61 B4
Potters Field Rd GL2 ..138 C3
Potters Pond GL12 ..68 C7
Pound Cl Ledbury HR8 ..178 E8
  Siddington GL7 ...150 E2
Pound Dr BS16 ...19 F5
Pound Farm Ctyd GL3 ..120 E5
Pound Farm La HR9 ..170 B5
Pound Hill GL8 ..140 B8
Pound La Arlingham GL2 ..157 B5
  Bristol BS16 .....109 F4
  Hardwicke GL2 ...119 C4
  Little Rissington GL54 ..169 C6
  Mickleton GL55 ..189 A6
Pound Mdw HR8 ..178 E8
Pound Rd Bristol BS15 ..20 F2
  Highworth SN6 ...145 C4
Pound The
  Almondsbury BS32 ..40 A5
  Ampney Crucis GL7 ..151 B5
  Little Rissington GL54 ..169 C6
  Oldbury-on-S BS35 ..63 B6
Pountney Dr BS5 ..9 D8
Pow's Rd BS15 ...10 D7
Powell's CE Prim Sch
  GL7 ....190 C5
Powells Way GL8 ..140 D3
Powis La GL8 ...140 B8
Poynard Cl BS30 ..10 F3
Poyntz Ct BS30 ...4 F2
Poyntz Rd BS4 ...2 B8
Pratten's La 1 BS16 ..20 D4
Preacher Cl BS5 ..10 A6
Preddy's La BS5 ..10 A6
Prescott BS37 ...32 D8
Prescott Ave GL4 ..119 B4
Prescott Cl BS22 ..134 C4
Press Moor Dr BS30 ..10 F4
Prestbury BS37 ..32 D8
Prestbury Green Dr
  GL52 ....134 C4
Prestbury Manor Ho
  GL52 ....134 C5
Prestbury Rd GL52 ..134 A4
Prestbury St Mary's CE Jun
  Sch GL52 ....134 B3
Preston Cl NP16 ..60 F4
Preston Cross HR8 ..178 B6
Preston Wlk GL4 ..9 A1
Prestwick Cl BS4 ..9 D1
Pretoria Rd BS34 ..28 E5
Prewett St BS1 ..195 B1
Prices Ground GL4 ..119 D6
Priddy Ct BS14 ...3 B5
Priddy Dr BS14 ...3 B5
Priestley Rd 10 GL20 ..192 C4
Priestwood Cl BS10 ..28 A3
Primrose Cl Bristol BS32 ..40 D2
  Bristol,St George BS15 ..10 A8
  Gloucester GL4 ...119 A4
Primrose Ct GL56 ..187 A3
Primrose Dr
  Milkwall GL16 ...155 B4
  Thornbury BS35 ..64 D2
Primrose Hill CE Prim Sch
  GL15 ....92 B5
Primrose Hill Rd GL15 ..92 A5
Primrose La BS15 ..20 C1
Primrose Terr BS15 ..20 C1
Primrose Way
  Cirencester GL7 ..190 E1
  Lydney GL15 .....92 B5
Prince Albert Ct GL2 ..120 C6
Prince Charles Rd 6
  GL8 ....152 E4
Prince Cres 12 GL8 ..172 A8
Prince Ct 12 BS8 ..10 F5
Prince Of Wales Row 17
  GL8 ....140 B4
Prince St Bristol BS1 ..195 A1
  Gloucester GL1 ...196 C4
Prince Street Rdbt BS1 ..195 A2
Prince's Bldgs BS8 ..7 F6
Prince's Rd GL50 ..133 B1
Prince's St Bristol BS2 ..195 C4
  Cheltenham GL52 ..133 F1
Princes Ct BS30 ..195 C4
Princes Mews BS8 ..127 F7
Princes' La BS8 ..7 F6
Princess Elizabeth Way
  GL51 ....132 C3
Princess Gdns BS16 ..19 D6
Princess Row BS2 ..195 A4
Princess Royal Ind Est
  GL15 ....155 E1

Princess Royal Rd [7]
GL15 ....155 D1
Princess St
Bristol,Newton BS2 ....9 A7
Bristol,Windmill Hill BS3 ....8 E4
Princess Victoria St BS8 ....7 F6
Prinknash Abbey* GL4 ..112 B8
Prinknash Bird & Deer Pk*
GL4 ....112 B8
Prinknash Cl [7] GL4 ....119 C4
Prinknash Rd [6] BS37 ...32 D7
Prinknash Pottery*
GL4 ....112 C8
Prinknash Rd [8] GL4 ...119 C4
Prior Park Prep Sch
SN6 ....143 F4
Prior's Hill [1] BS6 ....18 D1
Priors Ct Baunton GL7 ...150 D7
Cheltenham GL52 ....134 B3
[4] Tewkesbury GL20 ....192 C4
Priors Lea BS37 ....43 E1
Priors Lo [5] BS52 ......133 F2
Priors Rd GL52 ....134 B3
Priors Wlk GL7 ....153 F2
Priory Ave BS9 ....18 A7
Priory Cl
Chepstow/Cas-Gwent NP16 ..72 D1
Cirencester GL7 ....190 C5
Priory Court Rd BS9 .....18 A7
Priory Ct
Bristol,Hanham BS15 ......10 C3
Bristol,Upper Knowle BS4 ...9 B2
Churchdown GL3 ....128 D5
Dursley GL11 ....88 A3
Leonard Stanley GL10 ....97 E3
Priory Dene BS9 ....18 A7
Priory Fields GL6 ....82 F8
Priory Gdns
Bristol,Horfield BS7 ......18 F8
Bristol,Shirehampton BS11 ..16 D7
Easton-in-G BS20 ....16 B4
Priory Gn SN6 ....145 D3
Priory Ho GL1 ....196 B2
Priory Ind Est GL8 ....140 C4
Priory La
Bishop's Cleeve GL52 .....138 A4
Monmouth NP25 ....162 A1
Priory Lea HR9 ....163 C8
Priory Lea Ho HR9 ....163 C8
Priory Mews GL52 ....193 C3
Priory Pl
Cheltenham GL52 ....193 C2
Gloucester GL1 ....196 B2
Priory Rd
Bristol,Shirehampton BS8 ..16 D6
Bristol,Tyndall's Park
BS8 ....194 C4
Easton-in-G BS20 ....16 B4
Gloucester GL1 ....196 A3
Gloucester GL1 ....196 B4
Keynsham BS31 ....4 E7
Priory St GL12 ....193 C3
Priory Terr GL52 ....133 F1
Priory The SN6 ....143 F5
Priory Way [7] GL8 .....140 C4
Priory Wlk GL7 ....133 F1
Pritchard St BS2 ....195 B4
Private Rd GL5 ....99 C2
Pro-Catherdral La BS8 ...194 B3
Probersbarn La GL17 ....163 C3
Probyn Cl BS16 ....20 A7
Proctor Cl BS4 ....9 D1
Proctor Ho BS1 ....195 B1
Promenade GL50 ....193 B3
Promenade The BS7 ......18 D2
Prospect Ave Bristol BS15 ..20 B1
Bristol,Kingsdown BS2 ...195 A4
Prospect Cl
Coleford GL16 ....155 A5
Easter Compton BS35 .....39 A2
Frampton Cotterell BS36 ..30 F8
Winterbourne BS36 ....30 E4
Prospect Cres BS15 ....20 F2
Prospect La
Frampton Cotterell BS36 ..30 F8
Llangrove HR9 ....162 B6
Prospect Pl
[7] Bristol,Bedminster BS3 ..8 C3
[1] Bristol,Montpelier BS6 ..18 D2
Bristol,Moorfields BS5 .....9 C8
Cirencester GL7 ....190 D3
Dursley GL11 ....88 A1
Prospect Rd
Cinderford GL14 ....191 D4
Severn Beach BS35 ....38 A5
Prospect Row HR9 ....170 B4
Prospect Terr
Chalford GL6 ....148 C5
[2] Cheltenham GL52 ....133 F2
Prosper La GL10 ....155 B5
Prothereos Ho BS1 ......194 C2
Providence La BS41 ....7 A1
Providence Pl BS2 ....195 C2
Providence View BS41 ....7 A1
Prowse Cl BS35 ....64 C1
Prudham St [7] BS5 ......19 C1
Pry La WR12 ....185 A8
Puck Pit La GL54 ....174 A7
Pucklechurch CE Prim Sch
BS16 ....22 C6
Pucklechurch Trad Est
BS16 ....22 B4
Puckrup GL20 ....181 E7
Puckrup La GL20 ....181 E7

Pudlicott La GL55 ....189 D1
Pullar Cl GL52 ....137 F4
Pullar Ct GL52 ....137 F4
Pullen Ct GL52 ....138 A7
Pullens Rd GL6 ....111 F1
Pullin Ct BS30 ....11 D4
Pullins Gn [3] BS35 ......64 B1
Pullman Ct GL1 ....196 C3
Pullnoggin Pool La
HR9 ....162 D3
Pump La Bristol BS1 ....195 B1
Tetbury GL8 ....140 E3
Tockington BS32 ....50 D4
Pump Row GL6 ....91 C5
Pump Sq BS20 ....16 D5
Pumphreys Cl BS31 ....131 A5
Pumphreys Rd GL31 ....131 A5
Purbeck Way GL52 .....134 C4
Purcell Rd GL2 ....128 A8
Purcell Wlk BS4 ....2 D7
Purdown Rd BS7 ....18 F5
Purdy Ct BS16 ....20 A4
Purley Ave GL7 ....190 D4
Purley Rd GL7 ....190 D4
Pursey Dr BS32 ....29 F6
Purslane Cl GL4 ....119 B4
Purton Cl BS15 ....10 E6
Purton Pl GL15 ....92 C2
Purton Rd BS7 ....18 D2
Puxley Cl BS14 ....3 E6
Puzzle Cl [4] GL15 ......147 D8
Puzzle Wood* GL16 .....155 A4
Pwllmeyric Cl NP16 .....60 B5
Pyart Ct GL16 ....155 A5
Pye Croft BS32 ....40 E3
Pyecroft Ave BS9 ....18 C7
Pyghtell The
Luckington SN14 ....47 E5
Stratton GL7 ....190 B7
Pyke Rd GL20 ....192 F4
Pylers Way GL15 ....90 E7
Pylle Hill Cres BS3 ....8 F4
Pynne Cl BS14 ....3 F5
Pynne Rd BS14 ....3 F5
Pyracantha Wlk BS14 ....3 A6
Pyrton Mews [2] GL15 ..129 C5
Pystol La GL15 ....146 E7

Q

Quabbs Rd GL17 ....164 B4
Quadrangle The
Naunton GL54 ....175 D2
Westerleigh BS37 ....32 C4
Quadrant BS32 ....40 B3
Quadrant E BS16 ....20 C3
Quadrant The
Bristol BS32 ....40 A3
Bristol,Westbury Park BS6 ..18 B3
Quadrant W BS16 ....20 C3
Quail Cl GL4 ....119 E7
Quail Mdws GL8 ....140 B4
Tewkesbury GL20 ....64 B1
Quaker La BS35 ....64 B1
Quaker's Cl BS16 ....20 D8
Quaker's Rd BS16 ....20 E8
Quakers Row GL7 ......149 E4
Quakers' Friars BS1 .....195 B3
Quantock Cl BS30 ....11 C5
Quantock Rd Bristol BS3 ..8 D3
Quedgeley GL2 ....109 D8
Quarries The BS32 ....40 C6
Quarrington Rd BS7 .....18 E5
Quarry Barton BS16 .....20 D4
Quarry Cl Hartpury GL19 ..172 C3
Stratton GL7 ....190 B8
Quarry Cres SN6 ....145 C3
Quarry Gdns GL11 ....87 D4
Quarry La Bristol GL11 ...27 C1
Gorsley HR9 ....170 B4
Winterbourne BS36 ....30 E4
Quarry Mead BS35 ....50 F5
Quarry Rd Alveston BS35 ..50 F5
Bristol BS8 ....18 A2
Bristol,Frenchay BS16 ....20 C7
Bristol,Kingswood BS15 ..10 D6
Chipping Sodbury BS37 ...44 A1
Quarry Steps [3] BS8 ....18 A2
Quarry The Ablington GL7 ..159 F1
Bristol BS11 ....27 C1
Dursley GL11 ....87 D4
[10] Fairford GL7 ....152 E4
Quarry View GL7 ....153 C6
Quarry Way
Bristol,Emerson's Green
BS16 ....31 A1
Bristol,Fishponds BS16 ...20 C7
Quat Goose La GL51 ....133 B7
Quay St Bristol BS1 .....195 A3
Gloucester GL1 ....196 A3
Tewkesbury GL20 ....192 C4
Quay The GL1 ....196 A3
Quays The BS1 ....194 C1
Quayside BS8 ....194 B2
Quayside La [4] BS5 .....9 F6
Tintern Parva NP16 .....146 C4
Quebec Dr GL15 ....132 E3
Quedgeley BS37 ....32 C8
Quedgeley Ent Ctr GL2 ..110 B8
Quedgeley Enterprise Ctr
GL2 ....118 A1
Quedgeley Trad Est
GL10 ....109 F3
Quedgeley Trad Est W
GL2 ....109 D2
Queen Ann Rd GL2 ......9 B6

Queen Anne's Rd GL7 ...190 E5
Queen Charlotte St BS1 ..195 A2
Queen Charlton La BS14 ...3 F2
Queen Elizabeth Rd
GL7 ....190 E4
Queen Elizabeth's Hospital
Sch BS8 ....194 B3
Queen Margaret Prim Sch
GL20 ....192 C2
Queen Quay BS1 ....195 A2
Queen St Bristol BS1 ....195 A2
Salford BS31 ....5 F3
Queen Square Ave [7]
BS1 ....195 A2
Queen St BS2 ....195 B3
Queen St Avonmouth BS11 ..26 A1
Bristol BS2 ....195 B3
Bristol,Eastville BS5 .....19 D3
Bristol,St George BS15 ...10 B8
Chedworth GL54 ....159 A7
Cheltenham GL51 ....133 C3
Cirencester GL7 ....190 D3
Lydney GL15 ....92 B4
Queen Victoria Rd BS6 ...18 A4
Queen Victoria St BS2 ....9 A6
Queen's Ave BS8 ....194 B3
Queen's Cir GL53 ....193 B2
Queen's Ct
Brimscombe GL5 ....148 A5
Bristol BS4 ....194 B3
Ledbury HR8 ....178 E8
Queen's Dr Bristol BS7 ...18 C5
Stroud GL5 ....98 E8
Queen's Rd
Bristol,Ashley Down BS7 ..18 F5
Bristol,Bishopsworth BS13,
BS41 ....1 F4
Bristol,Cadbury Heath BS30 ..11 B4
Bristol,Crew's Hole BS5 ....9 F7
Bristol,Victoria Park BS8 ..194 B3
Cheltenham GL50 ....130 B8
Chepstow/Cas-Gwent NP16 ..60 E6
Pucklechurch BS16 ....22 B5
Stonehouse GL10 ....97 F7
Stroud GL5 ....99 B6
Queen's Retreat GL51 ...133 B2
Queen's Way HR8 ......178 E8
Queens Acre GL14 ......156 F6
Queens Ave SN6 ....145 D3
Queens Cl GL3 ....128 A1
Queens Ct
Cheltenham GL50 ....130 A8
[18] Tewkesbury GL20 ...192 C4
Queens Down Ct BS4 .....9 C3
Queens Down Gdns BS4 ...9 C3
Queens Dr BS15 ....10 A1
Queens Field GL7 ....152 E4
Queens Gate BS9 ....17 D5
Queens La GL7 ....193 A2
Queens Par Bristol BS1 ..194 C2
Cheltenham GL50 ....193 A2
Queens Rd Bristol BS4 .....9 C2
Hannington SN6 ....145 A4
Keynsham BS31 ....4 C2
[21] Winchcombe GL54 ...174 A7
Queens Way GL12 ....68 B7
Queens Wlk BS35 ....64 B3
Queens Wood Forest Trails*
GL18 ....170 B7
Queensdale Cres BS4 .....9 A1
Queensdown Gdns BS4 ...9 C2
Queenshill Rd BS4 ....9 B1
Queensholm Ave BS16 ...30 E1
Queensholm Cl BS16 ....30 D1
Queensholm Cres BS16 ..30 D1
Queensholm Dr BS16 ....30 D1
Queensmead
Bredon GL20 ....182 D7
Painswick GL6 ....103 E7
Queensway Bristol BS34 ..29 D6
Coleford GL16 ....155 B5
Queenwood Gr GL52 ....134 D5
Quenneys Cl GL4 ....119 C3
Querns La GL7 ....190 C4
Querns Rd GL7 ....190 C3
Querns Westonbirt Sch
GL8 ....58 F8
Quickthorn Cl BS14 ......3 A6
Quietways GL10 ....97 E8
Quilter Gr BS4 ....2 D7
Quinton Cl GL3 ....128 B6

Ragnal La GL6 ....91 A3
Ragnall GL12 ....68 D8
Raikes Rd GL1 ....118 D6
Railton Jones Ct BS34 ....29 C3
Railway Arches BS2 .....195 C2
Railway Cotts BS37 ......33 E8
Railway Dr [3] GL16 ....155 A5
Railway Rd GL14 ....191 C1
Railway Terr Bristol BS16 ..20 C4
Kemble GL7 ....141 F8
Lechlade on T GL7 .....153 E3
Lydney GL15 ....84 A8
Railway View GL5 ......148 A5
Rainbow Ct BS37 ....43 B3
Ralegh Ct Innsworth GL3 ..127 F8
Stroud GL5 ....5 D2
Raleigh Rd BS3 ....8 B4
Ralph Rd BS7 ....18 F4
Ram Hill BS36 ....31 D4
Ram Hill Bsns Pk BS36 ..31 D5
Ramsdale Rd GL2 ....118 B4
Ramsey Rd BS7 ....18 F4
Rance Pitch GL4 ....119 E2
Randall Cl BS15 ....20 F2
Randall Rd Bristol BS8 ..194 B2
Upper Rissington GL54 ..169 D6
Randalls Field GL6 ......103 F7
Randalls Gn GL6 ....148 C5
Randolph Ave Bristol BS13 ..2 B5
Yate BS37 ....43 D4
Randolph Cl Bristol BS13 ..2 B5
Cheltenham GL53 ....130 F6
Randwick CE Prim Sch
GL6 ....102 D3
Randwick Rd GL4 ....118 D3
Range The GL2 ....125 D5
Rangers Ave GL11 ....80 C7
Rangers The GL11 ....80 C7
Rangers Wlk BS15 ....10 C4
Rangeworthy CE Prim Sch
BS37 ....52 F1
Ranmoor GL4 ....119 D3
Rannoch Rd BS7 ....28 F1
Raphael Ct BS1 ....195 B1
Ratcliff Lawns GL52 ....134 B8
Ratcliffe Dr BS34 ....29 F5
Rathbone Cl BS36 ....31 C5
Rathmore Ct [5] GL54 ..174 A7
Raven Ct BS9 ....17 F8
Ravendale Dr BS30 ......11 B2
Ravenglass Cres BS10 ...28 D2
Ravenhead Dr BS14 ......3 B8
Ravenhill Ave BS3 ....8 F2
Ravenhill Rd BS3 ....8 F2
Ravens Wood BS30 ......11 B3
Ravenscourt Rd BS34 ....29 B7
Ravensgate Rd GL53 ....131 B4
Ravenswood Rd BS6 ....18 C1
Ravis Cl GL4 ....119 B6
Rawnsley Ho [18] BS5 ....19 A1
Rayleigh Rd BS9 ....17 E7
Raymend Rd BS3 ....8 E3
Raymend Wlk BS3 ....8 E2
Raymill BS4 ....10 A2
Raymond Ho BS16 ....20 F4
Raynes Rd BS3 ....8 A3
Raysfield Inf Sch BS37 ...32 F8
Raysfield Jun Sch BS37 ..32 F8
Rea La GL4 ....119 B5
Rea The GL2 ....117 F5
Reaburn Ct [1] GL52 ....131 B6
Read Way GL52 ....137 F2
Reade St [12] NP25 .....154 A7
Reades Piece WR11 .....188 C6
Reading St BS15 ....10 B8
Ready Token GL7 ....151 F7
Rectory Barns GL54 ....176 D4
Rectory Cl
Lower Swell GL54 ......176 D4
Upton St Leonards GL4 ..119 E2
Yate BS37 ....43 F3
Rectory Cotts GL54 .....176 D4
Rectory Ct GL52 ....138 A4
Rectory La Avening GL8 ..148 B1
Bristol BS34 ....29 A3
Cricklade SN6 ....143 F6
Cromhall GL12 ....53 A8
Gloucester GL2 ....118 A6
Rectory Mdw GL7 ......164 F6
Rectory Rd
Easton-in-G BS20 ....16 B3
Frampton Cotterell BS36 ..31 A8
Gloucester GL4 ....119 C4
Red Admiral Dr GL4 ....119 E4
Red Cliff La GL19 ....179 D1
Red House La
Almondsbury BS32 ....40 B4
Bristol BS9 ....17 E6
Red La GL20 ....192 C5
Red Lion Ct [2] GL1 ....119 A8
Red Lion La SN6 ....143 F4
Red Maids Jun Sch The
BS9 ....18 A6
Red Maids Sch The BS9 ..18 A6
Red Rower Cl GL50 .....133 C5
Red Well Rd GL4 ....119 E2
Redbrook CE Prim Sch
NP25 ....154 C4
Redcar Ct BS16 ....30 F1
Redcatch Rd BS4 ....9 B3
Redcliff Backs BS1 ......195 B2
Redcliff Cres BS3 ....8 E4
Redcliff Hill BS1 ....195 B1
Redcliff Mead La BS1 ...195 B1
Redcliff St BS1 ....195 B2
Redcliffe Coll GL1 ......127 A2
Redcliffe Par E BS1 .....195 A1
Redcliffe Par W BS1 ....195 A1

Redcliffe Way BS1 ......195 B1
Redcross Mews [16] BS2 ..195 C3
Redcross St BS2 ....195 C3
Redding Cl GL2 ....117 E1
Reddings Cl GL15 ....147 C8
Reddings La GL14 ......191 E4
Reddings La GL51 ......129 C3
Reddings Rd GL51 ......129 C3
Reddings The Bristol BS15 ..20 B1
Cheltenham GL51 ....129 C3
Chepstow/Cas-Gwent NP16 ..60 F7
Pendock WR13 ....180 A7
Redesdale Mews [6]
GL56 ....187 A6
Redesdale Pl GL56 .....187 A6
Redfield Edge Prim Sch
BS30 ....11 C5
Redfield Hill BS30 ....11 D1
Redfield Rd BS34 ....29 E1
Redford Cres BS13 ......1 C3
Redford La BS16 ....22 C6
Redford Wlk BS13 ....1 C3
Redgrove Cotts GL51 ...129 C4
Redgrove Pk GL51 ......129 C4
Redgrove Rd GL51 .....132 C8
Redham La BS35 ....19 D8
Redhill Cl BS16 ....19 D8
Redhill Dr BS16 ....19 D8
Redhill Farm Bsns Pk
BS35 ....49 B4
Redhill La BS35 ....49 B4
Redhouse La
English Bicknor GL16 ...163 C6
Stroud GL5,GL6 ....98 E8
Redland Cl GL2 ....18 B1
Redland Court Rd BS6 ...18 B1
Redland Gr BS6 ....18 B1
Redland Green Rd BS6 ..18 A1
Redland High Sch BS6 ..18 B2
Redland Hill BS6 ....18 A1
Redland Pk BS6 ....18 A1
Redland Rd BS6 ....18 B1
Redland Sta BS6 ....18 B2
Redland Terr [8] BS6 ...18 B1
Redlands Cl SN6 ....145 D5
Redlynch La BS31 ....4 E1
Redmarley CE Prim Sch
GL19 ....179 A1
Redmarley Rd GL18 ....171 E5
Rednock Dr GL11 ....88 A5
Rednock Sch GL11 ......88 A5
Redpoll Way GL4 ....119 E4
Redshelf Wlk BS10 ......28 B1
Redstart Way GL4 ......119 E4
Redthorne Way GL51 ..129 A4
Redwick & Northwick CE
Prim Sch BS35 ....48 B8
Redwick Cl BS11 ....27 C3
Redwick Crossroads
BS35 ....38 E6
Redwick Gdns BS11 ......38 E6
Redwick Rd Pilning BS35 ..38 E4
Redwick BS35 ....38 E6
Redwing Way GL4 ......127 F6
Redwing Gdns BS16 .....11 A1
Redwood Cl Bristol BS30 ..11 B5
Chepstow/Cas-Gwent NP16 ..60 F7
Gloucester GL2 ....118 A3
Redwood Ct
[4] Cheltenham GL51 ...132 C8
Northway GL20 ....182 A1
Redwood Ho Bristol BS13 ..2 D4
Brookthorpe GL4 ....110 B2
Reed Cl BS10 ....18 B7
Reed Ct BS30 ....18 B3
Reed's Row GL12 ....55 A8
Reedley Rd BS9 ....17 F5
Reedling Cl BS16 ....11 A1
Reeds Sch The SN6 .....145 A4
Reema Hos The SN6 ....145 A4
Reevers Rd [23] GL18 ...171 E4
Reeves Cl GL7 ....190 B6
Regency Dr BS4 ....10 A4
Regent Apartments BS6 ..18 F1
Regent Arc GL50 ....133 C2
Regent Chambers GL50 ..193 A1
Regent Ct GL51 ....130 C2
Regent Ho [3] GL52 ....130 C2
Regent Rd BS3 ....8 E3
Regent St
Bristol,Clifton Wood BS8 ..194 B2
Bristol,Kingswood BS15 ...10 B8
Cheltenham GL50 ....193 A1
Lydney GL15 ....92 C5
Stonehouse GL10 ....97 E8
Regent Way NP16 ....60 B4
Regents Cl BS35 ....38 C8
Regents The BS31 ....4 E1
Regents Wlk [5] GL15 ...92 C5
Regis Cl GL53 ....133 F1
Reine Barnes Cl GL11 ...58 D1
Remenham Dr BS9 ......18 A4
Remenham Pk BS9 ......18 A4
Remus Cl GL4 ....119 E7
Rendcomb Cl GL4 ......119 B6
Rendcomb Coll GL7 ....158 A8
Rendcomb Dr GL2 ......190 B6
Rendle Ho BS16 ....19 B5
Renishaw Rd BS4 ....9 A1
Repton Hall BS10 ....28 A4
Repton Rd BS4 ....9 B4
Reservoir Cl GL15 ....99 F8
Reservoir Rd
Gloucester GL4 ....118 E1
Stroud GL5 ....99 B7
Restway Wall [11] NP16 ...60 B5
Retort Rd BS11 ....26 A6

Retreat The
3 Broadway WR12 .....185 B8
Gloucester GL4 .....118 D2
Highworth SN6 .....145 C3
4 Tetbury GL8 .....140 C4
Reynold's Wlk BS7 .....19 A7
Reynolds Cl BS31 .....5 A5
Rhode Cl BS31 .....5 A3
Rhodesia Ho 1 GL51 .....132 F4
Rhodfa Wyesham/Wyesham Ave 4 NP25 .....154 A7
Ribble Cl GL3 .....120 F5
Ribblesdale BS35 .....51 D8
Ribston Hall GL1 .....196 A2
Ribston Hall High Sch GL1 .....118 E5
Ribston Mews GL1 .....118 E5
Ricardo Rd GL6 .....91 F7
Richard Pate Sch The GL53 .....130 E4
Richard Pl GL20 .....192 D1
Richards Rd GL51 .....133 B4
Richeson Cl BS10 .....27 F2
Richeson Wlk BS10 .....27 F2
Richmond Apartments BS6 .....18 C3
Richmond Ave
Bristol,Montpelier BS6 .....18 F2
Bristol,Stoke Gifford BS34 .....29 E5
Gloucester GL4 .....119 C6
Richmond Bldgs GL5 .....98 D6
Richmond Cl BS31 .....4 D4
Richmond Ct
1 Ashton Keynes SN6 .....142 F5
Bristol BS34 .....39 F1
7 Bristol,Clifton BS8 .....18 A2
2 Bristol,Windmill Hill BS3 .....8 F4
Richmond Dale 6 BS8 .....18 A2
Richmond Dr 4 GL52 .....134 A1
Richmond Gdns GL2 .....127 D5
Richmond Hill BS8 .....194 B3
Richmond Hill Ave BS8 .....194 B3
Richmond Hts BS8 .....194 B3
Richmond La BS8 .....194 B3
Richmond Mews BS8 .....194 A3
Richmond Park Rd BS8 .....194 A3
Richmond Rd
Bristol,Mangotsfield BS16 .....21 A5
Bristol,Montpelier BS6 .....18 E1
Bristol,Pile Marsh BS5 .....9 E7
Tewkesbury GL20 .....192 E1
Richmond St BS3 .....8 F4
Richmond Terr
Avonmouth BS11 .....26 B1
Bristol BS8 .....194 A3
Richmonds The GL4 .....119 D4
Rickfield The NP25 .....162 A1
Rickyard Way GL2 .....100 E5
Riddle St GL13 .....94 B3
Ride The BS15 .....21 A2
Ridge Jun Sch The BS37 .....43 F2
Ridge Pl GL17 .....163 D1
Ridge The Bristol BS11 .....16 E7
Broad Blunsdon SN26 .....144 D1
Bussage GL6 .....148 B6
Coalpit Heath BS36 .....31 C7
Ridge Wlk GL17 .....164 A4
Ridge's La GL8 .....140 C7
Ridgehill BS9 .....18 C6
Ridgemeade BS14 .....3 B4
Ridgemont Rd GL5 .....99 E6
Ridgemount Cl GL3 .....120 E5
Ridgemount Gdns BS14 .....3 B5
Ridgeview BS41 .....7 B2
Ridgeway
Coalpit Heath BS36 .....31 D7
Eastnor HR8 .....179 B8
Monmouth/Trefynwy NP25 .....154 A7
Yate BS37 .....44 A2
Yorkley GL15 .....156 B2
Ridgeway Cres HR9 .....162 D4
Ridgeway Ct
Bristol,Henbury BS10 .....28 A1
Bristol,Hengrove BS14 .....3 C5
Ridgeway Gdns BS14 .....3 C5
Ridgeway Ind Ctr BS5 .....19 E2
Ridgeway La Bristol BS14 .....3 B5
Marston Meysey SN6 .....144 B6
Ridgeway Par BS5 .....19 E3
Ridgeway Rd Bristol BS16 .....19 F3
Long Ashton BS41 .....7 A2
Ridgeway The
Bristol BS10 .....28 A1
Bussage GL6 .....148 B6
Crudwell SN16 .....141 C3
Ridgeways GL56 .....177 C8
Ridgewood BS9 .....17 D3
Riding Barn Hill BS30 .....12 A6
Ridingleaze BS11 .....27 A1
Ridings Cl BS37 .....44 D1
Ridings High Sch The BS36 .....30 D6
Ridings Rd BS36 .....31 C6
Ridings The Bristol BS13 .....1 E4
Coalpit Heath BS36 .....31 C6
Maisemore GL2 .....126 A7
Nailsworth GL6 .....91 C3
Ridler Rd GL15 .....92 C2
Rigsby's La SN16 .....142 D3
Ring Fence GL15 .....147 B3
Ringer's Cl GL19 .....173 C7
Ringfield Cl GL6 .....91 C3
Ringspit La BS14 .....3 E1
Ringswell SN14 .....15 A7
Ringwood Cres BS10 .....28 D1
Ripley Rd BS5 .....20 A1
Ripon Ct BS16 .....30 F2
Ripon Rd BS4 .....9 E6
Rippledale Cl GL51 .....129 E7
Risdale Rd BS3 .....7 F1
Rise The GL54 .....166 E5
Risedale Ho BS15 .....10 D5
Rising Sun La GL52 .....138 E2
Rissington Cl GL51 .....129 E8
Rissington Rd
Bourton-on-t-W GL54 .....169 A6
Gloucester GL4 .....118 E3
Rivelands Rd GL51 .....133 B7
River Leys GL51 .....132 F5
River Mead BS37 .....43 C3
River Rd BS37 .....44 A1
River St BS2 .....195 C3
River Terr BS31 .....4 F5
River View Bristol BS16 .....19 E5
Chepstow/Cas-Gwent NP16 .....60 E8
River Way GL7 .....142 F8
Riverdale GL14 .....157 A6
Rivergate BS1 .....195 C2
Riverland Dr BS13 .....1 F5
Riverleaze BS9 .....17 C5
Rivermead Cl GL2 .....126 E4
Rivers Way SN6 .....145 C3
Riverside GL54 .....174 A7
Riverside Bsns Pk BS4 .....9 D6
Riverside Cl Bristol BS11 .....16 F5
Charlton Kings GL52 .....131 B6
Riverside Cotts
Bristol BS15 .....10 B1
Brockworth GL3 .....120 E5
Riverside Ct 2 Bristol BS4 .....9 F6
Tewkesbury GL20 .....192 C5
Riverside Dr BS16 .....20 C7
Riverside Mews BS4 .....9 F6
Riverside Pk
Eastington GL10 .....97 A8
23 Monmouth/Trefynwy NP25 .....154 A7
Severn Beach BS35 .....37 F6
Riverside Stps BS4 .....9 E7
Riverside Way BS15 .....10 C3
Riverside Wlk 6 BS5 .....9 F6
Riversley Rd GL2 .....127 C2
Riversmeet GL3 .....120 F5
Riversmill GL11 .....80 D8
Riversmill Ct GL11 .....80 D8
Riversmill Wlk GL11 .....80 D8
Riverview Way GL51 .....133 A4
Riverwood Ho BS16 .....30 C1
Riverwood Rd BS16 .....30 C1
Riviera Cres BS16 .....20 E4
Riviera Way BS34 .....30 A4
Rixon Gate SN6 .....143 A5
Roach's La GL9 .....46 D2
Road Hill SN14 .....15 D1
Road Two BS10 .....38 A3
Robbers Rd GL6 .....102 C2
Robbins Cl Bristol BS32 .....29 F6
Marshfield SN14 .....14 F8
Stroud GL5 .....98 C6
Robbins Ct BS16 .....21 B6
Robel Ave BS36 .....31 A8
Robert Burns Ave GL51 .....129 D7
Robert Ct Bristol BS16 .....21 B7
Leigh Woods BS8 .....7 D7
Robert Franklin Way GL7 .....143 A8
Robert Harvey Ho 4 GL52 .....193 C4
Robert Raikes Ave
Gloucester GL4 .....118 D2
Gloucester GL4 .....118 E2
Robert St
Bristol,Baptist Mills BS5 .....19 B2
16 Bristol,Russell Town BS5 .....9 B7
Roberts Cl
Bishop's Cleeve GL52 .....137 F4
Stratton GL7 .....190 B8
Roberts Rd
Cheltenham GL52 .....134 D3
Innsworth GL3 .....127 E7
Robertson Dr BS4 .....9 F6
Robertson Rd Bristol BS5 .....19 C2
Shurdington GL51 .....129 D2
Robin Cl
Bristol,Brentry BS10 .....28 B2
Bristol,Stockwood BS14 .....3 D6
2 Chalford GL6 .....148 C6
Northway GL20 .....182 B5
Robin Ct GL10 .....97 F8
Robin Hood Junc GL16 .....154 F6
Robin Way BS37 .....33 A7
Robinhood St GL1 .....118 D7
Robinia Cl GL53 .....131 B5
Robinia Wlk BS14 .....3 A7
Robins Cl GL52 .....134 A2
Robins End GL3 .....127 D7
Robins Wood Hill Ctry Pk* GL4 .....119 A2
Robinson Cl GL18 .....171 A5
Robinson Dr BS5 .....9 A8
Robinson La
Upper Lydbrook GL17 .....163 D2
Woodmancote GL7 .....158 B4
Robinson Rd GL1 .....118 E7
Robinswood Gdns GL4 .....119 A4
Robinswood Hill Ctry Pk* GL4 .....118 F3
Robinswood Pl 11 GL4 .....119 C4
Robinswood Prim Sch GL4 .....119 C3
Rochester Cl GL51 .....130 A5
Rochester Rd BS4 .....9 F5
Rock & Fountain La GL14 .....157 E8
Rock Cl BS4 .....9 E2
Rock Cotts Pill BS20 .....16 E4
Stroud GL5 .....99 C8
Rock Ho BS10 .....28 C3
Rock La Bristol BS34 .....29 F4
Coleford GL16 .....155 A5
Elton GL14 .....157 E8
Northwood Green GL14 .....165 E1
Rock Rd Dursley GL11 .....87 D4
Keynsham BS31 .....4 E5
Wick BS30 .....12 D8
Rock St Chaceley GL19 .....181 B1
Thornbury BS35 .....51 B8
Rock The BS4 .....9 E3
Rock Villa La NP16 .....72 F1
Rockhill Est BS31 .....4 F4
Rockhill Ho BS31 .....4 F4
Rockingham Gdns BS11 .....17 A8
Rockingham Rdbt BS11 .....26 D6
Rockland Gr BS16 .....19 D5
Rockland Rd BS16 .....20 D7
Rockleaze Bristol BS9 .....17 E2
9 Thornbury BS35 .....64 B1
Rockleaze Ave BS9 .....17 E3
Rockleaze Ct BS9 .....17 E3
Rockleaze Rd BS9 .....17 E3
Rockleigh Cl GL4 .....118 E3
Rockness Hill GL6 .....91 A2
Rocks Rd GL17 .....163 D3
Rocks The GL16 .....155 A3
Rockside Ave BS16 .....20 F8
Rockside Dr BS9 .....18 C6
Rockside Gdns
Bristol BS16 .....20 F8
Frampton Cotterell BS36 .....31 C8
Rockstowes Way BS10 .....28 D3
Rockwell Ave BS11 .....27 B1
Rockwood Ho BS37 .....44 A4
Rockwood Rd NP16 .....60 E7
Rodborough BS37 .....32 C7
Rodborough Ave GL5 .....99 B6
Rodborough Com Prim Sch GL5 .....99 B6
Rodborough Hill GL5 .....99 B6
Rodborough La GL5 .....99 C5
Rodborough Terr GL5 .....99 B5
Rodborough Way BS15 .....11 A7
Rodbourne Rd BS10 .....18 E6
Rodford Prim Sch BS37 .....32 D7
Rodford Way BS37 .....32 D7
Rodfords Mead BS14 .....3 A7
Rodley Rd GL15 .....92 C3
Rodley Sq GL15 .....92 C3
Rodmarton Sch GL7 .....149 B1
Rodmead Wlk BS13 .....2 A4
Rodney Ave BS15 .....10 A8
Rodney Cl GL2 .....127 B4
Rodney Cres BS34 .....29 A4
Rodney Pl BS8 .....194 A3
Rodney Rd Bristol BS15 .....10 A8
Cheltenham GL50 .....193 B3
Saltford BS31 .....5 E2
Rodney Wlk BS15 .....20 A1
Rodway Ct BS16 .....21 A5
Rodway Hill BS16 .....21 B3
Rodway Hill Rd BS16 .....21 A4
Rodway La GL19,GL2 .....172 E3
Rodway Rd Bristol BS34 .....29 A8
Bristol,Mangotsfield BS16 .....21 A5
Bristol,Patchway BS34 .....28 F7
Rodway View BS15 .....20 F3
Roebuck Mdws GL17 .....163 F3
Roegate Dr BS4 .....9 E6
Roegate Ho BS5 .....20 A1
Roel Gate GL54 .....174 D3
Rogers Cl BS30 .....11 B5
Rogers Ct BS37 .....44 C1
Rogers Wlk BS30 .....11 D7
Rokeby Ave BS6 .....18 C1
Rollers The GL6 .....91 B4
Rolleston Way GL51 .....129 F7
Rolling Stones 4 GL55 .....189 A2
Rolph Ct 8 GL56 .....187 A2
Roman Amphitheatre* GL7 .....190 B4
Roman Farm Ct BS11 .....27 C2
Roman Farm Rd BS4 .....2 E7
Roman Hackle Ave GL50 .....133 C5
Roman Rd Bristol BS5 .....19 B1
Cheltenham GL51 .....133 A1
Gloucester GL4 .....119 E6
Roman Way
Bourton-on-t-W GL54 .....169 A8
Bristol BS9 .....17 C4
Brockworth GL3 .....120 E6
Coleford GL16 .....155 A5
Highworth SN6 .....145 C3
Lechlade on T GL7 .....153 E3
Littledean GL14 .....191 F4
Roman Wlk
Bristol,Kensington Park BS4 .....9 C3
Bristol,Stoke Gifford BS34 .....29 E5
Romney Ave BS7 .....19 B6
Romney Avenue Jun & Inf Schs BS7 .....19 B6
Romney Cl GL1 .....118 E5
Romney Rd GL8 .....140 B4
Romo Ct BS16 .....20 C4
Ron Jones Ho 3 BS1 .....195 B4
Ronald Rd BS16 .....19 F6
Ronayne Wlk BS16 .....20 C6
Rookery La Newton GL13 .....85 E7
Pilning BS35 .....39 A6
Pucklechurch BS30,SN14 .....22 F4
St Briavels GL15 .....154 F2
Rookery Rd Bristol BS4 .....9 A3
Innsworth GL3 .....127 D6
Rookery The GL54 .....159 A6
Rookery Villas GL2 .....116 A3
Rookery Way BS14 .....2 F4
Rooksmoor Hill GL5 .....99 A3
Roosevelt Ave GL52 .....131 A8
Rope Walk Ho BS2 .....195 C3
Rope Wlk 3 GL12 .....68 B7
Rope Wlk The GL5 .....99 E3
Ropewalk GL20 .....192 D4
Rosary RC Prim Sch The GL5 .....99 B7
Rosary Rdbt The BS16 .....21 D7
Rosary The Bristol BS16 .....21 D7
Chepstow/Cas-Gwent NP16 .....72 D1
Rose & Crown Ho GL50 .....193 B4
Rose & Crown Pas GL50 .....193 B4
Rose Acre BS10 .....28 A3
Rose Cl BS36 .....30 E4
Rose Green Cl BS5 .....19 E2
Rose Green Rd BS5 .....19 D2
Rose Hill Sch GL12 .....68 D2
Rose La BS36 .....31 D6
Rose Mead BS7 .....19 A7
Rose Meare Gdns BS13 .....1 E7
Rose Oak Dr BS36 .....31 D7
Rose Oak Gdns BS36 .....31 D7
Rose Oak La BS36 .....31 D7
Rose Rd BS5 .....9 E7
Rose Row GL54 .....176 B2
Rose Terr BS8 .....194 B3
Rose Tree Ho BS16 .....20 F4
Rose Way GL7 .....190 E2
Rose Willis Ct 10 GL18 .....171 A4
Rose Wlk BS16 .....20 C3
Rosebank BS5 .....19 D2
Rosebay Gdns GL51 .....132 E5
Rosebay Mead BS16 .....19 E5
Roseberry Pk BS5 .....9 D8
Roseberry Rd BS5 .....9 C7
Roseberry Terr GL6 .....148 C5
Rosebery Ave Bristol BS2 .....19 A1
Gloucester GL1 .....118 E6
Rosebery Mount GL11 .....80 C8
Rosebery Pk GL11 .....80 C8
Rosebery Rd GL11 .....80 C8
Rosebery Terr BS8 .....194 B2
Rosedale Ave GL10 .....98 A7
Rosedale Cl GL2 .....109 D8
Rosedale Rd BS16 .....20 C3
Rosefield Cres GL20 .....192 F4
Rosehill Ct GL7 .....190 C7
Rosehill St GL52 .....130 F8
Rosehill Terr 6 GL52 .....130 F8
Rosehip Ct GL51 .....130 A4
Rosehip Way GL52 .....137 E4
Roselarge Gdns BS10 .....28 A2
Rosemary Cl Bristol BS32 .....29 F7
Gloucester GL4 .....119 D4
Rosemary La Bristol BS5 .....19 C2
Stroat NP16 .....146 F1
Rosemary Terr GL12 .....68 B7
Rosemont Terr BS8 .....194 A2
Rosemount Ct BS15 .....10 B8
Rosery Cl BS9 .....18 A8
Rosery The BS16 .....20 C3
Rosevear BS2 .....9 A7
Roseville Ave BS30 .....11 A2
Rosewood Ave BS35 .....50 F5
Rosewood Wlk GL52 .....138 B4
Roshni Gar E 16 BS5 .....19 B1
Roshni Gar W 15 BS5 .....19 B1
Rosling Rd BS7 .....18 E6
Roslyn Rd BS6 .....18 C1
Ross Cl BS37 .....44 B1
Ross Rd Berry Hill GL16 .....155 A8
Mitcheldean GL17 .....164 D6
Newent GL18 .....170 F5
Rossall Ave BS34 .....29 C6
Rossall Rd BS4 .....9 D3
Rossiter Wood Ct BS11 .....27 B2
Rossiter's La BS5 .....10 A6
Rosslyn Way BS35 .....64 C3
Rothermere Cl GL51 .....129 F5
Rothleigh GL51 .....129 E5
Rotunda Terr GL50 .....193 A2
Rougemont Gr NP16 .....60 F4
Rounceval St BS37 .....44 A1
Roundabouts The GL5 .....99 F1
Roundhills Mead SN6 .....145 D4
Roundhouse Mews 7 GL56 .....187 A3
Roundmoor Cl BS31 .....5 D3
Roundmoor Gdns BS14 .....3 D7
Roundways BS36 .....31 D6
Rousham Rd BS5 .....19 A3
Roves La SN6 .....145 D1
Row The Aust BS35 .....49 A7
Donnington GL56 .....176 F7
Lechlade on T GL7 .....153 F4
Southrop GL7 .....153 C6
St Arvans NP16 .....72 B6
Rowacres BS14 .....2 F6
Rowan Cl BS16 .....20 A2
Rowan Ct 10 Bristol BS5 .....9 B7
Yate BS37 .....43 C3
Rowan Dr NP16 .....60 E5
Rowan Gdns GL3 .....120 D6
Rowan Gr GL11 .....88 A3
Rowan Ho BS13 .....2 D4
Rowan Tree Ho BS16 .....20 F4
Rowan Way Bristol BS15 .....10 B3
15 Cheltenham GL51 .....129 E5
Nailsworth GL6 .....90 F5
Rowan Wlk BS31 .....4 C4
Rowandean GL14 .....191 C5
Rowanfield Exchange GL51 .....133 A2
Rowanfield Inf & Jun Schs GL51 .....133 A2
Rowanfield Rd GL51 .....133 A1
Rowans The Bristol BS16 .....30 B1
Pontshill HR9 .....164 B8
Woodmancote GL52 .....138 B3
Rowberrow BS14 .....2 F7
Rowcroft GL5 .....99 B7
Rowcroft Retreat GL5 .....99 B7
Rowe Ct GL50 .....193 A3
Rowena Cade Ave GL50 .....130 B6
Rowland Ave BS16 .....19 D4
Rowlandson Gdns BS7 .....19 B6
Rowley GL11 .....88 A5
Rowley Mews GL11 .....88 A5
Rowley St BS3 .....8 C3
Rownham Cl BS3 .....7 E4
Rownham Ct BS8 .....194 A1
Rownham Hill BS8 .....7 E6
Rownham Mead BS8 .....194 A1
Rows The GL55 .....188 D4
Roxburgh BS8 .....7 F8
Roxton Dr GL51 .....129 C7
Roy King Gdns BS30 .....11 C6
Royal Agricultural Coll GL7 .....150 B4
Royal Albert Rd BS6 .....18 A4
Royal Cl BS10 .....27 D3
Royal Cres GL50 .....193 B3
Royal Ct 9 GL51 .....132 D2
Royal Forest of Dean Coll GL16 .....155 B7
Royal Fort Rd BS2,BS8 .....194 C3
Royal La GL1 .....127 A2
Royal Oak Mews GL50 .....193 B4
Royal Oak Rd
Gloucester GL1 .....196 A3
Upper Lydbrook GL17 .....163 E3
Royal Oak Terr GL55 .....188 F1
Royal Par BS8 .....194 B3
Royal Parade Mews GL50 .....193 A2
Royal Park Mews 3 BS8 .....194 A3
Royal Pk BS8 .....194 A3
Royal Prom BS8 .....194 B3
Royal Rd BS16 .....21 A6
Royal Spring GL17 .....165 A5
Royal Victoria Pk BS10 .....28 B2
Royal Well La GL50 .....193 B3
Royal Well Pl GL50 .....193 B3
Royal Well Rd GL50 .....193 B3
Royal West of England Acad* BS8 .....194 B3
Royal York Cres BS8 .....7 F6
Royal York Ho BS8 .....194 A2
Royal York Mews BS8 .....194 A2
Royal York Villas BS8 .....194 A2
Royate Hill BS5 .....19 D2
Roycroft Rd BS34 .....29 B2
Royston Wlk BS10 .....28 D2
Rozel Rd BS7 .....18 E5
Ruardean CE Prim Sch GL17 .....163 E4
Ruardean Garden Pottery* GL17 .....163 E4
Ruardean Rd GL17 .....163 F3
Rubens Cl BS31 .....5 A5
Ruby St BS3 .....8 B3
Rudford Cl BS34 .....40 B1
Rudge Cl BS15 .....20 F2
Rudge The GL2 .....126 B8
Rudgeway Pk BS35 .....50 F1
Rudgewood Cl BS13 .....2 D4
Rudgleigh Ave BS20 .....16 C4
Rudgleigh Rd BS20 .....16 C4
Rudhall Ct GL1 .....196 A3
Rudhall Gr BS10 .....18 E7
Rudhall View HR9 .....164 D8
Rudthorpe Rd BS7 .....18 E5
Ruffet Cl GL16 .....155 B4
Ruffet Rd BS36 .....31 B4
Ruffet's Cl NP16 .....60 D8
Ruffitt The GL14 .....191 F5
Rugby Rd BS4 .....9 D3
Rumsey Cl GL4 .....119 E4
Runnings Rd GL51 .....133 A5
Runnings The GL51 .....133 A6
Runnymead Ave BS4 .....9 D2
Runnymede Bristol BS15 .....20 E1
Cheltenham GL51 .....129 E5
Runswick Rd BS4 .....9 C3
Rupert St
Bristol,Kingsdown BS1 .....195 A3
Bristol,Redfield BS5 .....9 C7
Ruscombe Rd GL6 .....102 E2
Rush Cl BS32 .....40 D2
Rusham BS13 .....1 F4
Rushley La GL54 .....174 A7
Rushmead La SN14 .....24 F2
Rushton Dr BS36 .....31 D7
Rushworth Cl GL51 .....132 D2
Rushworth Ho GL51 .....132 D2
Rushy BS30 .....11 A4
Rushy Ho GL52 .....134 A4
Rushy Mews GL52 .....134 A4
Rushy Way BS16 .....31 A1
Rushyleaze GL15 .....92 B2
Ruskin Gr BS7 .....19 A8
Ruskin Ho BS34 .....29 A8
Ruspidge Cl GL4 .....119 E5
Ruspidge Rd GL14 .....156 C6
Russ St BS2 .....195 C2
Russell Almshouses GL20 .....192 C3
Russell Ave BS15 .....10 E7
Russell Cl GL9 .....57 B3

Russell Gr BS6 . . . . .18 C5
Russell Pl GL51 . . . . .133 C3
Russell Rd
  Bristol,Chester Park BS16 . .20 B2
  Bristol,Westbury Park BS6 . .18 B4
Russell St
  Cheltenham GL51 . . . . . . .133 C3
  Gloucester GL1 . . . . .196 B2
  Stroud GL5 . . . . .99 C7
Russell Town Ave BS5 . . . . .9 B8
Russell Town Ind Pk 18
  BS5 .9 C7
Russet Ave GL7 . . . . .153 F2
Russet Cl Bredon GL20 . . . .182 C7
  Gloucester GL4 . . . . .118 B3
  2 Ledbury HR8 . . . . .178 E7
  Olveston BS35 . . . . .50 A3
Russet Ct GL12 . . . . .67 F4
Russet Rd GL51 . . . . .132 F3
Russett Way 24 GL18 . . . .171 A4
Rustic Cl GL4 . . . . .119 C4
Rustic Pk BS35 . . . . .38 A6
Rutherford Cl BS30 . . . . . .11 A3
Rutherford Way GL51 . . . .133 A5
Ruthven Rd BS4 . . . . .9 D5
Rutland Ave BS30 . . . . .11 A2
Rutland Ct 4 GL50 . . . . . .133 B1
Rutland Pl GL7 . . . . .190 C3
Rutland Rd BS7 . . . . .18 E3
Ryalls La GL2 . . . . .95 E5
Rydal Ho BS34 . . . . .29 A8
Rydal Rd GL2 . . . . .227 A4
Rydal Wlk GL51 . . . . .129 E7
Ryde Rd BS4 . . . . .9 B2
Ryder Cl GL11 . . . . .88 A4
Ryder Row GL3 . . . . .127 E6
Rye Ave GL4 . . . . .132 D5
Rye Cl BS13 . . . . .1 E6
Rye Close Bglws GL54 . . . .169 A7
Rye Cres GL54 . . . . .169 A7
Rye St WR13 . . . . .180 A6
Ryeclose GL54 . . . . .169 A7
Ryecroft Cl BS36 . . . . .31 C7
Ryecroft Rd BS36 . . . . .31 C8
Ryecroft Rise BS41 . . . . .7 B1
Ryecroft St GL1 . . . . .196 C5
Ryedown La BS30 . . . . .11 D2
Ryeford Ind Est GL10 . . . . .98 A6
Ryelands GL3 . . . . .118 C3
Ryelands Cl GL10 . . . . .97 E8
Ryelands Rd
  7 Bream GL15 . . . . .147 D8
  Stonehouse GL10 . . . . .97 E8
Ryelands The GL6 . . . . . . .102 D1
Ryeleaze BS30 . . . . .9 C7
Ryeleaze Rd GL5 . . . . .99 C7
Ryeworth Dr GL52 . . . . . . .131 B7
Ryeworth Rd GL52 . . . . . . .131 B7
Ryland Cl GL4 . . . . .140 C5
Ryland Pl 1 BS2 . . . . .19 A2
Rylestone Cl BS36 . . . . .30 F8
Rylestone Gr BS9 . . . . .17 F5
Rysdale Rd BS9 . . . . .17 F6

S

Sabre Cl GL2 . . . . .118 A3
Sabrina Way Bristol BS9 . .17 C4
  Lydney GL15 . . . . .92 B4
Sackville App GL50 . . . . . .133 D4
Saco Ho BS1 . . . . .195 B2
Saddlers La GL50 . . . . .193 A1
Saddlers Rd GL2 . . . . .117 F2
Sadlers Ct 8 GL52 . . . . . . .133 F2
Sadlers Field 4 SN6 . . . . .142 F5
Sadlier Cl BS11 . . . . .17 A8
Saffron Cl GL4 . . . . .119 A5
Saffron Rd GL20 . . . . .192 C4
Sage Cl GL3 . . . . .127 F6
Sages Mead BS32 . . . . .29 E8
Saint Andrews Mews
  BS6 . . . . .18 E3
Saint Way BS34 . . . . .30 A4
Saintbridge Cl GL4 . . . . . .119 B5
Saintbridge Pl GL4 . . . . . .119 B5
SS St Britain* BS1 . . . . . .194 B1
SS Peter & Paul RC Prim Sch
  BS8 . . . . .194 C4
St Agnes Ave BS4 . . . . .8 F2
St Agnes Gdns BS4 . . . . .8 F2
St Agnes Wlk BS4 . . . . .8 F2
St Aidan's Cl BS5 . . . . .10 B6
St Aidan's Rd BS5 . . . . .10 B6
St Alban's Cl GL51 . . . . . . .132 C2
St Alban's Rd BS6 . . . . .18 B8
St Albans Cl BS31 . . . . . . .130 A5
St Albans Rd GL2 . . . . . . .192 C4
St Aldams Dr BS16 . . . . .22 B5
St Aldate St GL1 . . . . .196 B3
St Aldwyn Rd GL1 . . . . . . .118 F6
St Aldwyn's Cl BS7 . . . . . . .18 F4
St Andrew CE Prim Sch
  SN26 . . . . .144 E1
St Andrew's Ave NP16 . . . . .60 E7
St Andrew's CE Prim Sch
  GL54 . . . . .159 A6
St Andrew's CE Prim Sch
  GL12 . . . . .66 A1
St Andrew's Rd
  Avonmouth BS11 . . . . .26 B1
  Avonmouth BS11 . . . . .26 B2
  Bristol BS6 . . . . .18 E2
St Andrews
  Ashleworth GL19 . . . . .172 D4

St Andrews *continued*
  Bristol BS30 . . . . .11 B6
  Yate BS37 . . . . .43 F1
St Andrews Cl GL20 . . . . . .182 C4
St Andrews Gate Rdbt
  BS11 . . . . .26 B2
St Andrews Gn GL3 . . . . . .128 B5
St Andrews Road Sta
  BS11 . . . . .26 B4
St Andrews Trad Est
  BS11 . . . . .26 C2
St Ann St NP16 . . . . .72 F1
St Ann Way GL1 . . . . .196 A1
St Ann's Cross 10 GL15 . .147 D8
St Annal's Rd GL14 . . . . . .191 E4
St Anne's 15 GL52 . . . . . . .133 F2
St Anne's Ave BS31 . . . . .4 D6
St Anne's CE Prim Sch
  BS30 . . . . .11 C3
St Anne's Cl Bristol BS30 . .11 B4
  Cheltenham GL52 . . . . .133 F2
St Anne's Ct BS31 . . . . .4 D6
St Anne's Dr
  Coalpit Heath BS36 . . . . . . .31 C5
  Wick BS30 . . . . .11 F8
St Anne's Inf Sch BS4 . . . . .9 D5
St Anne's Jun Sch BS4 . . . . .9 D5
St Anne's Park Prim Sch
  BS4 . . . . .9 E5
St Anne's Park Rd BS4 . . . . .9 E5
St Anne's Rd
  Bristol,St Anne's Park BS4 . . .9 F6
  Bristol,St George BS5 . . . . .10 B6
  Cheltenham GL52 . . . . .193 C3
St Anne's Terr Bristol BS4 . .9 E5
  Cheltenham GL52 . . . . .193 C3
St Annes Cl 7 Bristol BS5 . . .9 F6
  Brockworth GL3 . . . . .120 E6
St Annes Ct BS4 . . . . .9 D5
St Annes Dr BS30 . . . . .11 C2
St Annes Way GL15 . . . . . .146 E7
St Anthony's Cl BS30 . . . . .12 B7
St Anthony's Sch GL14 . . .191 D4
St Arild's Rd GL17 . . . . .57 B4
St Aubin's Ave BS4 . . . . .9 F3
St Augustine's Par BS1 . . .195 A2
St Augustine's Pl 1
  BS1 . . . . .195 A2
St Augustine's Working
  Farm* GL2 . . . . .157 B6
St Augustines of Canterbury
  RC Sch BS16 . . . . .20 F7
St Barbara's Cl GL20 . . . . .182 D4
St Barnabas CE Prim Sch
  BS11 . . . . .17 C5
  Bristol,North Common BS30 .11 C6
St Barnabas Cl
  Bristol,Lower Knowle BS4 . . .8 F1
  Bristol,Warmley BS30 . . . . .11 C7
  Gloucester GL1 . . . . .118 E4
St Barnabas Ho BS30 . . . . .11 C7
St Bartholomew's Rd
  BS7 . . . . .18 F3
St Bartholomews 12
  GL18 . . . . .171 A4
St Bartholomews Cl GL11 .87 F5
St Bede's RC Coll BS11 . . .26 C1
St Bede's Rd BS15 . . . . . . .20 D2
St Benedict's RC Sch &
  Sports Coll GL15 . . . . . .133 A3
St Bernadette RC Prim Sch
  BS10 .3 B6
St Bernadette RC Sec Sch
  BS10 .3 A6
St Bernard's RC Sch
  BS11 . . . . .16 E6
St Bernard's Rd BS11 . . . . .16 E6
St Birinus Ct GL7 . . . . .153 E3
St Blaize Ct GL7 . . . . .190 C4
St Bonaventure's RC Prim
  Sch BS7 . . . . .18 D4
St Brelades Gr BS4 . . . . .9 F5
St Brenda's Ct 1 BS8 . . . .194 A3
St Brendan's Rd GL5 . . . . . .99 E7
St Brendan's Sixth Form Coll
  BS4 . . . . .10 A1
St Brendan's Way BS11 . . .26 F5
St Brendans Rdbt BS11 . . .26 C1
St Briavels Castle*
  GL15 . . . . .146 E7
St Briavels Ct BS37 . . . . . . .32 D8
St Briavels Parochial CE Prim
  Sch GL15 . . . . .146 E7
St Briavels Rd GL15 . . . . . .147 B2
St Bruel's Cl GL15 . . . . . . .146 F7
St Cadoc Ho BS31 . . . . .4 F5
St Catharine's RC Prim Sch
  GL55 . . . . .188 F2
St Catherine Ct GL11 . . . . .118 E7
St Catherine St GL1 . . . . . .196 B4
St Catherine's Ind Est BS3 .8 D3
St Catherine's Mead
  BS20 . . . . .16 D3
St Catherine's Terr BS3 . . . .8 D3
St Catherines Pl 7 BS3 . . . .8 D3
St Chloe Mead GL5 . . . . . . .91 B8
St Christopher's Sch BS6 . .18 B4
St Clair Cotts GL51 . . . . . .173 F2
St Clement's Wlk GL7 . . . .190 C5
St Clements Ct
  6 Bristol BS16 . . . . .20 D3
  Keynsham BS31 . . . . .4 E4
St Clements Rd BS31 . . . . . . .4 E4
St Cyril's Rd GL10 . . . . .97 F7
St David's Ave BS30 . . . . . .11 B5
St David's Cl
  Chepstow/Cas-Gwent NP16 .60 E7
  Gloucester GL4 . . . . .118 D3

St David's Cres BS4 . . . . .9 F6
St David's Ct GL56 . . . . . . .187 A3
St David's Rd BS35 . . . . . . .64 C1
St David's Sch GL56 . . . . . .187 A3
St Davids Cl GL51 . . . . . . .130 A6
St Davids Rd GL20 . . . . . . .182 C4
St Dominics RC Prim Sch
  GL5 .91 A7
St Dunstan's Rd BS3 . . . . . . .8 C2
St Dunstans Cl BS31 . . . . . . .4 E6
St Edward's RC Prim Sch
  BS8 . . . . .194 B2
St Edward's Sch GL52 . . . .131 A7
St Edwards Dr GL52 . . . . . .176 F4
St Edwards Jun Sch
  GL52 . . . . .131 B7
St Edwards Rd BS4 . . . . . . .176 F4
St Edwards Wlk GL53 . . . . .131 A6
St Edyth's Rd BS9 . . . . .17 C6
St Ewens Rd NP16 . . . . .60 E6
St Fagans Ct BS30 . . . . .11 B2
St Francis Dr Wick BS30 . . .12 B7
  Winterbourne BS36 . . . . .30 F6
St Francis Rd
  6 Bristol BS3 . . . . .8 A4
  Keynsham BS31 . . . . .4 D6
St Gabriel's Bsns Pk 24
  BS5 . . . . .9 B8
St Gabriel's Rd BS5 . . . . .9 B8
St George CE Prim Sch
  BS1 . . . . .195 B2
St George Pl NP16 . . . . . . .194 C2
St George's Rd GL51 . . . . . .88 B3
  Gloucester GL4 . . . . .118 C3
  21 Moreton-in-M GL56 . . . .187 A3
St George's Dr GL51 . . . . . .133 B2
  Gloucester GL4 . . . . .118 C3
St George's Hill BS20 . . . . .16 A2
St George's Ho BS1 . . . . . . .194 B2
St George's Hts 12 BS5 . . . .9 C7
St George's Prim Sch BS1 .193 B3
St George's Rd
  Cheltenham GL50 . . . . .193 A3
  Dursley GL11 . . . . .88 A3
  Keynsham BS31 . . . . .4 D6
St George's Sq GL50 . . . . . .193 B4
St George's Sch GL51 . . . . . .93 B4
St George's Terr GL56 . . . .186 C6
St Georges Ct BS45 . . . . .9 F6
St Georges Bsns Pk
  GL51 . . . . .133 A2
St Georges Cl GL10 . . . . . . .97 F4
St Georges Ho BS5 . . . . .9 B8
St Georges Ind Est BS11 . .26 B3
St Georges Rd
  Ashchurch GL20 . . . . .182 C4
  Bristol BS1 . . . . .194 C2
  Watermead GL20 . . . . .120 E5
St Georges Twr 5 GL50 . . .193 B4
St Georges Way NP16 . . . . .61 B4
St Giles Barton GL12 . . . . . .55 D8
St Giles Ct Bristol GL20 . . .182 C7
St Gregory's Rd BS7 . . . . . . .18 F8
St Helen's Wlk BS5 . . . . . . .20 A1
St Helena Rd BS5 . . . . .9 C7
St Helens CE Prim Sch
  BS35 . . . . .51 A4
St Helens Dr Bristol BS30 . .11 C2
  Wick BS30 . . . . .12 C7
St Helier Ave BS4 . . . . .9 F3
St Hilary Ct GL9 . . . . .17 D5
St Ivel Way BS30 . . . . .11 C6
St Ives Ct GL52 . . . . .133 F4
St James CE Prim Sch
  Cheltenham GL50 . . . . .130 B6
  Chipping Campden GL55 . . .189 A1
St James Cl BS35 . . . . .64 A3
  4 Cheltenham GL50 . . . . .193 A4
  1 Moreton-in-M GL56 . . . .187 A2
St James Cvn Pk GL16 . . . .155 B3
St James Mews 3 GL1 . . . .119 A8
St James Pl BS16 . . . . .21 A5
St James Sq GL15 . . . . .147 D8
St James St
  Cheltenham GL52 . . . . .193 C3
  Gloucester GL1 . . . . .119 A8
St James Trad Est 4
  GL1 . . . . .119 A8
St James' Cl GL2 . . . . .117 F1
St James' Ct GL1 . . . . .117 F1
St James' Pl GL50 . . . . . . .193 A1
St James' Rdbt GL50 . . . . .193 A4
St James' Sq
  Cheltenham GL50 . . . . .193 B3
  20 Monmouth/Trefynwy
  NP25 . . . . .154 A7
St James' Terr GL50 . . . . . .193 B2
St James's Pk SN14 . . . . . . .14 F8
St James's Rd BS8 . . . . . . .18 B1
St James's St GL15 . . . . . . .21 A5
St John St
  Hawkesbury Upton GL9 . . . .56 A3
  2 Thornbury BS35 . . . . . . .64 B1
St John's Bridge BS1 . . . . .194 C1
St John's CE Prim Sch
  Bristol BS8 . . . . .18 A2
  Cheltenham GL52 . . . . .193 C3
  Coleford GL16 . . . . .155 A5

St John's CE Prim Sch
  BS31 .4 E5
St John's Cl
  Bishop's Cleeve GL52 . . . . .137 F4
  Stratton GL7 . . . . .190 B7
St John's Cres BS3 . . . . .8 E2
St John's Ct 3 GL50 . . . . .133 B2
St John's Ct GL20 . . . . .136 A8
St John's Ho BS5 . . . . .9 D8
St John's La Bristol BS3 . . . .8 E2
  Gloucester GL1 . . . . .196 B3
St John's Mead CE Prim Sch
  BS37 . . . . .44 B1
St John's Rd Bristol BS8 . . .18 A1
  Bristol,Bedminster BS3 . . . . .8 E2
  Cirencester GL7 . . . . .190 C6
  Ruardean GL17 . . . . .163 F4
  Slimbridge GL2 . . . . .95 E3
St John's St Bristol BS3 . . . .8 C3
  12 Coleford GL16 . . . . . . .155 A5
  Lechlade on T GL7 . . . . . . .153 E2
St John's-on-the-Hill Sch
  NP16 . . . . .72 F2
St Johns Ave
  Cheltenham GL52 . . . . .193 C3
  Churchdown GL3 . . . . .128 A6
St Johns Ct Bristol BS16 . . .20 A3
  Bristol,Bedminster BS3 . . . . .8 D2
  7 Coleford GL16 . . . . .155 A5
  Keynsham BS31 . . . . .4 E6
St Johns Sq GL14 . . . . .191 C2
St Johns Way BS37 . . . . . . .44 C2
St Joseph's RC Prim Sch
  BS16 . . . . .20 B3
St Joseph's Rd BS10 . . . . . .28 E6
St Jude's Wlk GL53 . . . . . .130 F6
St Katherine's Hospl The
  Alms Houses 7 HR8 . . . . .178 F8
St Katherine's Sch BS20 . .16 E3
St Kenya Ct BS31 . . . . .4 F5
St Keyna Rd BS31 . . . . .4 E5
St Kilda Par GL1 . . . . .196 C2
St Kingsmark Ave NP16 . . .72 D1
St Ladoc Rd BS31 . . . . .4 D6
St Laud Ct GL9 . . . . .17 D5
St Lawrence Cl
  Cheltenham GL51 . . . . .190 B5
  Sandhurst GL2 . . . . .172 F2
St Lawrence La NP16 . . . . . .60 C7
St Lawrence Rd NP16 . . . . . .60 C7
St Lawrence Rd
  Chepstow/Cas-Gwent NP16 .60 C8
  Gloucester GL4 . . . . .119 D8
  Lechlade on T GL7 . . . . . . .153 E2
St Lawrence's CE Prim Sch
  GL7 . . . . .153 E2
St Leonard's Ct OX7 . . . . . .177 E1
St Leonard's Rd
  Bristol,Horfield BS7 . . . . . . .18 E5
  Bristol,Lower Easton BS5 . . .19 C2
St Leonard's Row SN16 . . .142 B2
St Leonards
  Cheltenham GL50 . . . . .142 B2
  Upton St Leonards GL4 . . . .119 E2
St Loe Cl BS14 . . . . .2 E3
St Loes Pitch GL5 . . . . .91 A8
St Lucia Cl BS7 . . . . .18 E7
St Lucia Cres BS7 . . . . .18 E7
St Luke St BS5 . . . . .196 B4
St Luke's Cres BS3 . . . . .8 B7
St Luke's Ct BS3 . . . . .8 B7
St Luke's Gdns BS4 . . . . .9 E2
St Luke's Mews BS4 . . . . . . .9 E2
St Luke's Pl GL53 . . . . .193 C2
St Luke's Rd Bristol BS3 . . . .8 E4
  Cheltenham GL53 . . . . .193 C2
St Lukes Cl BS16 . . . . .21 C7
St Lukes St GL1 . . . . .119 A1
St Margaret's Cl BS31 . . . . . .4 D6
St Margaret's Dr BS7 . . . . . .18 E5
St Margaret's Par 6
  GL50 . . . . .193 B4
St Margaret's Rd
  Cheltenham GL50 . . . . .193 B4
  Ruardean GL17 . . . . .163 F4
St Margarets Cl GL2 . . . . . .117 A2
St Margarets Dr GL20 . . . .183 E4
St Margarets Rd
  Alderton GL20 . . . . .139 E4
  Gloucester GL3 . . . . .119 A8
St Mark St GL1 . . . . .196 B4
St Mark's Ave 1 BS5 . . . . . .19 B1
St Mark's Cl GL51 . . . . .129 D7
St Mark's Ct GL1 . . . . .196 B4
St Mark's Gr 8 BS5 . . . . . . .19 B1
St Mark's Ho 18 BS5 . . . . . .19 B1
St Mark's Rd
  Bristol BS5 . . . . .19 B1
St Mark's Terr 11 BS5 . . . . .19 B1
St Marks Church Ho 4
  BS5 .19 B1
St Marks Cl BS31 . . . . .4 E6
St Martin's Gdns BS4 . . . . . .9 B1
St Martin's La SN14 . . . . . .14 F8
St Martin's Pk SN14 . . . . . . .14 F8
St Martin's Rd BS4 . . . . .9 B2
St Martin's Wlk BS4 . . . . .9 B2
St Martins Cl BS4 . . . . .9 B1
St Martins Terr GL50 . . . . .133 E3
St Mary Redcliffe & Temple
  CE Sch BS1 . . . . .195 B1
St Mary Redcliffe CE Prim
  Sch BS3 . . . . .8 E4

St Mary St
  8 Chepstow/Cas-Gwent
  NP16 . . . . .60 E8
  Thornbury BS35 . . . . .51 B8
St Mary Street Arc 9
  NP16 . . . . .60 E8
St Mary's Abbey Church*
  GL20 . . . . .192 C3
St Mary's CE Inf Sch
  GL52 . . . . .134 B3
St Mary's CE Prim Sch
  Bromesberrow Heath HR8 .179 C5
  Tetbury GL8 . . . . .140 B4
  Thornbury BS35 . . . . .64 C2
St Mary's CE Prim Sch
  BS37 . . . . .43 E2
St Mary's Cl
  Kempsford GL7 . . . . .144 F7
  Lower Swell GL54 . . . . .176 D4
St Mary's Halt* GL15 . . . . .92 A2
St Mary's Hill GL5 . . . . .91 A7
St Mary's Hospl BS8 . . . . .194 B2
St Mary's La GL20 . . . . . . .192 C4
St Mary's Mead GL6 . . . . . .103 F7
St Mary's RC Prim Sch
  NP16 . . . . .60 E7
St Mary's Rd Bristol BS11 .16 B7
  Cirencester GL7 . . . . .190 C4
  Leigh Woods BS8 . . . . .7 D2
  Tetbury GL8 . . . . .140 B4
  Tewkesbury GL20 . . . . .192 B4
St Mary's Sq
  Gloucester GL1 . . . . .196 A3
  Lydney GL15 . . . . .92 C3
St Mary's St
  Gloucester GL1 . . . . .196 A3
  Painswick GL6 . . . . .103 F8
St Mary's Way BS37 . . . . . . .43 F2
St Mary's Wlk BS11 . . . . . . .16 C6
St Marys Cl Bristol BS30 . . .11 B5
  Dymock GL18 . . . . .178 D2
St Marys Dr GL7 . . . . .152 E4
St Marys Field GL7 . . . . . . .152 A3
St Marys RC Prim Sch
  Bristol BS34 . . . . .30 A7
  Innsworth GL3 . . . . .127 F6
St Marys Way 6 BS5 . . . . . .19 B1
St Matthew's Ave 10 BS6 . .18 D1
St Matthew's CE Prim Sch
  GL5 .9 B8
St Matthew's Rd BS6 . . . . .195 A4
St Matthews Cl BS5 . . . . . . .98 E6
St Matthias & Dr Bell's CE
  Prim Sch BS16 . . . . .20 A4
St Matthias Ho BS2 . . . . . .195 C3
St Matthias Pk BS2 . . . . . .195 C3
St Maur Gdns NP16 . . . . . . .72 D1
St Michael On The Mount CE
  Prim Sch BS2 . . . . .194 C3
St Michael's Ave SN6 . . . . .145 C3
St Michael's CE Prim Sch
  BS34 . . . . .29 E5
St Michael's Cl GL17 . . . . .165 B4
St Michael's Cl
  Mitcheldean GL17 . . . . .164 D5
  Winterbourne BS36 . . . . .30 F7
St Michael's Hill BS2 . . . . .194 C4
St Michael's Hospl BS2 . . .194 C4
St Michael's Pk BS2 . . . . . .194 C4
St Michaels Ave GL52 . . . . .138 B4
St Michaels CE Prim Sch
  BS36 . . . . .30 E6
St Michaels Cl BS7 . . . . .18 E4
St Michaels Pk GL14 . . . . .191 C1
St Michaels Rd
  Cheltenham GL51 . . . . .130 B5
  Cirencester GL7 . . . . .190 C3
St Monica Ct BS9 . . . . .18 A5
St Nicholas Cl GL20 . . . . . .183 A3
St Nicholas Ct
  Gloucester GL1 . . . . .196 A3
  Hardwicke GL2 . . . . .109 F7
St Nicholas Dr GL54 . . . . . .133 D5
St Nicholas of Tolentine RC
  Prim Sch BS5 . . . . .9 A8
St Nicholas Pk 10 BS5 . . . .19 B1
St Nicholas Rd BS14 . . . . . . .3 C4
St Nicholas Sq GL1 . . . . . . .196 A3
St Nicholas St BS1 . . . . . . .195 A2
St Nicholas' Rd BS2 . . . . . . .19 B1
St Oswald's Cl BS13 . . . . . . .2 A8
St Oswald's Ct BS13 . . . . . . .2 A8
St Oswald's Rd Bristol BS6 .18 B2
  Gloucester GL1 . . . . .196 A4
St Oswalds Ret Pk GL1 . . .120 C4
St Patrick's Ct GL3 . . . . . . .120 D5
St Patrick's RC Prim Sch
  BS5 .9 D7
St Patricks Ct BS31 . . . . .4 E5
St Patricks Rd GL20 . . . . . .182 C4
St Paul St BS2 . . . . .195 B4
St Paul's La BS8 . . . . .194 A3
St Paul's Par GL50 . . . . . . .133 C2
St Paul's Prim Sch
  GL1 . . . . .196 A1
St Paul's RC Prim Sch
  BS37 . . . . .32 E8
St Paul's Rd
  2 Bristol,Southville BS3 . . . .8 D4
  Bristol,Victoria Park BS8 . . .194 B4
  Cheltenham GL50 . . . . .133 D1

Paul's Rd continued
Gloucester GL1 . . . . .118 E7
Paul's St N GL50 . . . . . . .133 D3
Paul's St S GL50 . . . . . . .193 B4
Paul's Terr GL50 . . . . . . .193 B4
Pauls Ct 5 GL56 . . . . . .187 A2
Peter's Cl 10 GL14 . . . .157 A6
Peter's Cres BS36 . . . . .31 B8
Peter's Ct GL7 . . . . .190 C4
Peter's Ho BS8 . . . . .194 B2
Peter's RC High Sch &
Sixth Form Ctr GL4 . . . .118 E1
Peter's RC Prim Sch
GL1 . . . . .127 B2
Peter's Rd GL4 . . . . .119 C3
Peter's Rise BS13 . . . . . . .2 B7
Peter's Sq GL51 . . . . . . .133 A4
Peter's Wlk 3 BS9 . . . . .18 B6
Peters Cl
Cheltenham GL51 . . . . . .133 B4
Rodmarton GL7 . . . . .149 B1
Peters Ct 3 GL56 . . . .187 A2
Peters Rd GL7 . . . . .190 C4
Peters Way 12 GL54 . .174 A7
Philip's Cl GL3 . . . . .120 A8
Philip's Ct GL1 . . . . .118 D7
Philips Central BS2 . . . . . .9 A5
Philips Cswy BS2 . . . . . . .9 B5
Philips Trad Pk BS2 . . . . .9 B4
Phillip's St GL50 . . . . . .193 B1
Phillips Rd BS2 . . . . .9 A7
Pierre Dr BS30 . . . . .11 B6
Pius X RC Prim Sch
BS13 . . . . .2 A5
Ronan's Ave BS6 . . . . .18 C1
Rose's Specl Sch GL5 . .99 B7
Sampson's CE Jun Sch
SN6 . . . . .143 E4
Sampson's Inf Sch
SN6 . . . . .143 E4
Saviour's Rise BS36 . .31 B6
Saviours Ho BS4 . . . . . .8 F2
Stephen's Ave 3
BS1 . . . . .195 A2
Stephen's CE Jun Sch
BS15 . . . . .20 D2
Stephen's Ct GL1 . . . .118 D7
Stephen's Manor
GL51 . . . . .130 B7
Stephen's Rd
Bristol BS16 . . . . .20 D2
Cheltenham GL51 . . . . . .130 B7
Stephen's St BS1 . . . .195 A2
Stephens Bsns Ctr
BS30 . . . . .11 C5
Stephens Cl
2 Bristol,Brentry BS10 . .28 C2
Bristol,Upper Soundwell
BS16 . . . . .20 E3
Cheltenham GL51 . . . . . .130 B7
Swithin's GL10 . . . . . .97 E4
Swithins Rd GL15 . . . .156 B1
Swithuns Rd GL2 . . . .118 A6
Tecla Rd NP16 . . . . . . .60 E6
Teresa's RC Prim Sch
BS7 . . . . .28 E1
Tewdric Rd NP16 . . . . .60 E7
Tewdrics Pl NP16 . . . .60 B4
Thomas More RC Prim Sch
GL51 . . . . .132 D2
Thomas More RC Sch
BS7 . . . . .19 A3
Thomas Pl BS1 . . . . . .195 B2
Thomas Rd BS1 . . . . .195 B2
Thomas St E BS1 . . . .195 B2
Ursula's High Sch BS9 .18 A6
Vincent Way GL3 . . . .128 A8
Vincent's Hill 1 BS6 . .18 A2
Vincent's Rd BS4 . . . .194 A2
Vincents Trad Est BS2 . .9 B6
Werburgh's Pk BS2 . . .19 A2
Werburgh's RC Prim Sch
BS2 . . . . .19 A2
Werburgh's Rd BS2 . . .18 F2
Whites Cl GL14 . . . . . .191 C2
Whites Prim Sch
GL14 . . . . .191 C2
Whites Rd GL14 . . . . .191 D3
Whites Terr GL14 . . . .191 C2
Whytes Rd BS4 . . . . . . .2 D8
Wulfstans Ave BS10 . .18 A8
alamanca Rd GL2 . . . .134 B2
alcombe Rd BS4 . . . . . .9 A1
alem Rd BS36 . . . . . . .30 F7
alisbury Ave Bristol BS15 .10 B8
Cheltenham GL51 . . . . . .130 A5
alisbury Dr BS16 . . . . .20 E6
alisbury Gdns BS16 . . .20 E5
alisbury Ho GL1 . . . . .119 A8
alisbury Pk BS16 . . . . .20 E6
alisbury Rd
Bristol,Mangotsfield BS16 .20 E6
Bristol,St Anne's BS4 . . . .9 D5
Gloucester GL1 . . . . . . .119 A8
alisbury St
Bristol,Pile Marsh BS5 . . .9 E7
Bristol,Russell Town BS5 . .9 B6
alix Cl GL51 . . . . .130 A4
allis Cl GL20 . . . . .182 B5
alm Rd BS36 . . . . .30 F7
alsbury Cl BS13 . . . . . . .2 B4
almon Cl GL54 . . . . . . .9 B8
almon's Spring Ind Est
GL6 . . . . .103 B1
almons Way BS16 . . . .21 B8

Salmonsbury Cotts
GL54 . . . . .169 A8
Salt Way
Coln St Aldwyns GL7 . . . .152 D8
Compton Abdale GL54 . .167 D3
Salter St GL13 . . . . .85 E3
Salter's La GL54 . . . . . .174 C8
Salterley Grange GL53 .122 D7
Salford CE Prim Sch
BS31 . . . . .5 E2
Saltford Ct BS31 . . . . . .5 E3
Salthouse Farm Pk BS35 .38 A7
Salthrop Rd BS7 . . . . . .18 E4
Saltmarsh Dr BS11 . . . .27 A1
Saltwell Ave BS14 . . . . .3 C5
Salvia Cl GL3 . . . . .127 F6
Sambourne La BS20 . . . .16 C4
Sambourne Rd SN16 . . .142 E1
Samian Way BS34 . . . . .29 E5
Sampson House Bsns Pk
BS10 . . . . .27 D7
Sampsons Rd BS13 . . . . .2 D4
Sams La SN26 . . . . . . .144 E1
Samuel St 3 BS5 . . . . . .9 C8
Samuel White Rd BS15 .10 C4
Samuel White's Inf Sch
BS15 . . . . .10 C4
Samuel Wright Cl BS30 .11 D5
San Andreas BS34 . . . . .28 E6
San Remo GL1 . . . . . . .118 C6
Sanctuary Gdns BS9 . . .17 D3
Sand Hill BS4 . . . . .9 C4
Sandalwood Dr GL2 . . .118 B7
Sandbach Rd BS4 . . . . . .9 D4
Sandbed Rd BS2 . . . . . .19 A2
Sandburrows Rd BS13 . . .1 F6
Sandburrows Wlk BS13 . .1 F6
Sandcroft BS14 . . . . .2 F6
Sandfield Cres GL2 . . . .100 A7
Sandfield Rd GL3 . . . . .128 D5
Sandfield The GL20 . . . .182 C5
Sandfields GL18 . . . . . .179 B3
Sandford Leaze GL8 . . .148 B1
Sandford Mill Cl GL53 . .130 F7
Sandford Mill Rd GL53 .130 F7
Sandford Park Pl GL52 .193 C2
Sandford Rd
Aylburton GL15 . . . . . . .147 D4
Bristol BS8 . . . . .194 A1
Cheltenham GL53 . . . . . .193 C1
Sandford Sch GL53 . . . .123 B7
Sandford St GL53 . . . . .193 C2
Sandford Terr GL15 . . . .147 D4
Sandford Way GL4 . . . .118 B1
Sandgate Rd BS4 . . . . . .9 D3
Sandgrove Rd GL6 . . . . .82 F8
Sandholme Cl BS16 . . . .20 E8
Sandholme Rd BS4 . . . . .9 D4
Sandhurst BS37 . . . . . . .32 D8
Sandhurst Cl BS34 . . . . .40 B1
Sandhurst La
Down Hatherley GL2 . . . .173 A2
Gloucester GL2 . . . . . . .126 E5
Sandhurst Rd Bristol BS4 .9 D4
Charlton Kings GL52 . . . .131 B6
Gloucester GL1 . . . . . . .118 D4
Sandiway La HR9 . . . . .162 D3
Sandling Ave BS7 . . . . . .19 A7
Sandown Cl BS16 . . . . . .30 F1
Sandown Rd
Bishop's Cleeve GL52 . . .137 F4
Bristol,Filton BS34 . . . . .29 C3
Bristol,Kensington Park BS4 .9 D4
Sandpiper Cl 2 GL2 . . .117 D1
Sandpits La
Hawkesbury Upton GL9 . . .56 A2
Randwick GL6 . . . . .102 C1
Sherston SN16 . . . . .58 C1
Stroud GL6 . . . . .98 C8
Sandpool La GL7 . . . . .149 C2
Sandringham Ave
Bristol BS16 . . . . .20 E8
Gloucester GL2 . . . . . . .118 C1
Sandringham Ct GL53 . .130 F7
Sandringham Pk BS16 . .20 E8
Sandringham Rd
Bristol,Kensington Park BS4 .9 D4
Bristol,Longwell Green
BS30 . . . . .11 D7
Bristol,Stoke Gifford BS34 .29 D4
Sands Cl WR12 . . . . . . .188 A1
Sands Croft Ave WR12 .188 B1
Sands Hill SN14 . . . . . . .23 E3
Sands La BS36 . . . . .43 F1
Sands The 11 WR12 . . .185 B8
Sandstar Cl GL2 . . . . . .118 A7
Sandstone Rise BS36 . . .30 E4
Sandtumps GL15 . . . . . .147 B4
Sandwich Rd BS4 . . . . . .9 D4
Sandy Cl BS32 . . . . .29 E6
Sandy La Aust BS35 . . . .49 A6
Aust BS35 . . . . .49 A8
Bristol BS5 . . . . .9 F8
Cheltenham GL53 . . . . . .130 F4
Coleford-in-GL20 . . . . . .163 A1
Hewelsfield GL15 . . . . . .146 E5
Upper Rissington GL54 . .169 D6
Sandy Lane Cl GL54 . . .169 D5
Sandy Lane Rd GL53 . .130 F5
Sandy Lodge BS37 . . . . .32 E8
Sandy Park Rd BS4 . . . . .9 C3
Sandy Pluck La GL51 . . .129 B5
Sandycroft Rd GL13 . . .128 A7
Sandydaze Bristol BS37 . .17 E7
Gloucester GL2 . . . . . . .127 D3
Sandyleaze GL54 . . . . .166 C2
Saniger La Berkeley GL13 . .85 D6
Newton GL13 . . . . .85 C7

Sankey Gr 9 GL56 . . . .187 A2
Sappercombe La GL53 .131 B5
Sapperton CE Prim Sch
GL7 . . . . .149 B6
Sapperton Rd GL4 . . . .118 F5
Sapphire Cl GL4 . . . . . .118 C2
Sarah Siddons Wlk 1
GL50 . . . . .130 B6
Sarah St BS3 . . . . .9 B7
Sargent St BS3 . . . . . . .9 B7
Sargent's La HR9,GL18 .170 B4
Sarn Hill Grange GL20 .181 C5
Sarnedy Rd 3 GL16 . . .155 A5
Sarum Cl BS16 . . . . .21 C6
Sarum Cres BS10 . . . . . .28 C1
Sassoon Ct BS30 . . . . . .10 F5
Satchfield Cl BS10 . . . . .27 F2
Satchfield Cres BS10 . . .27 F2
Satellite Bsns Pk BS5 . . .9 D6
Sates Way BS9 . . . . .18 C6
Saturn Cl GL4 . . . . .119 F6
Saunders Cl
Huntley GL17 . . . . .165 A7
Lea HR9 . . . . .164 D8
Saunders Rd BS16 . . . . .20 E4
Saunton Wlk BS4 . . . . . .2 E8
Savage Hill GL6 . . . . . .154 E4
Savages Wood BS32 . . .29 E8
Savages Wood Rd BS32 .29 D8
Savernake Rd GL4 . . . .119 A7
Saville Cl GL50 . . . . . . .133 E4
Saville Gate Cl BS9 . . . .17 F4
Saville Mews BS6 . . . . .195 A4
Saville Pl BS8 . . . . .194 A2
Saville Rd BS9 . . . . .18 E3
Savoy Rd BS4 . . . . .9 E4
Savoy The BS11 . . . . . . .16 E6
Saw Mill La 5 BS35 . . .64 B1
Saw Mills End GL4 . . . .127 D1
Sawpit La GL19 . . . . . .173 C7
Sawpits La BS36 . . . . . .177 D5
Sawpits La HR9 . . . . . .162 E4
Sawyers Cl SN16 . . . . .142 D1
Sawyers Hill SN16 . . . .142 D1
Sawyers Rise
Ashleworth GL19 . . . . . .172 D4
Minety SN16 . . . . .142 D1
Saxon Cl Cricklade SN6 .143 E4
Gloucester GL2 . . . . . . .127 C5
Sherston SN16 . . . . .58 C1
Saxon Pl NP16 . . . . .61 A7
Saxon Rd Bristol BS2 . . .19 A2
Cirencester GL7 . . . . . . .117 B6
Saxon Way Bristol BS32 . .40 C1
Cheltenham GL52 . . . . . .152 D4
Fairford GL7 . . . . .152 D4
Say Wlk BS30 . . . . .11 D7
Sayers Cres GL2 . . . . . .129 C1
Saylittle Mews GL2 . . .127 E5
Sayth Ho GL7 . . . . .190 D5
Sbtl Ctr BS15 . . . . .195 D4
Scandrett Cl BS10 . . . . .27 E2
Scantleberry Cl BS14 . . .3 A7
Scar Hill GL6 . . . . .80 F3
Scarr Rd GL18 . . . . . . .171 A7
Scarr Rd GL18 . . . . . . .171 A7
Scholars Ct GL51 . . . . .133 B2
School Cl
Bristol,Eastville BS5 . . . .19 D2
Bristol,Patchway BS34 . . .29 C8
Bristol,Whitchurch BS14 . . .3 A5
5 Coleford GL16 . . . . . .155 B5
Dursley GL11 . . . . .87 B8
Hillesley GL12 . . . . .58 E8
School Cnr Corse GL19 .172 B7
Joy's Green GL17 . . . . . .163 D3
Lydney GL15 . . . . .92 B5
School Ct BS34 . . . . . . .40 A5
School Hill
Bourton-on-t-W GL54 . . .168 F7
Chepstow/Cas-Gwent NP16 .50 F8
Stratton GL7 . . . . .190 A8
Winstone GL7 . . . . .107 A8
School Hill Ind Est 10
NP16 . . . . .29 D6
School Ho GL50 . . . . . .193 B4
School La
Ampney Crucis GL7 . . . .124 C5
Badminton GL9 . . . . .46 E2
Bishop's Cleeve GL52 . . .137 E4
Blockley GL56 . . . . .186 C5
Bretforton WR11 . . . . . .188 A2
2 Bristol BS16 . . . . .19 E5
Castle Eaton SN6 . . . . . .144 D4
Cirencester GL7 . . . . . . .117 B4
Edgeworth GL6 . . . . . . .105 D1
Hardwicke GL2 . . . . . . .109 E8
Longhope GL17 . . . . . . .164 D6
Meysey Hampton GL7 . . .152 A1
North The NP25 . . . . . . .154 C1
Overbury GL20 . . . . . . .182 F8
Ruardean GL17 . . . . . . .163 A1
Shipton GL54 . . . . .166 F5
Shurdington GL51 . . . . .121 A4
South Cerney GL7 . . . . .142 F8
Sevenleaze La Edge GL6 .111 B2
Gloucester GL4,GL51 . . .129 B1
School Mead GL11 . . . . .87 B8
School Mews GL4 . . . . .119 B4
School Rd Alderton GL20 .182 A4
Appperley GL19 . . . . . . .173 C6
Bishop's Cleeve GL52 . . .137 F2
Bisley GL6 . . . . .105 A1
Bristol BS15 . . . . .10 D6

School Rd continued
Bristol,Totterdown BS4 . . .9 A3
Charlton Kings GL53 . . . .131 B6
Dursley GL11 . . . . .80 C8
Frampton Cotterell BS36 . .31 A8
Joy's Green GL17 . . . . . .163 D3
Kemble GL7 . . . . .141 F8
Minchinhampton GL6 . . . .148 A3
Ruardean GL17 . . . . . . .163 F4
Upper Lydbrook GL17 . . .163 D2
Wotherill GL15 . . . . . . .155 F1
Wotton-y-E GL12 . . . . . .68 B7
School Road Flats 3
GL53 . . . . .131 B6
School Row GL7 . . . . . .149 E3
School Sq GL5 . . . . .98 F5
School St WR11 . . . . . .188 C6
School Terr GL5 . . . . . . .98 D6
School Way BS35 . . . . . .38 A6
School Wlk Bristol BS11 . .27 B1
School St BS37 . . . . . . .43 E2
Schooler's La GL56 . . . .177 E6
Scop The BS32 . . . . .40 B5
Scotland La BS4,BS14 . . .4 A7
Scott Ave GL2 . . . . .118 C4
Scott Ct BS30 . . . . .11 B3
Scott Ho GL51 . . . . . . .132 E3
Scott Lawrence Cl BS16 . .20 A7
Scott Way BS37 . . . . . . .32 F8
Scowles Rd GL16 . . . . .154 F6
Scrubbett's La GL8 . . . . .69 FB
Sea Mills Inf Sch BS9 . . .17 C7
Sea Mills La BS9 . . . . . .17 C8
Sea Mills Prim Sch BS9 .17 B4
Sea Mills Sta BS9 . . . . .17 C5
Seabright Cl GL51 . . . .132 E5
Seabroke Rd GL1 . . . . .196 C4
Seacole Rd GL51 . . . . .132 D2
Seagry Cl BS10 . . . . . . .28 E1
Searle Court Ave BS4 . . .9 E4
Sawyers Cl SN16 . . . . .142 D1
Seaton Rd BS5 . . . . .19 C1
Seawalls BS9 . . . . .17 D2
Seawalls Rd BS9 . . . . . .17 D2
Sebert St GL1 . . . . .196 C4
Second Ave Bristol BS14 . .3 B7
Dursley GL11 . . . . .80 C8
Second Chance Touring Site
SN6 . . . . .144 C7
Secret La GL1 . . . . .196 B4
Secunda Way (Hempsted
By-Pass) GL2 . . . . .192 C3
Sedbury Bsns Pk NP16 . .61 B8
Sedbury Chase NP16 . . .73 A1
Sedbury La NP16 . . . . . .73 A1
Seddon Rd 8 BS2 . . . . .19 A3
Sedgefield Gdns BS16 . .30 F2
Sedgewick Gdns GL51 .129 D6
Sedgley Cl GL52 . . . . . .137 F4
Sedley Ho GL50 . . . . . .133 E4
Sedum Ho 1 GL50 . . . .133 B4
Sefton Park Jun & Inf Schs
BS7 . . . . .18 F3
Sefton Park Rd BS7 . . . .18 F3
Segrove Cl GL1 . . . . . . .109 D7
Selborne Rd
Bishop's Cleeve GL52 . . .137 E4
Bristol BS7 . . . . .18 E5
Selbrooke Cres BS16 . . .20 D6
Selby Rd BS5 . . . . .19 F1
Selkirk Ct GL52 . . . . . .133 F2
Selkirk Ct 3 GL52 . . . .133 F2
Selkirk Gdns GL52 . . . .133 F2
Selkirk Rd BS15 . . . . . . .20 C1
Selkirk St GL52 . . . . . . .133 F2
Sellars Rd GL2 . . . . . . .109 D7
Sellars Way BS16 . . . . . .20 D6
Selsey Cl BS4 . . . . .2 E8
Selsley Hill GL5 . . . . . . .98 E4
Selworthy Bristol BS31 . . .4 D5
Cheltenham GL51 . . . . . .129 E5
Selworthy Rd BS31 . . . . .9 B2
Seneca Pl 11 BS5 . . . . . .9 D7
Seneca St BS5 . . . . .9 D7
Seneca Way GL50 . . . . .133 E2
Serlo Rd GL1 . . . . .196 B4
Serridge La BS36 . . . . . .38 B8
Serts Row GL17 . . . . . .165 C6
Setts Rd GL17 . . . . .165 C6
Seven Acres GL14 . . . . .191 D3
Seven Bridges Cotts
SN6 . . . . .144 B3
Seven Stars Rd GL14 . .191 C6
Seven Waters GL10 . . . .91 A4
Sevenacres Rd GL51 . . .91 A4
Sevenleaze La Edge GL6 .111 B2
Gloucester GL4,GL51 . . .129 B1
Seventh Ave
Bristol,Filton BS7 . . . . . .29 B1
Bristol,Hengrove BS14 . . .3 C7
Severn Ave GL2 . . . . . . .118 C2
Severn Beach Prim Sch
BS35 . . . . .38 A6
Severn Bridge Pk NP16 . .61 B5
Severn Cl Charfield GL12 . .67 A4
Maisemore GL2 . . . . . . .126 B7

Severn Cres NP16 . . . . .60 F7
Severn Dr Berkeley GL13 . .85 E4
Tewkesbury GL20 . . . . . .182 B5
Thornbury BS35 . . . . . . .64 B2
Severn Grange BS10 . . .27 D3
Severn Ho BS10 . . . . . . .27 D3
Severn La Berkeley GL13 . .84 E1
Bevington GL13 . . . . . . .76 F8
Severn Lodge 3 GL4 . .119 C4
Severn Oaks GL7 . . . . .109 F7
Severn Rd
Avonmouth BS11 . . . . . .26 C4
Bristol BS11 . . . . .16 D6
Cheltenham GL52 . . . . . .134 A3
Dursley GL11 . . . . .87 E4
Gloucester GL1 . . . . . . .196 B8
Hallen BS10 . . . . .27 A7
Lydney GL15 . . . . .92 B2
Newton GL13 . . . . .85 B8
Pill BS20 . . . . .16 C5
Severn Beach BS35 . . . . .37 F3
Stonehouse GL10 . . . . . .97 E8
Severn St 6 GL14 . . . .157 A6
Severn Terr GL14 . . . . .157 A6
Severn Vale Sch GL2 . .109 E8
Severn View Bristol BS10 . .27 C1
Cinderford GL14 . . . . . .191 E5
Severn View Par GL13 . .85 C8
Severn View Rd
Thornbury BS35 . . . . . . .64 C2
Woolaston GL15 . . . . . .147 B3
Yorkley GL15 . . . . .156 B2
Severn Way
Apperley GL19 . . . . . . .173 C2
Bristol BS34 . . . . .39 F1
Keynsham BS31 . . . . .5 A5
Severnbank Ave GL15 . .92 C3
Severnbanks Prim Sch
GL15 . . . . .92 B3
Severnleigh Gdns BS9 . .17 F3
Severnleigh Ho BS9 . . . .17 F3
Severnside Trad Est
Avonmouth BS11 . . . . . .26 C5
Gloucester GL2 . . . . . . .126 C1
Severnvale Dr GL2 . . . .117 E2
Severnwood Gdns BS35 .38 A5
Sevier St BS2 . . . . .19 A4
Seymour Cl BS37 . . . . . .18 E4
Seymour Cl 3 GL16 . . .155 A7
Seymour Pl
Tewkesbury GL20 . . . . . .192 C3
10 Winchcombe GL54 . .174 A7
Seymour Rd
Bristol,Ashley Down BS7 . .18 E4
Bristol,Kingswood BS15 . .20 C1
Bristol,Upper Easton BS5 . .19 A1
Gloucester GL1 . . . . . . .118 D7
Seyton Wlk BS34 . . . . . .29 E5
Sezincote Cl GL54 . . . . .148 B6
Sezincote House & Gdns*
GL56 . . . . .186 D2
Shackel Hendy Mews
BS16 . . . . .21 B5
Shackleton Ave GL53 . .137 E8
Shackleton Cl GL3 . . . .128 C5
Shadwell GL11 . . . . .81 A8
Shadwell Rd BS7 . . . . . .18 D3
Shaft BS35 . . . . .38 A8
Shaftesbury Ave GL51 . .18 E1
Shaftesbury Hall 4
GL50 . . . . .193 B4
Shaftesbury Rd
BS1 . . . . .133 B6
Shaftesbury Pl 1 GL51 .132 D2
Shaftesbury Terr BS5 . . .9 D7
Shakespeare Ave
Bristol BS7 . . . . .18 C4
Cheltenham GL51 . . . . . .132 E1
Shakespeare Cotts
Cheltenham GL51 . . . . . .132 E1
Dursley GL11 . . . . .80 C7
Shakespeare Ct GL20 . .192 C4
Shaldon Rd BS7 . . . . . . .18 E4
Shalford Cl GL7 . . . . . .190 B3
Shallowbrooks La SN14 . .47 F8
Shallows The BS31 . . . . .5 F3
Shambles Mus The*
GL18 . . . . .171 A4
Shambles The 12 GL5 . .99 C7
Shamrock Cl GL52 . . . .127 F6
Shamrock Rd BS5 . . . . .19 D3
Shanklin Dr BS34 . . . . . .29 B3
Shannon Cl BS35 . . . . . .51 D8
Shannon Ct BS35 . . . . . .51 D8
Shannon Way GL20 . . . .182 B6
Shapcott Cl BS4 . . . . . . .9 B1
Shaplands BS9 . . . . .17 F4
Shard The GL6 . . . . . . .102 F3
Sharland Cl BS9 . . . . . . .17 F1
Sharland Gr BS13 . . . . . .2 C5
Sharman Pitch HR9 . . . .163 C2
Sharpness Prim Sch
GL13 . . . . .85 D8
Sharps Way NP16 . . . . .60 F5
Shaw Cl Bristol BS5 . . . .19 C1
3 Bristol,Upper Easton BS5 . .9 B8
Shaw Gn La GL51 . . . . .133 C4
Shaw Rd GL51 . . . . . . .133 C4
Shawfield La GL56 . . . .134 C5
Shaymoor La BS35 . . . . .39 A4
Shear Ho 7 WR12 . . . .185 C8
Shearmore Cl BS7 . . . . .19 A7

Shearwater Ct BS16 ......19 F6
Shearwater Gr GL3 ......127 E6
Sheene Ct **17** BS3 ....8 C3
Sheene La BS3 ....8 C3
Sheene Way BS3 ....8 C3
Sheenhill Rd WR11 ......188 B8
Sheens Mdw GL14 ....156 F7
Sheep St Cirencester GL7 .190 C4
Highworth SN6 ....145 D3
Stow-on-t-W GL54 ......176 F4
Sheepfair La SN14 ....14 F8
Sheeps Croft BS13 ....2 A1
Sheepscombe Cl GL51 ..129 E8
Sheepscombe Prim Sch
GL6 ....112 E1
Sheepwash The BS35 ....63 D5
Sheepwood Cl BS10 .....28 A2
Sheepwood Rd BS10 ....28 A2
Sheevaun Cl GL2 ....127 D5
Sheiling StS BS35 ....64 B2
Shelburne Rd GL51 .....129 F8
Sheldare Barton BS5 ....10 B7
Sheldon Ave WR12 .....188 B1
Sheldons Ct GL52 ....193 C4
Sheldrake Dr BS16 ......19 E6
Shelduck Rd GL2 ....117 D1
Shellard Rd BS34 ....29 A2
Shellards La BS35 ....51 E2
Shellards Rd BS30 ....10 F3
Shelley Ave
Cheltenham GL51 ....132 E1
Gloucester GL2 ....118 C4
Shelley Cl BS5 ....9 F8
Shelley Ho BS34 ....40 A1
Shelley Rd
Cheltenham GL51 ....132 E1
Dursley GL11 ....80 C7
Shelley Way BS7 ....19 A8
Shellmor Ave BS34 ......40 B1
Shellmor Cl BS32 ....40 D1
Shephard Mead GL20 ...192 B3
Shepherd Rd GL2 ....118 B3
Shepherd's Cl GL55 .....188 F1
Shepherd's Leaze GL12 .68 C6
Shepherdine Cl GL15 ....92 C3
Shepherds Cl Bristol BS16 .20 E5
Cheltenham GL51 ....132 D4
5 Ledbury HR8 ....178 E7
Stroud GL5 ....99 D8
Shepherds Croft GL5 ...99 D8
Shepherds Mead **3**
GL8 ....140 C5
Shepherds Row **4** GL54 .176 F4
Shepherds Way
Cirencester GL7 ....190 C6
Innsworth GL3 ....127 F7
Northleach GL54 ....167 F1
10 Stow-on-t-W GL54 ..176 F4
Shepherds Well GL5 .....99 D1
Shepherds Wlk GL20 ....68 C6
Sheppard Rd BS16 ......20 C6
Sheppard Way
Minchinhampton GL6 ....91 F7
Newent GL18 ....171 A4
Shepperdine Rd BS35 ...75 D2
Sheppey Cnr WR12 .....184 F5
Shepton Wlk BS3 ....8 C2
Sherborne CE Prim Sch
GL54 ....169 A1
Sherborne Cl GL10 .....97 F8
Sherborne Ho
Gloucester GL1 ....196 C3
1 Stonehouse GL10 ....97 F8
Sherborne La GL54 ....169 C3
Sherborne Park Nature
Trail* GL54 ....168 E1
Sherborne Pl GL52 .....193 C3
Sherborne St
Bourton-on-t-W GL54 ..168 F7
Cheltenham GL52 ......193 C4
Gloucester GL1 ....196 C4
Lechlade on T GL7 .....153 E2
Sherborne Stables GL54 .168 F1
Sherborne Terr **4** GL54 .168 F7
Sherbourne Ave BS32 ..29 E7
Sherbourne Cl BS15 ....20 F2
Sherbourne St BS5 .....9 F7
Sherbourne's Brake
BS32 ....29 E6
Shergar Cl GL4 ....119 D4
Sheridan Rd BS7 ....19 A8
Sheridan Way BS30 .....11 A2
Sherrin Way BS13 ....1 A3
Sherrings The BS34 .....29 B8
Sherry The GL54 ....175 B7
Sherston Cl BS16 ....18 E8
Sherston Rd Bristol BS7 ..18 E8
Luckington SN14 ....47 F5
Sherwell Rd BS4 ....9 F3
Sherwood Cl BS31 ......29 E2
Sherwood Gn GL2 .....126 F6
Sherwood Rd Bristol BS15 .20 B1
Keynsham BS31 ....4 E5
Tetbury GL8 ....140 B4
Shetland Rd BS10 ....28 D1
Shield Rd Ctr BS34 ......29 A3
Shield Road Prim Sch
BS7 ....29 A1
Shields Ave BS7 ....29 A1
Shiels Dr BS32 ....29 D7
Shilton Cl BS15 ....10 F7
Shimsey Cl **2** BS16 ....20 C6
Ship La BS1 ....195 B1
Shipham Cl BS14 ....3 B5
Shipley Mow BS16 ......21 B6

Shipley Rd BS9 ....18 A8
Shipman Ct BS16 ....20 C1
Shipton's Grave La GL6 .91 C1
Shipway Ct GL52 ....137 F4
Shire Gdns BS11 ....16 D8
Shire Hill SN14 ....25 A7
Shire Way BS37 ....32 D6
Shirehampton Prim Sch
BS11 ....16 D6
Shirehampton Rd BS9 ..17 C6
Shirehampton Sta BS11 .16 D5
Shirreff Ct **8** BS6 .....18 B1
Shooters End GL5 ......99 C8
Shop La Badminton GL9 .46 E2
Bretforton WR11 ....188 A7
Shophouse Rd GL15,
GL16 ....155 A2
Shorland Ho BS8 ....18 A1
Short Hedges Cl **18**
GL54 ....168 A1
Short La BS41 ....7 A2
Short St Bristol BS2 .....9 A5
Cheltenham GL53 ......130 C6
Short Way BS35 ....51 B7
Shorthill Rd BS37 ......32 C4
Shortlands Rd BS11 ....27 A1
Shortwood Hill BS16 ...22 E4
Shortwood Rd Bristol BS13 .2 E3
Nailsworth GL6 ....91 A3
Pucklechurch BS16 .....22 A4
Shortwood View BS15 ..10 F8
Shortwood Wlk BS13 ...2 E3
Shotts La GL18 ....170 C3
Showering Cl BS14 ......3 D5
Showering Rd BS14 .....3 D5
Shrivenham Rd SN6 ...145 D2
Shrubberies Sch The
GL10 ....97 E8
Shrubbery Cotts **4** BS6 .18 B2
Shrubbery Ct BS16 .....20 D5
Shrubbery Rd BS16 ....20 D5
Shrublands GL53 ......130 F5
Shrubbery The GL7 ....153 E2
Shurdington CE Prim Sch
GL51 ....129 D1
Shurdington Rd
Cheltenham GL50,GL51,
GL53 ....130 B5
Little Shurdington GL3,
GL51 ....121 B7
Shurdington GL51 .....129 E2
Shute St GL10 ....98 A3
Shutehay Dr GL11 ......87 F5
Shuter Rd BS13 ....1 E5
Shuthonger Manor
GL20 ....181 E6
Shutter La GL52 ....137 F8
Sibland BS35 ....51 D8
Sibland Cl **5** BS35 ....51 D8
Sibland Rd BS35 ....51 D8
Sibland Way BS35 ......51 D8
Sibree Cl GL6 ....148 B6
Sidcot BS4 ....10 A2
Siddington CE Prim Sch
GL7 ....190 D1
Siddington Hall GL7 ...150 E2
Sideland Cl BS14 ....3 E6
Sidelands Rd BS16 .....20 D2
Sidings The Bristol BS34 .29 F2
Charfield GL12 ....67 B5
Sidmouth Ct BS3 ....8 D2
Sidmouth Gdns BS3 .....8 D2
Sidmouth Rd BS3 ....8 E2
Sidney St
Cheltenham GL52 ......193 C3
Gloucester GL1 ....127 A1
Signal Rd BS16 ....20 F4
Silbury Rd BS3 ....8 A3
Silbury Rise BS31 ....5 A2
Silcock Cl GL2 ....127 F7
Silcox Rd BS13 ....2 C4
Silk Mill Ct **18** GL54 ..174 A7
Silk Mill La GL54 ......174 A7
Silklands Gr BS9 ....17 C6
Silley's Cl NP16 ....72 F2
Silver Birch Cl
Bristol BS34 ....29 D7
Quedgeley GL2 ....117 E1
Silver Cl Gloucester GL4 .118 C3
Minety SN16 ....142 D6
Silver St Arlingham GL2 .157 C6
Bristol BS1 ....195 A3
Cirencester GL7 ....190 C5
Coaley GL11 ....88 A1
Dursley GL11 ....88 B1
Littledean GL14 ....156 E8
Minety SN16 ....142 D1
Nailsworth GL6 ....164 D5
Nailsworth GL17 ......164 D5
15 Tetbury GL8 ....140 C4
17 Thornbury BS35 ....64 B1
Silverdale Par GL1 ....119 F8
Silverhill Brake BS35 ...10 E7
Silverhill Rd BS10 .....27 E4
Silverhill Sch BS16 ....10 E7
Silverthorne Cl GL53 ..130 B3
Silverthorne La BS2 .....9 A6
Silverthorne Wharf BS2 ..9 B6
Silverton Ct BS35 ....8 F1
Silvertree Gdns GL53 ..99 E3
Silverwood Way GL51 .129 E5
Simmonds Cl GL6 .....148 A3
Simmonds Rd GL11 ....88 B7
Simmons View BS34 ...29 F5
Simms Bldgs BS16 ......21 D7
Simon Rd GL54 ....122 C5
Simplex Ind Est The
BS30 ....11 D4

Sims La GL2 ....117 F4
Sinclair Ho
Bristol,Clifton Wood BS8 .194 A2
Bristol,Filton BS34 .....29 A2
Sinclair Rd GL51 ......129 D1
Sinderberry Dr GL20 ..182 C5
Sinope St GL1 ....196 C2
Sion Hill BS8 ....7 F7
Sion La BS8 ....7 F7
Sion Pl BS8 ....7 F7
Sion Rd **8** BS3 ....8 C3
Sir Bernard Lovell Sch
BS30 ....11 C4
Sir Bernard Lovell Sch
(annexe) BS30 ....11 D5
Sir Bevil Grenville's Mon*
BA1 ....13 A1
Sir John's La Bristol BS7 .19 B5
Bristol,Eastville BS5 ...19 B4
Sir Thomas Rich's Sch
GL2 ....127 D3
Sir Walter Montague
Almshouses NP16 ......72 E1
Sir William Romney's Sch
GL8 ....140 C5
Siston Rd GL54 ....190 D7
Sissinghurst Gr GL51 ..130 A5
Sisson End GL2 ....127 D2
Sisson Rd GL2 ....127 C2
Siston Cl BS15 ....21 A2
Siston Comm Bristol BS15 .21 A2
Siston Ctr The BS15 ...21 A2
Siston Hill BS30 ....21 B2
Siston Hill Rdbt BS15 ..21 B2
Siston La BS30 ....21 F2
Siston Pk BS15 ....21 A2
Sivell Cl GL2 ....127 A6
Six Acres GL4 ....119 F3
Sixth Ave Bristol,Filton BS7 .29 B1
Bristol,Hengrove BS14 ...3 A7
Skillicorne Mews GL50 .130 B8
Skinner St GL1 ....196 B4
Skinner's Cl SN6 ......145 A4
Skippon Ct BS15 ....10 E5
Skye Cl SN6 ....145 C4
Skylark Way GL4 ......119 B6
Slad La GL5,GL6 ....99 F8
Slad Mill GL5 ....99 D8
Slad The GL11 ....80 B8
Slad The Longhope GL17 .165 B5
Popes Hill GL14 ....156 E8
Slade Brook GL5 ....99 E8
Slade Rd Woolaston GL15 .147 A3
Yorkley GL15 ....156 B2
Slade The GL11 ....80 B8
Sladbrook Cl GL51 ....129 D1
Slateleigh Cl BS37 .....32 F7
Slimbridge La GL13 ....94 D2
Slimbridge Prim Sch
GL2 ....95 E2
Slimbridge Rd GL4 ....118 D3
Sloan St BS5 ....9 D8
Slough La SN14 ....3 D3
Slymbridge Ave BS10 ..28 A3
Small La BS16 ....19 E5
Small Mead BS37 ....1 A1
Small St Bristol BS1 ...195 A3
Bristol,St Philip's Marsh BS2 ..9 A5
Smallbrook Rd WR12 ..188 A1
Smarts Gn BS37 ....33 C8
Smeaton Rd BS1 ....7 A6
Smith Barry Cir GL54 ..169 E6
Smith Barry Cres GL54 .169 D6
Smith Barry Rd GL54 ..169 D6
Smith's Field GL7 .....190 A3
Smith's La GL14 ....192 C4
Smithcourt Dr BS34 ...29 D6
Smithmead BS13 ....2 B5
Smiths Ct Bristol BS34 ..29 A8
Nailsworth GL6 ....164 D8
Smithville GL15 ....146 F7
Smithville Cl GL15 ....146 F7
Smithwood Gr GL53 ..131 A4
Smithy Cl GL16 ....163 A2
Smithy La GL54 ....184 A1
Smithy The
Blakeney GL15 ....156 E2
Cirencester GL7 ......190 E3
Smithyman Ct **1** GL14 .157 A6
Smoke La BS11 ....26 D6
Smooth Stones NP16 ..60 A7
Smyth Rd BS3 ....8 A3
Smyth Terr **3** BS3 .....8 A3
Smythe Croft BS14 ......3 A3
Smythe Mdw GL6 .....148 B5
Smythe Rd GL51 ......133 B6
Smyths Cl BS11 ....16 A7
Snake Dr GL7 ....152 D7
Snead Rd GL54 ....119 F5
Sneedhams Rd GL4 ...119 B2
Sneyd Park Ho BS9 ....17 D3
Snipe Rd GL54 ....169 D6
Snowberry Cl BS32 ....24 B2
Snowberry Wlk BS5 ...19 E1
Snowden Ho BS16 .....19 A4
Snowdon Cl BS16 .....19 A4
Snowdonia Rd GL20 ..182 C5
Snowdrop Cl **1** GL14 ..119 E5
Snowshill Cl BS38 .....51 D8
Snowshill Dr GL52 ....137 F3
Snowshill Manor*
WR12 ....185 B4

Snowhill Rd
Broadway WR12 ....185 B7
Gloucester GL4 ....119 E7
Snowswick La SN7 .....51 F8
Soapers La BS35 ....51 B8
Soaphouse Ind Est BS5 ..9 E8
Sochi Mews **17** GL51 ..132 E2
Sodbury Rd
Acton Turville GL9 ......35 F7
Wickwar GL12 ....53 F7
Soldiers of Gloucester Mus*
GL1 ....196 A2
Solent Way BS35 ....51 D7
Solon Ct BS13 ....1 F5
Solway Rd GL51 ......132 D4
Somerby St BS32 ....29 D7
Somerdale Ave BS4 .....9 A1
Somerdale Rd N BS30,BS31 ..4 F8
Somerford Ct BS10 ....27 F1
Somerford Rd GL7 ...190 C2
Somergate Rd GL51 ..132 D4
Somermead BS3 ....8 C1
Somerset Ave
Cheltenham GL51 .....133 A2
Dursley GL11 ....80 C7
Yate BS37 ....43 F3
Somerset Cl GL12 ......67 F4
Somerset Cres BS34 ...29 F5
Somerset Ho
18 Bristol BS2 ....195 C3
3 Cheltenham GL50 ..193 B4
Somerset Pl
Gloucester GL1,GL2 ...196 A1
Tewkesbury GL20 .....192 D1
Somerset Rd Bristol BS4 ..9 B3
Cinderford GL14 ......191 C4
Somerset Sq BS1 .....195 B1
Somerset St Bristol BS1 .195 B1
Bristol,Kingsdown BS2 .195 A4
Somerset Terr BS3 .....8 D3
Somerset Way NP16 ..107 F4
Somerton Cl BS15 .....10 E7
Somerton Rd BS7 .....18 E6
Somerville Cl BS31 .....5 E2
Somerville Ct GL7 ....190 B2
Somerville Ho BS10 ...18 A4
Somme Rd GL52 ....134 B2
Sommerville Rd BS7 ...18 E3
Sommerville Rd S **1** BS6 .18 F2
Soper Gdns BS4 ....10 A2
Sopwith Rd GL54 .....169 D7
Sopworth Rd SN14 ....47 E7
Soren Larsen Way GL2 .118 C6
Sorrel Cl Gloucester GL4 .118 C4
Thornbury BS35 ....64 D2
South Africa Ho **2**
GL51 ....132 C4
South Ave
Ashchurch GL20 ......182 D4
Yate BS37 ....43 B1
South Bank GL51 ......132 F3
South Bristol Ret Pk BS3 ..8 A2
South Bristol Trad Pk BS3 ..7 F2
South Cerney GL7 .....150 E2
South Cerney Rd GL54 .150 E2
South Cl GL2 ....127 B4
South Croft BS9 ....18 C7
South Dene BS9 ....17 D3
South Down Rd BS9 ...17 C
South Gate Cotts GL54 .54 E2
South Gn GL54 ....50 A4
South Gloucestershire
Central Teaching Unit
BS16 ....21 A5
South Gr Bristol BS6 ...18 C4
Pill BS20 ....16 C4
South Green St **9** BS8 ..7 F6
South Hayes BS35 ......19 B4
South Liberty La
2 Bristol BS13 ....8 B2
Bristol BS3 ....8 A1
South Mdw La SN5 ...144 D3
South Meadow La SN5 .144 A2
South Par
1 Ledbury HR8 ......178 F8
Yate BS37 ....43 E1
South Rd
Bristol,Bedminster BS3 ..8 C3
Bristol,Kingswood BS15 .10 D8
Bristol,Redland BS6 ...18 C4
3 Coleford GL16 .....155 D4
Lydney GL15 ....92 A4
Woodside Down BS37 ..43 B3
South Sea Rd GL53 ....89 C1
South Side Sch GL15 ..146 E4
South Street Prim Sch
BS3 ....8 B3
South Terr **8** BS23 ...43 E1
South View
Blockley GL56 ....186 C6
Frampton Cotterell BS36 .31 E2
Ripple GL20 ....181 D8
Stroud GL5 ....98 C7
South View Bsns Pk
BS16 ....21 A5
South View Cotts GL51 ..98 B8
South View Rise BS36 .31 D6
South Villas GL54 .....190 C4
South Wlk
Mitcheldean GL17 ....164 D5
Yate BS37 ....43 E1

Southall Terr GL18 ....170 E
Southam La GL52 .....134 B
Southampton Gdns BS7 .18 F
Southampton Mews BS7 .18 F
Southbank GL5 ....99 A
Southbow Ho **2** BS3 ....8 B
Southbrook Rd GL4 ...127 C
Southcourt Cl GL53 ...130 D
Southcourt Dr GL53 ..130 D
Southend Ho BS9 ....17 F
Southend Ho GL12 .....54 A
Southend La GL18 ....171 A
Southend The HR8 ....178 F
Southern Ave GL4 ....118 E
Southern Rd GL53 ....130 E
Southernhay
Bristol,Clifton Wood BS8 ..194 B
Bristol,Staple Hill BS16 ..20 D
Southernhay Ave BS8 .194 B
Southernhay Cres BS8 .194 B
Southey Ave BS15 .....20 D
Southey Cl BS15 ....20 D
Southey St BS2 ....20 D
Southfield
Minchinhampton GL6 ...91 F
Southfield Cl GL53 ....130 E
Southfield App GL53 ..130 E
Southfield Ave BS15 ...20 D
Southfield Cl GL53 ....130 E
Southfield Ct BS9 ......18 A
Southfield Jun Sch SN6 .145 D
Southfield Manor Pk
GL53 ....130 F
Southfield Rd
Bristol,Clifton BS6 ....18 D
Bristol,Knowle Park BS4 ..9 B
Tytherington GL12 ....53 A
Southleigh Mews BS8 .194 B
Southleigh Rd BS8 ....194 B
Southmead GL7 ....190 E
Southmead Hospl BS10 .18 A
Southmead La GL6 ....105 B
Southmead Rd BS10,BS34 .28 C
Southmere Ct BS10 ....28 C
Southover Cl BS9 ......18 B
Southrop CE Prim Sch
GL7 ....153 De
Southsea Rd BS34 .....29 A
Southside Cl BS9 ....59 E
Southside Cl BS37 .....17 B
Southville Prim Sch BS3 ..8 B
Southville Rd BS3 ......8 C
Southway Dr BS15 .....11 D
Southwood Ave BS9 ...17 C
Southwood Dr BS9 ....17 B
Southwood Dr E BS9 ..17 C
Southwood La GL50 ..193 A
Sovereign Chase GL19 .178 A
Sovereign Cl BS22 ....192 B
Spa Cl SN6 ....145 D
Spa Ct GL50 ....192 F
Spa Gdns GL52 ....192 F
Spa Mews GL11 ....98 A
Spa Rd GL1 ....196 B
Spa Villas GL1 ....196 B
Spalding Cl BS7 ....19 A
Spaniorum View GL53 .38 F
Spar Rd Avonmouth BS11 .26 D
Yate BS37 ....43 D
Spark Hill GL14 ....119 E
Sparrow Cl **1** GL6 ...148 C
Sparrow La HR9,GL18 .170 Be
Sparrows La HR9,GL18 .170 Be
Spartan Cl **2** GL4 .....19 E
Spartley Dr BS13 ....1 F
Spartley Wlk BS13 ......1 F
Speculation Rd GL14 ..191 De
Speech House Rd
Cinderford GL14,GL16 ..156 A
Coleford,Broadwell GL16 .155 E
Speedwell **5** BS35 .....9 A
Speedwell Ave **5** BS5 ...9 D
Speedwell Cl
Gloucester GL4 ....119 E
Thornbury BS35 ....64 D
Speedwell Rd BS5,BS15 .20 A
Speedwell Tech Coll
BS15 ....20 A
Spencer Cl GL3 ....107 E
Spencer Ct BS30 .....193 A
Spencer Ho **6** BS1 ...195 B
Spencer's Ct BS35 ....51 B
Spenser Ave GL2 .....118 D
Spenser Rd GL51 .....132 E
Sperringate GL7 .....190 D
Spetchley Cl **3** GL51 .132 F
Thornbury BS35 ....64 B
Spider La GL5 ....99 D
Spillman's Pitch GL5 ..99 A
Spillman's Rd GL5 .....99 Aa
Spindles The GL53 ....130 A

pine Rd W GL7 . . . . .142 D5
pine Road E GL7 . . . . . .143 B7
pinnaker Ho GL2 . . . . . . .118 C8
pinnaker Rd GL2 . . . . . . .118 C8
pinners Cotts GL6 . . . . . . .91 F3
pinners Ho 10 GL5 . . . . . . .99 C7
pinners Croft BS13 . . . . . . .1 F5
pinney Ct GL5 . . . . .99 F1
pinney Rd GL4 . . . . .119 E7
pinney The Bristol BS32 . . .29 E7
Cheltenham GL52 . . . . . . .133 E4
Frampton Cotterell BS36 . . .31 B7
Lechlade on T GL7 . . . . . .153 E2
Stroud GL6 . . . . .105 C7
pinning Wheel Ct GL5 . .98 E7
pire Way GL4 . . . . .119 D8
pires View 4 BS16 . . . . . .19 E5
pital La SN6 . . . . .143 F4
pitalgate La GL7 . . . . . .190 C5
pittle Leys 5 GL54 . . . . .174 A7
poonbill CI GL2 . . . . . . .117 D1
pout Hill GL15 . . . . .147 C3
pout La GL17 . . . . .164 A4
pouthouse La GL11 . . . . . .88 A5
pratsgate La GL7 . . . . . .142 D6
pread Eagle Rd GL1 . .196 B3
pring Cotts
Stonehouse GL10 . . . . . . .98 A6
Stroud GL6 . . . . .104 A2
pring Dale GL2 . . . . . . .165 F5
pring Field Terr GL5 . . . .99 A6
pring Gdns Bristol BS4 . . .9 A1
Lechlade on T GL7 . . . . . .153 E2
Quenington GL7 . . . . . . .152 D7
Stow-on-t-W GL54 . . . . . .176 F4
Tewkesbury GL20 . . . . . .192 D4
pring Gr 6 HR8 . . . . . . .178 F7
pring Hill
Bristol,Kingsdown BS2 . . .195 A4
Bristol,Upper Soundwell
BS15 . . . . .20 E2
Eastington GL10 . . . . . . .97 A8
Nailsworth GL6 . . . . .91 B4
pring Ho 2 BS35 . . . . . . .51 C8
pring La
Cheltenham GL52 . . . . . .134 B6
Cleeve Hill GL52 . . . . . . .138 E2
Dundry BS41 . . . . .2 A1
Stroud GL5 . . . . .99 D6
Thrupp GL5 . . . . .99 D6
pring Meadow Rd GL15 .92 A4
pring Ind Est GL6 . . . . . .91 D3
pring PI GL17 . . . . .163 E4
pring St BS3 . . . . .8 E4
pring Street PI BS3 . . . . . .8 E4
springbank CI GL51 . . . .132 C4
springbank Dr GL51 . . . .132 C3
springbank Gr GL51 . . . .132 C3
springbank Rd GL51 . . . .132 C3
springbank Way GL51 . . .132 D4
springbank HR9 . . . . . . .170 B4
springdale CI GL2 . . . . .109 D8
springfield
Blockley GL56 . . . . .186 C6
Bourton-on-t-W GL54 . . . .168 F7
Dursley GL11 . . . . .87 E4
Hardwicke GL2 . . . . .109 E7
Tewkesbury GL20 . . . . . .192 F5
Thornbury BS35 . . . . . . .51 D8
springfield Ave
Bristol,Horfield BS7 . . . . .18 F5
Bristol,Mangotsfield BS16 . .21 A7
Bristol,Shirehampton BS11 . .16 D6
springfield PI GL4 . . . . .121 F1
springfield Rd
Bristol,Cotham BS6 . . . . .18 D1
Bristol,Mangotsfield BS16 . .21 A7
Cirencester GL7 . . . . . . .190 B2
Lydney GL15 . . . . .92 A6
Pill BS20 . . . . .16 C4
Quenington GL7 . . . . . . .152 D7
Stroud GL5 . . . . .99 C8
Stroud,Westrip GL5 . . . . .98 D8
springfield Terr GL51 . . . .51 B8
springfields Bristol BS34 . .29 A2
Tetbury GL8 . . . . .140 C4
springfields Ct GL11 . . . .87 E4
springfort BS9 . . . . .17 F3
springhill Dursley GL11 . .88 C3
Sandhurst GL2 . . . . .172 F2
Stroud GL5 . . . . .99 C8
springhill (Old Court)
GL11 . . . . .88 B3
springhill CI GL6 . . . . . .91 B4
springhill Cotts WR12 . . .185 B4
springhill Cres GL6 . . . . .91 B4
springhill Ct GL2 . . . . . .172 F1
springleaze
Bristol,Knowle Park BS4 . . .9 A1
Bristol,Mangotsfield BS16 . .21 A7
springly Ct BS15 . . . . . .11 A8
springs The GL5 . . . . . . .92 A4
springvale GL54 . . . . . . .168 F8
springville CI BS30 . . . . . .11 A3

Springwater CI GL20 . . . .182 C5
Springwater Pk Trad Est
BS5 . . . . .9 E7
Springwell Gdns GL3 . . .128 B6
Springwood Dr BS10 . . . . .27 D3
Spruce Rd GL16 . . . . . . .155 C6
Spruce Ride
Cinderford GL14,GL16 . . .156 A5
Coleford GL16 . . . . .155 F6
Spruce Way BS34 . . . . . . .28 F7
Square The Alveston BS35 . .51 A4
Bibury GL7 . . . . .160 A1
Bristol BS1 . . . . .142 B3
Bristol,Knowle Park BS4 . . .9 A1
Bristol,Staple Hill BS16 . . .20 E4
6 Chipping Campden
GL55 . . . . .189 A2
Goodrich HR9 . . . . .163 A6
Guiting Power GL54 . . . . .175 B3
Ruardean GL17 . . . . . . .163 E4
St Briavels GL15 . . . . . . .146 F7
8 Stonehouse GL10 . . . .97 F8
Stroud GL5 . . . . .99 C8
Toddington GL54 . . . . . .184 B3
Wotton-u-E GL12 . . . . . . .68 C6
Squires CI GL6 . . . . .148 B6
Squires Ct
Bretforton WR11 . . . . . . .188 A6
Bristol BS30 . . . . .10 F4
Squires Leaze BS35 . . . . .64 D2
Squirrel CI GL2 . . . . . . .109 E7
Stable Cotts
Adlestrop GL56 . . . . . . .177 E5
Bromesberrow Heath HR8 .179 C5
Stable Yd GL5 . . . . .99 C8
Stable Yd The GL9 . . . . . .46 B7
Stables The
Cheltenham GL52 . . . . . .134 C4
Lechlade on T GL7 . . . . . .153 E3
Stow-on-t-W GL7 . . . . . .176 F5
Stackpool Rd BS3 . . . . . . .8 C4
Stadium Rd BS6 . . . . . . .18 C5
Stafford CI 8 GL6 . . . . .155 B8
Stafford Cres BS35 . . . . . .64 B1
Stafford Rd BS2 . . . . .19 A2
Stafford St BS3 . . . . .8 D4
Staffords Ct BS30 . . . . . . .11 A6
Stag Hill GL15 . . . . .156 A2
Stainer CI BS4 . . . . .2 D7
Staites Orch GL4 . . . . . . .119 E3
Stamage's La GL6 . . . . . .103 F7
Stambourne La GL13 . . . . .85 E8
Stambourne Villas GL13 . . .85 E8
Stamp's Mdw GL2 . . . . . .126 F5
Stanborough La GL4 . . . . .167 F8
Stanbridge CI BS16 . . . . . .20 F6
Stanbridge Prim Sch
BS16 . . . . .20 F6
Stanbridge Rd BS16 . . . . .20 C5
Stanbury Ave BS16 . . . . . .20 C5
Stanbury Mews GL3 . . . .128 B6
Stanbury Rd BS3 . . . . .8 E3
Stancombe La
Bisley GL7 . . . . .104 F2
Winchcombe GL54 . . . . . .174 B7
Stancombe View
North Nibley GL11 . . . . . .79 D5
2 Winchcombe GL54 . . . .174 B7
Standfast Rd BS10 . . . . . .27 F3
Standish Ave BS34 . . . . . .40 C1
Standish CI BS10 . . . . . . .27 F3
Standish Ct GL10 . . . . . . .101 E5
Standish Hospl GL10 . . . .102 B2
Standish La GL2,GL10 . . .101 C6
Standish Park Cotts
GL10 . . . . .102 C4
Standle La GL11 . . . . .87 A4
Standon Way BS10 . . . . . .28 C2
Stane Way BS11 . . . . .16 C7
Stanfield CI BS7 . . . . . . .19 C6
Stanford Ct BS36 . . . . . . .30 F8
Stanford Rd BS7 . . . . .2 D7
Stanford Rd Lydney GL15 . .92 A3
Northway GL20 . . . . .182 C4
Stanhope Rd BS30 . . . . . .11 B7
Stanhope St BS2 . . . . .9 A5
Stank La GL2 . . . . .99 C8
Stanleigh Terr GL2 . . . . .126 A7
Stanley Ave
Bristol,Bishopston BS7 . . .18 E3
Bristol,Filton BS34 . . . . . .29 B2
Stanley Chase BS5 . . . . . .19 E2
Stanley Cotts
Gloucester GL1 . . . . . . .196 C1
Gretton GL54 . . . . .183 E1
Stanley Gdns BS30 . . . . . .11 B4
Stanley Hill BS4 . . . . .9 A4
Stanley Mead BS32 . . . . . .40 E2
Stanley Mills Cotts GL10 . .98 A5
Stanley Park Rd BS16 . . . .20 E3
Stanley Pk Bristol BS5 . . .19 C1
Stanley PI GL51 . . . . . . .132 D3
Stanley Rd
Bristol,Cotham BS6 . . . . .18 C1
Bristol,Warmley BS15 . . . .11 B8
Cheltenham GL52 . . . . . .134 B1
Stanley St
5 Bristol,Bedminster BS3 . .8 C3
Bristol,Upper Easton BS5 . .9 A8
Stanley St N 16 BS3 . . . . .8 C3
Stanley St S BS3 . . . . .8 C2
Stanley Terr Bristol GL1 . . .8 C2
Gloucester GL1 . . . . . . .196 C1
Stanley The GL4 . . . . . . .119 F2
Stanley View GL5 . . . . . .99 C8

Stanley Wlk GL4 . . . . . . .119 F1
Stanmoor GL4 . . . . .119 E3
Stansby Cres GL3 . . . . . .128 A6
Stansby Park Cvn Pk
GL5 . . . . .129 B6
Stansby Touring Pk
GL51 . . . . .129 B6
Stanshaw CI BS16 . . . . . . .20 A7
Stanshaw Rd BS16 . . . . . .20 A7
Stanshawe Cres BS37 . . . .43 E1
Stanshawes Court Dr
BS37 . . . . .43 E1
Stanshawes Dr BS37 . . . . .43 D1
Stanshaws CI BS32 . . . . . .40 C2
Stansted Ho GL1 . . . . . .196 A3
Stanthill Dr GL11 . . . . . . .80 C8
Stanton CI BS15 . . . . .20 F1
Stanton Rd Bristol BS10 . .28 E2
Stroud GL5 . . . . .98 E8
Tewkesbury GL20 . . . . . .192 D5
Stanton Way GL51 . . . . .129 E8
Stantons Dr GL51 . . . . . .133 A7
Stantway La GL14 . . . . . .157 E8
Stanway BS30 . . . . .11 C1
Stanway House & Water
Gdns* GL54 . . . . .184 E3
Stanway Rd
Cheltenham GL51 . . . . . .129 D8
Gloucester GL4 . . . . . . .119 C7
Stanton WR12 . . . . .184 D5
Stanway Wood Dr GL52 .137 E3
Stanwick Cres GL51 . . . .133 B5
Stanwick Dr GL51 . . . . . .133 B5
Stanwick Gdns GL51 . . . .133 B5
Staple Gr BS31 . . . . .4 D5
Staple Grove Cres BS5 . . .10 A7
Staple Hill Prim Sch
BS16 . . . . .20 D4
Staple Hill Rd BS16 . . . . .20 B6
Staples Rd BS37 . . . . .43 D2
Stapleton CI Bristol BS16 . .19 D5
Highworth SN6 . . . . .145 C3
Stapleton Rd
Bristol,Baptist Mills BS5 . . .19 B1
Bristol,Eastville BS5 . . . . .19 C2
Stapleton Road Sta BS5 . . .19 B1
Star Ave BS34 . . . . .30 A4
Star Barn Rd BS36 . . . . . .30 E7
Star Beech Hill GL17,
GL2 . . . . .126 A8
Star Ct 10 GL52 . . . . . . .133 F2
Star Hill GL6 . . . . .91 A5
Star La Avening GL8 . . . .140 B8
Bristol BS16 . . . . .19 F5
Pill BS20 . . . . .16 C7
Starling CI 7 GL10 . . . . . .97 F8
Stars Pitch GL17 . . . . . . .144 D2
Station App Bristol BS1 . .195 C1
Gloucester GL1 . . . . . . .196 C2
Minety SN16 . . . . .142 E1
Station Ave S 9
BS16 . . . . .20 A4
Station CI Bristol BS15 . . .11 C8
Chipping Sodbury BS37 . . .40 B8
Station Cotts GL20 . . . . .182 C7
Station Ct BS5 . . . . .9 E8
Station Dr GL20 . . . . . . .182 C7
Station Ind Est NP16 . . . . .60 F8
Station La Bristol BS5 . . . . .9 D7
Longhope GL17 . . . . . . .164 F5
Tewkesbury GL20 . . . . . .192 C4
Station Mdw GL16 . . . . . .168 F8
Station Rd
Acton Turville GL9 . . . . . .35 F8
Andoversford GL54 . . . . .130 A6
Avonmouth,St Andrew WR11 .183 E8
Beckford GL20 . . . . .183 B6
Berkeley GL13 . . . . .85 E5
Bishop's Cleeve GL52 . . . .138 B6
Bledington OX7 . . . . . . .177 B6
Blockley GL56 . . . . .186 D6
Bourton-on-t-W GL54 . . . .168 A7
Bristol,Ashley Down BS7 . .18 E4
Bristol,Filton BS34 . . . . . .29 A4
Bristol,Fishponds BS16 . . .20 A5
Bristol,Henbury BS10 . . . . .27 C2
Bristol,Montpelier BS6 . . .18 C2
Bristol,Shirehampton BS11 . .16 D6
Bristol,Stapleton BS16 . . . .19 C6
Bristol,Staple Hill BS16 . . .20 B6
Bristol,Warmley BS30 . . . .11 C7
Broadway WR12 . . . . . . .185 B8
Charfield GL12 . . . . .67 B5
Chepstow/Cas-Gwent NP16 .60 F8
Chipping Campden GL55 . .189 A2
Churchdown GL3 . . . . . .129 A7
Coalpit Heath BS36 . . . . . .31 A8
Dursley GL11 . . . . .88 A5
Gloucester GL1 . . . . . . .196 C2
Highworth SN6 . . . . .145 D4
Honeybourne WR11 . . . . .188 C1
Iron Acton BS37 . . . . .42 D1
Kemble GL7 . . . . .141 B8
Kempsham BS31 . . . . .4 F6
Kingham OX7 . . . . .177 F2
Lechlade on T GL7 . . . . . .153 B2
Lydney GL15 . . . . .84 A8
Milkwall GL16 . . . . .165 E5
Minety SN16 . . . . .142 E1
11 Moreton-in-M GL56 . . .187 A3
Nailsworth GL6 . . . . .91 C4
Newnham GL14 . . . . . . .156 F7

Station Rd continued
Pill BS20 . . . . .16 C4
Pilning BS35 . . . . .38 F4
Ripple GL20 . . . . .181 D8
Severn Beach BS35 . . . . . .38 A6
South Cerney GL7 . . . . . .143 A7
Stroud GL5 . . . . .99 B7
Tewkesbury GL20 . . . . . .192 D5
Wickwar GL12 . . . . .54 B7
Winterbourne BS36 . . . . . .30 E4
Woodchester GL5 . . . . . . .99 A1
Woolaston GL15 . . . . . . .147 C2
Yate BS37 . . . . .43 C2
Station Road Bsns Ctr
BS15 . . . . .21 A3
Station Road Link BS15 . .21 A2
Station Road Workshops
BS15 . . . . .21 A3
Station St
Cheltenham GL50 . . . . . .193 A4
Cinderford GL14 . . . . . . .191 C5
Tewkesbury GL20 . . . . . .192 D4
Station Terr
Cinderford GL14 . . . . . . .191 C5
Dymock GL18 . . . . .178 D2
Staunton & Corse CE Prim
Sch GL19 . . . . .172 B8
Staunton CI GL4 . . . . . . .119 E4
Staunton Ct Bsns Pk
GL19 . . . . .172 A8
Staunton Fields BS14 . . . . .3 C4
Staunton Ho GL16 . . . . . .154 D7
Staunton La BS14 . . . . . . .3 D3
Staunton Rd
Coleford GL16 . . . . .154 F6
Monmth/Trefynwy GL16,
NP25 . . . . .154 C7
Staunton Way BS14 . . . . . .3 D4
Staveley Cres BS10 . . . . . .27 E3
Staverton CI BS32 . . . . . .40 C1
Staverton Connection
GL51 . . . . .173 F1
Staverton Tech Pk GL51 . .173 F1
Staverton Way GL51 . . . . .11 A7
Staverdale Gr BS14 . . . . . .3 B6
Staynes Cres BS15 . . . . . .10 E8
Steadings Bsns Ctr The
GL2 . . . . .126 A8
Steam Mills GL14 . . . . . .191 B8
Steam Mills Prim Sch
GL14 . . . . .191 B8
Steel Ave GL15 . . . . .92 B3
Steel CI BS30 . . . . .4 F3
Steel Mills BS31 . . . . .4 F4
Steep St NP16 . . . . .60 E8
Steeple CI GL4 . . . . .118 A7
Steeple View GL15 . . . . . .92 A2
Steevens Ho (almshouses) 1
BS16 . . . . .195 C3
Stella Ave BS3 . . . . .8 A2
Stella Way GL52 . . . . . . .137 A6
Stenders Bsns Pk GL17 . .164 C5
Stenders CI GL17 . . . . . .164 D5
Stenders Rd GL17 . . . . . .164 D5
Step La GL6,GL8 . . . . . .148 B1
Step'n'a La GL6 . . . . .91 D1
Stepbridge Rd GL16 . . . .155 B4
Stephens Dr BS30 . . . . . . .10 F5
Stephens PI GL16 . . . . . .155 B5
Stephenson Way WR11 . . .188 A7
Stepney Rd BS5 . . . . .9 A8
Stepney Wlk BS5 . . . . .9 A8
Stepping Stone La GL6 . .103 E6
Stepping Stones The BS4 . .9 E6
Steps CI GL17 . . . . .187 F6
Steptairs CI GL17 . . . . . .164 D5
Steptairs La GL17 . . . . . .190 D3
Sterling CI GL54 . . . . . . .132 B2
Stern Ct GL15 . . . . .133 B2
Sterrys Cnr WR7 . . . . . . .170 C4
Sterrys Rd WR7 . . . . . . .170 C4
Stevens CI BS32 . . . . .40 E2
Stevens Way GL16 . . . . . .90 F1
Stevens Wlk BS30 . . . . . .20 A3
Stibbs Ct BS30 . . . . .10 F4
Stibbs Hill BS5 . . . . .10 A8
Sticky La GL7 . . . . .190 A1
Stidcote La GL12 . . . . . . .66 F5
Stidcote La GL12 . . . . . . .66 F5
Stile Acres BS11 . . . . .16 C8
Stillingfleet Rd BS13 . . . . . .2 C5
Stillman CI BS13 . . . . .1 B4
Stinchcombe Rd GL51 . . .133 A7
Stinchcombe Rd GL51 . . .133 A7
Stirling CI BS37 . . . . .43 D4
Stirling Rd BS4 . . . . .9 B2
Stirling Way BS31 . . . . . . .4 F5
Stirrup CI BS14 . . . . .91 D1
Stock Hill BS35 . . . . .38 B3
Stock Hill GL13 . . . . .85 E5
Stockdale CI GL2 . . . . . .118 B3
Stocken CI GL17 . . . . . . .164 D5
Stockholm PI HR9 . . . . . .164 D8
Stockley Way GL4,GL6 . .111 D6

Stocks The GL6 . . . . . . .102 D2
Stockton CI
Bristol,Oldland BS30 . . . .11 B3
Bristol,Whitchurch BS14 . . .2 F4
Cheltenham GL53 . . . . . .130 F4
Stockwell Ave BS16 . . . . .21 A6
Stockwell CI BS16 . . . . . .20 F7
Stockwell Dr BS16 . . . . . .21 A6
Stockwell Gn GL14 . . . . .191 D3
Stockwell La
Aylburton GL15 . . . . . . .147 E4
Woodmancote GL52 . . . .138 D3
Stockwells GL56 . . . . . . .187 A3
Stockwood Chambers 9 .7 C7
Stockwood Cres BS4 . . . . .8 F2
Stockwood Green Prim Sch
BS14 . . . . .3 E4
Stockwood Hill BS31 . . . . .4 B3
Stockwood La BS14 . . . . . .3 E5
Stockwood Mews BS4 . . . .9 F5
Stockwood Rd BS4 . . . . . .9 F1
Stoke Bishop CE Prim Sch
BS9 . . . . .17 D5
Stoke Bridge Ave BS34 . .29 C8
Stoke Common La SN5 .143 D1
Stoke Cotts BS9 . . . . . . .17 E6
Stoke Gr BS9 . . . . .17 E6
Stoke Hamlet BS9 . . . . . .17 F6
Stoke Hill BS9 . . . . .17 E3
Stoke La
Bristol,Broomhill BS16 . . . .19 E7
Bristol,Patchway BS34 . . . .29 C8
Bristol,Westbury on Trym
BS9 . . . . .17 F6
Stoke Lodge Prim Sch
BS34 . . . . .29 C8
Stoke Mdws BS32 . . . . . .40 D1
Stoke Paddock Rd BS9 . . .17 E6
Stoke Park Rd BS9 . . . . . .17 F4
Stoke Park Rd S BS9 . . . .17 F4
Stoke Rd
Bishop's Cleeve GL52 . . . .137 E4
Bristol BS8 . . . . .18 A2
Stoke Orchard Rd GL52 . .137 C4
Stoke View Bsns Pk 6
BS16 . . . . .19 A4
Stoke View Rd BS16 . . . . .19 F3
Stokefield CI BS35 . . . . . .64 B1
Stokeleigh Wlk BS9 . . . . .17 C5
Stokemead BS34 . . . . . . .29 C8
Stokes Croft BS1 . . . . . . .195 A4
Stokes CI 1 Bristol BS30 . .11 A4
17 Tewkesbury GL20 . . . .192 C4
Stokes Rd GL20 . . . . . . .181 D5
Stone Bridge GL56 . . . . . .187 A3
Stone CI GL4 . . . . .119 E7
Stone Cotts GL16 . . . . . . .91 B3
Stone House Mews BS37 .44 B1
Stone La BS36 . . . . .30 C3
Stone Manor GL1 . . . . . . .99 E6
Stone Manor Ct GL5 . . . . .99 E6
Stone Monolith BS34 . . . .29 C8
Stone Rd GL14 . . . . .172 A7
Stone Vale Bridge GL14 . .191 C5
Stonebberow Rd GL18 . . .178 D2
Stonebrack Piece GL4 . . .3 B3
Stonebridge Rd GL14 . . . .19 B6
Stonechat Ave GL4 . . . . . .118 F2
Stonechat Gdns BS16 . . . .19 C5
Stonecote Ridge 8
GL6 . . . . .148 C6
Stonecroft CI GL52 . . . . .137 E4
Stonedale Rd GL10 . . . . . .97 D8
Stonefern CI 18 GL16 . . .187 A3
Stonefield Dr SN5 . . . . . .183 A6
Stonehall WR11 . . . . . . .188 A7
Stonehenge Rd GL4 . . . . .118 F2
Stonehill BS15 . . . . .21 B7
Stonehill Farm GL14 . . . .141 B7
Stonehouse CI GL54 . . . .176 D4
Stoneleigh BS37 . . . . . . .43 B8
Stoneleigh Cres BS4 . . . . .8 F3
Stoneleigh Dr BS30 . . . . .11 A4
Stoneleigh Rd BS4 . . . . . .8 F3
Stoneleigh Wlk BS4 . . . . .8 F3
Stonepits La WR11 . . . . . .188 B2
Stones Ct 11 GL13 . . . . . .85 D8
Stoney Hill BS36 . . . . .31 A1
Stoney Pool GL17 . . . . . .144 D2
Stoney Stile Rd GL5 . . . . .51 A5
Stoney Stoke GL6 . . . . . . .91 A4
Stoneyhills Ind Est HR9 .162 D4
Stoodley CI GL54 . . . . . .174 A7
Stores Rd BS11 . . . . .26 C4
Storrington CI 8 GL10 . . .97 F7
Stothard Rd BS7 . . . . . . .19 A4
Stottbury Rd BS7 . . . . . . .19 A3
Stoulgrove La NP16 . . . . . .73 A4

Stoulton Gr BS10 . . . . .28 A3
Stourden Cl BS16 . . . . .20 A7
Stourton Dr BS30 . . . . .10 F4
Stover Rd BS37 . . . . .43 B2
Stover Trad Est BS37 . . . .43 B2
Stow Cl GL4 . . . . .118 F6
Stow Ct GL51 . . . . .133 A1
Stow Gn **18** GL54 . . . . .176 F4
Stow Hill Rd GL12 . . . . .52 B6
Stow Ho BS11 . . . . .16 E5
Stow Rd Baunton GL7 . . . .150 E7
 Bledington OX7 . . . . .177 E1
 Moreton-in-M GL56 . . . . . .187 A2
Stow-on-the-Wold Prim Sch
 GL54 . . . . .176 F4
Stowe La GL15 . . . . .154 E1
Stowe Rd GL15 . . . . .146 D8
Stowell Hill Rd GL12 . . . . . .52 B6
Stowell Mews GL4 . . . . . . .119 D7
Stowell Pk GL54 . . . . .159 D8
Stowfield Rd GL17 . . . . . . .163 C4
Stowick Gdns BS11 . . . . . . .27 C2
Strachans Cl GL5 . . . . .99 A7
Stradbrook Ave BS5 . . . . . .10 B7
Stradling La BS16 . . . . .27 C2
Stradlings Yd BS2 . . . . . . .194 C4
Straight La GL19 . . . . .172 B8
Straight St BS2 . . . . .195 C2
Straits Par BS16 . . . . .20 B5
Strand Ct GL53 . . . . .193 C3
Strand La GL14 . . . . .157 C8
Strand The GL50 . . . . .193 C3
Stranks Cl SN6 . . . . .145 D2
Stratford Bridge GL20 . . . .180 E9
Stratford Cl Bristol BS14 . . .2 F3
 Gloucester GL2 . . . . .118 C4
Stratford Ct BS9 . . . . .17 F8
Stratford Rd
 Honeybourne WR11 . . . . . .188 D7
 Mickleton GL55 . . . . .189 A7
 Stroud GL5 . . . . .99 A8
Strathearn Dr BS10 . . . . . . .28 B2
Strathedon BS8 . . . . .194 A4
Strathmore Rd BS7 . . . . . . .18 F5
Stratmore Est GL16 . . . . . .155 B3
Stratton CE Prim Sch
 GL7 . . . . .190 A8
Stratton Cl BS34 . . . . .29 C7
Stratton Cnr GL1 . . . . .196 C1
Stratton Ct GL20 . . . . .192 D5
Stratton Hts GL7 . . . . .190 B8
Stratton Mills GL7 . . . . . . .190 C7
Stratton Rd
 Gloucester GL1 . . . . .196 C1
 Saltford BS31 . . . . .5 E3
Stratton St BS2 . . . . .195 C3
Strawberry Field **2**
 GL16 . . . . .155 C5
Strawberry Hill GL18 . . . . .171 A6
Strawberry La Bristol BS5 . . .9 E7
 Dundry BS13,BS41 . . . . .1 E3
 Meysey Hampton GL7 . . . .152 B2
Strawbridge Rd **11** BS5 . . . .9 B7
Stream Cl BS10 . . . . .28 D3
Stream La GL18 . . . . .171 B5
Stream Side BS16 . . . . .20 F6
Stream The BS16 . . . . .30 B2
Streamfield GL12 . . . . .68 B8
Streamleaze BS31 . . . . .51 C8
Streamleaze Ct BS35 . . . . . .51 B8
Streamside
 Bishop's Cleeve GL52 . . . .137 F4
 Gloucester GL4 . . . . .118 A2
 Stroud GL5 . . . . .99 C7
Streamside Rd BS37 . . . . . .44 A1
Streamside Wlk BS4 . . . . . . .9 E3
Street Cotts SN16 . . . . . . .142 A4
Street The
 Acton Turville GL9 . . . . .35 F6
 Alveston BS35 . . . . .51 B5
 Burton SN14 . . . . .36 B4
 Castle Eaton SN6 . . . . . . .144 D6
 Coaley GL11 . . . . .88 E8
 Crudwell SN16 . . . . .141 C3
 Didmarton GL9 . . . . .57 C3
 Frampton on Severn GL2 . .157 F2
 Horsley GL6 . . . . .90 F1
 Latton SN6 . . . . .143 E6
 Leighterton GL8 . . . . .70 C3
 Leonard Stanley GL10 . . . . .97 E3
 Luckington SN14 . . . . .47 E4
 Marston Meysey SN6 . . . .144 B8
 North Nibley GL11 . . . . .79 D4
 Oaksey SN16 . . . . .142 A4
 Olveston BS35 . . . . .50 A3
 Shipton Moyne GL8 . . . . . .59 D8
 Uley GL11 . . . . .89 C4
 Woodchester GL5 . . . . .99 B3
Strensham Bsns Pk
 WR8 . . . . .180 A9
Strensham Court Mews
 WR8 . . . . .180 A10
Strensham Gate WR8 . .180 A10
Stretford Ave BS5 . . . . .9 D8
Stretford Rd BS5 . . . . .9 D8
Strickland Homes **5**
 GL52 . . . . .130 F8
Strickland Rd GL52 . . . . . .130 F8
Stride Cl BS35 . . . . .38 A6
Striguil Rd NP16 . . . . .60 E6
Stringer's Cl GL51 . . . . .99 A5
Stringer's Dr GL51 . . . . .99 A5
Strode Comm BS35 . . . . . . .50 F5
Strode Gdns BS35 . . . . .50 F5

Stroma Way SN6 . . . . .145 C4
Strongbow Rd NP16 . . . . . . .60 E6
Stroud Coll GL5 . . . . .99 A8
Stroud Ent Ctr GL15 . . . . . .98 F4
Stroud General Hospl
 GL5 . . . . .99 D6
Stroud Girls' High Sch
 GL5 . . . . .99 A7
Stroud Maternity Hospl
 GL5 . . . . .99 D6
Stroud Rd Bisley GL6 . . . . .105 A1
 Bristol,Patchway BS34 . . . .28 F8
 Bristol,Shirehampton BS11 . .16 E7
 Cirencester GL7 . . . . .150 B4
 Gloucester GL1,GL4 . . . . . .118 E6
 Nailsworth GL6 . . . . .91 B5
 Painswick GL6 . . . . .103 D6
Stroud Sta GL5 . . . . .99 B7
Stroud Valley Com Prim Sch
 Stroud GL5 . . . . .99 C7
 Stroud GL5 . . . . .99 C7
Stuart Ave NP16 . . . . .72 D1
Stuart St BS5 . . . . .9 C7
Studland Cl BS9 . . . . .18 B6
Studland Dr GL52 . . . . . . .134 C4
Stump La GL3 . . . . .120 B8
Stumpwell La GL12 . . . . . . .79 E2
Sturden La BS16 . . . . .30 C3
Sturdon Rd BS3 . . . . .8 A3
Sturmer Cl BS37 . . . . .43 E4
Sturmey Way BS20 . . . . . . .16 E3
Sturminster Cl BS14 . . . . . . .3 D6
Sturminster Rd BS14 . . . . . . .3 D7
Sturmeys Rd GL6 . . . . .148 D6
Sudbrook Trad Est GL2 . .196 A1
Sudbrook Way GL4 . . . . . . .119 C5
Sudeley Castle & Gdns*
 GL54 . . . . .174 B6
Sudeley Dr GL7 . . . . .142 F7
Sudeley Ho **5** GL51 . . . . . .132 E3
Sudeley View GL54 . . . . . .139 F5
Sudgrove Pk GL4 . . . . .119 E5
Sudmeadow Rd GL2 . . . . . .126 C1
Suffolk Cl **2** GL8 . . . . .140 C5
Suffolk Ho GL50 . . . . .193 A2
Suffolk Mews GL50 . . . . . .193 B1
Suffolk Par GL50 . . . . .193 B2
Suffolk Rd GL50 . . . . .193 A1
Suffolk Sq GL50 . . . . .193 A2
Suffolk St GL50 . . . . .193 B1
Suffolk Villas GL50 . . . . . . .193 B1
Sugley La GL6 . . . . .90 F2
Sulgrave Cl GL4 . . . . .118 C1
Sullivan Cl BS4 . . . . .2 D6
Summer Cl GL5 . . . . .99 E7
Summer Cres GL5 . . . . .99 E7
Summer Ct BS8 . . . . .194 B3
Summer Hill BS4 . . . . .9 A4
Summer House Way
 BS30 . . . . .11 B7
Summer La SN14 . . . . .36 F3
Summer Mdw GL4 . . . . . . .119 B4
Summer St **4** Bristol BS3 . . .8 C4
 Stroud GL5 . . . . .99 E7
Summerfield Cl
 Blockley GL56 . . . . .186 C6
 Cheltenham GL51 . . . . . . .132 F5
Summerhayes BS30 . . . . . . .11 D5
Summerhill Jun & Inf Schs
 BS5 . . . . .9 E8
Summerhill Rd BS5 . . . . .9 F8
Summerhill Terr BS5 . . . . . . .9 F7
Summerhouse La NP16 . . . .60 F4
Summerland Dr GL3 . . . . . .128 C5
Summerleaze
 Bristol BS16 . . . . .20 C3
 Keynsham BS31 . . . . .4 E7
 Lydney GL15 . . . . .92 B2
Summerleaze Rd GL5 . . . . . .92 B2
Summers Dr BS30 . . . . .23 A1
Summers Mead BS37 . . . . . .43 E4
Summers Rd
 4 Bristol BS2 . . . . .19 A1
 13 Winchcombe GL54 . . . .174 A7
Summers Terr **3** BS2 . . . . . .19 A1
Summersfield Cl GL4 . . . . . .148 A3
Summersfield Rd GL4 . . . . .148 A3
Sun Green Cl **2** GL15 . . . .155 D1
Sun Green Rd **3** GL15 . . . .155 D1
Sun La GL16 . . . . .155 B3
Sun Rise Rd **1** GL15 . . . . . .155 D1
Sun Tump GL15 . . . . .147 D8
Sundale HR9 . . . . .170 B4
Sundays Hill BS32 . . . . .40 A4
Sundayshill La GL12 . . . . . . .65 D7
Sunderland Cl GL53 . . . . . .137 B4
Sunderland Pl BS8 . . . . . . .194 B3
Sundridge Pk BS37 . . . . . . .32 E8
Sunground The GL4 . . . . . . .148 B5
Sunningdale Bristol BS8 . . .194 B4
Sunningdale Dr BS30 . . . . . .11 B6
Sunny Bank Bristol BS15 . . .20 B1
 14 Coleford GL16 . . . . . . .155 A5
 Wick BS30 . . . . .11 D2
Sunny View GL4 . . . . .90 F4
Sunny Wlk BS15 . . . . .20 B1
Sunnybank Bristol BS16 . . . .20 E6
Sunnybank Rd GL16 . . . . . .155 A6
Sunnybrook Terr GL13 . . . . .93 D2
Sunnycroft GL52 . . . . .138 A2
Sunnycroft Mews GL11 . . . .91 C5

Sunnydene BS4 . . . . .9 D4
Sunnyfield La GL51 . . . . . . .129 C5
Sunnyfield Rd GL2 . . . . . . .109 D8
Sunnyhill GL5 . . . . .98 E8
Sunnyhill Dr BS11 . . . . .16 E6
Sunnyhill Ho E BS11 . . . . . .16 E6
Sunnyhill Ho W BS11 . . . . . .16 E6
Sunnymead Bristol BS30 . . .11 D6
 Keynsham BS31 . . . . .4 F7
Sunnymead Cl GL17 . . . . . .164 B4
Sunnyside Bristol BS9 . . . . . .17 C5
 Frampton Cotterell BS36 . . .31 B8
Sunnyside Farm Trad Est
 BS20 . . . . .16 C2
Sunnyside La Bristol BS16 . .30 C2
 Yate BS37 . . . . .43 C1
Sunnyvale Dr BS30 . . . . . . .11 B3
Sunridge BS16 . . . . .20 D6
Sunrise Gr BS4 . . . . .9 D4
Sunset La GL52 . . . . .134 C8
Sunset Pl GL19 . . . . .165 D6
Surrey Ave GL51 . . . . .132 F2
Surrey Rd BS7 . . . . .18 E3
Surrey St BS2 . . . . .195 B4
Sussex Ave GL51 . . . . .133 A2
Sussex Gdns GL3 . . . . .120 B7
Sussex Pl BS2 . . . . .18 F1
Sussex St BS2 . . . . .9 A6
Sutherland Ave
 Bristol BS16 . . . . .20 E7
 Yate BS37 . . . . .43 D4
Sutton Ave BS4 . . . . .9 D4
Sutton Cl GL11 . . . . .80 B8
Sutton Pk SN26 . . . . .144 E1
Sutton Pl GL5 . . . . .99 D7
Sutton Rd
 Littledean GL14 . . . . .191 F3
 Upper Soudley GL14 . . . . .156 C5
Swagwater La HR9 . . . . . . .170 C5
Swainswick BS14 . . . . .2 F6
Swaish Dr **2** BS30 . . . . . . .11 A4
Swallow Cres GL3 . . . . . . .127 D6
Swallow Croft GL10 . . . . . . .96 F7
Swallow Ct BS14 . . . . .2 F4
Swallow Dr BS34 . . . . .28 E8
Swallow Pk BS35 . . . . .64 D3
Swallows Ct BS34 . . . . .29 E4
Swallowtail Ct **6** GL51 . .132 D2
Swan Cl
 Lechlade on T GL7 . . . . . . .153 E2
 Moreton-in-M GL56 . . . . . .187 A3
Swan Ct GL5 . . . . .196 A3
Swan Field BS37 . . . . .43 F2
Swan La Blakeney GL15 . . .156 E2
 Leigh SN6 . . . . .143 A3
 Stoke Orchard GL52 . . . . .136 D5
Swan Rd Gloucester GL1 . .196 C4
 Lydney GL15 . . . . .92 A3
Swan Yd GL7 . . . . .190 C5
Swane Rd BS14 . . . . .3 E6
Swanley La GL13 . . . . .78 B5
Swanmoor Cres BS10 . . . . .28 A4
Swanscombe Pl **14**
 GL51 . . . . .129 E5
Swansfield GL7 . . . . .153 E3
Swanswell Dr GL51 . . . . . .129 E8
Sweden La GL20 . . . . .183 B5
Sweetbriar GL52 . . . . .137 E4
Sweetbriar St GL1 . . . . . . .196 C4
Sweetmore Cl GL56 . . . . . .177 C5
Sweets Cl BS15 . . . . .20 E2
Sweets Rd BS15 . . . . .20 D2
Swell CE Prim Sch
 GL54 . . . . .176 D4
Swells Hill GL6 . . . . .99 E1
Swift Rd GL4 . . . . .119 D5
Swifts Hill View GL6 . . . . . .103 E1
Swilgate Rd GL20 . . . . . . .192 C3
Swindon & Cricklade Rly*
 SN5 . . . . .143 F1
Swindon Cl GL4 . . . . .133 C3
Swindon La GL50 . . . . .133 D5
Swindon Manor GL51 . . . .133 A6
Swindon Rd
 Bristol,Hanham BS15 . . . . .20 C1
 Cheltenham,St Peter's
 GL50 . . . . .133 B4
 Cirencester GL7 . . . . .190 E3
 Cricklade SN6 . . . . .143 F4
 Highworth SN6 . . . . .145 C2
Swindon St
 Highworth SN6 . . . . .145 D3
Swindon Village Prim Sch
 GL51 . . . . .133 B7
Swinhay La GL12 . . . . .66 B1
Swish La GL12 . . . . .164 A4
Swiss Dr BS3 . . . . .7 F1
Swiss Rd BS3 . . . . .7 F1
Swordfish Cl GL3 . . . . .128 C5
Swynford Cl GL7 . . . . .191 F8
Sybil Rd GL1 . . . . .119 A6
Sycamore Ave NP16 . . . . . . .60 E5
Sycamore Cl
 Bristol,Hanham BS15 . . . . .10 B3
 Bristol,Whitehall BS5 . . . . . .9 E8
 Gloucester GL1 . . . . .118 D5
Sycamore Cres Bristol GL52 .138 B4
 St Arvans NP16 . . . . .72 B5
Sycamore Dr Bristol BS34 . .28 F4
 Stroud GL5 . . . . .91 D8
 Thornbury BS35 . . . . .64 C1

Sycamore Ho **6** BS16 . . . .20 C6
Sycamore Rd
 Harrow Hill GL17 . . . . .164 B3
 Northway GL20 . . . . .182 C4
Sydenham Hill BS6 . . . . . . .18 D1
Sydenham Hill Rd BS6 . . . . .18 D1
Sydenham La BS6 . . . . .18 E1
Sydenham Pl **15** BS6 . . . . .18 E1
Sydenham Rd
 Bristol,Cotham BS6 . . . . . . .18 E1
 Bristol,Totterdown BS4 . . . . .9 A3
 8 Cheltenham GL52 . . . .130 F8
Sydenham Sch **5** GL52 . .130 F8
Sydenham Terr GL1 . . . . . .118 E7
Sydenham Villas Rd
 GL52 . . . . .130 F8
Sydenham Way BS15 . . . . . .10 C3
Sydney GL10 . . . . .101 C1
Sydney Row BS1 . . . . .194 B1
Sylvan Cl **3** GL16 . . . . . . .155 A5
Sylvan La GL52 . . . . .146 B4
Sylvan Way BS9 . . . . .17 B7
Sylvia Ave BS3 . . . . .8 F3
Symes Ave BS13 . . . . .2 C4
Symington Rd BS16 . . . . . . .20 B5
Symn La GL7 . . . . .68 C7
Synwell La GL12 . . . . .68 C7
Syon Rd GL6 . . . . .148 A3
Syston View BS15 . . . . .11 A8
Syston Way BS15 . . . . .20 D1

T

T T Trad Est BS37 . . . . .44 C1
Tabernacle Pitch GL12 . . . .68 B7
Tabernacle Rd
 Bristol BS15 . . . . .10 C6
 Wotton-u-E GL12 . . . . .68 B8
Tabernacle Wlk GL5 . . . . . . .99 B5
Tabrams Pitch GL6 . . . . . . .91 C4
Tackley Rd BS5 . . . . .19 B3
Tadwick La BA1 . . . . .13 E1
Taena Pottery* GL4 . . . . . .120 B2
Tailor's Ct BS1 . . . . .195 A3
Tainmor Cl GL2 . . . . .127 E5
Tait's Hill GL11 . . . . .87 C4
Tait's Hill Rd GL11 . . . . . . .87 C4
Taits Hill Ind Est GL11 . . . . .87 C4
Talbot Ave BS15 . . . . .20 C1
Talbot Cl BS34 . . . . .176 F4
Talbot Mews GL51 . . . . . . .130 D6
Talbot Pl GL17 . . . . .164 D5
Talbot Rd BS2 . . . . .9 C2
 Cheltenham GL51 . . . . . . .130 A8
Talbot Sq GL54 . . . . .176 F4
Talboy's Wlk **6** GL8 . . . . .140 C5
Talgarth Rd BS7 . . . . .18 F4
Tall Elms Cl GL3 . . . . .128 B5
Tallard's Pl NP16 . . . . .61 A8
Tallis Gr BS4 . . . . .2 D6
Tallis Rd GL3 . . . . .127 F8
Tally Ho La GL54 . . . . .159 C3
Talybont Ave HR9 . . . . .162 C3
Tamar Cl BS35 . . . . .51 D7
Tamar Dr BS31 . . . . .5 A4
Tamar Rd Bristol BS2 . . . . . .9 C6
 Brockworth GL3 . . . . .127 A3
Tamarisk Cl GL51 . . . . .134 A2
Tamesis Dr GL7 . . . . .141 F8
Tamsin Ct BS31 . . . . .4 E4
Tamworth Rd BS31 . . . . .4 E4
Tandey Wlk GL3 . . . . .127 D6
Tanglewood Way GL6 . . . .148 B6
Tanhouse La BS37 . . . . .44 A3
Tankard's Cl BS8 . . . . .194 C3
Tanner Cl BS30 . . . . .11 A5
Tanner Ct **4** BS31 . . . . . . .4 D4
Tanner's Cl GL56 . . . . .187 E5
Tanner's La GL51 . . . . .132 F3
Tanner's Piece GL16 . . . . . .155 F7
Tanner's Rd GL51 . . . . .132 F3
Tanners Ct
 Bristol,Frenchay BS16 . . . . .30 B1
 4 Bristol,Two Mile Hill
 BS15 . . . . .20 C1
 Thornbury BS35 . . . . .51 F8
Tanners La SN14 . . . . .14 F8
Tannery Rd GL10 . . . . .97 E3
Tannery Gdns GL16 . . . . . .155 B8
Tanorth Cl BS14 . . . . .2 A3
Tanorth Rd GL14 . . . . .168 A1
Tansy Cl GL4 . . . . .119 F5
Tanyard The BS37 . . . . .43 B6
Tapscott Cl GL12 . . . . .68 A7
Tapsters BS30 . . . . .11 A4
Tara Cl BS36 . . . . .37 F5
Taragon Cl GL4 . . . . .119 F5
Tarlton Cl GL4 . . . . .118 C1
Tarn Ho BS34 . . . . .29 B1
Tarnock Ave GL4 . . . . .118 A1
Tarragon Pl BS32 . . . . .36 D7
Tasmania Ho **7** GL51 . . . .118 C7
Tatchley La GL52 . . . . .137 B4
Taunton Wlk BS7 . . . . .19 A6
Taurus Cl BS14 . . . . .2 E6
Taut The GL4 . . . . .148 A6
Taverner Cl BS4 . . . . .2 D7
Tavistock Rd BS4 . . . . .8 F1
Tavistock Wlk BS4 . . . . .8 F1
Tawny Cl GL51 . . . . .132 D2
Tayberry Gr GL51 . . . . .129 F4
Taylor Cl BS15 . . . . .10 F1
Taylor Dr Bristol BS34 . . . . .29 C7
Taylor Gdns BS13 . . . . .1 E4

Taylors End GL50 . . . . .130 B
Taylors Ground GL2 . . . . . .117 F2
Taylors Row **62** GL54 . . . .176 F4
Tayman Cl BS10 . . . . .28 B1
Tayman Ridge BS30 . . . . .5 D8
Taynton Cl BS30 . . . . .11 C7
Teal Cl Bristol BS32 . . . . . . .40 D7
 Quedgeley GL2 . . . . .117 D3
Teasel Cl GL2 . . . . .126 F6
Teasel Mead GL52 . . . . .29 E1
Tebbit Mews **8** GL52 . . . .193 C4
Ted Preston Cl GL20 . . . . . .192 D2
Teddington Gdns GL4 . . . . .119 B6
Teewell Ave BS16 . . . . .20 E5
Teewell Cl BS16 . . . . .20 E5
Teewell Ct BS16 . . . . .20 E5
Teewell Hill BS16 . . . . .20 E5
Teignmouth Rd BS4 . . . . .8 F1
Telephone Ave BS1 . . . . . . .195 A2
Telford Ho Bristol BS8 . . . . . .7 E3
 Cheltenham GL51 . . . . . . .132 F3
Telford Way GL2 . . . . .109 F4
Telford Wlk BS5 . . . . .9 F4
Tellings Orch SN16 . . . . . . .142 B3
Teme Rd GL52 . . . . .134 A2
Tempest Dr NP16 . . . . .60 D8
Templar Rd BS37 . . . . .43 E2
Temple Back BS1 . . . . .195 B2
Temple Back E BS1 . . . . . . .195 C2
Temple Circle Gyratory
 BS1 . . . . .195 B1
Temple Cl
 Gloucester GL4 . . . . .119 A1
 Lydney GL15 . . . . .147 F6
Temple Ct BS31 . . . . .4 E5
Temple Gate BS1 . . . . .195 B1
Temple Gate District Ctr
 BS3 . . . . .8 F4
Temple Guiting CE Prim Sch
 GL54 . . . . .175 A4
Temple Hill Inf Sch BS31 . . .4 F7
Temple Jun Sch BS31 . . . . . .4 F7
Temple Meads Sta BS1 . . .195 C2
Temple Rose St BS1 . . . . . .195 B2
Temple St Bristol BS1 . . . . .195 B2
 Bristol,Bedminster BS3 . . . . .8 B2
 Keynsham BS31 . . . . .4 E5
Temple Trad Est BS2 . . . . . . .9 E5
Temple Way BS2 . . . . .195 B2
Temple Way Underpass
 BS2 . . . . .195 C2
Templefields GL4 . . . . .166 C2
Templefields Cl GL4 . . . . . .166 C2
Templeland Rd BS13 . . . . . . .1 F5
Templeway GL15 . . . . .147 F6
Templeway W GL15 . . . . . .147 F6
Tenby St BS5 . . . . .9 B7
Tenby St BS5 . . . . .9 B7
Tennessee Dr BS36 . . . . . . .37 B8
Tennis Rd BS4 . . . . .9 A1
Tenniscourt Rd BS15 . . . . . .21 A3
Tennyson Ave GL2 . . . . . . .118 C4
Tennyson Rd Bristol BS7 . . .18 E5
 Cheltenham GL51 . . . . . . .132 E3
 Dursley GL11 . . . . .80 C1
Tensing Rd GL53 . . . . .130 E4
Terrace The
 Nailsworth GL6 . . . . .92 A3
 Wotton-u-E GL12 . . . . .68 D8
Terrell St BS2 . . . . .195 A4
Terrets Ct BS34 . . . . .29 A1
Terry Ho BS1 . . . . .194 C3
Terry Ruck Cl GL51 . . . . . . .132 D2
Tesco Rdbt GL2 . . . . .117 F1
Tetbury Cl BS34 . . . . .29 C7
Tetbury Hill GL8 . . . . .140 D8
Tetbury Hospl GL8 . . . . . . .140 C3
Tetbury La
 Crudwell SN16 . . . . .141 B3
 Leighterton GL8 . . . . .70 C3
 Nailsworth GL6 . . . . .91 C2
Tetbury Police Mus*
 GL8 . . . . .140 B4
Tetbury Rd Bristol BS15 . . . .10 C3
 Cirencester GL7 . . . . .150 B3
 Gloucester GL4 . . . . .190 B4
 Sherston SN16 . . . . .40 C4
 Stow-on-t-W GL54 . . . . . .176 F5
 Uckington GL51 . . . . .129 C2
Teviot Rd BS31 . . . . .5 A4
Tewkesbury CE Prim Sch
 GL20 . . . . .192 D4
Tewkesbury Hospl
 GL20 . . . . .192 F6
Tewkesbury Mus*
 GL20 . . . . .192 C4
Tewkesbury Rd
 11 Ashchurch GL20 . . . . .19 A2
 Cheltenham GL51 . . . . . . .133 A4
 Gloucester GL2 . . . . .126 F5
 Longford GL2 . . . . .126 F6
 Newent GL18 . . . . .153 F8
 Northway GL20 . . . . .182 C3
 Stow-on-t-W GL54 . . . . . .176 F5
 Twyning GL20 . . . . .182 A4
Tewther Rd BS13 . . . . .2 B4
Texas Cl GL7 . . . . .152 E2
Teyfant Com Sch BS13 . . . . .2 E4
Teyfant Rd BS13 . . . . .2 E4
Teyfant Wlk BS13 . . . . .2 E4

Thackeray BS7 . . . . .19 A8
Thames Cl Charfield GL12 . .67 A4
Cricklade SN6 . . . . .143 E4
Thames Ho 3 BS35 . . . . . .51 C8
Thames La SN6 . . . . .143 F4
Thames Rd GL52 . . . . . . .134 A2
Thames St GL7 . . . . .153 E2
Thames View 2 SN6 . . . . .142 F4
Thamesmead Cotts SN6 .143 E4
Thanet Rd BS3 . . . . .8 B2
Thatcham Rd GL20 . . . . . .192 E1
Thatchers Cl BS5 . . . . .10 B7
Thatchers End GL52 . . . . .138 B3
Theatre Royal* BS1 . . . . .195 A2
Theescombe Hill GL5 . . . . .91 B6
Theocs Cl GL20 . . . . .192 C2
There-and-Back-Again La
BS1 . . . . .194 C3
Theresa Ave BS7 . . . . .18 E4
Theresa St GL1 . . . . .118 D7
Thessaly Gate GL7 . . . . . .190 A8
Thessaly Rd GL7 . . . . . . .190 B8
Theyer Cl GL3 . . . . .120 E5
Theynes Croft BS41 . . . . . . .7 B1
Thicket Ave BS16 . . . . . . .20 C3
Thicket Rd BS16 . . . . .64 C1
Thicket Wlk BS35 . . . . . . .64 F1
Thiery Rd BS4 . . . . .9 C2
Thingwall Pk BS16 . . . . . .19 E3
Third Ave
Bristol,Filton BS7 . . . . . . .29 A1
Bristol,Hengrove BS14 . . . .3 B7
Dursley GL11 . . . . .80 C8
Third Way BS11 . . . . .26 C2
Thirlebrook Cotts GL20 .182 E4
Thirlestaine House Cotts
GL53 . . . . .193 B1
Thirlestaine Rd GL53 . . .193 C1
Thirlmere Ct BS30 . . . . . .11 D6
Thirlmere Rd Bristol BS34 .29 A8
Cheltenham GL51 . . . . . .129 E7
Thistle Downs GL20 . . . . .182 C5
Thistle St 1 BS3 . . . . .8 B3
Thistlebank GL2 . . . . .127 B5
Thistledown Cl GL51 . . . .132 C4
Thomas Ave BS16 . . . . . . .21 B8
Thomas Ct BS1 . . . . .195 B2
Thomas La BS1 . . . . .195 B2
Thomas Moore Cl GL3 . . .128 A8
Thomas Pring Wlk 1
BS5 . . . . .20 A1
Thomas St
Bristol,Kingsdown BS2 . .195 B4
8 Bristol,Russell Town BS5 . .9 F8
Bristol,St Pauls BS2 . . . . .18 F1
Chepstow/Cas-Gwent NP16 .66 D8
Cirencester GL7 . . . . . . .190 C5
Gloucester GL1 . . . . .196 C1
Thomas St N 12 BS2 . . . . .18 D1
Thomas Stock Gdns
GL4 . . . . .119 E6
Thomas Way BS16 . . . . . .19 E7
Thomond Cl GL11 . . . . . .133 C4
Thompson Dr GL53 . . . . .130 D4
Thompson Rd Bristol BS14 .3 E6
Siddington GL7 . . . . .150 F2
Stroud GL5 . . . . .9 D8
Thomson Way GL3 . . . . . .127 E6
Thomson Rd 7 BS5 . . . . . . .9 B8
Thoresby GL52 . . . . .133 E5
Thoresby Ave GL4 . . . . . .110 C8
Thorn Cl BS37 . . . . .43 D1
Thorn Tree Dr NP16 . . . . .60 F4
Thornbury Cl GL51 . . . . . .133 B2
Thornbury Hospl BS35 . . . .64 C1
Thornbury Ind Pk BS35 . . .51 B7
Thornbury Mus* BS35 . . .51 B8
Thornbury Rd BS35 . . . . . .51 A5
Thorncliffe 10 GL51 . . . .130 B8
Thorncliffe Dr GL51 . . . .130 B8
Thorndale BS8 . . . . .194 A4
Thorndale Mews BS8 . . . .194 A4
Thorough Mews 5
GL51 . . . . .129 E5
Thornhayes Cl BS36 . . . . .31 A8
Thornhill Cl GL1 . . . . . . .118 D5
Thornhills The BS16 . . . . .20 B6
Thornleigh Rd BS7 . . . . . .18 E5
Thornmead Gr BS10 . . . . .28 A2
Thorns Farm BS37 . . . . . .43 E1
Thornwell Prim Sch
NP16 . . . . .60 F5
Thornwell Rd NP16 . . . . . .60 F5
Thornycroft Cl BS7 . . . . . .19 B7
Thorpe Lodge 3 BS8 . . . . .8 A1
Threadneedle St 10 GL5 .99 C7
Three Ashes La GL18 . . . .171 A6
Three Brooks La BS32 . . . .29 E8
Three Choirs Vineyard*
GL18 . . . . .170 F7
Three Cocks La GL1 . . . . .196 A3
Three Counties Pk
WR13 . . . . .180 C5
Three Oaks Cl BS16 . . . . .20 C4
Three Queens' La BS1 . . .195 B2
Three Sisters La GL3 . . . .133 D3
Three Wells Rd BS13 . . . . .1 F4
Thrissell St BS5 . . . . .9 A8
Throat The GL6 . . . . .102 F4
Throgmorton Rd BS4 . . . . .2 F1
Thrupp La GL5 . . . . .99 E3
Thrupp Sch GL5 . . . . .99 E3
Thrush Cl GL4 . . . . .119 D6
Thurlestone BS14 . . . . .3 A6
Thurlow Rd BS5 . . . . .9 C2
Thurston's Barton BS5 . . .19 E1
Tibberton BS15 . . . . .11 A8

Tibberton Com Prim Sch
GL19 . . . . .171 E1
Tibberton Dr GL51 . . . . .129 B7
Tibberton La GL19 . . . . . .165 D6
Tibbiwell Gdns GL6 . . . . .103 F8
Tibbiwell La GL6 . . . . . . .103 F8
Tibbott Rd BS14 . . . . .3 D5
Tibbott Wlk BS14 . . . . .3 D5
Tiberius Ave GL15 . . . . . . .92 B4
Tichborne Rd BS5 . . . . .9 C7
Tide Gr BS11 . . . . .17 A8
Tidenham Way BS34 . . . . .39 F1
Tidling Cnr SN16 . . . . . . .142 B3
Tidswell Cl GL2 . . . . .109 F8
Tiffany Cl BS1 . . . . .195 B1
Tilley Cl BS3 . . . . .5 A2
Tilling Rd BS10 . . . . .18 E7
Tilling Wlk BS10 . . . . .18 E7
Tillis View GL11 . . . . .64 B7
Tilney Rd GL50 . . . . .133 D4
Tilnor Cres GL11 . . . . .87 F4
Tilsdown GL11 . . . . .87 F4
Tilsdown Cl GL11 . . . . .87 F4
Tilting Rd BS35 . . . . .64 B2
Timber Dene BS16 . . . . . .19 D4
Timbercombe La GL53 . . .131 B3
Timbercombe Mews
GL53 . . . . .131 B4
Timberscombe Wlk BS14 . .3 C5
Timbrells Cl GL7 . . . . . . .142 B8
Timbrells The GL7 . . . . . .142 B8
Timmis Cl GL4 . . . . .119 C4
Timms Gn WR12 . . . . . . .188 B2
Timperley Way GL51 . . . .129 E5
Timsbury Rd BS3 . . . . .8 E2
Timsbury Wlk BS3 . . . . . . .8 E2
Tindell Ct 12 BS30 . . . . . .10 F4
Tinglesfield GL7 . . . . .190 B8
Tinker's Cl 7 GL56 . . . . .187 A3
Tinkley La GL10 . . . . .90 B5
Tinmans Gn NP25 . . . . . .154 C4
Tintagel Cl BS31 . . . . .4 D4
Tintern Abbey* NP16 . . .146 C2
Tintern Ave BS5 . . . . .9 D8
Tintern Cl BS30 . . . . .10 F6
Tintern Hts NP16 . . . . . . .146 A5
Tintern Old Sta* NP16 . .146 A3
Tintern Rd GL14 . . . . . . .118 E3
Tippetts Rd BS15 . . . . .10 D6
Tirle Bank Way GL20 . . . .192 F4
Tirlebrook Grange
GL20 . . . . .182 D4
Tirlebrook Prim Sch
GL20 . . . . .192 F4
Tirley Cl GL2 . . . . .117 C7
Tirley Ho BS34 . . . . .39 F1
Tirley Knowle GL19 . . . . .172 F8
Tirley St GL19 . . . . .172 F7
Tithe Farm La GL19 . . . . .165 E6
Tiverton Cl GL11 . . . . . . .132 D3
Tiverton Wlk BS16 . . . . . .20 A2
Tivoli La GL50 . . . . .193 A1
Tivoli Mews GL50 . . . . . .193 A2
Tivoli Pl GL50 . . . . .193 A1
Tivoli St GL50 . . . . .193 A1
Tivoli Wlk 16 GL50 . . . . .130 B8
Toadsmoor Rd GL5 . . . . .148 A5
Tobacco Cl GL54 . . . . . . .139 F4
Tobacconist Rd GL6 . . . . .148 A3
Tobias Gdns BS37 . . . . . . .43 D1
Tobyfield Cl GL52 . . . . . .138 A3
Tobyfield La GL52 . . . . . .138 A3
Tobyfield Rd GL52 . . . . . .138 A3
Tockington Gn BS32 . . . . .50 B2
Tockington La BS32 . . . . . .40 A7
Tockington Manor Sch
BS32 . . . . .50 C2
Tockington Park La BS32 . .40 E8
Tocknell Ct GL11 . . . . .87 F8
Toddington Cl BS37 . . . . .32 D8
Toddington Prim Sch
GL54 . . . . .184 C3
Toddington Sta* GL54 . . .184 D3
Toghill La BS30 . . . . .13 A8
Toll Down Way SN14 . . . . .36 A3
Toll House Ct 5 BS3 . . . . . .8 A4
Tolsey La GL2 . . . . .192 C4
Tom Price Cl GL52 . . . . . .138 A3
Tomlin Pl GL15 . . . . .156 B1
Tommy Taylor's La
GL50 . . . . .133 D4
Tone Dr GL1 . . . . .120 F5
Tooke Rd GL6 . . . . .91 E7
Top Rd Kempsford GL7 . . .144 E8
Upper Soudley GL14 . . . .156 C5
Torchacre Rise GL11 . . . . .88 A1
Tormarton Cres BS10 . . . .27 F4
Tormarton Intc BS37 . . . . .34 B1
Tormarton Rd
Acton Turville GL9 . . . . . .35 E6
Marshfield SN14 . . . . . . .25 A4
Marshfield,East End SN14 . .15 A8
Toronto Rd GL3 . . . . .19 A8
Torpoint Rd BS3 . . . . .8 D2
Torrance Cl BS30 . . . . .11 D6
Torwood House Sch BS6 . .18 A3
Torrington Ave BS4 . . . . . .2 F8
Tortworth Farming Mus*
GL12 . . . . .66 B6
Tortworth Prim Sch
GL12 . . . . .66 C7
Tortworth Rd BS7 . . . . . . .18 E5
Totshall Dr BS13 . . . . .2 E4
Totshill Gr BS13 . . . . .2 E4
Tottenham Pl BS8 . . . . . .194 B3

Totterdown Bridge Ind Est
BS2 . . . . .9 A4
Totterdown La GL7 . . . . .152 E2
Touching End La SN14 . . .14 F8
Touchstone Ave BS34 . . . .29 F5
Tower Cl GL4 . . . . .119 D8
Tower Hill BS2 . . . . .195 B3
Tower Ho
10 Cheltenham GL52 . . . .193 C4
Woodchester GL5 . . . . . . .98 F1
Tower House Dr GL19 . . .179 F2
Tower La Bristol BS1 . . . .195 A3
Bristol,Cadbury Heath BS30 . .11 B6
Tower Rd Bristol BS15 . . . .20 C1
Yorkley GL15 . . . . .156 A2
Tower Rd N BS30 . . . . . . .11 B7
Tower Rd S BS30 . . . . .11 B5
Tower St Bristol BS1 . . . .195 B2
Cirencester GL7 . . . . . . .190 D4
Tower The BS1 . . . . .195 B2
Towerleaze BS9 . . . . .17 D3
Town St GL19 . . . . .173 A8
Townsend
Almondsbury BS32 . . . . . .39 F4
Mitcheldean GL17 . . . . . .164 D5
Ruardean GL17 . . . . .163 E4
Townsend Cl Bristol BS14 . .3 F5
St Briavels GL15 . . . . . . .146 F7
Townsend La BS32 . . . . . .40 A5
Townsend Rd BS14 . . . . . . .3 F5
Townsend St GL51 . . . . . .133 C3
Townwell GL12 . . . . .66 B2
Tozers Hill BS4 . . . . .9 C2
Tracy Cl BS14 . . . . .2 F7
Tracy Row GL20 . . . . . . .192 D5
Trafalgar Dr GL3 . . . . . . .127 F8
Trafalgar St GL50 . . . . . .193 B2
Trafalgar Terr 3 BS3 . . . . .8 B2
Traherne Cl 5 HR8 . . . . .178 F7
Trajan Cl GL4 . . . . .119 F5
Tralee Wlk BS4 . . . . .8 D1
Tram Rd The 8 GL14 . . . .155 A5
Tramway Rd Bristol BS4 . . .9 E2
Cinderford GL14 . . . . . . .156 C6
Upper Soudley GL14 . . . .156 C6
Tranmere Ave BS10 . . . . . .28 A4
Tranmere Gr BS10 . . . . . . .28 A3
Transom Rd BS1 . . . . . . .195 B2
Transport Mus* GL1 . . . .196 A3
Tranton La GL11 . . . . .76 C4
Tratman Wlk BS10 . . . . . .27 F3
Tredegar Rd BS16 . . . . . . .20 B3
Tredington Com Prim Sch
GL20 . . . . .136 B6
Tredington Pk GL20 . . . . .173 F8
Tredworth Jun & Inf Schs
GL1 . . . . .118 E7
Tredworth Rd GL1 . . . . . .118 F6
Tree Leaze BS37 . . . . .43 F2
Treefield Pl 5 BS2 . . . . . . .9 A2
Treelands Cl GL20 . . . . . .192 D1
Treelands Dr GL53 . . . . . .130 D5
Tregarth Rd BS3 . . . . .7 F3
Trelawney Ave BS5 . . . . . . .9 D8
Trelawney Rd BS6 . . . . . . .18 C1
Trelawney Rd BS6 . . . . . . .9 D3
Trelleck Rd NP16 . . . . . . .146 B4
Trellick Wlk BS16 . . . . . . .19 F8
Tremes Cl SN14 . . . . .14 F8
Trench La BS32 . . . . .30 C3
Trenchard Gdns GL7 . . . .150 F2
Trenchard Rd
8 Bream GL15 . . . . .147 D8
Saltford BS31 . . . . .5 D3
Trenchard St BS1 . . . . . . .194 C3
Trendlewood Pk BS16 . . . .19 E7
Trenley Rd GL11 . . . . .88 F7
Trent Cl BS37 . . . . .40 A8
Trent Gr BS31 . . . . .4 E2
Trent Rd GL3 . . . . .20 F5
Trentham Cl 7 BS2 . . . . . .19 A2
Tresham Cl BS32 . . . . .40 D2
Tresmore Cl GL52 . . . . . .133 F2
Tretawn Gdns GL20 . . . . .192 F4
Trevanna Rd BS3 . . . . .7 F1
Trevelyan Wlk
Bristol,Henbury BS10 . . . .27 F3
Bristol,Stoke Gifford BS34 . .30 A5
Treverdowe Wlk BS10 . . . .27 A2
Trevethin Cl BS15 . . . . . . .10 F1
Trevisa Cres GL13 . . . . . . .85 E3
Trevisa Gr BS10 . . . . .27 F3
Trevor Rd GL3 . . . . .119 F7
Trewint Gdns BS4 . . . . .9 E8
Trewsbury Rd GL7 . . . . . .149 E3
Triangle S BS8 . . . . .194 B3
Triangle The
Hewelsfield GL15 . . . . . .146 D4
Longlevens GL2 . . . . .117 C8
Triangle W BS8 . . . . .194 B3
Tribune Pl GL4 . . . . .110 C8
Trident Cl BS16 . . . . .31 A1
Trier Way GL1 . . . . .196 B1
Trim Mills BS1 . . . . .195 A2
Trinder Rd BS20 . . . . .16 A4
Trinity CE Prim Sch GL1 . .36 A6
Trinity Coll BS9 . . . . .17 E3
Trinity Dr GL6 . . . . .148 A3
Trinity La GL52 . . . . .193 C4
Trinity Mews 17 BS2 . . . . .19 A2
Trinity Pl BS8 . . . . .194 B3
Trinity Rd BS2 . . . . .9 A7
Cirencester GL7 . . . . . . .190 C3
Gloucester GL4 . . . . .119 F6

Trinity Rd continued
Harrow Hill GL17 . . . . . .164 B3
Stroud GL5 . . . . .99 D6
Trinity School La GL19 . .193 C4
Trinity St Bristol BS2 . . . . . .9 A7
Tewkesbury GL20 . . . . . .192 C4
Trinity Way GL14 . . . . . . .191 D5
Trinity Wlk Bristol BS2 . . .195 C3
Bristol,Newton BS2 . . . . . . .9 A7
Tewkesbury GL20 . . . . . .192 D4
Tripps Row BS41 . . . . .7 A1
Triscombe Way GL51 . . . .132 D3
Troon BS37 . . . . .32 E4
Troon Dr BS30 . . . . .11 B6
Troopers' Hill Rd BS5 . . . .10 A7
Trotman Ave GL11 . . . . . . .87 F5
Troughton Pl GL20 . . . . . .192 E4
Trowbridge Rd BS10 . . . . .28 C1
Trowbridge Wlk BS10 . . . .28 C1
Trowscoed Ave GL53 . . . .130 D6
Trubodys Yd BS30 . . . . . . .11 E7
Trubshaw Ct GL3 . . . . . . .128 C5
Truit Cotts GL8 . . . . .140 F7
Truro Rd BS3 . . . . .8 B3
Tryes Rd GL50 . . . . .130 C6
Trygrove GL4 . . . . .119 D6
Trym Bank BS9 . . . . .17 D7
Trym Cross Rd BS9 . . . . . .17 C5
Trym Rd BS9 . . . . .18 A7
Trym Side BS9 . . . . .17 C5
Trymleaze BS9 . . . . .17 C5
Trymwood Cl BS10 . . . . . .27 F2
Trymwood Par BS9 . . . . . .17 D6
Tubbar Cotts NP16 . . . . . .73 A1
Tucker St BS2 . . . . .195 C3
Tuckett Ho BS16 . . . . .20 C7
Tuckett La BS16 . . . . .20 C7
Tuckwell Rd GL7 . . . . . . .144 F7
Tudor Cl BS30 . . . . .11 C3
Tudor Ct Gloucester GL1 . .127 A3
Leonard Stanley GL10 . . . .78 C5
Tudor Dr NP16 . . . . .72 C1
Tudor Lo GL50 . . . . .130 C6
Tudor Lodge Dr GL50 . . .193 A1
Tudor Lodge Rd GL50 . . .130 C6
Tudor Pl GL20 . . . . .192 D2
Tudor Rd
Bristol,Hanham BS15 . . . .10 C5
Bristol,Lower Easton BS5 . .19 C1
Bristol,St Pauls BS2 . . . . .18 F1
Cirencester GL7 . . . . . . .190 E5
Monmouth/Trefynwy
NP25 . . . . .154 B7
Tudor St GL1 . . . . .118 C6
Tudor Wlk GL16 . . . . .155 A4
Tuffley Ave GL1 . . . . .118 D5
Tuffley Cres GL1 . . . . . . .118 C8
Tuffley La GL4 . . . . .118 C3
Tuffley Pk GL1 . . . . .118 E4
Tuffley Prim Sch GL4 . . .118 D1
Tuffley Rd GL1 . . . . .118 C6
Tufthorn Ave GL16 . . . . . .155 A4
Tufthorn Ind Est GL16 . . .155 B4
Tufthorn Rd GL16 . . . . . .155 A4
Tufton Ave BS11 . . . . .17 A8
Tufts The GL15 . . . . .147 C8
Tug Wilson Cl GL20 . . . . .182 C5
Tugela Rd BS13 . . . . .1 F7
Tulworths The GL2 . . . . . .127 B5
Tunacre GL2 . . . . .125 D6
Tunbridge Way BS16 . . . . .21 A8
Tunnel La GL15 . . . . .141 C3
Tunstall Cl BS9 . . . . .17 C5
Turkdean Rd GL51 . . . . . .129 E8
Turley Rd BS5 . . . . .9 D1
Turnberry Bristol BS30 . . . .11 H4
Yate BS37 . . . . .32 E8
Turnberry Wlk 3 BS4 . . . . .9 E8
Turnbridge Rd BS10 . . . . .28 C2
Turnbury Cl GL51 . . . . . . .132 D3
Turner Cl BS31 . . . . .5 A5
Turner Dr BS37 . . . . .43 B1
Turner Gdns BS7 . . . . .19 B6
Turner Rd GL11 . . . . .87 F4
Turner's Ct 8 GL20 . . . . .192 C4
Turners Cl GL2 . . . . .125 D4
Turners Ct BS30 . . . . .10 F4
Turnpike Ave GL12 . . . . . .30 F4
Turnpike Cl
Chepstow/Cas-Gwent NP16 . .72 C1
15 Moreton-in-M GL56 . .187 A3
Turnpike Gate GL12 . . . . .54 B6
Turnpike Ho GL12 . . . . . . .30 F5
Turnstone Dr GL2 . . . . . . .117 D1
Turtlegate Ave BS13 . . . . . .1 E4
Turtlegate Wlk BS13 . . . . . .1 E4
Turville Barns GL7 . . . . . .153 C8
Turville Dr BS7 . . . . .19 A6
Tuscany Ho BS6 . . . . .18 A3
Tusculum Way GL17 . . . .164 D5
Tuthill Rise GL15 . . . . .92 B3
Tutnalls St GL15 . . . . .92 B3
Tutshill Gdns GL16 . . . . . .73 A1
Tweed Cl BS35 . . . . .51 C8
Tweenbrook Ave GL1 . . . .118 E6
Tweeny La GL53 . . . . .130 F3
Twenties The GL2 . . . . . . .150 E2
Twenty Acres Rd BS10 . . . .28 A2
Twigworth CE Prim Sch
GL2 . . . . .127 A8
Twigworth Ct GL2 . . . . . .173 A1
Twinberrow La GL11 . . . . .80 B7

Twinnell Ho 5 BS5 . . . . . . .9 A8
Twixtbears GL20 . . . . . . .192 C5
Two Acres Rd BS14 . . . . . . .3 A7
Two Hedges Rd GL52 . . . .138 A3
Two Mile Ct BS15 . . . . . . .10 C8
Two Mile Hill Jun & Inf Schs
BS15 . . . . .10 C8
Two Mile La GL2 . . . . . . .125 B4
Twomile Hill Rd BS15 . . . .10 B8
Twyning Manor GL20 . . . .181 F8
Twyning Rd WR8 . . . . . . .180 A10
Twyning Sch GL20 . . . . . .182 A7
Twynings The BS15 . . . . . .20 E2
Tyler Cl BS15 . . . . .10 E5
Tyler Ct 3 GL51 . . . . .132 E2
Tyler St BS2 . . . . .9 A6
Tyler's La BS16 . . . . .20 D5
Tylers Farm BS37 . . . . . . .43 F4
Tylers Way Chalford GL6 . .81 B8
Sedbury NP16 . . . . .61 B8
Yate BS37 . . . . .43 F5
Yorkley GL15 . . . . .156 B2
Tyndale Ave Bristol BS16 . .20 A4
Yate BS37 . . . . .43 D3
Tyndale Cl GL11 . . . . .79 E4
Tyndale Ct 7 BS6 . . . . . . .18 B1
Tyndale Mon The* GL11 . .79 E4
Tyndale Rd Bristol BS2 . . . .20 E2
Dursley GL11 . . . . .87 E4
Gloucester GL3 . . . . .120 A8
Slimbridge GL2 . . . . .95 B1
Tyndale View BS35 . . . . . .51 B8
Tyndall Ho 6 BS2 . . . . . . .195 C3
Tyndall Rd BS5 . . . . .9 B8
Tyndall's Park Mews BS2 . .194 C4
Tyndalls Park Rd
BS2 . . . . .194 C4
Tyndalls Way BS10 . . . . . .18 E8
Tyne Ho 8 BS35 . . . . .51 C8
Tyne St BS2 . . . . .19 A2
Tyne St Bristol BS14 . . . . . .3 A7
Salisbury BS31 . . . . .5 E2
Tynings Cl GL3 . . . . .128 D5
Tynings Rd GL6 . . . . .91 A4
Tynings Sch The BS16 . . . .20 E6
Tynings The GL6 . . . . . . .148 A4
Tynte Ave BS13 . . . . .2 E3
Tyntesfield Rd BS13 . . . . . .2 A8
Tyrone Wlk BS4 . . . . .2 E8
Tyrrel Way BS34 . . . . .29 E5
Tythe Ct Dursley GL11 . . . .87 F5
Tythe Rd WR12 . . . . .188 A1
Tythe Terr 19 GL54 . . . . .174 A7
Tytherington Rd BS35 . . . .52 A6
Tythings Cres GL18 . . . . .170 F4
Tythings Mews GL18 . . . .170 F4
Tythings The GL18 . . . . . .170 F4

U
Uley CE Prim Sch GL11 . . .89 C1
Uley Long Barrow (Hetty
Pegler's Tump)* GL11 . . .89 B5
Uley Rd GL11 . . . . .80 E8
Ullenwood Court Bsns Pk
GL53 . . . . .122 B7
Ullenwood Rd GL4 . . . . . .119 D7
Ullswater Cl Bristol BS30 . .11 D6
Yate BS37 . . . . .33 A8
Ullswater Rd Bristol BS10 . .28 C1
Cheltenham GL51 . . . . . .129 E7
Underbanks BS20 . . . . . . .16 D4
Undercliff Ave GL53 . . . . .130 D3
Undercliff Terr GL53 . . . . .130 D3
Underdown Ho BS1 . . . . .195 A1
Underhill NP16 . . . . .146 C4
Underhill Dr 12 GL54 . . . .119 C4
Underhill Rd
Charfield GL12 . . . . .67 A5
Gloucester GL4 . . . . .119 C4
Underwood Cl BS35 . . . . . .51 A4
Underwood End NP25 . . .154 B7
Unicorn Bsns Pk BS4 . . . . .9 D5
Unicorn Ho GL50 . . . . . . .193 B3
Union Pl GL20 . . . . .192 D4
Union Rd 2 Bristol BS2 . . . .9 A2
Coleford GL16 . . . . .155 B6
Union St Bristol BS1 . . . . .195 B3
Bristol,Brandon Hill BS1 . .194 C2
Bristol,Kingswood BS15 . . .10 C8
Dursley GL11 . . . . .80 B8
Gloucester GL1 . . . . .196 C4
Stow-on-t-W GL54 . . . . .176 F4
Stroud GL5 . . . . .99 C2
Unite Ho BS1 . . . . .194 C2
Unity Ct BS31 . . . . .5 A5
Unity Rd BS31 . . . . .5 A6
Unity St
Bristol,Brandon Hill BS1 . .194 C2
Bristol,Kingswood BS15 . . .10 C8
Univ of Bristol BS8 . . . . . .194 C3

Univ of Bristol Dept of
Economics BS8 ......194 C4
Univ of Bristol Dept of Ed
BS8 ....194 C3
Univ of Bristol Sch of
Veterinary Science
BS2 ....194 A4
Univ of Gloucestershire
(Hardwick Campus)
GL50,GL51 ....133 C3
Univ of Gloucestershire
(Oxstalls Campus) GL2 .127 B3
Univ of Gloucestershire (Park
Campus) GL53 ......130 C6
Univ of Gloucestershire
(Pittville Campus)
GL52 ....133 F4
Univ of
Gloucestershire(Francis
Close Hall) GL50 ....133 D3
Univ of the West of England
BS3 ....7 E4
Univ of the West of England
Faculty of Health & Social
Care BS16 ....19 E5
Univ of the West of England
Frenchay Campus BS16 .29 E1
Univ of the West of England,
St Matthias Campus
BS16 ....20 A5
University Cl BS30 ....1 C3
University Farm 17
GL56 ....187 A3
University Rd BS8 ....194 C3
University Wlk BS8 ....194 C3
Unlawater Ho GL14 ....157 A7
Unlawater La GL14 ....157 A7
Unwin Cl GL51 ....129 C7
Unwin Rd GL51 ....129 C7
Up Hatherley Way GL51 .129 E5
Upcott SN6 ....143 E6
Upfield Cl GL5 ....98 F8
Upfield Prep Sch GL5 ..98 F8
Uphill Pl GL1 ....118 D5
Uphill Rd Bristol BS7 ..18 F5
Upper Lydbrook GL17 ..163 D2
Upjohn Cres BS13 ....2 D3
Uplands Com Prim Sch
GL5 ....99 D8
Uplands Dr BS31 ......5 F2
Uplands Rd Bristol BS16 .20 D3
Saltford BS31 ....5 F2
Stroud GL5 ....99 D8
Uplands View Terr GL5 ..99 D7
Upper Bath Rd BS35 ....51 B8
Upper Bath St GL50 ..193 B1
Upper Belgrave Rd BS8 .18 A2
Upper Belmont Rd BS7 ..18 E3
Upper Berkeley Pl BS8 .194 B3
Upper Bilson Rd GL14 .191 C6
Upper Byron Pl BS8 ....194 B3
Upper Chapel La BS36 ..31 C7
Upper Cheltenham Pl
BS6 ....18 E1
Upper Church La BS2 ..194 C3
Upper Church Rd GL5 ..98 E7
Upper Church St NP16 ..60 F8
Upper Comm GL15 ....147 D5
Upper Conham Vale
BS15 ....10 D8
Upper Cranbrook Rd BS6 .18 B4
Upper Cross 6 HR8 ....178 F8
Upper Dorrington Terr
GL5 ....99 D6
Upper End Ct WR11 ..188 A6
Upper Hayes Rd GL6 ..91 A4
Upper Horfield Prim Sch
BS7 ....19 A8
Upper Kitesnest La GL6 .102 F4
Upper Leazes GL5 ......99 D7
Upper Lynch Rd GL6 ..148 D6
Upper Maudlin St BS2 .195 A3
Upper Mill La GL52 ..134 E5
Upper Mills Ind Est GL10 .98 F4
Upper Myrtle Hill BS20 .16 C4
Upper Nelson St NP16 ..60 E8
Upper Norwood St
GL5 ....130 C6
Upper Park Rd GL6 ....91 C3
Upper Park St GL52 ..130 F8
Upper Perry Hill BS3 ..8 C4
Upper Poole Rd GL11 ..80 B8
Upper Quay Ho GL1 ..196 A3
Upper Quay St GL1 ..196 A3
Upper Queen's Rd 2
GL10 ....97 F7
Upper Rd Eastnor HR8 ..179 F8
Pillowell GL15 ......155 F1
Upper Rissington Bsns Pk
GL54 ....169 D6
Upper Rodley Rd GL14 .157 F8
Upper Sandhurst Rd BS4 .9 D4
Upper Springfield Rd
GL5 ....99 C8
Upper St Bristol BS4 ..9 A4
Dyrham SN14 ....23 D4
Upper Station Rd BS16 .20 D4
Upper Stone Cl BS36 ..31 C7
Upper Stowfield Rd
GL17 ....163 C4
Upper Sydney St BS3 ..8 B3
Upper Terr BS11 ......27 B1
Upper Tockington Rd
BS32 ....50 A2
Upper Tynings GL6 ....91 A4

Upper Tynings The GL5 ..98 D8
Upper Washwell GL6 ..111 F1
Upper Wells St BS1 ..194 C3
Upper York St BS2 ..195 B4
Upperfield Rd GL51 ..133 A5
Upperhall Cl 8 HR8 ..178 F8
Upthorpe GL11 ....88 B5
Upthorpe La GL11 ....88 B6
Upton Cl GL4 ....119 E7
Upton Gdns GL8 ......140 B5
Upton Hill GL4 ......119 D1
Upton La
Brookthorpe GL4 ....111 B6
Gloucester GL4 ......119 F4
Maiden Head BS41 ....1 F1
Upton Rd BS3 ....8 B4
Upton St GL1 ....119 A8
Upton St Leonards CE Prim
Sch GL4 ....119 F3
Upton's Gdn GL2 ....100 E5
Urdords Dr 1 BS16 ..20 C8
Usk Cl 5 BS35 ......51 C8
Usk Way GL3 ....120 F5
Utah Dr GL7 ....152 E2

V

Vaisey Field GL2 ....100 F5
Vaisey Rd GL7 ......190 B8
Vale Bank GL2 ......157 B6
Vale Ct Bristol BS8 ..194 A4
9 Cricklade SN6 ....143 E4
Vale La BS3 ....2 C8
Vale Rd GL7 ....190 B8
Vale St BS4 ....9 A4
Vale The BS16 ......21 F6
Valentine Cl Bristol BS14 .1 A6
Chepstow NP16 ......61 A4
Valerian Cl Bristol BS11 .16 F6
Gloucester GL4 ......119 E7
Valiant Way GL3 ....120 C7
Vallenders Rd GL20 ..182 C7
Valley Cl GL5 ....148 A5
Valley Cotts GL51 ..173 F1
Valley Gdns BS16 ....20 F8
Valley La GL4 ......120 A1
Valley Pk GL2 ......128 F8
Valley Rd
Bristol,Bedminster Down
BS13 ....2 A8
Bristol,Mangotsfield BS16 .21 A5
Bristol,Warmley BS30 ..11 D6
Cinderford GL14 ....191 C3
Leigh Woods BS8 ....7 C2
Lydney GL15 ....92 C2
Wotton-u-E GL12 ....68 C8
Valley View
Chedworth GL54 ....159 A6
Dursley GL11 ....87 F4
Valley View Pk GL54 ..168 E7
Valley View Rd GL5 ..99 F6
Valls The BS32 ......29 F6
Valma Rocks BS5 ....10 A6
Van Der Breen St GL6 .105 B1
Vanbrugh La BS16 ....19 E7
Vandyck Ave BS31 ....4 D2
Vantage Point Bsns Village
GL17 ....164 D5
Varley Ave GL3 ......120 B6
Varnister La GL17 ..163 F4
Varnister Rd GL17 ..163 F4
Vassall Ct BS16 ......20 B5
Vassall Rd BS16 ......20 B5
Vatch La GL5 ....148 B7
Vatch View GL5 ......148 B7
Vattingstone Ho BS35 .50 F5
Vattingstone La BS35 .50 F5
Vaughan Cl BS10 ....27 F3
Vauxhall GL18 ......170 F4
Vauxhall Rd
Chepstow/Cas-Gwent NP16 .60 D8
Gloucester GL1 ....196 C1
Vauxhall Terr
3 Bristol BS3 ......8 A4
Gloucester GL1 ....196 C1
Vayre Cl BS37 ......44 C1
Veldt House Barns HR8 .178 B5
Velhurst Dr 1 GL6 ..148 B6
Velthouse La GL17 ..165 A5
Vennings The GL11 ..87 F6
Venns Acre GL12 ....68 B6
Vensfield Rd GL2 ..117 E2
Vention La GL17 ....163 D3
Ventnor Ave 1 BS5 ..9 F8
Ventnor Rd
Bristol,Filton BS34 ..29 B3
Bristol,St George BS5 .11 F7
Venton Ct 8 BS15 ..10 B5
Vera Rd BS16 ....20 E3
Verbena Cl 2 GL14 ..119 E5
Vernal Cl GL14 ......119 A4
Verney Cl GL53 ......130 E6
Verney Rd GL10 ......97 F7
Verneys The GL53 ....130 E6
Vernon Ct BS31 ......5 B3
Vernon Pl GL53 ......193 C3
Vernon St 5 BS3 ......8 B4
Vernon Terr BS5 ......7 F1
Vertican Rd GL3 ....127 D6
Vervain Cl GL4 ......128 A2
Verwood Dr BS30 ....11 C2
Vestry Gdns GL14 ..191 E5
Vetch Cl GL4 ....119 A4
Viburnum Way BS13 ..130 B6

Viburnum View 4 GL4 ..119 F5
Vicarage Cl
Churchdown GL3 ....128 C4
Lydney GL15 ....92 A2
Shurdington GL51 ..129 E2
Vicarage Cotts
12 Chipping Campden
GL55 ....189 A2
Vicarage Ct Bristol BS15 ..10 B5
Brockworth GL3 ....120 E5
Vicarage La
Arlingham GL2 ......157 B5
Brockworth GL3 ....120 E6
Frampton on Severn GL2 .157 F1
Highworth SN6 ......145 D3
Hillesley GL12 ......55 D8
Olveston BS35 ......50 B3
Vicarage Rd
Bristol,Bishopsworth BS13 ..2 A6
Bristol,Hanham BS15 ..10 B5
Bristol,Southville BS3 ..9 C8
Bristol,Southville BS3 ..8 B4
Coalpit Heath BS36 ..31 C6
Gloucester GL1 ......119 A7
Leigh Woods BS8 ....7 D6
Pilning BS35 ....38 C7
Vicarage St GL6 ....104 A8
Vicars Cl BS16 ......22 D8
Viceroy Cnr 7 GL50 ..193 A4
Vickers Rd GL4 ......169 D7
Victor Ho BS4 ....9 C8
Victor Rd BS3 ....8 C3
Victor St
9 Bristol,Russell Town BS5 ..9 B6
Bristol,St Philip's Marsh BS2 ..9 A4
Victoria Ave GL51 ....9 C7
Victoria Cl BS35 ....64 B3
Victoria Cotts
Quedgeley GL2 ....117 E3
4 Stonehouse GL10 ..97 F8
Victoria Cres BS35 ..38 A6
Victoria Ct
6 Bristol,Cotham BS6 ..18 D1
Bristol,Redland BS6 ..18 D3
Bristol,Russell Town GL52 ..126 F6
Victoria Dr GL10 ....96 F7
Victoria Gdns 7 BS6 ..18 D1
Victoria Gr BS16 ....30 B1
Victoria Ho BS31 ....4 F4
Victoria Mans GL50 ..193 A3
Victoria Par BS5 ....9 C7
Victoria Park Com Inf Sch
BS3 ....8 E3
Victoria Park Com Jun Sch
BS3 ....8 E3
Victoria Pk
Bristol,Fishponds BS16 ..20 A5
Bristol,Kingswood BS15 ..20 D1
Victoria Rd
Bristol,Avonmouth BS11 ..16 B7
Cheltenham GL52 ..133 F1
Stonehouse GL15 ....99 F1
Bristol,Hanham BS15 ..10 C5
Bristol,St Philip's Marsh BS2 ..9 A4
Bristol,Warmley BS30 ..11 D5
Chepstow/Cas-Gwent NP16 ..60 F5
Cirencester GL7 ....190 D4
Coleford GL16 ......155 A5
Gloucester GL2 ....126 F6
Ledbury HR8 ......178 E8
Lydney GL15 ....92 A3
Quenington GL7 ....152 D7
Saltford BS31 ....5 D3
Victoria Retreat GL50 .193 B1
Victoria Sq
6 Bourton-on-t-W GL54 .168 F7
Bristol,Staple Hill BS16 ..20 D5
Cinderford GL14 ....191 C3
Cinderford GL14 ....191 C4
Painswick GL6 ......103 F8
Victoria Terr
9 Bourton-on-t-W GL54 .168 F7
Bretforton WR11 ..188 A7
15 Bristol,Clifton BS8 ....7 F6
Bristol,St Philip's Marsh BS5 ..9 B6
Cheltenham GL52 ..133 F1
Victoria Villas BS20 ..14 F5
Victory Rd
Gloucester GL7 ......103 A3
Whiteshill GL6 ......103 A3
Victory Villas GL4 ..152 F4
Vigor Rd BS13 ....2 A6
Vilda The GL14 ......191 C2
Villa Way HR8 ......178 E7
Village Green La GL54 .168 E7
Village Mews GL4 ..152 F1
Village Rd GL11 ......132 B8
Village St Bristol BS16 ..21 C7
Westbury-on-S GL14 ..165 C1
Vilner La BS35 ......51 B7
Vilverie Mead GL52 ..137 D4
Vimpany Cl BS10 ....27 F3
Vimpennys La BS35 ..63 F5
Vincent Ave GL4 ....118 D1
Vincent Cl BS11 ......27 C2

Vincent Ct 2 BS16 ....20 D3
Vine Cotts NP16 ......60 E8
Vine Ct GL50 ....133 C3
Vine Hall GL15 ......147 E4
Vine Terr GL1 ......196 C4
Vine Way GL20 ......192 D1
Vinecroft GL13 ......85 E8
Viner's La GL9 ......36 B5
Vineries GL51 ......130 C4
Vines The GL3 ......120 B7
Vineyard La GL12 ....67 F5
Vineyard St GL54 ..174 A7
Vineyard The WR12 ..184 E5
Vineyards Cl GL53 ..131 B4
Vineyards The GL51 ..133 A1
Vining Wlk 4 BS5 ....9 B8
Vinney La BS37 ......44 F8
Vinny Ave BS16 ......21 A7
Vintery Leys BS9 ....18 B7
Virginia Ave GL7 ....152 E2
Virginia Cl BS37 ....44 A1
Virginia Rd GL20 ..182 C4
Vittoria Wlk GL50 ..193 B2
Vivian St BS3 ....8 D3
Vizard Cl GL11 ......80 B8
Vorda Rd SN6 ......145 D4
Vowell Cl BS13 ......2 B4
Voxwell La GL52 ....137 C3
Voyager Ct BS34 ....30 A4
Voyce Cl GL4 ......118 D2
Vulcan Way GL4 ..119 F6
Vyners Cl GL7 ......190 C2
Vyvian Ct GL1 ......196 B2
Vyvyan Rd BS8 ......194 A3
Vyvyan Terr BS8 ..194 A3

W

Wad La GL19 ....180 F2
Wade Cl GL51 ......129 C7
Wade Hill SN6 ......145 C3
Wade Rd BS37 ......43 A3
Wade St BS2 ....195 C3
Wadehurst Ind Pk BS2 ..9 A7
Wadham Cl GL7 ......153 C6
Wadham Dr BS16 ....30 B1
Wadham Gr BS16 ....21 B5
Waggons La GL19 ..172 C4
Wagtail Dr GL20 ....182 B5
Wainbridge Cres BS35 .39 D2
Wainbrook Dr BS5 ..10 C8
Wainland Pl GL16 ..154 F3
Wainlode La GL2 ..173 A3
Wakefield Cl GL7 ..144 F7
Wakefield Rd BS30 ..11 A7
Wakeford Way BS30 ..11 A7
Wakeman Cl GL20 ..192 E2
Wakeman Rd GL20 ..192 E2
Waldist Cl BS11 ....132 F5
Walford Prim Sch HR9 .163 C7
Walham Cl GL2 ....126 E4
Walk Mill La GL12 ....67 E5
Walk The GL12 ......67 F5
Walker Cl
Bristol,Downend BS16 ..20 D3
Bristol,Upper Easton BS5 ..9 B8
Walker Ct BS16 ......20 F5
Walker Rd BS34 ....194 C4
Walker's La GL17 ..155 B7
Walkers Gdn 14 GL54 .168 A1
Walkley Hill GL5 ..130 B6
Walkley Rd GL20 ..192 D5
Wallace Apartments 11
GL52 ....193 C4
Wallace Rd GL4 ....133 D6
Wallbank Ho GL1 ..127 A3
Wallbridge BS9 ......9 B2
Wallbridge Ind Est GL5 .99 B6
Wallcroft Ho BS34 ..29 B1
Walled Gdn The
Kingscote GL8 ......82 B5
Ledbury HR8 ......178 F8
Wallingford Rd BS4 ..2 D7
Walliscote Ave BS9 ..18 C6
Walliscote Rd BS9 ..18 C6
Wallscourt Rd BS34 ..29 B1
Wallscourt Rd S BS34 ..29 B1
Wallsend La SN14 ....24 C5
Wallsworth Hall Nature in Art
Mus* GL2 ....173 A1
Wallwern Wood/Coed
Wallwern NP16 ......72 C1
Walmer's View GL11 ..56 D6
Walmore Hill Prim Sch
GL2 ....165 F1
Walnut Ave BS37 ....28 D1
Walnut Bank Dr GL20 .183 A4
Walnut Cl Bristol BS31 ..5 C5
Easton-in-G BS20 ..14 F1
Frampton Cotterell BS36 .31 B4
Gloucester GL4 ....119 E6
Keynsham BS31 ......5 C5
Yate BS37 ....27 F1
Walnut Cres BS15 ....10 F8
Walnut Ct GL20 ....183 A4
Walnut Dr SN14 ......31 F6
Walnut La BS15 ......11 F7
Walnut Tree Cl BS32 ..40 A5
Walnut Wlk Bristol BS13 ..2 A6

Walnut Wlk continued
Keynsham BS31 ......4 C4
Walsh Ave BS14 ......3 A2
Walshe Ave BS37 ....44 C1
Walsingham Rd BS6 ..18 E2
Walter Preston Ct GL5 ..99 B6
Walter Reynold Homes
GL54 ....176 E5
Walter St BS3 ....8 A4
Walton Cl Bristol BS30 ..11 C2
Keynsham BS31 ......4 B8
Walton Ct GL54 ......119 E1
Walton Dr GL20 ....192 F5
Walton Gdns GL20 ..192 F4
Walton Heath BS37 ..43 F1
Walton Ho
Cheltenham GL51 ..132 E2
Tewkesbury GL20 ..192 F4
Walton House Bglws 8
GL54 ....168 A1
Walton St Leonards GL54 ..9 F7
GL54 ....168 A1
Walton Rd BS11 ......16 D6
Walton Rise BS9 ......18 A2
Walton St BS5 ....19 B1
Walwyn Cl GL17 ....164 D5
Walwyn Gdns BS13 ....2 C1
Wandsdyke Prim Sch
BS14 ....2 A6
Wansbeck Rd BS31 ....5 A4
Wanscow Wlk BS9 ..18 B6
Wansdyke Ct BS14 ....3 A5
Wansdyke Workshops
BS31 ....5 A6
Wantridge GL18 ....170 B8
Wapley Bank BS37 ..32 D5
Wapley La BS37 ......32 E4
Wapley Rd BS37 ......33 B3
Wapping Rd BS1 ..195 A1
Ward Ave GL3 ......127 E6
Ward Cl GL52 ......138 A4
Ward Ind Est GL15 ..34 A2
Wardens Cl BS15 ....8 A4
Warden Hill Cl GL51 ..168 A4
Warden Hill Prim Sch
GL51 ....130 A5
Warden Hill Rd GL53 ..130 A4
Warden Rd BS3 ......8 C4
Wardour Rd BS4 ......9 A1
Wards Rd GL51 ......129 D6
Ware Ct BS36 ....30 D5
Warend Hill Dursley GL11 .80 A4
North Nibley GL11 ....79 F6
Waring Ho BS1 ......195 A3
Warman Cl BS14 ......3 F6
Warman Rd BS14 ....3 F6
Warmington Rd BS14 ..3 E8
Warminster Rd BS2 ..19 B1
Warmley Park Sch BS30 .11 B7
Warmley Park Sch BS30 .11 B7
Warnbrook Cl GL14 ..187 A3
Warner Cl BS15 ......10 E5
Warns Ct 11 GL53 ..140 B4
Warns The BS30 ......11 C2
Warren Cl Bristol BS32 ..28 C3
Cheltenham GL51 ..128 A1
Churchdown GL3 ..128 A2
Warren Ct GL8 ......179 F4
Warren Dr 18 HR8 ..178 F8
Warren Dr BS5 ....9 F8
Warren Gdns BS14 ....3 F5
Warren La HR9 ......170 A1
Warren Rd Bristol BS34 ..29 B3
Northway GL20 ......182 B4
Warren Slade NP16 ..60 F5
Warren Way BS37 ....43 F1
Warrens Gorse Cotts
GL7 ....150 B8
Warrington Rd BS4 ..9 F3
Warren La Arlingham GL2 ..157 C6
Northwick BS35 ......48 D3
Warwick Ave
7 Bristol BS5 ....19 B1
Gloucester GL4 ......118 C1
Warwick Cl Bristol BS31 ..5 A4
Chepstow/Cas-Gwent NP16 ..60 D6
Coleford GL17 ......152 E4
Stroud GL5 ....99 A7
Warwick Cres GL53 ..131 B6
Warwick Pl
Cheltenham GL52 ..193 C4
Tewkesbury GL20 ..192 D3
Thornbury BS35 ......64 A1
Warwick Rd
Bristol,Baptist Mills BS5 ..19 A3
Bristol,Redland BS6 ..18 B3
Keynsham BS31 ......4 D4
Washing Pound La BS14 ..3 A4
Washingpool Hill BS35 .50 E1
Washingpool Hill Rd
BS32 ....50 F7
Washingpool La BS11 ..26 C7
Washington Ave BS5 ..19 C1
Washpool La
Fairford GL7 ....152 F7
Kempsford GL7 ....144 F8
Wasley Rd GL51 ..130 A6
Watch Elm Cl BS32 ..39 A3
Watch House Rd BS20 .16 E1
Watchill Cl BS13 ......1 F6
Watchill Rd BS13 ......1 F6
Water La Brimscombe GL5 .99 E1
Bristol BS1 ....195 B2
Bristol,Hanham Green BS15 ..10 B3
Bristol,Upper Knowle BS4 ..9 D2
Bristol,Windmill Hill BS3 ..9 D7
Charlton Kings GL52 ..179 C4

Water La *continued*
Pill BS20 . . . . .16 C4
Woodchester GL5 . . . . . . .98 F3
Wotton-u-E GL12 . . . . . . .68 B6
Water Mdw GL2 . . . . . . .109 E7
Water St GL11 . . . . .88 B1
Water Wheel Cl **7** GL2 . .117 D1
Water's La BS9 . . . . .18 A7
Waterbridge Rd BS13 . . . . .1 F4
Watercress Rd BS2 . . . . .18 F3
Waterdale Cl Bristol BS9 . .18 C7
Hardwicke GL2 . . . . . . .109 D8
Waterdale Gdns BS9 . . . .18 C7
Waterfield Cl GL53 . . . . .193 B1
Waterford Cl BS35 . . . . . . .51 D8
Waterford Ct GL53 . . . . .130 C6
Waterford Rd BS9 . . . . . .18 B6
Watergrip La GL20 . . . . .183 A8
Waterloo Bsns Pk GL17 .163 D2
Waterloo Cl GL20 . . . . . .182 D7
Waterloo Ho BS20 . . . . . .16 D5
Waterloo La GL7 . . . . . . .152 E3
Waterloo Pl **2** BS2 . . . .195 C3
Waterloo Rd BS2 . . . . . .195 C3
Waterloo St Bristol BS2 . .195 C3
11 Bristol,Clifton BS8 . . . . . .7 F7
Cheltenham GL51 . . . . .133 B3
Waterloo The GL7 . . . . . .190 D5
Waterlow Rd GL20 . . . . .182 D7
Watermans Ct **4** GL2 . . .117 D1
Watermead GL1 . . . . .92 A3
Watermill Cl GL12 . . . . . .65 E7
Watermoor CE Prim Sch
GL7 . . . . .190 D3
Watermoor Cl GL51 . . . .132 D4
Watermoor Ct GL3 . . . . .128 B5
Watermoor Rd GL7 . . . .190 D3
Watermoor Way GL7 . . . .190 D3
Watermore Cl BS36 . . . . .31 C7
Waters Rd BS15 . . . . .10 C8
Waters Reach GL2 . . . . .118 B6
Waters Way NP16 . . . . . . .60 D7
Watershoot Cl GL52 . . . .134 A5
Waterside **3** GL20 . . . . .192 C4
Waterside Cl
Andoversford GL54 . . . . .166 D6
Quedgeley GL2 . . . . . . .117 D1
Waterside Dr GL2 . . . . . .40 A1
Waterton Cl GL3 . . . . . . .120 B6
Waterwells Dr GL2 . . . . .110 A6
Watery La Doynton BS30 . .13 A8
Frampton on Severn GL2 . .157 F2
Gloucester GL4 . . . . . . .111 B8
Kinsham GL20 . . . . .182 D6
Lea HR9 . . . . .164 C8
Lydney GL15 . . . . .147 F5
Minsterworth GL2 . . . . . .117 B7
Newent GL18 . . . . .170 F4
Wathen Rd BS6 . . . . .18 F3
Watkins Cnr SN5 . . . . . .143 E1
Watkins Terr GL11 . . . . . .88 E8
Watkins Yd BS9 . . . . .18 A8
Watledge Bank GL6 . . . . .91 B5
Watledge Cl GL20 . . . . . .192 D4
Watledge Rd GL6 . . . . . . .91 B5
Watley's End Rd BS36 . . . .30 F7
Watling Way BS11 . . . . . .16 D7
Watson Ave BS4 . . . . .9 D4
Watson Gr GL4 . . . . .119 F5
Watson Ho **4** GL52 . . . .193 C4
Watson's Rd BS30 . . . . . .10 F3
Watters Cl BS36 . . . . .31 D6
Watts Cl Berkeley GL13 . . .85 E4
Gloucester GL3 . . . . . . .120 B7
Wavell Cl BS37 . . . . .43 D3
Waveney Rd BS31 . . . . . . .5 A3
Waverley Rd
Bristol,Cotham BS6 . . . . . .18 C1
Bristol,Shirehampton BS11 . .16 E6
Gloucester GL2 . . . . . . .127 C2
Yate BS37 . . . . .43 B2
Waverley St **8** BS5 . . . . .19 A1
Waycroft Prim Sch BS14 . . .3 E5
Wayend St HR8 . . . . .179 C7
Wayford Cl BS31 . . . . .5 A3
Wayland Ct **7** BS16 . . . .20 A4
Waylands SN6 . . . . .143 F4
Wayleaze
Coalpit Heath BS36 . . . . . .31 D7
Wapley BS37 . . . . .32 F3
Wayridge The GL4 . . . . . .119 D4
Wayside Cl BS36 . . . . .31 B7
WCA Ho BS1 . . . . .195 A2
Weald Cl GL4 . . . . .119 C5
Weare Ct BS1 . . . . .194 A1
Weavers La Dursley GL11 . .80 B8
Kingswood GL12 . . . . . . .67 F4
Weavers Dr GL11 . . . . . . .89 B1
Weavers Ho **17** GL5 . . . .99 C7
Weavers Rd
Cirencester GL7 . . . . . . .190 E4
Quedgeley GL2 . . . . . . .117 F2
Weavers Row GL5 . . . . . .99 F1
Webb Rd GL4 . . . . .140 B5
Webb St BS5 . . . . .9 A8
Webber Rd GL20 . . . . . . .192 B3
Webbs Heath BS36 . . . . . .11 E8
Webbs Wood BS32 . . . . . .29 F7
Webbley Rd GL2 . . . . . . .163 F3
Wedgewood Cotts
WR12 . . . . .184 E5
Wedgewood Cres GL14 . .191 D6
Wedgewood Rd BS16 . . . .30 D1
Wedgwood Cl BS14 . . . . . .3 B5
Wedgwood Dr GL2 . . . . .127 C4
Wedlock Way BS3 . . . . . . .7 F3
Wedmore Cl BS15 . . . . . .10 F7

Wedmore Rd BS31 . . . . . . .5 D4
Wedmore Vale BS3 . . . . . .8 E2
Weedon Cl **6** BS2 . . . . .19 A2
Weigh Bridge Ct GL55 . . .189 A2
Weight Rd **2** BS5 . . . . . . .9 C7
Weir Bridge Cl GL4 . . . . .119 E8
Weir La SN14 . . . . .14 F8
Welch Ho GL51 . . . . .129 D2
Welch Rd GL51 . . . . .132 E4
Welcomyn **11** GL6 . . . . .148 C6
Well Alley GL20 . . . . .192 C5
Well Cl
Chepstow/Cas-Gwent NP16 . .60 F4
Long Ashton BS41 . . . . . . .7 B1
Northway GL20 . . . . .182 C5
Well Cross Rd GL4 . . . . .119 A4
Well End GL5 . . . . .99 E8
Well Hill GL6 . . . . .148 A3
Well House Ct BS9 . . . . . .17 E3
Well La Badminton GL9 . . . .46 E5
Drybrook GL17 . . . . .164 A4
Guiting Power GL54 . . . . .175 B3
Stow-on-t-W GL54 . . . . . .176 F4
Well Pl GL50 . . . . .133 B1
Well Vale La HR9 . . . . . . .162 D3
Welland Ct GL52 . . . . . . .134 A4
Welland Dr GL52 . . . . . . .134 A4
Welland Lodge Rd GL52 . .134 A4
Welland Rd Keynsham BS31 . .4 E5
Tewkesbury GL20 . . . . . .117 F2
Wellbrook Rd GL52 . . . . .137 F5
Weller Bglws GL2 . . . . . .118 C4
Wellesley Prim Sch BS37 . .32 D6
Wellesley Rd GL50 . . . . .133 E3
Wellesley St GL1 . . . . . . .118 F6
Wellfield GL20 . . . . .192 F5
Wellgarth Ct BS4 . . . . .9 A2
Wellgarth Rd BS4 . . . . . . .9 A2
Wellgarth Wlk BS4 . . . . . .9 A2
Welling Cl GL11 . . . . .80 C7
Wellington Ave BS6 . . . . .18 E1
Wellington Aviation Mus*
GL56 . . . . .187 A3
Wellington Cres BS7 . . . . .18 E6
Wellington Ct **1** BS6 . . . .18 E1
Wellington Dr Bristol BS9 . .18 D6
Yate BS37 . . . . .43 B2
Wellington Hill BS7 . . . . .18 E6
Wellington Hill W BS9 . . . .18 D7
Wellington Ho GL7 . . . . .190 D5
Wellington La **6** BS6 . . . .18 E1
Cheltenham GL52 . . . . . .133 F2
Wellington Lodge Cl
GL20 . . . . .182 D7
Wellington Mews BS11 . . .16 D5
Wellington Par GL11 . . . .196 C3
Wellington Pk BS8 . . . . . .18 A2
Wellington Pl Bristol BS16 . .30 B1
Cheltenham GL52 . . . . . .193 C2
Wellington Rd
Bristol BS2 . . . . .195 C4
Bristol,Kingswood BS15 . . .20 D2
Cheltenham GL52 . . . . . .133 F2
10 Moreton-in-M GL56 . .187 B3
Upper Rissington GL54 . . .169 D6
Yate BS37 . . . . .43 B2
Wellington Sq
Cheltenham GL50 . . . . . .193 C3
Gloucester GL1 . . . . .196 B2
Wellington St
Cheltenham GL50 . . . . . .193 C3
Gloucester GL1 . . . . .196 B2
Wellington Terr
18 Bristol BS8 . . . . .7 F6
2 Moreton-in-M GL56 . . .187 B3
Newnham GL14 . . . . . . .156 F6
Wellington Wlk BS10 . . . .18 C7
Wellmeadow GL16 . . . . .154 D7
Wellmeadow La GL16 . . .154 D7
Wells Cl Bristol BS14 . . . . .3 C5
Cheltenham GL51 . . . . . .129 F5
Wells Gdns **5** WR12 . . . .185 C8
Wells Rd Bisley GL6 . . . . .148 D8
Bristol BS4 . . . . .9 B2
Gloucester GL4 . . . . .119 C8
Maiden Head BS41 . . . . . . .1 E1
Wells St BS3 . . . . .8 A4
Wellsprings Ho GL2 . . . .127 C3
Wellsprings Rd GL2 . . . .127 C3
Wellstead Ave BS37 . . . . .43 D1
Wellswood BS31 . . . . .4 F3
Wellway Sec Sch BS31 . . . .5 A5
Welsford Ave BS16 . . . . . .19 C4
Welsford Rd BS16 . . . . . .19 C4
Welsh Back BS1 . . . . . . .195 A2
Welsh House La GL18 . . .170 F8
Welsh St GL17 . . . . .72 D1
Welsh Way
Bagendon GL7 . . . . .158 D1
Fairford GL7 . . . . .152 B5
Sunhill GL7 . . . . .151 F7
Welton Wlk BS15 . . . . . . .20 C2
Welveland La GL14 . . . . .129 E5
Welwyn Mews **4** GL51 . .129 E5
Wenchford Forest Trail*
GL15 . . . . .156 C2
Wend The GL17 . . . . .164 F5
Wendover Gdns GL50 . . .133 B1
Wenlock Rd GL20 . . . . . .192 D3
Wenmore Ct BS16 . . . . . .30 D1
Wentforth Dr **2** BS15 . . . .20 D1
Wentsfield GL10 . . . . .96 F7
Wentworth Bristol BS30 . . .11 A6
Yate BS37 . . . . .43 C1
Wentworth Cl
Cheltenham GL51 . . . . . .132 D4
Gloucester GL2 . . . . . . .127 B5
Wentworth Rd BS7 . . . . . .18 D3
Cheltenham GL51 . . . . . .132 D3
Werth La GL19 . . . . .181 B1

Wescott Gr BS11 . . . . . . .27 C2
Wesley Ave BS15 . . . . . . .10 D5
Wesley Cl Aylburton GL15 . .147 E4
7 Bristol,Upper Soundwell
BS16 . . . . .20 D3
Bristol,Whitehall BS5 . . . . .19 D1
Wesley Ct
Gloucester GL1 . . . . .196 C2
18 Stroud GL5 . . . . .99 C7
Wesley Hill BS15 . . . . . . .20 D1
Wesley Ho GL50 . . . . . . .193 B4
Wesley La BS30 . . . . .11 B5
Wesley Pl GL5 . . . . .99 B4
Wesley Rd Bristol BS7 . . . .18 E4
Cinderford GL14 . . . . . . .191 D5
Leonard Stanley GL10 . . . .97 E3
Whitecroft GL15 . . . . .155 F1
Wesley St BS3 . . . . .8 C3
Wesley Theological Coll
BS10 . . . . .27 F1
Wessex Ave BS7 . . . . .18 F7
Wessex Cl BS7 . . . . .18 F7
Wessex Dr GL52 . . . . . . .134 B2
Wessex Ho **11** BS2 . . . . .195 C3
Wessex Way SN6 . . . . . . .145 D4
West Allcourt GL7 . . . . . .153 C2
West Approach Dr GL52 . .133 E4
West Ave GL7 . . . . .164 B4
West Dene BS9 . . . . .17 D6
West Coombe BS9 . . . . . .17 D6
West Country Water Pk*
BS36 . . . . .40 F2
West Croft BS9 . . . . .18 C7
West Dene BS9 . . . . .17 C6
West Dr GL50 . . . . .133 E3
West Dundry La BS41 . . . . .1 E2
West End Avening GL8 . . .140 A8
Bristol,Kingsdown BS2 . . . .195 A4
Bristol,Southville BS3 . . . . .7 F2
Coaley GL11 . . . . .96 D1
Kingham OX7 . . . . .187 F2
Minchinhampton GL6 . . . .148 A3
Northleach GL54 . . . . . . .169 B4
Oldbury-on-S BS35 . . . . . .63 C6
Ruardean GL17 . . . . .163 D4
West End Gdns GL7 . . . . .152 D4
West End La
Broadway WR12 . . . . . . .185 B7
Gloucester GL2 . . . . .120 B8
West Fields GL7 . . . . .190 D6
West Gr BS6 . . . . .18 E1
West Grange Ct GL5 . . . . .99 F8
West Hay Gr GL7 . . . . . . .141 F8
West Hill SN26 . . . . .144 D2
West La GL17 . . . . .141 F8
West Leaze **3** BS37 . . . .29 E6
West Littleton Rd SN14 . . .24 E2
West Lodge Dr GL4 . . . . .119 D6
West Mall BS8 . . . . .7 F7
West Market Pl GL7 . . . . .190 C5
West Mill La SN6 . . . . . . .143 F4
West Par BS9 . . . . .17 C7
West Park Rd BS16 . . . . . .20 C5
West Pk BS8 . . . . .194 B4
West Point Row BS32 . . . .40 C7
West Priory Cl BS9 . . . . . .17 F8
West Ridge BS36 . . . . . . .31 C7
West Rocke Ave BS9 . . . . .17 F7
West Shrubbery **2** BS6 . .18 B2
West Town Ave BS4 . . . . . .9 E3
West St Bristol BS2 . . . . .195 C3
Bristol,Bedminster BS3 . . . . .8 A4
2 Bristol,Kingswood BS15 . .10 D8
Bristol,Oldland Common
BS30 . . . . .11 C4
Kingham OX7 . . . . .187 F3
Tetbury GL8 . . . . .140 B4
Tytherington GL12 . . . . . . .52 B5
West Town Cl BS4 . . . . . . .9 D1
West Town Dr **2** BS4 . . . .9 D1
West Town Gr BS4 . . . . . . .9 D1
West Town La BS4 . . . . . . .9 D1
West Town Lane Inf Sch
BS4 . . . . .9 C1
West Town Lane Jun Sch
BS4 . . . . .9 C1
West Town Pk BS4 . . . . . . .9 D1
West Town Rd BS11 . . . . .16 B7
West Tynings GL6 . . . . . . .91 A4
West View Alveston BS35 . .50 F4
Bristol BS16 . . . . .21 A6
Cinderford GL14 . . . . . . .191 D5
Joy's Green GL17 . . . . . . .163 D3
Newent GL18 . . . . .156 F7
Pouton GL7 . . . . .151 F3
Wotton-u-E GL12 . . . . . . .68 C7
West View Rd Bristol BS3 . . .7 F3
Keynsham BS31 . . . . .4 E5
West Way
Bristol BS10,BS34 . . . . . . .28 E4
Cirencester GL7 . . . . . . .190 C4
Lechlade on T GL7 . . . . . .153 C2
West Wlk BS37 . . . . .43 E1
Westacre Cl BS10 . . . . . . .28 A2
Westal Gn **15** GL50 . . . .133 B2
Westal Pk GL50 . . . . .130 B7
Westbourne Ave BS31 . . . . .4 E5
Westbourne Cl **3** BS15 . .21 A7
Westbourne Dr
Cheltenham GL52 . . . . . .133 F2
Hardwicke GL2 . . . . .109 E7
Westbourne Gr **3** BS3 . . .8 B3
Westbourne Ho **12** GL52 . .133 F2
Westbourne Pl BS8 . . . . .194 B3
Westbourne Rd
Bristol,Downend BS16 . . . .20 F8

Westbourne Rd *continued*
8 Bristol,Upper Easton BS5 . .9 B8
Westbourne Terr BS16 . . .20 B7
Westbrook Rd BS4 . . . . . . .3 D8
Westbrooke Ct BS1 . . . . .194 A1
Westbury Court Gdns*
GL14 . . . . .157 C8
Westbury Court Rd BS9 . .18 A7
Westbury Ct BS9 . . . . . . .18 A7
Westbury Hill BS9 . . . . . .18 A7
Westbury La BS9 . . . . . . .17 F7
Westbury Mews **6** BS9 . .18 A7
Westbury Park Prim Sch
BS6 . . . . .18 B3
Westbury Pk BS6 . . . . . . .18 B3
Westbury Rd Bristol BS9 . .18 A4
Cheltenham GL53 . . . . . .130 E4
Gloucester GL4 . . . . .118 D3
Westbury-on-Severn CE
Prim Sch GL14 . . . . . . .165 C1
Westcote Rd GL4 . . . . . . .118 E1
Westcourt Dr BS30 . . . . . .11 B4
Westdown Gdns GL52 . . .133 F1
Westend GL11 . . . . .87 D4
Westend Cross GL10 . . . .101 A2
Westend La BS35 . . . . . . .63 A6
Westend Par GL1 . . . . . . .126 C3
Westend Rd GL12 . . . . . . .53 E5
Westend Terr
Chipping Campden GL55 . .188 F7
Gloucester GL1 . . . . .126 C3
Westering GL21 . . . . .21 A5
Westerleigh Bsns Pk
BS37 . . . . .43 B1
Westerleigh Cl BS16 . . . . .20 F7
Westerleigh Rd
Bristol BS16 . . . . .20 F6
Coalpit Heath BS36 . . . . . .31 D2
Pucklechurch BS16 . . . . . .22 C7
Westerleigh BS36,BS37 . . .32 B5
Yate BS37 . . . . .43 B4
Western Approach
Distribution Pk BS35 . . .38 C4
Western Ave
Chepstow/Cas-Gwent NP16 . .60 F5
Frampton Cotterell BS36 . . .42 A1
Mitcheldean GL17 . . . . . .163 A6
Western Ct
6 Cheltenham GL50 . . .133 B1
Western Dr BS14 . . . . .2 D2
Western Grange Ct GL4 . .118 D2
Western Rd Bristol BS7 . . .18 B5
Cheltenham GL50 . . . . . .133 B1
Western Way GL18 . . . . .178 D2
Westfield Dursley GL11 . . . .89 F3
Llangrove HR9 . . . . .162 B6
Westfield Ave
Brockworth GL3 . . . . . . .132 C6
Northway GL20 . . . . .182 C4
Westfield Cl Bristol BS15 . .10 D5
Keynsham BS31 . . . . .4 C5
Westfield Cotts GL51 . . . .132 B5
Westfield Ct GL14 . . . . . .191 D5
Westfield Ho BS9 . . . . . . .17 F5
Westfield La GL52 . . . . . . .43 A3
Westfield Pl BS8 . . . . .7 F7
Westfield Rd Bristol BS9 . .18 A4
Brockworth GL3 . . . . . . .120 D6
Cinderford GL14 . . . . . . .191 D5
Westfield Terr GL14 . . . . .126 E5
Westfield Way BS32 . . . . .24 D2
Westgate BS1 . . . . .194 B1
Westgate St GL1 . . . . . . .196 A3
Westhill Cl SN6 . . . . .145 C3
Westland Ave BS30 . . . . . .11 E5
Westland Rd GL2 . . . . . . .109 D7
Westleigh Cl Bristol BS10 . .28 D1
Yate BS37 . . . . .43 A2
Westleigh Pk BS14 . . . . . . .3 A7
Westleigh Rd BS10 . . . . . .28 D1
Westmarsh BS35 . . . . . . .63 B5
Westmarsh La BS35 . . . . .63 B5
Westmead GL20 . . . . . . .183 A8
Westmead Rd Bristol BS5 . .10 B8
Gloucester GL2 . . . . .127 D5
Westminster Cl
1 Bristol BS9 . . . . .18 C6
Cheltenham GL53 . . . . . .130 F7
Westminster Ct **3** GL52 . .127 B2
Westminster Rd BS4 . . . . . .9 C4
Westmoreland Rd BS6 . . .18 A3
Westmorland Ho GL51 . . .130 A3
Westmorland Terr BS37 . . .34 D7
Weston Ave BS5 . . . . .19 E3
Weston Cl BS9 . . . . .17 C7
Weston Cotts SN7 . . . . . .145 E8
Weston Cres BS7 . . . . . . .18 D3
Weston Ind Est WR11 . . .188 D4
Weston Park Prim Sch
BS10 . . . . .28 B3
Weston Rd
Bretforton WR11 . . . . . . .188 F3
Honeybourne WR11 . . . . .188 D6
Long Ashton BS41 . . . . . . .7 A1
Westonbirt Arboretum*
GL8 . . . . .68 E8
Westonbirt Sch GL8 . . . . .58 E8
Westonian Ct BS9 . . . . . .17 B7
Westons Brake BS16 . . . . .31 A1
Westons Hill Dr BS16 . . . .31 A1

Wat – Whi **239**

Westons Way BS15 . . . . . .10 F7
Westover Cl BS9 . . . . .27 F1
Westover Ct GL3 . . . . . . .128 B7
Westover Dr BS9 . . . . .28 A1
Westover Gdns BS9 . . . . .17 F8
Westover Rd BS9 . . . . . . .28 A1
Westover Rise BS9 . . . . . .28 A1
Westpoint Trad Est BS15 . .10 D7
Westridge Rd GL12 . . . . . .68 A8
Westrip Pl GL5 . . . . .98 D8
Westrop SN6 . . . . .145 C3
Westrop Prim Sch SN6 . . .145 C3
Westview GL19 . . . . .173 C7
Westward GL51 . . . . .7 B2
Westward Cl GL5 . . . . . . .98 D6
Westward Dr BS20 . . . . . .16 C4
Westward Gdns BS41 . . . . .1 C1
Westward Rd Bristol BS13 . .1 F7
Stroud GL5 . . . . .98 D6
Westwick Rd GL2 . . . . . .165 D6
Westwood Cres BS4 . . . . . .9 D5
Westwood La GL52 . . . . .134 D3
Westwood Rd BS4 . . . . . . .3 D8
Wetherby Ct BS16 . . . . . . .9 E4
Wetherby Gr **1** BS16 . . . .30 F1
Wetherell Pl BS8 . . . . . . .194 B3
Wetherleigh Dr GL4 . . . . .125 C6
Wexford Rd BS4 . . . . .9 A4
Weyhouse Cl GL6 . . . . . . .99 D5
Weymouth Rd BS3 . . . . . . .8 D2
Whaddon Ave GL52 . . . . .134 A2
Whaddon Dr GL52 . . . . . .133 F2
Whaddon Prim Sch
GL52 . . . . .134 B2
Whaddon Rd GL52 . . . . . .134 B2
Whaddon Road (Cheltenham
Town FC) GL52 . . . . . . .133 F3
Wharf La Kempsford GL7 . .144 E2
Lechlade on T GL7 . . . . . .153 C2
Wharf Rd **5** BS16 . . . . . .19 F4
Wharf Rd GL19 . . . . .173 E6
Wharfdale Sq GL51 . . . . .132 F3
Wharfdale Way
Hardwicke GL2 . . . . .109 D8
Stonehouse GL10 . . . . . . .97 E6
Wharfedale BS35 . . . . . . .51 D8
Wharfings The GL7 . . . . .144 E7
Wharnecliffe Cl BS14 . . . . .3 B5
Wharnecliffe Gdns BS14 . . .3 B5
Whatley Rd **3** BS8 . . . . . .18 B1
Wheal Cl GL20 . . . . .182 C4
Wheal Rd GL20 . . . . .182 C4
Wheat Hill **2** GL4 . . . . .140 B4
Wheatfield Cl BS35 . . . . .189 A6
Wheatfield Dr BS32 . . . . . .40 D1
Wheathill CE Prim Sch
BS35 . . . . .40 D1
Wheathill Cl GL52 . . . . . .132 D4
Wheatland Dr GL51 . . . . .132 D4
Wheatridge E The GL4 . . .119 E4
Wheatsheaf Dr GL52 . . . .137 D4
Wheatstone Rd GL1 . . . . .126 C5
Wheatstone Rd GL1 . . . . .182 C5
Wheatway GL4 . . . . .118 E7
Wheelers Patch BS16 . . . .21 B5
Wheelers Rd GL5 . . . . . . .99 F8
Wheelers Wlk GL5 . . . . . .99 F8
Whelford Cnr **3**
GL6 . . . . .91 B4
Whelford Rd GL7 . . . . . . .144 E8
Whetstones GL14 . . . . . .157 A2
Whimbrel Rd GL14 . . . . . .117 D1
Whimsey BS16 . . . . .191 B6
Whinchat Gdns BS16 . . . .19 F6
Whippington Ct BS1 . . . . .195 B3
Whippington's Cnr
GL6 . . . . .154 E7
Whitby Rd BS4 . . . . .9 C4
Whitchurch CE Prim Sch
HR9 . . . . .162 E4
Whitchurch District Ctr
BS14 . . . . .3 A5
Whitchurch La
Bristol,Bishopsworth BS13 . .2 B5
Bristol,Hartcliffe BS13 . . . . .2 C1
Bristol,Whitchurch BS14 . . . .2 C1
Dundry BS41 . . . . .1 F3
Whitchurch Under Fives
BS14 . . . . .2 E4
White Cotts GL5 . . . . .92 E6
White Cross Rd GL14 . . . . .98 A1
White Hart Cl GL7 . . . . . .172 D4
White Hart Ct GL7 . . . . . .152 E3
White Hart La **15** GL54 . .176 F4
White Hart Rd GL15 . . . . .128 C3
White Horse Rd SN6 . . . . .143 E4
White House Bsns Ctr The
BS14 . . . . .3 D6
White Lodge Rd BS16 . . . .20 F7
White St BS5 . . . . .195 C4
White Tree Rd BS9 . . . . . .18 A4
Whitebeam Cl GL2 . . . . . .127 B5
Whitebeam Ho **7** BS16 . .20 C6

Whitechapel Rd 🎱
GL15 . . . . .155 D1
Whitecourt GL11 . . . . .89 A1
Whitecroft GL6 . . . . .91 B4
Whitecroft Rd GL15 . . . . . .155 E1
Whitecroft Sta* GL15 . . .155 F1
Whitecroft Way BS15 . . . . .11 A7
Whitecross Ave BS14 . . . . . .3 C6
Whitecross Sch GL15 . . . . .92 A2
Whitecross Sch GL53 . . . .193 C1
Whitecross St 🔟 NP25 . . .154 A7
Whitefield Ave
Bristol,Hanham BS15 . . . . . .10 D5
Bristol,Speedwell BS5 . . . . .20 A1
Whitefield Cl
🎱 Bristol BS16 . . . . .20 D3
Stonehouse BS16 . . . . .20 D3
Whitefield Fishponds Com
Sch BS16 . . . . .19 F4
Whitefield Rd BS5 . . . . . . .20 A2
Whitefields BS37 . . . . .44 C1
Whitefields Rd GL52 . . . .137 D4
Whitefriars La SN6 . . . . . .142 F6
Whitegates BS36 . . . . .30 D6
Whitehall GL5 . . . . .99 D7
Whitehall Ave BS5 . . . . . . .19 E1
Whitehall Gdns BS5 . . . . . .19 E1
Whitehall La GL2 . . . . .124 E6
Whitehall Prim Sch BS5 . . .19 D1
Whitehall Rd BS5 . . . . .9 C8
Whitehall Trad Est 🎲 BS5 . .9 C8
Whitehart Ho GL51 . . . . . .133 C3
Whitehill La GL17 . . . . . . .164 B4
Whitehouse Ctr BS13 . . . . . .2 C5
Whitehouse Farm GL14 . .165 D1
Whitehouse La Bristol BS3 . .8 D4
Gorsley HR9,GL18 . . . . . . .170 C5
Pilning BS35 . . . . .38 C7
Tetbury GL8 . . . . .140 C1
Whitehouse Pk GL5 . . . . . . .98 E7
Whitehouse Pl BS3 . . . . .8 E4
Whitehouse St BS3 . . . . .8 E4
Whitehouse Way GL52 . . .138 B3
Whitelades Rd BS58 . . . . . .194 B4
Whitelands
Little Shurdington GL51 . . . .121 C8
Little Shurdington GL51 . . . .121 D8
Whitelands Rd GL7 . . . . . .190 E5
Whiteleaze BS10 . . . . .18 C8
Whitemarsh Cl GL51 . . . .132 D4
Whitemead Ho 🎱 BS3 . . . . .8 A3
Whites Hill BS5 . . . . .10 A6
Whiteshill BS16 . . . . .30 D3
Whiteshill Prim Sch
GL6 . . . . .102 F3
Whitethorn Cotts GL51 . . .133 A7
Whitethorn Dr GL52 . . . . .134 C3
Whitewall La BS35 . . . . . . .64 F1
Whitewall Rd GL8 . . . . . . .70 C4
Whiteway GL11 . . . . .80 C6
Whiteway Cl
Bristol,St Anne's Park BS4 . . . .9 E6
Bristol,St George BS5 . . . . . .10 A8
Dursley GL11 . . . . .80 C7
Whiteway Ct
🎱 Bristol BS5 . . . . .10 A8
Dursley GL11 . . . . .190 D6
Whiteway Mews BS5 . . . . .10 A8
Whiteway Rd
Bristol BS5,BS15 . . . . .20 A1
Gloucester GL4 . . . . .119 B5
Whiteway View GL7 . . . . .190 B7
Whitewell Cl GL4 . . . . .119 E7
Whitewood Rd BS15 . . . . . .19 F1
Whitfield Ho 🎱 BS15 . . . .10 D8
Whitfield Rd BS35 . . . . . . .64 C2
Whitfield St GL1 . . . . .196 B2
Whitford Cl WR11 . . . . . . .188 A6
Whiting Rd BS13 . . . . .2 A4
Whitland Ave BS13 . . . . . . .2 B5
Whitland Rd BS13 . . . . .2 B5
Whitley Cl BS37 . . . . .43 C3
Whitley Mead BS34 . . . . . .29 E3
Whitlow La GL19 . . . . .165 E5
Whitmead Gdns BS13 . . . . . .2 C4
Whitminster CE Prim Sch
GL2 . . . . .100 E5
Whitminster La GL2 . . . . .100 A4
Whitmore Ave BS4 . . . . . . .10 A3
Whitmore Rd GL54 . . . . . .174 A8
Whitmores The GL54 . . . .176 C1
Whitson Ho 🎲 BS2 . . . . . .195 C3
Whitson St BS1 . . . . .195 B4
Whittingham Hall GL14 . .156 E5
Whittington Ct* GL54 . . .166 C7
Whittington Ho GL5 . . . . . .99 A7
Whittington Rd
Bristol BS16 . . . . .20 C6
Cheltenham GL51 . . . . .129 D8
Whittington Way GL15 . . . .147 D8
Whittington Wlk 🔞
GL18 . . . . .171 A4
Whittle Ave GL4 . . . . .118 D2
Whittle Cl GL51 . . . . .129 C8
Whittles La GL2 . . . . .157 F2
Whittlestone Cl GL54 . . . .176 D4
Whittlestone Hollow
GL54 . . . . .176 D4
Whittock Rd BS14 . . . . .3 D6
Whittock Sq BS14 . . . . .3 D7
Whittucks Cl BS15 . . . . . . .10 C4
Whittucks Rd BS15 . . . . . . .10 C4
Whitwell Rd BS14 . . . . .3 A6
Whitworth Mews GL3 . . . .120 C6
Whitworth Rd GL7 . . . . . .190 C3

Whornes Orch GL4 . . . . . .119 F3
Whytes Cl BS9 . . . . .18 A8
Wick CE Prim Sch BS30 . .12 B6
Wick Cres BS4 . . . . .9 D3
Wick House Cl BS31 . . . . . . .5 D3
Wick La
Lower Apperley GL19 . . . . . .173 C6
Upton Cheyney BS30 . . . . . . .12 A2
Wick Rd Bristol BS4 . . . . . . .9 D4
Oaksey SN16 . . . . .142 A4
Pilning BS35 . . . . .38 C7
Wick St GL6 . . . . .103 E4
Wick Wick Cl BS16,BS36 . .31 A2
Wickets The
Bristol,Filton BS7 . . . . .28 F1
Bristol,Upper Soundwell
BS15 . . . . .20 D2
Wicketts The BS7 . . . . .28 F2
Wickfield La GL52 . . . . . . .138 F4
Wickham Cl BS37 . . . . .33 D8
Wickham Glen BS16 . . . . . .19 D5
Wickham Hill BS16 . . . . . . .19 D5
Wickham View BS16 . . . . . .19 D4
Wicklow Rd BS4 . . . . .2 E8
Wickridge Cl GL5 . . . . .99 C8
Wickwar Rd
Kingswood GL12 . . . . .67 E4
Rangeworthy BS37 . . . . .53 B1
Wickwar La GL7 . . . . .143 B6
Widcombe BS14 . . . . .3 A6
Widcombe Cl 🎲 BS5 . . . . . .10 A7
Widden Prim Sch GL1 . . . .196 C2
Widden St GL1 . . . . .196 C2
Widdicomb La GL11 . . . . . .144 D1
Widmore Gr BS13 . . . . .2 B5
Wigeon La GL20 . . . . .192 E3
Wigmore Cl GL4 . . . . .119 E6
Wigton Cres BS10 . . . . .28 C2
Wilbye Gr BS4 . . . . .2 D7
Wilcox Cl BS15 . . . . .10 C6
Wildcroft Ho BS9 . . . . .18 A4
Wildcroft Rd BS9 . . . . .18 A4
Wilder Cl BS2 . . . . .195 B4
Wilder St BS2 . . . . .195 B4
Wilder Way BS2 . . . . .195 B4
Wilder St BS2 . . . . .195 B4
Wildfowl & Wetlands Trust
Slimbridge* GL2 . . . . .95 A6
Wildlife Wlk GL3 . . . . .120 E4
Wildmoorway La GL7 . . . .143 A8
Wildwood Residential Cvn Pk
GL7 . . . . .190 F2
Wilkes Ave GL3 . . . . .120 A8
Wilkes Mdw GL16 . . . . . . .155 B6
Wilkinson Rd GL7 . . . . . . .190 D1
Willada Cl BS3 . . . . .8 B2
Willcox Dr GL52 . . . . .138 B3
Willersey Bsns Pk
WR12 . . . . .188 B3
Willersey CE Prim Sch
WR12 . . . . .188 B2
Willersey Rd GL51 . . . . . . .129 E8
William Emes Gdn GL56 . .186 F7
William Gough Cl GL51 . .132 D5
William Mason Cl 🔞 BS5 . . .9 B7
William St
🎱 Bristol,Fishponds BS16 . . .20 B3
Bristol,Moorfields BS5 . . . . . .9 C8
Bristol,Newton BS2 . . . . .9 A6
Bristol,Windmill Hill BS3 . . . .8 E4
Williams Cl BS30 . . . . .10 F3
Williams Orch GL2 . . . . . .125 D5
Williamson Rd GL7 . . . . . .190 C4
Williamstrip Farm Cotts
GL7 . . . . .160 F1
Willis Ho BS4 . . . . .2 F8
Willis Est BS2 . . . . .18 F3
Willis Rd BS15 . . . . .20 F2
Willis Wlk GL20 . . . . .182 C5
Willmott Way BS11 . . . . . . .26 D1
Willmott Cl BS14 . . . . .2 F3
Willoughby Cl
Alveston BS35 . . . . .51 A4
Bristol BS13 . . . . .2 B7
Willoughby Rd BS7 . . . . . . .18 E5
Willow Ave GL4 . . . . .119 B7
Willow Bank BS10 . . . . .18 C7
Willow Bank Rd GL20 . . . .183 D4
Willow Bed Cl BS16 . . . . . .20 B6
Willow Cl
Ashton under Hill WR11 . . . .183 D8
Bristol,Patchway BS34 . . . . . .28 F7
Bristol,Warmley BS30 . . . . . .11 D6
Charfield GL12 . . . . .9 A8
Chepstow/Cas-Gwent NP16 . .60 D6
Dursley GL11 . . . . .88 A3
Wick BS30 . . . . .12 B6
Woodmancote GL52 . . . . . . .138 B3
Willow Ct BS7 . . . . .19 A7
Willow Cvn Site GL2 . . . .126 D5
Willow Dr GL2 . . . . .138 B4
South Cerney GL7 . . . . .143 A8
Willow Gn 🎱 Bristol BS16 . .20 C2
Willow Gr Dursley GL11 . . . .81 A8
Willow Ho BS13 . . . . .2 D4
Willow Hts GL15 . . . . .92 B5
Willow Park Dr GL52 . . . .137 F4
Willow Rd BS15 . . . . .10 C3
Charlton Kings GL53 . . . . . .131 C5
King's Stanley GL10 . . . . . . .99 F2
Stonehouse GL10 . . . . .97 F2
Willersey WR12 . . . . .188 B2
Willow Sh Ctr The BS16 . .20 E6
Willow Way
Coalpit Heath BS36 . . . . .31 C6
Gloucester GL4 . . . . .119 B7
Willow Wlk Bristol BS10 . . .28 B3

Willow Wlk *continued*
Keynsham BS31 . . . . .4 D4
Willowbrook Dr GL51 . . . .132 D4
Willowcroft Cl GL4 . . . . . .119 D3
Willowdean GL14 . . . . .191 C5
Willowherb Cl GL52 . . . . .134 C3
Willowleaze GL2 . . . . .127 D3
Willows The Bristol BS16 . .20 E4
Bristol,Bradley Stoke BS32 . .29 D8
Bristol,Frenchay BS16 . . . . . .30 B1
Coalpit Heath BS36 . . . . .31 F7
Dymock GL18 . . . . .178 D2
Willsbridge GL12 . . . . .196 C4
Wills Dr BS5 . . . . .9 A8
Wills Way BS13 . . . . .3 D6
Willsbridge Hill BS30 . . . .11 A2
Willsbridge Mill* BS30 . .11 A2
Willway St BS3 . . . . .8 D4
Wilmot Ct BS30 . . . . .11 A6
Wilmots Way BS20 . . . . . . .16 D4
Wilshire Ave BS15 . . . . .10 D5
Wilson Pl BS2 . . . . .195 C4
Wilson Rd BS15 . . . . .10 C5
Wilson St BS2 . . . . .195 C4
Wilton Cl Bristol BS10 . . . .28 C1
Gloucester GL4 . . . . .118 D6
Wilton Rd GL1 . . . . .118 D6
Wiltshire Ave BS37 . . . . . . .44 A3
Wiltshire Pl BS15 . . . . .20 E3
Wilverley Ind Est BS4 . . . . .9 E1
Wimbledon Rd BS6 . . . . . . .18 C5
Wimborne Cl GL51 . . . . . .129 E6
Wimborne Rd BS34 . . . . . . .29 E6
Winash Cl BS14 . . . . .3 D7
Wincanton Cl BS16 . . . . . . .30 F1
Wincel Rd GL54 . . . . .174 A7
Winchcombe Abbey CE Prim
Sch GL54 . . . . .174 A7
Winchcombe Folk & Police
Mus* GL54 . . . . .174 A7
Winchcombe Gr BS11 . . . . .16 F5
Winchcombe Hospl
GL54 . . . . .139 F4
Winchcombe Rd
Dumbleton WR11 . . . . .184 A8
Frampton Cotterell BS36 . . . .31 B8
Gloucester GL4 . . . . .118 C2
Winchcombe Sch GL54 . . . .174 A8
Winchcombe Sta GL54 . . . .174 A8
Winchester Ct BS16 . . . . . .19 E6
Winchester Rd BS4 . . . . . . .118 E3
Winchester Way BS37 . . . . .43 D8
Wincombe Trad Est BS2 . . .9 A4
Wincroft BS30 . . . . .11 C4
Windcliff Cres BS11 . . . . . .129 E7
Windermere Rd
Bristol BS34 . . . . .29 A8
Cheltenham GL51 . . . . .129 E7
Windermere Way BS30 . . . .11 D6
Windfall Way GL2 . . . . . . .127 D2
Windmill Cl BS3 . . . . .8 E4
Windmill Cotts GL8 . . . . . . .82 A6
Windmill Farm Bsns Ctr
BS3 .8 D4
Windmill Field GL4 . . . . . .119 D7
Windmill Hill BS3 . . . . .8 D3
Windmill La Bristol BS10 . . .27 D3
Kingscote GL8 . . . . .82 A6
Windmill Rd Kemble GL7 . .141 F8
Minchinhampton GL6 . . . . . .129 E7
Windrush Ct
Temple Guiting GL54 . . . . . .175 A8
Thornbury BS35 . . . . .51 C8
Windrush Gn BS31 . . . . .5 A4
Windrush Rd
Bristol BS31 . . . . .134 A2
Gloucester GL4 . . . . .118 E2
Keynsham BS31 . . . . .5 A4
Windrush View GL54 . . . . .175 D2
Windscreens Ave BS2 . . . . . .9 A4
Windsor Ave Bristol BS5 . . .10 B6
Keynsham BS31 . . . . .4 E6
Windsor Cl BS34 . . . . .29 E4
Windsor Cres BS10 . . . . . . .27 C4
Windsor Ct
🔞 Bristol,Clifton BS8 . . . . .7 F6
Bristol,Downend BS16 . . . . .20 E7
Wick BS30 . . . . .12 B6
Yate BS37 . . . . .27 F3
Windsor Gr GL53 . . . . .92 B6
Windsor Gr 🔳 GL2 . . . . . . .43 D2
Windsor Pl
Bristol BS8 . . . . .7 F6
Bristol,Mangotsfield BS16 . . .21 A5
Stroud GL6 . . . . .103 B1
Windsor Rd
Bristol,Longwell Green
BS30 . . . . .10 F2
Bristol,Montpelier BS6 . . . . .18 E2
Dursley GL11 . . . . .88 A3
🎱 Tetbury GL8 . . . . .140 B4
Windsor Terr
Bristol,Clifton BS8 . . . . .7 F6

Windsor Terr *continued*
Bristol,Windmill Hill BS3 . . . .8 F4
Cirencester GL7 . . . . .190 E4
Windsoredge La GL6 . . . . . .91 A6
Windyridge GL6 . . . . .105 A1
Windyridge Gdns GL50 . . .133 C5
Windyridge Rd GL50 . . . . .133 C5
Wine St BS1 . . . . .195 A3
Wineberry Cl BS5 . . . . .19 D1
Winfield Cl GL18 . . . . .170 F4
Winfield Rd BS30 . . . . .11 C7
Winford Ct BS6 . . . . .18 A5
Winford Gr BS13 . . . . .2 A8
Winford La BS41 . . . . .1 C1
Winford Terr BS41 . . . . .1 C5
Wing La GL20 . . . . .182 E8
Wingfield Rd BS3 . . . . .8 E2
Winkworth Pl 🎲 BS2 . . . . .18 F1
Winniecroft Cotts GL4 . . .119 D2
Winnycroft La GL4 . . . . . . .119 C1
Winsbury Way BS32 . . . . . . .40 D1
Winscombe Cl BS31 . . . . . . .4 D6
Winsdor Dr GL4 . . . . .118 C2
Winsford St 🎲 BS5 . . . . . . .9 A8
Winsham Cl BS14 . . . . .3 B5
Winsley Ct 🔟 GL4 . . . . . . .119 C4
Winsley Rd Bristol BS6 . . . .18 D1
Gloucester GL4 . . . . .119 C4
Winstanley Ho 🎲 BS5 . . . . .9 B6
Winston Cl 🔳 HR8 . . . . . . .178 F7
Winston Rd GL3 . . . . .128 B5
Winstone Cl BS2 . . . . .194 C5
Winstonian Rd GL52 . . . . .133 F2
Winterbotham Rd
Cheltenham GL51 . . . . .132 D2
Dursley GL11 . . . . .80 A1
Winterbourne Hill BS36 . . .30 D5
Winterbourne Rd BS34 . . . .29 E6
Wintersfield GL2 . . . . .144 F8
Winterspring La GL12 . . . .138 F3
Winterstoke Cl 🎲 BS3 . . . . .8 B2
Winterstoke Ctr 🔟 BS3 . . . .8 B2
Winterstoke Ho 🚹 BS3 . . . . .8 A3
Winterstoke Rd BS3 . . . . . . .8 A2
Winterstoke Underpass
BS3 .7 F4
Winterway GL56 . . . . .186 C6
Wintle's Hill GL54 . . . . . . .174 A6
Wintles Cl GL17 . . . . .164 D5
Wintles La GL14 . . . . .165 C3
Winton Cl GL51 . . . . .130 A7
Winton Rd GL51 . . . . .130 A7
Winton St BS2 . . . . .8 E4
Wintour Cl NP16 . . . . .72 D1
Wirewood Cl NP16 . . . . . . .73 A2
Wirewood Cres NP16 . . . . .73 A2
Wishford Cl GL2 . . . . .127 B3
Wisloe Rd GL2 . . . . .95 F2
Wistaria Ave BS37 . . . . .27 E1
Wistaria Rd 🔳 GL18 . . . . . .140 B4
Wistaria Way GL13 . . . . . .128 A3
Wistley Rd GL53 . . . . .131 B4
Witch Hazel Rd BS13 . . . . . .2 E3
Witchell Rd BS5 . . . . .9 C7
Witcombe BS37 . . . . .32 C7
Witcombe Cl BS15 . . . . .20 F1
Witcombe Pl GL52 . . . . . . .193 C3
Witham Rd BS31 . . . . .14 A3
Witherlies Rd BS16 . . . . . . .19 F4
Withers The GL54 . . . . .137 F4
Withey Cl W BS9 . . . . .17 F5
Witheys The BS20 . . . . .3 C4
Withington CE Prim Sch
GL54 . . . . .166 A7
Withington Cl BS30 . . . . . . .11 C2
Withpool Cl BS14 . . . . .3 A6
Withy Cl BS9 . . . . .17 F6
Withy Mews GL4 . . . . .119 C2
Withy Trees Rd WR11 . . . .188 A8
Withy Way GL11 . . . . .97 F5
Withybridge Gdns GL51 . .132 A7
Withybridge La GL51 . . . . .132 A6
Withyfield Rd GL52 . . . . . .138 A6
Withyholt Cl GL53 . . . . . . .130 F5
Withyholt Ct GL53 . . . . . . .130 F5
Withymead Rd SN14 . . . . . .15 A8
Withypool 🎱 GL51 . . . . . . .129 C5
Withypool Gdns BS14 . . . . . .3 B5
Withys The BS20 . . . . .16 D4
Withywood Com Sch BS13 . .2 A4
Withywood Gdns BS13 . . . . . .1 F4
Withywood Rd BS13 . . . . . . .1 F4
Witley Cl BS31 . . . . .129 D6
Witney Cl BS32 . . . . .28 F1
Witney Mead BS36 . . . . . . .31 F8
Witpit La GL7 . . . . .91 C5
Woburn Ave GL4 . . . . .118 C1
Woburn Cl BS30 . . . . .10 A7
Woburn Rd BS5 . . . . .19 D1
Wolds End Cl 🎲 GL51 . . . .189 A2
Wolferton Rd GL52 . . . . . . .178 F7
Wolford Rd GL56 . . . . .187 D6
Wolfridge Gdns BS10 . . . . .28 F8
Wolfridge La BS35 . . . . .50 F4
Wolfridge Ride BS35 . . . . . .50 F4
Wolseley Lodge GL2 . . . . .127 B2
Wolseley Rd Bristol BS7 . . .18 D3
Gloucester GL2 . . . . .127 B2
Wood Edge Rd GL16 . . . . . .155 B3
Wood End St GL18 . . . . .59 B4
Wood End Wlk BS9 . . . . . . .17 C6
Wood La
Down Hatherley GL2 . . . . . .173 D1
Gorsley GL18 . . . . .170 D4

Wood La *continued*
Horton BS37 . . . . .55 A1
Nailsworth GL6 . . . . .91 C5
Wood Mews GL2 . . . . .126 A4
Wood Rd Bristol BS15 . . . . .10 D8
Mile End GL16 . . . . .155 B6
Wood St Bristol BS5 . . . . . . .19 B2
Bushley GL20 . . . . .181 C5
Stroud GL5 . . . . .99 D7
Woodbine Cl GL4 . . . . .119 E5
Woodbine Rd BS5 . . . . .9 D8
Woodbines Park Mobile
Home Pk GL51 . . . . .129 C6
Woodborough Cl GL6 . . . . .103 F7
Woodborough St BS5 . . . . . .19 B1
Woodbridge La GL54 . . . . .166 E1
Woodbridge Rd BS4 . . . . . . .9 A2
Woodbury La BS8 . . . . .7 D8
Woodchester Bristol BS15 . .20 E3
Yate BS37 . . . . .32 E7
Woodchester CE Prim Sch
GL5 . . . . .99 A2
Woodchester Mansion*
GL10 . . . . .89 F7
Woodchester Park Walks*
GL10 . . . . .89 D7
Woodchester Pk* GL10 . . .90 B7
Woodchester Rd BS10 . . . . .18 C7
Woodcock Cl
Gloucester GL4 . . . . .119 D5
Stonehouse GL10 . . . . .101 F1
Woodcock La GL10 . . . . .97 F8
Woodcote Bristol BS15 . . . . .10 D6
Gloucester GL2 . . . . .127 B5
Woodcote Rd BS16 . . . . . . .20 B3
Woodcote Wlk BS16 . . . . . .20 B3
Woodcroft Ave BS5 . . . . . . .19 D1
Woodcroft Cl Bristol BS4 . . .9 E4
Woodcroft Rd BS34 . . . . . . .9 E4
Woodcroft La NP16 . . . . . . .73 A4
Woodcroft Terr NP16 . . . . .73 B4
Woodend BS15 . . . . .10 D6
Woodend Cl GL4 . . . . .119 E8
Dursley GL11 . . . . .87 F6
Woodend La Awre GL14 . . .157 B2
Dursley GL11 . . . . .87 F6
Gorsley HR9 . . . . .170 A4
Rockhampton BS35 . . . . .76 D1
Woodend Rd
Frampton Cotterell BS36 . . . .31 C7
Harrow Hill GL17 . . . . .164 B3
Woodfield Rd Bristol BS6 . . .18 C3
Mile End GL16 . . . . .155 B6
🎱 Ledbury HR8 . . . . .178 F7
Woodford Ct GL4 . . . . .119 B7
Woodgate Cl
Charlton Kings GL52 . . . . . .131 C5
Gloucester GL4 . . . . .119 B6
Woodgate Rd
Cinderford GL14 . . . . .191 D5
Mile End GL16 . . . . .155 B7
Woodgrove Rd BS10 . . . . . .27 D2
Woodhall Cl BS16 . . . . .20 B6
Woodhouse Ave GL2 . . . . . .40 D7
Woodhouse Cl
Cirencester GL7 . . . . .190 B3
Woodhouse Down BS32 . . . .40 E7
Woodhouse Gr BS7 . . . . . . .18 B4
Woodhouse La BS57 . . . . . . .9 B6
Woodington Ct 🔳 BS30 . . . .10 F7
Woodland Ave
Bristol BS15 . . . . .10 E6
Dursley GL11 . . . . .88 A2
Woodland Cl BS15 . . . . .20 C2
Woodland Ct
🔞 Bristol BS9 . . . . .17 C3
Woodland Dr GL14 . . . . . . .191 C5
Woodland Gr BS9 . . . . .17 D6
Bristol BS15 . . . . .10 E6
Woodland Rd
Berry Hill GL16 . . . . .155 A7
Bream GL15 . . . . .155 D1
Bristol BS8 . . . . .194 C4
Coleford GL16 . . . . .154 F8
Gloucester GL4 . . . . .118 E7
Leyhill GL12 . . . . .164 B7
Parkend GL15 . . . . .155 C3
Woodland Rise
Lydney GL15 . . . . .92 B4
Parkend GL15 . . . . .155 C3
Woodland Terr
Bristol,Kingswood BS15 . . . . .10 E7
Bristol BS15 . . . . .18 B2
Woodland View
Joy's Green GL17 . . . . .163 D3
Leonard Stanley GL10 . . . . . .97 F3
Monmouth/Trefynwy
NP25 . . . . .154 A7
Ruspidge GL14 . . . . .156 C6
Woodmancote GL7 . . . . .158 B4
Bristol GL12 . . . . .10 E7
Woodlands
Bristol,Downend BS16 . . . . .20 E6
Bristol,Patchway BS32 . . . . .28 F4
Bristol,Sneyd Park BS9 . . . . .17 E3
North The NP25 . . . . .154 B1
Shirehampton BS11 . . . . .27 A8
Woodlands Ct
St Arvans NP16 . . . . .72 B6
Whitecroft GL15 . . . . .92 B5
Woodlands Dr GL5 . . . . . . .119 C8
Woodlands La
Berkeley GL13 . . . . .85 A1
Bristol BS32 . . . . .40 C1

Woodlands Park Cvn Pk
  GL50 . . . . .133 D5
Woodlands Pk
  Bristol BS32 . . . . .40 C3
  Quedgeley GL2 . . . . .117 D1
Woodlands Rd
  Charfield GL12 . . . . .67 A4
  Cheltenham GL51 . . . . .130 B5
  Cirencester GL7 . . . . .190 B2
  Tytherington GL12 . . . . .52 B6
Woodlands Reach
  GL14 . . . . .191 D4
Woodlands Rise BS16 . . . .20 D6
Woodlands The
  Llandogo NP25 . . . . .146 B2
  Stroud GL5 . . . . .99 D8
Woodleaze BS9 . . . . .17 B6
Woodleigh BS35 . . . . .64 C1
Woodleigh Ci 9 HR8 . . . .178 E8
Woodleigh Field GL2 . . . .125 E6
Woodleigh Gdns BS14 . . .3 C6
Woodleigh Rd HR8 . . . . .178 E8
Woodmancote
  Dursley GL11 . . . . .80 B7
  Yate BS37 . . . . .32 D8
Woodmancote Rd 7 BS6 .18 E1
Woodmancote Sch
  GL52 . . . . .138 B4
Woodmancote Vale
  GL52 . . . . .138 B3
Woodmans Cl BS37 . . . . . .33 B8
Woodmans Rd BS37 . . . .33 C8
Woodmans Vale BS37 . . .33 C8
Woodmarsh Cl BS14 . . . .3 A4
Woodmead Gdns BS13 . . . .2 C4
Woodmead La BS30 . . . . .23 A1
Woodnook The BS10 . . . .28 C2
Woodpecker Cres BS16 . .32 C2
Woodpecker Rd GL2 . . . .118 C5
Woodpecker Wlk GL6 . . . .90 F5
Woodpeckers Cl GL19 . . .172 D5
Woodrow Way GL2 . . . . .118 A3
Woodruff Cl GL4 . . . . . . .119 B4
Woodrush Rd GL20 . . . . .192 E2
Woods Cl SN16 . . . . .58 C1
Woods Orch GL4 . . . . . . .118 F2
Woods Orchard Rd GL4 . .118 E2
Woodside Bristol BS9 . . . . . .17 D3
  Stroud GL5 . . . . .99 F8
  Turkdean GL54 . . . . .167 F4
  Woolaston GL15 . . . . .147 B3
Woodside Ave GL14 . . . .191 D3
Woodside Gr BS10 . . . . . .27 D3
Woodside Prim Sch
  GL17 . . . . .163 F3
Woodside Rd
  Bristol,Downend BS16 . . . . .20 C7
  Bristol,Kingswood BS15 . . . .10 C7
  Bristol,St Anne's Park BS4 . . . .9 E6
  Coalpit Heath BS36 . . . . . . .31 E6
  Woolaston GL15 . . . . .147 B3
Woodside St GL14 . . . . .191 D4
Woodside Terr GL6 . . . . .102 F3
Woodstock Ave BS6 . . . . .18 C1
Woodstock Cl
  Avening GL8 . . . . .148 A1
  Bristol BS15 . . . . .10 F8
Woodstock La GL8 . . . . .148 A1
Woodstock Rd
  Bristol,Kingswood BS15 . . . .10 F7
  Bristol,Redland BS6 . . . . . . .18 C2

Woodstock Sch BS10 . . . .27 E2
Woodstock Terr GL11 . . . .89 C1
Woodview
  Four Oaks GL18 . . . . .170 D7
  Frampton Mansell GL6 . . . .148 E5
Woodview Cl BS11 . . . . . . .16 E7
Woodview Rd GL11 . . . . . .88 A4
Woodville Ave GL16 . . . .155 C6
Woodville Rd
  Cinderford GL14 . . . . .191 E4
  Tewkesbury GL20 . . . . .192 D1
Woodville Rd W GL14 . . .191 E4
Woodward Ave BS37 . . . . .43 B1
Woodward Cl GL8 . . . . . .140 B5
Woodward Dr BS30 . . . . . .10 F4
Woodwell Rd BS11 . . . . . .16 E5
Woodyleaze Dr BS15 . . . .10 D6
Woolaston Comm GL15 . .147 C3
Woolaston Prim Sch
  GL15 . . . . .147 C3
Woolaway Bglws GL56 . .187 A6
Woolcot St BS6 . . . . .18 B2
Woollard La BS14 . . . . .3 E1
Woolley Rd BS14 . . . . .3 E5
Woolmarket The GL7 . . . .190 D5
Woolpitch Wood/Coed
  Woolpitch NP16 . . . . .60 C8
Woolridge Hill GL19 . . . .172 C2
Woolstone La GL52 . . . . .137 F8
Woolstrop Way GL2 . . . . .118 A3
Woolthorpe La GL2 . . . . .157 C6
Wootton Cres BS4 . . . . .9 E6
Wootton Pk BS14,BS4 . . . . .9 B1
Wootton Rd BS4 . . . . .9 F6
Worcester Cl BS16 . . . . . .20 B2
Worcester Cres BS8 . . . .194 A4
Worcester Ct BS8 . . . . . .194 A4
Worcester Par GL1 . . . . .196 B4
Worcester Rd
  Bristol,Clifton BS8 . . . . . . .194 A4
  Bristol,Kingswood BS15 . . . .20 D1
  Cinderford GL14 . . . . .191 E5
  Ledbury HR8 . . . . .178 F8
Worcester St GL1 . . . . . .196 B3
Worcester Terr BS8 . . . .194 A4
Worcester Wlk GL16 . . . .155 C6
Wordens The GL5 . . . . . . .98 D8
Wordings Mount GL6 . . .104 E8
Wordsworth Ave GL51 . .132 E1
Wordsworth Ho BS34 . . . .29 A8
Wordsworth Rd
  Bristol BS7 . . . . .19 B7
  Dursley GL11 . . . . .80 C7
Working La GL54 . . . . . . .183 E1
Workshop Rd BS11 . . . . . .26 C4
World of Mechanical Music
  Mus* GL54 . . . . .168 A1
World's End La BS31 . . . . . .5 C5
World's End La GL12 . . . . .68 C7
Worldsend La GL13 . . . . . . .78 E7
Worley Ridge GL6 . . . . . . .91 A4
Wormwood Hill GL6 . . . . .91 A1
Worrall Mews 10 BS8 . . . .18 A2
Worrall Pl 11 BS8 . . . . . . .18 A2
Worrall Rd BS8 . . . . .18 A2
Worrel's La BS16 . . . . .30 D3
Worsley St BS5 . . . . .9 D7
Worthing Rd BS34 . . . . . .28 F8
Worthy Cl BS15 . . . . .10 F6
Worthy Rd BS11 . . . . .26 C4
Worthys The BS34 . . . . . .30 A6
Wortley Rd GL12 . . . . .68 C6

Wortley Terr GL12 . . . . . . .68 C6
Wotton Cres GL12 . . . . . . .68 C6
Wotton Ct GL4 . . . . .127 D1
Wotton Elms Ct 4 GL2 . .127 B2
Wotton Heritage Ctr*
  GL12 . . . . .68 B7
Wotton Lawn Hospl
  GL1 . . . . .127 A2
Wotton Rd Charfield GL12 . .68 F5
  Iron Acton BS37 . . . . .42 F5
  Kingswood GL12 . . . . .67 F5
Wragg Castle La GL6 . . .103 C6
Wragg Ct GL11 . . . . .88 A5
Wraggs Row 23 GL54 . . .176 F4
Wraxall Gr BS13 . . . . .2 A8
Wraxall Rd BS30 . . . . .11 A6
Wren Cl Bristol BS16 . . . . . .19 E7
  Gloucester GL4 . . . . .119 B6
Wren Dr BS16 . . . . .20 A6
Wren Terr GL3 . . . . .127 D6
Wrenbert Rd BS16 . . . . . .20 D5
Wright Cl GL54 . . . . .169 D7
Wright Rd GL54 . . . . .169 D7
Wright Way BS16 . . . . .19 E8
Wrington Cl BS34 . . . . . . .29 C7
Wrington Cres BS13 . . . . . .2 A7
Wroughton Dr BS13 . . . . . .2 D4
Wroughton Gdns BS13 . . .2 D4
Wroxham Dr BS34 . . . . . . .29 C8
Wyatt Ave BS13 . . . . .1 F5
Wyatt Cl BS13 . . . . .1 F5
Wyatt Ct GL54 . . . . .166 E5
Wyatts View BS4 . . . . .9 E6
Wychbury Cl GL53 . . . . . .130 D5
Wychwood BS15 . . . . .10 E6
Wychwood Ct GL56 . . . . .187 B3
Wyck Beck Rd BS10 . . . . . .28 A3
Wyck Rissington GL54 . . .169 C8
Wycliffe Coll GL10 . . . . . . .79 F2
Wycliffe Prep Sch GL10 . .98 A6
Wycliffe Rd BS9 . . . . .18 B7
Wycliffe Row 9 BS3 . . . . . . .8 F4
Wycombe Gr BS4 . . . . .9 D2
Wydelands GL56 . . . . . . .186 E6
Wye Cres NP16 . . . . .60 E7
Wye Croft Cl BS10 . . . . . .28 D3
Wye Ct BS35 . . . . .51 C8
Wye Rapids Cotts HR9 . .162 E7
Wye Rd GL3 . . . . .120 F5
Wye Valley Link Rd NP16 . .60 E5
Wye View Ho NP16 . . . . . .61 A7
Wye View La HR9 . . . . . . .162 E3
Wye View Terr NP16 . . . .154 C4
Wye's Gn NP25 . . . . .154 C4
Wyebank Ave NP16 . . . . . .73 A1
Wyebank Cl NP16 . . . . . . .61 A8
Wyebank Cres NP16 . . . . .73 A1
Wyebank Pl NP16 . . . . . . .61 A8
Wyebank Rise NP16 . . . . .61 A8
Wyebank View NP16 . . . . .61 A8
Wyebank Way NP16 . . . . .61 A7
Wyebridge St 17 NP25 . .154 A7
Wyedale Ave BS9 . . . . .17 C7
Wyedean Cl GL15 . . . . . . .92 C2
Wyedean Sch NP16 . . . . .61 A8
Wyelands Pk GL17 . . . . .163 D4
Wyelands View NP16 . . . .60 B4
Wyesham Ave/Rhodfa
  Wyesham 4 NP25 . . . . .154 A7
Wyesham Inf Sch NP25 . .154 A7

Wyesham Jun Sch
  NP25 . . . . .154 A7
Wyesham La (Sky Farm La)
Wyesham Rd NP25 . . . . .154 B7
Wyeside Commercial Ctr 25
  NP25 . . . . .154 A7
Wyeside Pk HR9 . . . . . . .163 C5
Wykis Ct BS15 . . . . .10 E5
Wyman's La GL51 . . . . . .133 B6
Wyman's Rd GL52 . . . . . .134 A3
Wymans Ct GL50 . . . . . . .133 C5
Wymbush Cres BS13 . . . . .2 C5
Wymbush Gdns BS13 . . . . .2 C5
Wyndbrook La GL19 . . . .179 F4
Wyndcliffe View NP16 . . . .72 B5
Wyndcliffe Ho NP16 . . . . .61 A7
Wyndham Cres
  Bristol BS4 . . . . .10 A3
  Easton-in-G BS20 . . . . .16 B4
Wyndham Ct BS2 . . . . . .195 B4
Wynford Villas GL19 . . . .171 C1
Wynols Cl 6 GL16 . . . . . .155 B5
Wynols Ct 7 GL16 . . . . . .155 B5
Wynols Hill La GL16 . . . .155 B5
Wynols Rd GL16 . . . . . . .155 B5
Wynstones Dr GL4 . . . . . .110 F5
Wynstones Sch GL4 . . . .110 C8
Wynstones The BS15 . . . . .10 D7
Wyntour Ho NP16 . . . . . . .61 A8
Wyntour's Par GL15 . . . . .92 A2
Wynyards Cl GL20 . . . . . .192 D4
Wyvern Rd NP16 . . . . .61 B1
Wyvern Villas BS9 . . . . . . .18 A8

Y

Y Paddgau/The Paddocks 6
  NP25 . . . . .154 A7
Yalta Cl 16 GL51 . . . . . . .132 E2
Yanleigh Cl BS13 . . . . .1 D6
Yanley La BS41,BS13 . . . . . .1 C7
Yard The BS2 . . . . .19 A3
Yarlington Cl GL52 . . . . . .137 E4
Yarnells Alley GL4 . . . . . .192 C4
Yarnold Terr GL51 . . . . . .133 A4
Yarnolds GL51 . . . . .129 E1
Yarrow Cl GL4 . . . . .119 A4
Yartleton La GL17 . . . . . .165 A7
Yate Her Ctr* BS37 . . . . . . .43 E2
Yate Rd BS37 . . . . .42 F3
Yate Rocks BS37 . . . . .43 C7
Yate Sta BS37 . . . . .43 C2
Yatton Cl BS13 . . . . .1 F8
Yeaman's Ho BS1 . . . . . .195 B1
Yeldham Mews GL52 . . .133 F4
Yellow Hundred Cl GL11 . .80 C8
Yelverton Rd BS4 . . . . .9 E1
Yeomans Cl BS9 . . . . .17 C5
Yeomanside Cl BS14 . . . . . .3 C5
Yeomeads BS41 . . . . .7 A1
Yetts The NP16 . . . . .61 B8
Yew Tree Cl
  Cheltenham GL50 . . . . . . .133 C5
  Shipton GL54 . . . . .166 E5
  Whitchurch HR9 . . . . .162 D4
Yew Tree Cott 10 GL6 . . . .90 B8
Yew Tree Cotts 16 GL54 . .176 F4
Yew Tree Ct Bristol BS13 . . . .3 B5
  8 Broadway WR12 . . . . .185 C8

Yew Tree Dr Bristol BS15 . . .20 F3
  Gotherington GL52 . . . . . .138 A8
Yew Tree Gdns BS20 . . . .16 C4
Yew Tree Way
  Churchdown GL3 . . . . .128 A5
  Thrupp GL5 . . . . .99 E3
Yew Tree Wood NP16 . . . .60 B8
Yewcroft Cl BS14 . . . . .3 A4
Yewtree Cl GL11 . . . . .87 D3
Yokehouse La GL6 . . . . . .104 A6
York Ave BS7 . . . . .18 F4
York Bldgs BS3 . . . . .8 E4
York Cl
  Bristol,Bromley Heath BS16 . .30 F1
  Bristol,Stoke Gifford BS34 . .29 D4
  Yate BS37 . . . . .43 E4
York Ct BS2 . . . . .195 B4
York Gdns Bristol BS8 . . . . .7 F6
  Winterbourne BS36 . . . . . . .30 F8
York Pl
  Bristol,Brandon Hill BS1 . . .194 C2
  Bristol,Victoria Park BS8 . .194 B3
York Rd
  Bristol,Lower Easton BS5 . . .19 C1
  Bristol,Montpelier BS6 . . . . .18 E1
  Bristol,Staple Hill BS3 . . . . .20 E4
  Bristol,Windmill Hill BS3 . . . .8 E4
  Cinderford GL14 . . . . .191 E5
  Gloucester GL4 . . . . .119 C8
  Tewkesbury GL20 . . . . . . .192 C2
York Row GL52 . . . . .134 A4
York St
  Bristol,Baptist Mills BS2 . . . .19 A2
  2 Bristol,Clifton BS8 . . . . .18 A2
  3 Bristol,Redfield BS5 . . . . . .9 C7
  Bristol,St Pauls BS2 . . . . .195 B4
  Cheltenham GL52 . . . . . . .193 C4
Yorkley La GL15 . . . . .156 A1
Yorkley Prim Sch GL15 . .156 A1
Yorkley Wood Rd GL15 . .156 A1
Youngs Cotts GL6 . . . . . .148 B4
Youngs Ct BS16 . . . . .21 B8
Youngs Orch
  Brimscombe GL5 . . . . .148 A5
  Gloucester GL4 . . . . .119 D6
Yr Hen Heol/The Old Rd 22
  NP25 . . . . .154 A7

Z

Zetland Rd BS6 . . . . .18 D2
Zinc Rd BS11 . . . . .26 C3
Zinnia Cl GL3 . . . . .127 F7
Zion Apartments 12
  GL16 . . . . .155 A7
Zion Hill GL6 . . . . .102 F3
Zoons Rd GL3 . . . . .120 A8

Name and Address	Telephone	Page	Grid reference

Addresses

Name and Address	Telephone	Page	Grid reference

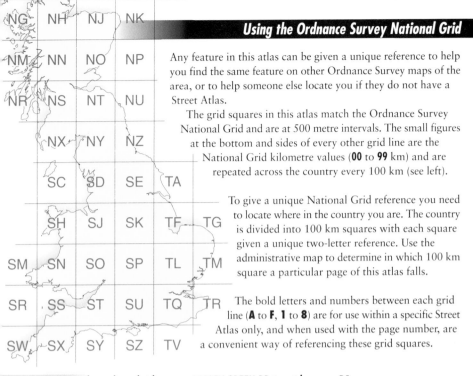

Any feature in this atlas can be given a unique reference to help you find the same feature on other Ordnance Survey maps of the area, or to help someone else locate you if they do not have a Street Atlas.

The grid squares in this atlas match the Ordnance Survey National Grid and are at 500 metre intervals. The small figures at the bottom and sides of every other grid line are the National Grid kilometre values (**00** to **99** km) and are repeated across the country every 100 km (see left).

To give a unique National Grid reference you need to locate where in the country you are. The country is divided into 100 km squares with each square given a unique two-letter reference. Use the administrative map to determine in which 100 km square a particular page of this atlas falls.

The bold letters and numbers between each grid line (**A** to **F**, **1** to **8**) are for use within a specific Street Atlas only, and when used with the page number, are a convenient way of referencing these grid squares.

Example *The railway bridge over DARLEY GREEN RD in grid square B1*

Step 1: Identify the two-letter reference, in this example the page is in **SP**

Step 2: Identify the 1 km square in which the railway bridge falls. Use the figures in the southwest corner of this square: Eastings **17**, Northings **74**. This gives a unique reference: **SP 17 74**, accurate to 1 km.

Step 3: To give a more precise reference accurate to 100 m you need to estimate how many tenths along and how many tenths up this 1 km square the feature is (to help with this the 1 km square is divided into four 500 m squares). This makes the bridge about **8** tenths along and about **1** tenth up from the southwest corner.

This gives a unique reference: **SP 178 741**, accurate to 100 m.

Eastings (read from left to right along the bottom) come before Northings (read from bottom to top). If you have trouble remembering say to yourself "Along the hall, THEN up the stairs"!

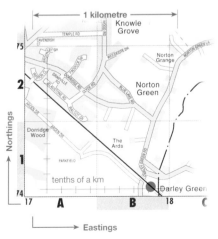

PHILIP'S MAPS
the Gold Standard for drivers

◆ **Philip's street atlases cover every county in England, Wales, Northern Ireland and much of Scotland**

◆ Every named street is shown, including alleys, lanes and walkways

◆ Thousands of additional features marked: stations, public buildings, car parks, places of interest

◆ Route-planning maps to get you close to your destination

◆ Postcodes on the maps and in the index

◆ Widely used by the emergency services, transport companies and local authorities

Street atlases currently available

England
Bedfordshire
Berkshire
Birmingham and West Midlands
Bristol and Bath
Buckinghamshire
Cambridgeshire
Cheshire
Cornwall
Cumbria
Derbyshire
Devon
Dorset
County Durham and Teesside
Essex
North Essex
South Essex
Gloucestershire
Hampshire
North Hampshire
South Hampshire
Herefordshire Monmouthshire
Hertfordshire
Isle of Wight
Kent
East Kent
West Kent
Lancashire
Leicestershire and Rutland
Lincolnshire
London
Greater Manchester
Merseyside
Norfolk
Northamptonshire
Northumberland
Nottinghamshire
Oxfordshire
Shropshire
Somerset
Staffordshire
Suffolk
Surrey

East Sussex
West Sussex
Tyne and Wear
Warwickshire
Birmingham and West Midlands
Wiltshire and Swindon
Worcestershire
East Yorkshire
Northern Lincolnshire
North Yorkshire
South Yorkshire
West Yorkshire

Wales
Anglesey, Conwy and Gwynedd
Cardiff, Swansea and The Valleys
Carmarthenshire, Pembrokeshire and Swansea
Ceredigion and South Gwynedd
Denbighshire, Flintshire, Wrexham
Herefordshire Monmouthshire
Powys

Scotland
Aberdeenshire
Ayrshire
Dumfries and Galloway
Edinburgh and East Central Scotland
Fife and Tayside
Glasgow and West Central Scotland
Inverness and Moray
Lanarkshire
Scottish Borders

Northern Ireland
County Antrim and County Londonderry
County Armagh and County Down
Belfast
County Tyrone and County Fermanagh

For national mapping, choose
Philip's Navigator Britain
the most detailed road atlas available of England, Wales and Scotland. Hailed by Auto Express as 'the ultimate road atlas', this is the only one-volume atlas to show every road and lane in Britain.

How to order Philip's maps and atlases are available from bookshops, motorway services and petrol stations. You can order direct from the publisher by phoning **0190 828503** or online at **www.philips-maps.co.uk** For bulk orders only, e-mail philips@philips-maps.co.uk